Turkish Migration Conference 2015
Selected Proceedings

TRANSNATIONAL PRESS LONDON

Overeducated and Over Here

Turkish Migration Series
Politics and Law in Turkish Migration
Family and Human Capital in Turkish Migration
Göç ve Uyum
Turkish Migration, Identity and Integration
Little Turkey in Great Britain (forthcoming)

Journals by TPL
Migration Letters
Remittances Review
Göç Dergisi
Journal of Gypsy Studies
Kurdish Studies
International Economics Letters
Border Crossing TWP
Transnational Marketing Journal

Turkish Migration Conference 2015
Selected Proceedings

Editors:

Güven **Şeker**, Ali **Tilbe**, Mustafa **Ökmen**,

Pınar **Yazgan**, Deniz **Eroğlu**, Ibrahim **Sirkeci**

TRANSNATIONAL PRESS LONDON
2015

Turkish Migration Conference 2015 Selected Proceedings
Co-edited by Güven Şeker, Ali Tilbe, Mustafa Ökmen, Pınar Yazgan, Deniz Eroğlu, Ibrahim Sirkeci

First Printing: 2015

Paperback

ISBN: 978-1-910781-01-2

London, United Kingdom
www.tplondon.com
www.turkishmigration.com

Cover Photo: Tuncay BİLECEN

TRANSNATIONAL PRESS LONDON
12 Ridgeway Gardens, London, N6 5XR, United Kingdom
www.tplondon.com

Contents

TÜRK GÖÇ KONFERANSI 2015 - TÜRKÇE BİLDİRİLER

Turkish Migration Conference 2015
Selected Proceedings

TMC 2015 was hosted by Charles University Prague, Czech Republic from 25 to 27 June 2015. The TMC 2015 was the third event in the series that we were proud to organise and host at Charles University Prague. This selection of papers presented at the conference are only a small portion of contributions. Many other papers are included in edited books and submitted to refereed journals in due course. There were a total of about 146 papers by over 200 authors presented in 40 parallel sessions and three plenary sessions at Jinonice Campus of Charles University Prague. About a fifth of the sessions at the conference were in Turkish language although the main language was English. Therefore some of the proceedings are in Turkish too.

The TMC 2015 was a specialist event bringing researchers, scholars, and students investigating Turkish migrant dynamics and patterns, migrant experiences, the costs of migration, as well as the economic, social, educational and cultural outcomes. Including contributions from scholars and students from anthropology, demography, business, economics, psychology, sociology, political science, geography, development studies, law and other disciplines, the conference provided a forum through which to consider all aspect's related to Turkish migration around the world. Adopting an interdisciplinary approach to migration dynamics and patterns, and by drawing on comparative studies of international and internal migration process, the TMC 2015 included contributions covering country of origin, transit and destination countries focusing on human mobility from, to and in Turkey as well as studies on other migration cases from around the world.

We would like to thank all our colleagues who served on the conference committee, hundreds of authors who contributed by presenting their papers but they also reviewed substantial number of abstracts and papers. Once again, we thank to Charles University Prague for hosting the event, the University of California Davis Gifford Centre for Population Studies, Manisa Celal Bayar University Faculty of Economics and Administrative Sciences and Center for Population and Migration Studies, Regent's University London Centre for Transnational Studies, Univerziti Publishing, Transnational Press London, for their support and contribution to the Conference. Our local hosts and co-chairs Inna Cabelkova and Wadim Strielkowski deserve a big thank you for their year long effort and hospitality during the three days in Prague. We thank to our great team of assistants, Burcu Oskay, Tereza Kalinová, Sonja Lovrentjev, Therese Svensson and Emine Akman who were heroes behind the scenes as well as smiling faces at the front desk.

We thank to the keynote speakers Douglas Massey of Princeton University, Caroline Brettell of Southern Methodist University, Nedim Gürsel of CNRS, and co-chairs Jeffrey Cohen of Ohio State University and Philip Martin of University of California Davis.

Among many other colleagues, we would like to thank M. Rauf Kesici and Tuncay Bilecen of Kocaeli University, Gizem Özgür of Karadeniz Technical

University, Veysel Gelberi from Middle East Technical University for their efforts in the editing process of the proceedings.

We are looking forward to seeing all at the TMC 2016 in Vienna, Austria.

Güven Şeker
Ali Tilbe
Mustafa Ökmen
Pınar Yazgan
Deniz Eroğlu
Ibrahim Sirkeci

Conference Committee

- Prof Ibrahim Sirkeci (Chair), Regent's Centre for Transnational Studies, Regent's University London, UK
- Prof Philip L. Martin (Co-Chair), Dept. of Agricultural & Resource Economics, University of California, Davis, USA
- Dr Wadim Strielkowski (Co-Chair), Faculty of Social Sciences(Co-chair), Charles University Prague, Czech Republic
- Dr Inna Čábelková (Co-Chair), Faculty of Humanities, Charles University Prague, Czech Republic
- Prof Ali T. Akarca, Department of Economics, University of Illinois, Chicago, USA
- Dr Bahar Baser, University of Coventry, UK
- Prof Gudrun Biffl, Department of Migration and Globalization, Danube University Krems, Austria
- Dr Elias Boukrami, Regent's Centre for Transnational Studies, Regent's University London
- Prof Jeffrey H. Cohen, Department of Anthropology, Ohio State University, USA
- Prof Dilek Cindoğlu, Department of Sociology, Artuklu University, Turkey
- Prof Ali Caglar, Department of Political Science, Hacettepe University, Turkey
- Dr Mehmet Ali Dikerdem, Institute for Work Based Learning, Middlesex University, UK
- Dr M. Murat Erdoğan, Migration and Politics Research Centre, Hacettepe University, Turkey
- Dr Tahire Erman, Department of Political Science, Bilkent University, Turkey
- Prof Sibel Kalaycıoğlu, Department of Sociology, Middle East Technical University, Turkey
- Dr Altay Manco, l'Institut de Recherche, Formation et Action sur les Migrations, Belgium
- Luisa Morettin, Regent's Centre for Transnational Studies, Regent's University London
- Dr Assia S. Rolls, Faculty of Business and Management, Regent's University London
- Dr B. Dilara Seker, Department of Psychology, Celal Bayar University, Turkey
- Dr Levent Soysal, Faculty of Communications, Kadir Has University, Turkey
- Prof Aysit Tansel, Department of Economics, Middle East Technical University, Turkey
- Dr Ali Tilbe, Namik Kemal University, Turkey and Regent's University London, UK
- Dr Östen Wahlbeck, School of Social Science, University of Helsinki, Finland

- ❖ Dr Pinar Yazgan-Hepgul, Department of Sociology, Sakarya University, Turkey
- ❖ Dr M. Murat Yüceşahin, Department of Geography, Ankara University, Turkey
- ❖ Dr Welat Zeydanlıoğlu, Kurdish Studies Network, Sweden
- ❖ Dr Sinan Zeyneloğlu, Department of City and Regional Planning, University of Gaziantep, Turkey

Local Organisation Committee
- ❖ Dr Wadim Strielkowski (Co-Chair), Faculty of Social Sciences, Charles University Prague
- ❖ Dr Inna Čábelková (Co-Chair), Faculty of Humanities, Charles University Prague
- ❖ Dr Tuncay Bilecen, Regent's Centre for Transnational Studies, Regent's University London
- ❖ Dr M. Rauf Kesici, Regent's Centre for Transnational Studies, Regent's University London
- ❖ Burcu Oskay, Regent's Centre for Transnational Studies, Regent's University London
- ❖ Prof Ibrahim Sirkeci, Conference Chair & Director of RCTS, Regent's University London
- ❖ Dr Güven Şeker, Population and Migration Research Centre (NUGAM), Celal Bayar University, Turkey
- ❖ Therese Svensson, Regent's Centre for Transnational Studies, Regent's University London
- ❖ Fethiye Tilbe, Namik Kemal University, Turkey and Regent's Centre for Transnational Studies, Regent's University London

Supporting Organisations
- ❖ Charles University Prague, Faculty of Humanities
- ❖ University of California Davis Gifford Center for Population Studies
- ❖ Regent's University Centre for Transnational Studies
- ❖ Manisa Celal Bayar University, Population and Migration Research Centre
- ❖ Manisa Celal Bayar University, Faculty of Economics and Administrative Sciences
- ❖ Migration Letters journal
- ❖ Göç Dergisi journal
- ❖ Kurdish Studies journal
- ❖ International Economics Letters
- ❖ Ria Financial
- ❖ University Servis Publishing
- ❖ Transnational Press London

Programme Summary

THURSDAY 25th June

Parallel Sessions 1. 13:20 - 15:20
A. Integration Processes
B. Business, Economics and Immigrants
C. Göç ve Edebiyat
D. Syrian Movers in Turkey

Parallel Sessions 2. 15:40 - 17:10
A. Europe in Turkish Migration Policy
B. Irregular Migration and Remittance
C. Göç ve Sürgün Edebiyatı
D. Migrant Identity

Parallel Sessions 3. 17:30 - 19:00
A. Integration, Harmonization, Marginalization
B. Family Formation and Migration
C. Göç ve Uyum
D. Migration Policy and Perceptions
E. Internal Migration

FRIDAY 26th June

Parallel Sessions 4. 09:00 - 10:30
A. Return Movements
B. Circassian Diaspora
C. Kamu Yönetimi Açısından Göç
D. Gender and Sexuality

Parallel Sessions 5. 10:50 - 12:20
A. Counter-Hegemonic Migrant Spaces, Place-Making and Resistance
B. Demographic Analysis of Migration
C. Yeni Göç Eğilimleri
D. Migration in Literature

Parallel Sessions 6. 16:20 - 18:20
A. Migration and Religious Identity
B. Kamu Hizmetleri ve Göç
C. Türkiye'de Göç ve İşgücü Piyasaları
D. Integration and Identity

SATURDAY 27th June

Parallel Sessions 7. 09:30 - 11:00
A. Between Naturalization and Irregularity: Migrants and (Il)legal Membership in Turkey
B. Politics and Migration
C. Integration and Identity
D. Spatial Productions of the Social: Identity, Subjectivity and Power

Parallel Sessions 8. 11:20- 12:50
A. Integration in Europe
B. Migrants of Istanbul
C. Migration and Literature

Public services for asylum seekers in Turkey within the perspective of new migratory movements

Tülin Canbay[1]

Introduction

Since the beginning of humanity, countless number of people have had to leave their places and homelands due to various reasons such as climate conditions, natural disasters, wars, economic crises, human rights violations, and security. Unfortunately, this international migratory movements still continue.

Due to its geographical location, Turkey lies between unstable and poor countries on its eastern borders and stable and wealthy countries on its western borders. For this reason, it is both a transition and a target country for asylum-seekers and refugees (tbmm.gov.tr, 2010). Thus, Turkey has become an important actor in terms of global migration in the last two decades, and while it was a source country before, now it has become a `target` and `transit country`.

There is a substantial increase in the number of asylum seekers, refugees, and migrants who are caught crossing borders illegally and the number of those involved in asylum procedures compared to previous years, especially due to the civil wars in the Middle East. Statistical data shows that Iraqi and Iranian asylum seekers and refugees have the highest numbers in the last years, and the number of Afghani origin refugees and asylum seekers was very high in 2012. Syrian refugees have become the biggest mass refugee group that has been trying to survive in the refugee camps in Turkey since 2012-2013 war (Yıldız, Ünlü,Sezer,2014,p.44).

This paper mainly deals with the immigration from Syria to Turkey, which has caused complex and multi-dimensional humanitarian, legal, political, social and financial problems. This paper aims to understand the public services given to Syrian asylum seekers, especially in health and education fields, to discuss the costs of these services, and to analyse the support by international community and actors.

Syrian asylum seekers in Turkey

Following the anti-government protests that started in March 2011, the events in Syria have caused one of the biggest humanitarian crises of the World. Due to the civil war in Syria, 11 million out of 23 million people have become dependent on humanitarian assistance; 7 million people have been internally displaced, and over 3 million Syrian refugees fled to neighbouring countries. Since March 2011, Syrian civil war and mass immigration movement have affected domestic political, economic and social dynamics of all countries in the region, especially Turkey. One of the most important outcomes of the war is the number of Syrian refugees, which is close to 4 million. Every month, this figure increases 100,000 on average

[1] Tülin Canbay is Professor of Celal Bayar University Faculty of Economic and Administrative Sciences Department of Finance, Turkey. E-mail: tcanbay@hotmail/com

(Kap,2015). Among the neighbouring countries, Turkey hosts the largest number of refugees.

As Turkey ratified Geneva Convention of 1951 with geographical restrictions, Syrian citizens are not considered refugees. According to the geographical restrictions, Turkey extends refugee status to only those coming from European countries, who seek asylum with fear of prosecution due to religion, race, nationality, membership of certain social group and political ideas. The status of those who seek asylum in Turkey are determined in coordination with the UNHCR and, if deemed suitable, are transferred to third countries. For this reason, asylum seekers coming to Turkey from Syria are not here as refugees, they are referred to as "guests" (ORSAM-TESEV, 2015, p.12)

As of February 11, 2015, the official number of Syrians who are registered by AFAD in all Turkey is 1,629,000 (Milliyet,02.03.2015). Unofficial numbers are claimed to be over 2 million. There are many refugees, who have yet to be registered and entered Turkey illegally, in many provinces of Turkey, especially those close to the border (ORSAM-TESEV, 2015, p.10). Most of the Syrian refugees in Turkey come from border regions with conflicts.

As of March 6, 2015, 243,692 asylum seekers reside in 25 shelters in 10 provinces (Milliyet, 09.03.2015). The remaining Syrian guests, which constitute the biggest group of Syrians, are trying to survive all over Turkey. Over 53% of Syrians in Turkey are below 18 years old and over 75% are children and women in need of protection (Erdoğan,2014,p.4). In the current situation, Turkey is hosting a whole lot more than its critical threshold permits and is facing a wide range of refugee problem (ORSAM-TESEV, 2015, p.12).

Turkey announced that its Syrian "guests" are under "temporary protection regime" in accordance with the Article 10 of Regulation 1994 of the Ministry of Internal Affairs as of October 2011. This regime is in compliance with minimum international standards and comprises principles such as open door policy, non-refoulment policy, individual refugee status determination, provision of services such as settlement in camps, and other services (Ihlamur,2014, p.44). Within this scope, Turkey has undertaken an important obligation to Syrian asylum seekers, which is admired by the international community.

Public services given to asylum seekers and problems

Syrians are in search of meeting their basic needs such as security, nutrition, accomodation, and health much more than leading a good life in their host countries (ORSAM-TESEV,2015, p.10). However, they cannot meet these needs on their own as they cannot enter labour force or find jobs legally due to educational differences, language problems, and current employment laws in effect. For this reason, protection and care of asylum seekers have to be through public services given by the state.

Turkish Government has assumed the role of giving the best possible life conditions and the most comprehensive humanitarian aid possible, in addition to shelter. The Republic of Turkey Prime Ministry Disaster and Emergency Management Authority (AFAD), together with the Turkish Red Crescent, has been actively involved in establishing refugee camps and orderly settlements (http://www.mavikalem.org/ 2013,p.9). In 25 shelters under the coordination of

AFAD, there are market, heating, security, religious service, infrastructure, communication, firefighting, interpretation, psychosocial support, and banking services. In addition to these, laundry, dish washing, and personal cleaning needs are met. There are educational and vocational classes. The refugees are given three meals in their camps aas well as electronic cards, which contain a certain amount of money so that they can purchase their personal needs (Milliyet,09.03.2015).

Most of those staying in camps are better off, in terms of welfare and social means, compared to those who live outside of camps. Approximately 85% of the refugees live outside of camps. Thus, the refugees living outside of camps face most of the problems (ORSAM-TESEV,2015,p.10). Although, those who live in the camps have been registered systematically since the beginning of the crisis, we cannot say the same for the others. Registrations are made both in parallel and differing systems and they have not been completed due to problems in reaching the population outside of camps (Velieceoğlu,2014,p.28). It is necessary to generalize registration services so that refugees can reach public services, and their safety and protection are ensured. If a document that could be used instead of ID is issued, it will be easier for them to access many public services such as health care and education. Furthermore, their needs will be determined and aids will be sent much more easily.

The asylum seekers outside of camps, though they are covered by the temporary protection regime, cannot benefit from services and aids given by the AFAD. Asylum seekers in provinces also have limited access to aids of domestic and international NGOs (Ihlamur,2014,p.45). Most of Syrian refugees outside of camps, who do not have access to suitable shelter, food or even clean water and survive in inhumane conditions, do not have regular incomes. The rate of those who obtain food thanks to public aid is only 3.7%. This is an important indicator for the limited public support to the families outside the camps.

The Ministry of Labour and Social Security (MoLSS) has been working on a way to issue work permits to Syrians to prevent illegal employment. However, there is not any information on if Syrians can obtain work permits (Ihlamur, 2014, p.45).

One of the most important services that the state needs to give to the asylum seekers is adaptation service. When we take into consideration that Syrian refugees are staying longer than initially forecasted and that there is a possibility that an important part of them might end up staying permanently, adoption of adaptation policies for co-existence is very important in terms of social integration. National Action Plan emphasizes that an integration program for adaptation of candidates of refugees and asylum seekers and an integration system should be formed within the framework of regulatory and supervisory responsibilities of the state.

Education and health services are the two biggest problems within the scope of public services given to Syrian refugees. For this reason, this study will focus more on these two basic services.

Health services given to Syrian refugees could be analysed under three basic topics: 1. Emergency health services given to wounded refugees at the borders 2. Health services given at the temporary settlement centres, and 3. Health services given to the patients transferred from camps and those who live outside of camps on their own means in second and third care hospitals. There are preventive health services as well as diagnosis and treatment services at the camps.

As of January 18, 2013, all Syrian refugees who live in the border cities were given the right to access to free health and this right was extended to all Syrian refugees, who live in Turkey and are registered, on September 9, 2013 (Söylemez,2014). In theory, those who are unregistered can apply to health centres and they are immediately registered and given health care and the cost of treatments should be billed to the governorship of the province that the health centre is located. Although, free access to health services have been secured in theory, we could say that hospitals follow different pricing in practice and there is no single practice. Plus, even if examination is free, they have problems in paying for the medications due to limited funds.

As of January 6, 2015, the number of patients treated by in-camp policlinic services was 3,164,164, and patients from out of camp was 3,366,804, and general total was 6,530,968. Number of the patients transferred from camps to hospitals, until now, has been 576,748. A total of 249,230 Syrians have received in-patient treatment until now. A total of 199,165 Syrian patients were operated. A total of 40,823 children were born in our hospitals (Arıkan,2015,s.80). We can see that approximately 60% of Syrians, who live outside of camps, benefit from health care in Turkey and 97% of the children who are born outside of camps are born in hospitals or health centres (AFAD, 2013,p.44).

Another important service in health care field is vaccination. Following influx of refugees, some diseases, previously non-existent in Turkey, unfolded and cases of polio, for which Turkey did not even have vaccination anymore, arose in border provinces. Within this scope, all children within 0-5 age group have been vaccinated against polio. In addition to this, measles and aleppo boil group diseases are seen again (ORSAM-TESEV, 2015, p.20). Syrian children are vaccinated for free at Family Health Centre and Community Health centres and this does not require a special registration.

State hospitals in the border provinces give 30% to 40% of their overall service to Syrian patients. For this reason, there are some capacity problems in those hospitals. These hospitals treat not only asylum seekers in Turkey but also those, who live in Syria and are wounded in the conflicts. And this leads to a capacity problem in terms of both physical conditions and number of health sector workers (ORSAM-TESEV, 2015, p.20).

One of the most important problems is provision of health services (X-ray, operations, continuous use of medication, cancer, and diabetes patients). Pregnant refugee women, infants, and children need to be regularly monitored and treated. The fact that all Syrian citizens in Turkey are not registered, their lack of permanent addresses, and language problems are important barriers to access to public health and protective health care and to proper treatment.

Over 53% of Syrians in Turkey are children under 18. When this young age group stays in Turkey longer, they lose their chances for education and they turn into lost generations. An important part of the Syrian refugee children do not have access to primary education. Although the situation is better for children in camps than for those outside, schooling rate is still low at the camps. The situation is even worse for those outside of camps. An important part of them have to work to support their families or girls are married off at early ages and are deprived of education. Another factor for low schooling age is that the education language is Turkish.

Looking at the figures, we see that 80% of children who live in the camps receive education. UNICEF states that it is only 26% for Syrian children who live outside of camps, who are in school age group (UNICEF,2014,p.19). According to the statement of AFAD on December 16, 2013, approximately 50,000 Syrian children receive education services of kindergarten, primary education and high school levels in 693 classrooms from 1,923 teachers, 377 Turkish and 1,546 Arab, within the scope of education services in the camps. It is stated that, in addition to humanitarian needs in shelters, there are vocational and educational classes tailored for social needs of Syrian guests and that over 27,000 people took classes in 139 vocational training classes for adults until now (www.afad.gov.tr/TR, 2013).

Despite the efforts of Turkish government, the schooling rate for primary and high school education in state schools and the number of students sent to private schools with Arabic as the instruction language, are not at the desired level due to financial difficulty, bureaucratic obstacles, and unregistered refugees.

In terms of university education, those who were studying at the university in Syria and those who have a high school diploma have been given the opportunity to study for free and without an entrance exam at universities in Turkey. Furthermore, they are accommodated at state student lodgings, given monthly stipend, and not charged for university fees.

AFAD started building schools which will give education only to Syrians. But this is still at the initial phase. For this reason, approximately 10% of those education age group Syrians who live in cities receive education (ORSAM-TESEV, 2015,p.20). But if we consider that this number will increase in the future, there will be a considerable burden on the existing education capacity. On the other hand, lack of education among asylum seekers have long term social impacts.

Cost of services and scarcity of international support

In accordance with Article 14 of Universal Declaration of Human Rights "everyone has the right to seek and to enjoy in other countries asylum from persecution". For this reason, all countries need to act susceptive to this basic human right.

Nevertheless, the pressure of Europe on Turkey to "*Keep eastern border open, but close the western borders so they cannot reach us*" pushes the borders of ethics and consciousness. When 3.5 million Syrians have fled their country, those who have gone to or have been promised to be received by the developed countries are 123,000. This represents 3.5% of the group. Turkey and other neighbouring countries have been victimized by the "open door" policy (Erdoğan,2014,p.4).

Turkey is currently hosting 2 million asylum seekers and has spent 5.2 billion USD for them. However, international community has given only 300,000 million USD humanitarian aid to the refugees hosted in Turkey (Milliyet, 09.03.2015). As can be seen, Turkey is facing a massive cost because of Syrian refugee issue. Support from international community for this cost is very limited and Turkey has born almost all the cost. When the conflict started in Syria, Turkish government has refused aid from abroad for many reasons such as they thought the conflict would not last long and wanted to keep the camps under its control, but they changed their decision in April 2012 (ICG, 2014,p.15). However, it is not possible to say that there is a meaningful international aid.

International community, to a large extend, has been unresponsive to the international aid call, made by the UN, for raising 6.5 billion USD for millions of Syrian refugees who had to flee their country. As a result of this, the UN World Food Programme (WFP) ended its aid to 9 refugee camps in Turkey due to lack of funds. As of October 15, 2014, only 28% of 497 million USD, which was allocated to Turkey, from 2014 regional fund call for Syrian refugees. Foreign aid received as of August 2014 is 233 million USD, making it only 4,1% of the total spending (BMMYK, 2013,p.7. The developed-rich countries and organizations have not been responsive to the "emergency" calls made by the UN for meeting basic needs (Erdoğan, 2014,p.15).

Conclusion

Attitude of Turkish society towards asylum seekers and Turkish state's services in terms of establishment and management of camps are examples for the World and these are admired by international community. However, status of Syrian guests, which was assumed to be short-term, is becoming permanent as the war goes on and overstrains Turkey in terms of both its service capacity and costs and sustainability of social acceptance. For this reason, there is need for effective and permanent solutions and comprehensive migration governance that will be established through national and international organizations' cooperation for education, health, sheltering, work life, and municipality services.

Policies and procedures about the rights and services given to Syrian refugees in Turkey need to be announced effectively by the authorities. Especially majority of Syrian refugees are not aware of benefits of being registered. It is necessary to establish mobile registration centres and register every asylum seeker, for free and regardless of how they entered Turkey, for ensuring effective access to public services and realistic determination of their needs.

Within this framework, following suggestions need to be evaluated by authorities: registration of all Syrians, building additional capacity in education and health sectors, work permit issue, giving initiatives to local authorities, coordination between local and central authorities, building additional capacity and budget for municipality services, forming Syrian opinion leader groups in the border provinces, preparation of brochures and webpages in Arabic, opening new zoning areas in border provinces, increasing international aid, increasing border controls, building amenity spaces for Syrians, developing programmes for helping Turkish public to get used to presence of Syrians, establishing a database on demographic structure of Syrians and possible migratory movements, preventing begging, developing effective solutions to possible problem with public order, and realizing of capacity building projects for Syrians (ORSAM-TESEV,2015, p.9).

The biggest problem in terms of services given to asylum seekers is bearing the cost of these services. Especially failure of international community in assuming its responsibility in terms of costs and humanitarian aid, when the number of refugees increase daily, makes it hard for Turkey to bear these costs on its own.

References

AFAD (Republic Of Turkey Prime Ministry Disaster And Emergency Management Authority).(2013). Sixth Response Plan from AFAD & UN 16 December 2013, https://www.afad.gov.tr/TR/HaberDetay.aspx?ID=5&IcerikID=1651, available on: 19.02.2015.

AFAD. (2013). Syrian Refugees in Turkey 2013, Field Survey Results, Syrian Refugees in Turkey : 2013, Field Survey Results.

Arıkan N., O. (2015). Health Services Provided to Syrian Refugees, Sağlık Düşüncesi Ve Tıp Kültürü Dergisi, March – April – May 2015 Spring, No : 34.

UNHCR (The United Nations Refugee Agency) (2013). 2014 Syrian Refugees Regional Response Plan : Turkey , 18 December 2013, Received from http://data.unhcr.org/syrianrefugees/country.php?id=224, available on: 01.03. 2015.

UNHCR (The United Nations Refugee Agency).(2014) , Turkey: Syrian Refugees Regional Response Plan (2014), Received from http://www.unhcr.org/syriarrp6/docs/Syria-rrp6-full-report.pdf, sf. 34). available on: 01. 03.2015.

Erdoğan, M.M. (2014). Syrian in Turkey : Social Acceptance and İntegration , Hacettepe University Migration and Politics Research Center - MPRC, November 2014, Ankara.

ICG (International Crisis Group). (2014). İncreasing Costs of Syria Dilemma For Turkey , Europe Report No. 230, 30 April 2014.

Ihlamur, Ö., S. G. (2014). Turkey's Policy İntended Syrian Refugees , Ortadoğu Analiz, March -April Vol: 6 No: 61, April 2014.

Kap, D. (2015). Syrian Refugees : İntended Citizenship Of Turkey, Akademik Perspektif, 19 October 2015, http://akademikperspektif.com/2015/01/19/suriyeli-multeciler-turkiyenin-mustakbel-vatandaslari/, available on: 11.03. 2015.

Milliyet. (02.03.2015). "Number of Syrian Refugees Exceeded The Population of 11 City İn Turkey", Received from http://www.milliyet.com.tr/suriyeli-sayisi-11-ilin-nufus-gundem-2021373/ available on: 09.03.2015.

Milliyet. (09.03.2015). Excess Burden Of Syrian Refugee On Turkey , Received from http://www.milliyet.com.tr/suriyeli-multeci-yuku-turkiye-nin-gundem-2025109/ available on: 09.03.2015.

TBMM (2010). http://www.tbmm.gov.tr/komisyon/insanhaklari/belge/gocmen_raporu.pdf). available on: 01.06.2015.

Yıldız, K., Ünlü, Ü., Sezer, M. (2014). Refugee And Defector İnsanıtıes And The Socıety Every Human Beıng Has The Rıght To Dıe In Peace, In Hıs Own House, Among The People He Loves And In Hıs Own Country! Journal Of Social And Economic Research , KMÜ, 16 (Special Issue I): 42-50.

ORSAM (Center For Middle Eastern Strategic Studies), TESEV (The Turkish Economic and Social Studies Foundation). (2015). The Effects of the Syrian Refugees İn Turkey , ORSAM Report Number : 195, October 2015.

http://www.mavikalem.org/wp-content/uploads/2014/05/DURUM-ANALIZI-SURIYELI-SIGINMACILAR_SANLIURFA-2013-.pdf S.9, available on: 09.03.2015.

Söylemez, A. (2014). Deepest Refugee Crisis İn Recent Years , BİANET, 20 November 2014, http://www.bianet.org/bianet/insan-haklari/160092-son-yillarin-en-derin-multeci-krizi, available on: 09.04.2015.

UNICEF, Monthly Situation Report of Syria Humanitarian Crisis, 18 March -17 April 2014,

Velieceoğlu Y., A. (2014). Syrian Refuges İn Turkey , Regional Application , Monitoring and Research Center - Mersin University , Final Report : The İssues of The Syrian Refugees, MERSİN, 27 October 2014.

A Study on Relationship of Syrian Immigrants in Turkey and Their Tendency of Returning Home

Mehmet Emin Sönmez[†]

Introduction

Turkey is one of the countries which receives permanent migration and is situated on the route for transit migration to Europe due to its geographical location and cultural characteristics. Migration to Turkey is forced largely due to wars, internal conflicts and disputes rather than economic in nature. Starting due to cultural imperatives as a result of the Ottoman State's losing territories, such migration has accelerated during the construction of Turkey's nation states and the immigration continued to flow from particularly Balkans and other regions including the East Turkistan, Iran, Iraq and Afghanistan in the period of the Republic (İçduygu & Sirkeci, 1999, p. 259-265; Çakırer Özservet, 2013, p. 170). Many immigrants immigrate to Turkey temporarily or permanently due to economic and political instability in abovementioned countries as well as Turkey's being a bridge between East-West and North-South (İçduyu & Toktaş, 2005, p. 43). In addition, Turkey is in the "host country" position especially for those immigrants from the same culture since it took over the Ottoman legacy (Buz, 2008, p. 2).

The largest wave of immigration in the history of the Republic of Turkey happened due to the ongoing civil war in Syria which started in 2011. This is also closely related to the immigration policies of developed countries. In reality, Turkey was previously in the position of a transit country for immigration to Europe. However, the fact that the European countries blocked legal means to prevent mass migration consisting of asylum seekers/refugees and took preventive measures against immigrants pushed Turkey into the position of an immigration country. Besides, the difficulty of the distance to travel forces refugees/asylum seekers to mostly migrate to neighbouring countries. Indeed, 10.4 million refugees sought refuge in neighbouring countries in year 2011, only 17% migrated out of their own region (Ghosh & Enami, 2015, p. 2; UNHCR S. 2011). In reality, approximately 42.3% of the 3,834,584 Syrian refugees registered by the UNHCR migrated to Turkey, 30.8% to Lebanon, 16.3% to Jordan, 6.4% to Iraq, 3.6% to Egypt and the remaining 6 ‰ immigrated to Europe and other neighbouring countries (UNHCR, 2015). As seen, migration policies pursued by the developed countries and the shifting of the immigrants to close surrounding countries affected Turkey the most. Besides this, the growth and strengthening of Turkey's economy has created a separate attraction for those fleeing the civil war in close surrounding countries. As a result, despite being a transit point for international immigration until recently, Turkey has become one of the focuses of international immigration for its close vicinity. The most important and most difficult of these movements took place aftermaths of the civil war in Syria.

† Mehmet Emin Sönmez is Associate Professor in Geography Department, Gaziantep University, Gaziantep, 32103. E-mail: eminsonmez@gantep.edu.tr.

It is estimated that the number of Syrian refugees will reach 6,500,000 by the end of 2015 (UNHCR G. 2015). It is understood from the data that asylum seekers turn especially to neighbouring countries, mainly Turkey. According to official data by UNHCR, the number of Syrian refugees arriving in Turkey until 31 December 2014 is 1,552,839. Unofficial figures report that this figure exceeds 2,2. So, according to the official figures, approximately 2,1% of Turkey's population is composed of Syrian refugees, while it corresponds to 2,9% in unofficial sources. Indeed, according to the Ministry of Health, 35 thousand Syrian births took place in Turkey during this period (ORSAM, 2015, p. 7). This makes it necessary for Turkey to reconsider its emigration policy. In this context, Turkey signed the refugee definition subject to geographical restrictions in the Geneva Convention on the Legal Status of Refugees in 1951 and it has chosen to execute its own migration and asylum arrangements according to the Regulations on Asylum dated 1994. Consequently, those who come from European countries to Turkey are recognized as "refugee" and operations are carried out for entry to a third country, those coming from countries outside Europe (Middle East, Africa) are treated as "refugees" and can reside temporarily in Turkey. Turkey is a country which accepts more refugees from the second group being in our country temporarily (Buz, 2008, p. 2; İçduygu & Sirkeci, 1999, p. 165). But because of the uncertainty of the definition of "refugee", in October 1994, the Ministry of Domestic Affairs granted the status of "temporary protection" to Syrian refugees in accordance with Article 10 of the Regulation of 1994. Later, a legal regulation was made on this issue on 30 March 2012 and "the Instructions for Admission and Hosting of Syrian Arab Republic Citizens Incoming to Turkey for Mass Influx and Stateless Persons Residing in Syrian Arab Republic" numbered 62 was created. Thus, Syrian refugees were taken under "temporary protection" and in accordance with minimum international standards, they gained such rights as open door policy, not to force for return, to ensure no individual status determination, camps sheltering and provision of basic services (ORSAM, 2014, p. 11). This might be effective to varying degrees on Turkey's demographic, social, economic and cultural structures. As a matter of fact, according to the unofficial data, the number of Syrians in Turkey is more than population of several small ethnic groups and cultures (Zaza, Circassians, Armenians and Greeks). This situation may give rise to different risks in the future. Therefore, it is of utmost importance to determine the profile of Syrian refugees as well as their returning tendency and to produce policies based on these results. Related to this issue, field studies have been carried out including all of the Syrian refugees in Turkey (ORSAM, 2014; ORSAM, 2015; Güçer et al., 2013) apart from other studies in provinces like Kilis (Paksoy, 2013) and Hatay (Harunoğulları & Cengiz, 2014).

In present study, the relationship between the economic profile of Syrian asylum seekers and their return to Syria is discussed. To this end, a field study was performed in Gaziantep as one of the towns with the highest number of Syrian refuges since the beginning of 2015. During this study carried out on individual and household basis, questionnaires were given to 215 participants from 215 households. Also face to face interviews were held with 15 participants, 7 female and 8 male, accompanied by a translator. The questionnaires were analyzed with SPSS.

Data and method

Quantitative evaluations are usually criticized due to some shortcomings such as the oversights of details in social studies covering large groups and areas, snapshot varying of social events and failure to put out locality sufficiently (Çakırer Özservet, 2013, p. 165) and due to their descriptive nature (Sağlam Arıet al., 2009). Therefore, the survey neighbourhoods with different levels of development and individuals with different race, culture, economy and social features are selected in this study. During the field study, 215 individuals filled in questionnaires from 215 households and 15 people were interviewed face to face. Information was obtained about all individuals in the household at varying degrees with the questionnaire. In order to make a more healthy overall assessment, the proportional distribution of ethnicity in Syria was also taken into account and it was attempted to reach people of different races according to the proportions.

The questions in the questionnaire were prepared so as to cover the conditions in Turkey of Syrian refugees in Gaziantep since the survey relates to their economic profile in Syria and their trends of return. Thus, the relationship between the refugees' economic and living conditions in both Turkey and Syria is put forward in a much more meaningful way.

Return of Syrians who took refuge in Turkey seems likely under existing conditions or in the event of establishment of different states with different ethnic and cultural structures in fragmented Syria. On the other hand, accepting of Syrian refugees as citizens of the Republic of Turkey may also affect the trend of return of Syrian refugees. Therefore, the participants were asked a variety of questions in this context and the relationship between economic profile and a tendency to return of Syrian refugees is further elaborated.

The survey results were analyzed for frequency and cross tables by using SPSS. Then, the results of the SPSS were evaluated and discussed together with conclusions drawn from the interviews.

Economic profile of Syrian refugees in Turkey

A total of 1327 residents were found in 215 surveyed households. 37.3% of them (496 people) were below 18 years, 47.7% (634 people) were aged between 18 and 45 and the rest of 15% were above 45. According to the data about these households, 51.5% of Syrian refugees in Gaziantep are male, while 48.5 % are female. Of study participants, 72.5% are males and 27.5% are females. 42% of them are Arabs, 29% Turkmen, 24% are Kurdish, 2% Armenian and the remaining 3% are from other races. 70.1% of participants are in the 25-50 age range, 19.4% above 50 years of age and the remaining 10.5% are in the range of 18-25 years. 80.6% of them are married, 14.5% of single, 3.2% widowed and the remaining 1.7% are married but live separately from their spouse.

Looking at total income of the households in Syria, it is seen that 60.3% of them had an income of less than $ 375, while 19% earned between $ 375-750, 5.2% between $ 750-1000 and 15.5% earned more than $ 1000.

The total income of families in Turkey was found lower. As an evidence, 64.5% of the families earn less than $ 375, while 23.7% earn between $ 375-750; 10.1% earning $ 750-1000 dollars and the remaining 1.7% gain more than $ 1000.

4.8% of the asylum seeker families did not own a house in Syria. 77.4% owned at least 1 house, 11.3% owned 2-3 houses, 4.8% owned 4-5 houses and 1.7% had at least 6 houses in Syria. Of these households, 50% had no other land outside the home, whereas 65% had a land less than 1 acre, 24.1% had a land between 1-10 acres, 6.5% owned a land between 11-50 acres and 12.9% owned more than 50 acres of land. None of the families surveyed are property owners in Turkey.

In the survey, also the number of vehicles owned by asylum seekers in Syria was questioned. It was found out that 19.3% had no vehicles at all, 54.8% had one 1 vehicle, 24.2% had 2-3 vehicles and 1.7% owned at least 4 vehicles. Among the same families, 74.3% do not have any vehicles in Turkey, while 22.5% have 1 and 3.2% have more than 1 vehicle.

In relation with the issues the refugees are most uncomfortable, it was seen that economic shortcomings come to the fore. As an evidence, 67.3% of the respondents worry about the future and face economic problems in the first place. Another 16.4% see as a priority issue for them the unpleasant behaviours of people in Turkey and 9.8% social and cultural differences. Lastly, 6.5% of the Syrian refugees perceive Turkey's political regime as the biggest threat for themselves.

Findings regarding the relationship between economic profile of asylum seekers and their trend of return to Syria

This study aims at making predictions regarding the trend of returning to Syria after the civil war among Syrian immigrants according to their economic profile. In order to be able to make inferences to this end, cross-examination was applied relevant questions on the SPSS. As a result, it was found;

The Relationship between the Refugees' Trend to Return and Their Economic Profile under Former Regime Conditions (Assad regime), Assuming the Immediate Cease of the Syrian Civil

While there were found no respondents having no home in Syria who tend to return to Syria, 54% have the tendency to return with 1 house in homeland. The rate of those who tend to stay in Turkey is found to be 46%. 71% of the participants owning 2-3 homes in Syria have a tendency to return, whereas 29% of those tend to stay in Turkey. The proportion of those with availability of 4-5 homes who tend to return is found 66%, while 34% are found to have the tendency to stay in Turkey. Lastly, none of the households owning 6 or more homes in Syria tend to return to Syria under such an imaginary circumstance.

The percentage of those not owning a vehicle in Syria still tending to return is 32%, the proportion of those who tend to remain in Turkey is 68%. Of those having 1 vehicle in homeland, 61% is found to be likely to return to Syria, while 39% have an opposite tendency. 53% of the refugees with 2-3 vehicles in Syria want to return, but 57% seem to tend to remain in Turkey. Lastly, all of those with 4 or more vehicles tend to settle in Turkey.

In relation with monthly average income level, 42% of those with an income less than 375 dollars in Syria show tendency to return, while 58% have an opposite intention. Among those earning 375-750 dollars in Syria, 37% tend to return to Syria, whereas 63% want to stay. In the group with an income level of 750-1000 dollars in Syria, all have a tendency to return. Similarly, 78% of those earning more than 1000 dollars intend to go back to Syria, while only 22% think the opposite.

Regarding income level in Turkey, 63% of those with monthly income less than 375 dollars tend to return to their homeland, while 37% do not. The proportion of those who have a tendency to return with a monthly income of 375 to 750 dollars in Turkey is 42% and proportion of the others is found as 58%. All of those currently earning 750-1000 dollars and more than 1000 dollars are likely to stay permanently.

As for the land property outside home in Syria, 48% showed the tendency to return, while the others were 52%. None of those owning less than 1 acre of land in Syria have a tendency to return. However, % 66 of the refugees with a land of 1-10 acres want to migrate back. But, 34% are inclined to stay in Turkey. Among those having a land between 11-50 acres of land in Syria, as high as 75% were found likely to return the remaining having the opposite tendency. Again 62% of those with a land of more than 50 acres tend to return to Syria, while 38% do not want to go.

Among participants facing the future anxiety and economic shortcomings in Turkey, 59% have a tendency to go back to their country, while 41% want to stay. In the group composed of those uncomfortable with negative behaviours of Turkish people, 40% show the tendency to return, while 60% want to settle in Turkey. 17% of those suffering from social and cultural discrepancies tend to return to their homeland, but 83% show an opposite trend. Lastly, of those facing difficulties under Turkish regime, 75% want to migrate back leaving the 25% with the intention to stay.

Syrian Refugees Intentions of Returning Home

While there were having no home in Syria who tend to return to Syria 66%, the proportion of those who tend to remain in Turkey is 34%. Of those having 1 home in Syria, 85% is found to be likely to return to Syria, while 15% have an opposite tendency. All of the households owning 2 or more homes in Syria tend to return to Syria under such an imaginary circumstance.

The percentage of those not owning a vehicle in Syria still tending to return is 83%, the proportion of those who tend to remain in Turkey is 17%. Of those having 1 vehicle in homeland, 93% is found to be likely to return to Syria, while 7% have an opposite tendency. 73% of the refugees with 2-3 vehicles in Syria want to return, but 27% seem to tend to remain in Turkey. Lastly, all of those with 4 or more vehicles tend to return to Syria.

In the group with an income less than 375 dollars in Syria, 91% show tendency to return, while 9% have an opposite intention. Among those earning 375-750 dollars in Syria, 81% tend to return to Syria, whereas 19% want to stay in Turkey. In the group with an income level of 750-1000 dollars in Syria, 67% show tendency to return, 33% have an opposite intention. Similarly, 89% of those earning more than 1000 dollars intend to go back to Syria, while only 11% think the opposite.

Regarding income level in Turkey, 89% of those with monthly income less than 375 dollars tend to return to their homeland, while 11% do not. The proportion of those who have a tendency to return with a monthly income of 375 to 750 dollars in Turkey is 85% and proportion of the others is found as 15%. In the group with a monthly income of 750-1000 dollars in Turkey is 83% tend to return to Syria, whereas 17% tend to stay in Turkey. All of those currently earning more than 1000 dollars are likely to stay permanently.

As for the land property outside home in Syria, 90% showed the tendency to return, while the others were 10%. Among those owning less than 1 acre of land in Syria, 75% have a tendency to return, %25 want to stay in Turkey. However all of those with a land of more than 1 acre tend to return to Syria.

Among participants facing the future anxiety and economic shortcomings in Turkey, 95% have a tendency to go back to their country, while 5% want to stay. In the group composed of those uncomfortable with negative behaviours of Turkish people, 55% show the tendency to return, while 45% want to settle in Turkey. All of those suffering from social and cultural discrepancies tend to return to their homeland. Lastly, of those facing difficulties under Turkish regime, 50% want to migrate back leaving the 50% with the intention to stay.

Turkish Citizenship and Syrian Refugees Intentions of Return

While there were having no home in Syria who tend to return to Syria 66%, the proportion of those who tend to remain in Turkey is 34%. Of those having 1 home in Syria, 47% is found to be likely to return to Syria, while 53% have an opposite tendency. 58% of the participants owning 2-3 homes in Syria have a tendency to return, whereas 42% of those tend to stay in Turkey. The proportion of those with availability of 4-5 homes who tend to return is found 67%, while 33% are found to have the tendency to stay in Turkey. Lastly, none of the households owning 6 or more homes in Syria tend to return to Syria under such an imaginary circumstance.

The percentage of those not owning a vehicle in Syria still tending to return is 33%, the proportion of those who tend to remain in Turkey is 67%. Of those having 1 vehicle in homeland, 52% is found to be likely to return to Syria, while 48% have an opposite tendency. 60% of the refugees with 2-3 vehicles in Syria want to return, but 40% seem to tend to remain in Turkey. Lastly, all of those with 4 or more vehicles tend to return to Syria.

In the group with an income less than 375 dollars in Syria, 45% show tendency to return, while 55% have an opposite intention. Among those earning 375-750 dollars in Syria, 27% tend to return to Syria, whereas 73% want to stay in Turkey. All of the group with an income level of 750-1000 dollars in Syria, show tendency to return to Syria. Lastly, 89% of those earning more than 1000 dollars intend to go back to Syria, while only 11% think the opposite.

Regarding income level in Turkey, 61% of those with monthly income less than 375 dollars tend to return to their homeland, while 39% do not. The proportion of those who have a tendency to return with a monthly income of 375 to 750 dollars in Turkey is 35% and proportion of the others is found as 65%. In the group with a monthly income of 750-1000 dollars in Turkey is 50% tend to return to Syria, whereas 50% tend to stay in Turkey. All of those currently earning more than 1000 dollars are likely to return to Syria.

As for the land property outside home in Syria, 38% showed the tendency to return, while the others were 62%. Among those owning less than 1 acre of land in Syria, 50% have a tendency to return, 50% want to stay in Turkey. However, % 60 of the refugees with a land of 1-10 acres want to migrate back. But, 40% are inclined to stay in Turkey. Among those having a land more than 11 acres of land in Syria, as high as 75% were found likely to return the remaining having the opposite tendency.

Among participants facing the future anxiety and economic shortcomings in Turkey, 51% have a tendency to go back to their country, while 49% want to stay. In the group composed of those uncomfortable with negative behaviours of Turkish people, 60% show the tendency to return, while 40% want to settle in Turkey. All of those facing difficulties under Turkish regime want to migrate back to Syria. Lastly, of those suffering from social and cultural discrepancies, 16% show tendency to return to Syria, 84% want to stay in Turkey.

Conclusion and discussion

In this study, it was determined that Syrian refugees in Gaziantep have a tendency to return varying depending on their economic profile. In particular, it was seen that the tendency to return increases along with the amount of economic resources owned in homeland. Indeed, those with more economic power in Syria have predominant tendency to return even under the circumstances of the worst probable peace. The same was also noted during the face to face interviews. For example, all of the individuals interviewed often referred to "the existence of their possessions in Syria" throughout the interviews. In particular, it seems that the refugees' future anxiety in Turkey and belief in the Assad regime seems to affect their tendency to return to Syria.

In addition, among Syrian refugees with a high level of household income, the tendency to return decreases. While refugees with a high level of income as understood from the face-to-face interviews show a tendency to return in any case, the same cannot be said under today's conditions. Among the same refugees, the tendency is greatly reduced in case of granting of citizenship by Republic of Turkey. In case of probable giving of the Turkish citizenship, the tendency to return is seen to decrease among not only those with high household income but all refugees. As a proof, the individuals we interviewed face-to-face stated that such a status would give them at least a sense of confidence, though not in economic sense. In the case of Syrian refugees remain in Turkey is essential to ensure mutual compatibility. The integration process is consist such as health, communicative competence, awareness, a sense of acceptance, cultural behavioral skills and economic structure qualifications (Sam & Berry, 2010, s. 472; Şeker, 2015, p. 18). The integration process is not only of interest to immigrant groups. Because concord and cultural integration is achieved by the interaction between host and immigrant community groups (Şeker, 2015, p. 16). Therefore, the perspective of Syrian refugees in Turkey, where usually one-sided, so the citizens of the Republic of Turkey should also make an effort for adaption and integration.

Under the imaginary condition of emerging of new state(s) in Syria according to their ethnic and religious background, the tendency to return reaches the highest level. All of the interviewed refugees associate it with the feeling of confidence, not facing cultural conflicts and any possible war in the future rather than economic reasons. This is also supported with the findings that they face both economic and political uncertainty in Turkey as the most important problem in both questionnaires and interviews. According to these data and from the view of this perspective it can be said that the possibility of gathering the nations in Syria and the people from different sectarians under a single roof is very low in case of a probable piece.

As a conclusion, the Syrian immigrants in Turkey are found to be inclined to go back to their home country due to the reasons such as economic problems, future anxiety, social and cultural discrepancies and being treated improperly. On the other hand, they do not lean towards the same due to certain fears such as another war in Syria and exposure to oppression and atrocity. Nevertheless, it was found that they have the desire to return to a possible environment of confidence in Syria due to the economic facilities, spiritual and cultural bonds they have in the homeland. Besides, a large portion of the long-term or permanent asylum seekers should be evaluated for the possibility of staying in Turkey. For this purpose, as the host and refugee communities' social, psychological and economic integration, which will ensure compliance and integration policies and projects need to be made immediately.

References

Buz, S. (2008). Türkiye'deki Sığınmacıların Sosyal Profili. Polis Bilimleri Dergisi, 10(4), 1-14.

Çakırer Özservet, Y. (2013). İstanbul Zeytinburnu İlçesi'nde Afgan Türklerinin Ulusötesi Kentleşme Ağlarının Analizi. FSM İlmî Araştırmalar İnsan ve Toplum Bilimleri Dergisi(2), 163-181.

Ghosh, S., & Enami, A. (2015). Do refugee-immigrants affect international trade? Evidence from the world's largest refugee case. Journal of Policy Modeling.

Güçer, M., Karaca, S., & Dinçer, O. B. (2013). Sınırlar Arasında Yaşam Savaşı: Suriyeli Mülteciler. Ankara: USAK.

Harunoğulları, M., & Cengiz, D. (2014). Suriyeli Göçmenlerin Mekânsal Analizi: Hatay (Antakya) Örneği. TÜCAUM-VIII. Coğrafya Sempozyumu 23-24 Ekim, 2014. Ankara.

İçduygu, A., & Sirkeci, İ. (1999). Cumhuriyet Dönemi Türkiye'sinde Göç Hareketleri. 75 Yılda Köylerden Şehirlere (s. 249-268). içinde İstanbul: Tarih Vakfı Yurt Yayınları.

ORSAM, O. (2014). Suriye'ye Komşu Ülkelerde Suriyeli Mültecilerin Durumu: Bulgular Sonuçlar ve Öneriler. Ankara: ORSAM.

ORSAM, O. (2015). Suriyeli Sığınmacıların Türkiye'ye Etkileri. Ankara: ORSAM.

Paksoy, M. (2013). İç Savaştan Kaçarak Kilis'te Yaşamını Sürdüren Suriyelilerin Sosyo-Ekonomik Sorunları Üzerine Bir Araştırma Raporu. Kilis: Kilis 7 Aralık Üniversitesi Ortadoğu Araştırmaları Uygulama ve Araştırma Merkezi.

Sağlam Arı, G., Armutlu, C., Güneri Tosunoğlu, N., & Yücel Toy, B. (2009). Nicel Araştırmalarda Metodoloji Sorunları: Yüksek Lisans Tezleri Üzerine Bir Araştırma. Ankara Üniversitesi SBF Dergisi, 64(4), 15-37.

Sam, D. L., & Berry, J. W. (2010). Acculturation: When Individuals and Groups of Different Cultural Backgrounds Meet. Perspectives on Psychological Science, 5(4), 472–481.

Şeker, B. D. (2015). Göç ve Uyum Süreci: Sosyal Psikolojik Bir Değerlendirme. B. D. Şeker, İ. Sirkeci, & M. M. Yüceşahin içinde, Göç ve Uyum (s. 11-27). London: Transnational Press London.

UNHCR, B. (2015, 03 09). Syria Regional Refugee Response. 03 09, 2015 tarihinde unhcr.org: http://data.unhcr.org/syrianrefugees/country.php?id=224 adresinden alındı

UNHCR, G. (2015, 03 07). Syrian Arab Republic.

UNHCR, S. (2011). Trends in displacement, protection and solutions (11th ed.). United Nations High Commissioner for Refugees.

Economic and financial aspects of forced migration from Bulgaria in 1989

Mustafa Miynat, Öznur Akyol, Deniz Alçin Şahintürk

Introduction

The pressures that started with the name changes of Turkish villages in the 1930s began to rise even further with the "one nation" decision of the communist regime in 1956. By the year 1984, the Turks whose names were changed perforce due to the assimilation policy in Bulgaria and whose languages were banned started a resistance campaign, which was widely supported by the Turks in the resistance zone.

The Bulgarian government has forced the Turks to migrate in 1989 in order to avert Turkish people from gaining further power in the region. The then Prime Minister Turgut Ozal has offered the introduction of a migration law which the Bulgarian government rejected, declaring a forceful expulsion within twenty-four hours. The 1989 Bulgarian immigration went down in history as the largest migration movement in Europe after the Word War II. In our study, the economic and financial impacts of the tragedy that the Turks went through in Bulgaria are discussed.

Reasons and Characteristics of the Bulgarian Immigration in 1989

Migration is about moving from one place where circumstances have become harder for various reasons to another where living conditions are more convenient (TBMM, 2015).The essential motivations for the immigration to Turkey are political uncertainty in neighboring countries, Turkey's geographical location as a bridge between continents and the job opportunities (Deniz, 2014). Due to the aforementioned reasons migrations to Anatolia from many regions occurred throughout history. In this article, one of these migrations, the one from Bulgaria in 1989 is discussed.

As seen in Table 1, there has been a continuing wave of migrations to Anatolia from Bulgaria throughout history. Between January 1, 1950 through November 30, 1951, 154.393 of our compatriots came to Turkey (TBMM, 2015). Between 1969 to 1978, 130.000 Turkish citizens immigrated within the frame of Turkey-Bulgaria Agreement on Close Relative Migration (Gunduz, 2013).

The next wave of migration took place in 1989. The general characteristics and the distinctiveness of this wave are as follows (Kuyucuklu, 2015);.

• This migration which began in the middle of 1989 was not based on any agreement between the two countries.

• Migration took place very quickly and the number of immigrants in a period of two and a half months exceeded 320.000

• Immigrants couldn't sell their real estates and they could only bring some part of their movables along.

The reasons of this migration; the existence of large Turkish minority groups in Bulgaria, the name-changing of Turkish people, the ban on Turkish language, the growth of the solidarity and organization among the Turks, the organizational attempts of Bulgarian intellectuals on the basis of "Human Rights", resistance by the Turkish minority, the emergence of Glasnost and Perestroika movements in the Soviet Union and the Western pressure (Kuyucuklu, 2015). On June 2nd, 1989, President Todor Jivkov had declared on TV, "Open the border crossing Turkey and let them get out!" in the face of the resistance by the Republic of Turkey and international reactions (TBMM, 2015). From this date on, the Republic of Turkey has allowed visa-free movement of the Turks living in Bulgaria. Thus, from June 2nd, 1989 until August 22nd, 1989, some 311.862 Bulgarian Turks entered into the homeland (Atasoy, 2010). However, Turkey ended the visa-free travel agreement after August 22nd, 1989 in order to compel the Bulgarian government to a comprehensive migration agreement as well as to secure property and social rights of the Turkish compatriots living in Bulgaria. Until May 1990, 34.098 compatriots entered Turkey by visa (TBMM, 2015).

Table 1: Migration to Anatolia from Bulgaria in Republican Era

Years (between)	Number of Immigrants People (In thousands)
1950-1951	154.393
1969-1978	130.000*
1989-1991	320.000*

*Approximate figure

73.615 compatriots who were not welcomed by their relatives, who were unsure about permanent settlement, and who did not want to give up their social rights in Bulgaria were forced to return to Bulgaria until December 18th, 1989 (DPT, 1990).

Economic and Financial Aspect of Migration

The economic aspect of the immigration are discussed with a view to employment, labor force prices and general level of prices and financial aspect are discussed in terms of the amount of spending for immigrants and weight of these expenditures on the budget.

The unplanned and uncontrolled acceptance of 313.894 immigrants in a short period of time as six months affected the economy of Turkey more than expected (Cetin, 2008). 35% of immigrants are secondary school graduates, 17% of immigrants are high school graduates (Sirin (2014). The Turkish government placed the qualified immigrants to work in factories and made regulations for immigrants to get a job in government departments (Kemaloglu, 2012). 15.898 people were placed to jobs by the Turkish Employment Agency and 17.747 people by the provincial governor's offices (Cetin, 2008). Many factories and workplaces hired our compatriots at much lower prices by firing the existing senior workers (Kemaloglu, 2012). Bulgarian immigrants were preferred by employers due to their willingness to work, training, and differences on issues such as work discipline (Erder 2007). As immigrants worked at half the wage they earned in Bulgaria, this resulted in declining wages and increased unemployment. If we look at the supply side, low wage and well-trained immigrant workers have contributed to a reduction in labor costs. Uninsured women supported the home economics by sewing and doing embroidery and these activities have had culturally positive impacts on the local citizens.

In terms of the general level of prices; house and land quickly escalated in Bursa, İzmir, Tekirdağ, Çorlu, and rental houses were rented out (Atasoy, 2012).

In examining the financial aspect of immigration, qualities and quantities of expenditures and their respective weights in the budget are considered.

Cash and Real Aids

The real and cash benefits for immigrants from various institutions and organizations with the beginning of the migration are shown in Table 2. 50 thousand TL per person and the truck fees by the Poor and Destitute Fund, 100 million TL worth of drugs by Pharmaceutical Industry Employers' Association and the Ministry of Health, 1 billion 667 million TL monetary aid by Religious Affairs and the Meat and Fish Authority and 50 million TL worth of shoes, shirts, pants and coats by Sümerbank (Kemaloglu, 2012: 209, 213,214).

Table 2: Cash and Real Aids

Source of the Aid	Amount of Aid (TL)	Scope of Aid
The Poor Fund	50 thousand per person	Subsidy
The Poor and Destitute Fund	-	Truck Fee
Sümerbank	50 million	Shoes, pants, shirts, coats
Pharmaceutical Industry Employers' Union and the Ministry of Health	100 million	Drug aid
Religious Affairs and the Meat and Fish Institution	1 billion and 667 million	Subsidy

Apart from the aids listed in Table 2 and within the scope of an agreement between Turkey and UN Food and Agricultural Organization (FAO), 3,048,780 USD worth of food—mainly composed of wheat flour, crops, beans and sugar—were distributed to immigrants. Again, in line with the principle of social state, a commission established by provincial governors repeatedly visited immigrants' houses and helped them solve their various problems such as food, firewood and coal, education and health (Cetin, 2008:262).

In addition, following the introduction of a law to include a new item in the 2510 Housing Act in June 14th, 1934 citizenship processes of the compatriots were decided to be maintained as an accelerated procedure and they were considered to be free and settled immigrants (TBMM 2015) and exempt from customs duties for their possessions to be brought from Bulgaria from January 1, 1989 onwards (Cumhuriyet, 1989).

Temporary Housing

June and july 1989; 20.795 of the immigrants were placed in camps in Edirne and Kırklareli and some of them were placed in the school and dormitories (Kemaloglu, 2012). The tends in the Edirne and Kırklareli were changed because of the approaching winter, government had provided 400 units pole tents for family and camps belonging to all public institutions and organizations had been opened for compatriots since the date of September 1, 1989 (Kemaloglu, 2012:218-223). Ten billion TL had been spent on temporary housing until August 10, 1989 (Kuyucuklu, 2014:284).

Because of approaching winter a single type of 500 prefabricated house which were 60 to 72 square meters were decided to be done as of September (Kemaloglu, 2012:222). As a result, 900 house had been built for needs of immigrants (Sirin, 2014: 263).

Seven thousand families of our compatriots that were placed in 44 cities by year 1989, had been placed in home and the same period 14 billion TL had provided to them (Kemaloglu, 2012:225). Because of job opportinities immigrants settled mostly in Marmara Region.

Training Aids

In order to facilitate The Turks from Bulgaria to be employed, Ministry of National Education opened language and training courses and June 22, 1989 opened a school in order to educate the children living in tentcities in Edirne. UNICEF and Turkey Business Association had created a traditional Turkish crafts courses Project for women migrants such as ceramics and pottery, embroidery, lace, knitting, crochet ands ewing and the people who graduateed from the course had found various jobs (Cetin, Fall 2008:261). Kndreal Project which covered tourism, textiles, services, industry, manufacturing, construction and electricity sectors in collaboration with the UN Development Programme (relatives) was started, with this programme in 1989 25 courses, in 1990 85 courses, in 1991 345 courses, in 1992 64 courses and in 1993 12 courses were opened, a total of 9150 people had received a certificate from the setraining (Cetin, Fall 2008:261).

15 thousand quota was reserved for immigrant children in boarding schools. In addition, the Ministry of National Education prepared programs and provided job opportunities in Turkey for migrant teachers to ensure their compliance with the Turkish education system (Kemaloglu, 2012:226). In addition, 75 primary schools, 100 secondary schools and 150 university students were given grants by Social Assistance and Solidarity Fund (Cetin, Fall 2008:262) and important facilities were provided to the entrance to the university for students who continue their education. With the opening of schools, uniforms, shoes, stationery, tools and equipments were provided to our compatriots children by the Social Assistance and Solidarity Foundation. In addition to determining the educational and professional status of immigrants, surveys were carried out (Kuyucuklu, 2014: 287).

Job Opportunities and Social Security

In particular, Jobs were provided to 2 400 teachers and 3 000 health personnels in the public sector, 6500 also in agriculture (TBMM, 2015). According to official records as of October 1989, while the number of registered families who emigrated from Bulgaria to Turkey were 52 568, the total number of recruits was 39 847people (Kemaloglu, 2012:14).

Immigrants had not experienced problems with regard to health services, they had benefited from social security services and spending on public hospitals had been borne by the state (Sirin, 2014).

As a result, as shown in Table 3 as of March 1990, the total amount of assistance was made to the kin137 billion, 74 billion 777 million TL of this assistance was social assistance, 62 billion 147 million TL had been realized in the form of rental assistance (Kemaloglu, 2012: 225). 137 Billion TL is negligible number with in transfer spending figures of two years.

Table 3:Total Assistance Amount as of March 1990

Type of Aid	Amount
Social Aid	74 Billion 777 Million
Housing Benefit	62 Billion 147 Million
TOTAL	137 Billion

Table 4:Public Expenditure Type and Quantity in 1989-1990 (Billion TL)

Years	Total Expenditure	Current Expenditures	Personnel Expenditures	Other Current Expenditures	Capital Expenditures	Transfer Expenditures
1989	38.871	16.660	12.539	4.121	5.818	16.393
1990	68.527	33.452	26.465	6.987	10.055	25.020

Source: TUIK, İstatistik Göstergeler 1923-2013, Ankara, 2014, s.589.

Table 5: Government transfers in the years 1989-1990 Shares in Total Transfer Spending

Years	Participation Shares of the institution	Economic Transfer and Capital Formation and Assistance	Financial Transfers	Social Transfers	Debt Transfers	Other Debt Payments	Expropriation and Building Purchase	Others	Total
1989	7,9	3,8	12,2	8,6	56,7	8,7	1,7	0,4	100
1990	6,5	4,6	14,7	7,1	53,8	11,1	1,6	0,6	100

Source: TC. Maliye Bakanlığı, Bütçe Gerekçeleri, 1990, 1995., Aktaran: Aytac (2004): 73).

This situation stemed from Turkey's debt burden at the time. Because, as seen in Table 5, the maximum share of transfer spending in two years was devoted to interest payments.

Conclusion

The Turks who could not endure the assimilation policies of the Bulgarian government were subjected to a kind of forced immigration, and began to come to our country just after Turkey opened its doors in the summer of 1989 without any immigration agreement. 320.000 people came to Turkey under this forced migration.

Forced migration caught both immigrants and Turkey unprepared. Immigrants could not bring along any valuable goods. They left some of their family members in Bulgaria and they waited for long hours at border crossings. They lived in temporary settlement areas within schools, camps and tent cities. Those who were lucky settled to live with their relatives. Immigrants who were clearly expelled from Bulgaria and couldn't find exactly what they expected in Turkey began to work at low-wages. Given the fact that they were qualified and hardworking personnel, the employers had willingly chosen to employ them.

Looking at the situation in terms of Turkey, the management of this immigration has been a failure. Camps were established for the immigrants; houses were built; money, food, clothing, educational aids were provided and some immigrants were placed in public services and private sector. However, the number and nature of the camps had remained inadequate, house construction lagged and there had been problems in employment. The most significant reason for this lack of coordination is the shortage of necessary resources. At the time, the largest share of the budget transfers went to debt interest payments. This prevented the allocation of enough resources to social transfers. The share of the total aid to immigrants- 137.000 billion TL- even in the overall transfer spending is negligible.

These financial difficulties had inevitably reflected in the whole economy, as unemployment increased and employment rates decreased. Again, this mass migration raised house and rental prices. From the viewpoint of entrepreneurs, qualified, hard-working and low-wage workers helped reduce costs. Immigrants with their traditional handicrafts set examples to local public with many uninsured women living on their handicrafts.

As a result immigrants who received little support from the state are trying to maintain their lives in Turkey largely by their own efforts.

References

http://www.tbmm.gov.tr/kultursanat/yayinlar/yayin073/073_00_010.pdf (13.3.2015).

Atasoy, E. (2010). "Siyasi Coğrafya Işığında Bulgaristan Türklerinin 1989 Yılındaki Zorunlu Göçü", İstanbul Üniversitesi Edebiyat Fakültesi Coğrafya Bölümü Coğrafya Dergisi, Sayı 21, İstanbul.

Aytaç, D. (2004). "Türkiye'de Konsolide Bütçe Harcamalarının Gelişimi: Avrupa Birliği Ülkeleri ile Bir Karşılaştırma", Yayınlanmamış Yüksek Lisans Tezi, Ankara: Ankara Üniversitesi.

Çetin, T. (2008) (1). "Bulgaristan'daki Soydaşlarımızın Türkiye'ye Göç Etme Süreçlerini Etkileyen Bazı Değişkenlerin İncelenmesi", Türk Dünyası İncelemeleri Dergisi/Journal of Turkish World Studies, Cilt:VIII, Sayı 1, İzmir.

Çetin, T. (Fall 2008) (2). "Bulgaristan'dan Türkiye'ye Son Türk Göçünün (1989) Sosyo-Ekonomik Etkileri", International Periodical Fort he Languages, Literature and History of Turkish o Tukic, Volume 3/7/.

Deniz, T. "Uluslararası Göç Sorunu Perspektifinde Türkiye", TSA / YIL: 18 S: 1, Nisan 2014. http://www.tsadergisi.org/Makaleler/756705266_19_279_175-204.pdf (07.03.2015).

Cumhuriyet (1989). "Göçmenler İçin İki Tasarı", Cumhuriyet, 15 Haziran 1989.

Gündüz, A. O. "Bulgaristan'dan Türkiye'ye Türk Göçü (1989 Örneği)", Kırklareli Üniversitesi Balkan Araştırmaları Uygulama ve Araştırma Merkezi (Kasım 2013) http://acikerisim.kirklareli.edu.tr:8080/xmlui/bitstream/handle/123456789/225/2013-.html.pdf?sequence=1.

Erder, S. (2007). Yabancısız Kurgulanan Ülkenin Yabancıları, der: ARI A., Türkiye'de Yabancı İşçiler: Uluslararası Göç, İşgücü ve Nüfus Hareketleri, Derin Yayınları, İstanbul, 2007, s.62-66.

Kemaloğlu, Ayşegül İnginar (2012). Bulgaristan'dan Türk Göçü (1985-1989), Atatürk Araştırma Merkezi, Ankara, 2012.

Kuyucuklu, N. "Bulgaristan'dan 1989 Göçünün Nedenleri, Oluşumu ve Olası Sonuçları" http://webcache.googleusercontent.com/search?q=cache:-uhyjq42UPkJ:www.journals.istanbul.edu.tr/iusiyasal/article/download/1023011952/10230112 14+&cd=2&hl=tr&ct=clnk&gl=tr (16.03.2015).

Şirin, A. (2014). 1989 Zorunlu Göçü ve Göçmenlerin Sosyal Entegrasyonu: Tekirdağ'daki Bulgaristan Göçmenleri Üzerine Bir Çalışma, Uluslararası Balkan Kongresi, 28-29 Nisan 2014, Kocaeli.

TBMM Tutanak Dergisi, Dönem 18, Cilt 38, Yasama Yılı 3, 27 Aralık 1989.

TBMM Tutanak Dergisi, Dönem 18, Cilt 29, Yasama Yılı 2, 16 Haziran 1989.

TUİK, İstatistik Göstergeler 1923-2013, Ankara, 2014.

Continuity or Change in Turkey's Mass Migration Policy: From 1989 émigrés to Syrian "guests"

N. Aslı Şirin Öner* and Deniz Genç*

Introduction

As a country being a stage for a variety of migratory movements for many years, Turkey, until recently, did not have a comprehensive migration and asylum policy which takes into account of the realities of those movements and responds accordingly. The need for such policy has brought with it the efforts to develop a migration regime of which the new Law on Foreigners and International Protection (LFIP) is an essential element. The factors which played a role in the growing need for a migration and asylum policy are the increasing number of irregular migrants in the country and the deterioration of the Syrian refugee crisis. The lack of a comprehensive migration and asylum policy has loomed large when the country is a stage for mass migration movements.

The present paper examines Turkey's migration and asylum policy in the case of mass migration of two groups: 1989 émigrés considered as "kindreds" and "guests" fleeing the conflict in Syria since 2011. The main question is whether there has been a paradigmatic shift in the management of mass migrations in Turkey. It is argued in the paper that in the field of migration and asylum, rather than continuity or change in terms of policy, there is a newly emerging policy. The LFIP is quite important in that sense because until the adoption of the LFIP in April 2013, we cannot talk about a comprehensive migration policy in Turkey. For the immigrants of Turkish origin such as the émigrés from Bulgaria or specific groups like Ahıska Turks, *ad hoc* solutions have been developed.

As known, there are various studies on the mass migration from Bulgaria in the summer of 1989 and the recent flight of Syrians. In the latter case, there is a limited number of studies because it is an ongoing crisis. Yet those studies help us draw a picture of the situation both in Syria and the neighbouring countries hosting the Syrians, namely Turkey, Lebanon, Jordan and Iraq. The mass migration of Syrians is a sign of a new period in Turkey's migration management. In that sense, it makes a difference and thus is important in itself. Yet, examining the similarities and differences between the state's approach to these two groups is crucial since it will help us understand Turkey's policy in the case of mass migration. On the other hand, we can talk about neither migration management nor a comprehensive migration and asylum policy until the adoption of the LFIP and the establishment of the General Directorate of Migration Management. It is a gap in itself. Hence, there is a gap in the existing literature. In that sense, in this paper, we try to examine the emerging migration and asylum policy.

The present paper is based on two qualitative researches. The mass migration from Bulgaria in the summer of 1989 is in fact part of a broader research on comparing the migration and integration of 1989 émigrés and Ahıska Turks

* Assist. Prof. Dr., European Union Institute, Marmara University.
* Assist. Prof. Dr., Department of Political Science and International Relations, İstanbul Medipol University.

(Meskhetian Turks) in Turkey, carried out in the four cities of Marmara region, namely İstanbul, Bursa, Tekirdağ and Kocaeli (Gebze district) in the 2010-2013 period. The recent migration of Syrians is based on a research conducted in the neighborhoods of Istanbul.[2] In the research on Syrian migration, in order to understand the attitudes of Istanbulites towards Syrian migrants, 16 in-depth face-to-face and 214 phone interviews were conducted with the local governors of the neighborhoods in 21 counties of Istanbul. Backed up by secondary literature, the findings of these two researches are evaluated around same themes, such as entry, reception and registration, temporary accommodation, shelter and housing, employment, and education and healthcare in a comparative manner.

The paper is composed of three main parts. In the first part, the context of Turkey's experience with mass migration is set out. The fact of Turkey being a stage for numerous migration movements is underlined. The second part is about the legal and institutional arrangements in the migration and asylum field. The time is almost a century. It begins with the early years of the Turkish Republic and continues until today. The focus is the limited nature of what has been done in the migration and asylum field, particularly until 1990s and 2000s. The third and last part is about Turkey's approach in two cases of mass migration: the forced migration of Turks – the "kindreds" – from Bulgaria – taking place in the summer of 1989 and the migration of Syrian "guests" – currently "people with temporary protection status" – continuing since April 2011. The findings of two researches are evaluated in a comparative manner.

Turkey's Experience of Mass Migration: The Context

Migration and refugee movements are not new phenomena for Turkey. Historically, since the Ottoman times, the land of today's Turkey has received people coming with mass migrations and refugees (Latif, 2002). Early years of the Republic, in particular, were marked by mass migrations. While there was a huge volume of outflow of non–Muslim populations from Anatolia through forced migrations and deportations, Muslim populations were immigrating to Anatolia from the territories that belonged to Ottoman Empire no more. Autochthonous Christian people of Anatolia, Greeks and Armenians left in large numbers and Muslims from Balkans, Caucasus, Crimea and from other former Ottoman territories arrived to today's Turkey (Keyder, 2003; Kirişçi, 2003b; Şaul, 2013; Erder, 2000). As Şaul (2013) notes, immigration of Muslims from former Ottoman territories has become a recurrent movement in the history of Turkish Republic. According to Erder (2000), in the period between 1923 and 1997 more than 1.6 million such immigrants settled in Turkey and most of them arrived before the 1960s. Though the early years of the Republic were mainly marked by the mass migrations and refugee movements of these aforementioned groups, they have increasingly involved refugees and asylum-seekers other than these groups since the end of the 1970s. Turkey has received mass-influxes of Iranians, Turks of Bulgaria, Iraqis, Chechens, Bosniacs (Bosnian Muslims) and very recently Syrians. In line with these, this paper examines the migration policy of Turkey in

---

[2] This research is being conducted by Assist. Prof. Dr. Deniz Genç and Dr. Merve Özdemirkıran from Bahçeşehir University.

the case of mass migration of two groups: the ethnic Turks of Bulgaria who migrated forcefully to Turkey in the summer of 1989 and the Syrians, who are displaced as a result of the conflict in Syria and have been forced to migrate to Turkey in large numbers since 2011.

The ethnic Turks of Bulgaria migrated to Turkey in three waves in the post-1945 period. The first wave occurred in the 1949-51 period. In August 1950, it was announced by the Bulgarian government that 250.000 ethnic Turks had applied to leave for Turkey because of economic reasons. Turkey opened its borders. Yet, faced with a huge influx, it had to close its borders in November 1950. Two months later, the two governments reached an agreement that Bulgaria would allow only the Turks possessing a Turkish entry visa to leave. However, Bulgarian government acted contrarily and continued evicting Turks. So Turkey closed its border again in November 1951 (Poulton, 1991). In the period of 1949-51, about 156.000 ethnic Turks emigrated (Şimşir, 2009).

The second wave took place in the 1970s. Following the 1968 Agreement on the Emigration of Close Relatives signed between Turkey and Bulgaria, Turks started emigrating. The Agreement allowed the departure of close relatives of the Turks who had come to Turkey in the previous phase. The aim was the reunion of separated families. The Agreement expired in November 1978. In the period 1969-78, 130.000 Turks came.

The last wave is the mass exodus to Turkey in the 1989 summer taking place as a result of the Bulgarian government's assimilationist policy which had started in the 1960s and gained a violent dimension in the mid-1980s. The renaming campaign carried out in the last days of 1984 and early months of 1985 marked the beginning of assimilationist policies involving coercion (Bojkov, 2004).

By the end of the 1980s, the objections of the Turkish minority to the assimilationist policies grew. In May 1989, there were hunger strikes leading to mass protests in the Turkish districts of northeast Bulgaria.[3] The Turks demanded the return of their names and respect for their customs and traditions. The demonstrations which quickly spread throughout Bulgaria,[4] were brutally suppressed killing many demonstrators. Towards the end of the month, the President of Bulgaria, T. Zhivkov gave a speech on TV stating that "the Bulgarians who had forcefully become Muslims in the past, could go to Turkey as tourists if they wished". He also demanded Turkey to open its borders to receive all "Bulgarian Muslims", who wanted to live there. Upon Zhivkov's speech, the then Turkish President, T. Özal announced that the borders were open to the Turks of Bulgaria. In the June 2-August 22 period, 311.862 Turks migrated from Bulgaria.[5]

---

[3] On 20-27 May, mass demonstrations in which thousands of Turks participated, took place in numerous towns and cities such as Bohçalar, Akkadınlar (Dulovo), Vokil, Cerkovna, Vodno, Kemallar (Isperih), Cebel, Beli Lom, Osmanpazar, Şumnu (Shumen), Gradnica, Benkovski, Ezerçe, Razgrad, Mahmuzlar, Dobriç. The mass demonstrations started with the following statement: "Türklüğümüz'den asla vazgeçmeyiz, Bulgar isimlerini almayız" (We will never give up our Turkishness and we will not take Bulgarian names), see (Şimşir,2009).

[4] The demonstrations clearly indicated that the so-called "rebirth process" did not succeed.

[5] After August 22, 34.098 people came with visa until May 1990. In the meantime, some of the émigrés returned to Bulgaria after Zhivkov was ousted in November 1989. Among the Turks coming in the June 2-May 1990 period, the number of those who stayed is 212.688 (Şimşir, 2009: 447).

The influx of Syrians is the other case of mass migration that Turkey is still experiencing. Since the outbreak of the civil war in Syria in March 2011, 9 million Syrians are estimated to have fled their homes. According to the UNHCR (March 20, 2015), almost 4 million Syrians have taken refuge in Syria's immediate neighbours including Turkey. Fleeing from atrocities, the first group of 252 Syrian citizens sought refuge in Turkey by crossing into the province of Hatay on April 29, 2011. In the early phases of the Syrian crisis, Turkish government expected that the Assad regime would soon collapse and it estimated that the Syrians would stay 2 to 3 weeks with their number not exceeding a 100 thousand (Erdoğan, 2014). Thus, it declared, in October 2011, an *open-door policy* towards the refugees fleeing Syria (Kirişçi, 2014). However, when the crisis protracted and evolved into a civil war, the number of asylum-seekers increased. In addition, since September 19, 2014, ten thousands of Syrians from Kobane have fled to Turkey due to the offensive of Islamic State of Iraq and Syria (ISIS) to capture the city.[6] As a result of these unforeseen developments, as of March 20, 2015, the UNHCR reports that Turkey hosts more than 1.7 million registered Syrian refugees.

Different Legal & Institutional Frameworks

One of the most important points in comparing the management of mass migrations of ethnic Turks of Bulgaria and Syrian nationals to Turkey is the legal framework that regulates these migrations. In the period between 1934 and 2006, the formal settlement of foreigners in Turkey, including the ethnic Turks of Bulgaria in 1989, was regulated by the 1934 Law No.2510 on Settlement. The Law restricted the right of asylum and immigration only to the persons of 'Turkish descent and culture'. In other words, it restricted these rights to the individuals of those groups that were believed to assimilate into the Turkish identity (Kirişçi, 2003b). As the emphasis on 'Turkish descent and culture' is kept in the new Law No. 5543 on Settlement adopted in 2006, it is understood that in Turkey, the channel of facilitated formal settlement, which also leads to citizenship in a short period of time is still reserved for the individuals of such groups. The reference point of regulating the mass migration from Bulgaria in the summer of 1989 is the 1934 Law on Settlement.

Apart from the Law of 1934, Turkey did not have anything specific regarding migration management until the 1950s. The establishment of the United Nations High Commissioner for Refugees (UNHCR) and the creation of an international refugee regime in early 1950s laid down Turkey's refugee regime (Latif, 2002; Kirişçi, 2003a). Turkey became party to the UN Convention Relating to the Status of Refugees (known as the 1951 Geneva Convention) and its updating 1967 New York Protocol,[7] but maintained a 'geographical limitation' to the Convention and

---

[6] Kobane's siege by ISIS has come to an end on 26 January 2015 (New York Times, 26/01/2015). The cumulative number of admitted refugees fleeing Kobane stands at 192,147 persons (UNHCR, 2014). Since 13 November, when some 368 Syrian arrivals were recorded in Turkey, there have been no further recorded arrivals from the area of Kobane (UNHCR, 2014).

[7] The 1951 Convention was originally limited in scope to persons fleeing events taking place within Europe before 1 January 1951. With the 1967 Protocol, both the geographical and temporal limitations were removed and the Convention gained universal coverage (Convention and Protocol Relating to the Status of Refugees, http://www.unhcr.org/3b66c2aa10.html [Date of access 20/10/2014])

the Protocol under which "it applies the Convention only to persons who have become refugees as a result of events occurring in Europe". This means that Turkey does not grant refugee status to the non-European asylum-seekers.[8] In the face of mass refugee movement from Northern Iraq in the early 1990s, the first national legislation about the asylum claims in Turkey, namely the Regulation on Asylum[9] was introduced in 1994. With the Regulation, the asylum-seekers – both European and non-European – had to apply to the Turkish authorities besides the UNHCR. If an asylum-seeker had 'genuine' reasons for applying for refugee status, the applicant was granted temporary protection until his status was determined by the UNHCR (Suter, 2013:13). In line with this practice, an important implication of the Regulation came out to be that it concretized a two-tiered asylum policy. The first-tier would be applied to European asylum-seekers and people of Turkish descent, and the second-tier to non-European asylum seekers, who would file two asylum claims.

In the years following 1999, a turning point in Turkey's EU accession bid, new laws and policies were introduced. In 2005, before the accession negotiations started, the Turkish government prepared a National Action Plan for Adoption of *Acquis* on Asylum and Migration (NAPAA), according to which the existing legal structure concerning the migration area would be modernized. Following intensive work, the Law on Foreigners and International Protection (LFIP) was adopted in April 2013 and it entered into force in April 2014. The Law is the first inclusive and updated act about migration-related issues. The main migration-related issues elaborated in LFIP are visa policy, residence permits, asylum, deportation and administrative detention, and integration. Moreover, the Law established the Directorate General for Migration Management (DGMM) under the authority of the Ministry of Interior to become the single authority not only in issuing and approving visas but also in developing migration policy and managing all migration related issues. In line with these developments, Syrians' conditions in Turkey have been regulated by the Temporary Protection Regulation, which was adopted by the Turkish government on October 22, 2014 by taking the Article 91 of the LFIP as its basis. The Temporary Protection Regulation provides all registered Syrian nationals and stateless persons from Syria temporary protection and it grants Syrians the rights of access to health, to education, to social assistance and to the labor market. As UNHCR (January 2015) notes, the implementation of some of these rights such as access to the labor market will be clarified by the Ministry of Labor in the future.

Not only the laws and regulations, but also the institutions dealing with these two mass migrations are different. In the management of mass migration from Bulgaria in the 1989 summer, we come across with a "Coordination Committee" headed by a State Ministry established in the first days of the migration. State Ministry was authorized by the High Planning Agency, an agency directly affiliated

---

[8] Yet, as Kaya (2008: 3) notes, persons coming from the east are given a specific status, namely *de facto* status and these asylum-seekers are internationally protected.

[9] Its official name is 'Regulation on the Procedures and the Principles Related to Population Movements and Aliens Arriving in Turkey either as Individuals or in Groups Wishing to Seek Asylum either from Turkey or Requesting Residence Permission in order to Seek Asylum From another Country' (No. 1994/6169).

to the Prime Ministry. This "Coordination Committee" was responsible for coordinating the assistance to the "kindreds" coming *en masse*. The émigrés' first temporary accommodation and later on housing including housing benefit, their employment matching their professional skills, access to education and healthcare, food assistance and their adaptation to the social environment was carried out by the Coordination Committee (Şimşir, 2009: 445).

By the time Syrians' mass migration began, on the other hand, new institutions have been set up. Until 2014, when the LFIP entered into force, all issues related to foreigners, including their travels, visas, residence permits and the status-determination processes for their asylum applications were handled by the National Police in the Department of Foreigners, Borders and Asylum under the Directorate of General Security of the MoI. The Directorate was also responsible for the fight against human smuggling, human trafficking and irregular migration and for the orderly flow of movement in and out of the border-crossing points. As part of the EU accession process, in the mid-2000s, Turkey has started to take concrete steps to build institutional capacity that would help it in aligning with the related *acquis* in the fields of migration, asylum and borders. To these ends, Projects Directorate for Integrated Border Management (IBM) was set up under the authority of MoI in 2004, and following the adoption of the NAPAA in 2005, another Directorate on Asylum and Migration, again under the MoI, was set up. Both of these Directorates worked for the alignment processes and actively took part in the Twinning Projects. While the Projects Directorate for IBM concerted its efforts on the development of a legal and institutional framework to align with EU's IBM system, Directorate on Asylum and Migration worked hard to draft a new, comprehensive migration and asylum law for Turkey. In 2012, both Directorates have become Bureaus and with the entry into force of the LFIP, Asylum and Migration Bureau has ceased to exist as the Law established the Directorate General for Migration Management (DGMM) in April 2014.

Articles 103 and 104 of the LFIP are about DGMM. While the former one explains the establishment of the institution by noting that the body is responsible for implementing policies and strategies on migration, the latter details the responsibilities. According to the Article 104, DGMM is responsible for developing legislation and administrative capacity, for monitoring and coordinating the implementation of the policies and strategies on migration, for the tasks accorded to Law No. 5543 on Settlement, for the protection of the victims of human trafficking, about stateless persons, harmonization process, temporary protection and fight against irregular migration.

As these detailed responsibilities and tasks show, by the LFIP, DGMM has become almost the sole authority not only in devising the migration policies and strategies but also in implementing them. In line with this, since its establishment, the institution has been taking over the tasks that were used to be performed by the Department of Foreigners, Borders and Asylum under the Directorate of General Security (Emniyet Genel Müdürlüğü, 2012).[10]

---

[10] In line with this institutional building, the name of the Department has become Border-Crossing Points' Department (*Hudut Kapıları Daire Başkanlığı*) (Emniyet Genel Müdürlüğü, 2012).

In the management of Syrian migration to Turkey, in addition to the DGMM, Disaster and Emergency Management Presidency [*Afet ve Acil Durum Yönetimi Başkanlığı* (AFAD)] is the lead agency in dealing with the Syrian refugees. AFAD is affiliated to the Prime Ministry. It is responsible for setting up and managing the camps, for organizing the NGOs in the field and it also shares responsibility with the DGMM and the National Police in the registration process of the Syrian nationals.

Turkey's Policy in the case of Mass Migration: "kindreds" from Bulgaria and "guests" from Syria

In this part, we would like to examine – if there is any at all - Turkey's policy in the case of mass migration in terms of themes including the government's discourse on the migrants' status, their reception and registration, actual legal status, the issues of shelter, employment, education and healthcare.

To start with the government's discourse on the status of the migrants, we can say that 1989 émigrés are called as "kindreds" (*soydaşlar*) and in line with the Law on Settlement of 1934, they have the right to migrate to Turkey because they are of "Turkish descent and culture". In other words, they meet the criterion of migrating, settling in Turkey and acquiring Turkish citizenship.[11] As the 1934 Law and later 2006 Law recognized their entry and settlement to Turkey with facilitated access to citizenship, it can be put forth that, they have been dreamt of as part of the Turkish nation. In line with the legal framework applied to them, the governments have adopted the kindred discourse to make Turkish people accept and embrace them.

Syrians, on the other hand, have been called as 'guests' since the first entries began. Despite the calls from academia and NGOs, the government officials and agencies have continued to use the term 'guests' to describe the Syrians. The title of the latest AFAD report is a concrete example of this approach: '*Population Movements from Syria to Turkey: Being Guests in Fellow Territories*'. All speeches made by the government officials, all reports released by the government authorities and even the name of the regulation that apply to Syrians have reminded or connoted 'the *expected* temporariness' of the Syrian migration to Turkey. In line with such a discourse manifesting the unhidden expectations of the government, it is not realistic to wait for any improvement in the living conditions of the Syrians.

Entry, Reception and Registration

Regarding the reception and registration process of the émigrés, we need to note in the first place that on June 2, 1989, Turkey lifted the visa requirements temporarily so that the "kindreds" could enter the country without a visa (Şimşir, 2009: 440). As a response to the Turks' expulsion from Bulgaria, Turkey pursued an open-door policy but for a temporary period.

Migration *en masse* continued throughout the summer and as Turkey realized that it would not be able to sufficiently provide assistance to the "kindreds", the government had to reintroduce visa requirements on August 22, 1989.[12] It was

---

[11] Even though it is not a must to be of 'Turkish culture and descent' to acquire Turkish citizenship, being of Turkish descent acts as a facilitator in the process.

[12] The entry of the train carrying the "kindreds" was also banned.

not prepared enough even to provide shelter to the émigrés. The purpose of the reintroducing visa requirements was, as Şimşir (2009) notes, to exert pressure on Bulgaria so that it would agree to a detailed migration agreement. This migration agreement would guarantee the social rights of the Turks, who already migrated and who would migrate, as well as the preservation of their property in Bulgaria.

The ethnic Turks entering Turkey[13] were registered by the officials on the border. The officials asked the émigrés whether they wished to go anywhere specifically. The ones, who gave the names of their relatives/friends, were sent to stay near them. Others were provided temporary accommodation. The émigrés registered at the border were given temporary ID documents called "émigré paper" (*muhacir kağıdı*).

Concerning the legal status of 1989 émigrés, we may say that, with the help of an additional provision to the Law on Settlement of 1934 (dated 16/06/1989), they were considered as "independent or settled immigrants who are of Turkish descent and culture". So their immigration, settlement in Turkey and acquisition of Turkish citizenship and property were facilitated (Şirin, 2011: 364). They collectively acquired Turkish citizenship in a couple of years. In the meantime, they used their temporary ID documents.[14]

While this was the case for the 'kindreds', Syrians have been subject to different practices since their entry into the country. First of all, before the war, there was a very close relationship between Syria and Turkey and this close relationship had led to the reciprocal liberalization of visa policies in 2009. It is important to note that with the help of this liberalization, many Syrians could enter to Turkey with their valid passports without any problems when the crisis escalated (Kirişçi, 2014, 14). As UNHCR (2014) notes, Syrians who entered Turkey regularly with their passports, were able to receive a one-year residence permit by applying to the Foreigner's Department of the Ministry of Interior. Apart from these regular entries, asylum-seekers have started entering Turkey in April 2011. In the early phases of the crisis, the Turkish government stated that Turkey would maintain an open-border policy for the Syrians. According to AFAD (2014: 5), "no Syrian brother is returned from the door". Amnesty International (2014: 20), on the other hand, claims that "official border crossings have become […] accessible only to the small minority of refugees from Syria who possess valid passports [and that many Syrians] are being denied access to the Turkish territory." The institution continues to report that the Turkish authorities let refugees with passports and the individuals with urgent medical or humanitarian needs enter Turkey by referring to the limited capacity of the accommodation centers in the country (*ibid.*). Even if this is the case, the number of Syrians in Turkey, being more than 1.7 million, shows that Turkey has tried to keep its borders open as long as possible – especially during the most severe days of the civil war.

---

[13] Over 300.000 ethnic Turks forcefully migrated to Turkey in convoys (Şimşir, 2009: 441).

[14] Moreover, it is to be underlined that since the Bulgarian government sent the ethnic Turks to Turkey as tourists, they did not lose their Bulgarian citizenship. If they went to the Bulgarian police department with their birth documents, they could get their passports without any problem. So the 1989 émigrés, who claimed their Bulgarian passports, were able to acquire double citizenship.

Moreover, the registration of the Syrians has been far more protracted when compared with that of the 'kindreds'. Though there are many Syrian nationals who entered Turkey regularly in the earlier phases of the crisis, since April 2011, the Syrian movement to Turkey took place as a mass refugee movement. As a result of this influx, there have been problems in their registration process and their exact number in the country is still unknown to the relevant authorities. The registration of earlier asylum-seekers is going on. In addition to AFAD and DGMM, the police officers in the cities where the camps have been set up are responsible for registering the Syrians and providing ID Cards to them (Dinçer, et.al., 2013).[15] As noted above, as of April 1, 2015, the Directorate General for Migration Management reports that there are more than 1.7 million registered Syrian nationals in Turkey. According to AFAD President (AFAD, 2015: 2), there are "almost 2 million Syrian nationals" in the country and 1.8 million of them have been registered through biometric registration. In reality, as the registration process continues, it is understood that there are still many unregistered Syrians. The registered ones are provided with a foreigner identity number, which gives them access to the healthcare and education system (Nüfus ve Vatandaşlık İşleri Genel Müdürlüğü, 2015).

Temporary Accommodation, Shelter & Housing

In terms of temporary accommodation, it is to be noted that the émigrés were sent to cities such as Edirne, İzmir, Aydın etc. where they were settled in schools, dormitories and guesthouses of public agencies. Because it was summer, schools and dormitories were available at that time. When these were full, refugee camps named "tent-city" were set up in cities such as Kırklareli (Gaziosmanpaşa camp), Bursa, Adapazarı and İstanbul (Küçükçekmece and Kağıthane districts). Some of the émigrés were sent to the transit accommodation centre in Edirne. Assistance in the camps were provided by the Turkish Red Crescent (*Kızılay*).

In addition to providing temporary shelter to the émigrés, a dwelling-building project was initiated. 450 dwellings were built in Kırklareli, 200 in Edirne, 100 in Tekirdağ and 150 in Manisa (Devlet Planlama Teşkilatı, 1990). Starting from November 1990, we come across with another housing project, this time carried out by Emigre Dwelling Coordinatorship of Housing Development Administration (TOKİ).[16] The émigrés would pay fees (minimum amount of fee was 2.500.000 TL), and the houses built (dwellings) would be distributed by lot. The émigrés who did prepayment or who paid much more than the minimum amount (e.g. 8.000.000 TL) were given houses without any lot. The ones who paid their fees but could not get any house were given plots in the cities where émigré dwellings were built (about 4000 émigrés were given plots). The ones who got neither plot nor house were given the right to reclaim their fees. Furthermore, as Barutçugil (1990) notes, to assist the émigrés who rented flats in suburbs of Bursa and İstanbul, the Social Assistance and Solidarity Fund provided housing benefit (maximum amount was 300.000 TL) for a year (September 1989-September

---

[15] UNHCR is supporting AFAD and other authorities in this process with mobile registration units (UNHCR, 2014).
[16] Before TOKİ, the Emigre Dwelling Coordiinatorship was responsible to State Ministry dealing with the mass migration from Bulgaria.

1990).[17] In addition to housing benefit, there was food assistance. The émigrés were able to get food from the officials by showing their "émigré papers".

Syrians, on the other hand, express that their main problem is housing (Erdoğan, 2014). Together with the Turkish Red Crescent, AFAD provides shelter to the refugees; it sets up and runs refugee camps in the border provinces. According to DGMM, there are 25 accommodation centers located in 10 provinces near to the Turkish-Syrian border (Göç İdaresi Genel Müdürlüğü, 2015).[18] The camps were set up at a time when it was expected that the regime in Syria would soon collapse and that refugees would return to their homes in a short period of time. So, the conditions are not so favorable any longer as the war is entering its fifth year at the time of writing. As a matter of fact, the camp residents have many complaints about the conditions, and these complaints increase with the winter.[19] Moreover, the camps can host only 254.681 Syrian nationals with leaving 1.502.581 Syrians outside temporary accommodation centers (Göç İdaresi Genel Müdürlüğü, 2015). Compared to the camp refugees, the ones living in urban areas are faced with really tough conditions. With the influx of refugees, a housing shortage has emerged resulting in an increase in rents across the country.[20] In line with this, they come across problems in finding housing not only in the border cities but also in big cities.[21]

Employment

In terms of employment, as Scott (1991) notes, the government requested help from the International Labour Organisation (ILO) on conducting a research on the employment patterns of the émigrés and the effects of these patterns on their life conditions. The objective was to administer the labour market more efficiently. The research financed by the United Nations Development Program (UNDP) was carried out by the Ministry of Health.[22] Making use of the results of this research, the government provided assistance to the émigrés. For instance, they were provided vocational training courses. The ones who were teachers by profession attended adaptation classes. Moreover, the employers were required to employ a certain number of 1989 émigrés in their enterprises (Şirin, 2011).

---

[17] The ones who came with visa in December 1989 were also provided this benefit (Şirin 2012).

[18] The camps are reported to be relatively good in terms of the quality of shelter and services provided. There are medical centres, schools, recreational opportunities and vocational training programs in the camps. Due to the quality of accommodation, the International Crisis Group refers to the camps in Turkey as the "best refugee camps ever seen" (Intermational Crisis Group, 2013:8).

[19] For more on camp conditions both in Turkey and other countries hosting Syrian refugees see (ORSAM, 2014).

[20] For more on the problems of shelter and housing see (ORSAM, 2014; Amnesty International, 2014).

[21] For example, in Akçakale, a small town in Şanlıurfa, one of the provinces bordering Syria because the refugee camp was full, 150-200 people were living on the side of a highway (Amnesty International, 2014). In other border provinces such as Hatay, Gaziantep, many refugees talking to Amnesty International complained about being refused as tenants by Turkish landlords due to their national origin (ibid.).

[22] There are other researches on the employment of the 1989 émigrés. One of them is published in 1990. It is Prof. Dr. İsmet S. Barutçugil's research in Turkish titled "The Employment Problems of Kindreds who were Forced to Migrate from Bulgaria in 1989 Summer and Solutions" (1989 Yaz Aylarında Bulgaristan'dan Göçe Zorlanan Soydaşların İstihdam Sorunları ve Çözüm Önerileri).

Apart from the assistance provided by the government, the émigrés had access to the labour market in a relatively short period of time.[23] They found jobs either with the help of their relatives or on their own. One may say that they looked for jobs without being selective at all. They were ready to work in any place. Some of the émigrés were relatively lucky since they have found jobs in a short time. However, there was a mismatch between most of the jobs they have found and their professional skills. This situation did not matter for them because they did not have a chance to be selective.

When compared with the 'kindreds' access to the labor market, Syrians' access is more problematic. Article 29 of the Temporary Protection Regulation (October 22, 2014) notes that the principles and the conditions of the temporary protected people's access to the labor market is determined by the Council of Ministers (CoM) upon the proposal of the Ministry of Labor and Social Security. The Regulation continues by clarifying that the individuals with temporary protection IDs can apply to the Ministry of Labor and Social Security to obtain work permits to work in those sectors and geographical places determined by the CoM. In line with the Temporary Protection Regulation, the Ministry of Labor and Social Security has submitted a draft law on the employment of foreigners in Turkey (TBMM, 2015). Article 23 of the draft aims to regulate the temporary protected individuals' access to the labor market. Though the Commission of Health, Family, Labor and Social Security has brought many amendments to the draft before its submission to the Turkish Grand National Assembly, it is understood that when it is adopted, the draft is going to provide work permits to the temporary protected individuals six months after they register themselves.

As the draft is still being worked on, it is difficult to say that Syrians have legal access to the labor market in Turkey. According to the labor statistics provided by the Ministry of Labor and Social Security (Çalışma ve Sosyal Güvenlik Bakanlığı, 2015), the number of Syrians, who were able to obtain work permits since the crisis has begun, is very low: 118 Syrians in 2011; 220 in 2012 and 794 in 2013. As this is the case, Syrians work irregularly in the labor market and they are vulnerable to the exploitation of employers. As the findings of the ongoing research conducted by Deniz Genç and Merve Özdemirkıran in the neighborhoods of Istanbul show that they are paid half and sometimes one third of the minimum wage in Turkey.

Education & Healthcare

Lastly, in the fields of education and healthcare, we have to note that the children of the kindreds were provided adaptation classes including language classes. Turkish courses and courses on religion and history were taught. In Bulgaria, the children of the émigrés were speaking Turkish at home even though the Bulgarian authorities banned speaking Turkish in public places. So the children had problems in reading and writing in Turkish. Thus Turkish courses were indeed important for them (Şirin, 2011). The adaptation classes continued until the new academic year started in September.

---

[23] The Acts facilitating the émigrés' access to the labour market are the 1932 Law No. 2007 on Arts and Services Assigned to Turkish Citizens (abolished in 2003 with the Law No. 4817 on Work Permits of Foreigners) and the 1981 Law No. 2527 on Turkish Raced Foreigner's Freely Performing their Professions and Arts, Being Employed in Public, Private Institutions and Workplaces.

In addition to the classes in summer 1989, about 2000 students were enrolled in boarding schools and they did not pay any tuition fees (Devlet Planlama Teşkilatı, 1990); 75 primary school students, 100 secondary school students and 150 college students were given scholarship by the Social Assistance and Solidarity Fund (*Fak-Fuk-Fon*). Furthermore, the students who started university programs in Bulgaria but had to leave their schools due to the forced migration to Turkey were given the right to continue in the departments they were enrolled.

In the field of healthcare, we may underline the fact that the 1989 émigrés, like in the other fields, were not faced with any problems in this field. At the beginning, while the émigrés were staying in camps – the so-called "tent-cities" – they had free access to healthcare. Later on, they had right to social security. So their expenditures in public hospitals were covered by the Social Security System. In the first years following their migration to Turkey, they made use of the "Green Card" program[24] – health insurance scheme for the poor, as well.

Similar to the other fields, unlike the 'kindreds', the Syrians have had difficulties in accessing education system in Turkey. According to the Turkish national law, "all children in Turkey, including foreigners, have the right to receive primary and secondary school education free of charge" (UNHCR, January 2015: 4). However, as the Turkish government expected that the Syrian asylum-seekers would stay in the border camps for a very short period of time, the Ministry of National Education prepared itself only to offer schooling to 'the guest students' within the camps in Arabic in line with the Turkish curriculum (Seydi, 2014). As explained by the then Minister of National Education Ömer Dinçer, in these early phases of the crisis the aim was to "take care of the education needs of the Syrian children in the camps without adopting an encouraging attitude for the stay of their families in Turkey" (Dünya Bülteni, 31.07.2012). According to Seydi (2014) this attitude was kept until the mid-2013, when the Ministry started to issue successive circulars to work out the education needs of the Syrian children. It should be noted that by that time, the number of camp and non-camp Syrian asylum-seekers had increased in an unprecendented pace and reached to almost a million with more than two-thirds of them being non-camp refugees (AFAD, 2013).

The latest circular (Circular on Foreigners' Access to Education (No. 2014/21) was adopted in September 2014. According to this circular and the Temporary Protection Regulation, registration with the Turkish authorities is a pre-requisite to access education. In addition to this, Syrian children have to provide a document: a residence permit, temporary protection identification or the Foreigners' Identification Card to enroll the schools. In the absence of these documents, the children may be enrolled as 'guests'. However, there are several problems in schooling of the Syrian children in Turkey. The main one is the language barrier. The medium of instruction is Turkish in primary and secondary schools in Turkey. In addition to Turkish schools, temporary schools that teach in Arabic with a modified form of Syrian curriculum have been set up in the camps and in the cities with high number of Syrian settlers. However, these schools offer

---

[24]"Established in 1992, this program aimed to provide health benefits to the poor who are not covered through formal means of health insurance and are unable to pay for health services. It is funded through the national budget," (Menon et al, 2013: 7).

only an unofficial document, which states the students' attendance and successful completion of the school year (*ibid*). In the light of these, it is thought that very small number of Syrian children could access to the education system in Turkey.

The access to health services is also reported to be problematic for the Syrians. According to the Temporary Protection Regulation (October 22, 2014), all registered Syrians have access to healthcare system. While Amnesty International (2014: 19) reports that Syrians are "unable to access healthcare", AFAD (2014) notes that the 'guests' in the camps have uninterrupted access to the health services. AFAD continues to note that the number of urban Syrians, who have used health services, is very low when compared with the Syrians in the camps and according to the agency, this is related with their registration processes. According to DGMM, since the entry into force of the Temporary Protection Regulation, the conditions are getting better. Syrians are able to seek healthcare and the costs for their treatments are paid by the AFAD (Göç İdaresi Genel Müdürlüğü, 2015b). World Health Organization (2014:1), on the other hand, attracts attention to the "increased risk of communicable diseases, potential health service access limitations and an increased number of patients requiring psychosocial support" for the urban Syrians in Turkey.

Conclusion

In this paper, based on two separate qualitative researches, we examine Turkey's migration and asylum policy in the case of mass migration by comparing how the state treats two groups experiencing mass migration, namely 1989 émigrés from Bulgaria and Syrian nationals fleeing the conflict in their country and coming to Turkey since 2011. We departed with the following question: Is there a paradigmatic shift in the management of mass migration in Turkey when two cases of mass migration are compared? Or is there continuity or change in Turkey's mass migration policy when two cases of mass migration are compared? As we proceeded with our examination of 1989 émigrés and Syrian nationals, we came to the point of arguing that rather than continuity or change in Turkey's mass migration policy, there is a newly emerging policy in the field of migration and asylum. In other words, we cannot talk about a comprehensive migration policy until the harmonization efforts in the 2000s reaching its peak with the adoption of the LFIP in 2013. As Özer (2015: 39) notes, the LFIP is quite an important step in developing a consolidated migration policy since it draws the legal framework regarding the rights of "registered" migrants. Moreover, the regulations and arrangements based on the "right of asylum and immigration only to the persons of 'Turkish descent and culture" stated in the 1934 Law on Settlement, have been meaningless and ineffective in the cases of migration movements Turkey has been facing in the last two decades. Even the protection provided to the Syrians was in the form of ad hoc solution at the beginning (in 2011 spring) when the LFIP has not been in effect. The "temporary protection" regime was formed with the Art. 91 of the LFIP. Faced with various migration movements, Turkey was definitely in need of a comprehensive migration policy. Yet we do not know whether a migration regime would be formed if there was no Syrian refugee crisis.

Apart from the argument of the paper, there is another point we have to underline. It is about the difference in the state's discourse and treatment of two groups of migrants. 1989 émigrés were considered and called as "kindreds". Both the 1934 Law on Settlement and its revised form in 2006 recognized their entry and settlement in Turkey. The "kindred" discourse has been adopted to make Turkish people accept and embrace the 1989 émigrés. Differently from the Syrian nationals, they were not treated as "guests" and many steps were taken to ease their integration. Furthermore, there was no language barrier as in the case of Syrians. Since the Syrians are "guests" in the state's discourse and are provided "temporary protection" they are faced with many problems in various fields including the access to labour market, education and healthcare. On the one hand, the Syrians are expected to stay temporarily in Turkey. On the other hand, the picture of the civil war coming to an end in Syria and Syrians returning to their country in the short term is not a pink one. Therefore, it is perhaps better to stop the "guest" discourse in order to start thinking that the Syrians are here to stay until at least the war ends in Syria and solving the problems they are facing.

References

AFAD (2013), Türkiye'de Sığınmacılar: 2013 Saha Araştırması Sonuçları, Ankara.

AFAD (2014), Suriye'den Türkiye'ye Nüfus Hareketleri: Kardeş Topraklarındaki Misafirlik. Ankara: AFAD.

AFAD (April 30, 2015), 'AFAD President Guest of Leading US Think Tanks, Holds Meetings in Washington', Press Release, https://www.afad.gov.tr/en/HaberDetay.aspx-?IcerikID=4067&ID=5. (Accessed 12/05/2015).

Amnesty International (2014), Left Out In the Cold: Syrian Refugees Abandoned by the International Community. London: Amnesty International Peter Benenson House.

Barutçugil, İ. S. (1990). "1989 Yaz Aylarında Bulgaristan'dan Göç'e Zorlanan Soydaşların İstihdam Sorunları ve Çözüm Önerileri", İstanbul Ticaret Odası.

Bojkov, V. (2004), "Bulgaria's Turks in the 1980s: a minority endangered", Journal of Genocide Research, 6(3): 343-369.

Çalışma ve Sosyal Güvenlik Bakanlığı (2015), İstatistikler, http://www.csgb.gov.tr/csgb-Portal/csgb.portal?page=istatistik. (Accessed 12/05/2015).

Devlet Planlama Teşkilatı (1990), "Bulgaristan'dan Türk Göçleri", DPT Sosyal Planlama Başkanlığı Hizmete Özel Rapor, Ankara.

Dinçer, O. B.; Federici, V.; Ferris, E.; Karaca, S.; Kirişçi, K. and Çarmıklı, E. Ö. (2013) Turkey and Syrian Refugees: The Limits of Hospitality,Washington, DC and Ankara: Brookings Institute.

Dünya Bülteni (31.07.2012), 'Oyunun Kuralları Değişmemeli', http://www.dunyabulteni.net/-servisler/haberYazdir/221066/haber. (Accessed 10/04/2015).

Emniyet Genel Müdürlüğü (EGM). (2012). Yabancılar Hudut İltica Daire Başkanlığı. http://www.egm.gov.tr/Sayfalar/Yabanc%C4%B1lar-Hudut-%C4%B0ltica-Dairesi Ba%C5%9Fkanl%C4%B1%C4%9F%C4%B1-.aspx (Accessed 05/02/2015).

Erder, S. (2000). "Uluslararası Göçte Yeni Eğilimler: Türkiye "Göç Alan" Ülke mi?" içinde Fuat Ercan, Fulya Atacan, Hatice Kurtuluş ve Mehmet Türkay (der.), Mübeccel Kıray için Yazılar İstanbul: Bağlam Yayınları, 235-259.

Erdoğan, M. (2014). HUGO Report: Syrians in Turkey: Social Acceptance and Integration Research, Ankara: Hacettepe University.

Göç İdaresi Genel Müdürlüğü (2015), Göç İstatistikleri: Geçici Koruma Altında Bulunan Suriye Vatandaşları,http://www.goc.gov.tr/icerik6/temporary-protection_915_1024_474-8_icerik. (Accessed 12/05/2015).

Göç İdaresi Genel Müdürlüğü (2015b), I. Uluslararası Göç Çalıştayı 20-21 Aralık, Ankara.

International Crisis Group (2014), The Rising Costs of Turkey's Syrian Quagmire, Europe Report No.230

Kaya, İ. (2008). "Legal Aspects of Irregular Migration in Turkey", CARIM Analytic and Synthetic Notes 2008/73, Robert Schuman Center for Advanced Studies, San Domenico di Fiesole: European University Institute.

Keyder, Ç. (2003). Memalik-i Osmaniye'den Avrupa Birliği'ne, İstanbul: İletişim Yayınları.

Kirişçi, K. (1995). "Refugee Movements and Turkey in the Post-World War II Era", Boğaziçi Research Papers, ISS/POLS 95-01.

Kirişçi, K. (2003a), 'The Question of Asylum and Illegal Migration in European Union-Turkish Relations', Turkish Studies, 4:1, 79-106.

Kirişçi, K. (2003b), 'Turkey: A Transformation from Emigration to Immigration', Migration Policy Institute, http://www.migrationpolicy.org/article/turkey-transformation-emigration-immigration. (Accessed 15/10/2014).

Kirişçi, K. (2013). Syrian Refugees in Turkey: The Limits of an Open Door Policy, Brookings Institution,

Kirişçi, K. (2014). "Will the readmission agreement bring the EU and Turkey together or pull them apart?", CEPS Commentary, 04/02/2014, www.ceps.eu/book/will-readmission-agreement-bring-eu-and-turkey-together-or-pull-them-apart. (Accessed 10/09/2014).

Kirişçi, K. (2014b). Syrian Refugees and Turkey's Challenges: Going Beyond Hospitality, Brookings Institution,

Latif, D. (2002). 'Refugee Policy of the Turkish Republic", The Turkish Yearbook of International Relations, Ankara University Press, Number XXXIII.

Menon R., Salih M., and Iryna P. (2013). Toward Universal Coverage: Turkey's Green Card Program for the Poor, UNICO Studies Series 18, http://wwwwds.worldbank.org/external/default/WDSContent-Server/WDSP/IB/2013-/02/04/000333037_20130204152023/Rendered/PDF/750120NWP0Box300for0the0Poor0T URKEY.pdf. (Accessed 23/04/2015).

Nüfus ve Vatandaşlık İşleri Genel Müdürlüğü (2015), Sık Sorulan Sorular: Yabancı No Kimlik İşlemleri,http://www.nvi.gov.tr/Sik_Sor-ulan_Sorular,Sorular.html?pageindex=16. (Accessed 12/05/2015).

ORSAM (2014) Türkiye'ye Komşu Ülkelerde Suriyeli Mültecilerin Durumu: Bulgular, Sonuçlar, Öneriler, Rapor No. 189, Ankara.

Özer, Y. (2015). Türkiye ve Fransa Örnekleriyle Uluslararası Göç ve Yabancı Düşmanlığı, İstanbul: Derin Yayınevi

Poulton, H. (1991). Balkans: minorities and states in conflict, Great Britan: Minority Rights Group

Regulation No. 1994/6169 on the Procedures and Principles related to Possible Population Movements and Aliens Arriving in Turkey either as Individuals or in Groups Wishing to Seek Asylum either from Turkey or Requesting Residence Permission in order to Seek Asylum From Another Country', Official Gazzette, November 30, 1994, No. 22127, http://www.resmigazete.gov.tr/arsiv/22127.pdf. (Accessed 24/06/2014).

Scott, W. (1991). "Ethnic Turks from Bulgaria: An Assessment of their Employment and Living Conditions in Turkey", World Employment Programme ResearchWorking Paper, Geneva: International Labour Office.

Seydi, A. R. (2014). 'Türkiye'nin Suriyeli Sığınmacıların Eğitim Sorununun Çözümüne Yönelik İzlediği Politikalar', SDÜ Fen Edebiyat Fakültesi Sosyal Bilimler Dergisi, Nisan, Sayı 31, ss. 267-305.

Suter, B. (2013). 'Asylum and Migration Policy in Turkey: An Overview of Developments in the Field 1990 – 2013' Mim Working Paper Series, No.13:3, Malmö University: Malmö.

Şaul, M. (2013). 'Sahra-altı Afrika Ülkelerinden Türkiye'ye İş Göçü', Ankara Üniversitesi SBF Dergisi, Vol. 68, No. 1, pp. 83-121.

Şimşir, B. (2009). Bulgaristan Türkleri, İstanbul: Bilgi Yayınları, Genişletilmiş II. Baskı.

Şirin, N. A. (2011). "1989 Zorunlu Göçü ve Göçmenlerin Sosyal Entegrasyonu: Tekirdağ'daki Bulgaristan Göçmenleri Üzerine Bir Çalışma", içinde Hasret Çomak ve Caner Sancaktar (der.), Uluslararası Balkan Kongresi 28-29 Nisan 2011, Bildiriler Kitabı, Kocaeli: Kocaeli Üniversitesi Yayınları

Şirin, N. A. (2012). "1989 Göçü ve Sonrası ile İlgili Türkiye'de Yapılan Sosyolojik Araştırmalarla İlgili Bir Değerlendirme" içinde N. Ersoy-Hacısalihoğlu ve Mehmet Hacısalihoğlu (der.), 89 Göçü: Bulgaristan'da 1984-89 Azınlık Politikaları ve Türkiye'ye Zorunlu Göç, İstanbul: Yıldız Teknik Üniversitesi.

TBMM (2015). Yabancı İstihdamı Kanunu Tasarısı ile Sağlık, Aile, Çalışma ve Sosyal İşler Komisyonu Raporu (1/1035).

UNHCR (January, 2015) 'Syrian Refugees in Turkey: Frequently Asked Questions', http://w-ww.unhcr.org.tr/uploads/root/frequently-_asked_questions.pdf. (Accessed 10/04/2015).

UNHCR (March 20, 2015) 'Syria Regional Refugee Response', http://data.unhcr.org/syrian-refugees/country.php?id=224 (Accessed 09/04/2015).

UNHCR (2014) Syrian Refugees - Inter-Agency Regional Update, (December 16, 2014) http://www.refworld.org/docid/5492bc514.html (Accessed 7/1/2015)

World Health Organization (2014) 'WHO Denor Sanpshot-Turkey', http://www.who-.int/hac/donorinfo/syria_turkey_donor_snapshot_1july2014.pdf. (Accessed 20/05/2015).

The fundamental parameters of Turkey's new migration policy and management within the terms of new legislation

Ali Zafer Sağıroğlu[25]

Introduction

Turkey has developed into the sending, transiting and receiving position in regard of migration throughout the republic's history. These characteristics have differed from time to time depending on the global migration trends.

In the early period of the republic, ethnic concerns became the main influence of the policies. Like the other contemporary nation states, Turkey used migration as an instrument of "homogenization" and building the nation-state (Kirişçi, 2007; Erder, 2007, p:6). İskan Kanunu (settlement law), issued in 1934, is important to show a typical policy of the early period. Turkey maintained the iskân kanunu and was in force until recently. The iskan kanunu deteremined that only the Turks or people of Turkic origins including the Muslims coming from the ex-territories of the Ottoman Empire were accepted as an "immigrant" (İçduygu, 2007, p: 206).

The 1950s indicates another period. The acceleration of Turkey's integration with the World System and intensifying the relations with "the Western block" led Turkey to become a signatory to the Geneva Agreement in 1951. Then, the migration of workers in the 1960s consolidated the process (Toksöz, 2012, p:44)

In the 1980s, Turkey faced great immigrant waves for the first time in its history and became a migrant receiving country (Kirişçi, 2007). This is related to both the integration of Turkey with the global world and the changes around it (İçduygu, 2014, p:57). Newcomers intensified from former Soviet Union countries while the asylum seeker numbers from the near region like Afghanistan, Iran and Iraq had increased sharply. After the 1990s, mass influxes begin to appear rather frequently from Balkans and the Middle East.

In all these periods, Turkey put various regulations into force. These regulations were issued according to different necessities and needs of the governmental institutions. With the new law number 6458 on foreigners and international protection brought all these regulations, besides new ones, together in one law.

The path to the new law

There are two main arguments about the motivation that led Turkey to make new regulations on migration. The first argument asserts that the turn of mind whose roots goes to 1980s and accelerated in the 1990s. Turkey has intended to be not only a regional, but also a global "trading state" for last thirty years (Kirişçi, 2009, 38). It has been implementing its policies in many areas to integrate itself

---

[25] Ali Zafer Sağıroğlu is the Assistant Professor in the Sociology Department and Director of Migration Policy Center, Yıldırım Beyazıt University, Güvenevler Mah. Cinnah Cad. No: 16 Çankaya Ankara, Turkey. Email: alizaferus@yahoo.com

into the world system. The "soft visa regime," which has been in force in recent years, shows the same intention.

The other argument asserts that the motivation of the new regulations on migration stands purely as the process within the framework of EU integration. EU has forced Turkey to adapt its legislative system since the beginning of 2000's (İçduygu, 2014, 14). On the other hand, one source of hesitation for admitting Turkey for EU stemmed from the geopolitical position with regard to migration (Martin, 2015, 38). Thus, the migration issues hase come into question during every attempt Turkey had mad efor EU accession.

Although both arguments seem convincing, they are inadequate today. In fact, Turkey's strives to be a global actor and has taken into considereing the forcing factor's from EU. On the other hand, the stimulus for new regulations about migration like the many others is not limited with economic motivations. The pressure from EU is not something uncontrollable or irresistible. Moreover, just at the peak moment of EU demands for regulating migration area, Turkey faced one of the most severe mass migration influxs in its borders onwards from 2011. In such a situation, Turkey could postpone some regulations and have rebuttals to the comments being made globally. Although such action would be justifiable, Turkey did not do it. In the middle of the most traumatic chaos around it, Turkey put a brave new law into force in 2013.

Another reason that forced Turkey to make new legislative reforms is the changing global migration trends. Turkey has been a net immigrant country since 2010 (Duvell, 2015, 37). Although mostly the illegal and mass influx migration movements come out, the legal movements have also showed inreasing trends in Turkey. The relative political stability and flourishing economy in the last years must be taken into consideration to explain this situation.

From "national action plan" to the "lfip"

It is clear that the new legislative arrangements have progressed in parallel with EU process. The first wave began in 1999 in line with Turkey being accpeted for negotiating with EU for accession. In 2001 "the accession partnership document" was signed, which turned into a "national program" in 2003 after a review.

The expectations of "the accession partnership document" could be summarized into two headings: In the short-term, strengthening the struggle with illegal migration and approving the readmission agreement was expected. In the long-term, accepting and implementation of EU regulations and "acquis communitaire" about the struggle with illegal migration; initiating to abolish geographical restrictions accepted in the Geneva agreement in 1951; assessment and strengthening of the determined system of asylum applications; providing accommodation and social support for asylum seekers and refugees was expected (Eylem Planı, 2005).

Meanwhile, EU forced not only Turkey but also the other member countries to implement some new regulations. The purpose of these arrangements is to meet on a common ground about the migration management (Güner, 2007, 86). Therefore, the second wave came in 2001, at a time Turkey was already engaged in its own planning and preparation and was doing its own homework. One more step in 2002, the Turkish government formed a new task force among the different public agencies to determine a new migration strategy. The new task force concentrated on mainly three topics and shaped three different working groups which are border, migration and asylum.

The works ended in October 2003 and "the strategy paper which will contribute to the action plan on migration management in Turkey" was declared. Meanwhile on 24th July "Turkey National Program" was published in the official gazette in which the Turkish government clearly announced some commitment about the area of migration and asylum. Then, these works continued with a series of seminars and turned into a module of training for various governmental staff during 2004.

The year of 2005 was a crucial point with regard of the acceleration of the migration management. "The Turkish National Action Plan for the adaptation of the EU acquis in the field of asylum and migration" was declared by the government. As stated in the action plan, Turkey accepted to prepare a new law on foreign and asylum until 2012.

In 2008, "the bureau of implementation and development for administrative capacity and legislation of asylum and migration" was founded to coordinate the establishment and functioning for basic facilities and infrastructures. This bureau would be the main core of new legislation and organization in Turkey.

The works were accelerated with the bureau and ended with the introduction of the Law number 6458 on Foreign and International Protection coming into force on 11 April 2013. One year later, as the new law dictated, 11 April 2014, the Directorate General for Migration Management became operative.

The Law mainly consists of four chapters and regulates mainly three areas. The first one is about entrance, exit and residence affairs of foreigners, including stateless person and deportation. The second area is about the kinds of international protection and general procedures with the exceptional positions for international protection. The last area is the foundation and organization of Directorate General of Migration Management (DGMM).

The New Regulations about Foreigners

With regards to legal migration, an efficient and systematic structure with reduced bureaucracy and informality was created. The scattered regulations were gathered under the same structure. This change is important for an active and efficient migration management system. Residence permits are classified; specific conditions and charge for each type are specified. Residence permits are able to be issued prior to entering the country. It is provided that the work permit will substitute a residence permit. Foreign students have the right to work while studying. Any person who lost his Turkish spouse and victims of domestic violence can obtain independent residence permits. Anyone who resides in Turkey continuously for 8 years can take temporary residence permit which is bringing rights very close to citizenship.

Residence permits for human trafficking victims and the rights of stateless persons are regulated for the first time. Procedural guarantees, in addition to the efficient appeal procedures regarding return procedures and detention, are formed by the law. Non refoulement principle is granted by the law for the first time. The right for appeal to deportation is provided.

The New Regulations for International Protection

The international protection area is being regulated by the law for the first time. The regulations are in accordance with the EU legislation (Özer, 2011, 78). The basic human rights standards and needs of international protection for individuals are guaranteed. For mass influx situations, temporary protection gains a legal basis. Subsidiary protection and special protection mechanisms for vulnerable groups are brought in line with the international standards for the first time. Nonrefoulement principle gained a legal basis. Detailed regulations are in place for deportation and detention procedures in the law.

The New Migration Management Organization

The widest part of the law is about the new administrative unit, Directorate General of Migration Management (DGMM). DGMM is a concrete and broad policy making institution. It is also responsible and authorised to report, analyse and conduct research in relation to the administrative, legal and social dimensions of migration.

DGMM is organized in 81 provinces and 148 districts with the central unit. Over 100 representative units abroad are being also planned. There is one director general, three deputy director generals and twelve departments.

The prominent ones are the Department of Foreigners and Department of International Protection. The Department of Foreigners is conducting many procedures including the preparation of residence permits. The department of International Protection is evaluating and classifying the individual and massive claims for protection. Another unit is Harmonization and Communication Department that is to work to the harmonization of foreigners within the society. Here, the emphasis is that the concept of harmonization is something new and remarkable. By this concept, the new policy makers try to state its new perspective which has an emphasis to the interaction between the host communities and newcomers. The Department of Protecting Victims of Human Trafficking is also important to show that combating human trafficking is seen as a separate and significant issue. Department of Migration Policies and Projects is also responsible for determining, implementing and coordinating policy and strategies in the migration management.

The law establishes new boards and commissions. The Migration Policies Board was formed to develop, determine and monitor the implementation of Turkey's migration policies and strategies. The board consists of various governmental institutions and organizations to provide coordination between different actors and to determine common migration policies.

The Migration Advisory Board was also formed to consult with different national and international institutions, organizations, civil societies and academics. The board indicates that the policy and management of migration would be shaped by taking various actors' views into consideration.

The Coordination Board on Combat against Irregular Migration has the mission to coordinate civil, military and police forces to plan against Irregular Migration.

The International Protection Assessment Commission brings the representatives of different ministries to assess the protection claims.

Moreover, many new Removal Centers, Reception and Accommodation Centers and Shelters for Victims of Human Trafficking are under construction to strengthen the administrative capacity of migration management in Turkey.

Conclusion

Turkey has stepped in a new area in migration management with the enactment of the new law. It is not the end of the road, it is not a revolution. The results of the implementation have not appeared yet. However, as many experts stated, even though Turkey was in the midst of a huge mass influx of migrants from Syria during the current crisis, Turkey did not step back on the process which begin in 2005.

The new law has filled many gaps in the legislative structure by collecting scattered regulations and introduced new ones. Thus, Turkey has gained new legislative and administrative body in accordance with the universal standard.

In the new area, Turkey's approach to migration has shifted from an ethnocentric dimension to the universal perspective. Therefore, the main concern for Turkey relating to the migration phenomenon has been basic human rights rather than security.

The new law has been shaped not only by the entrance and exit of foreigners, but also relevance to their residence in Turkey. The concept of harmonization, on which new administrative units emphasize the importance, is a concrete signal of the new policy about foreigners. Many changes stimulate not only foreigners, but also the host community to interact on a common ground.

All these remarkable developments have been mentioned with praise in EU development report of 2013. Last but not least, while almost every country in the world has been approaching the migration phenomenon with a security concerns, Turkey has launched a new law which possibly extended the consideration of human rights.

References

Çelikel A., Gelgel G. (2004). Yabancılar Hukuku (Law of Foreigners) 11. Baskı, Beta Yayınları, İstanbul,. (in Turkish).

Duvell, F. (2014). International Relations and Migration Management: The Case of Turkey, Insight Turkey, V. 16, No. 1, 35-44.

Erder, S. (2007). Türkiye'de Yabancı İşçiler (Foreign Workers in Turkey). Arı, A. (Eds.) 'Yabancısız' Kurgulunan Ülkenin 'Yabancıları'. Derin yay. Istanbul, 1-83. (in Turkish).

Güner, C. (2007). İltica Konusunda Türkiye'nin Yol Haritası: Ulusal Eylem Planı (The Road Map of Turkey About Assylum: National Act). AÜHFD V.56, N.4, 81-109. (in Turkish).

İçduygu, A. (2007). Europenization of National Policies and Politics of Immigration. T. Faistand & A. Ette (Eds.). EU-ization matters: Changes in Immigration and Asylum Practices in Turkey. Palgrave Macmillan. The New York.

İçduygu, A., Erder S., Gençkaya Ö. F. (2014). Türkiye'nin Uluslararası Göç Politikaları, 1923-2023 (International Migration Politics of Turkey, 1923-2023). Mirekoç Proje Raporları (Project Reports Of Mirekoc), İstanbul. (in Turkish).

İltica Ve Göç Alanındaki Avrupa Birliği Müktesebatının Üstlenilmesine İlişkin Türkiye Ulusal Eylem Planı (2005). http://www.goc.gov.tr/files/files/turkiye_ulusal_eylem_plani(3).pdf available on 01/ 04/2015. (in Turkish).

Kaya, A. (2014). Türkiye'de Göç ve Uyum Tartışmaları: Geçmişe Dönük Bir Bakış (The Debates on Migration and Harmonization in Turkey: A Retrospective). İdeal Kent Dergisi Göç I, 11-28, Ankara. (in Turkish).

Kirişçi, K. (2007). Turkey: A Country of Transition From Emigration to Immigration, Mediterranean Politics. 12(1), 91-97.

Kirişçi, K. (2009). The Transformation of Turkish Foreign Policy: The Rise of the Trading State, New Perspectives on Turkey. 40, 29-47.

Kirişçi, K. (2011). Turkey's "Demonstrative Effect" and Transformation in the Middle East, Insight Turkey, 13 (29), 33-55.

Martin, P. (2012) Turkey – EU Migration: The Road Ahead. Perceptions, Summer, V. XVII, N. 2, 125-144.

Özer, Y. (2011). Türk Kamu yönetiminde Yeni Bir Çalışma Alanı Olarak Uluslararası Göç: Kanunlaşma ve İdari Yapılanma Sürecinin Değerlendirilmesi (International Migration As a New Study Area in Turkish Public Administration: Legalization and Evaluation of Administrative Restructuring Process). İ.Ü. Siyasal Bilgiler Fakültesi Dergisi No: 45, 73-88. (in Turkish).

Toksöz, G., Erdoğdu S., Kaşka S. (2012). Türkiye'de Düzensiz Emek Göçü ve Göçmenlerin İşgücü Piyasasındaki Durumları (The Status of Irregular Workers in the Labor Market and Irregular Migrant Labor n Turkey). IOM Pub., Ankara. (in Turkish).

Yabancılar ve Uluslararası Koruma Kanunu(Law on Foreigners and International Protection). (in Turkish). http://www.goc.gov.tr/files/files/YUKK_I%CC%87NGI%CC%87LI%CC%87ZCE_BASK I(1)(1).pdf available on 01/ 04/2015.

European Union and Turkish Migration Policy Reform: From Accession to Policy Conditionality

Birce Demiryontar[26]

Introduction

The EU typically exerts influence on domestic policy change in Turkey through accession conditionality. The main shortcoming of this reform framework is its interconnectedness to the country's accession process, when the country's prospects for membership are losing their credibility. This loss of credibility, leads to a halt in the EU induced policy change, though migration policy area presents a deviation from this trend. In the absence of a credible membership prospect, in 2011, the Law on Foreigners and International Protection was drafted, and ratified by the Parliament on April 2013. Subsequently, in December 2013 Turkey and the EU have signed the readmission agreement in parallel to the introduction of the road-map to visa liberalization. The main reason behind this commitment to the EU induced reform agenda, is the successful detachment of the migration policy area, from the accession conditionality by establishing its own policy conditionality. This paper claims that in the EU accession negotiations where the parties were stuck in a deadlock, persistence in using the accession conditionality as an incentive has been counterproductive. With the visa liberalization road map, the EU introduced an external incentive specific to migration and set a more approachable target than accession, which ensured the sustainability of the reforms.

Selection of readmission for establishing such an elaborate policy conditionality is not coincidental. Readmission agreements were initially introduced as the EU policy responses to the irregular migration. With the increasing salience of the issue, the Commission sought for a faster and more efficient way to conclude a readmission agreement with Turkey. The main concerns of the EU are related to Turkey's status as a transit country for irregular immigrants from the Middle East and North Africa, on their route to Europe. Available data shows that their apprehensions are not unfounded. An up to date data on irregular migration was provided by the Turkish General Staff, on the total number of immigrants who were detained in the country's border areas[27]. These borders can be categorized under two headings as: (a) borders of entrance to Turkey: Syria, Iran and Iraq and; (b) borders of exit from Turkey: Greece, Bulgaria, the Aegean Sea and the Mediterranean. The data show an increase in the number of persons detained in Turkish border areas, between the years 2004 and 2014. For this period, the data suggest an annual number of 7867 attempted entrances and 6697 attempted exists. This means, for every 117 immigrants attempting to enter the country another 100 attempts to leave. This is not the exact number of

---

[26] Birce Demiryontar is currently a PhD student at the Sussex Centre for Migration Research, University of Sussex, Falmer, Brighton, BN1 9RH, United Kingdom. E-mail: b.demiryontar@sussex.ac.uk.
[27] This data set have been provided by the Turkish General Staff upon my online request in the framework of the Law on Right to Obtain Information (Law No. 5432 and 6495).

the scale of immigration through Turkey but it is indicative of Turkey's status as a transit country. When the politicization of irregular migration in the EU member countries and the discourse of crisis related with it, is considered, these figures increase the sense of emergency for a readmission agreement. Moreover, since 2011, Turkey has been facing a refugee crisis in its south-eastern border with the entrance of Syrian asylum seekers. By March 2015, the number of the Syrian asylum seekers, who were registered by Turkish authorities, was around 1,623,000[28]. Turkey is still following an open borders policy towards Syria and it is another source of concern for the EU as the transit migration of the Syrians is expected to increase as well.

With respect to the increased salience of irregular migration, this paper aims to explain the shift from the accession conditionality to policy conditionality in the issue area migration, focusing on the case of readmission and visa liberalization road map. Using the data I have obtained for my doctoral research, the paper seeks to illustrate the negotiation process of this policy conditionality, through analysing twenty-one expert interviews. These interviewees were chosen among the policy making and implementing bodies of the Turkish Ministries of Interior, Foreign Affairs and the EU Affairs, Turkish National Police, involved international organizations and non-governmental organizations. Another five meetings were conducted in Brussels, with the high and middle rank officials from the Directorate General for Home Affairs and Directorate General for Enlargement[29]. In light of these interviews, the final aim of the paper is to demonstrate the possibility and the significance of a relation between Turkey and EU beyond accession, like the one in the migration policy change.

External incentives and decline of accession conditionality

External Incentives Model and Policy Conditionality

According to the *external incentives model,* the EU exerts influence on domestic policy change in third countries by facilitating conditionality. External incentives model recognizes the material benefits of the EU membership as the main incentives for compliance. The model presumes, EU induced domestic policy change is anticipated in the countries and policy areas where conditionality is credible and size and speed of the rewards meet the domestic adaptation costs (Schimmelfenning & Sedelmeier, 2005). The instrument of conditionality is categorized under two headings: (a) accession conditionality; (b) policy conditionality.

Accession conditionality refers to the structured and extensive EU conditionality presented to the candidate countries during their accession negotiations, while policy conditionality is applicable to all third countries with the attachment of policy-specific rewards to certain areas of reform (Langbein & Börzel, 2013). Policy conditionality takes the form of neighbourhood policies, association agreements and partnerships (Vachudova, 2005). The strongest and

---

[28] The data is obtained from the UNHCR Turkey: http://data.unhcr.org/syrianrefugees/country.php?id=224 (Consulted in 20.08.2014).
[29] As a prerequisite of the ethical review process undertaken by the University of Sussex, anonymity was guaranteed to the interviewees, though they will be stated with their positions and affiliations.

most effective form of conditionality is the accession. However, considering the limits of the EU's enlargement capacity, the Union introduced alternative forms of conditionality, without presenting the accession as a final aim. Thus, above mentioned policy conditionalities were introduced, for influencing policy change in the third countries. With the policy conditionality there is a likelihood of an increase in the level of policy convergence in parallel to the rewards attached to the specific policy (Lavenex, 2008; Schimmelfenning, 2008). Moreover, as the outcomes of the policy conditionality are shorter-term, they are politically more valuable for government actors with electoral concerns (Kelley, 2006).

Decline of the Accession Conditionality and Rise of the Policy Conditionality

Although Turkey's Europeanization efforts were framed around accession conditionality, in the last decade, it is difficult to state a substantial progress towards accession. One of the main reasons for this disengagement is Turkey's Cyprus policy, which generated complications in the accession process following Cyprus' accession to the Union in 2004 (Esfahani & Çeviker-Gürakar, 2013). In December 2006, the EU froze the accession negotiations due to Turkey's failure to fully implement the Customs Union Agreement by opening its ports and airports to Cypriot traffic. After this decision, readmission negotiations were abandoned, in the absence of an alternative incentive to membership. In 2009, Cyprus unilaterally blocked the opening of six chapters in Turkish accession negotiations, including Chapter 24, Justice Freedom and Security. This blockage further weakened Turkey's incentives, considering the chapter covering readmission was blocked and a progress in the agreement would not result in progress in the accession negotiations (Bürgin, 2013).

In 2007, the Commission offered Turkey to negotiate visa facilitations, on the condition that Turkey signs the readmission agreement at first. Turkey did not respond to this offer, due to the limited scope of the proposed visa facilitations. Some Turkish officials suggested that these facilitations were already granted to, but not implemented for, Turkey in the framework of its Association Agreement. Moreover, introduction of procedures different from the Balkan countries, raised concerns over unequal treatment to Turkey (Bürgin, 2013). With these claims, Turkish policy makers refused to settle for anything other than visa liberalisations for concluding a readmission agreement. Aiming to obtain visa liberalisations, negotiations were re-launched in 2010. After a period of negotiations between 2004 and 2010, parties agreed upon a draft agreement in January 2011, and agreement was concluded in December 2013 with the introduction of the visa liberalisation road map in parallel to the agreement.

Significance of policy conditionality: readmission agreement and visa liberalisation road map

Initial point for this paper, came from a statement made by a high-rank official working in the Turkey unit of the European Commission's DG Enlargement.[30]

---

[30] The meetings with the officials from the Commission were held between 24 and 30th April 2014 at DG Home, Rue de Luxembourg 46 and at DG Enlargement Rue de la Loi, 15, Brussels, Belgium.

He stressed upon the possibilities of cooperation between the EU and Turkey detached from the accession process:

"... Enlargement and migration, are in two different strands. We have readmission agreements and visa liberalisation with countries, who have no prospect of accession to the EU. .... Beyond the accession, we need to cooperate. Readmission and visa liberalisation process confirmed there is room for cooperation outside of the accession process."

With this statement, this official not only stressed upon the significance of keeping migration related issues immune from the complexities related with the accession process, he also signalled the suitability of readmission for establishing a negotiation process beyond accession, considering it is an international agreement, negotiable with any third country. After a long negotiation process lasted from 2004 to 2012, the EU recognized the significance of presenting a policy conditionality independent from the accession. A high-rank policy officer from the Commission's DG Home Affairs have stated the significance of the continuation of relations and a need for a balanced shorter term deal by stating the following:

"Turkey is a very important country, for migration reasons. It is a transit country for irregular migration as well...This road is one of the biggest, bringing the irregular migrants to the EU ... In any case, migration management is a joint endeavour. So, we need to always look for convergence, this is important for us to address irregular channel. But Turkey also has its priorities, so hence we end up with visa dialogue."

Visa liberalisations have notable political significance in Turkish domestic arena. In July 2012, at a time of declining public support for the EU membership and Turkish public demanding visa-free EU, rather than accession, the then Turkish Minister of the EU Affairs, Egemen Bağış, stated that *"the readmission agreement will be indexed to our citizens' visa-free travel ... For our citizens, visa-free travel is more important than accession."*[31] While in the past, Turkish Ministries emphasized membership, this approach highlighted a notion of being close to the EU, as the accession prospects were declining. And the main indication of being close to the EU is presented as visa liberalisations. Introduction of the full implementation of the EU-Turkey readmission agreement as the primary condition in the visa liberalisation road map, is therefore presented as a balanced deal. As a senior official from the European Commission, DG Home affairs stated: *"...I see the deal is balanced, visa dialogue was also something very dear to Turkey so I think we are both winners."*

Despite its political significance, visa liberalisation road map was not sufficient to overcome the implementing bodies' concerns. Turkish Ministry of Interior stressed its reservations over burden sharing, in the forms of financial and technical assistance. These reservations were addressed with the introduction of technical assistance clauses to the agreement. A senior policy advisor from the

---

[31] July 11, 2012. "Halk Üyelik Değil Vizesiz AB İstiyor (Public does not want Membership, They Prefer Visa-Free EU)", *Radikal.* Consulted 31 July 2013.
<http://www.radikal.com.tr/Radikal.aspx?aType=RadikalDetayV3&ArticleID=1093806&CategoryID=78>

Turkish Ministry of Foreign Affairs have indicated that the forms this assistance will take by interpreting the clauses in the agreement:

"...This technical assistance clause implies financial assistance as well, without suggesting it implicitly. Between the lines, "general sources" of the EU are mentioned. This means Turkey would not only benefit from the funds related with its accession process to the EU, the funds we call as IPA funds, it would also get a contribution from a more general budget."

These assurances for assistance have been valuable for overcoming the implementing institutions' reservations. Moreover, much needed flexibility that was absent in the accession process was present in these negotiations. Draft text of the agreement have been negotiated thoroughly and amended for ensuring the elimination of practitioners' apprehensions. A joint declaration that was added to the agreement, which suggests "good faith" in implementation and guaranteeing that the EU would show an effort on sending the third country citizens to their countries of origin, before sending them to Turkey. The parties did not perceive these details as given and aimed to produce a definitive document for sufficient implementation.

With the introduction of the visa-liberalisation road-map[32], presenting a package for reforms and introducing a framework on their implementation, one of the most structured negotiation processes between EU and Turkey began. Almost all of the officials that were interviewed in the EU Commission have stated that Turkey had overcame a deadlock in the relations by signing the readmission agreement and by accepting a structured negotiation framework with the introduction of the visa liberalisation road map. Previously, Turkey was using a hard bargaining method with the facilitation of threats and retractions in its migration policy negotiations. In the end, this bargaining method proved to be counterproductive as the Council was presenting this lack of concessions from the Turkish side as a justification for using its power to block the negotiations. As soon as Turkey presented a concession by signing the readmission agreement, the Council was normatively trapped to act accordingly. As a senior official from the EU Commission, DG Home Affairs puts it:

"On our side, for a long time, the power has been in the Council who used this power to block the Commission. Turkey believed, by hard negotiations, they were doing on their best advantage, but they were supporting the blockage that the Council was so willingly implementing. When they have accepted the readmission agreement, they have liberated the Commission, who is their best friend within the EU, from the blockage. If Turkey plays a fair game in the negotiations, Turkey and the Commission can act as a team and in a few years' time, the Council will have to recognize Turkey's progress."

After the Council's blockage on the relations was lifted, the level of consultation and deliberation among the parties have increased. Since the establishment of the road map, the Commission officials take frequent visits to Turkey. The Commission also established two permanent missions in the country for the implementation of the road map. There are also relatively independent

---

[32] For more information see the Road Map towards a Visa-Free Regime with Turkey: http://ec.europa.eu/dgs/home-affairs/what-is-new/news/news/docs/20131216-roadmap_towards_the_visa-free_regime_with_turkey_en.pdf

technical experts who will contribute to the Communication that will be presented to the Council by the Commission, concerning the developments related with the implementation of the visa road map. Participation of these independent experts in the process is promising to reinforce trust among the parties, especially in the issues related with the assessment. Also, their involvement provides venues for unofficial socialization in the field, which is valuable for the progress of policy implementation. The scope of their task is explained by a senior official from the EU Commission, DG Enlargement, as the following:

"In these missions… we are accompanied by a member of experts from member states. The role of these experts will be to draft technical assessments, on the situation in Turkey … And on the bases of these assessments and on the bases of Commission's and EU Community's priorities, we will draft the Communication … We choose them on the bases of experience, of availability. We are trying to diversify."

Although involvement of these experts is significant for enhancing trust among the parties, it is not sufficient. A sufficient safeguard for enhancing trust is within the nature of the agreement. The readmission agreement that Turkey signed with the EU is an international agreement with provisions for denouncement and appeal. These clauses are significant for ensuring progress by the Council on visa liberalisation after Turkey has fulfilled the visa road map's benchmarks. In the absence of progress from the Council to grant Turkey visa liberalisation, the country may facilitate threats to denounce the agreement. A senior official from the DG Enlargement have stressed upon this clause as a last resort for Turkey:

"Turkey retains the right, if for instance we make the proposal to change the visa regulation and if say the Council drags its feet, the Parliament drags its feet, or member states oppose it, at the end of the day they don't really want to give visa-free access, Turkey then retains that it has the right to denounce the readmission agreement."

This clause also guarantees that for the continuity of the relations on migration policy, as the EU institutions need to show at least some progress on visa liberalisation, considering the accession prospect is no longer a credible term at the table and none of the parties can risk the severance of the relations in migration management.

Conclusion

In the case of the readmission agreement, the detachment of accession conditionality and the introduction of new terms and concessions peculiar to this negotiation process increased the chances to reach a negotiation agreement on five main grounds. Primarily, the introduction of the visa liberalisation road map is perceived as a balanced shorter-term deal by both parties which increased their commitment to the implementation of its benchmarks, including the readmission agreement. Secondly, such a structured negotiation process increased the interactions between the parties, which led to further flexibility for deliberation in a faster and more efficient manner. Thirdly, a step taken by Turkey, overcame a deadlock in the negotiations and prevented the Council from sustaining its uncompromising behaviour in these negotiations, though the member states' approach against Turkey's accession remained. Fourthly, the involvement of relatively independent technical staff increased the trust in the Turkish side, and especially relieved the practitioners in the Ministry of Interior, both in the process of implementation and afterwards for the assessment. Finally, the denouncement or appeal clauses in the readmission agreement have guaranteed progress and increased the confidence of Turkish negotiators. These clauses suggest, after the full implementation of visa liberalisation road map, if the Council continues to drag its feet in lifting the visa obligation for Turkish citizens, Turkish officials may return to methods of hard bargaining.

The negotiation process of EU-Turkey readmission agreement and visa liberalisation have revealed that when the parties are stuck in a deadlock, persisting in using the accession conditionality as a negotiation framework ends up being counterproductive. Instead, when the parties established a well-structured negotiation process, the process became more promising to reach a negotiated agreement. Further research is needed to see whether a similar shift in a different policy area would produce similar results. In the case of migration, the continuation of policy reform process was valuable for both parties, in a time when a discourse of immigration "crisis" have been dominating European political agenda, and visa-free Europe had a domestic electoral power in Turkey. Moreover, EU Commission was competent to negotiate migration policy, due to its trans-national nature. Thus, this kind of cooperation may remain limited to the scope of Justice, Freedom and Security chapter, as long as the priorities of the member states and the competences of the Commission remain as it is. However, in principle, other policy areas may as well be promoted to this level of urgency, provided that the conditions change in a way to lead the member states to adopt a state of imminence for cooperation in other issue areas and seek for a transnational solution by assigning competence to the Commission. For instance, the recent high level energy dialogue, launched between the EU and Turkey is promising for establishing such a structure.

References

Aydın, U., & Kirişci, K. (2013). With or Without the EU: Europeanization of Asylum and Competition Policies in Turkey. South European Society and Politics, 18(3), 375-395.

Bürgin, A. (2013). Salience, Path Dependency and the Coalition Between the European Commission and the Danish Council Presidency: Why the EU Opened a Visa Liberalisation Process with Turkey? European Integration Online Papers (EIOP), 17(9), 1-19.

Esfahani, H., & Çeviker-Gürakar, E. (2013). Fading Attraction: Turkey's Shifting Relationship with the European Union. The Quarterly Review of Economics and Finance, 53, 364-379.

Kelley, J. (2006, March). New Wine in Old Wineskins: Promoting Political Reforms through the New European Neighbourhood Policy. Journal of Common Market Studies, 44(1), 29-55.

Langbein, J., & Börzel, T. (2013). Introduction: Explaining Policy Change in the European Union's Eastern Neighbourhood. Europe-Asia Studies, 65(4), 571-580.

Lavenex, S. (2008). A Governance Perspective on the European Neighbourhood Policy: Integration beyond Conditionality? Journal of European Public Policy, 15(6), 938-955.

Nas, Ç. (2011). Turkey and the European Union: A Stumbling Accession Process under New Conditions. In Ö. Z. Oktav, Turkey in the 21st Century: Quest for a New Foreign Policy (pp. 159-184). Aldershot: Ashgate.

Schimmelfennig, F. (2008). EU Political Accession Conditionality after the 2004 Enlargement: Consistency and Effectiveness. Journal of European Public Policy, 15(6), 918-937.

Schimmelfenning, F., & Sedelmeier, U. (2005). Introduction: Conceptualizing the Europeanization of Central and Eastern Europe. In F. Schimmelfenning, & U. Sedelmeier, The Europeanization of Central and Eastern Europe (pp. 1-28). Ithaca, NY: Cornell University Press.

Vachudova, M. A. (2005). Europe Undivided: Democracy, Leverage and Integration after Communism. Oxford: Oxford University Press.

EU-Turkey readmission agreement: Not a *"carrot"* but more a '?'[33]

Ülkü Sezgi Sözen[34]

Introduction

"Migration has become global but there is no global regime to govern the international movement of persons." (Philippe Fargues)[35]

First of all, it is essential to point out the importance of the cooperation with the neighboring countries. Solely the protection of European Union's (hereinafter EU) borders cannot be successful unless neighboring countries cooperate in the fields of irregular migration[36] and the fight against cross-border criminality and terrorism. In order to do this, the EU should offer a certain level of compensatory measures that incentivize such cooperation, such as economic privileges or visa facilitation. As an incentivizing measure, the EU recently signed readmission agreements with its neighboring countries and offered economic advantages, such as access to the single market, free trade agreements or the possibility of easier visa acquisition, which can be considered a *"realistic option"*[37].

Alongside the accession negotiations with Turkey, the EU signed the Readmission Agreement with Turkey (henceforth, the Agreement)[38], after a long drawn negotiation process with the intention of reducing irregular migration to the EU. This agreement aims at strengthening their cooperation in order to combat irregular migration more effectively and to establish through reciprocity, an effective and swift procedure for the identification and safe and orderly return of persons; all of this to achieve domestic concerns while maintaining and facilitating a spirit of cooperation between the two countries.[39] Moreover, the Agreement provided Turkey with a transitional period of up to three years after the entry into force of the whole agreement, which will not oblige Turkey for accepting the third country nationals whose origin country has no readmission

---

[33] This paper is summarized from the original published paper Sözen, Ü.S., December 2014. Akademik Yaşamının 55. yılı Onuruna Rona Aybay'a Armağan (2. Cilt) [Special issue]. Legal Journal of Law, 2049-2074.

[34] Ülkü Sezgi Sözen, LL.M. is a PhD. Candidate at Law Faculty of Hamburg University - Albrecht Mendelssohn Bartholdy Graduate School of Law, Rothenbaumchaussee 33, 20148 Hamburg. E-mail: u.sezgisozen@gmail.com.

[35] See Trauner, F. & Wolff, S., 2014. *EJML,* 16(1), p. 5.

[36] Even if in the Readmission Agreement and in the Roadmap the term *"illegal migration/migrant"* is used, this article uses the term *"undocumented/irregular migration/migrants"* because the term *"illegal migration/migrant"* infers negative connotations equating the migrant directly with criminality and suggesting that the migrant person has no rights at all.

[37] For detailed information see Schieffer, M., 2003. *EJML,* 5, p. 356.

[38] The agreement signed in accordance with Council Decision 2012/499/EU, which is published in OJ L 244, 8.9.2012.

[39] Commission of the European Communities, COM (2012) 239 final., Proposal for a Council Decision of Concerning the Conclusion of the Agreement between the European Union and the Republic of Turkey on the Readmission of Persons Residing without Authorization (Brussels: EU Commission, 2012).

agreement with Turkey yet. Subsequently, the EU will facilitate the issuing of visas for Turkish citizens, if Turkey can fulfill its obligations under the Agreement successfully.

However, migration policy remains a big concern for Turkey domestically. Due to the regional instabilities especially in Syria, Iraq, Afghanistan, Palestine, Pakistan and China, irregular migration to Turkey increased significantly. Even if many of them try to continue their journey towards the EU, many others, especially Syrian people try to stay in Turkey because of the new economic opportunities there.

Therefore, the migration policy of the entire region is a major issue not only for the EU, but also for Turkey. Consequently, in January 2011, the first draft asylum law in Turkey was released and in April 2013, the Foreigners and International Protection Law[40] was adopted by the Turkish parliament, which partially came into force one year after from 11 April 2013. This new law shows finally a clear legal framework of Turkey extending protection to asylum seekers and refugees.

The aim of this paper is therefore to analyse the Agreement between the EU and Turkey and discuss the possible fallouts of this Agreement not only from the EU's perspective but also from Turkey's perspective. In order to do this legal interpretation, the hermeneutic method[41] will be used. In the literature there is not enough analyses, which give an overview from both parties of this agreement and make a connection to migration policy of the EU. In order to fill this gap, firstly, Turkey's EU journey will be explained. Secondly, the competence of the EU on signing a readmission agreement on behalf of its Member States will be clarified. Thirdly, the genesis and scope of the Agreement will be handled. Further, the Roadmap towards a visa-free regime will be examined. Finally, in conclusion, the likely impacts of this Agreement on migration policy will be analysed and discussed.

Turkey's EU journey

Since the early part of the 19th century, when Turkey chose to follow the Western Model for its economic, political and social structures, the desire for deeper cooperation with Europe has become increasingly entrenched in the Turkish State psyche, and this led to its first application to join the European Economic Community (hereinafter EEC)[42] shortly after its creation in 1958. After this application, in 1963 both sides signed the "Agreement Creating An Association Between the Republic of Turkey and the European Economic

---

[40] OJ from 11.4.2013 with the Number 28615.

[41] In hermeneutic discipline the main objects are legal texts, documents, agreements and their legal interpretation. The hermeneutic point of view preserves the classical scientific, i.e. objective, approach to the study of law. In other words, the hermeneutic approach is not just reporting facts or beliefs; it sets out normative standards. Moreover empirical facts are not ignored.

[42] European Economic Community, organization established by the Treaty establishing the European Economic Community, signed Rome in March 1957, brings together France, Germany, Italy and Benelux countries in a community whose aim is to achieve integration via trade with a view to economic expansion.

Community" (also known as the "Ankara Agreement"), which came into force in 1964.[43]

The Ankara Agreement intended to secure Turkey's full membership in the EEC through the establishment of a customs union in three phases, which would serve as an instrument of deeper integration between the EEC and Turkey. To get it working the Ankara Agreement provided the progressive establishment of a customs union, which would bring the parties closer together in economic and trade matters.

Moreover, despite the fact that the Ankara Agreement established the free movement of goods, persons, services and capital between the countries, it excluded Turkey from the EEC decision-making processes, which means that Turkey gained some benefits but membership, and made no provision for any recourse to the EEC for dispute settlement. In this respect, the customs union between the countries could just go through the abolition of tariff and quantitative barriers to trade and the application of Common External Tariff for imports from third countries, and supported harmonization with the EEC policies regarding the internal market. The legal basis of the relationship between Turkey and the EU is still the Ankara Agreement.[44]

Further it is important to point out more precisely the relationship between the EU and Turkey in relation to migration issues. Indeed, through the European Agreement on Regulations governing the Movement of Persons between Member States of the Council of Europe[45], which was opened to sign in 1957, and came into force in 1958, the nationals of States Parties were allowed to enter or leave the territory of another Party, in any manner, such right being restricted to visits that were less than three months in duration. Turkey became a party to this instrument only in 1961. In the meantime, the Ankara Agreement gave the opportunity to Turkish citizens to work in the Member States.

On the one hand, the decision of Council of Association in 1980, regarding the deeper integration of Turkish workers and as well as their family members[46] in the EU internal market, could be defined as a further step concerning free movement of workers for the Parties. Also, at the same time in order to prevent the abuse of political asylum[47], Germany introduced a visa requirement for Turkish citizens. Following the insistence of Germany, France and the Benelux followed suit imposed visa requirement in 1982. Afterwards through the EU Acquis all Member States accepted the requirements.[48]

---

[43] Groenendijk, K., Hoffmann, H., & Kuiten, M., 2013, p. 10.

[44] Peers, S., 1996. EJIL, p. 412.

[45] European Agreement on Regulations governing the Movement of Persons between Member States of the Council of Europe, 13 December 1957, Paris, available at http://conventions.coe.int/Treaty/en/Treaties/Html/025.htm, (12 March 2014).

[46] Concerning the family members of workers, see cases, Case 12/86 Demirel 30.9.1987, ECJ 1987; C-337/07 Altun 18.12.2008, ECJ 2008, I-10323.

[47] Needless to say that under the 1951 Geneva Convention Relating to the Status of Refugees, States are under an obligation to consider request for political asylum even if the applicant cannot show any document, even a passport. Indeed visa requirement would not be an effective device to prevent an asylum application.

[48] Kabaalioğlu, H., 2012. Müller-Graff, P.C. & Kabaalioğlu, H. (eds.), Turkey and the European Union, p. 18.

Taking into account the standstill clause, Article 41 of the Additional Protocol, which banned any imposition of new obstacles to free movement, it's fair to say that even though the Ankara Agreement and the Additional Protocol between the Parties is still the legal basis, its objective has not been achieved yet. The reason for this is the contrasting situation of EU citizens, who move freely with no restrictions and are allowed to enter Turkey without any further requirement whatsoever; on the other hand, Turkish citizens do not have the unrestricted right to move freely into the EU countries.

It's essential to point out the recent jurisprudence regarding the movement of Turkish citizens, in relation to the Ankara Agreement, in light of scholarly discourse the direct applicability of the Ankara Agreement to EU law, and they argue that Turkish nationals do not need to have a visa to enter the EU concerning to receive services there.[49] In this respect, free movement of persons relating to receipt services refers to passive freedom to provide services. Although the decisions of the ECJ related to association agreement between the EU and Turkey gave a positive impression about the free movement of Turkish citizens into the EU, it changed with the time. Particularly the *Demirkan* Decision on 24 September 2013[50] demonstrated that the argumentation of ECJ changed the direction for Turkish citizens, which expended the hope of Turkey in order to get visa-free regime through the case law.[51]

Competence of the EU

Considering legal basis of the competence of the EU, the Maastricht Treaty on the EU[52] of 1992 did not cover any harmonization of visa, asylum and immigration policies. In this context, the first step was to adopt two recommendations[53], which aimed at limiting the disparities between bilateral agreements concluded by the different Member States with a third State. Meantime the EC had no competence on migration but the Member States. The second step was the adoption of standard clauses on readmission for the Commission in order to insert in association or cooperation agreements.[54] Through these standard clauses the Commission gained competence to insert

---

[49] For more information about the legal effects of EU association agreements in the community legal order see Kellermann, A.E., 2008. *EJLR*, 10(3), 339-382; also Sarıibrahimoğlu, Y.S., 2011. *Ankara Bar Review*, 1, 96-103.

[50] EuGH (Grosse Kammer) Urt. v. 24.9.2013 AktZ C-221/11 abgedr. in: NVwZ 22/2013, pp. 1465-ff; also see Zeran, Ü., 2013. *Informationsbrief Ausländerrecht* 11(12), 405-464; and Sözen, Ü.S., 2014. *Istanbul Kültür Üniversitesi Hukuk Fakültesi Dergisi* 13(1), 171-185.

[51] Essential decisions of the ECJ related to the association law considering Turkish citizens began in 2000 with C-37/98 *Savaş* and in 2003 C-317/01 *Abatay/Şahin*, afterwards in 2007 C-16/05 *Tüm/Darr*; pursued in 2009 C-228/06 *Soysal/Savath* and C-242/06 *Şahin*, in 2010 C-300/09 *Toprak*; lastly in 2013 with C-221/11 *Demirkan* came to the end.

[52] The Treaty on European Union, signed in Maastricht on 7 February 1992, entered into force on 1 November 1993, OJ C 191 of 29.7.1992.

[53] Council Recommendation of 30 November 1994 concerning a specimen bilateral readmission agreement between a Member State and a third country, OJ C-274 of 19.09.1996, pp. 20-24 and Council Recommendation of 24 July 1995 on the guiding principles to be followed in drawing up protocols on the implementation of readmission agreements, OJ C-274 of 19.09.1996, pp. 25-33.

[54] Council Documents 12509/95 for community agreements and also 4272/96 for mixed agreements.

migration issues in the agreements with third countries, although the EC had no competence on migration issues.

The Treaty of Amsterdam[55] of 1999 conferred implicit and shared competences on the EU to conclude a readmission agreement with other non-member states. Additionally, it established the Area of Justice Freedom and Security (AJFS) in Title V and brought asylum and civil law issues from the third to the first pillar.[56] Through Article 63/3b of the Treaty Establishing the European Community[57], the EU is empowered to legislate on irregular immigration and irregular residence, including repatriation of irregular residents. Despite this legislation, the question of whether Member States have still the competence to conclude bilateral agreements on readmission was not clarified.[58]

In other words, the Commission received the competence with the Amsterdam Treaty to conclude readmission agreements on behalf of EU member states, except for the non-Schengen states. This competence did not allow the Commission much flexibility because it was based upon a draft model readmission agreement. Furthermore, the return of third-country nationals was explained as a *"principle of neighborliness and the responsibility of a state for those impairments to other states emanating from its territory"*.[59]

However while it was clear that the EU had an implied competence to conclude readmission agreement, it remained unclear whether this competence was to be exclusive or shared. Consequently, the legal basis of the EU's competence for readmission agreements is Article 79/3[60], in conjunction with Article 218 of Treaty on the Functioning of the European Union[61].

In a nutshell, EU's readmission agreements and bilateral readmission agreements of many EU Member States exist simultaneously. While the Readmission Agreement between Turkey and Greece exists as a bilateral agreement, the Readmission Agreement between Turkey and the EU functions at the EU level. In this respect, one can argue that the existence of simultaneous readmission agreements in bilateral and multilateral levels lead to greater overall functioning. On the other hand this could also influence their functions in a negative way. To clarify, we may take the readmission agreement between Greece and Turkey as an example.

---

[55] The Treaty of Amsterdam, signed on 2 October 1997, entered into force on 1 May 1999, OJ C 340 of 10.11.1997.

[56] This means that a large part of the former Third Pillar on the free movement of persons, covering visas, asylum, immigration, and judicial cooperation in civil matters incorporated into the Community Pillar. This title and that of the amended Third Pillar was aiming at establishing 'an area of freedom, justice and security'.

[57] Consolidated Version of the Treaty Establishing the European Community, OJ C 325/33, 24.12.2002.

[58] Panizzon, M., 2012. *Refugee Survey Quarterly*, 31(4), p. 111.

[59] Hailbronner, K., 1997. *ZaöRV*, p.31.

[60] According to Article 79/3, "[t]he Union may conclude agreements with third countries for the readmission to their countries of origin or provenance of third-country nationals who do not or who no longer fulfil the conditions for entry, presence or residence in the territory of one of the Member States."

[61] Treaty on the Functioning of the European Union of 7 February 1992, last amended by the Treaty of Lisbon on 13 December 2007, taking into account changes by the Protocol of adjustment to the Treaty of Lisbon, ABI. 2009 C 290.

Greece has become the main entry for irregular migrants seeking entry to the EU, while Turkey has become the main country of transit.[62] The bilateral readmission agreement between Greece and Turkey of 2001 being highly dysfunctional, in as much as Turkey rejects a high number of readmission requests issued by Greece. Firstly, the readmission agreement was slow to start; but afterwards by 2006, despite Turkey accepting some readmission requests, there were remarkable delays and problems.[63]

In this context, the readmission agreement between the EU and Turkey could be dysfunctional if Turkey is not able to accept the readmission requests issued by the EU Member States. Despite the fact that it is straightforward to assume that the function of the Readmission Agreement between the EU and Turkey will be questionable.

Genesis and scope of readmission agreement between EU-Turkey

In March 2003, the Commission invited Turkey to begin negotiations on a draft text of a readmission agreement, but Turkey did not formally acknowledge this invitation. Afterwards, in March 2004, Turkey agreed to negotiate a readmission agreement with the EU without any precise date. On 27 May 2005 began the negotiations officially. Due to some problems the negotiations were frozen. It took several years for both parties to restart talks. Eventually an official statement issued by the Justice and Home Affairs Council on 24 February 2011 about the conclusion of negotiations on the EU-Turkey Readmission Agreement.[64]

Due to the lack of a clear statement on a clear Roadmap for visa liberalisation for Turkish citizens, Turkey reacted and bargained for a visa facilitation process and other steps towards a visa-free regime. Consequently, the JHA Council held in February 2011 declined to authorize the European Commission to start a dialogue with Turkey on the visa liberalisation. This led to parties initial the agreed text on 21 June 2012 in Brussels. Finally almost one and half year later, the Readmission Agreement was signed on 16 December 2013[65].

The Agreement consists of 8 sections with 25 articles. Additionally, it contains 6 annexes, which form an integral part of it, and 6 joint declarations, which shall apply to persons who do not or who no longer, fulfill the conditions for entry to, presence in, or residence on the territories of Turkey or one of the Member States of the EU. The readmission obligations laid down in the Agreement between Articles 3 and 6 and comprise own nationals (Article 3 and 5) as well as third country nationals and stateless persons (Article 4 and 6).

---

[62] DOC 13106 of 23.01.2013, Parliamentary Assembly, "Migration and asylum: mounting tensions in the Eastern Mediterranean, p.1, available at http://assembly.coe.int/ASP/Doc/XrefViewPDF.asp?FileID=19349&Language=en, (last visited 20.05.2014).
[63] Baldwin-Edwards, M., 2006. *SEER*, Vol. 2006/3, p.5.
[64] See Council Conclusions on EU-Turkey Readmission Agreement and related issues, Justice and Home Affairs Council Meeting No.3071, Brussels, 24-25.02.2011.
[65] The agreement signed in accordance with Council Decision 2012/499/EU, which is published in OJ L 244, 8.9.2012, p.4.

The obligation to readmit own nationals includes also former own nationals who have refused or who have been deprived of their nationality without acquiring the nationality of another state. Moreover, the readmission obligation considering own nationals covers also family members (i.e. spouses -except the ones holding another nationality- and minor unmarried children) regardless of their place of birth or their nationality and not having an independent right of residence in the Requesting State[66].

Furthermore, the prerequisites of the readmission obligation with regard to third country nationals and stateless persons (Articles 3 and 5) is as follows: a) the person concerned holds, at the time of submission of the readmission application, a valid visa or residence permit issued by the requested State or b) the person concerned holds a residence permit issued by the requested State c) the person concerned illegally entered the territory of the Requesting State coming directly from the territory of the Requested State. Released from these obligations are persons in air transit, all persons to whom the Requesting State has issued a visa or residence permit before or after entry to its territory and all persons who enjoy visa-free access to the territory of the Requesting State.

It is essential to point out that the obligation considering third country nationals or stateless persons will be applied only three years after the entry into force of the whole Agreement. Nevertheless, during that period that obligation will be applicable to third country nationals and stateless persons coming from those third countries with which Turkey concluded readmission agreements. At the same time the bilateral agreements between Turkey and Member States maintain applicable in the relevant parts (Article 24/3).

The acceptance of travel documents for readmission differs between own nationals and third country nationals or stateless persons. For own nationals, in the event that there is no consular office of Turkey in a Member State or in case of the expiry of specified time limits for issuance of travel documents, Turkey accepts a positive reply to the readmission application issued by the state as a sufficient travel document for the readmission of the person concerned; however for third country nationals or stateless persons, Turkey accepts the use of the EU's standard travel documents for expulsion purposes (Article 4/3 and 4/4).

The technical provisions regarding the readmission procedure (readmission application, means of evidence, time limits, transfer modalities and modes of transportation) and readmission in error (Article 13) set out in the third Section. The fact that no readmission application will be needed in cases where the person to be readmitted is in possession of a valid travel document or identity card and, in case of third country nationals, valid visa or residence permit issues by the Requested State provides some procedural flexibility (Article 7/3).

In addition to these, the so-called accelerated procedure is set out in Article 7/4. This procedure has been agreed upon for persons apprehended in the border region[67]. Under these conditions, readmission applications have to be submitted

---

66 With regard to the Agreement, *'Requesting State'* shall mean the State (Turkey or one of the Member States) submitting a readmission application pursuant to Article 8 or a transit application pursuant to Article 15 of this Agreement.

67 Border region is an area within the Requesting State's territory extending inwards up to 20 kilometers from the external border of that State, regardless the border is shared between the Requesting State

within 3 working days, and replies have to be given within 5 working days. In normal circumstances, the time limit for replies to readmission applications is 25 calendar days (Article 11). If the Requesting State has a shorter initial detention period in its national legislation, then the shorter period will apply. With an exception of the Requesting State with the maximum detention period of less or equal to 60 days, the initial period may be extended up to 60 calendar days. Time limits begin to run with the date of receipt of the readmission request.

In the fourth Section, transit operations are set out in Articles 14 and 15 in conjunction with annex 6. The following Sections contain the necessary rules on costs, data protection and the relation to other International obligations and existing EU Directives as non-affection clause.

In order to put the Agreement into operation and control the process, the Joint Readmission Committee will be composed, and have the tasks and powers laid down in Article 19. The decisions of the Committee will be binding on the Member States and Turkey. In addition, Article 20 gives the possibility for Turkey and individual Member States to conclude bilateral implementing Protocols, which are clarified in Article 21.

All obligations will be mentioned and explained in the paper are reciprocal. The thing that should be kept in mind is that even though, in theory, the readmission agreements are reciprocal, in practice they usually introduce more obligations for third countries than for the EU.[68] Consequently, in this case, Turkey will carry more obligations than the EU. Considering the all Member States under the roof of the EU as one Contracting Party, will mean that Turkey as Requested State will get all readmission applications from all Member States under the EU's umbrella.

Roadmap towards a visa-free regime

In parallel with the Readmission Agreement, a Roadmap towards a visa-free regime was initiated. Still it does not mean that a visa-free regime will come into force simultaneously with the readmission agreement. In contrast to the general hope of Turkish citizens, in procedural terms, following Turkey accept the Readmission Agreement with the EU; the right to start a Visa Free Dialogue will be given. To make it clear, the way towards visa liberalisation will depend on Turkey's progress in adopting and implementing the measure and fulfilling the requirements set out in the Roadmap, including the consistent and effective implementation of the Readmission Agreement and effective cooperation *vis-á-vis* all Member States on JHA issues.[69]

The Roadmap comprises four blocks, which are documents security, migration and border management, public order and security, and fundamental rights. The first Block of the Roadmap sets out document security, particularly passports or travel documents, ID cards and breeder documents. The second Block of the Roadmap is about migration management, expressly border

---

and the Requested State as well as the sea pots including customs zones and international airports of the Requesting State.
[68] Kruse, I., 2006. *EJML*, 8, p.122.
[69] Trauner, F., & Manigrassi, E., 2014. *EJML*, 16, p.129.

management, visa policy, carriers' responsibility, international protection, and illegal migration.

Regarding visa policy Turkey should abolish issuance of visas at the borders as an ordinary procedure for the national of certain non-EU countries, and especially for countries representing a high migratory and secure risk to the EU, pursue the alignment of Turkish visa policy, legislation and administrative capacities towards the EU *Acquis*, and allow non-discriminatory visa-free access to the Turkish territory for citizens of all EU Member States.

The requirements mentioned above regarding visa policy aim to harmonize the visa regime. On the one hand, the requirements intend to harmonize and make the implementation of the EU *Acquis* easier for Turkey; on the other hand, especially in economic terms, some restrictive stances, for instance the harmonization of the visa regime, might damage economic ties with neighboring countries.[70]

Moreover, while the obligation of allowing non-discriminatory visa-free access to the Turkish territory for the citizens of all the EU Member States should be fulfilled though the Roadmap, instead of lifting the visa obligation for Turkish citizens, this will come to the stage first after fulfillment of all the requirements of the Roadmap. One can argue that in terms of time implementation, this obligation is not reciprocal.

Another essential point is about the international protection. Despite the fact that Turkey signed the 1951 Refugee Convention[71] and its 1967 protocol[72] with a 'geographical limitation' under Article 1(B) of the Convention, since Turkey is not obligated to apply the Convention to refugees from outside Europe. In other words, non-European asylum seekers cannot remain permanently in Turkey as refugees. Turkey only offers them a domestic status called "temporary asylum", which allows them to stay in Turkey only on a temporary basis until they find a long-term solution through the assistance of UNHCR.

According to the Roadmap, Turkey should adopt and effectively implement legislation and implementing provisions, with regard to the EU *Acquis* and with standards set by the Geneva Convention on Refugees from 1951 and its 1967 Protocol, thus especially excluding any geographical limitation, in order to ensure the respect of the principle of *non-refoulement*, also taking into account also the European Convention on Human Rights.

It is clear that lifting the geographical limitation intends to harmonize the EU's asylum policy. Nevertheless, Turkey prepared the legal basis through the Foreigners and International Protection Law, in order to improve the living conditions and rights of asylum seekers in Turkey; it still comprises the geographical limitation but renamed the "temporary asylum" as "conditional refugees". The reason is that Turkey was actually supposed to link lifting the

---

[70] The requirements will be analysed and discussed further in detail on the paper.
[71] United Nations General Assembly, Convention Relating to the Status of Refugees, 28 July 1951, United Nations, Treaty Series, Vol. 189, p.137, available at http://www.refworld.org/docid/3be01b964.html, (last visited 10.05.2014).
[72] United Nations General Assembly, Protocol Relating to the Status of Refugees, 31 January 1967, United Nations, Treaty Series, Vol. 606, p. 267, available http://www.refworld.org/cgi-bin/texis/vtx/rwmain?docid=3ae6b3ae4, (last visited 10.05.2014).

geographical limitation with its accession to the EU, in order to get more protection under the EU umbrella.[73]

In Turkey's point of view, lifting the geographical limitation exactly at this time can cause big problems, especially because of the mass flow of Syrian refugees, which means that Turkey would face a "refugee crisis". Moreover, although Turkey would have a membership status in the future, this would lead Turkey into a "first country of asylum" responsible for status determination because of its geographical situation.[74] In EU's point of view, this is an essential improvement to ensure the respect of the principle of *non-refoulement*.[75] In practice, this would support the will of not only Syrian refugees but also refugees from all neighboring countries to stay and apply for asylum in Turkey and they would not need to go to the EU, for instance. In this sense, Turkey's fear of becoming a 'buffer zone' is an appropriate attitude.

Apart from geographical limitation, it is also resolved that Turkey should establish a specialized body responsible for the refugee status determination procedures, provide adequate infrastructures and sufficient human resources and funds ensuring a decent reception and protection of the rights and dignity of asylum seekers and refugees, and give the possibility to persons who are granted a refugee status to self-sustain, to access to public services, enjoy social rights and be put in the condition to integrate in Turkey.

Even if the Agreement referred to international agreements considering human rights, in particular the European Convention of November 4, 1950 for the Protection of Human Rights and Fundamental Freedoms[76], the Convention of July 28, 1951 on the Status of Refugees[77] and the Protocol of January 31, 1967 on the Status of Refugees[78], the Convention of December 10, 1984 against Torture and other Cruel, Inhuman or Degrading Treatment or Punishment[79] in

---

[73] Ibid.

[74] Toğral, B., 2012. Alternatives Turkish Journal of International Relations, Vol. 11/2, p. 71.

[75] For further information of the EU's point of view see also Resolution 1918 (2013), "Migration and asylum: mounting tensions in the eastern Mediterranean", p. 4, available at http://assembly.coe.int/ASP/Doc/XrefViewPDF.asp?FileID=19467&Language=EN, (last visited 22.05.2014).

[76] Convention for the Protection of Human Rights and Fundamental Freedoms and Protocol of 4 November 1950, available at http://www.echr.coe.int/Documents/Collection_Convention_1950_ENG.pdf, (last visited 22.05.2014); the text of the Convention had been previously amended according to the provisions of Protocol No. 3 (ETS No. 45), which entered into force on 21 September 1970, of Protocol No. 5 (ETS No. 55), which entered into force on 20 December 1971 and of Protocol No. 8 (ETS No. 118), which entered into force on 1 January 1990, and comprised also the text of Protocol No.2 (ETS No. 44 which, in accordance with Article 5, paragraph 3 thereof, had been an integral part of the Convention since its entry into force on 21 September 1970. All provisions which had been amended or added by these Protocols were replaced by Protocol No. 11 (ETS No. 155), as from the date of its entry into force on 1 November 1998. As from that date, Protocol No. 9 (ETS No. 140), which entered into force on 1 October 1994, was repealed and Protocol No. 10 (ETS No. 146) had lost its purpose. The text of the Convention as amended by its Protocol No. 14 (CETS No. 194) as from the date of its entry into force on 1 June 2010, available at http://conventions.coe.int/treaty/en/treaties/html/005.htm, (last visited 22.05.2014).

[77] See Fn. 39.

[78] See Fn. 40.

[79] United Nations General Assembly, Convention against Torture and Other Cruel, Inhuman or Degrading Treatment or Punishment, New York, 10 December 1984, United Nations, Treaty Series,

the preamble and Article 18, it did not keep lots of scholars and human rights agencies from criticizing and drawing attention to the human rights violations considering the EU's readmission agreements. Although some human rights clauses are included into the readmission agreements, they are not enough to control all process considering human rights protection; especially the EU is not able to control what could happen to the readmitted migrants in the transit country or generally in country of origin. In other words, when a third country national or a stateless person, who used Turkey as a transit country in order to reach the EU, is readmitted to Turkey, this migrant will readmit again to the country of origin with which Turkey supposed to conclude a readmission agreement. Therefore, this could lead to a domino effect in which the EU would have no power to control anymore.[80]

Despite the fact that the implementation of the EU's readmission agreements with third states have resulted in frequent human rights violations, which comprise violation of the rights of refugees and asylum seekers, and the *non-refoulement* principle. Therefore, the practical implementation of the readmission agreement between the EU and Turkey is also not able to guarantee human rights, owing to the neighbouring countries of Turkey from where the migrants in general come from and transit Turkey.

In light of human rights, three aspects of the readmission agreement between the EU and Turkey seem problematic. Firstly, apart from generally international obligations considering human rights protection, there is no particular safeguard in connection with the treatment of third country nationals readmit by Turkey, who may be restrained or deported on account of meeting with a repulse for refugee status or the domestic 'temporary asylum' status. Secondly, there is the lack of exclusive mechanism or authority for examining protection claims and inconsistent respect of international obligations considering the treatment of intercepted irregular migrants for whom a readmission request is issued. Last but not the least, there is no transparency with regard to monitoring and being responsible over the drafting and the implementation of the readmission agreement and especially the Roadmap.[81]

The third block of the Roadmap laid out public order and security, especially preventing and fighting organized crime, terrorism and corruption, judicial co-operation, law enforcement co-operation, and data protection. The last block covers fundamental rights, in particular freedom of movement of the citizens of Turkey, conditions and procedures for the issue of identity documents, citizens' rights and respect for and protection of minorities, and some final remarks. These final remarks show the conditional way to lift the visa obligation for Turkish citizens.

Vol. 1465, p.85, available at https://treaties.un.org/doc/Publication/MTDSG/Volume I/Chapter IV/IV-9.en.pdf, (last visited 22.05.2014).

[80] Billet, C., 2010. *EJML*, 12, p. 74.

[81] *Euro-Mediterranean Human Rights Network*, Policy Brief: "An EU-Turkey Readmission Agreement - Undermining the rights of migrants, refugees and asylum seekers?", p.7, available at http://www.euromedrights.org/eng/wp-content/uploads/2013/06/En_TurkeyReadmis_Pb_web.pdf, (last visited 22.05.2014).

Upon fulfillment of all the requirements of the Roadmap, the Commission will present a proposal to the European Parliament and the Council for the lifting of the visa obligations, by amending Council Regulation (EC) 539/2001[82]. The problem here is that the timetable set for the fulfillment of requirements, which is essential for lifting visa obligation for Turkish citizens, was not clarified. This explains why this can lead some misunderstanding between the EU and Turkey. In Turkey's point of view, Turkish citizens would be able to visa-free travel to the EU within maximum three and a half years. Conversely a strict timetable named neither in the Readmission Agreement nor in the Roadmap.

Therefore, in accordance with the ordinary decision making procedure, the Council of the EU and the European Parliament will vote upon by a qualified majority in order to lift the visa obligation. Therefore, this case will be again questionable, whether a qualified majority will support the lifting of the visa obligation.

Conclusion

According to Article 24/3, three years after the Agreement will have been ratified and come into force, Turkey will not be obligated to accept irregular migrants who used Turkey as a transit country *en route* the EU, nevertheless an exception is made for the third country nationals, whose come from the countries, which Turkey have already signed readmission agreements[83]. In addition, during this transitional period of three years Turkey will accept own nationals who do not or who no longer, fulfill the conditions for entry to, presence in, or residence on the territories one of the Member States.

During the last three years Turkey has been increasingly seen as a destination country by asylum seekers, and immigrants rather than a transit country, especially through a mass flow of Syrian refugees. This explains why, apart from all problematic issues, it is questionable whether Turkey will be able to handle all migrants, who are already in Turkey as refugees or guests, and additionally whom the EU to Turkey will readmit.

Moreover, a readmission agreement with a state like Turkey, which already has the candidate country status, is in fact contradictory to the EU's criteria[84], which are used for choosing third countries in order to negotiate new readmission agreements. These criteria excluded the countries with which the EU has ongoing accession negotiations.[85]

As already mentioned above, in the case of the visa liberalisation, the readmission agreement has to come into force and work properly. So the readmission agreement and the visa liberalisation will not come into force simultaneously. Subsequently, it is not straightforward to indicate the Agreement

---

[82] Council Regulation (EC) 539/2001, OJ L 81 of 21.3.2001.

[83] Turkey signed readmission agreements with Syria (2001), Kyrgyzstan (2003), Nigeria (2011), Bosnia Herzegovina (2012), Romania (2004), Ukraine (2005), Russia (2011), Pakistan (2010), Yemen (2011), Moldova (2012) and Greece (2001) to fight against irregular migration.

[84] "Criteria for the identification of third countries with which new readmission agreements need to be negotiated" see for details DOC 7990/02 of 15 April 2002, approved by JHA Council of 25/26 April 2002.

[85] Billet, C., 2010. *EJML*, 12, p. 54.

between the EU and Turkey as a *"carrot"*, as the EU usually gives this name to readmission agreements.

Due to the fact that compensatory measures on visas have been used as a *"carrot"* because of their nature, which are interconnected each other. To make it clear, in this sense, the readmission agreement signature in parallel with the agreement on visa facilitation, which has happened for the first time with Russia[86]. However this has been applied usually for readmission agreements for the EU's neighboring countries, with Turkey is not the same situation. Except that in the case of the readmission agreement between the EU and Pakistan[87], *"carrot"* turned to a *"stick"*, in as much as there was no sign for a visa facilitation agreement involved.

In this context, nevertheless in the future there is a sign for visa-free regime for Turkish citizens; it does not mean that this sign gives the guarantee. That's why, paving the way towards the visa-free regime seems rough. In a nutshell, neither with a *"carrot"* nor with a *"stick"* the right picture for the Readmission Agreement between the EU and Turkey could be drawn.

References

Baldwin-Edwards, M. (2006). Migration between Greece and Turkey: From the 'Exchange of Populations' to the Non-Recognition of Borders. *South-East Europe Review for Labour and Social Affairs*, Vol. 2006/3, 115-122.

Billet, C. (2010). EC Readmission Agreements: A Prime Instruments of the External Dimension of the EU's Fight Against Irregular Immigration. *European Journal of Migration and Law*, 12, 45-79.

Groenendijk, K., Hoffmann, H., & Kuiten, M. (2013). Das Assoziationsrecht EWG/Türkei: Rechte türkischer Staatsangehöriger in der EuGH-Rechtsprechung [The Association Law EC/Turkey: Rights of Turkish Citizens through the ECJ Jurisprudence]. Baden-Baden (in German).

Hailbronner, Kay (1997). Readmission Agreements and the Obligation on States under Public International Law to Readmit their Own and Foreign Nationals. *Zeitschrift für ausländisches öffentliches Recht und Völkerrecht*, 57, 1-50.

Kabaalioğlu, H. (2012). Turkey's Relations with the European Union: Customs Union and Accession Negotiations. *Müller-Graff, P.C. and Kabaalioğlu, H. (eds.) Turkey and the European Union.* Baden-Baden, pp. 11-23.

Kellermann, A.E. (2008). The Rights of Non-Member State Nationals under the EU Association Agreements. *European Journal of Law Reform*, 3, 339-382.

Kruse, I., (2006). EU Readmission Policy and its Effects on Transit Countries: The Case of Albania. *European Journal of Migration and Law*, 8, 115-142.

Panizzon, M. (2012). Readmission Agreements of EU Member States: A Case for EU Subsidiarity or Dualism?. *Refugee Survey Quaterly*, 31(4), 101-133.

Peers, S. (1996). Living in Sin: Legal Integration Under the EC-Turkey Customs Union. *European Journal of International Law*, 411-430.

Sarıibrahimoğlu, Y.S. (2011). Turkey's Mistakes and Legal Rights in Framework of EU-Turkey Relations. *Ankara Bar Review*, 1, 96-103.

Sözen, Ü.S. (2014). Avrupa Birliği Adalet Divanı'nın 24.09.2013 Tarihli C-221/11 Demirkan Kararı [The Demirkan Decision C-221/11 from 24.09.2013 of European Court of Justice]. *Istanbul*

---

[86] See Council Decision 2007/341/EC of 19 April 2007 on the conclusion of the Agreement between the European Community and the Russian Federation on readmission, published in OJ L 129 of 17.5.2007.

[87] See Council Decision 2010/649/EU of 7 October 2010 on the conclusion of the Agreement between the European Community and the Islamic Republic of Pakistan on the readmission of persons residing without authorisation, published in OJ L 287 of 4.11.2010.

Kültür Üniversitesi Hukuk Fakültesi Dergisi [Law Faculty Journal of Istanbul Culture University], 13(1), 171-185 (in Turkish).

Toğral, B. (2012). Securitization of Migration in Europe: Critical Reflections on Turkish Migration Practices. *Alternatives Turkish Journal of International Relations*, 11(2), 65-77.

Trauner, F., & Manigrassi, E. (2014). When Visa-free Travel Becomes Difficult to Achieve and Easy to Lose: The EU Visa Free Dialogues after the EU's Experience with the Western Balkans. *European Journal of Migration and Law*, 16, 125-146.

Trauner, F., & Wolff, S. (2014). The Negotiation and Contestation of EU Migration Policy Instruments: A Research Framework. *European Journal of Migration and Law*, 16, 1-18.

Zeran, Ü. (2013). Die Demirkan Entscheidung: eine nicht überzeugende Neujustierung des Assoziationsvertrages mit der Türkei [The Demirkan Decision: an unconvincing readjustment of the Association Agreement with Turkey]. Informationsbrief Ausländerrecht, 11(12), 405-464 (in German).

Combatting fraud as a disincentive of an unintended economic migrant: a comparative of the direct Turkish model and the indirect Australian model

Sherene Özyürek[88] and Rodger Fernandez[89]

Introduction

As Turkey has moved from a state of emigration to immigration, lawmakers have identified the need to combat fraud within its migration framework. Its new framework has distinct similarities to the Australian model, a country which has been shaped by immigration but has shifted its policies to that of a protective objective. This paper provides a platform for comparing policies in determining the more effective measures for migration planning in relation to combatting fraud to effectively deter unintended economic migrants in both countries.

Under Article 54 of the *Law on Foreigners and International Protection* ("Law No. 6458")[90], which came into effect in April 2013 (RTMIDGMM, 2013), a removal decision may be issued against foreigners who use false information and fraudulent documents in procedures concerning entry into Turkey. The foreigner, or his or her legal representative may appeal to the administrative court against the deportation decision within fifteen days and applications to the court is concluded in fifteen days and the decision of the administrative court on the issue is final (RTMIDGMM, 2013, p. 30).[91]

In contrast, the Public Interest Criteria 4020 ("PIC 4020") otherwise known as "the Fraud Principal", was introduced in April 2011 (Migration Regulations 1994 (Cth), Schedule 4, PIC 4020; Select Legislative Instrument No. 13, 2011)[92] into Australian Migration Law which was later amended to specifically deal with identity fraud in 2014 (Migration Amendment (2014 Measures No. 1) Regulation 2014 (Cth), *Select Legislative Instrument No. 32, 2014*).[93] The policy decision surrounding PIC 4020 was to significantly increase the level of integrity in visa applications by providing a *strong disincentive* to those considering giving, or causing to be given, a bogus document or information that is false or

---

[88] Senior Lawyer, FCG PTY LTD, Melbourne, Australia; Accredited Immigration Law Specialist, Law Institute of Victoria, Australia; Lecturer, Postgraduate Immigration Law Program, Victoria University, Australia; Undertaking Masters of Law by Research, Victoria University, Australia. FCG Legal Pty Ltd, 18 Drummond Street, Carlton, Victoria, Australia 3053; sherene@fcglegal.com

[89] Senior Lawyer, FCG PTY LTD, Melbourne, Australia; Accredited Immigration Law Specialist, Law Institute of Victoria, Australia; Adjunct Professor of Law, Victoria University, Australia; Director, Postgraduate Immigration Law Program, Victoria University, Australia. FCG Legal Pty Ltd, 18 Drummond Street, Carlton, Victoria, Australia 3053; rodger@fcglegal.com

[90] http://gocdergisi.com/kaynak/2013_yabancilar_ve_uluslararasi_koruma_kanunu.pdf

[91] Migration Regulations 1994 (Cth), Schedule 4, PIC 4020; Select Legislative Instrument No. 13, 2011.

[92] Migration Regulations 1994 (Cth), Schedule 4, PIC 4020; Select Legislative Instrument No. 13, 2011.

[93] Migration Amendment (2014 Measures No. 1) Regulation 2014 (Cth), Select Legislative Instrument No. 32, 2014.

misleading in a material particular, or in recent amendments, not providing their true identity. The applicant is subsequently banned for three years from applying for another visa (Commonwealth Consolidated Regulations, 2011).[94] However, in the time their application is being processed (up to 3 years in some cases), they are able to build up working experience and earn money and can then rely on this experience in their future application for permanent residency via the General Skilled Migration ("GSM") pathway. Evidence will be provided to support such a proposition and to indicate that the misuse of PIC 4020 as an unintended pathway for an unintended economic migrant could be partly attributed to the lengthy processing times. This supports the notion that the inclusion of the Fraud Principal into Australian Migration Law has not been an effective tool to combat unintended economic migrants, as it is not supported by other policies in the migration program, as demonstrated in the Turkish model, but rather is used as a procrastinating tool to remain in Australia.

In view of the evolving nature the immigration law in both countries, it is worth noting that the authors will continue to undertake further analysis to compare the effectiveness of Turkey's and Australia's models subsequent to the implementation of the new laws in each country that were introduced in 2014.

The current analysis of retrospective data (2011-2014) (Australian Government Migration Review Tribunal, MRT-RRT Caseload Reports [AGMRT], 2010-2014)[95] provides a background of the inefficiencies of the Australian model in comparison to the practicality of the current Turkish model that combats fraud in alignment with all policies of the migration program and not "in isolation", an important variable that contributes to the reported ineffectiveness of the Australian model.

Methods

This paper undertook a quantitative approach to analyse retrospective data (2010-2014) produced by the Australian Government Migration Review Tribunal ("MRT"), caseload statistics data presented over a 4 year period (one year prior to the introduction of the Fraud Principal and 3 years afterwards) (Australian Government Migration Review Tribunal [AGMRT], MRT-RRT Caseload Reports 2010-2014).

The focus of this inquiry is on economic migrants (skill linked migrants), however, since the introduction of policy changes impacts on different interlinked migration sectors, a comparative analysis was also included to encompass the Partner visa sector.

Results and discussion

Public Interest Criteria 4020 ("the Fraud Principal") was introduced in April 2011 into Australian Migration Law (Migration Regulations 1994 (Cth), Schedule 4, PIC 4020; Select Legislative Instrument No. 13, 2011).[96] However it

---

[94] Migration Regulations (Cth) 1994, Schedule 4, item 4020(2).
[95] Migration Review Tribunal caseload statistics (2010 – 2014)
[96] Migration Regulations 1994 (Cth), Schedule 4, PIC 4020; Select Legislative Instrument No. 13, 2011.

was amended to specifically deal with identity fraud in 2014 (Migration Amendment (2014 Measures No. 1) Regulation 2014 (Cth), Select Legislative Instrument No. 32, 2014).[97]

The policy decision surrounding PIC 4020 was to significantly increase the level of integrity in visa applications by providing a *strong disincentive* to those considering giving, or causing to be given, a bogus document or information that is false or misleading in a material particular, or in recent amendments, not providing their true identity.

The intended pathway for economic migrants, including Turkish incoming migrants is through the GSM scheme. This paper will focus on the unintended pathway and consequential burden on the migration program through the unintended use of the Fraud Principal.

PIC 4020 (the Fraud Principal) was first introduced into Australian Migration Law affecting initially the GSM program in April 2011(Migration Regulations 1994 (Cth), Schedule 4, PIC 4020; Select Legislative Instrument No. 13, 2011).[98] This was a response to the lack of effective refusal provisions in the legislation on the basis of providing fraudulent documents in relation to work experience, a necessary requirement for any visa criterion in the GSM scheme.

The pathway for GSM, particularly for students, including students of Turkish origin, at the time the PIC 4020 was introduced, required a skills assessment, which, depending on the occupation, required a component of practical work experience. This work experience was hard to obtain by recent graduates during their studies as they had yet to attain their qualification. This difficulty led to the facilitation of false documents in relation to work experience, consequently resulting in an extraordinary number of students having their visa's cancelled, which led to a three year ban on any temporary visas (Law Institute of Victoria Legal Policy and Practice, 2009).[99] It is noted that Turkey adopts a similar approach in cancellation, however also extends the consequence of cancellation to possible removal (RTMIDGMM, 2013, p. 14).[100]

The introduction of PIC 4020 was to combat fraud at the initial application stage. In theory, PIC 4020 worked as a parallel to the cancellation provision and extended the ban to both temporary and permanent visas. However, the ineffectiveness of PIC 4020 was highlighted in a case study of two registered Australian migration agents who sold a "three-year working visa", which in reality, were only encouraging onshore international graduate students with no alternative pathways to lodge applications onshore for General Skilled Migration (GSM) which would ultimately be refused due to the lack of work experience (McKenzie & Baker, 2014).[101] The reason they were three-year visas is that the

---

[97] Migration Amendment (2014 Measures No. 1) Regulation 2014 (Cth), Select Legislative Instrument No. 32, 2014

[98] Migration Regulations 1994 (Cth), Schedule 4, PIC 4020; Select Legislative Instrument No. 13, 2011.

[99] 'Inquiry into the welfare of International students, Submission to the Senate Education, Employment and Workplace Relations Committee' (2009) Law Institute of Victoria Legal Policy and Practice 21 August 2009.

[100] Law on Foreigners and International Protection No. 6458, Article 16.

[101] McKenzie and Baker, The Sydney Morning Herald, Visa fraud suspects fled after wiring $1m overseas (August 2014).

time to process the application through the Immigration Department and to then review the decision at the MRT equated to an average of three years (McKenzie & Baker, 2014). The fishing for alternative pathways for an economic migrant is not uncommon, however, the introduction at the time when students were applying for these "three-year working visas" was the same time these graduates would be rejected on PIC 4020 and consequently faced a three-year ban. PIC 4020, therefore, clearly did not provide a disincentive to apply.

This unintended pathway would be particularly attractive with students who had no alternative pathway, such as Turkish students (other than in a postgraduate level) who are subject to stricter evidentiary requirements in their initial student visa application stage as they are viewed as a higher risk in not abiding by their student visa requirements (Australian Government, Federal Register of Legislative Instruments, 2014).[102]

Data analysis showed that while the migration planning numbers for GSM stream over the period from 2011 to 2014 were consistent, there was a substantial increase of reviews at the MRT with an increase of 580% of applications lodged at the MRT for GSM in 2012 and a further 120% increase over 2013 (a total increase of 700% compared to 2011) (see Figure 1) (*Source: AGMRT, 2010-2014*).[103]

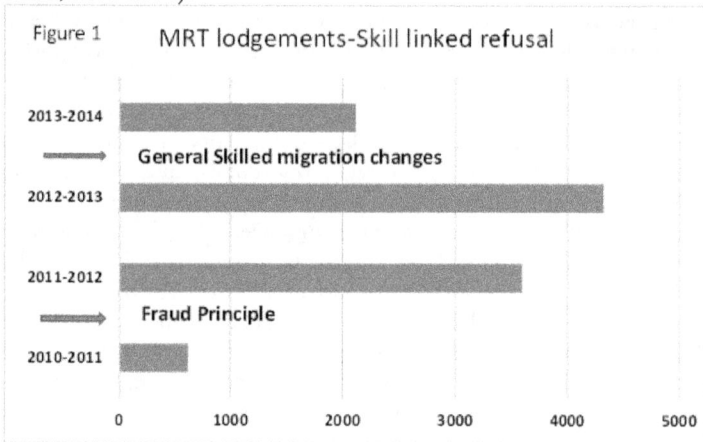

Figure 1   MRT lodgements-Skill linked refusal

---

[102] Migration Regulations (Cth)1994, Select Legislative Instrument 2014 No. 14.
[103] Migration Review Tribunal caseload statistics (2010 – 2014).

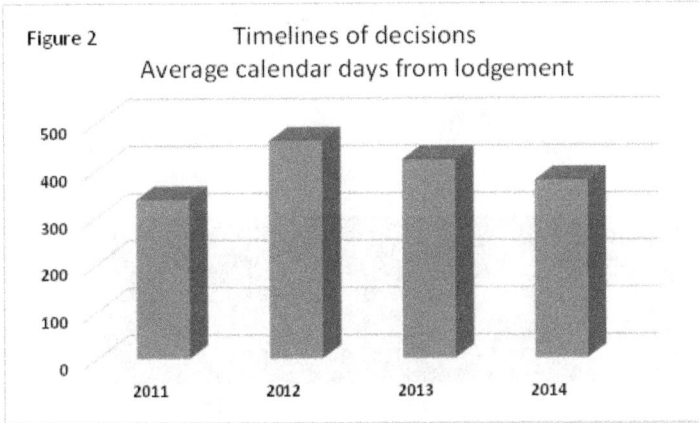

Figure 2
Timelines of decisions
Average calendar days from lodgement

Such a considerable increase in MRT lodgements for GSM in 2012 (shown in Figure 1) could be mainly attributed to the introduction of PIC 4020. What is concerning, is in addition to PIC 4020 not realising its disincentive intentions, it has only added to the issue of lengthy processing times (Figure 2) (*Source: AGMRT, 2010-2014*)[104] and subsequently the misuse of this as a pathway for an unintended economic migrant (AGMRT, 2010-2014).[105] This case study is representative of the attitude of applicants in relation to PIC 4020, when an unintended economic migrant is faced with no alternative pathways.

In July 2013, the 485 visa in the general skilled migration program was changed to include graduate work and post study streams, providing that if a student studied a bachelor degree or higher they do not require a skills assessment nor an occupation off a skills list if they obtained their first student visa after 5 November 2011 and therefore provided a pathway for a certain group. Therefore, such changes could have resulted in the limited observed drop in GSM refusal to 340% in 2014 (Australian Government, Department of Immigration and Border Protection [AGDIBP], 2011).[106] However, all of the remaining students not in this sector still required a skills assessment, experience and an occupation off a skills list and were left in the same position (AGDIBP, 2011).[107]

Secondly, in the same year, the alternative pathway for GSM was also stagnated by the introduction of an "invite system" based on a points test, which most graduates after completing their studies did not have enough points to even lodge an expression of interest to be invited to apply, again due to their inability to attain practical work experience during their studies or attain a visa that

---

[104] Migration Review Tribunal caseload statistics (2010 – 2014).
[105] Migration Review Tribunal caseload statistics (2010 – 2014).
[106] Migration Amendment Regulation (Cth) 2011 (No. 1), Explanatory Statement, Select Legislative Instrument 2011 No. 33.
[107] Migration Amendment Regulation (Cth) 2011 (No. 1), Explanatory Statement, Select Legislative Instrument 2011 No. 33.

would allow them to, after their studies (Migration Amendment Regulation (Cth) 2012 (No. 2)).[108]

Figure 3 Skill linked as a % of total migration program

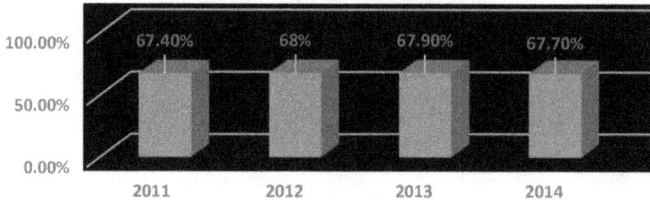

(Source: AGMRT, 2010-2014).[109]

As a result and despite the changes in GSM program, the data still showed a substantial 340% increase in MRT lodgement cases in 2014 compared to 2011, with the consistent variable being PIC 4020 despite the numbers in migration planning staying consistent (Figure 3)

It is interesting to note that while all these changes took place in GSM, another stream, namely, the Partner visa, where the PIC 4020 principal came into effect in 2013, showed an increase of 160% rate of refusal (Figure 4) *(Source: AGMRT, 2010-2014).*[110] That was the biggest increase in the last five years and happened at the same time GSM stream got stagnated, regardless of whether the PIC 4020 was introduced as a disincentive in the stream or not. It is worth noting here that the migration planning numbers were also consistent during these years in this stream (Australian Government, Department of Immigration and Border Protection [AGDIBP], 2015a).[111]

---

[108] Migration Amendment Regulation (Cth) 2012 (No. 2), Explanatory Statement, Select Legislative Instrument 2012 No. 82.
[109] Migration Review Tribunal caseload statistics (2010 – 2014).
[110] Migration Review Tribunal caseload statistics (2010 – 2014).
[111] Department of Immigration and Border Protection, Migration program statistics (2015a).

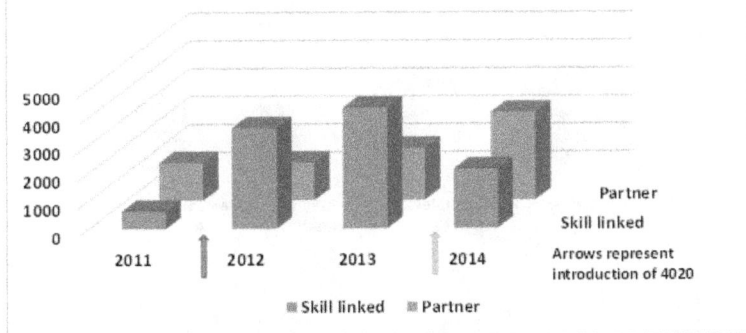

Figure 4   The Fraud factor impacted on skill linked and partner visas but not student visas

This supports the hypothesis that PIC 4020 does not provide a deterrent for economic migrants from seeking alternative pathways. It relates back to the case study that unintended economic migrants are looking at pathways regardless of the ultimate consequence and Partner visas have one of the highest processing times second to GSM to enable the applicant to work while their visa was getting processed and during review (AGDIBP, 2015b).[112] It is noted that Turkey also takes a strong stance on the unintended use of the Partner visa pathway based on false premises which consequence is also removal (RTMIDGMM, 2013, p. 23).[113]

Further analysis has shown that since the introduction of PIC 4020 and over the period from 2011 to 2014, the MRT has affirmed 75% of the total skill linked refusal cases to be based on a refusal under PIC 4020 (Figure 5) *(Source: AGMRT, 2010-2014).*[114]

This further strengthens the merit of the proposition that the sharp increase of skill-linked lodgements of MRT reviews over that period was mainly attributed to the introduction of the PIC 4020 (AGDIBP, 2014).[115] Furthermore, the system set up for GSM does not support the disincentive aim of PIC 4020. This current permanent pathway for GSM is based on a points test and provides points based on work experience in Australia for a 10 year period. Secondly, one year of work experience in Australia provides the same number of points for three years of overseas experience, three years of experience in Australia equates to five years overseas (Commonwealth Consolidated Regulations, 2012).[116]

---

[112] Department of Immigration and Border Protection, Family Visa processing times statistics (2015).
[113] Law on Foreigners and International Protection No. 6458, Article 36.
[114] Migration Review Tribunal caseload statistics (2010 – 2014).
[115] Annual Report 2013 – 2014, (2014) Australia Government, Department of Immigration and Border Protection.
[116] Migration Regulations (Cth) 1994, Schedule 6D.

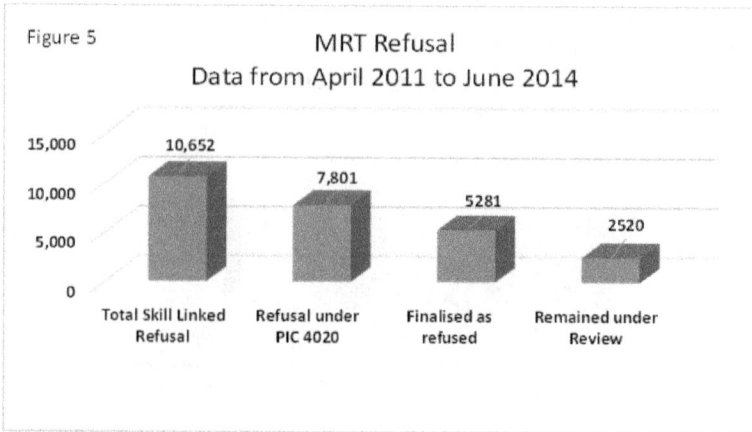

Figure 5 MRT Refusal Data from April 2011 to June 2014

Therefore, even If the applicants are banned for three years, by the time their applications are processed due to the inefficiencies of the Australian model, they can obtain experience and money in the processing period, which can then be relied on in their future applications for permanent residency via the GSM pathway. Therefore, in theory, the applicants still see themselves in a better position, having gained the experience, being banned for three years and then being able to apply after that, in comparison to facing no ban, gaining no experience, no wealth and not being able to apply within the same time frame. Hence, the system set up for GSM does not support the disincentive aim of PIC 4020. Therefore, in comparison, the Turkish approach of a possible ban of up to five years and no points system which is applied in the same circumstance may be a more effective long-term deterrent (RTMIDGMM, 2013, p. 5).[117]

What does the future hold? Australia and Turkey implemented changes in 2014 to take more measures to combat fraud. However, statistical analysis of MRT caseload statistics of retrospective data (2010-2014) produced by the Australian Government clearly supports the proposition that the PIC 4020 does not deter unintended economic migrants but rather is a procrastinating tool to allow GSM applicants to obtain experience for both short-term and long-term gain on their pathway to permanent residency. It can be predicted that the immediate consequential approach of the Turkish model of removal is the underlying variable to each countries' future success in combatting fraud as it removes the unintended pathway that unintended economic migrants are able to access through the Australian model.

References

Australian Government Migration Review Tribunal (2010-2014). MRT-RRT caseload statistics (2010–2014). Retrieved from http://www.mrt-rrt.gov.au/Forms-and-publications/Statistics.aspx

Australian Government, Department of Immigration and Border Protection. (2011). Migration Amendment Regulations 2011 (No. 1), Explanatory Statement, Select Legislative Instrument 2011 No.13; Policy Advice Manual 3-PAM – Sch4 - 4020 – The integrity PIC. Retrieved from http://www.austlii.edu.au/au/legis/cth/num_reg_es/mar20111n13o2011417.html

---

[117] Law on Foreigners and International Protection No. 6458, Article(9)(3).

Australian Government, Department of Immigration and Border Protection. (2014). Annual Report 2013 – 2014. Retrieved from https://www.immi.gov.au/about/reports/annual/2013-14/versions.htm

Australian Government, Department of Immigration and Border Protection, Migration program statistics (2015a). https://www.immi.gov.au/media/statistics/statistical-info/visa-grants/migrant.htm

Australian Government, Department of Immigration and Border Protection, Family Visa processing times statistics (2015b). Retrieved from https://www.immi.gov.au/about/charters/client-services-charter/visas/5.0.htm

Commonwealth Consolidated Regulations. (2011). Migration Regulations (Cth) 1994, Schedule 4, item 4020. Public interest criteria and related provisions. Retrieved from http://www.austlii.edu.au/au/legis/cth/consol_reg/mr1994227/sch4.html

Commonwealth Consolidated Regulations. (2012). Migration Regulations (Cth) 1994, Schedule 6D. Retreived from http://www.austlii.edu.au/au/legis/cth/consol_reg/mr1994227/sch6d.html

Australian Government, Federal Register of Legislative Instruments F2014L00837. (2014). Education Services for Overseas Students Amendment (Student Visas and Other Measures) Regulation 2014. Select Legislative Instrument 2014 No. 94. Retrieved from https://www.google.com.au/#q=Migration+Regulations+(Cth)1994%2C+Select+Legislative+Instrument+2014+No.+94.+

Law Institute of Victoria Legal Policy and Practice. (2009). Inquiry into the welfare of International students, Submission to the Senate Education, Employment and Workplace Relations Committee, 21 August 2009.

Retrieved from http://www.liv.asn.au/getattachment/dd9960d9-ad77-490d-9ef8-3dc5f56d75da/Inquiry-into-the-Welfare-of-International-Students.aspx

McKenzie, N. & Baker, R. (2014). Visa fraud suspects fled after wiring $1m overseas. The Sydney Morning Herald, (8 August 2014). Retrieved from http://www.smh.com.au/federal-politics/political-news/visa-fraud-suspects-fled-after- wiring-1m-overseas-20140807-3dbmu.html

Migration Amendment Regulation (Cth) 2012 (No. 2), Explanatory Statement, Select Legislative Instrument No. 82, 2012. Retrieved from http://www5.austlii.edu.au/au/legis/cth/num_reg_es/mar20122n82o2012399.html

Migration Amendment Regulation (Cth) 2014 (No. 1), Explanatory Statement, Select Legislative Instrument No. 32, 2014. Retrieved from https://www.comlaw.gov.au/Details/F2014L00286

Migration Regulations 1994 (Cth), Schedule 4, PIC 4020; Migration Amendment Regulations (2011 Measures No. 1), Select Legislative Instrument No. 13, 2011. Retrieved from http://www.austlii.edu.au/au/legis/cth/num_reg_es/ mar20111n13o2011417.html

Republic of Turkey Ministry of Interior Directorate General of Migration Management. (2013). Law on Foreigners and International Protection, Law No. 6458. Published in Official Gazette on 11 of April, 2013, NO: 28615:1-82. Retrieved from http://www.goc.gov.tr/files/files/YUKK_I%CC%87NGI%CC%87LI%CC%87ZCE_BASKI%281%29%281%29.pdf

Post-Immigration Policies in Turkey: Integration versus Harmonization

Gülay Uğur Göksel[118]

Introduction

Turkey has been perceived and studied as an emigration country for decades in the policy and the academic circles. However, due to its growing economy, geopolitical location, and EU accession process, Turkey is slowly turning into an immigrant receiving country (Kirisci, 2009; Icduygu et al., 2014 and Tolay, 2012). "From the very first waves of Iranians (after the 1979 revolution) and Iraqis (in 1988 and 1991) to the much diversified migratory field of the early twenty-first century (refugees, illegal migrants, circular migrants, transit migrants of different origins), Turkey has become a country of large-scale, continuous and complex immigration" (Tolay, 2012, p.2).

This "new" immigrant population can be characterized as having non-Turkish origin and coming from diverse ethnic and religious backgrounds. Turkey's rapidly growing "new" immigrant population will definitely bring economic benefits together with socio-political challenges to its social cohesion, security and national identity. In this sense, Turkey's newly minted role, as an immigration hub for its neighboring countries is indicative of the start of a new era for the Turkish immigration scholarship on the politics of post-immigration. While the integration of immigrants has been a widely contested issue, which is studied vigorously within the Western context, "it tends to be seen as a non- existent or minor issue by most Turkish people, as well as by some migration scholars" (Tolay, 2012, p.3). However, recent immigration law reforms including the adoption of the Law on Foreigners and International Protection (YUKK) and the establishment of a Directorate General of Migration Management (DGMM) in 2013 signal that there is a growing state level awareness for the issue of integration of immigrants.

In this paper, I aim to answer this one question: How is the term "integration" of new immigrants understood institutionally in Turkey? As immigration to Turkey is a relatively new phenomenon and the newly established Directorate General is active only for more than a year, this preliminary research is mainly based on a critical discursive analysis of the related article (96) of the YUKK, official speeches by the high level state officials, and the Directorate's website.

This paper consists of three parts. First I will give a brief historical introduction to the Turkish immigration and post-immigration policies. This section will reveal that there is a conceptual shift from "assimilation" to "harmonization" in the Turkish institutional discourse on immigration. In the second part, I will discuss the importance of the theoretical support and the role of the second order interpretations by the state institutions for the analysis of the integration of immigrants. In the third part, the term "harmonization" will come to the forefront and the discussion will revolve around how and why this term has

---

[118] Gulay Ugur Goksel is Assistant Professor in Political Science and International Relations Department, Istanbul Aydin University, Besyol Mah. Inonu Cad. No.38, Sefakoy, Istanbul Turkey. E-mail: gulaygoksel@aydin.edu.tr.

been interpreted in particular ways especially different than the term "integration". Finally, I will conclude my paper with a discussion of the apparent contradictions within the institutional discourse on immigration in Turkey.

"Old immigration" versus "new immigration"

Kirisci (2009) has coined these terms of "old" and "new" to signify the changes that the politics of immigration in Turkey has gone through for the last decade. Accordingly, the "new immigration" is completely different from the "old immigration" that the Turkish administration and immigration scholars are acquainted with. Turkey's official focus in the "old immigration" era was on the immigrants to Turkey with a Turkish ethnic descent and culture. According to the Settlement Law (Iskan Kanunu) of June 1934, "only persons of 'Turkish ethnic descent and Turkish culture' could immigrate, settle in Turkey and eventually receive Turkish citizenship" (Kirisci, 2009, p.6). There were some changes to the Settlement Law of 1934 but the "Turkishness" emphasis for the admission of immigrants into Turkey remained unchanged till 2013.

In theory, "Turkishness" has always been closely associated with the Turkish language. However, when we look at the practice of admission, we observe that the task of identifying who belongs to Turkish ethnic descent and culture had been left to the state authorities. With this regard, the concept of "Turkishness" has been interpreted and reinterpreted intermittently as the historical conjectures concerning the state of Turkish minority populations living outside of Turkey namely in Balkans, former Soviet Union, Iraq and Afghanistan changed due to specific historical events such as civil conflicts, dissolution of Soviet Union and Iraqi wars (Kirisci, 2009, Icduygu et al., 2014).

This apparent discriminatory standard for the admission of immigrants into Turkey emanates from the newly established Republic's ambition to create citizens with a fixed national and religious identity (Kirisci, 2009). For about 70 years, this nation-building project had been translated into the immigration policies as assimilationist practices which were relatively easy to sustain without a major opposition from the immigrant groups in Turkey. This is not surprising if we consider the scope of the rights of ethnic and religious minority groups in Turkey. The discrimination and assimilationist practices by the state and societal agents to these minority groups have been well documented in the literature and are major determinants for the explanation of many emigration trends in Turkey. Thus, the integration of immigrants into Turkish society has been treated as identical with assimilation, since the end result of the integration of an immigrant is expected to be an agent who behaves and speaks in exactly the same way as 'Turkish' nationals.

Whereas "old immigration" trends had been handled within a nationalistic and assimilationist framework by the state authorities in a vague and incoherent legal context, changing immigration trends together with Turkey's desire to fulfill the EU membership criteria[119] have brought a new institutional discourse of

---

[119] Moreover, the role of the single AKP regime and the changing dynamics of the state's relationship with Kurdish and Alevi minorities on this shift are also important determinants of this discursive shift (Kirisci 2006, Icduygu et al. 2009). The discussion of how this shift exactly happened is out of the

"harmonization" on the issue of immigrant integration into Turkey. The most important immigration reform that deconstructs the understanding of immigrant integration is the adoption of the Law on Foreigners and International Protection (YUKK), which was approved on 4 April 2013 by Turkey's Parliament. "The YUKK is expected to put an end to the lack of a comprehensive legal structure that has persisted for the past 63 years" (Elitok, 2013, p.167).

In general, the YUKK specifies the rules regarding the entry, stay and exit from Turkey for non-nationals in addition to the information on the organization, responsibilities and competences of the Directorate General of Migration Management (DGMM). The YUKK is also exemplary in the sense that the leading immigration and law experts, domestic NGOs and the international agents such as IOM were included in the process of making and discussions of its draft. The YUKK is recognized as in line with "international human rights, international agreements and the European Union legislation" (Bilgili, 2012, p.10). Under the Article 96 of the YUKK, Turkey's immigrant integration strategy is identified as "harmonization". Accordingly, the YUKK assigns the Directorate General to fulfill some duties on harmonization activities. I will discuss these in detail in the third part of this paper. Before venturing on this topic, I would like to briefly introduce the importance of institutional discourse for just integration of immigrants.

The integration of immigrants and institutional discourse

The integration of immigrants in Turkey has rarely been discussed in the literature except some exemplary reports (Tolay, 2011; Kirisci 2009; Icduygu & Sert, 2009; Erdoğan, 2014, Bilgili, 2012). The approach of these reports to the issue of integration is mostly descriptive and lacks the support of a theory of minority rights and democracy. The lack of theory in the Turkish immigration literature might be "typical of fields that are still in an early phase of development, when scholars are required to identify and define the studied social phenomenon" (Tolay, 2012, p.11). However, I contend that without a sophisticated theoretical framework for addressing the injustices faced by immigrants—which I believe have a profound impact on the immigrant integration— the analysis of the post-immigration policies falls short of producing healthy assumptions, concepts and just policy prescriptions.

Moreover, in political theory literature, the term "integration" has an ambivalent character, which makes it very difficult to study without a theoretical foundation. A critical survey of the use of the term "integration" in Western countries reveals that the term "integration" is a highly abstract concept. In elsewhere, I observe that the discourses on the integration policy has been historically moving on the axis of assimilation and multiculturalism as the degree of anxiety over social stability and national security changes in the face of real or perceived threats from a specific immigrant group at a certain time (Goksel, 2014). Thus the meaning of integration has continuously been reconstructed either to nullify or to celebrate the effects of immigrants on social stability and national

---

scope of this paper as the basic focus will be on the interpretation of the term "harmonization" on institutional level.

security of their host society. Whereas, I propose to approach the ideal of just integration as a concrete and transformative process through which collective individuals change societal values as equal members of society in the face of misrecognition.

In order to make this important perspectival shift, we need to understand the conditions of the existing institutional order that immigrants are being asked to integrate into. This recognition theoretical understanding of the institutional order necessitates questioning the validity of specific institutional interpretations of integration norms. According to Honneth (2004), *individualization* together with *inclusion* should constitute the value horizon with which we can analyze and criticize the existing norms of integration. These standards introduce how essential it is for immigrants to have equal rights to participate in public negotiations on an equal footing. In the spirit of Honneth's idea of recognition and immanent critique, I believe that it is a very fruitful practice to critically analyze the newly adapted YUKK and established DGMM's discourse on integration[120]. This practice will not only allow us to reveal how institutional interpretation may inhibit or help immigrants' adaptation process in Turkey but also shape public opinion on the perception of these people. In the following part of the paper, I will, first focus on the term "harmonization" and then try to reveal the contradictory character of the Turkish immigration discourse in my concluding remarks.

Harmonization

The Article 96 of the YUKK[121], defines some duties of the DGMM to facilitate "the mutual harmonization of the society and of foreigner, applicant or beneficiary of international protection" such as the provision of informative programs on the political, economic and social rights and obligations to empower immigrants' self-reliance. The Law also encourages the DGMM to take advantage of the third party support from NGOs, universities and international organizations for the preparation of these programs. The Department of Harmonization and Communication has already organized several meetings in Istanbul, Bursa and Didim where immigrants, local officials, NGO leaders and the DGMM officials came together to discuss the rights and obligations of immigrants and the new immigration law[122].

Moreover, in the DGMM's website, a letter[123] to the immigrant parents introduces MUYU (Harmony Child) as the mascot of the DGMM's

---

[120] I acknowledge the danger of applying concepts and theories of Western canon to the Turkish context, but there has always been a reference to universal assumptions about inclusion and democracy in the discussion of the integration of minority groups including immigrant groups. As many scholars and international organizations celebrate the YUKK for its rights-based approach to the pre and post-immigration policies, a discussion of the institutional understanding of individual and group rights and societal and political inclusion in Turkey becomes more relevant now than ever before.

[121] Refer to the Directorates website for the full draft of the YUKK at http://www.goc.gov.tr/icerik/yabancilar-ve-uluslararasi-koruma-kanunu_327_328 last accessed on 01.05.2015.

[122] For more information on these events: http://www.goc.gov.tr/icerik6/istanbul-bulusmalari_389_390_874_icerik last accessed on 1.05. 2015.

[123] For more information on MUYU and the DGMM's letter to the immigrant parents:

harmonization program for the immigrant children. It is stated in the letter that MUYU's website is designed "to ease the thousands of migrant children's harmonization and cohesion living in our country". In the letter, the DGMM acknowledges the fact that harmonization should be reciprocal and is only possible through an awareness of migrant children's possible problems by the children living in Turkey.

Finally, at the DGMM website[124], the term "harmonization" is defined neither as an assimilation nor as an integration. "It is rather a voluntary harmonization resulting from mutual understanding of each other between the migrants and the society. Two-way active interaction and voluntary actions are aimed within the scope of harmonization arrangements and efforts, and a migrant-oriented approach will be embraced".

As can be seen from these written documents, there is a major emphasis on the transformative, reciprocal and voluntary qualities of the harmonization process between the immigrants and the host society. This very definition of the term "harmonization" is also exemplary as it points out the institutional shift from assimilation to a more inclusive and reciprocal process. I believe that the official acknowledgment of mutually transformative character of the immigrant integration is a very important institutional step. However, as of now, the harmonization programs are seem to be limited to the programs that introduce Turkish institutional structure to the new-comer immigrants and their children. As I mentioned in the second part of the paper, for the integration of immigrants to be voluntary and reciprocal, the host state and society should provide fair and just conditions for the political participation of the immigrants on equal and free basis—without creating feelings of shame about their identity. Thus, Turkish state and society should be ready to open up public spaces for its immigrants as productive full members of Turkish society where interpretation of the rules of integration can be discussed. Creating these pre-conditions for the integration of immigrants necessitates active involvement of local governments and NGOs together with a change towards a multicultural education and workplace practices. Thus, an institutional focus on group and language rights will also become a necessity in the near future.

Moreover, it is very interesting to see how the DGMM insists that harmonization is different than integration. Integration is an abstract concept but it mainly signifies the opposite of assimilation in the immigration discourses of many Western countries—take for example Canadian official policy of multiculturalism and integration. I believe that this discursive move has two implications. First, there is a serious official effort to distance Turkey from European immigration policies. Second, there is an institutional struggle to represent Turkish immigration policy as being more liberal and democratic than its European counterparts. This discursive move might seem necessary by the state officials to take a critical official stand against the issue of integration of Muslim immigrants in Europe and Europe's strict policy towards refugees from conflict ridden neighbors of Turkey. Bombarded with criticism for its minority

---

http://www.uyumcocuk.gov.tr/ last accessed on 01.05.2015.

[124] http://www.goc.gov.tr/icerik6/about-harmonisation_917_1066_1411_icerik last accessed on 1.05. 2015.

rights throughout its accession process, it looks like Turkey has found an opportunity to appear as more democratic than European countries. This might be true as of now but the state officials should not forget that Turkey's new immigration is still very new and Turkey is not exempt from the challenges that ethnic diversity that immigrants bring in the future.

Even though there is a serious positive change with regard to the institutional understanding of the immigrant integration, Turkish post-immigration discourse is still riddled with contradictions. Some speeches of public officials reveal how the rights-based institutional logic of the new immigration discourse does not reflect on the representation of the issue of integration of immigrants to the Turkish society. On the one hand, Turkish state officials put forward a very liberal, rights-based and democratic stand for the post-immigration policies. On the other hand, the same Turkish state officials use Turkish culture of hospitality, tolerance and generosity and Pan-Ottoman cards to prove how Turkish society has always been ready for the cultural and religious diversity that this new wave of immigration brings.

To illustrate, one of the most fascinating written pieces of this discourse is the official letter signed by the current Minister of the Interior, Mr. Efkan Ala to the applicants of the approved resident permits in Turkey. In the letter, after giving reference to poet Rumi, it is stated "you will feel a great tolerance in this land, where people of various cultures have lived in peace and serenity for thousands of years"[125]. Such statements by state officials give assurance to the new residents of Turkey that Turkish society is also itself a culturally diverse society for centuries. They also help to remind Turkish citizens their stable and peaceful relationship with people who belong to diverse ethnic and cultural background for centuries.

In contrast to this emphasis on plurality, during the official reception for the celebration of the international migrants day on 18th of December 2014 in Ankara, Mr. Enver Salihoglu, the deputy secretary of Ministry of the Interior, stated "we are the grandchildren of Mevlana. There is a place of everyone in this country…. we perceive our immigrants as our guests. Approximately 5 billion dollars from the government budget is spent to make our guests to feel more comfortable. Turkish Republic is carrying this heavy burden without feeling any hesitations without the help of EU countries…"[126] While there is not any mention of right-based approach of the YUKK, Mr. Salihoglu's speech revolves around the Turkish nationalistic value of hospitality and generosity towards its guesses. This emphasis is in direct contradiction with the multicultural emphasis on diverse Turkish society.

These contradictions might be caused by two basic reasons. First, it is normal to see confusion of old and new discourses in the newly established institutions. Ideas are fluid but institutionally accepted ones can be quite rigid and hard to erase from the minds of the state officials and the public. The old assimilationist discourse creeps in to the official speeches on immigration due to its connection with highly ingrained nation building project, which is still dominant when one

---

[125] For the full version of Efkan Ala's letter: http://www.goc.gov.tr/icerik6/icisleri-bakanimizdan-yabancilara--ikamet-izni-mektubu_350_361_2580_icerik last accessed on 01.05.2015.
[126] http://goc.gov.tr/icerik6/18-aralik-uluslararasi-gocmenler-gunu-resepsiyonu-duzenlendi_350_361_2579_icerik last accessed on 01.05.2015.

considers the situation of minority rights in Turkey. Moreover, especially during Syrian refugee crisis, state officials prefer to use the hospitality and Pan-Ottoman card to increase the social acceptance rates of these refugees within the Turkish society. However, I believe that the contradictory use of national discourse if continued will cause more harm than good in the long run. Nationalistic discourse might help to persuade the society to mobilize its economic resources to help foreigners but it cannot go further than that. The very idea of belonging to a one nation is one of the major determinants of the ethnic conflicts in Turkey. This discourse creates rigid in-group and out-group identifications and it blocks the harmonization possibilities of the immigrants. Thus I strongly argue that the state officials should abandon this kind of nationalistic discourse completely. There is yet be a clear public opinion towards immigrants in Turkey, hence the role of the DGMM is very important in creating inclusive public perception towards immigrants.

References

Bilgili, O. (2012). Turkeys Multifarious Attitude towards Migration and its Migrants *MPC Research Report 2012/02*. San Domenico Di Fiesole (FI): Robert Schuman Centre for Advanced Studies.

Elitok Paçacı, Seçil & Straubhaar. (2011). Turkey as a Migration Hub in the Middle East. *Insight Turkey, 13*(2), 107-128.

Elitok Paçacı, S. (2013). Turkish Migration Policy Over The Last Decade: A Gradual Shift Towards Better Management And Good Governance. *Turkish Policy Quarterly, 12*(1).

Erdogan, M. (2014). Türkiye'deki Suriyeliler: Toplumsal Kabul ve Uyum Araştırması *HUGO*. Ankara.

Goksel, G. U. (2014). *The Theory of Immigration and the Integration of Immigrants.* (Ph.D), University of Colorado at Boulder.

Icduygu, A, Erder, S. & Genckaya, O. F. (2014). Türkiye'nin Uluslararsı Göç Politikaları, 1923-2023: Ulus Devlet Oluşumundan-Ulus-Ötesi Dönüşümlere *Mirekoç Proje Raporları*. İstanbul.

Içduygu, A. and Sert, D. (2009) Turkey Country Profile, *Focus Migration No.5.*, Hamburg Institute for International Economics (HWWI).

Honneth, A. (2004). Recognition and Justice: Outline of a Plural Theory of Justice *Acta Sociologica, 47*(351).

Kirisci, K. (2009). Mirage or Reality: Post-National Turkey and its Implication for Immigration *CARIM Research Reports* (Vol. 14). San Domenico Di Fiesole (FI): Robert Schuman Centre for Advanced Studies.

Tolay, J. (2011). In Ö. a. T. Çelebi (Ed.), İltica, Uluslararası Göç ve Vatansızlık: Kuram, Gözlem ve Politika: UNHCR publications.

Tolay, J. (2012). Discovering Immigration into Turkey: The Emergence of a Dynamic Field. *International Migration.*

Politically Motivated Migration: The Case of Turkish Migration to Northern Cyprus

Yücel Vural, Başak Ekenoğlu and Sertaç Sonan[127]

Introduction

The political relations between Turkey and Turkish Cypriot community intensified in the mid-1950s before the violent eruption of inter-communal conflict in Cyprus. The involvement of Turkey in the Cyprus dispute took place amidst the Cold War, which resulted in a process of transforming the major conflict between the Greek-Cypriot nationalist movement and British colonial administration into a Greek-Turkish politico-military confrontation at regional level and a Greek Cypriot-Turkish Cypriot contradiction at local-national level. The issue of 'Cyprus population' was introduced into the Cyprus politics by the Turkish Cypriot nationalists who demanded that regardless of the minority position of the Turkish Cypriots on the island the Turkish nation (Turks in Turkey and Turks in Cyprus) constitute the majority group[128] in the region and thus Turkish nation has the right to control Cyprus. This Turkish nationalist perspective was primarily a reaction to the Greek-Cypriot demand for Enosis (Union of Cyprus with Greece). Greek Cypriot nationalist perspective developed the argument that the 'majority of Cyprus population' had the right to self-determination. Until 1974, however, contradictory perspectives on the issue of population did not dominate the political discourses of the relevant actors of the Cyprus dispute. Turkey increased its political influence among Turkish Cypriots amidst the Cold War through providing political and military support for the establishment of the paramilitary organization called TMT[129] (Turkish abbreviation of Turkish Resistance Organization) which later managed to take control in the Turkish Cypriot population of the island. In addition to the diplomatic, political and military support to TMT, the special units of Turkey also assisted cadres of TMT with personnel and organizational instruments. Turkey became one of the three guarantor powers of the Republic of Cyprus established in 1960 and sponsored the 'Provisional Cyprus Turkish Administration' as an alternative authority to the Greek-Cypriot led Republic of Cyprus after 1964.

---

[127] Yücel Vural is Associate Professor of political science, Department of Political Science and International Relations, Eastern Mediterranean University, Salamis Yolu, Famagusta, Mersin 10 Turkey. E-mail: yucel.vural@emu.edu.tr

Başak Ekenoğlu is PhD candidate at the Department of Political Science and International Relations, Eastern Mediterranean University, Salamis Yolu, Famagusta, Mersin 10 Turkey. E-mail: basakekenoglu@gmail.com

Sertaç Sonan is Doctor of Political science, Department of Political Science and International Relations, Eastern Mediterranean University, Salamis Yolu, Famagusta, Mersin 10 Turkey. E-mail: sertac.sonan@emu.edu.tr

[128] See for example, Cyprus is Turkish Party (1956), Greek Atrocities against Turks, Nicosia: Bozkurt, p. 4.

[129]TMT was established as the counterpart of the Greek-Cypriot semi-military organization EOKA. While EOKA demanded unification of Cyprus with Greece (Enosis), TMT demanded partition of island between Greece and Turkey.

As a reaction to Greek-Junta-led military quo against the government of Cyprus on 15th of July 1974 Turkey launched a military operation on 20th of July 1974 to restore constitutional order on the basis of the Treaty of Guaranty. Turkish military intervention, however, culminated in the territorial division of the island followed by the proclamation of the 'Turkish Federated State of Cyprus' by the Turkish Cypriots in the areas controlled by the Turkish military in February 1975. Massive population transfers from Turkey to northern part of Cyprus started in this period and continued afterwards. With regard to Cyprus politics it seems that problems created by population transfers are two-dimensional, namely the humanitarian and the political dimensions. Humanitarian dimension refers to the feelings and expectations of second and third generations of the Turkish migrants/settlers who were born and socialized in Cyprus towards being accepted as a part of (Turkish-) Cypriot community with full citizenship rights in a proposed Federal Republic of Cyprus. The political dimension, on the other hand, can be associated with the argument that Turkey/Turkish Cypriot authorities involved in a series of conscious efforts towards changing the demographic structure of the northern part of Cyprus that constitutes a violation of Fourth Geneva Convention of 1949.[130] The increasing number of Turkish immigrants in the northern part of Cyprus and their influence in politics has become a sensitive and controversial issue both at intra-communal and inter-communal level of politics in Cyprus since 1974. While this has led to a fear of assimilation among a large portion of Turkish Cypriots, it provoked the Greek Cypriots who see these immigrants as settlers, to accuse Turkey of following a policy of colonization. Nevertheless, there is no official 'migration policy' employed by the current government in the northern part of Cyprus. Indeed there have been public policies aiming at regulating the unexpected results of migration rather than identifying the preferred conditions of migration.

In the literature, 'political migration' has usually been associated with forced migrations including such categories as refugees, displaced persons, asylum seekers etc. The case of northern Cyprus, however, seems to represent a distinct category where 'politically motivated migration' is a result of a combination of domestic policies of the host country and foreign policy objectives of the home country. Furthermore, unlike the related literature that concentrates on the general economic or political reasons behind migration to 'economically developed' countries, this paper intends to analyze migration through classifying the reactions of a 'developing host country'. By focusing on three different waves of Turkish immigration, this paper argues that 'politically motivated' immigration has generated three different types of reactions in the Turkish-Cypriot community: (1) clientelist reaction, which sees immigration from a nationalistic-opportunistic perspective; (2) protectionist reaction, which sees immigration as a threat to the Turkish-Cypriot identity and political stability; and (3) legalist reaction, which sees immigration as a human rights issue.

The paper argues that there has been a distinct policy of 'clientelism' of the host country (northern Cyprus) which overlaps with the foreign policy objectives

---

[130] According the abovementioned international convention "The Occupying Power shall not deport or transfer parts of its own civilian population into the territory it occupies."

of the home country (Turkey) which promoted Turkish migration to northern Cyprus. This hypothesis is analyzed through three sections. The remaining section of this part elaborates on the theories of migration and host country reactions. The second part focuses on the history and dynamics of immigration to Northern Cyprus through analyzing three different waves. The third part deals with the host country reactions through analyzing legal, economic and socio-political means used to regulate migration. The conclusion attempts to deepen theoretical understanding of politically motivated migration and develop specific policy suggestions aiming at reducing intra- and inter-communal tensions with regard to Turkish migration to the northern part of Cyprus.

Immigration usually activates dynamics of change both in sending and receiving countries, and shapes every dimension of social existence (Castles & Miller, 2009,p.21). Parallel to its wide range of influence, it is hard to mention a coherent theory of migration (Massey et al. 1993,p.432). Migration literature has identified various types of migration including *economic migration, force migration*, and *health migration* or *student mobility*. Most of the theories focus on the economic aspects of migration aiming at explaining economic, social and political factors that encourage migration. As the oldest and most influential theory of migration, *neo-classical economic theory* analyse individual choices to migrate on the basis of economic inequalities, or 'wage-differences' among countries (Massey et al., 1993; 1998; Jennissen, 2007). Due to the economic inequalities labour tends to immigrate from low-wage to high-wage countries (Borjas, 1989; Massey et al., 1993;1998). Nevertheless, this theory fails to analyze the migratory process fully and as a result 'the new economics of labor migration' emerged in order to fill this gap which focuses on families and households to analyze immigration choices (Stark, 1991). This theory suggests that immigration is not only an individual choice because the wider family and social networks have an impact on it. Although, economic theories on migration provide significant insights on the migratory process through different levels of analyses, they are insufficient to analyze the reasons of immigration (Massey et al., 1998,p.50-59). Furthermore, such theories concentrate on migration to *'economically developed'* countries only. Unlike the existing literature, this paper intends to analyze migration through classifying the reactions of a 'host country' against increasing immigration. Moreover, the paper concentrates both on economic and political reasons behind the migration.

When analyzing the migratory process, it is crucial to distinguish between the *voluntary* and *forced migration*. The abovementioned theories on the economic aspect of migration aimed at explaining the voluntary migration that is generally promoted by push and pull factors that usually originated from the demand for new economic and social benefits. Forced migration, on the other hand, occurs when "an element of coercion exists, including threats to life and livelihood, whether arising from natural or man-made causes."[131] Alternatively, forced migrants can be described as 'political migrants' mobilized due to humanitarian

---

[131] For further information see key migration terms in the web page of The International Organization for Migration; available at: http://www.iom.int/cms/en/sites/iom/home/about-migration/key-migration-terms-1.html

push factors (Stalker, 1999; Cornelius & Rosenblum, 2005). As stated above *political migration* has usually been associated with forced migration. The case of Northern Cyprus, however, seems to represent a distinct category where 'politically motivated migration' is a result of a combination of domestic policies of the host country and foreign policy objectives of the home country. In this sense the conceptual framework and theoretical assumptions of this study differ considerably from the conventional migration literature.

Beyond the reasons of why immigration occurs, it is necessary to focus on its outputs. From a general perspective it is possible to identify specific influences of immigration such as influences on economy, demography, culture and/or national identity within the host countries. Under specific circumstances such influences may result in reactions by the native population with the fear of losing their jobs, culture, identity and unity. In receiving countries, there is fear among the native people the unskilled immigrants reduce the jobs available for the former and drop the wages in labor market by providing cheap and often illegal work force Moreover, immigrant population usually seen as a threat to the unity of the receiving country with their own culture, language and/or social characteristics, and threatens the identity of the nation. Moreover, high levels of immigration may create security threats (Teitelbaum & Weiner, 1995). Therefore, immigration may create a debate among political actors culminating in the adoption of an immigration policy that consists of socio-political strategies aiming at controlling/regulating immigration and its undesirable effects on the host country. Massey sees immigration policy as:

"the outcome of a political process through which, competing interests interact with bureaucratic, legislative, judicial, and public arenas to construct and implement policies that encourage, discourage, or otherwise regulate the flow of immigrants" (1999, p.307).

In general, migration policies categorize migrants into such groups as legal residents, undocumented immigrants, temporary migrants and humanitarian migrants. These categories differ from one another by the rights of the migrants. Illegal or undocumented immigrants are the ones who entered a country unlawfully and remains in the country without fulfilling the legal procedures that obliged by the country such as valid visa, work/residential permit etc. The main distinction between legal residents and illegal/undocumented migrants is that the latter cannot benefit from the social rights associated with citizenship. Temporary migrants could be skilled, semi-skilled or untrained migrant workers who stay in the receiving country for defined periods as determined in a work contract (for further information see International Organization of Migration website) or students who came for education in a specific period of time. Temporary migrants can benefit from the social rights granted them through their contracts and regulations of the host country. Most of the developed countries receive humanitarian migrants through different national regulations with respect to the UN Conventions and protocols on human and refugees rights. Nevertheless, different policies are introduced in order to regulate voluntary migration.

The reactions of host countries can be classified into three distinct models. These are *multiculturalism, civic-integrationist* and *assimilationist* models. In general, multiculturalism holds the idea that "immigrants should be able to participate as equals in all spheres of society, without being expected to give up their own culture, religion and language" (Catles & Miller, p.247). In this respect, host countries recognize the cultural, religious or linguistic identities of immigrants. *Civic-integration model* on the other hand, represents the attempts by the host country to incorporate migrants into the existing socio-political values through being culturally, ethnically and linguistically indifferent to differences and through allocating common status on the basis of individual rights. The *Assimilationist* model can be defined as a forced integration in which "immigrants were to be incorporated into society through a one-sided of adaptation" (Ibid). It can be argued that there have been attempts by receiving countries to replace the assimilationist policies with the civic integrationist policies. For instance, European countries adopted common policies on migration, especially about humanitarian migrants, and most of them liberalized their assimilationist policies through civic integration. European Council adopted 'Common Basic Principles' (CBP 4) on immigrant integration in 2004 and some EU countries started to introduce programs to integrate their migrant populations.[132] According to CBP 4 "(…) *basic knowledge of the host society's language, history, and institutions is indispensable to integration; enabling immigrants to acquire the basic knowledge is essential to successful integration".*[133] As Bauböck (1996) argued, multiculturalism trend flourished in democratic societies since 1990's on the basis of the idea that it is a requirement of democracy (Castles & Miller, p.274).

Such countries as Australia and Canada have usually been ranked as the most open countries to immigration among Western states (Markus, 2014). In such advanced developed states immigration is encouraged because of its contributions to the economic life in the hos country. Migration policies of these states tend to promote various categories of migrant groups to enter and settle easily through allowing family unifications, which increased the bases of multiculturalism. On the other hand, the process of accepting immigrants is based on a number of criteria including those of age, skills, and job qualifications (Miller, 1999). In these countries, multicultural social policies are justified with the view that immigrants need services that address their special needs with regard to education, language and housing (Castles & Miller, p.262). Moreover, there are active policies to improve the position of immigrants in the labor market. The number of acquisition of citizenship is also higher in these countries since newcomers are encouraged to become citizens (Ibid.,p.269-70).

Most European countries, however, try to deal with the issues of immigration either through integrationist or assimilationist policies as defined above. It is argued that civic-integration policies go parallel with the perception that immigrants constitute a threat to the national identity and culture of the host country. Pakulski (2014,p.24) argues that this threat perception is base on three factors: *'the recent intensification of uncontrolled migrations,' 'accompanying high unemployment and financial austerities,'* and *'the political mobilization of nationalistic movements hostile to 'foreigners'*. In most of these countries acquisition of citizenship requires the

---

[132] See Policy Briefing on Introduction programmes and language courses for refugees and migrants in Europe, http://www.ecre.org/
[133] Ibid.

migrants to follow a tough procedure including their involvement in specific integration programs. For instance, in Germany long and complex bureaucratic process is being enforced. Although, the German governments sustained a kind of multicultural policy towards the immigrants, this policy had shifted to a sort of civic-integration policies bordering on an assimilationist strategy in 1980s and 1990s (Joppke, 2007).

Northern Cyprus has no legal immigration policy despite increasing immigration since 1974. Nevertheless, it is argued in this paper that having no legal policy is the official policy of the state since the immigrants (Turkish immigrants) are not recognized as 'immigrants'. The political situation in the northern part of Cyprus created a distinct policy of *clientalism*, which also generated a politically motivated immigration from Turkey.

History and dynamics of immigration in northern cyprus

This part analyses the migration movements from Turkey to northern part of Cyprus after the territorial division of the island in July 1974. In this regard, it is crucial to distinguish between three different immigration flows. The first immigration flow was initiated through a top-secret protocol, named as the *Protocol for Agricultural Labor Force.*[134] This protocol began to be implemented in the few months just after the military operation of the Turkish army, which started on 20th July 1974 and continued until 16th August 1974. The methods and motives of the first wave resemble the Ottoman massive migration policy and practice very closely. The Ottoman *sürgün*[135] policy was a politically motivated 'post-conquest arrangement' aiming at transforming Moslem population into the newly captured territories to enable the Ottoman rulers to establish and secure their political control. The expectation of Ottoman Sultan was both practical and ideological, namely, the blend of religious communities would create a basis for political loyalties to the Ottoman socio-political order and help to transform religious identity of the newly captured areas through peaceful ways. The Ottoman migration policy was systematic, compulsory and massive in character; based on a political decision by the supreme authority (*the Sultan*); and implemented by official units. Especially in 1975 organized groups of Turkish families from specific villages in Turkey were transferred to specific villages evacuated by the original Greek-Cypriot residents in the north Cyprus. This first wave was completed in few years.

The second wave of Turkish migration which took place in the period of 1980-1999, have some similar characteristics with that of the first wave in the sense that it was highly influenced by the several legal arrangements between the two governments such as *Labor Force Agreement* in 1987, and agreement signed in 1991 that allowed the use of National ID Cards as substitute of a passport for both states' citizens for entering into both countries.[136] However there is a difference between the first and second wave migrations. As Kurtulus and Purkis (2014)

---

[134] The protocol came out with the "top secret" inscription and only fifty copies reproduced for the second time. For crosscheck the information see, Birand, 1979, p.85 and Mutluyakalı, 2011a, p.18.
[135] Turkish word for 'compulsory population transfer.'
[136] TRNC Official Gazette, Date: 30.07.1991, Issue: 20945

stated during the second wave, educated people and skilled workers also migrated to the island rather than unskilled labor force from rural areas. Unlike the conclusion of Kurtulus and Purkis, however, an important finding of this paper is that the major difference between the first and second waves is the lack of economic and political privileges[137] to the second wave immigrants that were available to those of the first wave.

The third wave of immigration started in 2000's and continued to the present day. This wave differs from the first two and in a sense it can be asserted as the 'real labor migration flow' to the island. It is not directly influenced from agreements between the two governments. In addition third wave neither constituted a massive immigration nor resulted in automatic citizenship status of TRNC. Nevertheless, this immigration flow highly influenced from the policies and economic dynamic in both countries. On the one hand, this immigration flow was highly influenced from the neo-liberal economic transformation in Turkey, which leads to unemployment within the country, together with the policy of displacement of people in Eastern and South-eastern Anatolia (Kurtulus & Purkis, 2014,p.125). On the other hand, the internal socio-economic dynamics of the northern part of the island such as increase in the education level of Cypriot people, the rapid growth of construction industry during Annan Plan period, and the increase in the demand for unskilled labor force attracted Turkish population to come to the island. Turkish immigrants are seen as 'cheap labor' who can work in these sectors that are not preferred by the native population. Moreover, native workforce found better conditions in and therefore moved to the southern part of the island to work in construction sector after the opening up of the 'check points'[138] in 2003 (Kurtuluş & Purkis, 2014,p.132; Mehmet et al., 2007). On the one hand, this wave created a dilemma of providing cheap labor for specific sectors creating unemployment among native Turkish Cypriots.

These three immigration flows are interconnected and each provided a pathway to the following one. Moreover, the continuing immigration and its economic, political and social consequences created reactions towards immigration and immigrant population. This article focuses on the first wave since it constituted a massive population transfer to northern Cyprus. Together with this movement, massive Turkish population came with a special status through some economic and political incentives such as complimentary property (properties abandoned by the Greek Cypriots), employment and citizenship (Hatay, 2005; Kurtulus & Purkis, 2010; 2014; Mutluyakali, 2011a; 2011b). Regarding the first wave of migration although it is argued that the top secret protocol was signed in order to provide thirty thousand agricultural labors it is not possible to identify the number of people migrated to the island since there were no strict control or legal records kept for that period. In accordance with the quasi-official information given by Ismet Kotak, who was the first minister responsible for 'Public Development and Settlement' in 1975, 82.500 migrants

---

[137] Among such privileges it is necessary to state that the first wave migrants were settled collectively in the houses and provided with land originally belonged to the Greek Cypriots residents.
[138] 'Check points' are the crossing points on the Green Line which have functioned as cease fire line separating Greek-Cypriot and Turkish-Cypriot de-facto areas.

came to the island during the period between 1975-79 however; %20-25 of them turned back to their homeland (Kurtulus & Purkis, 2010,p.479). On the other hand, the significant Turkish Cypriot politicians and public officials of the period including R. R. Denktaş and Hakkı Atun stated that thirty thousand labor force was requested from Turkey by Turkish Federated State of Cyprus (TFSC) government (Ibid.,p.476-479). Moreover, Mete Hatay (2007,p.31) put forward the idea that only 11.925 people had immigrated to northern part of Cyprus in this period. It is obvious that different studies and several official sources presented different figures of the population who immigrated in the first wave.

The nature of the first wave is incompatible with the motives of labor migration for supplying urgent agricultural labor as it strived to be justified by the officials of Turkish Cypriots and Turkey (Inanc, 2007; Mutluyakali, 2011a). Some scholars like Kurtulus and Purkis (2013,p.6) stated that the primary reasons for the first wave Turkish immigrants were the dramatic labor gap emerged in northern part of Cyprus after the war in 1974. Unlike this conventional official perspective, however, this paper argues that the first wave immigration movement cannot be identified with an 'economic logic'. In classical understanding, labor migration is based on the mobilization of the male work force to get better economic conditions. But in the case of northern Cyprus, there was a 'massive mobilization' of various selected families and villagers rather than the mobilization of male labor force individually. Additionally, it is not a temporary development program since these people were provided with Greek Cypriot lands and houses, migrated and settled collectively and encouraged to move to the island to settle permanently. Moreover, migration was not based on individual decisions but rather a political decision of the official authorities. In light of this event, the first wave immigration aimed at providing ethnic-religious homogeneity in the northern Cyprus as a foreign policy objective of Turkey's government/Turkish Cypriot administration of the time.

Host country policies and reactions

Citizenship

Gaining citizenship status of the host country is one of the essential processes for immigrant population in order to benefit from some civic, economic, political and social rights (Castles & Miller, p.268). As argued in the first section, a group of states tend to encourage and celebrate citizenship status for immigrants while another group make it difficult through implementing complex bureaucratic procedures. In northern Cyprus, the increasing number of immigrants since 1974 and granting them the status of citizenship have become one of the most sensitive issues for the Turkish Cypriot politics. Socio-cultural differences between the Turkish migrants and the native Turkish Cypriots and reactions of the latter to the consequences of migration have resulted in an *anti-migrant language* by which immigrants are depicted as a "physical threat, potential criminals, and carriers of disease" (Hatay, 2008, p.161). The socio-political and cultural impacts of immigrant population on several aspects of the Turkish-Cypriot conventional ways of life created a *fear of assimilation*. The unlawful administrative practices of

Turkish-Cypriot authorities,[139] the nationalist policies towards integrating northern Cyprus into Turkey,[140] the nationalist propaganda that nothing is Cypriot except the 'donkeys of Karpasia,'[141] uncontrolled entries of Turkish nationals into northern Cyprus[142], the policy of Islamization, 'adoptee crisis' and other pejorative statements by Turkish authorities[143] and the continual motherland-babyland political discourses provided a real ground for the fear of assimilation among Turkish-Cypriots. The existence of a group of Turkish migrants' population also affected the Cyprus negotiation process between the two communities.[144] Moreover, there is a political opposition consisting mostly the left-wing parties and liberal cycles towards the immigration policy of the

---

[139] For instance, during the Annan Plan period Turkish nationals began to be given new IDs as if they were from Cypriot families (see Yenidüzen, 1.09.2003; 23.10.2003). Moreover 854 Turkish citizens were arbitrarily registered as citizens of TRNC with the motive that one of their family members got the TRNC citizenship (see Yenidüzen, 13.09.2003). During the period between July 2002and February 2003, another group of 3000 Turkish nationals obtained the citizenship of TRNC with an unlawful decision of the government (see Yenidüzen, 13.09.2003; 25.09.2003; 15.11.2007). For the elections in 14 April 2003, it is appeared that there were 20 Turkish nationals registered as TRNC citizens whose residence was the same address (the home address of Mustafa Tokay undersecretary of the prime minister of the time (see Yenidüzen, 30.10.2003). It is important to state that as a result of suing by the main opposition party of the time and some civil society organizations 156 unlawful 'citizens' lost their citizenship in November 2007 with the decision of the Court (see Yenidüzen, 15.11.2007). On the other hand, The Turkish Embassy of Cyprus has an influential role in the elections since 1983 through influencing the immigrant population's voting behavior. Some political parties established in different periods concentrated on the support from the immigrant population and tried to act as the representatives of that segment of population. To this end *Türk Birliği Partisi* (Turkish Union Party) was established in 1982 and *Yeni Doğuş Partisi* (YDP) *was* established in February 1984 by former military officer Aytaç Beşeşler. These parties announced their unconditional loyalty to Turkey and received incentives from the Turkish embassy in Nicosia (for further information see Fevzioglu, 1998, p.343). Moreover, Nuri Çevikel (Chairman of the TRNC Immigrant Association of the time) stated in October 29, 2003 that the immigrants gave up supporting Mr. Denktaş in the following elections and voted for the solution with the guidance of Ankara (Yenidüzen, 30.10.2003).

[140]See the statement of Denktaş who saw Cyprus as a province of Turkey like Aydın, Bursa (Yenidüzen, 5.12.2003) or Mümtaz Soysal's statements who demanded annexation of island into Turkey (for further information see http://t24.com.tr/yazarlar/tayfun-atay/kibrista-dil-yaresi,3221).

[141] Denktaş developed this perspective to encourage integration between Turkey and northern Cyprus as an alternative to Turkish Cypriot civil society demand: "Cyprus belongs to Cypriots" (for further information see Yenidüzen, 18.10.2003; 23.10.2003; 24.10.2003).

[142]There was strong opposition to the decision of the government on July 1991 that allowed the use of National ID Cards as substitute of a passport for both states' citizens for entering into both countries. Opposition parties, CTP and TKP, objected this decision that it cause more problems and harm the society; and increase illegal labor force from Turkey (for further information see Yenidüzen, 31.07.1991; Halkın Sesi, 31.07.1991).

[143]See Pejorative expressions by Turkey's Prime Minister Recep Tayyip Erdoğan about Turkish Cypriots: "We are feeding you" and reactions from Turkish Cypriot political parties and civil society organization against Recep Tayyip Erdoğan statements; "We are the ones that feeding Turkey since Turkey has huge number of population in island," (for further information see http://www.milliyet.com.tr/kktc-de-sen-kimsin-be-adam-bombasi/siyaset/haberdetay/05.02.2011/1348534/default.htm).

[144]The number and status of the immigrant population is one of the most problematic issues in the negotiation table between the two communities. For instance, in the last UN proposal known as the *Annan Plan*, a solution suggested a limitation on the number of population of Turkish origin that can be given citizenship of the 'United Cyprus Republic' at 45.000, and allowed settlers from Turkey and Greece to be able to stay who migrated a period up to 19 years.

Turkey-Turkish Cypriot authorities (Cuco, 1994; Hatay, 2005). For instance, Alpay Durduran (the chairman of the New Cyprus Party (YKP)) argued that the "Turkish-Cypriot community was being turned into a minority by the growing number of Turks who were settled on the island." In the absence of an official census, the YKP estimated that 55000 Turks had been naturalized since 1974" (Cuco, 1994, p.14). Ferdi Sabit Soyer (Secretary General of Republican Turkish Party (CTP) in 1991) stated that "It [migration] had been presented as an economic necessity, but it functioned as an instrument to change the Turkish-Cypriot cultural identity" (Ibid., p.15).

As presented in the previous part, the immigrant population of the first wave got the 'Turkish Federated State of Cyprus' citizenship simply when they arrived (Birand, 1979; Hatay, 2005; Mutluyakali, 2011b; Kurtulus and Purkis, 2010; 2014). According to the *Article 6/1* of the law of citizenship of the TFSC, which took force in 1975[145], the Minister of Internal Affairs could give citizenship discretionary upon request. Moreover, according to *Article 6/2* of the law, family members of the Turkish armed forces who took part in war in 1974 were granted citizenship status without subjecting to any condition with the decision of the Minister (see also Hatay, 2005, p.11). Nevertheless, internal opposition to citizenship policy[146] and international pressure ended up with the amendments in the law related to the privileges given to the Turkish migrant population on the island. For instance a complementary provision applied to the law of citizenship in 1981 which stated that Turkish-Cypriot citizenship could be granted to individuals who permanently reside in the north Cyprus for at least one year and for those "who made or could make an important contribution to the economy, or social and cultural life, and those who have rendered services to the security forces" (Ronen, 2008, p.27; also see Laakso Report, 2003).

It is stated in the constitution of 'Turkish Republic of Northern Cyprus'[147] that the citizens of TFSC and the Republic of Cyprus are the citizens of the newly established TRNC (Article 67). In 1993, the TFSC law of citizenship was abolished and a new citizenship law was passed by the parliament. The new law required the foreign citizens to reside in the island for at least five years" in order to gain TRNC citizenship (*Article 8(1)B*). Nevertheless, this article has an

---

[145] For Further information see Law 3/1975 of Turkish Cypriot Administration and also Laakso Report 2003.

[146] According to A. Cuco's Report "the communiqués of the Commonwealth Heads of Government (Vancouver 1987, Kuala Lumpur 1989 and Harare 1991) contain explicit references to the need for a speedy withdrawal of all foreign troops and settlers from Cyprus. A similar anxiety was expressed at various ministerial meetings of the non-aligned countries, which likewise called for the immediate withdrawal of the occupying forces and settlers (New York 1987, Belgrade 1989 and Algiers 1990). The European Parliament, in a resolution adopted in May 1988 on the situation on Cyprus, was also in favour of establishing a precise timetable for the withdrawal of the Turkish troops and settlers." (1994,p.24)

[147] After the division of the island Autonomous Turkish Administration was established in the north and it by succeeded by the Turkish Federated State of Cyprus (TFSC) in 1975. In 15 November 1983 the legislative assembly of TFSC proclaimed the Turkish Republic of Northern Cyprus (TRNC). After this decision UN Security Council passed a resolution (no.541) that declared that the TRNC is an illegal entity, its existence is against international law and condemned Turkey for its decision to recognize an illegal entity.

exception of some categories such as people who served in army in 1974 and their families (*Article 9(1)*). It can be argued that after 2004 the acquisitions of TRNC citizenship required more complicated process compared to the previous period (Ronen, 2008). Various proposals were offered by different governments to manage uncontrolled acquisition of citizenship.

Ordinary And Extraordinary Economic Benefits

In the first wave of migration from Turkey to Cyprus, the clear incentive for the newcomers was the promise of a livelihood. Each immigrant family was offered a generous package including a fully furnished house, enough land to cultivate, other various subsidies as well as full citizenship rights. Their transportation expenses were also covered (Sahin et.al. 2013: 614). In the words of an immigrant based in Yedikonuk village,

When we came here they gave us land. One hundred ? decaresof land were distributed households with under six members and for each additional child ten decareswere given. ... They gave us a house with two bedrooms and a sitting room and for one year our living expenses were paid. In addition they gave us seeds and fertilizers. Tractors were sold at very cheap prices - $800 to $1780 (1977 prices). A tractor was sold to every three households, which was affordable, but later we all bought our own tractors (cited in Morvaridi 1993, p.229).

This scheme, which had started in the mid-1975, lasted for around seven years and came to an end in 1982 (Hatay 2008,p.168). Until then according to one account, around 20,000 Turkish citizens moved to the northern part of Cyprus and benefited from this program (Gurel 2012,p.10). According to another one, the figure is around 30,000 (Bryant and Yakinthou 2012, p.27). In the second and third waves, such direct material benefits were not present. However, the flow of migrants was promoted and facilitated by bilateral agreements between the Turkish and Turkish Cypriot governments such as the Labor Force Agreement dated 1987 and the agreement, which lifted passport requirement for the travelers among the two countries signed in 1990. According to the former, for instance, the employer would incur all expenses including the transportation of the guest workers (except passport fees) and provide free of charge accommodation, while the second one effectively turned the northern part of Cyprus into a province of Turkey for Turkish job-seekers.

Social and Political Reactions

Clientelistic Reaction

Following the geographical division of the island in 1974, the northern part of Cyprus was ruled for three decades by governments dominated by right-wing political parties i.e. the Nationalist Unity Party (Ulusal Birlik Partisi, UBP) and its splinter party Democratic Party (Demokrat Parti, DP), whose main distinguishing characteristic is their preference for the continuation of the status quo in the island. While, the pro-reunification left approached the migration policy of Denktaş with suspicion and opposed it, these parties actively supported the flow of migrants from Turkey. Yet, if we put aside a small minority who were ideologically committed to the idea of the sameness of the "Turks of Cyprus" and the mainland Turks, looking from the perspective of the ruling nationalist elite, the immigrant/settler population was nothing but a clientele or a natural vote base against the parties in favor of the reunification of the island, which would be remembered when the election period came. The threat, "they will put you in boats and send back to Turkey" was regularly used by these parties to dissuade the voters of mainland Turkey origin, from voting for the pro-reunification parties –indeed this tactic was resorted to once again even in the most recent presidential election by the leader of the UBP against the pro-reunification candidate. Outright vote-buying has also been an important instrument of political clientelism to gain this group's electoral support.

In fact, the election periods were only times that the Turkish immigrants had some leverage on these parties. Until very recently, in every election period, the ministry of interior worked overtime to grant citizenship to the Turkish citizens so that they could vote for the nationalist parties. In the 1990 general election, for instance, as it was later confirmed by the report of a parliamentary enquiry committee, "even on the day of election (which was a Sunday), the ministry of interior was opened to grant citizenship" (Sonan 2014,p.182) In a similar vein, in the wake of 2003 election, the TRNC citizenship was granted to thousands of people. Curiously, some of them were not even resident in Cyprus; 20 of them were registered in the address of the undersecretary of the prime minister's office!

Furthermore, these carrots used to attract their votes were sometimes complemented with coercion too. The 1981 election is a good case in point. In an article entitled "I'm coming from the jungle," Ismet Kotak, who was on the field as the secretary general of the Democratic People's Party (another splinter party of the UBP), gives a good account of how these people were forced to vote for the UBP or another small party, which was established by the settlers.

"Armed groups surrounded villages populated mainly by the settlers ... in the last 48 hours before the polling day" ... Furthermore, on the day of election, "the voters were not allowed to go out; they were picked up from their houses and driven to the polling stations and then back to their houses" (cited in Sonan 2014, p.171).

It should be added that the newly emerging Turkish Cypriot economic elites were also in favor of the flow of migration from Turkey because of two obvious reasons. Firstly, they have provided cheap and abundant labor force and hence boost profits, and secondly they have created additional demand in the domestic market for the goods they produced or imported. It is no wonder that for a very long time, the Turkish Cypriot Chamber of Commerce was a staunch supporter of the UBP governments.

Protectionist Reaction

The intense Turkish migration to northern Cyprus also stipulated a political reaction implicitly or explicitly aired by the leftist and liberal circles. This is a protectionist reaction in the sense that   migrant groups are seen as a threat on Turkish Cypriot identity and political stability. Through using a historical perspective the protectionist reaction presents Turkish migration as a result of socio-political factors, namely the increasing economic and political influence of Turkey. It focuses on pre-immigration as well as post immigration processes. Regarding the pre-immigration processes the protectionists suggest that the northern Cyprus should adopt European laws and principles to regulate and limit migration. This argument is based on the belief that the status of northern Cyprus and Turkish Cypriot community has been politically attractive to Turkish nationals since gaining the TRNC citizenship would be legal instrument to benefit from specific facilities[148] available to the citizens of the Republic of Cyprus at least after the settlement of the Cyprus dispute. The protectionists believe that this misinterpretation of the status of northern Cyprus should be corrected and that legal limitation on citizenship and residential rights should be implemented to protect the distinct identity and culture of northern Cyprus.

Legalist Reaction

Legalist reaction sees immigration as a human right issue without connecting the political influence of Turkey to the intense Turkish immigration to northern Cyprus. Therefore it sees Turkey's government and its policies either as neutral or indifferent factors on the issue. Turkish immigration is perceived through classical economic perspective concentrating on pull and push factors. They argue that as job-seekers the Turkish migrants in northern Cyprus should be treated independently of what Turkey desires to see in northern Cyprus. The natural consequence of this perspective is the concentration only on the post immigration issues and policies. The suggestions of this perspective therefore focus on anti-discrimination legislation and the appropriate models of legal incorporation of Turkish migrants through providing them with TRNC citizenship and accepting them as potential citizens of the proposed federal Cypriot state.

Conclusion

The northern Cyprus represents a distinct case and category in the international migration studies. Its distinctiveness derives from such factors as the de-facto status of northern Cyprus, the ethno-nationalist conflict on the island, geostrategic perspectives of Turkey which shape its foreign policy instruments and the specific relations between Turkey and northern Cyprus. It is possible to argue that there are at least other potential cases which could be grouped in the same category together with north Cyprus. Such cases as Kosova, Estonia Crimea and some post-socialist countries demonstrate similar characteristic with regard to the reasons of migration and reactions to it. The case of Cyprus underline the fact that unlike what is suggested by conventional theories on international migration political dimensions of migration and various reactions to migration need to be refocused. Particularly, it is obvious that politically motivated migration creates effects beyond the conventional results of economic migration and necessitates further attention. It is also interesting to note that various reactions to migration culminated in the creation of a major area of debate between the political forces. Moreover, politically motivated migration seems to encourage new international regulations. Although the fourth Geneva Convention prohibit population transfers by the occupying state into occupied territories it does not provide any explicit model to deal with the consequences of such state acts. This paper suggests that the results of a politically motivated migration to northern Cyprus

---

[148] Turkish Cypriots who are registered as the citizens of the Republic of Cyprus began to travel, settle and work in EU countries freely. The Turkish migrants also want to be accepted as having the right to be identified as permanent and legal residents of the island of Cyprus to gain the same benefits.

have both a humanitarian and a political dimension. The humanitarian dimension requires explicit rules and criteria to regulate the consequences of migration through the application of universal human rights principles while the political dimension necessitates a clear identification of responsibility of the state involving in such activities towards sponsoring migration on the basis of political reasons.

References

Akgun, M., Gurel, A., Hatay, M. & Tiryaki, S. (2005). Quo Vadis Kıbrıs, TESEV Working Paper.

Atay, T. Kıbrıs'ta Dil Yaresi. T24 Online Newspaper (08 February 2011). Received from http://t24.com.tr/yazarlar/tayfun-atay/kibrista-dil-yaresi,3221 available on: 25.04.2015

Birand, M. A. (1979). Diyet. 5th Edition. Istanbul: Milliyet Yayınları A.Ş.

Borjas, G. J. (1989). Economic Theory and International Migration [Special Silver Anniversary Issue]. International Migration Review, 23(3), 457:485.

Bryant R. & Yakinthou, C. (2012). Cypriot Perceptions of Turkey. İstanbul: TESEV.

Castles, S. (2003a). The International Politics of Forced Migration. Society for International Development, 46(3), 11-20.

Castles, S. (2003b). Towards a Sociology of Forced Migration and Social Transformation. Sociology, 37(1), 13-34.

Castles, S. & Miller, M. J. (2009). The Age of Migration: International Population Movements In The Modern World, 4th Edition. N.Y: Palgrave Macmillan.

Cornelius, W. A., & Rosenblum M. R. (2005). Immigration and Politics. Annual Review of Political Science, 8, 99-119.

Cuco, A. (1994). Report on the Demographic Structure of the Cypriot Communities, Press and Information Office: Republic of Cyprus. Received from http://www.moa.gov.cy/MOI/pio/pio.nsf/All/20C7614D06858E9FC2256DC200380113/$file/cuco%20report.pdf?OpenElement available on: 26.11.2014

Fevzioğlu, B. (1998). Kıraathane-i Osmani 'den, Cumhuriyet Meclisi'ne (1886-1996): Olaylar ve Seçimler/Seçilenler. Lefkoşa: KKTC Cumhuriyet Meclisi (in Turkish).

Gürel, A. (2012). Displacement in Cyprus, Consequences of Civil and Military Strife: Turkish Cypriot Legal Framework. Oslo: PRIO.

Hatay, M. (2005). Beyond Numbers: An Inquiry into The Political Integration of The Turkish 'Settlers' in North Cyprus. PRIO Cyprus Centre Reports.

Hatay, M. (2007). Is the Turkish Cypriot Population Shrinking?- An Overview of the Ethno-Demography of Cyprus in the Light of the Preliminary Results of 2006 Turkish-Cypriot Census. PRIO Cyprus Centre Reports.

Hatay, M. (2008). The problem of pigeons: orientalism, xenophobia and a rhetoric of the 'local' in North Cyprus. The Cyprus Review, 20(2), 145-171.

Inalcık, H. (1997). A Note on Population of Cyprus. Journal for Cypriot Studies, 3(1).

Inanc, G. (2007). Büyükelçiler Anlatıyor: Türk Demokrasisinde Kıbrıs (1970-1991) [Ambassadors Telling: Cyprus in Turkish Democracy]. Istanbul: Türk İş Bankası Kültür Yayınları (in Turkish).

International Organization for Migration. Received from http://www.iom.int/cms/en/sites/iom/home/about-migration/key-migration-terms-1.html available on: 26.02.2015

Jennisen, R. (2007). Causality Chains in the International Migration System Approaches. Population Research and Policy Review, 26, 411-436.

Joppke, C. (2007). Transformation of Immigrant Integration in Western Europe: Civic Integration and Antidiscrimination Policies in the Netherlands, France, and Germany. World Politics, 59 (2), 243-273.

Karahasan, S. (2011, February 05). KKTC'de 'Sen Kimsin be adam!' bombası". Milliyet. Received from http://www.milliyet.com.tr/kktc-de-sen-kimsin-be-adam-bombasi/siyaset/haberdetay/05.02.2011/1348534/default.htm available on: 25.04.2015 (in Turkish).

Kurtulus, H. & Purkis, S. (2010). Gocmenlerin vatandaslık, kimlik ve aidiyeti uzerinden sosyal dıslanması: Kuzey Kıbrıs'ta T.C'li olmak! Ali Ekber Dogan and Besime Sen (eds.) Tarih, Sınıflar ve Kent. Ankara: Dipnot Publications, 465-506 (in Turkish).

Kurtulus, H. & Purkis, S. (2013). Spatially Segregated and Socially Excluded Turkish Immigrants in Northern Cyprus: An Alternative Perspective. İ.Ü. Siyasal Bilgiler Fakültesi Dergisi, 48.

Kurtulus, H. & Purkis, S. (2014). Kuzey Kıbrıs'ta Türkiyeli Göçmenler [Be A Turkish Immigrant in North Cyprus]. Istanbul: Turkiye Is Bankası Kultur Yayınları (in Turkish).

Laakso, J. (2003). Report on the Colonization by Turkish Settlers of the Occupied Part of Cyprus. Council of Europe Committee on Migration, Refugees and Demography. Received from http://assembly.coe.int/ASP/Doc/ XrefViewHTML.asp?FileID=10153&Language=en available on: 05.04.2015

Massey, D. S. (1999). International Migration at the Dawn of the Twenty-First Century: The Role of the State. Population and Development Review, 25(2), 302-322.

Massey, D. S., et al. (1993). Theories of International Migration: A Review and Appraisal. Population and Development Review, 19 (3), 431-466.

Massey, D. S., et al. (1998). Worlds in Motion: Understanding International Migration at the End of The Millennium. Oxford: Clarendon Press.

Markus, A. (2014). Attitudes in Immigration and Cultural Diversity in Australia. Journal of Sociology, 50(1), 10-22.

Mehmet, O. et al., (2007). Labor Mobility and Labor Market Convergence in Cyprus. Turkish Studies, 8(1), 43-69.

Miller, P. W. (1999). Immigration Policy and Immigrant Quality: The Australian Points System. American Economic Association, 89(2), 192-197.

Morvardi, B. (1993). Demographic Change, Resettlement and Resource Use. Clement Dodd, (eds.) The Political Social and Economic Development of Northern Cyprus. Cambridgeshire: The Eothen Press.

Mutluyakali, C. (2011a). Sene 1975, Kıbrıs'a Nüfus Gerek! [1975: Population Needed for Cyprus]. Adres Kıbrıs, 1(28), 16-21 (in Turkish).

Mutluyakali, C. (2011b). 1975'te Nüfus Nasıl Taşındı? [How Turkish Population Mobilized in 1975]. Adres Kıbrıs, 1(29), 24-27 (in Turkish).

Pakulski, J. (2014). Confusions about multiculturalism. J. of Sociology, 50 (1), 23-36.

Policy Briefing on Introduction programmes and language courses for refugees and migrants in Europe. Received from http://www.ecre.org/ available on:10.03.2015

Ronen, Y. (2008). STATUS OF SETTLERS IMPLANTED BY ILLEGAL REGIMES UNDER INTERNATIONAL LAW. International Law Forum of the Hebrew University of Jerusalem Law Faculty, Research Paper No. 11-08.

Sahin, I et al., (2013). Barış Harekatı Sonrasında Türkiye'den Kıbrıs'a Yapılan Göçler ve Tatbik Edilen İskan Politikası. Turkish Studies International Periodical For the Languages, Literature and History of Turkish or Turkic 8(7), 599-630 (in Turkish).

Sonan, S. (2014). In the Grip of Political Clientelism: The Post-1974 Turkish Cypriot Politics and the Politico-Economic Foundations of Pro-Taksim Consensus. Unpublished doctoral dissertation, University of Duisburg-Essen, Germany.

Stark, O. (1991). The Migration of Labour. Oxford: Blackwell.

Stalker, P. (1999). Workers Without Frontiers: The Impact of Globalization on International Migration. Boulder, CO: Lynne Rienner

Teitelbaum, M.S. & Weiner, M., (Ed.). (1995). Threatened Peoples, Threatened Borders: World Migration and U.S. Policy. New York: Norton

The Law of Citizenship of Autonomous Turkish Administration (Law 3/1975)

The Law of Citizenship, TRNC. Received from http://www.mahkemeler.net/cgi-bin/elektroks.aspx available on: 10.03.2015

TRNC Constitution. Received from http://www.mahkemeler.net/cgi-bin/elektroks.aspx available on: 10.03.2015

Turkish Cypriot Newspapers: Yenidüzen, Halkın Sesi

Migration Policy and Migration Management of Syrians in Turkey[149]

Michelle Dromgold[150]

Introduction

Since the outbreak of the Syrian Civil War in the spring of 2011, the number of Syrian nationals seeking refuge within the borders of Turkey has surged, and the recent intensified threat of the Islamic State of Iraq and Syria (ISIS) has only caused the number of Syrians fleeing to Turkey for safety to rise further. Today, Turkey hosts more Syrians than any other country in the world; according to official United Nations Refugee Association (UNHCR) registration statistics as of April 10, 2015, there are 1,758,092 registered Syrians in Turkey (UNHCR 2015) although estimates among academics, representatives from non-governmental organizations (NGOs) and others predict the actual number of Syrians in the country as closer to 2.5 million. However, the legal status of Syrians in Turkey is unique. Not legally recognized as refugees due to Turkey's historic and current migration policies, Syrians in Turkey are considered as 'guests' in the country and remain here under the legal status of temporary protection. Although this status provides for many basic rights - including shelter, food, education, medical support and the possibility of employment - Syrians often remain uninformed of and unable to access their rights-based provisions. Additionally, as the governmental and societal discourse of 'guests' suggests, Syrians are expected to be 'hosted' by the Turkish government and society and subsequently return home. Although governmental policy and many Turkish humanitarian aid-based NGOs continue to convey this discourse of Syrians as 'guests' under temporary protection, Turkish society is becoming tense - the Syrian 'guests' have overstayed their welcome.

As the Syrian conflict enters its fifth year and in the absence of a long-term plan for Syrians in the country, Syrians are now the normalized 'other' in Turkey. This research aims to illustrate how Turkey's migration policy and the provision of temporary protection, while legally including Syrians into Turkish society, continues to exclude Syrians in the reality of their everyday lives in Turkey. Following an overview of methodology, a legal outline of Turkey's historic and current migration policy is provided. Subsequently, the critical problems for Syrians in Turkey and their links to Syrians' legal status of 'temporary protection' are analyzed and discussed.

[149] I would like to acknowledge the input and insight of Professor Besim Can Zırh in advising the Masters thesis of which this research is a part.
[150] Michelle Dromgold is a second year Masters student, Department of Middle East Studies, Middle East Technical University, Dumlupınar Bulvarı 06800 Çankaya/Ankara E-mail: michelle.dromgold@gmail.com

Methodology

This research is based on data gathered from thirty-one interviews with NGOs and government employees in Ankara, Gaziantep, Istanbul and Şanliurfa. The interviews were conducted between February and May 2015 in person by the author; one interview was conducted over the phone. Four interviews were informal, but the remaining twenty-seven were semi-structured in-depth interviews in which the same questions were asked. Twenty-two interviews with NGOs included interviews with fourteen Turkey-based NGOs,[151] one Syrian-based NGO and five international NGOs. The remaining eight interviews ranged from government employees to religious leaders.[152] In all of the formal interviews and many of the informal interviews, interviewees were asked questions regarding their organization's overall mission and work, their work with Syrians in Turkey, their coordination with other NGOs and governmental organizations and their role in Turkey's migration management system. Here, I draw on relevant literature from the field and interview responses to questions regarding critical problems of the Syrian flows in Turkey to analyze how Syrians are legally included and excluded from Turkish society in various aspects of their everyday lives.

Turkey's migration policy and the law on foreigners and international protection

Turkey's 2014 Law on Foreigners and International Protection can be considered a benchmark as "the first law of its kind in Turkey" (Soykan 2012, p. 42). The law, "in many ways represents a vast step forward towards the transformation and regulation of asylum and migration for Turkey since the country ratified the 1951 Refugee Convention" (Soykan 2012, p. 41). The law's introduction of a human rights based legislative and legal framework represents a shift from the former national policies that were security centered.[153] Furthermore, the law is a significant initiative in Europeanization of Turkish immigration law, as "the law meets practically all the European Union's (EU) requirements, including the establishment of a specialised agency to deal with the reception of asylum-seekers and process their applications as well as the incorporation of the existing EU acquis in this area" (Aydin and Kirisci 2013, p.375-376). The only EU requirement left unfulfilled by the new law is the lifting of the geographical limitation of the 1951 Geneva Convention that restricts refugees to people displaced from Europe. The law has two main parts, the section on 'Foreigners' and the section on 'International Protection.' The law's legal framework for four types of international protection - refugee, conditional refugee, subsidiary protection and temporary protection - will be the focus of this paper. In the subsequent subsections, Turkey's historic refugee and asylum

---

[151] Interviews with two Turkey-based NGOs occurred in two cities, thus the discrepancy in numbers.
[152] See the 'List of Organizations Interviewed' at the end of this article.
[153] Although the law introduces a new human rights framework, it is still criticized for its remaining legal shortcomings, including allowance for administrative immigration detention in Turkey, detention for irregular migrants, and its adoption of concepts of "first country of asylum or a safe third country" (Soykan 2012, p.43).

policies are briefly overviewed, followed by the policies of the current Law on Foreigners and International Protection regarding international protection.

Turkey's Historical Refugee and Asylum Policy

As a signatory to the Universal Declaration of Human Rights (UDHR) and having ratified the 1951 Geneva Convention Relating to the Status of Refugees, Turkey's policy on asylum was based solely on the 1951 Convention until 2014. Turkey actively advocated for the Convention, including how to define a refugee and the inclusion of a geographical limitation that recognized only Europeans as refugees and ratified the convention in 1962. Accession to the 1967 Protocol occurred in 1968 (Kirisci 2002, p.13-14), when Turkey opted to maintain the geographical limitation, which restricts asylum seekers to "persons who have become refugees as a result of events occurring in Europe."

Therefore, the Convention establishes a two-tiered asylum system in Turkey (Kirisci 2002, p.14). The first tier relates to asylum seekers from European countries (under the Convention's geographic limitations) and those "to whom Turkey has upheld the Convention...with the understanding that recognized refugees would, eventually, be resettled in third countries" (Kirisci 2002, p.14). Historically, asylum seekers arriving from Europe have been considered first-tier asylum seekers and are resettled in other countries. Turkey's second-tier of the asylum system refers to 'non-convention' refugees, those refugees coming from countries outside of Europe (Kirisci 2002, p.17-18). Azeris, Ahiska Turks, Chechens and Uzbeks were common immigrants comprised in this second-tier in the early Republic. Until 1994, Turkish authorities generally "refrained from granting refugee status" to these groups and they were instead "allowed to stay in the country on an unofficial basis or have been allowed to benefit from the laws that allow people considered to be of Turkish descent to settle, work, and eventually obtain Turkish citizenship" (Kirisci 2002, p.15). Today, "the majority of asylum seekers in Turkey originate from non-European states, notably from Iraq, Iran, Afghanistan, Somalia and Sudan" (Soykan 2012, p.39).

In response to the influx of migrants and displaced persons from the Gulf War conflict in the early 1990s, Turkey's first asylum law was introduced in 1994. The 'Regulation on the Procedures and Principles Related to Mass Influx and Foreigners Arriving in Turkey or Requesting Residence Permits with the Intention of Seeking Asylum from a Third Country' placed a number of pre-conditions for asylum applicants as well as requiring both Europeans and non-Europeans to apply for residence permits during their stay (Kirisci 2002, p.20; Kirisci 2014, p.7). As Soykan (2012) explains, the law "created its own 'temporary' protection mechanism" that allowed non-Europeans to receive valid residence permits to remain in Turkey for the short-term (Soykan 2012, p. 39). Under this law, both the UNHCR and the Turkish government conducted Refugee Status Determination interviews for non-European asylum seekers; when both institutions recognized an individual as a 'refugee,' they were then eligible for resettlement (Soykan 2012, p. 39).

In the 2000s, Turkey began initial reform of its overall migration policies as required in the process of EU accession negotiations, particularly including signing readmission and visa liberalization agreements with a number of countries and ratifying international conventions and introducing new national laws regarding migration. Steps towards reforming asylum law began with a 2004 Asylum-Migration Twinning Project with Denmark and England that resulted in a 'National Action Plan on Asylum and Migration (NAP)' and a subsequent Action Plan in 2005 to align Turkey's migration and asylum legislation with European standards (Soykan 2012, p.38). In 2008, a new Bureau for the Development and Implementation of Asylum and Migration Legislation and Strengthening the Administrative Capacity was founded under the Ministry of the Interior (Soykan 2012, p.38). Together with leadership of the UNHCR and IOM and with input from Turkish NGOs working with refugees, such as Mülteci-Der, the Bureau completed the initial drafting process of the current law in 2010. The Law on Foreigners and International Protection was adopted in April 2013 and entered into force one year later in April 2014.

International Protection under the Law on Foreigners and International Protection

The Law on Foreigners and International Protection subcategorizes international protection in terms of: refugees, conditional refugees (previous called ex-asylum seekers), subsidiary protection, and temporary protection. A refugee is defined as a person originating from European countries who "shall be granted refugee status upon completion of the refugee status determination process" (Article 61). A conditional refugee is contrastingly a person originating from a non-European country, but who "shall be allowed to reside in Turkey temporarily until they are resettled to a third country" (Article 62). Subsidiary protection is granted to "a foreigner or stateless person, who…is unable or for the reason of such threat is unwilling, to avail himself or herself of the protection of his country of origin or country of [former] habitual residence" (Article 63).

Temporary protection is the legal stipulation under which Syrians are protected in Turkey. According to Article 91(1), "Temporary protection may be provided for foreigners who have been forced to leave their country, cannot return to the country that they have left, and have arrived at or crossed the borders of Turkey in a mass influx situation seeking immediate and temporary protection." However, as outlined in Article 91(2), the specifics of "the reception of such foreigners into Turkey; their stay in Turkey and rights and obligations; their exit from Turkey…shall be stipulated in a Directive to be issued by the Council of Ministers." The first directive regarding the rights of Syrians was issued on October 22, 2014. This Regulation on Temporary Protection specifies Syrians' admission to Turkish territory as unobstructed, forced returns as not permitted and Syrians' rights to access to basic needs - including shelter in camps, food and medical support and psychosocial services, education, and "the possibility to apply for work permits in certain sectors and regions" - with the issuance of temporary protection identification documents by the Turkish government (Malkin and Danforth 2014; Refugee Solidarity Network 2014). Unlike the status of 'refugee' or 'conditional refugee,' temporary protection does not allow for the possibility of resettlement, except in special cases, such as for lesbians, gay, bisexual, transgender and intersex (LGBTI) refugees who face "multiple layers of discrimination" and "are often marginalized in society and isolated from their communities and families" (UNHCR 2012, p.2; Kaos GL).

Syrians in Turkey - life under temporary protection

Due to the mass influx of Syrians into Turkey over the past four years, Syrians are granted temporary protection to stay in Turkey. As outlined in the 2014 Regulation on Temporary Protection, registered Syrians are legally granted rights regarding basic needs and services. However, the implementation of these rights is "still in flux" (Malkin and Danforth 2014), particularly due to "a lack of knowledge among the Syrian population [outside the camps] on how and where to access the services that are available to them" (Turkmen Sanduvac 2013, 6). Ineligible for resettlement and unable to return to Syria, the majority of Syrians in Turkey remain in limbo, waiting and trying to survive. This "indefinite waiting, limited knowledge" and unforeseen future of temporary protection can be included under the umbrella term of what Biehl (2015) considers a normalised 'protracted uncertainty' accompanying temporary asylum (Biehl 2015, p.57).

When twenty-five interviewees were questioned regarding the most critical problems for Syrians in Turkey, fourteen noted the problem of unemployment and lack of access to employment, nine mentioned shelter and rent, nine mentioned language, seven mentioned education, and six each mentioned nourishment and healthcare as the main problems for Syrians. Of thirteen responses to the question "What are the most critical problems of the Syrian flows for Turkish society," eight mentioned some form of exclusion, discrimination or underlying tensions between Turkish residents and Syrians; the stated grounds for these tensions were related mainly to the perception of many Turkish citizens that Syrians cause unemployment and the rise in rental prices, as well as a fear of multiple marriages with Syrian girls. Here, these main problems identified by the respondents - basic needs of shelter and nourishment, un/underemployment, discrimination, language and education and healthcare - are examined with regards to Syrians' legal rights in Turkey and how these problems contribute to Syrians continuing exclusion and 'othering' from Turkish society.

Shelter and Nourishment

Although Syrians residing in camps are adequately provided with shelter and food-items, these two basic needs continue to be major concerns for Syrians living outside the camps, with many living in crowded, unsanitary and unsafe conditions. For example, in Şanliurfa, the average Syrian household size is eleven (Turkmen Sanduvac 2013, p.6). Particularly Syrians arriving more recently in Turkey continue to struggle with accessing adequate shelter and nourishment. This lack of access is largely related to the issue of unemployment - unable to work or provide a steady income, Syrians residing outside of the camps continue to struggle to meet these basic needs.

Unemployment and Legal Employment

Thus the majority of interviewees also identified unemployment and lack of access to an adequate and steady income as a major current problem for Syrians.

Due to the inability to work legally with their status of temporary protection, many Syrians work illegally, with women frequently working in the textile industries and men generally working in heavy industries, while children and youth collect plastic on the streets (Anonymous Interview; Interview with family health center employee). This work is performed at wages significantly lower than required by law and in unsafe conditions. For example, a resident of Suruç or Akçakale would be paid 50TL per day, but a Syrian may work for only 20TL a day (Anonymous Interview). As a result, many employers hire Syrians to reduce their expenditures; this illegal employment, however only fuels mistrust of and discrimination towards Syrians among Turkish citizens, who increasingly blame high Turkish unemployment on Syrians' illegal work. Those Syrians who are unable to find illegal work often resort to begging or, in some cases, marrying off their young daughters. Although the October 2014 Regulation on Temporary Protection provides for "the possibility to apply for work permits in certain sectors and regions" (Malkin and Danforth 2014), this has not yet been consistently or nationally implemented. At the end of 2014, an additional proposal concerning working conditions for Syrians was submitted to the Council of Ministers; when approved, it must also be approved by the Parliament before entering into force (Yeginsu 2014). Although the approval of the additional proposal is seen by many as the best solution to Syrian illegal employment and reducing societal tension between Turkish citizens and Syrians, others worry that the new law may only allow camp residents to work, thus functioning merely as an incentive for Syrians to move to the camps and not actually improving the well-being of those Syrians residing outside the camps (Anonymous Interview).

Discrimination

Interviewees working in the field identified exclusion, discrimination or underlying tensions between Turkish residents and Syrians as a major problem of the Syrian flows for Turkish society. This discrimination is rooted in Turkish citizens' perception that unemployment and the recent rise in housing and food-item prices are results of Syrians' illegal employment and presence in the country. This discrimination is often subtle, but is very exclusionary for Syrians. Two common examples are hesitations and excuses to not rent to Syrians and children being told not to speak with Syrian children at their schools. As mentioned repeatedly in interviews in Gaziantep and Şanlıurfa, the fear of multiple marriages, particularly in the border region, is another source of tensions between Turkish citizens and Syrians. Without the ability to work, desperate Syrian families will sell their young daughters to Turkish men for second marriages. Many Turkish women and wives see this as a potentially invasive threat to their marriage and family stability, thus fueling further tension and providing a basis for discrimination of and distance from Syrians.

Language and Education

Although education is one of the rights provided to Syrians under temporary protection according to the October 2014 Directive, inability to access adequate education remains one of the main problems for Syrians in Turkey. Due to the 'protracted uncertainty' (Biehl 2015) of temporary protection, which education curriculum Syrian children should be taught, in which language this education should be offered and who should teach these classes remains a contested topic. There is a shortage of space in schools and a shortage of teachers, causing many urban schools to run double-shifts, with Turkish children attending in the morning and Syrian children in the afternoon. Additionally, high school and university certificates and diplomas often remain unrecognized in Turkey, excluding young Syrians from studying at Turkish universities and subsequently excluding them from the Turkish workforce. Language differences also remain a major hindrance to education, employment and social integration. Although Turkish and Arabic education is offered in AFAD camps, the majority of Syrians outside of camps do not have access to Turkish language courses. Additionally, education for non-Arab Syrians is not offered in their native language in the AFAD camps. This is particularly an issue for Kurdish Syrians, creating an incentive for Kurds to live in municipality camps or outside of the camps, even if their needs cannot be fully met outside of the camps (Suruç Municipality).

Health Care and Psychosocial Support

Access to health and adequate psychosocial support were also cited among interviewees as a major problem for Syrians. Particularly since Syrians must be registered to access medical support, unregistered Syrians remain unable to receive such care. Syrians' free access to Turkish medical support is however also a source of tension with Turkish society, in which Syrians are perceived as taking "everything for free," including healthcare (Anonymous Family Health Center). Just as there is a shortage of housing, of schools and of teachers, there is also a shortage of doctors and nurses (Anonymous Family Health Center).

Discussion

Although the legal status of temporary protection seems to be a benevolent governmental response to a mass influx of immigration, implementation of this legal status and migrants' access to their basic rights is not so easy. Although Syrians in Turkey have rights to basic needs of shelter, food, medical support and psychosocial services, education, and the future possibility for legal employment, knowledge of and access to these rights is not sufficient to fulfill the basic needs of the estimate 2.5 Syrians across the country. Although these rights are legally stipulated, Syrians' access and information regarding access to these rights outside of the camps remains insufficient. In addition to struggling to earn money to provide for their basic needs, Syrians additionally face subtle and direct discrimination from Turkish citizens and exclusion from Turkish society that reinforces the perception of Syrians as the 'other.'

Four years ago, Syrians were welcomed into Turkey as 'guests.' Now they are granted rights under the legal status of temporary protection. However, Syrians are increasingly normalized as the 'other' in Turkish society, the group for which unemployment, economic, education and health problems is scapegoated. Without a long-term plan for integration of Syrians into Turkish society, Syrians will continue to struggle to fulfill their basic needs and will remain the 'other' - the 'guest' who has overstayed their welcome.

List of organizations interviewed

Advisors to the Deputy Prime Minister (3), Anonymous Family Health Center, Anonymous NGOs (3), ASAM Gaziantep, ASAM Şanliurfa, Cansuyu Ankara, Göc Der, Helsinki Citizens Assembly, Human Rights Association Gaziantep, IHH, Imkander, IMPR, International Medical Corps, International Refugee Rights Association, Kaos-GL, Kimse Yok Mu, Mazlumder Ankara, Mazlumder Gaziantep, Mufti of Gaziantep, Mülteci Der, Police Academy, Support to Life, Suriye Nur-Der, Suruç municipality, Sanliurfa Sivil Toplumu Kuruluslar Platformu, World Food Programme

References

Aydin, U. and K. Kirişci (2013). With or Without the EU: Europeanisation of Asylum and Competition Policies in Turkey. *South European Society and Politics* 18(3), 375-395.

Biehl, K. S. (2015). Governing through Uncertainty: Experiences of being a Refugee in Turkey as a Country for Temporary Asylum. *Social Analysis* 59(1), 57-75.

Içduygu, A. et al (2014). Migration Policy Centre Migration Profile: Turkey. *Migration Policy Centre*. Received from www.migrationpolicycentre.eu available on: 17.08.2014.

Kirişci, K. (2002). Justice and Home Affairs Issues in Turkish-EU Relations. Istanbul: TESEV.

Kirişci, K. (2014). Syrian Refugees and Turkey's Challenges: Going beyond Hospitality. Washington: Brookings Institute.

Malkin, N. and N. Danforth (2014). Ghosts of the Future. *Middle East Research and Information Project*. Received from http://www.merip.org/mero/mero102414 available on: 29.04.2015.

Refugee Solidarity Network. Syrians in Turkey. Received from http://www.refugeesolidaritynetwork.org available on: 01.12.2014.

Soykan, C. (2012). The New Draft Law on Foreigners and International Protection in Turkey. *Oxford Monitor of Forced Migration*, 2(2), 38-47.

Soykan, C. (2010). The Impact of Common European Union Immigration Policy on Turkey. *Ethnologia Balkanica* 14, 207-225.

Turkmen Sanduvac, Z. (2013). Needs Assessment Report of Syrian non-camp refugees in Sanliurfa/Turkey. Concern WW and Mavi Kalem.

UNHCR (2012). Guidelines on International Protections No. 9: Claims to Refugee Status based on Sexual Orientation and/or Gender Identity within the context of Article 1 A(2) of the 1951 Convention and/or its 1967 Protocol relating to the Status of Refugees. *HCR/GIP/12/01* Received from http://www.refworld.org/cgi-bin/texis/vtx/rwmain?docid=50348afc2.html available on: 29.04.2015.

UNHCR (2015). Syria Regional Refugee Response: Turkey. Received from http://data.unhcr.org/syrianrefugees/country.php?id=224 available on: 29.04.2015.

Yeginsu, C. (2014). Turkey strengthens rights of Syrian refugees. *New York Times*. Received from http://www.nytimes.com/2014/12/30/world/europe/turkey-strengthens-rights-of-syrian-refugees.html?_r=0 available on: 29.04.2015.

Local perceptions on Syrian migration to Turkey: A case study of Istanbul neighborhoods

Deniz Genç* & Merve Özdemirkıran*

Introduction

Migration is not a new phenomenon for Turkey. Before and after the foundation of the Republic, the country has received waves of migration but since the 1970s, migration dynamics of the country has been changing. Turkey has increasingly become a destination country for asylum-seekers and a transit country for irregular migrants.[154] Mass influx of asylum-seekers and refugee movements in Turkey has originated mainly from its neighbours or former Ottoman territories. These movements have included Iranians, Turks of Bulgaria, Iraqis, Chechens, Bosniacs and very recently Syrians.

When the crisis in Syria evolved into civil war, along with Lebanon, Jordan, Iraq and Egypt, Turkey has become one of the main refuge countries for the Syrian Arab Republic citizens, who fled from the war. In the early phases of the crisis, Turkey declared that it would pursue and 'Open Door Policy' and admit fleeing Syrians. By the help of the visa –waiver agreement between the two countries in 2009, many Syrians entered Turkey regularly, as travellers and they later acquired residence permits. Many of them, on the other hand, entered Turkey irregularly in influx as asylum-seekers. They have crossed the borders into Turkey to seek asylum since April 2011. According to UNHCR (2015), as of March 20, 2015, Turkey hosts more than 1.7 million registered Syrian refugees. This number does not include the regular Syrians, who came to Turkey before April 2011. Though most of the Syrian asylum-seekers are reported to live in the cities, where the camps have been set up, they are now almost in every city of Turkey (AFAD, 2014; Erdoğan, 2014). Among these cities, Istanbul hosts the largest number of Syrians (Erdoğan, 2014).

Turkey has received very high number of asylum-seekers in a very short time. As a result, the government has had difficulties in managing this flow. Let alone the failures in registration of the asylees, we have very limited data on Syrian migration in the big cities: where do they live, what they do, how they are perceived, etc. In line with this lack of data on Syrian mass migration to Turkey, this study has aimed to take a picture of Syrian migration in the neighborhoods of Istanbul. In line with this main aim, the paper tries to answer two main questions: How do the Istanbulites perceive mass migration of Syrians to Turkey and to their neighborhoods and why do they have these perceptions? And how is this migration absorbed by the neighborhoods in Istanbul.

Besides giving us an instant picture of the Syrian migration in Istanbul (for the period between November 2014 and April 2015), these questions have increasingly led study to a field that has been exhausted by the scholars from

* Department of Political Science and International Relations, İstanbul Medipol University
* Department of Political Science and International Relations, Bahçeşehir University

diverse fields who have intensively worked on 'attitudes on immigrants, asylum seekers, refugees and foreigners'. In line with this direction, following the theoretical framework, the study continues with the methodology part and findings of the field research in Istanbul, preliminary findings of which show that the perceptions of the Istanbulites are marked by feelings of disturbance, worry and uneasiness.

Theoretical Framework

The volume of international migration has increased in the last decades and it has become a salient and a politicized issue. Academics from different disciplines within social sciences such as political science, sociology, social psychology, economy etc. have shown interest in the attitudes about immigrants. In line with this, a vast literature, which has been fed by both qualitative and quantitative research on attitudes towards foreigners, asylum seekers, refugees and immigrants, has emerged. In this literature, different theoretical approaches have been adopted to understand the dynamics of attitude formation processes and studies in different parts of the world have not only examined the attitudes towards out-groups - immigrants, foreigners, asylum-seekers or refugees in most of the cases; but they have also tried to understand how in-group members form them, when and why they change them. As Markaki and Longhi (2012: 4) note, theories on the formation of attitudes towards out-groups can be examined in two main groups: 'socio-psychological, affective or ideological explanations' and 'rational-based and labour market competition explanations'. In general lines, socio-psychological explanations focus on the groups' needs to mark themselves as different; their interests for social dominance; their belonging and identity formation or protection processes (Krysan, 2000; Stephan, et. al. 2005). In this vein, Herbst and Glynn (2004) note how belonging and identification lead to the formation of stereotypes as identification brings in-group favouritism and a belief of group superiority resulting in generalizations about negative out-group behaviours or characteristics. Moreover, socio-psychological explanations mention 'perceived threat' which in the end leads to irrational antipathy based on prejudices (Krysan, 2000; Stephan, et. al. 2005). It is argued that these feelings lead in-group to overreact to the 'perceived' negative consequences of immigration (Markaki and Longhi, 2012). Rational explanations, on the other hand, argue that in-group members make their opinions about out-group members by calculating the material and non-material costs and benefits for their group. This vein puts forth that no matter it is perceived or real, if the in-group members believe that the costs of the out-groupers exceed their benefits for the in-group, they tend to have negative opinions about them (Citrin et. al., 1997; Hempstead and Espenshade, 1996). As Markaki and Longhi (2012: 9) note rational interest explanations have different ramifications such as realistic conflict, deprivation theory and labor market competition theory but they all base their attitude formation analyses on the cost-benefit calculations for the group interests.

In line with these two main general theoretical explanation veins; in their review of almost 100 studies of immigration attitudes from more than 24 countries by Hainmuller and Hopkins (2013) categorize all these studies in two main groups: 'socio-political studies' and 'political economy studies'. According to the authors, while the studies in the first group emphasized "the role of group-related attitudes and symbols" and focused on the concerns of 'perceived threats to national identity', 'prejudice' and 'stereotyping', the studies in the second group mainly dealt with the economic impact of the immigration on society and they tried to explain attitude formation by examining the concerns on labor market competition and the fiscal burden. As the authors put forward, there is not only one factor in the attitude formation towards out-group members, but in general lines "the attitudes are driven by concerns about the nation as a whole, including symbolic or cultural threats as well as perceived economic threats" (*ibid*: 4). As the authors explain, symbolic threats "refer to threats to intangible social constructs such as the national economy or national identity" (*ibid*: 6). Similarly, Stephan *et al.* (2005, 2) note that fears and perceptions of threat play important role in prejudice towards out-groupers and they prepare the ground for attitude formation about immigration. Though the authors note that two main domains of threats are influential in this process - realistic threats and symbolic threats; they also add intergroup anxiety and negative stereotypes as influential determinants of attitude formation about out-group members. While the realistic threats are explained mainly as those threats to the political and economic power of the group, symbolic threats include threats to the values, beliefs, morals and attitudes of it. The authors do not pass without noting that symbolic or modern racism theories find their roots in those symbolic threats to the in-group. Negative out-group stereotypes, on the other hand, may pave the way for perceptions of threat and/or negative expectations about the behaviours or characteristics of the out-group members. Lastly, the authors explain intergroup anxiety as personal feelings of in-group members, who are concerned about their own self-beings in the event of interaction with out-group members.

In their review study of dozens of studies on attitudes on asylum-seekers and refugees, Finney and Peach (2004) also explain that prejudice, othering and factors such as demographic and economic factors, geographical factors and information sources influence the people's opinions on immigrants, asylum-seekers and refugees. In their analysis on the determinants of European attitudes towards foreigners, besides economic strain, Gang *et al.* (2002: 6) emphasize the influence of "increased concentration of immigrants in local neighborhoods" and they note that when combined with economic strain such a concentration leads to prejudice and likelihood of negative attitudes towards immigrants.

Though it shares parts of explanations with the main strands, 'politicized places hypothesis' of Hopkins (2010) departs from them by making 'sudden demographic changes' in the local communities its main emphasis. Hopkins (2010) focuses on national and local conditions, sudden demographic changes and rhetoric used at the national level and he puts forth that "hostile political reactions to neighboring immigrants are most likely when communities undergo sudden influxes of immigrants and when salient national rhetoric reinforces the threat." Hopkins (2010) explains that when the local communities receive high numbers of immigrants in a very short time, in other words when there is sudden demographic change in the local communities and when the immigration issues are being covered by the media as immigration is a nationally salient issue, people are informed by the media but they also observe the changes in their local communities. Combination of these events, lead them to form negative attitudes about immigrants and to take hostile political stance at the local level.

Methodology

Having an exploratory qualitative research design, the main aim of this study is to take a picture of mass migration of Syrians in the neighbourhoods of Istanbul and to make the Istanbul map of Syrians. In line with these aims, this paper is built on the analysis of primary data collected in the neighbourhoods of Istanbul by the help of two qualitative data collection techniques: face-to-face in-depth interviews guided by a semi-structured questionnaire and phone interviews to the neighbourhoods guided by a structured questionnaire.

The data of the study is collected from the local governors of neighbourhoods in Istanbul: the *Mukhtars*. There are several reasons for choosing *Mukhtars* as data source: Firstly, he/she is directly elected from the neighbourhood but he/she does what the state defines. There is confusion about their status in the law, they seem like a part of the local government but they take their signs/stamps from the *Kaimakam* and whenever they do this, they are thought to become part of the central government's administrative system. Interestingly, they are also considered to be the lowest level of directly elected local governments, the municipalities (Law No. 5393/2005 on Municipality, Article 9). Secondly, *Mukhtars* are directly elected on a party-independent basis. They cannot become members to any political party. It is thought that their controversial status in law and party-independent basis election might provide them a little more space to talk freely about the research questions of this study. Thirdly, according to the Article 9 of the Law on Municipalities, *Mukhtars* are "authorized to declare opinion on the matters which concern the neighborhood". Moreover, according to the same law, they have to be the residents of the neighborhoods they govern (for at least six months before the local elections). This makes them a real part of the local public opinion. Lastly, due to their work, *Mukhtars* are in direct contact with the inhabitants of the neighborhoods, they know their concerns, needs, problems, health issues and even marriage problems. For all these reasons, the researchers have thought that *Mukhtars* of Istanbul could say a lot about how the Istanbulites perceive Syrian migration, government policy on this issue, future of Syrians in Istanbul, the number of Syrians, their living and work conditions and registration processes.

In-depth Interviews

In-depth interviews are being conducted in 4 counties of Istanbul – Fatih, Başakşehir, Zeytinburnu and Bahçelievler. These counties have been chosen in the earlier phase of this study as they have been reported to involve very high number of Syrian residents at the time (Yılmaz, 2013). Until today, 16 in-depth interviews have been conducted.

Phone Interviews

Phone calls are being made to all neighbourhoods of all counties of Istanbul. The city has 39 counties with 782 neighbourhoods. The researchers are careful to reach more than half of the neighbourhoods in each county. Until today, 412 neighbourhoods in 21 counties have been called and 214 of them have been reached. During the research, 12 counties on the European side have been called.

These are Arnavutköy, Avcılar, Bahçelievler, Bağcılar, Başakşehir, Bayrampaşa, Çatalca, Fatih, Gaziosmanpaşa, Küçükçekmece, Şişli and Zeytinburnu. On the Anatolian side, the researchers have called 9 counties: Adalar, Beykoz, Çekmeköy, Kadıköy, Pendik, Sancaktepe, Şile, Ümraniye and Tuzla.

Istanbul Map of Syrians

Among all the counties called, only the *Mukhtars* in Çatalca report that they do not have any registered or unregistered Syrian residents. The other 20 counties have sizeable registered and unregistered Syrian residents. It is understood that the counties located on the European side have higher number of Syrians than those on the Anatolian side. Here, Şişli presents an exception as the *Mukhtars* in this county say that their neighborhoods either do not have or have very small number of Syrians. It is thought that Avcılar has received very small number of Syrians as the *Mukhtars* in this county say that they have not been 'that much' in interaction with them. Fatih, Başakşehir, Arnavutköy, Zeytinburnu and Küçükçekmece, on the other hand, are reported to have very high number of Syrian residents. Among these, with several of its *Mukhtars'* estimations, Fatih is reported to host more than 40.000 Syrian residents and Küçükçekmece is believed to have more than 30.000 Syrians. Başakşehir, Arnavutköy and Zeytinburnu are reported to host 10.000 to 15.000 Syrians. Bayrampaşa is reported to have a sizeable Syrian community. Bahçelievler and Gaziosmanpaşa host small number of Syrians, with the former being the residential area of wealthy Syrians.

On the Anatolian side, Ümraniye, Pendik and Sancaktepe are reported to have high number of Syrians by their *Mukhtars*. According to the *Mukhtars*, at least half of the Syrians in these counties are unregistered and many registered Syrians have changed their places since their registration. Ümraniye is believed to host more than 2000 Syrians, Pendik is reported to have around 1500 Syrians. The *Mukhtars* in Sancaktepe say that they have many registered and unregistered Syrian households with only one man and many women and children. Beykoz hosts small number of Syrians and its *Mukhtars* note that they do not have any complaints or problems with their Syrian inhabitants. In Şile there are only Syrian academics working for a private university in the county (*Mukhtar* No. 134, Şile) and in Adalar there are around 15-20 Syrians, who are working in touristic enterprises, as the county receives many tourists coming from Arabic speaking countries. Tuzla is reported to have a small number of Syrians, but the *Mukhtars* of the county have many complaints about them. Kadıköy, which can be considered as a middle-upper class district in Istanbul, hosts many Syrians during day time. But it is the residential area of wealthy Syrians who bought or rented flats when violence started in Syria, even before the visa liberalisation between Turkey and Syria was introduced in 2009. A *Mukhtar* (No. 182) in the county classifies these wealthy Syrians as "old Syrians" (*eski Suriyeli*) in order to emphasize that they are not asylum-seekers and that they have arrived before the war broke out in Syria.

Our ongoing field research shows that Syrians are settled "everywhere" in the biggest city of Turkey and the results allow us to make a preliminary map of Syrian population in Istanbul. Counties located on the European side (except Çatalca, Şişli and Avcılar), have higher number of Syrians than those on the Anatolian side (except Sancaktepe, Pendik, Ümraniye). Apart from numbers, *Mukhtars* are also able to provide data about the social profile of Syrians. Even though there are many similarities among different counties, some differences can be noted. In the counties with high number of Syrians, *Mukhtars* report that the majority of them have serious economic difficulties. They are crowded families and their principal activity is begging (especially in Fatih, city center, its proximity to many historical and touristic sites), working at workshops (textile in Zeytinburnu, shoe in Beykoz, light industries in Arnavutköy and Bayrampaşa), working at restaurants and small shops (in Küçükçekmece, in Fatih owned by Syrians), construction (Sancaktepe). Some Syrians own shops and workshops, some of them were wealthy in Syria and were able to transfer a part of their business. This is the case for textile workshop owners in Zeytinburnu, where in only one neighbourhood; they own 8 textile workshops and employ Syrians there. A second group of Syrians owns small shops or restaurants in the neighbourhoods highly populated by Syrians. In many neighbourhoods of Fatih, Zeytinburnu, Bahçelievler, Pendik, Arnavutköy and Küçükçekmece, it is not surprising to see these shops using only Arabic language on their boards and serving mostly Syrians. In Kadıköy, Şişli, Bahçelievler, Şile few different professions are reported by *Mukhtars* such as academics and engineers. It is complicated for *Mukhtars* to give clear indications about the professions of wealthy or middle-class Syrians in their neighborhoods; they classify them as "calm families, working properly". But they are clear that many of them don't work in İstanbul but live by the help of their wealth that they brought from Syria.

Istanbulites' Perception of Syrians

In general lines, our field work shows that the level of acceptance is low for Syrians in Istanbul; anti-immigration wordings and attitudes are not rare. In neighbourhoods with high number of Syrians there are many negative thoughts and complaints. It is understood that stereotyping and prejudices about Arab nationality play an influential role in the attitude formation about Syrians and their migration to Istanbul. Data collected from *Mukhtars* show that inhabitants in different parts of the city explain their perceptions of Syrian migration and attitudes towards Syrians by referring to common themes. The predominant theme that has been raised by many *Mukhtars* from different counties is Worry and uneasiness[155]. These words describe the general 'feeling' of local inhabitants about Syrian mass migration to Istanbul. They are followed by others: begging activities, hygiene questions, security problems (theft, fights).

Worry and Uneasiness

These themes are raised by all the *Mukhtars* contacted. Although there are many neighborhoods where no concrete complaint or incident have been reported and where the local inhabitants don't express any major criticism towards Syrians, local governors mentioned clearly that their Turkish inhabitants are "worried" about the arrival of Syrians to their neighborhood:

---

[155] Uneasiness is translated from the Turkish Word "*huzursuzluk*" which is used for a situation in which there is no peace and serenity and there is a general anxiety.

"There is no particular complaint but, you know, many people consider this situation negative, they don't think that it is a good thing. They don't want them here." (*Mukhtar* No. 114, Tuzla).

"Local inhabitants feel uncomfortable. [...] They don't want to live in the same building with Syrians. Actually, I agree, I wouldn't like to do so. You don't know who enters to the building." (*Mukhtar* No. 367- Şişli).

"They [local inhabitants] are worried. They worry about their daughters, their goods. Thanks God, no incident has been reported until now." (*Mukhtar* No. 327 - Pendik).

In the neighbourhoods with high number of Syrian population, the feeling of worry and uneasiness is reported in different ways; accompanied by prejudices and stereotypes in most of the times:

"Locals don't know who is who! There are doubts and uneasiness about them [Syrians]." (*Mukhtar* No. 318-Pendik).

"They [Syrians] are disharmonious with the society." (*Mukhtar* No. 20 - Fatih).

"They [Syrians] have uncontrolled behaviours, they think that they are still in Syria." (*Mukhtar* No.141-Arnavutköy).

"We are not in peace[156] anymore." (*Mukhtar* No. 80 - Gaziosmanpaşa).

"There is uneasiness…" (*Mukhtar* No. 106 - Başakşehir).

"Our neighbourhood has been affected negatively,, there is no peace." (*Mukhtar* No. 92 - Bahçelievler).

"They [Syrians] don't sleep until morning. They don't work. They are shouting all the night! [...] There is visual uneasiness." (*Mukhtar* No. 50 - Fatih).

Reasons of this main complaint on worry and uneasiness depend basically on the number, socio-economic status of Syrians settled in and the security questions. Moreover, it is understood that the local people are concerned over the exact number of Syrians in the country and in their counties. The interviewees almost always expressed their disturbance about this matter:

"Is there any neighbourhood in İstanbul without Syrians?" (*Mukhtar* No. 179– Bayrampaşa).

"Of course, we have Syrians!" (*Mukhtar* No. 203 - Sancaktepe)

Moreover, the perception or the belief that 'the Syrians ran away from fighting in their own country/homeland or defending their own country' strengthens the

---

[156] The word peace is used in order to describe the order and serenity in the neighborhood. This is the equivalent of the Turkish word: *huzur*.

stereotypes about Arab nationals in Turkey. Many *Mukhtars* expressed that if they were in their situation, they would return and fight for their own country whenever they found a safe place for their family in the neighbouring country. Again, in line with this thinking, many of them openly expressed that they did not believe the Syrians would be beneficial for Turkey. Apart from these, several common complaints have been raised by the *Mukhtars*. The most emphasized complaint is about the beggars.

Begging activities

Mukhtars from all counties emphasized the begging activities. Many *Mukhtars* call Syrians as 'beggars' and complain about their begging activities. The *Mukhtars* from the counties with the highest number of Syrian residents expresses that they see begging as the major source of problem in their neighborhoods. According to a Mukhtar (No. 50) from Fatih, Syrians caused "visual uneasiness" because of their begging activities. Beggars are also emphasized by those *Mukhtars* whose neighborhoods don't necessarily host Syrians; they say that they are "receiving Syrian beggars" especially on Fridays, in front of mosques before and after Friday prayer.

"Most of them [Syrians] *are begging here."(Mukhtar* No.56 - Fatih)

"There are many beggars. Especially children, they are always in front of mosques." (*Mukhtar* No.175 - Bayrampaşa)

"They [Syrians] *come to beg."* (*Mukhtar* No.385 - Şişli).

"They [Syrians] *are coming on marketplace day for begging. They are coming from the other side* [European side of Bosphorus] *"* (*Mukhtar* No.189-Kadıköy)

"An important number of beggars are coming on Fridays." (*Mukhtar* No. 190-Kadıköy).

"Inhabitants of my neighbourhood complain about beggars in front of the mosques. They want me to find a solution." (*Mukhtar* No. 321- Pendik).

"General complaint in the county is about begging activities in front of the mosques." (*Mukhtar* No.303 - Beykoz).

Furthermore begging is highly criticized by local inhabitants and *Mukhtars* as an "illegitimate and violent" economic activity:

"Their habit: free Money!." (*Mukhtar* No.145 - Arnavutköy)
"Beggars are stealing." (*Mukhtar* No.213 - Sancaktepe).
"We missed our beggars!" (*Mukhtar* No.80 - Gaziosmanpaşa)

Lack of hygiene and disorder in public places

The second main complaint is come as the second concrete complaints reported by *Mukhtars* that shape local inhabitant perceptions.

"They don't respect the cleanliness of the neighborhood, we are receiving complaints about this issue. We informed higher authorities such as the governorate but they don't do anything." (*Mukhtar* No.5 - Fatih)

"There is no hygiene!" (*Mukhtar* No.20 - Fatih)

"They go to marketplace with their children and their children mess up!" (*Mukhtar* No.108 - Pendik).

"They occupy parks!" (*Mukhtar* No.175 - Bayrampaşa)

Aggressive Behaviours

According to the *Mukhtars* of the neighbourhoods with high number of Syrian residents, Turkish inhabitants are worried about Syrians' 'aggressive behaviours' and they visit them to complain about this issue. They tell that from time to time, tensions among the Syrians and between the Syrians and Turks get high. Though they cannot provide any official document proving any incident; apparently there a few serious cases which necessitated the police involvement. However, it is obvious that local inhabitants perceive Syrians as aggressive:

"Quarrels take place very frequently. They [Syrians] *attack each other."* (*Mukhtar* No.56-Fatih)

"Their human relations are savage, violent." (*Mukhtar* No.59-Zeytinburnu)

"There are nice people among them, but they are mainly aggressive." (*Mukhtar* No.48-Fatih).

"They are aggressive! Quarrels, fights everyday!" (*Mukhtar* No. 147-Arnavutköy).

"They have weird habits, they swear a lot." (*Mukhtar* No.271- Ümraniye)

Housing

All the *Mukhtars* contacted, underlined the problem of housing. It is understood that Syrians have large families and they live together in small houses and flats in Istanbul. They don't have regular income and this fact leads them to share their flats with other Syrian families. The housing question provokes two sources of complaint that make locals' perception more negative: increase in rents and hygiene and security problems in buildings. The *Muhktars* blame mainly the real estate agencies but also the landlords. It is understood that the real estate agencies and landlords rented flats and houses to Syrians for very high prices when they first arrived. But this situation has turned out to be something very negative for everybody: the rents in those counties got higher and the landlords with Syrian tenants have had problems in collecting their rents:

"Rent prices were maximum at 400 TL, now you can't find a flat at 500." (*Mukhtar* No.145-Arnavutköy)

"Before the landlords were very happy. But now the Syrians started not to pay the rent. Owners are coming to complain. What can we do? Who told them to rent their house to Syrians!" (Mukhtar No. 271-Ümraniye)

Begging activities, aggressive behaviours, housing problems are also seen as security problems that make local inhabitants worried about the Syrian mass migration to Istanbul. The security problems seem to be more serious in a number of neighborhoods in Sancaktepe, Pendik, Ümraniye and Arnavutköy where theft, prostitution and drug dealing have been reported in relation with Syrians. Under these circumstances the image that the locals are building through their perceptions becomes more negative.

Too-many Syrians…

Mukhtars say that "there are too many Syrians" and think that their number is constantly increasing. The following expressions are not rare:

"There are too many Syrians. Their number increases. Their number increases all the time!" (Mukhtar No. 31 - Fatih).

"They walk trough the muhtarlik. I am saying to myself: Oh Dudullu is invaded by Syrians!" (Mukhtar No.255 - Ümraniye).

When the local management of Syrian mass migration to Istanbul is asked; they are generally perplexed and mention a lack of management. One of them explodes when he/she is asked how the neighbourhood absorbs the arrival of Syrians:

"Nobody absorbs! We cannot absorb!" (Mukhtar No.369 – Şişli)

Conclusion

Neither migrations nor migrants are new for Turkey. The country has received waves of migration before and after its foundation mainly from the former Ottoman territories. Besides these early migrations, which brought people of Turkish descent or of Turkish culture from these lands, Turkey has started to receive influx of asylum-seekers mainly from its neighbours in the late 1970s. Mass influx of Syrians is the latest of these movements. As it is elaborated in the introduction of this paper, Syrians have sought asylum in Turkey via regular or irregular entries to the country. Yet, despite the time passed since the first entries, there is still lack of data on the Syrian migration. Having been built on the findings of an exploratory qualitative field research, this paper aims to fill this gap partially and it aims to pave the way for further studies on the phenomenon.

As it is discussed in the paper, it is thought that the level of social acceptance is low for the Syrians in the neighbourhoods of Istanbul. According to the *Mukhtars* from different counties of the city, the Istanbulites feel themselves disturbed, they express that the Turkish inhabitants are worried and that there is uneasiness in their neighbourhood. The number of the Syrians seems to be an important source of anxiety, they frequently raise the question of what will happen if an unregistered Syrian Arab Republic citizen commits a crime in Turkey, they questioned the Syrians' flight from Syria and emphasize that they would not leave their country but stay and fight for it. When the main complaints and the way their expression are examined, it is understood that, many *Mukhtars* think of Syrians in Turkey as a homogenous group that is mainly made up of low – income, unqualified people, who mainly deal with begging activities in Turkey. It is unfortunate to reveal that the beggar Syrians have built an image for the all Syrians in Istanbul. Lack of hygiene, disorder in public places, the increase in the rents, their numbers and the way they live in the neighbourhoods are the other main complaints. It is interesting to note that these complaints are not raised only in the neighbourhoods with high number of Syrian residents. Several *Mukhtars* from neighbourhoods with low number of Syrian residents have also repeated these complaints. As a result, it is thought that many of these complaints and the *Mukhtars'* reactions to 'Syrians' flight from the war' are rooted in the general stereotypes and prejudices about the Arab nationals in Turkey – which have long depicted a picture of a dirty, coward and uncivilized person. As a result, we note that Istanbulites have negative attitudes towards Syrians and Syrian migration.

In line with these preliminary findings, it is thought that rather than rational-based labour market competition explanations, socio-psychological explanations seem to be more influential in Istanbulites' process of attitude formation towards Syrians. Labor market competition is emphasized as well; but only in 4 out of 214 neighbourhoods. It is understood that Istanbulites have fears, anxieties and perceptions of realistic and symbolic threats, rooted mainly in the stereotypes and prejudices about the Arab nationals. However, it is also thought that the pace of Syrian migration has played an influential role in this attitude formation. Therefore, in line with the Hopkins' (2010) 'politicized places hypothesis', it is believed that the 'sudden demographic change' caused by Syrians in many neighbourhoods of Istanbul is an important determinant of the attitude formation of Istanbulites towards Syrians. As it is observed during the field research, *Mukhtars* know a lot about the Syrian migration, about the state rhetoric, about the failures in the registration processes, about the negative incidents that have taken place in the Southeastern cities, about the camps in the bordering cities and at the same time they have been able to observe the Syrians, coming and going, quarrelling, etc. in their neighbourhoods.

It is believed that a migration-system has emerged between Syria and Turkey. If the war in Syria ends, many Syrians may return, but many of them will stay. As this paper puts forth, currently the attitudes of Istanbulites are negative towards Syrians for the reasons discussed; it is hoped that this research paves the way for further studies to work out this problem.

References

Ackermann, Maya and Markus Freitag. 2015. "What Actually Matters? Understanding Attitudes toward Immigration in Switzerland." *Swiss Political Science Review* 21: 36–47.

Afet ve Acil Durum Yönetimi Başkanlığı (AFAD). 2014. Suriye'den Türkiye'ye Nüfus Hareketleri: Kardeş Topraklarındaki Misafirlik. Ankara.

Barclay, Aileen, Alison Bowes, Iain Ferguson, Duncan Sim, Maggie Valenti, Soraya Fard and Sherry MacIntosh. 2003. *Asylum seekers in Scotland. Edinburgh: Scottish Executive Social Research.* Available at www.scotland.gov.uk/library5/social/asis-00.asp.

Berg, Justin Allen. 2015. "Explaining Attitudes toward Immigrants and Immigration Policy: A Review of the Theoretical Literature." *Sociology Compass* 9: 23-34.

Bridges, Sarah and Simona Mateut. 2014. "Should they stay or should they go? Attitudes towards immigrants in Europe." *Scottish Journal of Political Economy* 61: 397-429.

Duffy, Bobby. 2014. "Perceptions and Reality: Ten Things We Should Know About Attitudes to Immigration in the UK." *The Political Quarterly* 85: 259-266.

Erdoğan, M. (2014). HUGO Report: Syrians in Turkey: Social Acceptance and Integration Research. Ankara: Hacettepe University

Finney, Nissa and Esme Peach. 2004. Attitudes towards asylum seekers, refugees and other immigrants. London: ICAR.

Gand, Ira N., Fransisco L. Rivera-Batiz and Myeong-Su Yun. (2002). *Economic Strain, Ethnic Concentration and Attitudes Towards Foreigners in the European Union.* IZA Discussion Paper No. 578.

Hainmueller, Jens and Daniel J. Hopkins. (2013). *Public Attitudes toward Immigration.* CReAM Discussion Paper Series, No 15/13, London.

Herbst, S. and Glynn, C.J. (2004) *Public Opinion,* Westview Press.

Hopkins, Daniel, J. (2010). "Politicized Places: Explaining Where and When Immigrants Provoke Local Opposition." *American Political Science Review* 104: 40-60.

Krysan, M. (2000). Prejudice, Politics, and Public Opinion Understanding the Sources of   Racial Policy Attitudes. *Annual Review of Sociology* 26: 135-168.

Kuş, Elif. (2012). *Nicel-Nitel Araştırma Teknikleri.* Ankara: Anı Yayıncılık.

Kümbetoğlu, B. (2005). Sosyolojide ve Antropolojide Niteliksel Yöntem ve Araştırma. İstanbul: Bağlam.

Leong, C-H. (2008). "A multilevel research framework for the analyses of attitudes toward immigrants." *International Journal of Intercultural Relations* 32: 115–129.

Markaki, Y. and Simonetta L. (2012). What Determines Attitudes to Immigration in European Countries?: An Analysis at the Regional Level. Norface Migration Discussion Paper No. 2012-32, London.

McNabb, D. E. (2004). Research Methods for Political Science: Quantitative and Qualitative Methods. New York: M.E. Sharpe.

Pardos-Prado, S. (2011). "Framing Attitudes Towards Immigrants in Europe: When Competition Does Not Matter." *Journal of Ethnic and Migration Studies* 37 (7): 999-1015.

Sharan, M.(2013). Nitel Araştırma: Desen ve Uygulama İçin Bir Rehber. Ankara: Nobel Yayıncılık.

Stephan, W. G., C. L. Renfro, V. M. Esses, C. W. Stephan and T. Martin. (2005). "The effects of feeling threatened on attitudes toward immigrants."*International Journal of Intercultural Relations* 19: 1-19.

UNHCR. March 20, 2015. 'Syria Regional Refugee Response', retrieved on April 9, 2015, from http://data.unhcr.org/syrianrefugees/country.php?id=224

Ward, C. and A.-M. Masgoret. 2006. "An integrative model of attitudes toward immigrants." *International Journal of Intercultural Relations* 30: 671-682.

Refugees of a City: The socio-spatial impacts of those Syrian refugees who arrived in Izmir, Turkey

Arife Karadağ[157]

Introduction

In the last century, hundreds of thousands of people from the Balkan wars (1912-1913), from the population exchange between Turkey and Greece (1923-1924), from the Balkan countries (1950-1951 and 1978-1979), from Bulgaria (1989), from the Eastern and South-eastern Anatolia Region (the 1990s), and finally from Syria (as of 2012) left their homeland through forced migration and settled in Turkey. One of the cities most affected by this process is İzmir – the third biggest city of the country. Those people who venture migration merely to live and for a safe future deal with an inhumane life such as poverty, pressure, and otherization in the places where they go. There is no doubt that each migration flow also negatively affects the labor processes in cities, the urban infrastructure, and the socio-economic life of the city.

In this study, the socio-spatial impacts of migration on cities, particularly İzmir, were addressed, along with the dramatic migration stories of hundreds of thousands of people who had to migrate from Syria after 2012 due to the domestic turbulence and clashes. In the study, face-to-face interviews were made with 275 Syrians and with the same number of İzmirian families at the neighborhoods inhabited by the Syrian refugees who had settled in İzmir, and it was intended to reveal the reasons for, and dimensions of, the tension experienced in the city upon the arrival of the Syrians.

According to the records, there are 1 552 839 (as of December 2014) Syrian refugees in Turkey and 70 000 Syrian refugees wait for being recorded. Together with those who are unrecorded, their number has exceeded 2 million; however, it is predicted that the number will have reached 3 million by the end of the year (AFAD 2014). In light of the data by the UNHCR (December 2014), Turkey is still ranking first among the countries which house the Syrian refugees.

Only about 270 000 of them can be sheltered in the 21 camps built in 11 different provinces of Turkey. From time to time, some problems are experienced in the camps, which appear more advantageous in the senses of accommodation, security, food supply, health inspection, education, and rehabilitation services, due to the political threats of Syrian origin. Nevertheless, serious problems on this matter are actually experienced outside the camps between the Syrian refugees, most of whom have not been recorded yet and have hence remained out of inspection and who go on living as unrecorded refugees in such metropolitan cities as İstanbul, Ankara, İzmir, Adana, and Mersin besides the cities bordering Syria (Gaziantep, Urfa, Mardin, and Antakya) and the local people. The metropolitan cities which have to cope with many problems from security to the unfair competitive conditions experienced in the fields of business and

---

[157] Asssit. Prof. Dr., Ege University, Faculty of Arts, Department of Geography. E-mail: arife.karadag@ege.edu.tr

employment and to the gradually sharpening social and psychological problems that are caused by alienation & otherization have considerable difficulties in this process.

What is the general profile of the Syrians in İzmir?

Again according to the data by AFAD, it is expressed that there are about 75 thousand recorded Syrian refugees in İzmir – our study area – together with the recording studies which gained momentum as of early 2014. On the other hand, this number approached 150 thousand according to the data (2014) by the Society of Syrians, founded in İzmir in late 2012. In this case, about half the Syrian refugees in İzmir are still unrecorded. Besides, according to the data by TUIK, the number of Syrian citizens who have obtained a residence permit in Turkey also keeps growing apace. Likewise, the number of Syrians who obtained a residence permit in İzmir was 383 in 2012 but increased fivefold and reached 2 083 only at the end of a year.

The areas settled in the city by the Syrians who arrived in İzmir do not display any concentration in a single area; furthermore, there is a significant relationship between their ethnic structure and the place where they settle in the city. The same relationship is also present among the jobs they do in İzmir, the places in Syria from which they came, and the quarters they inhabit in İzmir. As it is known, there are three main groups of Syrian refugees in İzmir. The most crowded group comprises the Syrian refugees of Kurdish origin that live around Kadifekale, Agora, Çimentepe, and Ballıkuyu and that have settled here owing to their ties of kinship with our citizens who predominantly arrived from Mardin in particular and the other provinces of the South-eastern Anatolia Region. The majority of this group works as a tradesman. Besides, they work as workers at textile factories and building sites. The people that they work with and those who employ them or help them find a job also comprise their relatives, who settled in the city again from the south-eastern provinces, or their acquaintances. On the other hand, the Syrian Arabs have been concentrated at Gediz and Yıldız neighborhoods in Buca in the southern axis of the city in addition to Doğanlar neighborhood in Bornova. The textile workshops available in large numbers in this environment and the construction sector that has gained momentum recently are important job opportunities for them too. The third important group consists of Syrian Turkmens, who predominantly inhabit Pınarbaşı, Işıkkent, Doğanlar, and Mevlana Neighborhoods, located within the eastern industrial axis of the city. Almost all Turkmens came from Aleppo and work as shoe masters or workers at Shoemakers' Site. The Turkmens know Turkish. The Turkmens, who had also been shoe masters in Aleppo, therefore do not have any problems of finding a job in İzmir. Since they know Turkish, they can also communicate with the local people easily. However, when some refugees who suffer from the language problem go to the city, their relationship with the city is broken owing to the language problem.

In this study, the main question is concerned with whether there is a mutual inconvenience between the Syrian refugees and the local people in the city and with its socio-economic bases. As understood from the interviews during the fieldwork, it is clear that there are very serious inconveniences bilaterally. The current statuses of the parties according to each other are rather far from the expression "guest", which was included in the official discourse at the early stages of commencement of the arrival of Syrian refugees in Turkey. When considered in terms of the Syrian refugees, it is seen that before all, they are in a foreign place; there is no one who knows their language here; and they have no official entity in the city as most of them are unrecorded. Moreover, they lack a work permit. Hence, they have neither any defined identity in the city nor any favorable conditions under which they can make a living in this city. Furthermore, now that the domestic clashes in their country are ongoing, it does not seem so possible for them to return due to the perception and worry that it will take a long time for the economic and social conditions to improve even if the domestic clashes end. In summary, the new Syrian neighbors in İzmir in particular do not consider returning. The next main problem is whether a culture of coexistence can occur between the local people of İzmir and the Syrian refugees or how this process will take shape from now on. For them, İzmir is still a metropolitan city where alienation and otherization are experienced. They are treated as potential criminals due to the marginal sectors from which they make a living in this city (e.g. illegally-employed worker, begging, and theft & snatching). Moreover, they are regarded as a risk group in terms of urban security. As expressed by the Syrian refugees, "No matter what happens at the neighborhood, they knock at our door first." In addition, it is very difficult for them to find a job as they do not know the language; furthermore, most of them are unrecorded and fugitive. The case concerned is highly misused by employers as well. Their wages are low and their working hours are long at their workplaces; furthermore, most of the time, they cannot get their wages regularly. Especially the women express that they cannot go outside the neighborhood they inhabit owing to their language problem.

Regarding the perception of Syrians by the local people of İzmir, they also quite complain about their new Syrian neighbors whose number has suddenly increased immediately near them for the last three years, for even though they see that they are in a very difficult situation, for them, the Syrians are foreigners who have settled in their neighborhoods and this is not a safe situation for them at all. The rents have increased by five to one since the Syrians began to settle in their neighborhoods, and it is more difficult to find a house for rent than it used to be. Furthermore, the Syrians initially rent the house as 2 to 3 people; however, tens of people settle in the same house one week or two weeks later, which is unusual and threatening for the former inhabitants of the neighborhood.

Additionally, another problem frequently mentioned by the İzmirians is their concerns that the local workers no more have any job security with the arrival of the Syrians. They complain that they have lost their jobs because the Syrians agree to work at very low wages and that the employers prefer employing the Syrians for the same reason. In addition, the number of those who state that theft, snatching and beggars have increased in their environment and that they do not feel so safe at their neighborhoods after a specific hour as they used to do is not small at all. Nevertheless, the people of İzmir do not complain that "With the Syrians, their current family orders have been upset due to the increase in illegal marriages or because they have triggered polygamy", which is frequently expressed in the other provinces (e.g. Mardin, Gaziantep, and Antakya).

However, there is no remarkable increase in the events of theft and snatching for İzmir upon the arrival of the Syrians. The records in the security units also verify this information. Nevertheless, the increase in beggars at almost every quarter in the city, particularly at the junctions of transportation, at the squares, and around the shopping centers with high population circulation during the day is at striking dimensions. In summary, the Syrian refugees who have come to İzmir either work as illegally-employed workers at building sites and textile and shoe workshops or beg in the city. Thus, the İzmirians either regard the Syrians as beggars on the street or perceive them as people who share their bread and because of whom they can find a job in a more difficult way.

So, is this a just reaction? Notwithstanding all these inconveniences, there is still a case of conscience about the Syrian refugees in İzmir too. The İzmirians know that they fled from Syria with the fear of death, in order to save their families and then due to poverty. The first contact that Turks in general and the İzmirians in particular make with the Syrians is indeed a contact which develops within the framework of this sensitivity. Moreover, neither party hides the fact that they initially helped them acquire a house, put them up as guests, and provided them with food, clothing, and medication aid. Nevertheless, the problems which have arisen concerning job and security and the fact that the opinion on the extension of this guest (!) status for an uncertain period of time has become widespread have negatively affected the perception of Syrians by the local people of İzmir.

How do the practices of exclusion develop?

Doubtlessly, the process with respect to the settlement of the Syrian refugees in İzmir also develops practices of exclusion together with perceiving them as foreigners. For instance, there are very serious problems in the house acquisition processes. You suddenly become neighbors with people that you do not know, whom you do not know where, how, and when they came from, and whom you do not know what kind of a life they had in the places from which they had come; furthermore, you start to fail to select your neighbors. The house prices suddenly start to rise at your location. Likewise, the monthly rents which used to be TL 300 to 400 have now risen up to TL 700 to 800 at the neighborhoods where the Syrian refugees are tenants in İzmir today. While this is perceived as an opportunity by landlords and those in the real estate sector, this has increased the troubles of the local people about house acquisition.

In the working life, the Syrian refugees have agreed to work in return for much lower wages in order to make their living in this foreign city and this process has culminated in a decrease in the wages given in return for the same job in terms of the local workers. Likewise, the daily wages of construction workers in İzmir had been TL 90 to 120 until three years earlier, whereas the daily wage of the Syrian refugees has now decreased to TL 15 to 20. Furthermore, the Syrian refugees are not employed for 8 hours but up to 17 hours per day in return for these wages. What is worse is that this triggers an unsound process in which employers dismiss the local workers and, instead of them, employ the Syrian refugees without any insurance and with low wages and which increases the tension between both parties. Likewise, since 2012, there has been a serious escalation in the clashes and the tension, which has reached legal dimensions, particularly between the Syrian and local workers working at the workshops at the shoemakers' site in Işıkkent (Photo).

As the statements *"They have come here and been sharing our jobs, houses, and order and we no more have any security"* about Syrians increased among the local people, the initial attitude of conscience left its place to anger. Likewise, it was said that *"When they arrived, they were in a very difficult situation and we helped them. We have an ethnic tie with Syrians and all of us are Muslim societies and must help each other"*, while everything changed when the issue of job was opened and this time all İzmirians started to say in a common language: "if they do not go, what will happen from now on?" The people of İzmir think that the people who are actually responsible for these problems are local & central governors, employers, and politicians rather than their new Syrian neighbors and express that they have failed to manage this process properly. For instance, according to the İzmirians, employers misuse the unrecorded statuses of the Syrian refugees and have them work for long hours, under severe conditions, and at very low wages, whereas the fact that the Syrian refugees have no other choice in this foreign city creates an unfair competitive environment. What is more, this is also used as a pretext for dismissing the local workers. Subsequently, the Syrian refugee workers and the Turkish workers are confronted with each other in an undesired fashion.

So, by whom is this problem caused?

Even though the Republic of Turkey initially implemented the open-door policy for the Syrian refugees and defined them as guests, it granted them the temporary protection status in late 2011. In fact, the concept of being a guest is not a highly welcomed situation by the Syrian refugees, either; a guest (!) means "you will go when the day comes"; and our Syrian neighbors are not pleased with this expression at all. Especially those who have relatives/acquaintances in Turkey are very happy in İzmir, feel safe here, express this at every opportunity, and do not want to return. They express that they therefore go on remaining unrecorded and are safer in this way. They think that even if the domestic turbulence politically subsides in Syria, it will take a long time for the social life and the economy to recover. They know that they will not find their country, houses, and order as they left them. Hence, they do not want to go. **Likewise,** when asked *"Would you like to return if the conditions in your country improve?"* during the fieldwork, the Syrians first responded *"Of course, we would. It is our native country"*, although they immediately afterwards responded with *"yes"* – without exception – to the question *"Would you like to stay if favorable job and settlement opportunities are provided in İzmir?"*. In summary, another problem regarding the presence of the Syrian refugees in İzmir is that first of all they are unable to communicate with the urban people and that their children are unable to continue their education as they do not know Turkish. The Syrians will go on staying here in İzmir for some more unknown time. It appears a must for them to learn Turkish if they find a chance to go a step further than the neighborhoods they now live in. Nevertheless, there is no school in the city where the Syrian children of school age can continue their education and learn Turkish apart from a few state schools which have accepted them as visiting students. Although a preliminary study was carried out with respect to the opening of a school in Yenişehir for the Syrian refugee children with the support extended by the Society of Syrians in İzmir, the Governorship, the Directorate for National Education, and the NGOs, the opening of the school was not permitted in the last minute. The troubles with benefiting from health services have been substantially overcome with the support extended by AFAD and State Hospitals (e.g. diagnosis, treatment, medication, and operation). However, according to the expressions by the refugees, for instance, when they go to a hospital, there are still some hitches which are caused by the fact that their identity cards are in Arabic, by the unavailability of any employees at the hospitals who know Arabic, and by the fact that the documents cannot be understood by the employees at the hospitals. As a measure against this, the Syrian refugees are provided with translation services for these documents in a unit affiliated to the Police Headquarters, if they demand. The studies on the availability of work permits for the Syrian refugees for the period of their stay in Turkey have reached the final stage too. Studies are ongoing for the enrolment of those who certify that they were university students in Syria at the relevant departments of the universities in Turkey. Nevertheless, these two developments are followed by the local people in the cities with the concerns that they will trigger the unfair competitive environment.

In Lieu of Conclusion...

In fact, the problems which have arisen concerning the Syrians in İzmir are not problems which are merely about the present. For the future as well, the İzmirians have serious worries that the Syrian refugees will be granted a citizen status and that unfair competition will increase in the sense of the processes of benefiting from job, education, and urban services, which also lays the groundwork for a social clash among the urban people. Additionally, the rapid and uncontrolled rises in rents and in house acquisition costs in the city increase the costs of living in the city particularly for those İzmirians who are in the low- and middle-income groups. Truly, Basmane, Agora, Kadifekale and Mevlana neighborhoods around the city center each have been tending to turn into Syrian neighborhoods rapidly for the last three years. Moreover, according to the İzmirians, the city is rapidly getting crowded owing to this new migration flow. The inclusion of the Syrian refugees in the crowds at the hospitals is also regarded as a distinct trouble. Hence, the following are the new questions which are frequently expressed and which await an answer among the urban people of İzmir regarding their new Syrian neighbors:

• How will the aid and protection which are provided for the refugees whose number is gradually increasing be continued?

• What will be the next step about the security problems in the country which are caused by the gradually increasing presence of the Syrian refugees in cities and by the violence in Syria?

• When will the reality that the humane efforts will not be able to replace the political initiatives to be made so as to solve the Syrian crisis in a more comprehensive sense be realized?

• How will the language, education, health services, job & employment, security, social acceptance and integration process of the Syrians who undoubtedly go on living with us today be managed in this process?

• What do the local and central authorities tangibly plan for the settlement of the worries of Turkey in general and of the local people of İzmir in particular in this process? Because the clearest thing on this matter is again the uncertainties on this matter themselves.

Regarding the answer to be given to the question "Do the local authorities in İzmir and the central administration have any plans and preparations against possible problems?", AFAD, which works as being affiliated to the Governorship of İzmir, has made great progress in the recording of the Syrian refugees in İzmir particularly since 2014. There is no obstacle to refugees' benefiting from emergency health services at State hospitals. Furthermore, the Assembly is preparing a regulation on the granting of work permits to the Syrian refugees within the period of their stay here. Nevertheless, there is no study on how to manage the integration process despite the current problems and reactions between the Syrian refugees and the urban people of İzmir. The direct supporters of the Syrians do not go beyond a few NGOs in the senses of aid and solidarity in İzmir, as in our other metropolitan cities. There is no doubt that trying to solve each of these problems will not be possible through a broader fund than that provided so far, an organization which prioritizes the details or helping each other at the local level but through international cooperation.

Finally, another serious problem about the Syrian refugees in İzmir is the efforts of a large number of Syrians to pass to the EU countries via the Greek Islands through the illegal organizations by the human traffickers in the city. Unfortunately, the majority of them result in the losses of life and property. Regarding this matter, there is a need for a more realistic, organized, and internationally-based solution beyond the self-sacrificing efforts of the Police organization for prevention and rescuing.

However, the number of Syrians living in İzmir is gradually increasing today; they will go on staying here at least for an uncertain period of time; and it appears that the problems arising in the quality of urban life, urban security, the fields of house and job, and even the daily course of life in the city will go on increasingly.

References

AFAD- Afet ve Acil Durum Müdürlüğü (2013). Syrian Refugees in Turkey, 2013 Field Survey Results, https://www.afad.gov.tr/Dokuman/TR/61-2013123015505-syrian-refugees-in-turkey-2013_print_12.11.2013_eng.pdf adresinden 07.05.2014 tarihinde erişildi.

AFAD- Afet ve Acil Durum Müdürlüğü (2014a). Suriye'den Türkiye'ye Nüfus Hareketleri: Kardeş Topraklardaki Misafirlik. Afet ve Acil Durum Yönetimi Başkanlığı Yay. Ankara.

AFAD- Afet ve Acil Durum Müdürlüğü (2014b). Türkiye'deki Suriyeli Kadınlar. Afet ve Acil Durum Yönetimi Başkanlığı Yay. Ankara.

Buz, S. (2008). Türkiye'deki sığınmacıların sosyal profili. Polis Bilimleri Dergisi. 10 (4), 1-14.

Castles S. ve Miller M. J. (2008). Göçler Çağı: Modern Dünyada Uluslararası Göç Hareketleri (Çev. U.B. Bal ve İ. Akbulut). İstanbul: İstanbul Bilgi Üniversitesi Yayınları.

Danış, D. ve Bayraktar (2010). Irak'tan Irağa: 2003 Sonrası Iraktan Komşu Ülkelere ve Türkiye'ye Yönelik Göçler. Ortadoğu Stratejik Araştırmalar Merkezi. Rapor no: 21. Ankara.

Düvell F. (2014) "Avrupa'nın Suriyeli mülteciler konusundaki tavrı",Tüürkiye'deki Suriyeliler : toplumsal Kabul ve Uyum Çalıştayı, Hacettepe Üniv. Göç ve Siyaset Araşt. Merk. (HUGO), Ankara, 27 Mart 2014.

Erder, S. (2014). Küreselleşme ve Uluslararası Hukukun Zorunlu Göçle İmtihanı. İçinde: Sınır ve Sınırdışı, Türkiye'de Yabancılar, Göç ve Devlete Disiplinlerarası Bakışlar. Ed. D.Danışi İ.Soysüren.Nota Bene Yay. Ankara

Erdoğan M. M., 2015, Türkiye'deki Suriyeliler – Toplumsal Kabul ve Uyum, İstanbul Bilgi Üniversitesi Yay. 495, Göç Çalışmaları 6, İstanbul.

GÖÇDER (2013). Göz Ardı Edilenler: İstanbul'da Yaşayan Suriyeli Sığınmacılar. Göç Edenler Sosyal Yardımlaşma ve Kültür Derneği Eşit Haklar İçin İzleme Derneği. İstanbul.

Güçer, M., Karaca, S. ve Dinçer, B. (2013). Sınırlar Arasında Yaşam Savaşı 'Suriyeli Mülteciler' Alan Araştırması, Uluslararası Stratejik Araştırmalar Kurumu, Rapor No: 13-04.

Kirişçi, K. (1999). Türkiye'ye Yönelik Göç Hareketlerinin Değerlendirilmesi, içinde: Z. Bora (Ed.) Bilanço 1923-1998: Türkiye Cumhuriyeti'nin 75 Yılına Toplu Bakış (1). İstanbul. Tarih Vakfı Yay.

Kirişçi K. Dinçer B.Federici V. Ferris, Karaca S. Çarmıklı E. (2013) Suriyeli Mülteciler Krizi ve Türkiye : Sonu Gelmeyen Misafirlik, Brookings-USAK, Karınca Ajans Yay. Ankara.

Kirişçi, K. (2014). Misafirliğin Ötesine Geçerken: Türkiye'nin "Suriyeli Mülteciler" Sınavı. Çev: Sema Karaca. Brookings Enstitüsü. Uluslararası Stratejik Araştırmalar Kurumu (USAK). Ankara.

MAZLUMDER (2014). Kamp Dışında Yaşayan Suriyeli Kadın Sığınmacılar Raporu. İnsan Hakları ve Mazlumlar İçin Dayanışma Derneği Yay.
http://www.mazlumder.org/webimage/MAZLUMDER%20KAMP%20DI%C5%9EINDA%20YA%C5%9EAYAN%20SUR%C4%B0YEL%C4%B0%20KADIN%20SI%C4%9EINMAC ILAR%20RAPORU(2).pdf adresinden 27.02.2015 tarihinde erişildi.

ORSAM- Ortadoğu Stratejik Araştırmalar Müdürlüğü (2014). Suriye'ye Komşu Ülkelerde Suriyeli Mültecilerin Durumu: Bulgular, Sonuçlar ve Öneriler. Rapor No: 189. Ankara.

ORSAM- Ortadoğu Stratejik Araştırmalar Müdürlüğü (2015). Suriyeli Sığınmacıların Türkiye'ye Etkileri. Rapor No: 195. Ankara.

Paksoy, H.M., Paksoy, S., Memiş, H. ve Özçalıcı, M. (2012). Arap Baharı'nın Sosyo-Ekonomik Etkileri: Türkiye-Suriye Karşılaştırması. İçinde: A.H. Aydın, İ. Bakan ve M.Yardımcıoğlu (Editörler). II. Bölgesel Sorunlar ve Türkiye Sempozyumu Bildiriler Kitabı içinde (ss. 48-58) http://iibfdergisi.ksu.edu.tr/Imagesimages/files/8%281%29.pdf adresinden 17.12.2014 tarihinde erişildi.

Şeker B. D- Sirkeci İ.- Yüceşahin M. (Derleyen (2015). Göç ve Uyum, Turkish Migration Series, Transnational Press London, UK.

UNHCR (2014a) Syria Regional Refugee Response resmi web sitesi http://data.unhcr.org/syrianrefugees/country.php?id=224 adresinden 27 Şubat 2015 tarihinde erişildi.

UNHCR (2014b) Mid-Year Trends 2014. http://unhcr.org/54aa91d89.html adresinden 27 Şubat 2014 tarihinde erişildi.

Yıldız Ö. (2013) Türkiye Kamplarında Suriyeli Sığınmacılar: Sorunlar, Beklentiler, Türkiye ve Gelecek Algısı, Sosyoloji Araştırmaları Dergisi, Cilt: 16 Sayı: 1 - Bahar 2013: 141-169

Yılmaz H. (2013). Türkiye'de Suriyeli Mülteciler: İstanbul Örneği (Tespitler, İhtiyaçlar, Öneriler). İnsan Hakları ve Mazlumlar İçin Dayanışma Derneği Yay. İstanbul.

http://www.aljazeera.com.tr/haber/suriyeli-kizlar-yasamak-icin-evlendiriliyor 24.03.2015 tarihinde erişildi.

http://www.bbc.co.uk/turkce/haberler/2013/05/130510_suriye_multeci_kadinlar 24.03.2015 tarihinde erişildi.

http://www.cumhuriyet.com.tr/haber/turkiye/186333/Yarini_olmayan_kadinlar.html 24.03.2015 tarihinde erişildi.

http://www.haberturk.com/gundem/haber/1003940-neden-suriyeli-gelin 24.03.2015 tarihinde erişildi.

http://www.theguardian.com/world/2014/sep/08/syrian-refugee-brides-turkish-husbands-marriage 24.03.2015 tarihinde erişildi.

Gendered Citizenship: Experiences and Perceptions of the Bulgarian Turkish Immigrant Women

Özge Kaytan[158]

Introduction

The concept of citizenship, which is a multi-layered construct by itself, consists of diverse structures when it comes to the citizenship of immigrant women. The migration process itself is gendered not only because of the fact that men and women are differently affected; but it is also likely to affect how gender identity interacts with the new identity bestowed upon the migrant women. The gendered experiences of oppression directed towards minorities are transformed into gendered dynamics of migrating to a host country and integrating into the new society.

Ethnic Turks have been living in Bulgaria since the early years of the Ottoman Empire. Bulgarian Turkish minority in Bulgaria has had several migration processes towards Turkey. The Turkish minority was periodically exposed to ethnic discrimination in Bulgaria, which resulted in emigration to Turkey (Parla, 2009, p.757). The largest emigration flow of ethnic Turks took place during the mass exodus in 1989 with approximately 360.000 people fleeing to Turkey. This was the largest collective civilian migration after the Second World War, taking place due to the "revival process" of the Bulgarian state (Zhelyazkova, 1998), which included converting and assimilating ethnic Turks (Vasileva, 1992, p.346). When the ideal of a homogenous community peaked in 1984 with the "rebirth campaign", it continued with a systematic oppressive renaming campaign against Turks, strictly prohibiting the speaking of Turkish language, and denying the existence of ethnic Turks in Bulgaria (Parla, 2006, p.545).

Ethnic Turks from Bulgaria were considered as ethnic kins (soydaş) and were welcomed to the Turkish society with high degree of empathy for their situation. However, Bulgarian Turkish migrant women's citizenship experiences were subject to very few studies so far. The fact that there has not been much research on Bulgarian Turkish migrant women might be because of the submission and resignation culture they brought along from the communist system, as well as the misconception that the discrimination that they were faced with in Bulgaria as a minority had completely ended after migration to Turkey, and due to the illusion created by the existence of opportunities in Turkey that they had not enjoyed in Bulgaria. Migrant women underwent a process of adapting into the Turkish society where patriarchal structures more visibly constrain women's individual citizenship experiences than in the communist regimes.

This research underlines that, even those immigrant women who have gained certain citizenship rights by virtue of the fact that they are part of the ethnic majority in a host country are likely to have problems regarding the practice of

---

[158] Özge Kaytan is a Ph.D. Student of Sociology at Middle East Technical University, Üniversiteler Mah. Dumlupınar Bulvarı No:1, 06800 Çankaya-Ankara, Turkey. E-mail: ozgekaytan@gmail.com

their citizenship rights; as a result, their citizenship may be constructed incompletely. This research aims at contributing to feminist citizenship research by demonstrating the gendered experiences of a group of migrant women, which are like to share significant commonalities with migrant women in similar or different settings. The primary research technique used in this research was semi-structured in-depth interviews. 19 interviews were conducted with the Bulgarian Turkish immigrant women who immigrated to Turkey in 1989 and throughout 1990s.

Problematizing immigrant women's citizenship

Citizenship is not only about the identity certificates, nationality, and legal, political and social rights; citizenship covers multiple identities and socializations. Most of the time, the concept of citizenship is perceived only as political citizenship, which consists of political participation of citizens; or social citizenship, which covers economic dependence or independence of citizens (Prokhovnik, 1998, p.84). Nonetheless, citizenship is not necessarily constructed as 'neutral', 'abstract', 'universalized', 'genderless', which requires an equal membership of all in public sphere: rather it can include diversities of gender, ethnic and cultural bases in public and private spheres. Hence, the concept of citizenship is beyond the political and the social rights. As Walby (1994, p.391) contended, "access to citizenship is a highly gendered and ethnically structured process". It is important to point out that "engendering citizenship" should consist of subjective experiences of women, which are mostly ignored in issues of politics and perceived outside the domain of citizenship (Caldwell et al., 2009, p.7). Spirituality, emotions, family, kinship and sexuality are part of what constitutes citizenship (Caldwell et al. 2009, p.7). Gender is relevant to citizenship, because historically women, who comprised half the population, were denied from the full and active citizenship (Walby, 1994, p.391).

The public and private dichotomy has significantly shaped women's citizenship experiences and the power discrepancies among men and women. In addition to citizenship being a male-dominated notion, it is associated with the public space, which increases the gap between public and private domains, consequently rendering women invisible and subordinated in terms of being identified as figures of private sphere (Roy, 2005, p.28). In the private sphere, women are exposed to double burden while working outside home; they are also largely engaged in domestic chores and care work for elderly and children. Migration has a profound effect on women's labor force participation, which is a central element of migration research (Pedraza, 1991, p.313). Compared to migrant men, migrant women tend to enjoy a smaller scale of job opportunities. Migrant women mostly work in domestic service, garment industry, care work and more recently work in high-skilled occupations such as nursing; sometimes women can find jobs from hard labor, such as construction work, but they are few and mostly temporary (Pedraza, 1991, p.314).

Immigration is a contentious concept when considered in relation to citizenship, as the statuses and the life conditions of immigrants have often been problematic. Immigrant women construct their lives from scratch in the host country; so unlike other women's citizenship, their citizenship is reconstructed.

Phizacklea (1987 in Abraham et al.) argued that the relevance of migration to women's citizenship was about 'boundaries', 'rights' and 'unequal opportunities'. It reshapes and reconstitutes how women and men should be; gender is compromised with migration (Duran, 2011, p.77). Further, immigration generally comprises 'geographic movement' and 'linguistic and cultural displacement', which are not experienced in the same way for women and men; this displacement is very much related to 'belonging', 'citizenship' and 'inclusion/exclusion' (Duran, 2011, p.78). According to Pettman (2010, p.259), academic studies of migration do not reflect the stories of many migrant women, which include losses and gains, because many of them do not focus on women as a primary subject, but as victims and dependents. However, feminist studies have produced a better understanding of women's citizenship experiences by viewing them as the primary subjects in the immigration process (Pettman, 2010, p.259).

Bulgarian Turkish immigrant women in Turkey

The migration stories of women reveal that they had very difficult conditions in the first stages of the immigration, as well as in the following years of adaptation to a new country. Immigrant women remember the migration process with all details. One of the interviewees stated, "One morning the police came and wanted us to leave the country in three days. It was a shocking experience, because somebody forced you to leave your home country, and gave you only a couple of days for packing and leaving". The social and political environment in Bulgaria in 1989 was very problematic for Turks; as the interviewee stated that there were raids into houses to change the names of Turks, while people hid and run away, without coming home for several days. Turkish women in Bulgaria were afraid to speak Turkish in their workplaces due to the restrictions of the Bulgarian state. The Bulgarian Turkish immigrant women stated that they always had fear in their hearts in Bulgaria because of the forceful name changes and restrictions on speaking their mother tongue. The immigrant women's first years in Turkey were also difficult. All of the women stressed that they began everything from scratch in a new country. The first years of the immigration passed with difficulties, but all migrant women found a way to struggle. The first impressions of immigrant women about Turkey seem negative due to the prejudices against them and conservative gender norms and practices, which are especially imposed on women.

Ethnicity-based identity problems Bulgarian Turkish minority experienced in Bulgaria have also continued in Turkey. One interviewee[159] expressed her frustration in the following way: "People could hear our accent in the first years and understand that we are migrants, so they called us Bulgarians; but we are the grandchildren of Ottomans without any mixed race". Another interviewee[160] explained, "People in Turkey call us 'gavur'[161]; we are not gavur, we are real Turks". Similarly Fatma stated, "It was a real genocide, how do we go through such a genocide in 20th century?" Another woman expressed[162]; "Discrimination

---

[159] Fatma (55), university graduate, retired state officer. Migrated in 1989 with her husband.
[160] Zerrin (58), secondary school graduate, retired domestic worker in Turkey.
[161] Foreigner, infidel.
[162] Ganimet (64), retired nurse.

was very visible, they have called us 'nasty Turks' and it always created problems. I always felt humiliated and excluded in Bulgaria". Nevertheless, most of the immigrant women interviewed with expressed that they did not feel discriminated in Turkey.

The forced migration has some positive consequences for immigrant women, for which they all want to stay in Turkey. Some women declared that they never wanted to return to Bulgaria, despite the fact that there are negative aspects of Turkey as well. Living in big cities in Turkey, and earning higher wages compared to Bulgaria are important reasons why immigrant women prefer living in Turkey. Immigrant women asserted that they could live freely in Turkey without any restrictions about speaking their mother tongue and practicing their religion. One interviewee's[163] words clearly summarize how they felt about being in Turkey, as she stated, "If we have never seen Turkey, we would be content with what we had in Bulgaria". Almost all women highlighted that they were very happy to work and be able to get retirement in Turkey, as there is currently a high level of unemployment in Bulgaria. However, these positive sides of the migration came at the expense of increased domestic gender roles.

Bulgarian Turkish immigrant women have been exposed to marginalization and alienation in Turkey, initially because of their culture of work. Immigrant women argued that they received strong criticism about their work outside home. Fatma explained her experience in the following way: "Local people looked down upon us because immigrant women have been working outside; even women questioned how we dare to work. They were very narrow-minded; but now local women have begun working, after seeing it from us. People in Turkey cannot stand women's employment". In Turkey, men's limited engagement with private sphere and domestic works such as childcare captured immigrant women's attention. One interviewee[164] asserted that people rumor about a man if he takes his child to park, so she and her husband go to park together with their children in Turkey. This reflected the prevailing dominance of the male breadwinner idea in the Turkish society. In addition, Esma claimed that people in Turkey perceived every migrant woman who comes from Bulgaria, Russia or other Balkan countries as prostitutes: "Men in Turkey think that we -migrant women- are available for everything; because we come from a socialist country, they think we are common goods. Men in workplaces first test the waters to see if we are available for everything". Nimet made a similar point: "Being a woman in Bulgaria was easier compared to Turkey, because women could walk in the streets at nights without any fear, but in Turkey there are always rumors and gossips about women".

Immigrant women also suffered from the absence of certain social services in Turkey that were provided by the state in Bulgaria, such as childcare. Some women had to quit their jobs in order to look after their children, as there was nobody else to do it. Some of them sent their children to Bulgaria, so that their relatives can look after the children for some time. Immigrant women fled from an assimilation campaign while immigrating to Turkey; although they knew that the social and economic system is different in Turkey, they did not expect as much

---

[163] Nimet (44), high school graduate, subcontracted worker in a hospital in Turkey.
[164] Esma (47), university graduate, unemployed.

difference as they observed. The new social and economic system, combined with patriarchy in Turkey, resulted in negative conditions for immigrant women.

Discussion

The Bulgarian Turkish immigrants who fled to Turkey in 1989 were granted full Turkish citizenship; they enjoyed equal legal rights with Turkish citizens. In the eyes of the Turkish society, these immigrants had many advantages. They were not outsiders; on the contrary, they were welcomed by the Turkish government, and their settlement and employment were facilitated. They are "soydaş", who were provided refuge from the oppressive regime in Bulgaria at the time; however, immigrant women's conditions were never made an issue.

Bulgarian Turkish immigrant women's participation in public sphere remained limited in Turkey compared to Bulgaria. Immigrant women have been stuck visibly in private sphere in Turkey. Many immigrant women had to quit their jobs later to take care of their children, since there is not adequate and financially accessible state-provided childcare service in Turkey. This resulted in several years uncounted towards women's retirement insurance; in addition, some immigrant women could not go back to work. Most of the interviewees emphasized that they could not go out freely at nights in Turkey, which implies a limited presence in the urban space. Moreover, immigrant women had to change some of their domestic habits in Turkey because of the social oppression coming from the local women. More traditional and religious gender norms are reconstructed for the immigrant women in Turkey.

In Turkey, immigrant women are mostly employed in jobs that reproduce gender roles, such as children and elderly care work, domestic work, and nursery. Moreover, "failure to formally recognize the value of domestic work is itself a denial of citizenship" (Bosniak, 2009, p.131). When it comes to immigrant women, this issue gains a critical significance since adapting to a new country itself has proved to be a triple-burden on women's shoulders, **due to** their gender identity, migrant status and exploited laborer at home and in the employment market. Immigrant women's citizenship in Turkey required women's adaptation to flexible-overtime working hours, precarious conditions at work, and the lack of social security and retirement loans. This and all other circumstances regarding gendered work patterns in the private and public spheres effectively excluded immigrant women from equal and full citizenship. It seems like an illusion that the immigrant women consider Turkey as a country full of opportunities, where private sector dominates the economy; the opportunities immigrant women highlight do not provide full and equal citizenship for women. Although most of the immigrant women claimed that it was worth migrating to Turkey because they could now speak their language in Turkey and have achieved significant economic opportunities they never had in Bulgaria, these benefits came with the cost of increased gender inequality. Immigrant women sometimes seemed to underestimate the gender discrimination they faced in Turkey, because the issue of gender discrimination falls behind the issue of ethnic discrimination they experienced in Bulgaria. The ethnic discrimination Bulgarian Turkish immigrant women faced in Bulgaria was more dominant compared to the gendered one due to the gender equality myth in the communist system, which provided certain social rights to women, thereby making patriarchy less visible.

Conclusion

Immigrant women have been one of the most silenced groups in the society; as they have adapted to life in a new country, new rules, new gender norms, and a new citizenship. The Bulgarian Turkish immigrant women seem to underestimate the gender discrimination in Turkey, not only because they too seem to have integrated to the dominant gender norms and patriarchal culture in Turkish society, but also because the gendered discrimination the immigrant women experience in Turkey seems insignificant and invisible compared to the ethnic discrimination they experienced in Bulgaria. The new and ample economic opportunities the Bulgarian Turkish women found in Turkey, partly due to the capitalist system, may also have blinded them to the more traditional and religious gender roles they are subject to in their new country. The Bulgarian Turkish immigrant women define citizenship through having a national identity card, being employed, having access to wider economic opportunities, and a sense of belonging to the majority who speaks the same language and shares the same religion.

This research is conducted in order to indicate that even immigrant women who are the ethnic majority in a state and have certain citizenship rights may still have problems regarding citizenship, and their citizenship may be constructed in an incomplete manner. Full and equal citizenship does not necessarily mean being majority or having substantial rights. Citizenship consists of and intersects different factors including women's position in the public and private sphere, women's labor both inside and outside home, childcare, elderly care, how immigrant women's citizenship is subjectively constructed by the patriarchal prejudices, the stereotypes and critiques about them in the host country, and how they position themselves in the new country. Although the Bulgarian Turkish immigrant women are from the same ethnic kin with the majority of people in Turkey, it is important to recognize them as a different category of women who are excluded from citizenship, as their experiences during and after the immigration to the host country interacts with their gender identity and the other structural inequalities they have been exposed to in Turkey.

References

Abraham, M., Chow Ngan-ling, E., Maratou-Alipranti, L., Tastsoglou, E. (2010). "Rethinking Citizenship with Women in Focus". In M. Abraham, E. Tastsoglou, E. Chow (Eds.), *Contours of Citizenship: Women, Diversity and Practices of Citizenship*. Surrey: Ashgate Publishing.

Bosniak, L. (2009). "Citizenship, Noncitizenship and the Transnationalization of Domestic Work". In S. Benhabib & J. Resnik (Eds.), *Migrations and Mobilities: Citizenship, Borders and Gender*, New York, London: New York University Press. pp. 127-156.

Caldwell, K.L., Coll, K., Fisher, T., Ramirez, R.K., Siu, L. (2009). Gendered Citizenships, Transnational Perspectives on Knowledge Production, Political Activism and Culture. New York: Palgrave Macmillan.

Duran, M.G. (2011). "Gender, Migration and Identity". In S.P.C. Borrego & M.I.R. Ruiz (Eds.), *Cultural Migrations and Gendered Subjects: Colonial and Postcolonial Representations of the Female Body*. Newcastle: Cambridge Scholars Publishing.

Parla, A. (2006). "Longing, Belonging and Locations of Homeland among Turkish Immigrants from Bulgaria". *Southeast European and Black Sea Studies*, Vol.6, No.4, Routledge. pp. 543-557.

Parla, A. (2009). "Remembering Across Border: Postsocialist Nostalgia among Turkish Immigrants from Bulgaria". *American Ethnologist*, Vol. 36, No.4, American Anthropological Association. Pp. 750-767.

Pedraza, S. (1991). "Women and Migration: The Social Consequences of Gender". *Annual Review of Sociology*, Vol. 17. Annual Reviews Inc. pp. 303-325.

Pettman, J. (2010). "Migration". In L.J. Shepherd (Eds.), *Gender Matters in Global Politics* Routledge. pp. 251-264.

Prokhovnik, R. (1998). "Public and Private Citizenship: From Gender Invisibility to Feminist Inclusiveness". *Feminist Review*, No.6. pp. 84-104.

Roy, A. (2005). Gendered Citizenship: Historical and Conceptual Explorations, Orient Blackswan.

Vasileva, D. (1992). "Bulgarian Turkish Emigration and Return". *International Migration Review*, Vol. 26, No. 2. The Center for Migration Studies of New York. pp. 342-352.

Zhelyazkova, A. (1998). "The Social and Cultural Adaptation of Bulgarian Immigrants in Turkey". In A. Zhelyazkova (Eds.) *Between Adaptation and Nostalgia: The Bulgarian Turks in Turkey*. Sofia: International Center for Minority Research.

A Research on Psychosocial Support and Future Expectations of the Syrian Female Asylum-Seekers Living in Turkey

Veli Duyan, Elif Gökçearslan Çifçi, Fulya Akgül Gök and Ezgi Arslan[165]

Introduction

Migration is the phenomenon of people's leaving their areas of residence definitely or temporarily due to a number of reasons (IOM, 2009). Even though the term migration primarily connotes the movement of a particular population from one location to another, migration has a structure that is much more extensive and deep-rooted than mere geographic replacement (Aksu & Sevil, 2010). Today, rapidly changing environmental, economic, political, and social structures lead individuals and groups to migrating to settle in different regions. Based on classifications using different criteria, we may talk of types such as voluntary migration, forced migration, permanent or temporary migration, transit migration, illegal migration, and chain migration (Mutluer, 2003; Gündüz 1996 cited in Ilgaz & Tuzcu 2005). In the literature, internal migration is identified as the population movement between areas within the borders of the country and external migration is identified as movements of geographic replacement occurring towards neighbouring countries or even beyond (Şahin, 2001).

Due to regional conflicts continuing in her neighbours, Turkey is usually the scene to forced migration among types of external migration. Forced migration is defined as 'the migration movement that harbours a coercion element that includes threat on life and welfare due to natural or manmade causes.' (IOM, 2009). Related to the internal strife in Syria, approximately 5 million people were forced to leave their country (UNFPA 2014).

Considering migration routes and transit countries, it is seen that Turkey geographically occupies a central location and route. It should be particularly noted that a high number of asylum-seekers and immigrants from African, Asian, and Middle Eastern countries still choose Turkey both as a destination and as a transit country (Kolukırık, 2014).

Since we are a party to the Geneva Convention Relating to the Status of Refugees with geographic limitation the international protection statuses is accordingly stipulated as threefold in the law, namely refugee, conditional refugee, and secondary protection. Prior to the war in Syria, Turkey started to implement a new law for granting international protection and social rights to aliens and refugees and asylum-seekers with cooperation with UNHRC (RoT Ministry of Interior General Directorate of Migration Management, 2005).

The terms asylum-seeker and refugee are often confused: an asylum-seeker is someone who says he or she is a refugee, but whose claim has not yet been

---

[165] Veli Duyan is Professor at Social Work Department of Ankara University in Turkey; Elif Gökçearslan Çifci is Associate Professor at Social Work Department of Ankara University in Turkey; Fulya Akgül Gök is Research Assistant at Social Work Department of Ankara University in Turkey; Ezgi Arslan is Research Assistant at Social Work Department of Ankara University in Turkey (ezgiarslan88@hotmail.com).

definitively evaluated. A refugee is someone who "owing to a well-founded fear of being persecuted for reasons of race, religion, nationality, membership of a particular social group or political opinion, is outside the country of his nationality, and is unable to, or owing to such fear, is unwilling to avail himself of the protection of that country." (UNHRC 2012).

Right to asylum is underlined as a fundamental right by the expression '*Everyone has the right to seek and to enjoy in other countries asylum from persecution*' in the Article 14 of the Universal Declaration of Human Rights. By the start of the war in Syria, hundreds of thousands of Syrian nationals moved to the Turkish border, passed the border and sought asylum in our country. Turkish government followed an open door policy and it received the comers as guests, building camps for their accommodation (Yıldız, 2013).

According to the United Nations High Commissioner of Refugees (UNHCR), Turkey ranks the first among countries receiving Syrian asylum-seekers. Around 300-400 thousand Syrians took refuge in the country only in April 2012 (TBMM-İHİK, 2012) and this figure exceeded 500,000 in the year 2013 (UNHCR, 2013a).

Asylum-seekers that fled the Syrian civil war and arrived in Turkey are considered in the category of mass asylum and they stay as guests at the settlement units with the temporary protection principle. According to Çiçekli (2009 cited in Yıldız, 2013), the aim of temporary protection is to enable refugees and asylum-seekers urgently reach to a safe environment and to safeguard their fundamental human rights, most significantly against deportation to the home country.

According to a field study conducted in the year 2013, most of the Syrian asylum-seekers found in Turkey enter from the Turkish-Syrian border and half of the asylum-seekers living in camps and one fourth of asylum-seekers living outside camps made passage at an official border post without passport. Official figures give about 550,000 Syrian asylum-seekers formally registered (AFAD, 2013). About 70% of the Syrian asylum-seekers aged fifteen and older are married. Among Syrian asylum-seekers, around 17% of the householders living in camps and about 22% of the householders living outside camps are female.

Immigration, Women, and Psychosocial Support

Direct or indirect effects of globalization in the world, regional conflicts, poverty, and associated factors lead to an increase in the number of immigrants (OIM, 2012). External migration is a movement of individuals from their country to another one. This sudden and rapid movement causes environmental, physical, cultural, psychological, and social changes in the individual's life. Age, gender, and other personal attributes of the individual also affect the degree of exposure to such changes (Topçu & Başer, 2006).

Immigrant status leads to disintegration of the family, recession of social network links, and psychosocial stress. Stress experienced by individuals in the course of adapting to a new culture due to migration may lead to anxiety and depression in individuals. Among the reasons of the stress experienced are hardships faced in the course of adapting to a new culture, lack of access to health services, language barriers, and obstacles to education (Hiott et al., 2008).

Social networks, gender, age, language skills, level of education, religious beliefs, reasons of immigration, and the mode of reception in the host country are significant factors affecting the adaptation process. Factors with negative impact on health in the areas receiving immigrants include lack of sufficient health services and health professionals, low income level of the immigrants, economic hardships, poor nutrition, obstacles to transportation, lack of persons that may look after the children of working women, irregular working hours, language barriers, lack of health insurance, traditional ways of life, poor response of the local services to needs, status of being an alien, laws, and social and psychological stress (Başer, 2012 cited in İldam Çalım, Kavlak & Sevil, 2012).

One of the most significant changes experienced in immigration during the past half-century is that the women's migration is on increase compared to prior migrations. Women may also face forced migration due to exploitation or warfare in the countries they settle because of family problems or warfare. (UNFPA 2014).

One of the groups most deeply affected by the migration process is the women. Immigrant women are particularly affected in psychological sense because of their domestic roles and responsibilities and the hardships they encounter in their host countries. Nevertheless, a study by Kirmayer et al. emphasized that women do not act to seek help for their psychological problems and this results from factors such as lack of knowledge, their hesitation to share their emotional problems with individuals out of their (2011). It is known that most of the Syrian refugees experienced torture, rape, kidnap, murder and massacres; because of that these people's mental health have been affected severely (James et al., 2014).

It is also underlined that women, children, and the elderly require more protection among the immigrants (Hemmasi & Prorok, 2002). Problems of psychological health experienced by immigrants include depression, post-traumatic stress disorder, psychosomatic complaints, anxiety, and sleep disorders (Adanu & Johnson, 2009; Lindstrom & Munoz-Franco, 2006).

Women face multiple sources of stress such as social isolation, loneliness, language barriers, and cultural differences in this process. Depending on the negative impact of the stress on health and insufficient mechanisms of coping with stress, female immigrants suffer from various physiological and psychological health problems (Ilgaz & Tuzcu 2005). Today, the share of women among the international immigrant population is 50% but this figure may rise up to around 80% in certain countries (UNFPA 2014).

Women are placed in the high risk group concerning abuse, violence, and exploitation during immigration (UNFPA 2014). Migration usually brings a set of changes and stress in the individual's social interaction network and cultural structure. These changes and stress has a more intense impact on women and children. Female immigrants may encounter harassment, rape, and violence (Ilgaz & Tuzcu 2005).

Just like in other parts of the world, migrations experienced in our country, of whatsoever incentives, have physical, social, and psychological effects on all migrating individuals (İldam Çalım, Kavlak & Sevil, 2012).

Methodology

This study was designed as a qualitative research. It was implemented in the format of semi-structured interview. The study was conducted with Syrian women between the ages of 25 and 45 who immigrated to Turkey from Syria and resident in the Önder Mahallesi area of Ankara and receiving aid from the foundation Önder İlim ve Kültür Vakfı. Sound recording was made during interviews. Interviews were conducted with help from a Syrian interpreter who is continuing his university education in Turkey and can speak Turkish. Sound recordings taken were decoded and findings of the research were collected.

Since the Turkish government imposed a requisite of permission for researches with Syrian asylum-seekers during implementation of the research and because the said permission cannot be available by the date of the conference presentations, we were obliged to share only some results of this study and observations of the researchers.

Results and observations

As revealed by the aforementioned literature and the research, forced migration has an adverse effect on the psychosocial well-being of the people and, particularly in the context of this article, the women. In particular consideration of the Syrian asylum-seekers, in addition to psychological, economic, and social problems resulting from phenomena of migration and warfare that are encountered by individuals who left their country due to warfare, adaptation problems they face in the host country are considerably prominent.

The main reasons for Syrian female asylum-seekers' choice of Turkey for asylum include geographic proximity and cultural affinity. Women see Turkey as a familiar place in terms of way of life and prevailing cultural and religious values and believe that they shall encounter less significant problems in adaptation. Nevertheless, the language barrier appears as one of the most urgent and serious problems. Even though Syria and Turkey have similarities in cultural and religious sense, female asylum-seekers' lack of language skills hamper their efforts for adapting to social life and normalisation.

Another psychosocial problem to be considered for female asylum-seekers is that individuals with professional formation and who are students cannot continue with their work or studies in Turkey. It is particularly obvious that they have lack of information and guidance for continuing their education. Furthermore, as a bureaucratic obstacle, since they do not possess documentation in evidence of their education in Syria, which shall enable nostrification for university and lycée diplomas and lack of such mechanism, also the insufficient communication between the two countries prevent most women from continuing their studies. It is particularly observed that women who have school-age children do not have sufficient knowledge of these procedures and they are ignorant of authorities who may provide information.

It is seen that Syrian families living outside the camps particularly have problems in earning a living and accommodation. They lack sufficient information on where to apply for social or material support.

Another noteworthy aspect of the Syrian female asylum-seekers' processes of forced migration and afterwards is that they have received almost no help in terms of psychosocial and psychological support. Although women usually accept their bad experiences with maturity and keep hopeful for the future thanks to their religious beliefs, it is also observed that most of them go through episodes they have hardships in dealing with and sometimes causing emotional crises. It should not be surprising that the women, comparing their moods before the war with their current moods told that they were happier and calmer before the war but now more nervous and impatient. There is no formal psychosocial or psychological support services destined for asylum-seekers living outside camps in Turkey.

It is seen that female asylum-seekers who are unable to assess their psychosocial wellness status integrally give priority to needs such as food, accommodation, and clothing, as well as aids for children. Psychosocial or psychological support ranks among the last aids they require.

Aforementioned shortcomings constitute problems that should be urgently by the Turkish government that opened the doors and granted asylum to these asylum-seekers.

References

Adanu, R. M., and Johnson, T. R. (2009). Migration and women's health. International Journal of Gynecology and Obstetrics, 106(2), 179-181.

AFAD, Başbakanlık Afet ve Acil Durum Yönetimi Başkanlığı. (2013). Türkiyedeki Suriyeli Sığınmacılar, Saha araştırması sonuçları, Ankara. Received from https://www.afad.gov.tr/Dokuman/TR/60-2013123015491-syrian-refugees-in-turkey-2013_baski_30.12.2013_tr.pdf

Aksu, H. and Sevil, Ü. (2010). Göç ve kadın sağlığı. Maltepe Üniversitesi Hemşirelik Bilim ve Sanatı Dergisi, 2(3), 133-138.

Hemmasi, M.and Prorok, C.V. (2002). Women's Migration and Quality of Life in Turkey. Geoforum, 33(3), 399–411.

Hiott, A. E., Grzywacz, J. G., Davis, S. W., Quandt, S. A. and Arcury, T. A. (2008). Migrant farmworker stress: mental health implications. The Journal of Rural Health, 24(1), 32-39.

İldam Çalım, S., Kavlak, O. and Sevil, Ü. (2012). Evrensel bir sorun: Göç eden kadınların sağlığı ve sağlık hizmetlerinde yaşanan dil engeli. Sağlık ve Toplum Dergisi, 22(2), 11-19

Ilgaz, A. and Tuzcu, A. (2015). Göçün Kadın Ruh Sağlığı Üzerine Etkileri (çevirisi). Psikiyatride Güncel Yaklaşımlar (Current Approaches in Psychiatry) 7(1): 56-67 Doi: 10.5455/cap.20140503020915

IOM. (2009). Göç Terimleri Sözlüğü. Received from http://goc.gov.tr/files/files/goc_terimleri_sozlugu(1).pdf

IOM. World Migration Report 2010. The future of migration: building capacities for chance. Geneva: International Organization for Migration; 2010.

James, L., Sovcik, A., Garoff , F. and Abbasi, R. (2014) The mental health of Syrian refugee children and adolescents. Forced Migration Review, 42-44.

Kirmayer, L.J., Ryder, A.G. and Pottie, K. (2011). Common mental health problems in immigrants and refugees: General approach in primary care. Canadian Medical Association Journal, 183 (12), 959-967.

Kolukırık, S. (2014). Uluslararası Göç ve Türkiye: Yerel Uygulamalar ve Görünümler (International Migration and Turkey: Locak Applications and Outlook). Journal of World of Turks. Vol. 6, Nr. 2 : 37-53.

Lindstrom, D. P. and Munoz-Franco, E. (2006). Migration and maternal health services utilization in rural Guatemala. Social Science and Medicine, 63(3), 706-721.

Şahin C. (2001). Yurt dışı göçün bireyin psikolojik sağlığı üzerindeki etkisine ilişkin kuramsal bir inceleme. Gazi Üniversitesi Gazi Eğitim Fakültesi Dergisi, 21(2), 57-67

T.C. İçişleri Bakanlığı Göç İdaresi Genel Müdürlüğü. (2005). İltica ve Göç Alanındaki Avrupa Birliği Müktesebatının Üstlenilmesine İlişkin Türkiye Ulusal Eylem Planı. Ankara. Received from http://www.goc.gov.tr/files/files/turkiye_ulusal_eylem_plani%281%29.pdf

TBMM İHİK. (2012). Mülteci, Göçmen ve Sığınmacı Sorunları Raporu. Ankara. Received from http://madde14.org/images/f/f0/Tbmmihkraporu.pdf

Topçu, S. and Başer, A. (2006). Göç ve Sağlık. C.Ü.Hemşirelik Yüksekokulu Dergisi, 10(3), 37-42.

UNFPA. (2014). Crisis in Syria. Received from http://www.unfpa.org/emergencies/crisis-syria

UNHCR. (2013a). UNHCR Afghanistan Update on Volrep and Border Monitoring. Received from http://www.refworld.org/docid/52026e504.html

UNHRC. (2012). Syria Regional Refugee Response. Received from http//data.unhrc.org/syrianrefugees/reginal.php

Yıldız, Ö. (2013). Türkiye Kamplarında Suriyeli Sığınmacılar: Sorunlar, Beklentiler, Türkiye ve Gelecek Algısı. Sosyoloji Araştırmaları Dergisi, vol 16 No. 1 spring 2013

Child-Rearing Practices within Mixed European-Turkish Families in Istanbul: Setting Symbolic Boundaries

Nevena Gojkovic Turunz[166]

Introduction:

Once a typical emigration country, Turkey has since 1990s been established as a transit and receiving society. Furthermore, a significant number of foreigners live in Turkey not only for work, pleasure, or education but also for personal reasons. Hence, the article focuses on a particular group of migrants – 'love' migrants – men and women from several European countries, who settled in Istanbul due to their emotional ties with Turkish citizens and established families with them. The key questions of the article are: a) how foreign parents perceive family relations, a concept of a good mother and child-rearing practices in the Turkish society; and b) how on the basis of perceived differences, the foreign parents create symbolic boundaries specifically toward their Turkish in-laws, perceived typical Turkish "mothers", and Turkish society as a whole.

Literature review:

Distinctive parenting styles correspond to the socioeconomic contexts of particular societies. Parenting aims at installing appropriate values, and its final goal is a well-adjusted, functional, and culturally and socially competent child. According to Bornstein (2012) "culture- specific patterns of child-rearing can be expected to adapt to each society's specific setting and needs" (p. 213). In addition, "the context of the formation and the dynamics of a mixed union constitute a particularly active and complex sociocultural hybrid space, especially with respect to the upbringing of children" (Rodríguez García, 2006, p. 426).

This article takes a cross-national marriage in Lamont's understanding as a "group boundary crossing (Lamont: 2009: 152)." However, upon two people have crossed the boundaries of their ethnic or religious groups, the new boundaries are inevitably being created in many ways. As Bonjour and De Hart (2013) argue "the realm of the intimate – family life – is where the crucial boundary work is done; where the sharpest distinctions between 'us' and 'them' are drawn" (p. 73).

Lamont (1992) defines symbolic boundaries as "conceptual distinctions that we make to categorize objects, people, practices, and even time and space" (p. 9), and makes a distinction between moral, socioeconomic, and cultural boundaries. "Moral boundaries are drawn on the basis of moral character; they are centered around such qualities as honesty, work ethic, personal integrity and consideration for others" (p. 4). In Lamont's view "socioeconomic boundaries are drawn on the basis of judgments concerning people's social position as indicated by their wealth, power, or professional success." (p. 4). Finally, "cultural borders are drawn on the basis of education, intelligence, manners, tastes, and command of high

---

[166] Istanbul Sehir University, Adress: Dimitrija Tucovica 146/16, 11050 Belgrade, Serbia, Gojkovic.nena@gmail.com

culture" (p. 4). In my research, the cultural boundaries are created around issues of manners, hygiene and cleanliness, and education.

Methodology:

My research represents a qualitative micro level study, based on in-depth semi-structured interviews. Mason (2002) argues the usage of in-depth, semi-structured interviews is appropriate when an aim of the research is "understanding of depth and complexity in people's situated or contextual accounts and experiences" (p. 65). I conducted ten interviews in Istanbul 2014 with 3 participants from England, France, Ireland, Italy, Poland, Russia, Serbia, and Turkey. According to the research criteria, the participants are in Turkish/European marriage, have children and reside in Istanbul. Subsequently, I transcribed the interviews and coded them by "identifying appropriate blocks of text with a particular code" (Campbell et al., 2013, p. 297) and putting them into the coding scheme. Afterward, I linked grouped quotations to the relevant theoretical framework and analyzed them from the perspective of interpretivism. There is an over- representation of women, as I primarily focus on female experiences, following the argument of Yuval-Davis that mothers "embody boundaries of the cultural or national community" (cited in Bonjour & de Hart, 2013, p. 63).

Relationship between extended family members:

Kağıtçıbaşı (2005) argues that a concept of autonomy is comprised of two distinct dimensions. They are the degree of distancing of the self from others ("interpersonal distance") and the degree of autonomous functioning ("agency"). In Kağıtçıbaşı's words "Separate selves are distanced from others with well-defined self-boundaries, whereas the boundaries of connected selves may be fused with others. (Agency) extends from autonomy to heteronomy. Autonomy is the state of being a self-governing agent, whereas heteronomy is being governed from outside"

(p. 404). When individuals, who internalized different concepts of self, come into close contact, communication gaps occur, and disapproval of the actions and viewpoints of the others is frequent. The dimension of interpersonal distance has implications for the understanding of personal space and time. Besides, it refers to attitudes towards the intergenerational dependence. The dimension of agency, which distinguishes between autonomy and heteronomy, mostly affects the understanding of who has the authority over raising children.

Different family models and concepts of self, entitle family members various rights. However, these tacit rights provoke resentment in another sociocultural contexts. The following table, based on a case of Richard, an Englishmen, summarizes different understanding of various rights:

Rights presumed by the Turkish Family	Richard's perception	Quotation of Richard
A right to freely move about a daughter's house	Intrusion into	"When my mother comes into my house, she is a guest. But, when my

	personal space	mother-in-law comes, she takes over everything."
A right to decide on behalf of younger	Suppression	"There is no freedom, they suppress you. My parents in law bought us a house without us knowing!"
A right to rely on help of elders	Shame	"My brother in-law is nearly 30 years old and still takes an income from his parents. This is not shameful for him, but for me it is"
A right to know other's financial situation	Control	"They want to know your finances, everything. There is so much control the Turkish culture"

The words he chooses to describe his feelings and their actions, resulting from the different understanding of a degree of closeness between family members, bear a strong moral connotation (suppression, shame, intrusion). This case illustrates the depth of internalization of culturally determined concepts of family and self. Furthermore, different family models imply various power relations among the family members, exemplified through the issues of decision-making. Opposing the influences of in- laws, as a rule with the support of a Turkish husband or wife is another common issue in the participants' narratives. Commonly, the non-Turkish daughter in-law challenges the tacit authority of the Turkish grandparents. It is a process of asserting power over the child-rearingand a clash between different family models. Only one participant assesses family relations she encounters in Turkey as preferable over those in her native country. However, the harmonious relationship with in-laws is a decisive factor preventing the setting of symbolic boundaries toward Turkey.

What is a good mother?

Social, cultural, and economic factors all impact dominant mothering practices in one society. The cultural models of parenting and family correlate with motherhood ideologies and discourses. Along with the socioeconomic structure and cultural norms and values, the dominant political discourse in one society shapes the public perception of an ideal concept of a family and forms the expectations from the citizens. Melis and Parmaksız (2012) claim that in Turkey "each and every political power acted to constitute a specific gender regime and defined the motherhood accordingly" (p. 127). Eslen-Ziya and Korkut (2010) argue for Kemalist modernization project women are "sacred symbols or totems of modernization" (p. 312), whose "highest duty was defined as child rearing and motherhood, which epitomized 'republican motherhood'" (p. 318). It was followed by the conservative outlook of current AKP government. It is clear that the motherhood as a highest duty remains a constant in Turkish political discourse. The conducted researches demonstrate the impact of political discourses on motherhood ideologies and practices and suggest an exceptional child-centrism. According to Dedeoğlu (2010)

The mothering and consumption practices of mothers who reflect the "good mothering" discourse are centered on the themes of self-sacrifice and ultimate fulfillment, devotion and child-centeredness. Children reflect success of mothering practices and social and material status of their mothers (p. 13).

The non-Turkish research participants are frequently critical to self-sacrificing motherhood and losing of mother's personality and autonomy. The relationship between the mother and the child is related to the concept of self, particularly to the dimension of interpersonal distance. The understanding of the interpersonal distance influences both behaviors of the mother and the desired characteristics of the child, primarily how independent the child should be. When asked for her opinion about social expectations of a good mother in Turkey, Kassia (Polish) replied:

Good mother in Turkey – a child will always be clean and have ironed clothes. Nothing will ever force me to iron his clothes. Also, a mother here doesn't have a right to complain if she is tired. Her role is only to take care of this kid and meet all his needs, there is nothing else. In Turkey it is quite normal that after you have a child, you will just stay at home. Your social life will end. I go out in the evening and have a beer with my friends, for me it is normal and healthy (Kassia, personal communication, 4 June 2014).

At the practical level Kassia is fully devoted to her 3 years-old son, as she holds a part- time evening job and actively spends daytime with him. However, at the symbolical level she asserts her autonomy from her son through her wishes and her personal space. Besides, set her deliberate practices as opposite to those of an imagined, typical Turkish mother (it is expected to iron – I don't; your social life will end – I go out and have a beer).

Moral boundaries:

The issue of moral boundaries is strictly correlated with the individual understanding of good motherhood. The participants tend to set moral boundaries foremost in regard to the desired qualities they foster in children. The main issue is independence of children. In narratives of the European participants it is expressed in the children's ability to cope with the life on their own, to be self-confident, and freely speak up their mind. Participants frequently criticize what they perceive as excessive relying on Turkish, even adult, children on their parents. What is more, they consider it as an apparent lack of ability to take care of their life and take pride in the fact that their own children differ.

In addition, parents who take the independence as a crucial value tend to stress equality inintra-family relations and decision-making process, and encourage their children to express their opinions. Particularly, the decision-making reflects the nature of intra-family relations. Schönpflug (2001) considers the decision-making influence to be an important indicator of family structure. The author argues in traditional patriarchal Turkish family father is the maindecision-maker, followed by the mother, whereas "children are at the very end of the decision hierarchy" (p. 219).

The issue of respect that elders demand from younger ones is frequently reported in the interviews and closely related to the structure of the family. The respect younger pay to the elders is embedded in Turkish language. Words such as *teyze* (aunt), *amca* (uncle), *abi* (older brother) and *abla* (older sister) are commonly used with non-related people. This practice denotes intimacy and extends family relations to acquaintances, friends, and even people in shops and in the street. Nonetheless, when it is used among siblings, it introduces hierarchy. The older one, *abi* or *abla*, is entitled to respect and obedience of the younger. Hence, the usage of these words combines hierarchy and intimacy. This linguistic practice upset some non-Turkishparents, as they perceive it to be against equality. Whereas some participants considers a hierarchy established through linguistic practice to be connected with a lack of warmth among the family members, Sunar and Fisek argue hierarchy has a positive function. "They suggested that the strong hierarchy within the Turkish family offsets the high level of intimacy, interdependence, and proximity, providing differentiations between family members while still allowing for interconnectedness" (Sunar & Fisek: 2005, as quoted in Harwood et al., 2006 p. 12).

Socioeconomic boundaries

Primarily the participants from Eastern Europe link perceived negative aspects of child rearing in Turkey with its socioeconomic structural conditions. In their views, these conditions present obstacles for both good mothering and development of desired qualities in children. In Sanja's view, the parental active participation is decisive for raising an independent child:

> *In Turkey because of work no one can afford to stay with kids. Second, here children are forced to spend the entire day at school. They cannot play alone in the street or stay alone in the house. They get a very little education directly from the parents. Then after school they go to Dersane, do their homework there, they receive so much information, but don't learn anything concrete. (Sanja, personal communication, 8 February 2014).*

For Sanja, the Turkish socioeconomic system represents an obstacle to a "good motherhood", which means to spend an abundance of time with a child, to actively participate I his or her development, and to foster the independence and autonomous learning. She considers the structural reasons to prevent optimal parental involvement and influence. As children are most of the time directly supervised by unrelated adults and their activities are structured, it hinders the development of their independence and critical thinking.

Cultural boundaries:

In this research, cultural boundaries, defined as "cultural standards such as intelligence, refinement, curiosity, and aesthetic sophistication" (xxiii) as elaborated by Lamont (1992), are less prominent than moral and socioeconomic boundaries. Two issues Caroline raises, namely the importance of cleanness in

Turkish society and differences that she and her husband cases serve to create cultural boundaries in Lamont's sense.

> *You know, Turkish children are not allowed to get dirty. German children are allowed, we appreciate them getting dirty. Also, when they were older they wanted to attend hobbies, learn music, and play instruments. I would let them go, but my husband really objected. (Karolina, personal communication, 1 June 2014).*

In the second part of Karolina's account she is setting a typical cultural boundary in Lamont's sense. The disparity between her and her family on one hand (native in German, socially and culturally proficient, middle class membership) and the husband and his family on the other hand (low-skilled manual guest workers) enhances her sense of cultural superiority and conviction her approach to children is the right one. Additionally, the first part of Karolina's quotation resonates with those of the majority of other research participants, who have observed the significance of hygiene and cleanliness in Turkish society. Ger (1999) connects washing and cleaning practices to economic growth in Turkey and upward mobility. According to his findings, the participants tend to engage in high impact consumption, which include spending an abundance of cleaning products and hot water, once when they are affordable. Ger concludes, "There is a close association between cleanliness and aesthetics of the home. While "dirty" symbolizes poverty and backwardness, "clean" symbolizes a distance from poverty, modern civilization, respectability, religious virtue, beautification of the home, as well as hygiene."

Discussion:

According to Zerubavel (1999), "classifying is a universal mental act that we all perform as human beings" (p. 53). Thereupon, when participants want to explain family relations, motherhood, or child rearing practice they observe in Turkish society, they inevitably compare them to those in their home countries. Besides, at the core of all contrasting is the vision of what kind of adult children should become.

Studies on parenting of immigrants in individualistic countries show that immigrants' adoption of the host country's parenting styles largely correlates with their acculturation level (Yagmurlu & Sanson, 2009; Yaman et al., 2010, Steinbach, 2013). In this research it is true to a certain extent. The acceptance of and positive attitude the upbringing ways in the Turkish society depends on a combination of acculturation level and the harmonious relationship with the Turkish in-laws. When there is a common ground between a non-Turkish parent and Turkish in- laws on the direction of child rearing and crucial values, and when they are supportive and respectful of parent's decisions, the setting of symbolic boundaries is minimal. On the contrary, misunderstanding and conflicts with the in-laws greatly contribute to the disdain for Turkish society.

References

Bonjour, S & De Hart, B. (2013). A Proper Wife, a Proper Marriage: Construction of 'Us' and 'Them' in Dutch Family Migration Policy. *European Journal of Women's Studies*. 20 (I), 61-76

Bornstein, M. H. (2012). Cultural Approaches to Parenting. *Parenting: Science and Practice*, 12,212-221.

Dedeoglu, A. O. (2010). Discourses of Motherhood and Consumption Practices of Turkish Mothers. *Business and Economics Research Journal*, 1 (3), 1-15.

Eslen-Ziya, H. & Korkut, U. (2011). Political Religion and Politicized Women in Turkey: Hegemonic Republicanism Revisited. *Totalitarian Movements and Political Religions*, 11: 3,311-326.

Ger, G. (1999). Experiential Meanings of Consumption and Sustainability in Turkey in *NA- Advances in Consumer Research Vol. 26*, eds. Arnould E. J. & Scott, L. M, Provo, UT: Association for Consumer Research, 276-280

Harwood, R. L., Yalçinkaya, A., Citlak, B. & Leyendecker, B. (2006). Exploring the Concept of Respect among Turkish and Puerto Rican Migrant Mothers.*New Directions for Child and Adolescent Development*, No. 114, 9-24.

Kagitcibasi, C. (2005). Autonomy and Relatedness in Cultural Context: Implications for Self and Family. *Journal of Cross-Cultural Psychology*, 36 (4), 403-422.

Lamont, M. (1992). Money, Morals, and Manners:The Culture of the French and the AmericalUpper-Middle Class. The University of Chicago Press Books.

Mason, J. (2002). Qualitative Researching. SAGE

Melis, P. & Parmaksız, Y. (2012). Digital Opportunities for Social Transition: Blogosphere and Motherhood in Turkey, *Fe Dergi*, sayı 1, 123-134

Rodríguez García, D. (2006). Mixed Marriages and Transnational Families in the Intercultural Context: A Case Study of African-Spanish Couples in Catalonia. *Journal of Ethnic and Migration Studies*,Vol.32, No. 3, 403-433

Schönpflug, U. (2001). Decision-Making Influence in the Family: A Comparison of Turkish Families in Germany and in Turkey, *Journal of Comparative Family Studies*, Vol. 32, No.2, 219- 230.

Steinbach, A. (2013). Family Structure and Parent-Child Contact: A Comparison of Native and Migrant Families. *Journal of Marriage and Family*, Vol. 75, Issue 5, 1114-1129.

Zerubavel, E. (1999). Social Mindscapes: An Invitation to Cognitive Sociology. Cambridge: Harvard University Press.

Yagmurlu, B. & Sanson, A. (2009). Acculturation and Parenting Among the Turkish Mothers in Australia. *Journal of Cross-Cultural Psychology*, Vol. 40, no. 3, 361-380.

Yaman, A., Mesman, J., Van Ijzendoorn M. H.,Bakermans-Kranenburg, M. & Linting, M. (2010). Parenting in an Indivdualistic Culture with a Collectivistic Cultural Background: The Case of Turkish Immigrant Families with Toddlers in the Netherlands. *Journal of Child & Family Studies*, 19, 617-628.

Üstuner, T. & Holt, D. B. (2010). Toward a Theory of Status Consumption in Less Industrialized Countries. *Journal of Consumer Research*, Vol. 37, No. 1, 37-56.

The Fear of "What They Say": How Gossip Regulates Sexual Exploration among Migrants in Europe

Sherria Ayuandini and Oğuz Alyanak

Extant literature on gossip is vast. Since the earlier days of discussion on the topic, which divided anthropologists over functionalist and methodological individualist camps (Gluckman, 1963; Paine, 1967; Gilmore, 1978), there have been calls for clarification of the term. In this paper, we operationalize gossip as "the fear of what they say". Our approach to gossip reflects communal dynamics among the populations we study, Turks in Amsterdam and Strasbourg, where the fear of what other people might say ("elalem ne der?") constitutes a reality that shapes how one acts. As we take gossip as an effective controlling mechanism that works through fear, we also delve into the larger anxieties that are argued to threaten the communities in which we conduct our ethnographic fieldwork. One such anxiety emanates from the possibilities of sexual exploration that life in Amsterdam and Strasbourg brings. In both cities, the fear of young (and sometimes old and married) men and women "fooling around" puts the youth under the spotlight as potential candidates for misdemeanor. In both contexts, we witnessed a growing anxiety over second and third generation Turks' engagement with extra and pre marital affairs. The fear of becoming gossip material, which could not only tarnish one's reputation, but in some cases lead to more dire consequences, is a reality that our informants do not overlook. Both in Amsterdam and Strasbourg, the young Turkish women and men we talked to are well aware of moral boundaries that determine the do's and don'ts of communal life. However, rather than reorienting their actions in line with cultural norms, our informants invent tactics (de Certeau 1984) to navigate intra-community surveillance. How they continue to live their lives amidst surveillance is a topic that we look further into in this paper.

Our aim is to propose a way to analyze discussions on sexuality among Muslims in Europe that extends beyond emancipatory discourses. We are not interested, in this paper at least, in showing how Muslims' changing approaches to sexuality point to their accommodation of European norms and values. We are aware that these debates lie central to public discussions in the Netherlands and France. In the Netherlands, sexual freedom is taken as a token of women's emancipation. The "rhetoric of salvation" (Abu-Lughod 2002) very much shapes the Dutch doctors' relationship with their female Muslim patients. In France, the same rhetoric is embedded to the French principle of laicite (Fernando 2009; Scott 2010) where women's emancipation is seen as an end goal for maintaining *ordre public* (Bowen 2010:194) We are rather interested in examining the possible ways through which our informants navigate the much feared patriarchy. While gossip is a regulatory mechanism through which communities maintain their moral boundaries (i.e., proper ways of defining and performing sexuality), individuals also create ways of transgressing these moral boundaries while maintaining face as they participate in and present themselves to their communities (Goffman 1967).

In Amsterdam, discussions on sexuality are centralized around the topic of female virginity. In a context in which virginity is still seen as an important aspect of an unmarried person's life, gossip is often the direct driving forces that inform and shape decisions of intimacy and partner choice. Women of Turkish descent are still largely expected to be sexually untouched before marriage. A gossip that insinuates otherwise has proven to significantly affect a young woman's life unfavorably. To examine what young Turkish women in Amsterdam do to cope with gossip about their sexual life, the researcher [SA] looks at a hymen repair surgery known as hymenoplasty. Based on participant observation in doctors' consultation and in-depth interviews with female patients who are of Turkish origin, her research explores the opportunities and challenges emanating from medicalized procedure that provides Muslim Turkish women the possibility to evade gossip.

In Strasbourg, the case the researcher [OA] presents looks at how the issue of sexuality is problematized within the context of men's sexual exploration. The possibility of men's engagement in extra and premarital affairs, although often argued to be less problematic than that of women's, proves to be otherwise. While men may be more mobile or "freer" to explore the urban landscape, their movement is nonetheless regulated by moral frames that define the boundaries of proper sexual conduct. Strasbourg's location in a borderland geography that hosts one of Europe's largest leisure industries (nightclubs, brothels and casinos) further aggravates moral anxieties. Members of the community discuss men's bad habits and attempt to curb their excursions. Based on his preliminary research in Strasbourg, the researcher argues that Muslim Turkish men, too, encounter the burden of navigating moral norms.

The paper is based on the ethnographic research of two scholars who are at different stages in their research. As of the writing of this paper, the researcher in Amsterdam [SA] has been collecting data almost a year, where she has been conducting interviews with Dutch doctors and their Muslim female patients about hymenoplasty. The researcher in Strasbourg [OA] has conducted over two months of preliminary fieldwork in Strasbourg, and two additional months in the point of origin, Kayseri, where he collected data on the anxieties attached to Muslim men's everyday lives and movement around the Franco-German borderland.

Amsterdam: "Playing with Fire"

Turkish migrants first came to the Netherlands in the late 1960s and early 1970s as guest workers. In the current day Holland, there are about 400,000 people of Turkish descent living in the country, which makes up about 2.15% of the entire population. The youngest of them are now considered Dutch of the fourth generation immigrants, while those who are currently studying on high school and university levels are of the second and third generations. In its most classical definition, the second-generation immigrants are those who were born to immigrant parents (Levitt and Waters 2002) although those who migrated very young and attended school in the receiving country are also considered to be part of this category (Kasinitz, Mollenkopf and Waters 2004).

The second and third generation Turkish immigrants in the Netherlands, henceforth young Dutch Turkish, are in their formative years. Being both Turkish and Dutch, they often have to deal with two sets of cultural norms, which are often at odds with one another. Arguably, the conflicting expectations that are the most challenging to navigate are norms surrounding the issue of sexuality. Ever since the Dutch sexual revolution in the 1960s, the Dutch see sexuality as something that is innocent (*onschuldig*) (Schnabel 1990). Hence, explorations and expressions of sexuality are to be expected and even considered to be an integral part of Dutch society (Ketting 1990). Yet, the Turkish community values sexuality as something that is bound in the realm of marriage and engagements in any sexual act beforehand are to be discouraged. Based on a field research study conducted in the Netherlands on and off site since 2011, the young Dutch Turkish confirms their daily struggle with these conflicting sexual values. The expectation of being chaste before marriage is particularly strict on the young Dutch Turkish women while the young men are more lenient in exploring their sexuality. As one 20 something Dutch Turkish woman succinctly put it, "In Turkish culture if a woman does something before marriage she's like 'the ho' [prostitute] but if a man does everything, he's the man."

For Dutch Turkish women, the expectation to retain chastity is often conveyed through gossips, rumors, and hearsays. According to many young Dutch Turkish, gossip is indeed a significant part of life among people of Turkish background in the Netherlands. It is to an extent a part of the process of community building. The creations of new relationships are often built on the knowledge of a stranger received from a family member or an acquaintance. Hence, people of Turkish descent often make it their business to know a lot about other people of the same background, in the account that they might be asked of their opinion of those individuals. This is still particularly true in the case of marriage as people of Turkish background in the Netherlands still rely on people in their inner circle—family members, friends and neighbors—to find a potential suitor or to decide whether or not to continue a casual meeting to a matrimonial process "She is our neighbor. Several neighbors say, 'he is a good guy, she is a good girl'. You should talk to one another. A lot of people have said that. So he visited. And then they started to talk. And there's a click," explained a 22 year old Dutch Turkish woman as she detailed how her brother met his wife. This manner of finding a future spouse is still quite common among people of Turkish background in the Netherlands.

Hence, talking about other people is considered a common practice. Young Dutch Turkish often regret this, as many see gossiping to be a regrettable pastime and claim that they would not like to take part in it. Although they do acknowledge that they do talk about others and often, when they pass on the information to me, it is quite clear that judgment is also done on the person of interest. As one woman claimed, "… if I heard someone did something like that [sex], yeah, multiple times, I think not just once, but multiple times with different person, I would also think that it's not a good thing". Another added: "I live in Haarlem and we just hear from people you know,'oh my God, that girl is going to marry and stuff'. And I thought, 'oh the girl is 19!' You know? Very early, so it's kinda, uhh… I don't know."

This is how one's reputation is made or broken among the people of Turkish descent in the Netherlands. Reputation is still a significant aspect in a young Dutch Turkish's life as a question on one's character may compromise one's chance in finding a potential spouse to marry. One couple confided to me of their woe as the family of the woman refuses to give permission to marry the man of her choice. The man explained how he had some unfortunate past and her family learned about it and could not look pass it. Now, she is to marry someone else instead.

Particularly for women of Turkish background in the Netherlands, virginity is still a central aspect of their social reputation. Unmarried women are still expected to be virgins before marriage. The expectation of this is often conveyed through rumors and gossips. Stories of non-virgins who find it hard to marry are widespread and families worry about it happening to their daughters or sisters. "Yeah, for example my cousin. It's like a far family member. She did have a lot of boyfriends, and it kinda leaked out and now people are talking about her, 'oh that girl did that.' Very badly. Even her father said, 'oh no one is going to marry you.'" explained one young Dutch Turkish woman.

"What they say" has significant authority. It is often accepted as the truth regardless of what actually has come to pass. When I asked a young Dutch Turkish woman on how people could be sure that a woman was no longer a virgin, she replied: "They heard it. People talk about it. They gossip about it." This "talk" is enough to render a woman's character questionable and her undesirable. Hence to be linked to an unsavory gossip is something that is considered to be catastrophic to some. A young Turkish woman expressed her shock when she first learned how her mother really took gossips very seriously, "... I can remember that my mother said, 'I would rather see you die than hearing from other people that you'd be like... you know... [not virgin]' I was like... wow..."

Given the high importance placed on being or not being gossiped, how do young people, particularly young Dutch Turkish women, avoid it? Some simply avoid engaging in activities that might invite gossips. This, most of the time, means not engaging in sexual intimacies before marriage or even not dating all together albeit many young people claim that this is a decision that they made for themselves rather than because they are worried of tongue wagging. "I'm not choosing this because my mother was saying that. It's really something for me," explained the woman whose mother claimed she would rather her daughter dies than being gossiped.

For those who do "play with fire", their engagements are as discreet as possible. This often means going on a date in places that are far from home, even going to a different city altogether. This is possible to do so in the Netherlands where many cities are only located within two hour train away from one another and a lot of young people have free use of the mass transportation due to their enrollment in a higher education establishment. To ensure their secret escapade does not leak out to unwanted ears, young Dutch Turkish women rarely share with anyone that they are indeed intimate with their significant others. This is compounded by the fact that talking about sexuality is still considered a taboo. Only married people talk about such subject. An unmarried woman talking about sex might actually tempt a gossip to be started about her abstinence.

When they do choose to tell someone, they are being extra careful to make sure that the news would not at the very least reach their parents. Young people often claim that they barely care about being gossiped but their parents do. Hence their careful conducts are often intended to keep the good relationship they have with their parents. As one young Turkish woman explained: "I don't care about myself but I do care about my relationship with my mom. I would not want to see that get harmed." These young women then make sure not to share their stories with someone who is notorious for talking to others about salacious stories. "I also think you need to be careful about who you're gonna tell about it, because there are people who really like to see… They don't like to see you succeed. I also know in my neighborhood, okay, this girl is not trustworthy, don't tell her something. You know. You don't have to think about it. The next day you hear from another," added the same woman.

Some of the Dutch Turkish women take it to a somewhat more extreme measure. Many people of Turkish background in the Netherlands believe that virginity of a woman can be confirmed through whether or not she bleeds after coitus with a lawfully wedded husband. Women who believe that they are no longer a virgin and worry that they would not be able to produce blood during the first night take precautions so there would not be gossips about their purity. Some of them opt for a surgery called hymenoplasty, which medically alters the shape of the hymen membrane often believed to its virgin state. Women are afraid of the dissolution of marriage. Some even experience violence if they do not bleed during the wedding night. They are also concerned about what people might say or think. Having the surgery for them is a way to calm the mind as to not worry about these possible consequences. Two young women of Turkish background even came all the way from Belgium to a clinic in the Netherlands, spending seven long hours sitting in traffic in order to consult a doctor of the possibility of getting the operation. They lamented to me loudly, one after another, of how people talk really badly about girls who they think are no longer a virgin: "Sometimes even if you are just walking on the street with a guy they think you're a whore!" chimed one of them stating how easy it was for a woman's reputation to be damaged. When that is the case, when one's reputation is already damaged because of gossip, particularly when there is doubt about a woman's chastity, there is one solution: marriage. Marriage seems to be seen as an acceptable way to clear one's name of damaging whispers. Two mothers of Turkish background related their life story to me where they mentioned how their first marriage was short-lived and unwanted. They were both gossiped for having lost their virginity before marriage. To refute it, they were married off to a suitor who was not aware of the gossip. Both marriages ended in a divorce, lasted for about a year each. Nowadays, rumors abound about young Dutch Turkish women who are married off against their will to circumvent their ruined reputation. This often means being send to Turkey to marry a man who agrees to take the hand of the disgraced woman.

Strasbourg: "Buying Credits" for Freedom

Turkish migration to France dates back to 8 April 1965, which marks the signing of the labor force agreements between the two states that was in effect until 1974 (Abadan-Unat 1976). Similar to the Netherlands, the closing of the border for labor migration was no impediment to continuing migrant flow. As of mid 2000s, the number of Turks in France reached 208,000 (Fassman and İçduygu 2013: 354) making France the second most Turkish-populated state in Europe after Germany. The majority of Turks in France live in three departments—ile de France, Rhone Alpes and Alsace (de Tapia 2009). In Alsace, for which Strasbourg serves as the capital, one finds the largest concentration of Turks (ORIV 2003). Contrary to other French cities where North African immigrants constitute the largest minority group, in Strasbourg, approximately one in every five immigrant (étranger) is of Turkish origin (INSEE 2006). While official statistics remain unreliable, estimates of people of Turkish origin (including Kurdish) in Strasbourg metro area (pop~764,000) range between 12,305 immigrés (INSEE, 2011) and 134,139 people (ZamanFrance, 2014).

As in Amsterdam, in Strasbourg, too the second and third generation Turkish immigrants, hereafter the young French Turks, are in their formative years. On the one hand, they live in a community that is closely knit. Due to Strasbourg's small size, and high ratio of Muslim and Turkish institutions, kinship and communal ties, particularly among the Sunni Muslim Turks I studied are still strong. On the other hand, the generational divide between parents and their children are hard to ignore. Because the majority of second and almost all of the third generation children are born and/or raised in France, their ties to Turkey, and familiarity with religious norms and cultural mores, are either learned in the family, mosque associations and summer camps, or through the one month summer vacation in Turkey that they take with their families. The interest in learning about Turkish culture through acculturation in institutional settings, as opposed to the lived experience of the streets, is low. While parents speak of bearing the financial burden of building Turkish institutions, such as ethnic locales, mosque associations, and more recently, schools, to avoid cultural and moral disintegration, their kids, particularly those that are now young adults (18 and above), are less interested in the amenities that these institutions offer. Despite these institutions' efforts to appeal to the changing tastes of the younger generation, such as building indoor soccer fields, rooms equipped with PlayStation consoles, darts and foosball tables, Turkish institutions in Strasbourg are not the central venues for socialization for young French Turks. Parents sign up their primary, middle and high school aged kids to summer camps, extracurricular and opportunities offered by mosque associations. Those who are of working age (in their last years of high school and beyond), who gain their independence by earning money, however, only stop by the associations to attend the Friday prayer and to watch Turkish soccer league games. While attending the communal Friday prayer is a religious obligation, as one informant noted, it also serves the function to make the plans for the Friday night. Moreover, communal events, such as the Friday prayer, or religious and cultural festivities, are events where the youth, through their participation in them, gains symbolic capital. By appearing in public, attending communal gatherings or abiding by certain requests of their parents, such as taking the trip to Turkey every summer, which many of my informants half-heartedly attend, the youth, as an 18 year old Strasbourg-born informant put it, are "buying credits" towards their own freedom, such as obtaining th permission to go out with friends on a Friday night.

Nonetheless, these public appearances do not suffice to diminish parents' concerns. Parents' lack of control over their children, particularly their sons, leads to a growing anxiety in the community. During my preliminary research, the interviews conducted brought up the fear of male Muslims going astray (yoldan çıkmak) and acquiring bad habits (kötü alışkanlıklar edinmek). My older informants were wary of the "bad habits" that life in this bordertown offered to young men. The ease of access to street workers on the streets of Strasbourg, to brothels in Germany, as well as casinos and nightclubs in Strasbourg's German neighbor, Kehl, which, contrary to Strasbourg, were open until 5 AM during weekends and 3 AM during weekdays, were some of the factors that further perpetuated these fears.

Both parents and their sons were aware of the opportunities and challenges that living in a risky borderland geography brought to their doorstep. For the young French Turks I spoke with, living in a bordertown translated into different experiences. While many thought that engaging in sexual affairs with sex workers or gambling in German casinos was a thing that older men do—for they were young, and did not need to pay for sexual favors or lock themselves up in casinos—most benefited from the active nightlife that Strasbourg and Kehl offered them. With the exception of a few, almost all of my young male informants had a sexual experience at least once. Their partners were almost always French, or second and third generation young North African women whom they met in high school, nightclubs or house parties. However, as one young male informant noted, young Turkish women were also sexually active. This 19-year-old informant mentioned to me the names of certain bars in Strasbourg where one could meet younger Turkish women. Nonetheless, the fear of being sexually active with a young Turkish female was evident for the young men in the community. Not only were they concerned about the word spreading around, they also did not want to be in a committed relationship for they feared that taking things to the next step with a young Turkish girl in Strasbourg would most certainly lead to marriage. While most of the young men I spoke with wanted to get married at some point in their lives, preferably with a second or third generation Turk just like themselves, they did not have problems with "fooling around" before making such a life changing decision. However, marriage was not something that young Turkish men in Strasbourg postponed for too long. The fear was that the longer they waited, the more pressure they would have to endure from their parents who wanted to find a suitable bride for them—preferably, but not necessarily from Turkey. Hence, my oldest single informant was 22 years old. He was already in a committed relationship, and busy making plans for his wedding next year. Moreover, the community did not speak lightly of older single males. My single status as a then 28-year-old Turkish researcher was sometimes jokingly, other times, more seriously problematized. During an interview with an 18 year old Strasbourg-born Turkish female in her father's house in Kayseri, and under the watchful gaze of her father, the grandmother—who also lived in Strasbourg—who walked into the room made it clear that she was not happy about the scene she witnessed. Who was I, a young Turkish man, talking to her granddaughter in private! The father alleviated her fears by making clear that everything was fine. The scene, as my female informant also mentioned, was nothing out of ordinary. Such was the difference in attitude across three generations—the Turkey-born grandmother and father and the France-born daughter.

While young men fear the disclosure of their private lives, which involves the bad habits that their parents speak of in a disconcerted manner, and try to buy credit in the eyes of their parents by showing up in public events, their parents, and especially their fathers, do not themselves place very high on the moral pedestal. Interviews with older men show that Fatih Akin's portrayal of an older Black Sea man looking for companion in the red light district of a German city in his movie, *The Edge of Heaven*, is not an exception. Many of the first generation Muslim Turkish men, who left their hometowns in Central Anatolian villages to come to Europe and ended up settling in Strasbourg ended up spending years away from their families before bringing them to Europe for family unification. Some of my older male informants, who came to Strasbourg as "tourists" and overstayed their visa, mentioned living with French women which in some occasions led to short term marriages that granted them residency permits. With few exceptions, most of these men denied engaging in sexual intimacy with older French women, and argued that the marriage was "only on paper", that is, the result of a monetary exchange with a French woman to obtain an official marriage certificate. I did not get a chance to ask women whether they were aware of these deals. What I asked, however, was whether they knew about their husbands' bad habits. During one couple interview I conducted in one of Kayseri's highland villages with a first generation husband and wife now in their 60s, the wife, to my surprise, was quite forthcoming in speaking about her husband's gambling habits while he sat right next to her listening. The husband, with a grin on his face, nodded silently as his wife spoke bitterly about how he had spend most of his money gambling, bringing home little to make do. With time, the husband had come clean and now spends most of his free time in Strasbourg at a nearby mosque association.

It is easy to locate the older Turkish men in Europe. They spend the majority of their time either at work or in a mosque association socializing with friends. Younger men, however, are out exploring the city. Many own cars, which take them across the border to Germany. Unlike their parents, who spend their free time with other friends in mosques, what these young men do with their free time is relatively unknown. And the unknown generates the fear that they may be out doing bad things. The fear is not ungrounded. The increasing rate of divorces among members of the Turkish community in Strasbourg is a matter of grave anxiety. And as usual suspects of moral transgressions, fingers are easily pointed at men. I brought up this issue during my interviews with community leaders (imams and other high ranking administrative staff) in the four main mosque associations in Strasbourg. Without a surprise, all of them found moral degeneration as the reason behind families breaking apart. They blamed parents for not having taken good care of their kids, and not spending enough time with them to teach them about Islam and Turkish culture. The fathers I spoke with were also aware of their lack of engagement with family affairs, and criticized themselves for not having been more involved with their children. However, these interviews also brought to my attention that the stories circulating about men's bad habits have a practical social basis. It is no secret that in Strasbourg that the generations born and raised in Europe are sexually active, and engage in premarital affairs. The fear of what they say does not suffice to curb sexual exploration. It instead pushes these activities to the backstage. Young men's sexual exploration in Strasbourg, while a taboo, is a "public secret" (Taussig 1999). Everyone knows that young men do it but no one wants to point fingers at each other or do something about it other than talk about it. Until, of course, the gossip turns into a scandal, such as a girl getting pregnant outside of wedlock or family breaking apart. As we tried to show in this brief paper, both in Amsterdam and Strasbourg, the fear of what they say does not simply change young Turkish men and women's patterns of sexual exploration. Instead, it forces them to come up with tactics to hide their private lives, and present a public face that would leave others with little lead that they would be the protagonists of the word on the street.

References

Abadan-Unat, N. ed. (1976). Turkish Workers in Europe 1960-1975: A Socio-economic Reappraisal. Leiden: Brill.

Abu-Lughod, L. (2002). Do Muslim Women Really Need Saving? Anthropological Reflections on Cultural Relativism and its Others. American Anthropologist 104(3):783-790.

Bowen, J. R. (2009). Can Islam Be French?: Pluralism and Pragmatism in a Secularist State. Princeton: Princeton University Press.

de Certeau, M. The Practice of Everyday Life. Trans. Steven F. Rendall. Berkeley: University of California Press.

de Tapia, S. (2009). Permanences et Mutations de l'immigration turque en France. Hommes et Migrations 1280: 8-20.

Fassmann, H. and A. İçduygu. (2013). Turks in Europe: Migration Flows, Migrant Stocks and Demographic Structure. European Review 21(3): 349-361.

Fernando, M. (2010). Reconfiguring Freedom: Muslim Piety and the Limits of Secular Law and Public Discourse in France. American Ethnologist 37(1): 19–35.

Gluckman, M. (1963). Papers in Honor of Melville J. Herskovits: Gossip and Scandal. Current Anthropology 4(3):307-316.

Goffman, E. (1967)[1955]. Interaction Ritual. Garden City: Anchor Books.

Kasinitz, P. J. H. Mollenkopf and M. Waters, eds. (2004). Becoming New Yorkers: Ethnographies of the New Second Generation. Russell Sage Foundation.

Levitt, P. and M. C. Waters, eds. 2002. The Changing Face of Home: The Transnational Lives of the Second Generation. Russell Sage Foundation.

Paine, R. (1967). What is Gossip About? An Alternate Hypothesis. Man: The Journal of the Royal Anthropological Institute 2:278-285.

Gilmore, D. (1978). Varieties of Gossip in a Spanish Rural Community. Ethnology 17(1):88-99.

Scott, J. W. (2007). The Politics of the Veil. Princeton: Princeton University Press.

Schnabel, Paul. 1990. Het verlies van de seksuele onschuld. Amsterdams Sociologisch Tijdschrift 17(2):11-50.

Taussig, M. (1999). Defacement: Public Secrecy and the Labor of the Negative. Stanford University Press.

The research of internal migration in Turkey in the context of social exclusion (Case of Manisa)

Ramazan Temel and Hülya Yesilyurt Temel

Introduction

Migration movements that have many causes and effects is as old as human history. Migration is defined as changing of place. Migrations are mandatory or voluntarily according to the causes of migration. Movements of migration can also be classified as internal migration and international migration into two groups. Migration movements' causes, effects and consequences are diffirent from each other.

Due to a multidimensional phenomenon, internal migration has emerged in the light of social, economic, political and cultural reasons. Because of these reasons, immigrants face new challenges. These are poverty, urban poverty, squating, individuals not able to find a job in labor market where they migrate and turning towards informal employment and social exclusion which is the main theme of this study.

The concept of social exclusion has been the subject of quite a high number and different identification efforts by scientists. Walker A. and Walker C. define social exclusion as a dynamic process that determines individuals' socialization and excludes them from social, economic, political and cultural system partially or completely. Similarly, Oppenheim expresses social exclusion as an alienation and exclusion including informal support network from social, economic, political and cultural life (Oppenheim 1998 posted by Coşkun and Tireli, 2008: 42).

Besides social exclusion as we stated as both cause and consequence to internal migration; the discussion of poverty, social, economic and political issues has an importance in the terms of prosperity of our country. Because of not been addressing the size of the exclusion of native citizens who migrated from counties and villages besides immigrants Manisa where is one of the agricultural and industrial cities in the Aegean Region from Eastern Anatolia Region and Southeastern Anatolia Region, Manisa has been chosen for fieldwork.

Classification of Migration

Migration is a phenomenon that has existed since the beginning of human history. The concept of migration is able to explain in different ways. Migration is the movement of population of the process of changing geographical location by economical, cultural, social and politic aspects (Koçak and Terzi, 2012:165).

Migration in Turkey comes in two forms. The flow of migration takes place in the form of either into the final settlement directly or step-by-step migration. In the first type of migration, people directly go to big cities or their final settements. In the second type of migration people approach big cities step by step by starting from closest or smallest cities and settle in(Öztürk and Altuntepe, 2012: 1599).

The classification of migration can be grouped under two main headings as internal migration and external migration. External migtaions are divided itself as brain drain, labor migration, exchange migration. Internal migrations are divided as seasonal migration, continuous migration, labor-manpower migration and mandatory-voluntary migration (Koçak and Terzi, 2012:169). In this work, internal migration will be focused on.

Internal Migration

Internal migration is changing of place within the country. It is people' moving from one region to another or from one city to another. In a country by internal migrations, there in no any change in population but only population ratio of regions or cities change. As the reasons of internal migration in Turkey, that workforce who remain out of production migrate to the big cities in order to obtain new livelihoods because of the industrilization in the process of capitalization since 1950's, the rapid agricultural mechanization, the degradation of land-population balance in the rural areas can be shown.

According to the detection of Şen (2011), internal migration is a movement of population occuring under the effect of attractive and push forces. Push factors are the one that guide the population away their residences or economic lives. Attractive factors are economic and social factors that pull individuals who are ready and enthusiastic about leaving their residences in the cities. It has been stated that income differences between village and city, the possibility of a better and advanced education, the charm of the city, hope of finding a job, higher standard of living, transportation facilities and better health conditions are other attractive factors for immigrants.

According to the results of the researchs conducted by ILO in the villages selected from foru different from four different regions of Turkey, attractive factors are listed as follows: employment request, having better living conditions, catching up with better living standards and the thought of preparing and leaving a better future generations and children (Akgür, 1997: 70).

Social Exclusion

The concept of social exclusion appeared in France in the 1970's. When the concept of social exclusion was thrown out in 1974 by Lenoir for the first time, it was not defined depending on economic causation, it was mentioned as a process of exclusion and that excluded members only in the context of reduction of social relations (Tartanoğlu, 2013).

International Labour Organization, in the research done in a large number of developing countries has expanded the concept of social exclusion in a way that will include both individuals and groups. Social exclusion in the terms of individuals deals with the human nature directly. Social exclusion from a societal perspective, on the other hand, is a feature in relation to institutional framework and a result of the institutional arrangements on applicable law in which individuals and groups fulfill their day labors to earn their lives (Sapancalı, 2003: 18)

Social exclusion which means to be deprive of certain economic and social rights and resources that will be enable to social integration was built o deprivations (Durusoy Öztepe and Ünlütürk Ulutaş; 2013:309)

One of the most important reasons of social exclusion is migrations. Migration poses an important risk of social exclusion in different form and extent for developed and developing countries. Because point of origin of social exclusion is migrations. In this context, it is useful to examine the phenomenon of migration in terms of social exclusion.

The necessary research has not been done on the number of immigrants, its spatial distribution, its concentration in the cities and in the name of producing any qualitative and quantative data. Because it has not been carried out efficient and extensive studies on legal, politic and economic spaces, the problems has increased (Sürüel, 2008: 50).These increases in this issue effected social exclusion by deepening poverty and unemployment at the same time.

Migration is a phenomenon that emerges as a result of starting to not to be enough facilities and employment opportunities in rural areas and by impoverishment and because of the presence of the city attractiveness (Güler, 2014: 73) Also, migration has brought with both positive and negative consequences depending on the time period and the place of migration for individuals. From the perspective of social exclusion, the negative aspect of the study is that confronting with many problems such as discrimination, xenophobia and racism is inevitable for immigrants.

Immigrants have been pushed into a sense of loneliness because of language, cultural and social differences in the countries they migrate. Still in some countries, immigrant employment is preferred by employees because it meets the needs of the labor market, reduces costs and doesn't create an element of oppression in wages (Karataşoğlu, 2014: 12)

The case of Manisa

Manisa has raised to an important position in industrial, agricultural and service sector so it is a developed and developing city in terms of labor market and employment. Manisa is a city that allows numerous immigrants from its counties, villages and other regions and keeps let immigrants. The most important reason is that Manisa is a industry and agriculture-centric city.

In Manisa, the unemployment rate is lower compared to across Turkey. Especially in Turkey the unemployment rate range over %9 but in Manisa the rate is %45. Unemployment rate is less in Manisa. Besides which, the average of labor force participation rate is %50 in Turkey whereas, it is more than that in Manisa. In this context, in Manisa employment rate is above the the average of Turkey. Considering these reasons, it can be said that Manisa is a city allowing immigrants.

This work addresses the problem of social exclusion that the world countries have continued to struggle until todayh by incorporating our country and that people who turn towards migration and internal migration were exposed. The population of work were constitued by immigrants migrated to Manisa which is located geographically among Turkey's special organized industry is intense because of internal migration and developed in socio-economic sense. At the same time, another aim of this work is to determine whether immigrants are exposed to economic, social, cultural and politic problems such as unemployment, poverty or not and in order to propose necessary solutions.

Data and Method

Immigrants who migrated to city center of Manisa from Eastern Anatolia Region and Southeastern Anatolia Region besides county and rural areas constitues the unit of analysis of the work. For research data collection, it was used semi-structured interview which is a goal-oriented interview technique. The findings by in-depth interviews in fieldwork has been enriched by observation technique. Interviews were held with 25 immigrants. It was interviewed withthe authorities from the office of the Governor of Manisa and Associations of Immigrants in order to clarify the reasons of migration and problem faced.

In this research, previous studies has been guiding. But there has been amportant factors like that immigrants are seen a marginalized group in society, not been able to live in dignity, deepening of poverty every day and especially examining in the context of social exclusion.

In the scope of reseach, it has been interviewed with Manisa branch-Turkish Statistical Institute, Manisa Governor, Population and Immigration Applicationand Research Center Institution which established within Celal Bayar University and employees of the association who are also immigrants. According to the information obtained from The Statistical Office of Turkey, there are one hundred forty thousand immigrants from Eastern Anatolia Region and Southeastern Anatolia Region in Manisa. It has been also identified numcrous immigrants from districts and villages with the low level of economy and minimum employment opportunities.

In fieldwork, it has been interviewed with 25 representatives of migration who stay in Manisa and live in different neighborhoods. Ten of immigrants are female and fifteen are male. The lower age limit is 24 of individuals whereas upper age limit is 56. Eight of interviewers are single, seventeen are married. The respondents' educational status are different as follows: seven interviewer are literate, eight of them are primary school graduate, seven of them are secondary school graduate and three of the interviewers are high school graduate. It has been identified that school graduates work in more efficient and more regular jobs whereas primary and secondary school graduates work in irregular and informal jobs. It has been seen that immigrants from Eastern Anatolia and Southeastern Anatolia Region have no job cannot continue to work.

Accordingly, individuals with these characteristics work in unqualified works. A large part of individuals whose social securities changes as SSK (Social Insurance Institution) and BAĞKUR (Social security organization for artisans and the self-employed) have been benefit from General Health Insurance called as Green Card (health for uninsured people in Turkey). Besides income status are irregular, it changes between one thousand and two thousand Turkish lira. It has been seen that in families from Eastern Anatolia Region and Southeastern Anatolia Region the number of households is more than the families from rural areas or another regions.

Findings

Immigrants from Eastern Anatolia Region and Southeastern Anatolia Region migrated with their families, acquaintances, fellow citizens. But it has generally been seen that immigrants from rural areas of Manisa migrated alone. As the reasons of migrations these can be seen important factors: cultural values of whereabouts, family bonds, financial gain provided by city, unemployment, education and convenience in access to health, limited social and cultural activities and the charm of metropolitan cities. In this context, there are many economic, social and politic(terror) in order to occur the phenomenon of migration.

In findings, it has been found out that immigrants mostly migrated relative and fellow citizen-oriented. It has been an important role on immigrants that relatives and fellow citizens already stay in the city and help or give recommendation about find abode and job. Otherwise, it has been identified that immigrants generally found job by social ways through their relatives, fellow citizens.

With reference to findings, the conditions of immigrants varies between before migration and after. After migration, it has been identifies the convenience in access to basic needs such as education, health and transportation, increase in the level of welfare and especially the socialization of young population. In this context after migration, immigrants state that their revenues have increased and consequently their social lives have changed. They say that they can easily benefit from hospitals, develope their professional knowledge by attending to training courses, improve their educational levels and increase to participate social activities. Most of immigrants have no desire to return to their hometown. In this decision, economic return in place they migrated, the impact of terrorism for immigrants from Eastern Anatolia Region and Southeastern Anatolia Region, lack of job opportunities and lack easy access to basic needs in hometowns have great role. Besides having no desire to return, they state that they used to live in places they migrated and cannot do it there anymore if they return.

In findings, that most of immigrants have relatives and fellow citizens in places migrated is an important factor. Immigrants explain that they get financial and moral support from their relatives and fellow citizens besides they continue their traditions.

Considering the extent of the exclusion of migration, the main reason is economic reasons. Being unemployed and low level of icome leads immigrants to the poverty and accordingly to exclusion. Lack of employment opportunities in the place of living, being deprived of income push immigrants to migrate and continuing these problems after migration deepens poverty of immigrants. Therefore some situations that social exclusion is inevitable show up.

As a consequence of interviewers, it has been seen that immigrants face different types of social exclusion. Immigrants from Eastern Anatolia Region and Southeastern Anatolia Region have been excluded for the reasons like ethnic, cultural and terror at first as well as economic and labor reasons. Immigrants from counties and rural areas have been excluded from labor in addition to consumption and social welfare services because of being unskilled and lack of professional qualifications.

Conclusion

Migration is a constant phenomenon that all societies experience. In addition to this, by this time changes have occured in the structure of migration. These changes emerges as particularly the economy of the society, socio-culturel and political.

Migration is a social movements that people do together or seperately from a bounded settlement to a settlement near or far. Internal migration is generally defined as people living in a certain area transports their places of residence to the outside of the settlement in question by their own volution within a certain time frame. Migrating voluntarily signals for another point. Beyond the obvious, the phenomenon of internal migration can also be caused by acts of god (population prssure, concealed unemployment, underunemployment, low productivity, agricultural mechanization, lack of economic activities out of season, natural disasters, blood vengeances, characteristics of agricultural land, climatic conditions, erosion etc.)

Social exclusion we discussed in the context of both cause and result of internal migration is one of the important measures that should be taken to ensure social order. We confront social exclusion as one of the inevitable problems to describe, analyze and its consequences. The increasing significance of social exclusion day by day is another conspicuous factor.

Factors that do not provide a life in dignity such as the economic crisis in the country, natural disasters, warsand unemployment pave the way to migration. This shows that migration is experienced not only within country but also between countries. In this context, the results of migration may warm the society just as it may be helpful for society.

The main reason of migration is economic-centric so the main aim of immigrants is to fnd a job. The definition of migration in terms of labor is removing of unemployment from places where is unable to create demand for the supply of labor to the cities. Accordingly, immigrants say that they are exposed to social exclusion in order to find a job because of being unskilled and uneducated in labor market. They also say they apply İŞKUR (Turkish Employment Agency) and vocational courses in the name of eliminating this obstruct. In order to minimize the exclusion or abolish completely, more vocational courses should be opened and raise the awareness of society.

Another factor that forces individuals to migrate is having to live in places where they continue to live below the poverty line. Immigrants migrated to the cities hoping to increase the quality of living. Interviewers utter that after migration they benefit from the opportunities of the city such as health, education, transportation and social activities compared to the past. Besides that, in the literature search it has been also determined that even a little there are some immigrants who have returned to their hometowns because of not fitting in. It has been discussed that immigrants have risk of facing with problems like discrimination, xenophobia and racism. In interviews, it has been seen that these problems have been solved widely and immigrants warm towards local people more quickly. In this, settling in places where relatives, acquaintances and friends live may be the most efficient factor. However, they indicate that they are exposed to the social exclusion when they look for job, their children study at schools, they go to hospitals for health problems whereas they have no any trouble in their residences.

Especially immigrants from Eastern Anatolia Region and Southeastern Anatolia Region are perceived as pro-terror, hostile. But received responses from immigrants do not support this judgement. They state that at first they are regarded as guilty but in time they know each other by spending time together and this attitude is out now, they even migrate because of terrorism.

Social exclusion in the terms of individuals, a continuous accumulation of not being able to meet their needs bring long term outcomes with it like loss of connection with the society, stress, anxiety, decreasing self-esteem (Sürüel, 2008:107). In the terms of society, social exclusion might be a threat for the future of society. Due to the poverty in society, the occurance of social explosions are inevitable in the case of increasing tentation and crime rate, state creating fear on citizens because of not being able to provide security, the loss of the effectiveness of social institutions and alienation.

After all, as a result of social exclusion immigrants face with many problems. In this context, Migration Governance General Directorate related to the Ministry of Interior should direct the works in order to resolve the problems that immigrants face when they migrate to the country besides the Works done in the context of " Foreigners and International Protection Law".

References

Akgür, Z. (1997). *Rural-urban migration in Turkey and Interregional Instability (1970-1993)*, Turkish Republic, Publication of Ministry of Culture, Ankara.

Coşkun, T., & Tireli, M. (2008). *Poverty Reduction Strategies in European Union and Turkey*, Nobel Publishing, Ankara.

Durusoy Öztepe, N., Ünlütürk Ulutaş, Ç. (2013). Exclusion From Welfare Services in Turkey as a Type of Social Exclusion, *International Conference On Eurasian Economies*, s:308-313.

Güler, M. A. (2014,Aralık). "New Social Movements in the Context of Social Exclusion: Samples of Greece, Arab Spring, United States of America and Spain", Unpublished master thesis, Gazi University Institute of Social Sciences, Ankara.

Karataşoğlu, S.(2014). Effect of the Level of Income to Social Exclusion Sample of Mardin Province, Unpublished Doctoral Thesis, Sakarya University Institute of Social Sciences, Sakarya.

Koçak, Y. Terzi, E.(2012)" The Phenomenon of Migration in Turkey, The Effects of Immigrants for the City and Solution Proposals", *Kafkas University Faculty of Economics and Administrative Sciences Magazine, 3/3*, 163-184.

Öztürk, M., Altuntepe, N.(2008). Immigrants' Compliance Status to Work Life and the City in Turkey", *Journal of Yaşar University,3*(11),1587-1625.

Sakınç, S. (2014,March)."Studying on Professional Competences of Employees and the Ones Will Be Employed in Manisa", *Zafer Development Agency*, Manisa, 1-122.

Sapancalı, F. (2003). *Social Exclusion*, Dokuz Eylül University Rectorate Press, İzmir.

Sezal, İ. (1992). Urbanization, Ağaç Publishing, İstanbul.

Sürüel, T.(2008). The Analysis of Relation of Migration and Social Exclusion In the Terms of Social Politics: Sample of İstanbul Sultanbeyli, Unpublished Master Thesis, Kocaeli University, Institute of Social Sciences, Kocaeli.

Şen, M. (2014)." Searching of Internal Migrations In the Terms of Causes and Effects", *Work and Society Magazine, 40/1*, 231-256.

Tartanoğlu, Ş. (2010). "Social Exclusion: An Effort of Conceptualism From the Globalization Perspective ", *İstanbul Uniersity Sociology Conferences, 42*, 1-13.

Turkish Statistical Institute .(2012). Regional Consequences of Research of Household Labor Force 2012.

Walker, A., Walker, C. (1997). *Britain Divided: The Growth of Social Exclusion in the 1980s and 1990s*, Michigan University, Child Action Poverty Group, London.

Analysing Turkish Labour Migration to Europe via SWOT and STEEPLE

Hasan Akca[167]

Introduction

Turkish community living abroad amounts to more than 5 million people, around 4 million of which live in Western European countries, 300 thousand in North America, 200 thousand in the Middle East and 150 thousand in Australia (MFA, 2015). The common goal of first wave of Turkish "guest workers" was to collect capital to start a small business in Turkey. Most of the guest workers left their families behind in Turkey.

Bilateral agreements related to labor are as follows: Turkey-Germany Work Force Treaty (20 May 1964), Turkey-Austria Work Force Treaty (15 May 1964), Turkey- Belgium Work Force Treaty (16 July 1964), Turkey-Netherlands Work Force Treaty (19 August 1964), Turkey- France Work Force Treaty (8 April, 1965), Turkey-Sweden Work Force Treaty (10 March, 1967), Turkey- Australia Work Force Treaty (5 October, 1967), Turkey- Libya Work Force Treaty (5 January 1975), Turkey-Jordan Work Force Treaty (8 July 1982), Turkey-Turkish Republic of Northern Cyprus Work Force Treaty (9 March 1987), Turkey-Qatar Work Force Treaty (1 April 1986) (URL1). From 1974 onwards, Turkish labour force changed its destination towards North Africa, Middle East and Gulf countries. After collapse of Soviet Union, direction of Turkish labour force was changed towards Russian Federation and Central Asian Countries.

Geographical location would make the EU face the possibility of several economic and non-economic system shocks. One of the possible scenarios might represent massive migration inflows of labour from turkey to the EU (Strielkowski, Glazar & Duchac, 2014, p. 93).

According to Erzan, Kuzubaş & Yildiz (2014, p. 92) a successful accession period with high growth reduces and gradually eliminates the migration pressures. However, lower growth and higher unemployment associated with a suspension in Turkey's accession process might lead to more immigrants than a successful membership.

In the second half of 20th century, Turkey experienced substantial emigration flows. The 1960s and first half the 1970s presented the period of massive labour migration where Western Europe became the main destination for the Turkish migrants. This period was followed by a different type of migration characterized by the family reunifications, marriages migrations, politically motivated migrations, and migrations of illegal labourers (Akgunduz, 1993; Strielkowski, Glazar & Duchac, 2014, p. 96).

Historically, until 2004 Germany presented by far the most favourite destination for Turkish migrants. Most of the Turkish migrants lost their interest in Europe after the first wave of migration (from 1960s until the mid-1970s

[167] Hasan Akca is Professor in Economics Department, Faculty of Economics and Administrative Sciences, Cankiri Karatekin University, Cankiri, 18100, Turkey. E-mail: hasanakca@karatekin.edu.tr.

(Strielkowski, Glazar & Duchac, 2014, p. 102). There is visible decline in Turkish immigration to Germany at the brink of the 1980s. Since then, the Turkish migration remained low and stable (Strielkowski, Glazar & Duchac, 2014, p. 104).

Material and methods

Secondary data were used in the study. Data were obtained from TUIK, scientific articles, reports of Ministry of Foreign Affairs, etc.

In the first stage SWOT Analysis was used. The acronym SWOT stands for Strengths, Weaknesses, Opportunities, and Threats (Team FME, 2013, p. 8). It can be used as a brainstorming tool or to help focus your attention on key areas (Team FME, 2013, p. 29). STEEPLE analysis studies 7 dimensions of the investigated subject. It is an acronym which stands for Socio cultural, Technological, Economical, Education, Political, Legal, and European factors. Both techniques take a photo of Turkish labour migration to Europe from different aspects.

Research findings: Steeple analysis

According to 2009 Global Human Development Report, many people migrate from their hometown to other regions for survival or better life opportunities (Kandemir, 2012). Reasons why people migrate are not only economic (income and employment) but also better education and health facilities (Issah, Khan & Sasaki, 2005), security, etc (Table 1).

Turkish emigration to Western Europe dates back to the economic boom of the 1950s and resulting high demand for manual labour in Western European receiving countries. Signing of labour agreements was seen as an opportunity by Turkish government to decrease unemployment rate and develop Turkish economy via emigrant remittances (İcduygu & Sert, 2009: 2). Turkish authorities hoped that 'guest workers' would come back to Turkey with new skills and help transform its agricultural economy into an industrial one but majority of them settled in western countries and brought their families to live with them (İcduygu & Sert, 2009: 2-3). Turkish labour migration to Western Europe peaked in the late 1960s and early 1970s, and lost momentum with the economic decline that followed the 1973 oil crisis, and especially with Germany's decision to end its guest worker program. In the following era, emigration from Turkey to Western Europe instead took place via family reunification and marriage, and later, also asylum-seeking (İcduygu & Sert, 2009: 3).

Table 1: Highlights of STEEPLE Analysis

Socio-cultural factors	Migrating for survival or better life opportunities.
	Europe's demographic situation: low fertility and longevity.
Technological factors	Turkish labours have worked low tech jobs.
	"Guest workers" would return to Turkey with new skills.
Economic factors	Hope to find better job and have high income.
	They will help reorientation of the Turkish economy.

Educational factors	Better education facilities in Europe. In France only 11% of men and 3 percent of women of Turkish origin receive a university diploma. 26,5% percent of people of Turkish origin between the ages of 18 and 35 have no diploma at all. In Germany 21% of people of Turkish origin do not hold any diploma.
Political factors	Dual citizenship
Legal factors	Bilateral Labour Migration Agreement between Turkey and European countries EU Schengen visa system.
European factors	Being a full member to the EU and free movement of the labour.

For first wave Turkish migrants in European countries, educating their children was not the first priority. Their main aim was working of their children. In Germany 21% of people of Turkish origin do not hold any diploma, while for immigrants in general the percentage is 10,5. In France, only 11% of men and 3% of women of Turkish origin receive a university diploma and only one-fourth Turkish people between the ages of 18 and 35 have no diploma at all. However, the education levels of third-generation Chinese, Algerians, Senegalese and Malians are no different from those of the French population at large. Throughout Europe there are 144 thousand business owners of Turkish origin (URL2) (Table 1).

SWOT Analysis

Table 2: SWOT Analysis

Strengths	Weaknesses
* Signing bilateral labour agreements between Turkey and EU countries. * Establishment of SMEs by Turkish entrepreneurs in the EU * Economic boom of the 1950s, high demand for manual labour in European countries.	* Decreasing of population in European countries. * End of the guest worker program following the 1973 oil crisis. * Failure to benefit from the migration flows following the EU enlargement in 2004 and 2007. *Main characteristics of first migrant labours: village-born, having limited formal education.
Opportunities	Threats
* Location of Turkey at the crossroads of three continents: Asia, Europe and Africa. * Need for skilled-young labour in the EU in the future	* Threat of global terrorism (in the post September 11 period) * Illegal labour migration from Asian and African countries to Western countries over Turkey.

* In the 21st century, decreasing native work force in the EU (-44 million until 2050), but continuing growth of potentially active population in Turkey (+16 million until 2050).	* Stop of democracy in 1970 and 1980 in Turkey and political pressure to citizens * Increasing unemployment rate in the EU

The threat of global terrorism and its implications in the post 9/11 period posed new security challenges on the management of both irregular and regular migration. Accordingly, since the EU has become more actively involved in regulating migration in Europe, the issues of control-based, securitised migration policies have come under scrutiny for having been developed at the expense of a rights-based approach (Memişoğlu, 2014: 4) (Table 2). The commonly accepted view that Turkish immigrants who are already in Europe face integration difficulties, together with intensifying Islam phobia on the continent, have mad Turkey related migration issues a topic of critical debate in European circles (Kaya & Kentel, 2005).

Migration entails a number of risks for both the receiving and sending countries. Potential difficulties for receiving countries include compliance problems, including illegal visa overstays. For the sending country, outmigration can induce severe labour shortages and worsen poverty (Zimmermann, 2014: 3) (Table 1 and 2).

Throughout the 21st century, Western and Central Europe will be confronted with a rapidly decreasing native work force (-44 million until 2050) while potentially active population will continue to grow in Turkey (+16 million until 2050) (Table 2).

Conclusion

Important outcomes were derived from the results of the STEEPLE and SWOT analysis of labour force movement from Turkey to EU countries over 50 year period. These were summarised in the following paragraphs.

Turkey is located at the crossroads of three continents: Asia, Europe and Africa. This geographic position have shoulder important responsibility (i.e. preventing illegal labour movement) to Turkey due to being a bridge between the politically and economically unstable East and the prosperous West.

Main purpose of bilateral labour agreements was to find job for unemployed Turkish people and contribute to economies of European countries. Over the 50 year period of time, it can be said that the Turkish community has contributed to economic life and also political, social, cultural aspects of host countries not only as blue-collar labour force but also as professionals (academicians, doctors, journalists, lawyers, engineers, artisans, politicians, sports, etc.), traders, and representatives of NGOs.

In recent years, retired EU member-state citizens have been settled in Mediterranean costs of Turkey (especially Alanya-Antalya). Professionals have preferred Istanbul as settlement area. It is estimated that their numbers are about more than 100 thousand.

Some EU citizens afraid that if Turkey joined to the EU as full member a huge Turkish labour force would move to the EU countries but this afraid is not realistic because economically and politically strong Turkey is a chance for western Europe. Because low fertility, increasing life expectancy, and decreasing native population year by year can be main obstacles for EU economies in the future. Therefore, they need for skilled unemployed Turkish people in order to continue economic development.

References

Akgunduz, A. (1993). Labour migration from Turkey to Western Europe (1960-1974). *Capital & Class, 51*, 153-194.

Erzan, R., Kuzubaş, U., & Yıldız, N. (2006). Immigration scenarios: Turkey–EU. *Turkish Studies, 7*(1), 33–44.

İçduygu, A., & Sert, D. (2009). Country Profile: Turkey. Focus Migration, No: 5.

Ircah, I., Khan, T.Y., & Saoahi, K. (2005). Do migrants react to infrastructure difference between urban and rural areas? Development of an extended Harris-Todaro model. RURDS, 17(1), 68-88.

Kandemir, O. (2012). Human Development and International Migration. Procedia Social and Behavioral Sciences. 62(2012): 446-451.

Kaya, A., & Kentel, F. (2005). Euro-Turks: A Bridge or a breach between Turkey and European Union?: A comparative study of German-Turks and French-Turks. Centre for European Policy Studies: Brussels.

Memişoğlu, F. (2014). Management of Irregular Migration in the context of EU-Turkey Relations. TESEV Foreign Policy Programme, Istanbul.

MFA (2015). Turkish Citizens Living Abroad. Republic of Turkey, Ministry of Foreign Affairs.

Strielkowski, W., Glazar, O., & Duchac, T. (2014). Economic implications of Turkish migration in Europe: Lessons learned from Polish EU accession. Journal of Economic Cooperation and Development, 35(2), 91-120.

Team FME (2013). SWOT Analysis: Strategy Skills. www.free-management-ebooks.com.

URL1. Received from http://www.csgb.gov.tr/csgbPortal/diyih.portal?page=yv&id=2 available on: 23.04.2013.

URL2. European Turks: 50 years of labor migration from Turkey. Today's Zaman.

Zimmermann, K.F. (2014). Circular migration. IZA World of Labor. Received from http://wol.iza.org/articles/circular-migration.

Turkey's Immigration Reality and Evaluation of Labor Markets

Gülşen Sarı Gerşil[168]

Introduction

Considering the social and economic dimensions of migration, it is fact that both individuals who immigrated and community which is immigrated effect bilaterally from different perspectives. Migration describing as a demographic process in the sense of settlement changes between geographic region and / or the administrative areas, can also be described as population movements occurring with reasons such as economic, social, cultural, political, religious, natural disasters and so on. In other words, migration means that with better life expectancy individuals and communities leave theirs habitats and temporarily or permanently decide to go to new residential areas (Pazarlıoğlu, 2005:121).

Turkey has testified to internal migration with the process of industrialization and urbanization since 1950s. With rural population growth, agricultural mechanization, fragmentation of available land by inheritance, a large audience in rural areas do not get along either unemployed, migration has gained pace (Yenigül, 2004:273). Rural to urban migration rises its density with the transition from industry to the service sector and it has entered into a significant period in terms of economic development.

In light of this disclosure, considering social-economic and social consequences of internal migration, evaluating in terms of labor markets, unemployment and employment, it is inevitable to encounter some structural results. At this point, the part who are no experience working outside of the agriculture sector and have low levels of education sector, have forced to work in marginalized sectors or led to an increase in urban unemployment rate because of not being able to adapt to rapid advances in technology (Tatlıdil and Xantahco, 2002:8).

Migration and its types and causes

International migration, labor migration, overseas workers' remittances, international irregular migration, transit migration, lifestyle migration, environmental migration, human trafficking and smuggling, forced migration, forced human migration involve different issues such as the protection of refugees and asylum seekers. Each of these migration issues, as real, are shaped by articulation of local / national / regional and the global level (Toksöz, Erdoğdu, Kaşka; 2012:11).

The core of the migration movements is labor migration; due to the presence of global economic inequalities labor supply and demand are not only within national borders but also are determined beyond national borders. Migration in

---

[168] Gülşen Sarı Gerşil is Assistant Professor of Labor Economics and Industrial Relations Department, Faculty of Economics and Administrative Sciences, Celal Bayar University, Uncubozköy, Manisa, Turkey. E- mail: gulsen.gersil@cbu.edu.tr

the age of globalization is geographically widespread and the majority of the world countries take their places in the process of migration as destination countries, origin countries, transit countries, or all at the same time. With there is need for both skilled and unskilled labor, while orderly migration of highly skilled labor force has been promoting by governments, trying to prevent the migration of low-skilled labor has been effective in increasing irregular migration. Irregular migration is not only for developed countries, it is mainly prevalent in developing regions. It is estimated that there are 20-30 million irregular migrants worldwide. The reasons of this are the immigration policies of destination countries with strict regulations, increased migration pressures in the source countries, difficulties in the control of migration and the increase in the activities of criminal organizations engaged in smuggling of migrants (de Haas 2008, Bommes, Sciortino, 2011; Castles vd. 2012; OECD, 2012).

Another economic-based reason for migration is income distribution and hunger and poverty growing as paralel to it. Accordingly, disturbances in the distribution of income is one of the reasons for migration. Because of the injustice in income distribution, going to the town of remaining unemployed in villages; going to city on the grounds that not finding work in town; migration to big cities if not found work there; if there is no business, ultimately it has been faced with the emigration (Zaim, 2006: 328). In other words, due to the resulting income distribution imbalance, owing to the fact that individuals individuals learn opportunities elsewhere and want to take advantage of them, migration occurs (Tekeli, 1998:12).

In recent years, most of the population growth in many OECD countries – and a significant portion of those of working age population – come true as a result of international migration. If immigration rates continue at current levels working-age population in OECD countries, compared to the increase of 8.6% in the years between 2000-2010, has been forecasted to increase at the rate of 1.9% in the years between 2010-2020. While the immigrants form about one third of new recruits in the working age population, the arrival of children and older immigrants reduce this ratio. Only in France, the US and New Zealand, the main driving force of the population growth is natural increase, too. In some countries - in southern Europe, Austria and the Czech Republic - about 90% of population increase occurs in result of migration (SOPEMI, 2010).

Problems brought together by the immigration

According to the ILO a migrant worker in an irregular status; is a person who does not have valid authorization as required by law for entering, staying and employment in country where one lives or a person who cannot comply with the conditions governing the entry, stay and employment (ILO, 2005:96). At the beginning of the problems caused by irregular migration is from the vulnerability against violations of fundamental human and labor rights of migrant worker. Migrant workers have no social protection and faces with problems such as substandard wages and unpaid wages due to threats of deportation or the phenomenon. There are no facility to organize and seek right.

The ILO has noted that irregular migration is a management issue in terms of both sending and receiving countries. The growth of irregular migration makes it more profitable illegal activity, displaces of unskilled local labor, worsens working conditions by undermining collective bargaining, creates tension in society and leads to the growth of the economy's informal sectors. It creates problems in terms of sending country such as the exploitation and abuse of the citizens. Therefore, the states of the source and destination countries should make arrangements enabling regular migration, preventing irregular migration (ILO, 2005: 98).

Migrants are employed in labor-intensive and low-wage sectors, in manufacturing, particularly leather, including confection and food etc., construction, agriculture, tourism, entertainment and prostitution industries and in the home care services. In the fields of employment except for the construction sector would be assumed that the numbers of women are more than men. The relative height of the immigrants' education levels and work discipline, working without any problem in terms of their employers, the lack of any legal rights, and no agenda to avoid unionization makes them attractive to employers. But in the conditions which domestic labor will not accept: as uninsured, with long working hours without overtime pay more, because they can get run as deprived paying annual leave and other social rights, labor costs are lower and the domestic labor is preferred (Toksöz, Erdoğdu, Kaşka; 2012: 23).

Internal migration movements in Turkey

Explaining internal migration movements in Turkey only with the industrialization process is not possible. Internal migration speed is a population movement occurred under the influence of the repellent and attractive factors. Repellent factors pluck rather people from village and agriculture and pushes out of the village. Attractive factors are economic and social factors which pull those of being ready and willing to leave the villages to cities (Serter, 1994:79).

While internal migration movement beginning in 1950s and speeding up was defined as rather gaining momentum in the country's transformation in rural areas, in a sense "its repellency", then until at the end of 1960s, 1970s and at the beginning of 1980s it would define as rather the determination of the transformation in urban areas, in a sense "its appeal" (İçduygu ve Sirkeci, 1999:250).

There are economic, social, cultural, geographically demographic and political reasons between the main results of the internal migration movement in Turkey. However, the vast majority of people in Turkey tend to migrate for economic reasons. Hence, it has been seen that imbalances income in the local or personal dimension of migration are main reasons for internal migration (Yamak ve Yamak, 1999: 23-24). In the internal migration movements of the 1980s and the 1990s, the impact of negative developments because of terrorism has been an important driving factor besides the economic and political crisis. Another factor related to the social structure is about education. Still many villages in Turkey is experiencing a shortage of school. For this reason, it is observed that children wanting to study due to education migrate to the cities with their families. Another one family reasons can cause migrations with the scope of economic, political and cultural framework. Due to these feature migrations stemming from family reasons can be described as "the migration to legitimate movement" (Taşçı, 2009:190).

The nature events experienced in the countries can be addressed within the scope of the social structure. In this respect, natural phenomena such as earthquakes, floods, volcanic eruptions, erosion, desertification and drought are among the factors that cause migration.

Turkey and dimension of international migration

According to figures in the first five months of 2014 in some of the countries that accepted the most refugees, it has been a large increase in asylum seekers compared to the same period of the previous year. This was basically due to the clashes in Syria in 2011. While Germany adopted Fifty Three Thousand asylum seekers, 20 percent of them came from Syria. Second The US adopted Thirty Thousand Five Hundred Sixty asylum seekers besides France with Twenty Two Thousand Four Hundred, Sweden with Twenty Three Thousand Eighty Hundred, and Turkey also adopted Nineteen Thousand Thirty Hundred asylum seekers (OECD,2014).

In OECD countries in 2013 Five Hundred Fifty Six Thousand people applied for asylum. This is an increase of 20 percent compared to the previous year. The reason for the increase is due to immigration from the ongoing war in Syria. With Forty Seven Thousand Eight Hundred asylum applications from Syria, it has passed Afghanistan (Thirty Four Thousand Five Hundred applicants). With Russia, Iraq, Afghanistan, Serbia and Kosovo refugee applications have increased dramatically. Status of each application is currently reached Thirty Five-Forty thousand. Germany alone emerged as the country accepting the world's highest number of asylum applications field in 2013, the main countries of origin of application refugees to Germany are Russian Federation, Syria, Serbia and Kosovo. The United States, France, Sweden and Turkey following Germany received a large amount of asylum applications. The numbers of asylum seekers to Turkey have significantly risen due to coming from Iraq, Afghanistan, and Iran (OECD, 2014).

The number of international students increased significantly in Netherlands, Portugal and Turkey in 2012. Turkey attracts many foreigners with increased numbers in recent years. Foreign population in the last three years has increased Ninety Thousand. While in 2010, there were One Hundred Seventy Seven Thousand foreigners living on leave, the figure rose to Two Hundred Seventeen Thousand in 2011, to Two Hundred Sixty Seven Thousand Three Hundred in 2012. As the majority of permits were family reunification, a small portion was given in the form of a work permit. However, work-related permits are increasing. In 2012 the Turkish authorities issued Thirty Two Thousand Two Hundred Fifty work permits, this figure has showed the increase of 48% compared to the previous year. The number of residence permits issued is Thirty Two Thousand Eight Hundred Fifty and these are permissions granted for the first time. It has risen of 30% to the previous year. In 2013, the number of work permits issued was recorded as Forty Five Thousand Eight Hundred Fifty with the increase of 42% (OECD,2014).

The number of workers sent out by the Agency rose from Fifty Three Thousand Eight Hundred to Sixty Seven Thousand people between 2011-2012. But, in 2013 it fell to Fifty Five

Thousand Four Hundred. The majority of the Turkish contract workers has respectively worked in Iraq and in the Russian Federation (OECD, 2014).

Immigration and employment in Turkey

According to United Nations High Commissioner for Refugees (UNHCR), with 45 thousand applications in 2013, while Turkey is in the fifteenth queue among industrialized countries receiving individual asylum applications in the world in 2010, rose to fifth queue as increased suddenly ten queue (UNHCR, 2013:12). This picture has changed dramatically since April 2011. After 3 years from the date the country has become to host more than totally Nine Hundred Thousand Syrians, including about Two Hundred Twenty thousand of them in the refugee camps and about Seven Hundred thousand of them outside the camps. These figures reported by both the Turkish government and also UNHCR are thought to be "cautious data" (UNHCR,2014).

Although Syrians outside the camps spread all over the country, the vast majority of them concentrate in five provinces near the border with Syria that could be listed as Hatay, Kilis, Gaziantep, Sanliurfa and Mardin. Major cities in the western regions of Turkey such as Ankara, Izmir, Antalya, Istanbul, Konya and Mersin are among attractive residential areas for refugees. Unregistered number of Syrian refugees in Istanbul has exceeded Three Hundred Thousand (Yılmaz, 2014).

Graph 1. Registered Refugees and Total Estimated Figures in Turkey (2012-2014)

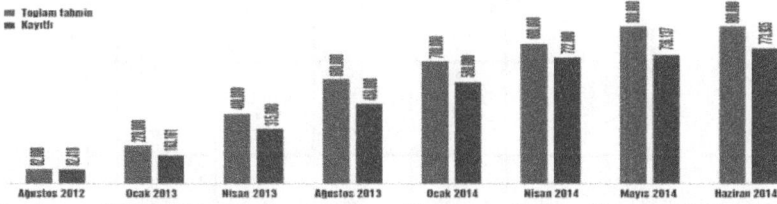

Source; "UNHCR Turkey Syrian Refugee Daily Sitrep 08.05.2014", http://reliefweb.int/report/turkey/unhcr-turkey-syrianrefugee-daily-sitrep-08-may-2014

Table 1: Distributions of reasons by years of residence in Turkey (*Source; TÜİK (2013).*)

	1Family Reunion	Research	Working	Other	Training-Education	Asylum	Short-term	Long-term	Total
2005	24.518	988	14.076	7.096	21.357	3.309	26.241	21.206	118.794
2006	28.728	1.095	12.704	7.636	23.314	3.383	26.706	34.898	138.464
2007	34.659	1.128	15.215	3.840	24.116	4.230	28.943	39.289	151.420
2008	43.122	1.222	19.093	3.767	27.327	8.623	29.495	33.555	166.204
2009	47.794	1.461	24.060	3.389	29.597	9.356	29.781	37.059	182.497
2010	52.186	1.437	26.616	3.709	34.418	9.049	21.243	33.520	182.178
2011	62.463	1.390	29.861	3.409	44.288	15.805	36.089	41.102	234.407
2012	61.963	1.553	42.238	14.381	57.567	20.890	80.442	43.180	322.214
2013	76.185	613	44.307	2.584	50.682	11.754	70.939	59.174	313.692

The Causes of migration to Turkey

Table 1 shows between the years 2005-2013 the distribution of the foreigners legally residing in Turkey for various reasons. When examined this chart, the attracting attention is the significant increase in the number of people receiving residence permits between 2011 and 2012. In order to obtain work permits of foreigners with the amendment of Law No. 5683 as the source of this increase must first apply for a residence permit within one month of entry in Turkey. Thanks to it, it is estimated that a lot of women working in foreign and domestic services apply for a work permit after taking the residence permit. Likewise, the number of residence permit in the area has increased at the rate of 44% compared to the previous year. This development is seen as a significant increase in the stock of legal immigrants in Turkey in recent years.

Work Permits of Foreigners Act No. 4817 regulating to participate in the labor markets of regular immigrants with a residence permit within the legal framework was enacted in 2003. The vast majority of immigrants working in the framework of this law are in position as technicians, craftsmen, workers and managers working in foreign organizations and institutions partnership operating in Turkey and their level of education is high (ÇSGB, 2011). The numerical rates of immigrants in this set is not affected the labor market, too. They have about two thousands of total nonfarm employment (TÜİK, 2013).

The first and second generation immigrants are playing an increasing role in the workforce. In addition to Western Europe, immigrants caused by the settlement of immigrants in countries like Australia, Canada, New Zealand and the United States are well rooted. It is considered an important political goal that in many OECD countries at least 15 years migrants and their families integrate with countries they settled. A range of policy approaches can help it to be implemented: Better dissemination of information on foreign diplomats and ensuring recognition of these diplomas, For immigrants, ensuring access of active labor market programs and benefit from them, Ensuring that immigrants get into more direct contact with employers, The provision of high quality early childhood care and education to immigrant children; and the provision of language training adapted to the skills of immigrants.

Results

Considering the different practices in the country, it has been observed that the process of legalization programs are on two different logic: 1) Humanistic; the legalization on rights-based reasoning are final goals and are organized to address the grievances immigrants arising from policy implementation in order to overcome deported. For example, the grievances may stem from the country's asylum system / policy 2) Non-rights-based, functioning regulatory purposes and labor market-oriented logic; the main goals of programs oriented labor markets functioning the regulatory logic are to obviate the unregistered employment under the irregular immigration and informal economy, to provide the fulfilment tax and social security obligations, such as to protect the social rights and workers' rights and to reach broader target. To sum up, the purpose is to solve social problems and grievances posed by unregistered employment with the increased irregular migration (Regıne 2009).

Examining the terms of employment of the sector is to provide information about the development of the country. While the share of agriculture in developed countries is low, the share of industry follows by a high course. Employment in the agricultural sector in Turkey is of still high rates. Enough increase in industry sector cannot be ensured. For this reason, service sector employment has increased more than expected and reached 50s% (Özpınar, Demir, Keskin, 2011:138).

The structure of employment in Turkey has undergone a significant change in the last 10 years. The transformation process is a natural reflection of three sectors law of Clark and is a transitional rather belatedly actually experienced in our country in this respect. On the one hand structural change simultaneously has supported urbanization, accordingly, on the other hand manufacturing and service sectors have been growing based in the city. In this case, both the role of rural areas the driving variables created by the contraction of the economic attractiveness(such as lack of agricultural productivity) and the attractive factors of urban areas created by the better working and living conditions are quite evident. In particular, it is clear that the structural stabilization program enacted in 2001 is an important factor in accelerating the transition of the sector (Karagöl ve Akgeyik, 2010:3).

Irregular migrants in Turkey are finding businesses through social networks or unauthorized agents. Private employment agencies mediating migrant workers to the businesses are not available. However, because of the fact that such offices are of high risk of abuse immigrants, it is known that public institutions in the source countries about settling to works help migrant workers. ILO Convention No. 97 stipulates that migrant workers free benefit from public employment services. İŞKUR (Turkey Business Organization) can provide employment opportunities to migrant workers and to establish an information system for regular work on legislation by cooperating with public employment offices of origin countries information pertaining and regular work.

References

ÇSGB (2011), received from: http://www.csgb.gov.tr/csgbPortal/ShowProperty
/WLP%20Repository/csgb/dosyalar/istatistikler/yabanciizin_2011, available on 10.05.2015
De Haas H.(2008) Irregular Migration from West Africa to the Magreph and the European Union, IOM.
Içduygu, A., & Sirkeci, I., (1999) "Cumhuriyet Dönemi Türkiye'sinde Göç Hareketleri", (ed.) Oya Baydar, 75 Yılda Köylerden Şehirlere, İstanbul: Tarih Vakfı Yayınları, 249-260 International Migration Outlook: SOPEMI (2010) –
Kirisci, K. (2014) Misafirliğin Ötesine Geçerken: Türkiye'nin "Suriyeli Mülteciler" Sınavı; Brookıngs Enstitüsü & Uluslararası Stratejik Araştırmalar Kurumu (USAK); ANKARA, http://madde14.org/images/4/43/USAKSuriyeKirisci2014.pdf12.05.2015
OECD(2014), International Migration Outlook Report, http://www.oecd.org/migration/international-migration-outlook-1999124x.htm20.04.2015
Pazarlıoglu, M. V. (2005), "İzmir Örneğinde İç Göç'ün Ekonometrik Analizi", Yönetim ve Ekonomi, Cilt 14, Sayı. 1.
Yenigül, S., B.(2004), "Göçün Kent Mekânı Üzerine Etkileri", G.Ü. Fen Bilimleri Dergisi, 18 (2), 2004:274

ILO (2005), Labor Migration Policy and Management –Training Modules. International Labor Office, Bangkok.

UNHCR Asylum Trends 2013: Levels and Trends in Industrialized Countries, pp.12, http://www.unhcr.org/5329b15a9.html 12.04.2015

UNHCR Turkey Syrian Refugee Daily Sitrep", BMMYK, 8 Mayıs 2014, http://reliefweb.int/report/turkey/unhcrturkey-syrian-refugee-daily-sitrep-08-may-2014

Karagol T., E., & Akgeyik T.,(2010) Türkiye'de İstihdam Durumu: Genel Eğilimler, SETA Analiz Dergisi, 21:4-27.

Ozpinar, S., Demir, O., & Keskin, S.,(2011), Türkiye'de İstihdamın Yapısının Değerlendirilmesi (2000-2010), Sosyal ve Beşeri Bilimler Dergisi, 3(2), 133,142.

Serter, N. (1994) Türkiye'nin Sosyal Yapısı, İstanbul: Filiz Kitabevi

Sen, M.(2014/1), Türkiye'de İç Göçlerin Neden ve Sonuç Kapsamında İncelenmesi, Çalışma ve Toplum,

Tekeli, I.(1998),"Türkiye'de İçgöç Sorunsalı Yeniden Tanımlanma Aşamasına Geldi", Konferans: Türkiye'de İçgöç; 6-8, Haziran 1997, İstanbul, Tarih Vakfı Yayınları, Ocak, pp.7-21.

Tasci, F.(2009) "Bir Sosyal Politika Sorunu Olarak Göç", Kamu-İş: İş Hukuku ve İktisat Dergisi, 10 (4), 177-205

Tatlıdil, E., & Xantahcou, Y.(2002), " Türk İşgücünün Yapısı ve Avrupa Birliği İstihdam Politikaları", Ege Akademik Bakış Dergisi, Cilt 2, Sayı 2

Toksoz,G.,Erdogdu,S.,& Kaşka, S.,(2012); Türkiye'ye Düzensiz Emek Göçü Ve Göçmenlerin İşgücü Piyasasındaki Durumları; IOM International Organization for Migration; İsveç Uluslararası Kalkınma ve İşbirliği Ajansı; SWEDEN.

Yamak, R. & Yamak N. "Türkiye'de Gelir Dağılımı ve İç Göç", Dokuz Eylül Üniversitesi Sosyal Bilimler Enstitüsü Dergisi, Cilt: 1, Sayı: 1, pp. 16-28

Yılmaz, H.(2013), Türkiye'de Suriyeli Mülteciler: İstanbul Örneği/Tespitler, İhtiyaçlar ve Öneriler, Mazlum-Der, 12 Eylül

Zaim, S. (2005), "IV. Oturum Değerlendirmesi: Türkiye'den Göçler," Uluslararası Göç Sempozyumu Bildiriler; 8-11 Aralık 2005, İstanbul, Zeytinburnu Belediyesi, pp. 327-330.

The Social Life of Remittance Houses: Scenes from Rural Kayseri

Oğuz Alyanak[169]

Hayra yorulmaz gurbetin düşü	The dream of *gurbet*[170], what good does it bring
Bitti tükendi Avrupa işi	Now that the Europe affair is complete
Koca koca evlerde hep iki kişi	In these big houses live only two
Aileleri parçaladı şu gurbet.	This *gurbet* has broken families apart
Gelip gide kaldım arada	Back and forth I am stuck in between
Hevesim kalmadı mülkte parada	Estate or money, I no longer have desire in
Gitmeyeceğim de yavrularım orada	I will not go back but my kids are over there
Aileleri parçaladı şu gurbet.	This *gurbet* has broken families apart

> Hamit Köşker, one of the first gastarbeiter in Germany, recited this poem to the author in Köşker's residence in Hayriye Mahallesi/Özvatan, Kayseri

It has been three years that the local *imam* of Karakaya [Black Rock] was assigned to this highland village of Kayseri by the Diyanet, Turkey's Directorate of Religious Affairs. What brought him to Kayseri in the first place was his graduate studies in the faculty of theology at Erciyes University. Himself a native of Adana, a Mediterranean city that is only a few hours driving away, coming to Kayseri was not a game changer. In the past three decades, Kayseri, a city that was once the hub of out-migration, has become a city in-migration that attracted population from the neighboring Central Anatolian cities. What he did not digest easily was his appointment to Karakaya, a village with two mosques and a barely any congregation to fill one. As one of Kayseri's main villages of outmigration, the village was empty for the majority of the year. In this village which was populated for the most part with the elderly and the retired, the imam argued that he would have a hard time gathering a congregation (*cemaat*) during the winter. Waking up at daybreak and battling his way through knee-high snow to recite the call to prayer in winter was not something he was used to back in his Mediterranean town. Moreover, serving to a non-existent congregation at this seemingly ghost town touched his nerves. The emptiness of the streets, and the presence of vacated houses was not something that he was familiar with.

The summers, however, were different. As the month of Ramadan came to an end, migrants from cities across Turkey and Europe—Kayseri, Izmir, Istanbul, Strasbourg, Munich, and Vienna, among others—returned back to the homeland for summer festivities. Around late June/early July, for a period of one month, the mosque would fill up to its full capacity once again. As the imam recalled,

---

[169] Oğuz Alyanak is currently a McDonnell International Scholars Academy scholar at Washington University and is pursuing his doctorate in sociocultural anthropology.

[170] The term, "gurbet" does not have a perfect one-word translation to English. It can best be translated as the experiential state of living in a foreign land/away from one's homeland. The poet requested his real name to be displayed next to this poem and I hereby respect his decision.

during these summer months, the village's population doubled, if not tripled. One could already see the immigrants, *gurbetçi,* starting to arrive Karakaya.

Not everyone returned to the homeland, though. Sometimes, it was gathering the money necessary to make the trip back home that proved problematic. Other times, there were other problems—troubles in the family, fighting amongst kin, economic downfalls, etc. And when migrants did not return, their houses would remain empty. Under the scorching sun of Karakaya, that particular day of Ramadan felt extraordinarily long. Here we were, the imam and I, sitting under the shade of the mosque passing time until the iftar. Only a few meters away from us was a three-storey apartment with its shutters locked tight. It was occupied by a dozen or so swallows under its roof. "Anyone lives there?" I asked the imam. "No, I haven't seen anyone in the last three years stop by," he replied and continued on with the story of this remittance house. Before, it used to be a one storey stone house, which was left in its dilapidated condition for years. Later the two brothers who inherited the house from their father got rid of the old house and built this three-story apartment. "The brothers were supposed to return", the imam continued. "Each brother would move in to a flat. Yet, no one returned for three years." When I asked him what sense he made of such a nice, yet empty apartment, he continued: "They built this three-story apartment in the village. With the money spent, they could have bought three different flats in the city." The imam was sympathetic to the owners of the apartment because as they replaced the rubbles of the old house, they opened up a lot of free space—which previous occupied much of the land that now serves as the mosque's courtyard. Nonetheless, the imam was as much surprised as I was by the unoccupied condition of this luxurious looking new apartment. Despite their lack of use, the brothers chose to invest in Karakaya instead. Perhaps, something happened to them, which would explain their absence. Or maybe, they were rich enough to not only built this apartment but also invested in land and housing in the city—a common practice among (particularly earlier wave) migrants who migrated to Europe. But the three-story apartment was nonetheless erected, watching over the imam and I on that very day.

The rationale behind this seemingly peculiar act, which, from an economic point of view could be described as "unproductive" investment" (Castles and Miller 2003), and which cannot be reduced to one *gurbetçi*'s practice alone, but is prevalent among many other immigrants living in cities around Turkey and Europe needs a closer look. In villages such as Karakaya, which continue to shrink as they lose their population by the year due to out-migration (to urban areas in Turkey and less so, to cities in Europe today), building a new, and apparently fully furnished house that is used for only a few months per year—granted that the owner(s) visit(s) the homeland at all—sounds counter-intuitive. Why, then, would immigrants engage in such a counter-intuitive practice? What, if anything at all, is to be gained by building these houses?

Migrants, their Remittance Houses and the Performance of Fatherhood

The practice of immigrants building houses in the homeland has been investigated by scholars who have conducted ethnographic fieldwork in various geographic contexts: Portugal (Brettell 2007), Ecuador (Codesal 2014), Mexico (Lopez 2010) Morocco (de Haas 2006), Nigeria (Osili 2004), Ghana (Grant 2005; Smith and Mazzucato 2009), Pakistan (Erdal 2012), Albania (Dalakloglou 2010), Madagascar (Thomas 1998; Freeman 2013), Turkey (van der Horst 2010), Bangladesh (Mand 2010), and the Philippines (Aguilar 2009), among others. More recently scholars have reoriented their focus on "social remittances" (Levitt 1998; 2001), bringing to fore the argument that remittance houses cannot be considered within the framework of economic investment alone. This leaves us with the following question: What kind of social or cultural investment do these houses signify. In this paper, based on a summer-long fieldwork conducted in the peripheral villages located in Kayseri, which are known to be points of departure/outmigration, I seek to understand what these houses represent particularly for the men who have built them. My findings show how masculine narratives of fatherhood complement the social life of remittance houses.

The remittance house serves two functions in consolidating the masculine self and endows one with the fatherly authority. On the one hand, returning to the father's home, or what in the vernacular is known as *baba ocağı* [father's hearth] even in instances when the father has passed away, comes out as an obligation for immigrants who may be temporarily or permanently living in the *gurbet*. By returning to the homeland, visiting the elderly either in person or through visits to cemeteries, investing in the homeland, and more importantly, dwelling in it by spending the summer vacation there, altogether with the family and kin, the father leaves his mark in the eyes of the others as someone who pays his dues.

On the other hand, the remittance house embodies values of national belonging and honor, which are central to the performance of masculinity, particularly in a rural context. In rural Turkey, the patriarchal code determines males as the breadwinners of the family (Kandiyoti 1988). The male's role as the head of the household, however, extends this economic function. Men, and especially those who are fathers, are responsible for regulating the values that their families present to the rest of the community. They are considered to be charge of making sure that their wive(s) and children do not transgress moral boundaries. In short, they are seen as regulators of a family's honor code. By bringing the kids along—many of whom may have been born outside of the "homeland", that is, the village, and may not even know most of the elderly to whom they may be tied through kinship—and uniting them under the same roof, the father performs the role of a responsible male who does not let his kids go astray, and instills in them the love of/attachment to the homeland.

Return to Baba Ocağı

The return to *baba ocağı* [father's hearth] in the homeland, even in instances when the father has long passed, is a duty that many first generation immigrants continued to comply. For Abdullah Bey, a 74-year-old retiree who lived in the Alsatian city of Selestat for over 30 years, the duty also had a pedagogic quality to it.

Coming here even for 15 days or a month is worth it. [Q: But is it worth the cost (of building a house)] But that was not why we built it! We built it because we would live in it. If I wanted to live in any other place, why would I even come to Turkey? I would travel around Lyon, Paris, Nice… However, to visit the cemetery of our ancestors, especially when one gets older… maybe, when you are old, you will remember this, but going to that cemetery is emotionally overwhelming… I have five kids and all five of them have started to share these feelings. I think that I have been a good teacher to them. I cry wondering what my dad's grave looks like, how my mom is doing [in her resting place], and I share these feelings as a part of a pleasant conversation with my kids. Because, let me repeat myself, if I want a vacation, I could very well go to Cannes or Nice. But, I rather come to my hometown.

The reason why Abdullah Bey chose to return to his homeland is to maintain his ties with the land of his ancestors, and more importantly, to instill a similar kind of emotional attachment in his kids. Filomeno Aguilar makes a similar point in his research on Filipino remittance houses. Immigrants' attachment to remittance houses—of not selling these houses despite not using them—is indicative of a different—non-utilitarian or non-economic—form of investment. For Aguilar, building a house is a form of cultural investment that reinforces the memory of the homeland as well as kinship ties. For immigrants overseas, such as the Filipino women subject to Aguilar's research, having a house built for parents—whom can also use upon return—shows immigrants' attentiveness to the members of the family left behind. By building a remittance house, the children "give face to parents… serving a living reminder to parents and to the wider community that migrant children have not forgotten their parents" (Aguilar 2009:107-108). Focusing on Italian immigrants, Susan Wessendorf makes a similar argument. In Wessendorf's analysis, the remittance house "provide[s] a symbolic site for the united family and an investment that link[s] the futures generations to the country of origin" (Wessendorf 2007: 1090). Resonating with Levi-Strauss' interpretation of Kwaiutl "house societies" (*sociétés a maison*), the Italians that Wessendorf studies see the house as a structure that symbolizes common belonging and continuation of lineage.

For Abdullah Bey, the return to the homeland provided the means to connect with the ancestors. It also gave him a chance to convey the same mentality to his children, whom he hoped would return to the homeland like he does, possibly visiting his grave after his passing. Nonetheless, the house that is so central to Claude Levi Strauss' theorization of kinship ties, which can be traced in the narratives of the elderly and retired immigrants, has a different meaning for children who left their hometowns either at a very early age, or who were born and raised in urban centers in Turkey or Europe. The elderly expect their kids to return some day, following their father's example, to the village and occupy the houses that their father's have built. The reason why they built two to three storey apartment complexes is to make sure that they could provide all of their children with a piece of the heritage that they themselves have inherited from their fathers.

Nonetheless, the elderly I spoke with were not blinded by the nostalgia of the homeland. Instead, all of my informants, Abdullah Bey included, were aware of the challenges that they were facing. When I asked them whether the houses would be occupied after their passing, and if the children, particularly those who were born and raised in other cities in Turkey and Europe would return to the village to live, many of them acknowledged the near-impossibility of attaining such an ideal. An informant who migrated to Germany, and worked there most of his life, who happened to be accompanying Abdullah Bey during our conversation intervened when I asked Abdullah Bey about his experience:

This place has turned into a holiday resort. The youth will not come here; there is nothing that would attract them to this place. No sea, no employment, no friends. Oguz Bey, our youth is strangers there and strangers here. They say, 'if I am a stranger to the lands that my father was born into, if I am not taken care of in these lands, then I would go to Antep or Mersin. I would go to the south, I would go to Izmir.'

And they do. The 18-year-old daughter of Hamit Bey, the man in his late 40s from Kermelik who traveled to Strasbourg after finishing his mandatory military service 20 years back, was counting down days to her return to Strasbourg. She was staying only for 15 days in Kermelik, and those 15 days were more than she needed.

I will be leaving soon, but they stay here for five weeks. I will be gone in three days. I will stay for 15 days overall. It has been 12 already, but three more, and then I am gone [Q: So you've had enough?] Enough, more than that! This place is not for me. They do not force me to be here, they want us to know this place. But they are also aware that if they do not put any pressure on me to come here, I would not. They are aware of that. [Q: But you still have to be here?] Yes, we need to comply. I do so because maybe when I am there [Strasbourg], they would not tell me not to go here or there. We are trying to find the middle ground. That is the way it goes, otherwise, they would make things really hard, and that is not good for me. There is also the fact that we are growing. The scene there is not the same as the scene here [Q: What's different?] The mentality here is different. Their thoughts... it is a given there to go out. Here, if you want to go out, after 8 PM, no way.

Changing Modes of Belonging to the Homeland

The children were aware of the reasons why they needed to be back in the villages. They did not object to the trip itself, but what they felt not too happy about was the extended (month-long) stay in the hometown. Despite the fact that the houses provided them with all the luxuries they could have asked for, including wireless Internet connection and satellite television, and despite having a car that they could drive around and go to the city with whenever they (the boys more than girls) wished, the second and third generation immigrants do not have the same friendship circles that their first generation parents do. Neither do they not know most of the inhabitants of these villages, nor do the inhabitants know who the kids are. Following the Friday Prayers, one of the questions that I often heard—which was also directed at me several times—was, "whose kid are you?" Rather than giving their own names, the children would give the names of their fathers and grandfathers, along with their surnames, to remind others that despite being strangers, they belong to a common ancestry.

The parents are aware of the changing modes of socialization of their children. That is why they try to make sure that the houses they built would accommodate their children's changing tastes and lifestyles. As houses become more oriented towards kids, and re-envisioned more than spaces that can be occupied during a migrant's retirement, the identity of the house also alters from a space of return to a space of vacation. Van der Horst's ethnography on Turks living in the Netherlands and traveling to their homeland every summer makes this point clear. According to the author, the practical side of the story weighs heavier than the nostalgic side for Turks today. Following Appadurai (1988), van der Horst treats remittance houses as objects with biographies. Houses have stories to tell. The biographies of remittance houses, according to the author, are representative of altered life plans of their owners (van der Horst 2010:1176). He argues that for Turkish migrants, the houses built in the homeland accommodate a different set of demands today. Whereas older dwellings were built with the idea of an ultimate return in mind, thereby facilitating the myth of return and addressing the needs of an ordinary life in a rural village, today, remittance houses are built and decorated to accommodate part-time residence needs.

Nonetheless, building big houses that are spacious enough to accommodate children still do not do the trick for the kids. And the parents are also aware that their children are not getting the same thrill from these visits to the homeland. I had two opportunities to converse with representatives of two generations (the parents and their children) around the same table, in Kermelik and Şıhbarak. In Kermelik, I talked to a father and mother, and their son and daughter in law, in the presence of their small (third generation) child, in their newly constructed house for which they spent over 100,000 Euros—an amount which by no means should be underestimated in Turkey. The mother complained that her husband buried all his investment in a house that kids do not want to live in:

There is no fun here, no stores. Kids do not stay... we should have built something much smaller instead. But once we started building the house, it was too late. Now we regret our decision... by regret, I mean... we are old now, we do not have as much [purchasing] power any more. The house is big, the kids do not come, and when they do, they do not stay. That is why I am regretful. [The house in] Kayseri is nice, it is great for me. It is clean, a small house, the doctor is nearby. If you get sick, no problems. But the Bey [husband] wants it here. The kids do not. He put in all our investment here and now we have nothing left. Just so that the kids would sleep comfortably, that they would live comfortably when they arrive. The older kid has not been here in years. The others [the son and daughter in law] have not been here in four years."

The son and the daughter in law came to Kermelik to visit their parents during the summer I was there. Thus far, they made the attempt to visit the homeland every other year. Yet, they knew that this was not the place to be for them. When I asked the bride what she thought about the situation, she wanted to play her cards safe and not upset her mother in law. She was wishful that her own kids would come to the village like they did. Yet, the mother in law intervened:

They would not come at all. [Q: Why?] The parents [the first generation mother's children] do not like it, let alone the kids [her grandchildren]. They [the children] always go outside [to places other than the village], they like it outside. I look at families in France, they always want vacation, no one cares about the village. They come for a few days, visit their families and leave. They stay here, they get bored tomorrow. Would the grandkids stay? They would not even come here.

The three-storey house that the father built on the land that he inherited from his own father was meant to bring the kids together. It was built with the kids' comfort in mind. Toilets in each room, separate master bedrooms, etc. Yet, as evident in the response given by the mother, the house failed to serve this function. The trend, as I was told in another interview, was not specific just to this village or to Turkey. In fact, houses built by the first generation parents in France were also left devoid of visits by the children. What is changing, perhaps, is kinship and conjugal ties which are expected to keep the kin and the families together, yet come short of living up to this expectation. The changing function the remittance house serves helps to make this visible.

Emotions were often high when I raised questions such as "what would become of these houses in 15-20 years", or "whether the kids would continue the tradition of returning to the homeland like their parents do, rather than spending the 'vacation' in some other place". In another house I visited in Kermelik, a father now in his late 50s broke into tears when he explained to me the current state of his relations with his children. He argued that he did everything he could to bring his children back to his house—a two-storey house that he built on the outskirts of the village overlooking a fascinating view of the valley. He used to take his kids to the stream nearby and go fishing with them when they were little. They seemed to enjoy the activities that pastoral life offered. However, once they grew older, fishing in the stream would no longer do the trick. His children drifted away gradually, leaving him and his wife alone in their house in Kermelik.

My conversation with a father and his two sons in Şıhbarak also brought up a similar issue. When I asked the three of them to compare life in Şıhbarak with life in Strasbourg, the father's description was by all means opposite of his two sons. Whereas the father found more things to do in the village, and considered Strasbourg to be too boring a place, the kids argued that their father did not know much about life in Strasbourg, other than his own house, the mosque and the workplace. I was later to learn that what the kids, who are in their early 20s, found missing in the village, as well as Kayseri, was the kind of social/night life that they enjoyed in Strasbourg. They enjoyed spending their vacation in bigger cities such as Istanbul or Antalya, which was more oriented towards the kind of high-paced life style they sought. Although these two youth were less skeptical of the time they spent in the village than the 18 year old French born young lady from Kermelik who was introduced in the pages above, their presence in the village, like that of the young lady, carried the intention to please their father than to please themselves.

Conclusion

Remittance houses which embody the return experience in paradoxical ways play an important role for immigrants. For elderly and retired, the house represents more than an (economic) investment, but an emotive one, often qualified as the return to the roots, the "father's hearth". That this return is rarely permanent, and the house, whether it is dwelled in for six months or nine, remains unoccupied for many months of the year (or in some cases, for many years), is where the problem lies. As my fieldwork shows, that the house cannot serve its envisioned function as the abode of a permanent return and that it does not unite the family under its roof troubles those who have invested in them. The remittance house becomes a summer house that may or may not unify the father with his children during vacation months. For the fathers, what remains heartbreaking is not the money invested in these houses. It is the emotional investment that fails to harvest its returns.

Class Disguised as Ethnicity: Association of *Turkishness* with Small Food Businesses in Germany

Anlam Filiz[171]

Introduction

"We Called for Manpower, but People Came Instead" (Max Frisch, 1965)

This famous line by Max Frisch is quoted frequently in articles dealing with the social and political lives and identities of *Gastarbeiter (guestworkers)* who later settled in Germany (e.g. Luft, 2002). These essays use this line to point out the surprise and the distress the West German society faced with its changing social landscape. This quote also shows the — mostly overlooked — ways migrant populations are understood in relation to their jobs. Migrants, more than most other groups, are defined by their labor. This article lays out the association between a migrant population, Turks, and a form of labor, small business ownership in Germany. It argues that the way Turks in Germany[172] are understood in the cultural imaginary of Germany shifted from "the guestworker" to "the small business owner" parallel to the changes in the labor patterns among them. The article argues so by analyzing two incidents, i.e. Thilo Sarrazin's interview about integration and the naming of NSU (*Nationalsozialistischer Untergrund*) murders as *"Döner-Morde"* ("döner murders") by the media.

The political and economic transformation of Germany is central to the ways Turks are represented in the German cultural imaginary. The largest migration wave from Turkey brought mainly blue collar workers to Germany starting in 1961. They were named as workers even before they arrived in their new homes. They worked in heavy industries and mines. With the cancellation of guest-worker agreements between Turkey and Germany in 1973 due to the oil crisis, many migrants started their own businesses to be able to extend their residence permits. The Turkish population in Germany continued to increase although the West German state encouraged migrants to return to Turkey by offering monetary incentives. Wives, husbands, children, and relatives rather migrated to Germany with family reunification visas. Germany also received many political refugees from Turkey in the 1980s and 1990s, during when Germany was the main receiver of refuge thanks to the changes undertaken as a reaction to the crimes of the Nazi Germany (Göktürk et. al., 2007, xviii). Reunification in 1989 increased unemployment among Turks because "ethnic Germans" who migrated to Germany from post-Soviet countries and eastern Germans were the first to be employed. In this process, entrepreneurship became more common among Turks than any other migrant group in Germany (Constant et al., 2007). Rising unemployment, and decreasing welfare benefits encourage increasing numbers of Turks to open their own businesses. There are approximately 130,000 Turkish

---

[171] Anlam Filiz is an anthropology PhD Candidate at Emory University, Atlanta, USA, 201 Dowman Drive, Atlanta, Georgia 30322 USA. E-mail: afiliz@emory.edu.

[172] The population defined as "Turks in Germany" is a diverse group with different ethnic and religious backgrounds, and migration stories. While recognizing the problematic nature of the concept, I use this term for the purposes of this paper, which evaluates how this population is *seen*.

owned businesses, 10,000 of which are in Berlin. Research shows that the growth of their number will continue to accelerate (TAVAK, 2012).

Today, Turks are associated with small businesses and with living on welfare. Despite the factual tendency among Turks to be self-employed, there are three critical aspects of the supposedly natural link between Turks and small businesses. 1) This association points out that migrant populations are linked with certain forms of labor in addition to cultural, national and ethnic elements such as clothing, music, and food as most of the literature focuses on (e.g. Baily & Collyer, 2006; Basu & Coleman, 2008). 2) In the case of Germany, this association between Turks and small business ownership reflects a derogatory outlook. As in the case of Sarrazin´s statements, the association considers small businesses as spaces of idleness and not of real value production. 3) The main small businesses that appear in these associations are in the gastronomy sector, such as döner and grocery stores. The owners of these businesses are seen as belonging to the lower classes. The job of owning and managing a business seems to not demand high levels of education and good German skills. Accordingly, those who manage small shops are seen as lacking the cultural capital to find white collar jobs. Through the association between small businesses and Turks, this image of the uneducated, lower class Turkish small business owner maps onto the idea of *Turkishness*.

The NSU case

Between September 2000 and April 2006, nine people with migration backgrounds were killed in Germany. Eight of those had migration stories from Turkey and one of them was from Greece. They were all murdered in small shops. The police looked for a cause within migrant communities. They investigated links to the drug trade and the football mafia. In 2011, those murders were revealed to be conducted by a Neo-Nazi group who call themselves NSU (*Nationalsozialistischer Untergrund*). Anti-racist activists, academicians and members of the media criticized the law enforcement after the revealing of the NSU because the police had not suspected a racist motive behind the murders. Activists and academics called for fighting against institutional racism within the law enforcement, which hinders the solving of racist crimes (e.g. Fekete, 2014, pp. 35).

Those anti-racist actors also criticized the mainstream media about their handling the case, for reinforcing the interpretations of the police, not being critical about police reports and for sustaining the racist attitudes against migrants. There was a big reaction against the media after the revealing of the NSU as the perpetrators of the murders because the mainstream media had labelled the murders as "döner murders." For instance, the influential weekly news magazine *der Spiegel* had introduced a police report about the serial murders with the title: "Mysterious Shootings: The Trace of Döner Murders Lead to the Football Mafia" (Neumann et. al., 2009). As the police investigated a hypothetical link between murders and mafia wars among migrants, the German tabloid *Bild-Zeitung*, had stated: "The police is chasing the uncanny döner killer since eleven years. He supposedly killed nine people between 2000 and 2006. Now, the unknown man might have struck again!" (Gaedt & Schmid, 2011). In 2010 when a döner stand owner got murdered, the center-left newspaper *Süddeutsche Zeitung* had written:

"An unknown man shot a Turkish vendor owner. The police has ruled out a connection with the "döner murders"" (Grassmann & Käppner, 2010).

The label "döner murders" became viral with other catch phrases such as *"Mauer des Schweigens"* ("the wall of silence), *"den noch nicht in unserer Gesellschaft angekommenen Türken"* ("the Turks who are not yet part of our society") and *"parallelwelt"* ("parallel world") (Virchow et. al., 2015). The unintegrated Turks, who were living in their parallel society, had ostensibly been killing each other. The silence wall was built around the issue to keep the German police from solving the cases and penetrating into the internal structures of illegal migrant organizations. According to this point of view within the police forces and the media, this silence wall was the reason why the investigation was not progressing. For the media, this was yet another proof that the multicultural societies of Europe had failed (ibid.). The supposed violence within the migrant communities were seen as an outlying cultural element that did not belong to Europe. As Virchow et. al. (2015) show the Turkish media also adopted this mindset. Newspapers named the murders as *"dönerci cinayetleri"* ("döner maker murders"), and *"kebap cinayetleri"* ("kebab murders") (pp. 23). For instance, the mainstream Turkish newspaper *Hürriyet* named the murders as "kebab murders" even in a news piece that pointed out different theories about the murders and the possibility of the existence of Neo-Nazis behind the killings (Hürriyet, 2006).

The revealing of the NSU as the organization behind the murders generated reactions against the concept of "döner murders" in the mainstream media. In these reactions, the representations of the murders are usually assessed as part of the racist attitudes towards Turks and migrants in general. These media representations are criticized for uncritically adopting existing social prejudices and for having the unethical intent to attract attention to the news at the expense of racism. Accordingly, the term *"Döner-Morde"* ("döner-murders") was selected as *"das Unwort,"* (the unpleasant word) in 2012 (Der Spiegel, 2012). In October 2012, Heribert Prantl, the head of the domestic policy department of *Süddeutsche Zeitung* in Germany, declared that the use of the term "döner murders" reflected discriminatory attitudes towards Turks (Prantl, 2012). Likewise, in a news piece in the center-left Turkish newspaper *Radikal*, Onur Yükçü, a journalist, and Belit Onay, a Green Party representative in the Lower Saxony Parliament, criticized the way the media had dealt with the serial murders. In this article, the authors state that the concept "döner murders" reproduces an orientalist attitude that assumes everyone from Turkey — and the East — to be döner makers and sellers. As the authors argue, the Turkish media had to translate "döner murders" into "döner maker murders" to avoid the even more problematic translation of "döner murders," which equates the murdered to a food product. They also point out that the initial commission set up to investigate the murders was named "the Bosphorus Commission." According to Yükçü and Onay, this name reflects the fact that rather than investigating the issue, the commission relied on preconceptions about the murders and looked for the perpetrators within the migrant community (Yükçü & Onay, 2013). As Virchow et. al. argue, the concept of "döner murders" also shows the misinterpretation and the neglecting of the political dimension of the murders. There was a racist motive behind the murders that remained unseen (Virchow et. al., 2015, pp. 7). The mainstream German media had failed to fulfill their duties of critical journalism but rather adopted and sustained the ongoing racist outlook.

Although these criticisms rightfully point out an important dimension of the issue, I argue that what brings the German and the Turkish media together is not only racism. The representations also point out the classed image of the Turkish population in Germany. Turks in Germany are associated with the lower classes both in Turkey and in Germany. Class in this sense is an achieved status, which is gained mainly through education and which does not necessarily reflect in economic capital. Today, the Turkish population in Germany is demographically very different from the so-called guestworkers of the 1960s. They are much more diverse in terms of age, migration histories, education levels, and occupation (Kaya & Kentel, 2005). Nevertheless, small businesses and especially small food businesses characterize the image of the Turkish population. At the same time, anti-migration discourses of today label the Turkish population as a burden on the German economic system. Increasing unemployment among Turks, seemingly low levels of education, and ostensibly poor German skills among the Turkish population heighten discussions about Turks' belonging to Germany and migrants' integration to Europe. The attitudes towards this population in Turkey are also discriminatory and classed in nature. "*Almancı*" ("German-like") has long been used as a derogatory term for migrants from Turkey in Germany and in Europe in general (Kaya, 2005). Many migrants report that they do not feel belonging to Turkey mainly because they are seen as unskilled peasants from Anatolia and an uneducated group of people with economic capital.

Sarrazin's interview

This derogatory approach to *guestworkers,* their families and other Turks in Germany became evident with an interview Thilo Sarrazin, a member of the Social Democratic Party of Germany (SPD), and former member of the Executive Board of the German Central Bank, gave about the economic problems of Berlin in the city's culture magazine *Lettre International.* As he stated:

"A large number of Arabs and Turks in this city [Berlin], whose numbers have risen due to wrong politics, have no productive function besides fruit and vegetable trade and they won't develop any other perspective other than this. This also applies to a part of the German underclass, whose members once turned magnetic coils in subsidized businesses or operated cigarette machines. These jobs do not exist anymore. Berlin has an economic problem with the size of its existing population" (Sarrazin, 2009, pp. 198).

Sarrazin's statements have been declared to be racist just like the term "döner murders" was regarded as racist. Sarrazin has been criticized by the public for ignoring educated and well-off Turks and Arabs, for making ungrounded generalizations about Turkish and Arabic cultures, and for not paying attention to the problems with migration policies in Germany. Although these criticisms are valid, just like in the case of "döner murders," the class aspect in Sarrazin's statements is overlooked. Sarrazin does not only criticize Turks and Arabs for not contributing to the society. He also likes them to the German underclass, whose members were unskilled workers and are now unemployed due to the changing production and labor market conditions. He does so despite the fact that he refers to Turks' and Arabs' vegetable and fruit trade, which have a big share in the gastronomy sector in Germany. Sarrazin's arguments about migrant communities' integration start with migrants' economic presence but Sarrazin's concern is not simply the economic contributions of migrant groups. His statements continue with a concern about integration into a pre-defined culture, which includes a certain lifestyle, education, and religion. In his interview in *Lettre International*, Sarrazin continues:

"I do not have to acknowledge anyone, who lives of state funds, rejects the state, does not worry about the education of their children and who constantly produces new small headscarved girls. This is true for 70 percent of the Turkish and 90 percent of the Arab population in Berlin" (Sarrazin, 2009, pp. 199).

Here, the Turkish and Arabic populations refer to an idle, almost homogenous group of people. They ostensibly live on welfare, do not contribute to the German economy and do not fit in the cultural landscape of Germany. They do not take good care of their children or of their children's integration into the German society through education. These parents also misdirect the new generations through religious imposition.

What is interesting in this outlook is that the supposedly welfare migrants of Germany fall into the same category with those who are involved in the vegetable and fruit trade. In other words both an economic activity, i.e. owning and managing grocery stores, and living on welfare represent the ethnic/national group of migrants from Turkey in Germany. What binds these two economic in/activities is the way they are associated with the lower class as defined through a lack of education, poor German skills and not doing jobs that are perceived to *actually* produce value. Both welfare recipients and business owners appear to lack the skills to be employed in white collar jobs in German companies or state institutions.

This approach ignores the structural problems in education and the labor market that disadvantage migrants as well as the large number of migrants in jobs that demand long term educational success. Cultural codes that are associated with lower classes get mapped onto the Turkish population while the upwardly mobile people within this group are either overlooked as a whole or are ignored as outliers. The reliance on the food industry to define Turks as a group is also misleading because Turkish and Arab businesses in Germany vary in size and are active in various different industries. For instance, in Berlin, in which ethnic fast food and grocery stores are on the rise, only 30 percent of Turkish businesses are in the restaurant and catering sector (Kaya & Kentel, 2005). Although the association of Turks with small food businesses is misdirected, a closer look will enrich our understanding of how ethnic and national groups are perceived in relation to class.

Conclusion

In this paper, I established the connection between small food businesses and the Turkish community in Germany by analyzing the handling of the NSU case in the media and Thilo Sarrazin's statements about integration. The NSU murdered 9 people with migrant backgrounds between 2000 and 2006. They were either small business owners or the place of murders were small businesses owned by migrants. The media named the serial murders as "döner murders" although the occupations of the murdered ranged from florist and locksmith to greengrocers. Both the Turkish and German media used pictures that showed döner shops as the quintessential reference to the murders. Sarrazin, whose books about integration are bestsellers in Germany, accused Turks and Arabs for not being able to integrate into the German society because they are only involved in food trade.

Food is a major representative of ethnic communities. Döner is the seemingly quintessential element of the Turkish culture. Therefore, it might seem only natural that the Turkish community in Germany is defined by this product and food trade at large. However, this outlook creates a false conception of a homogenous ethnic culture. Besides this analytical problem, the trade of food is not seen as a productive economic activity as Thilo Sarrazin's statements show. Accordingly, the equation made between Turks and food trade sustains the image of Turkish migrants as making no contribution to the German society. Moreover, the handling of the NSU case shows us that equating a population with a single occupation and a single cultural element creates political and practical problems by inhibiting the solving of a legal case and perpetuating the stigmatization of a group.

Scholars of migration have studied migrant identities and experiences in relation to different relations of power such as class and ethnicity (Herrera, 2013). Intersectionality has been used as a major theory to understand the experiences of people within the intersection of various power dynamics (Crenshaw, 1991). This body of scholarship has been helpful in exposing complex power relations. It has also been criticized for taking categories such as race, class, and gender for granted and not problematizing the adoption of such categories to varying contexts (e.g. Puar, 2007). The experiences of Turks in Germany and their representations in the news about NSU murders and in Sarrazin's statements, reveal that we also need to pay attention to how categories that we see as *intersecting* such as class, gender, and ethnicity might also be *disguised* as each other. In this case, Turks are understood as a group stuck in lower classes with poor education and language skills. This classed understanding represents itself in daily interactions, political speeches, and the media. These representations appear as if they are representations solely of an ethnic community. Our academic and political debates should not be limited to discussions about racism but should include various power relations, as in this case class, for us to gain a deeper and progressive understanding of minority experiences.

References

Baily, J., & Collyer, M. (2006). Introduction: Music and migration. Journal of Ethnic and Migration Studies, 32(2), 167-182.

Basu, P., & Coleman, S. (2008). Introduction: Migrant worlds, material cultures. Mobilities, 3(3), 313-330.

Constant, A., Shachmurove, Y., & Zimmermann, K. F. (2007). What makes an entrepreneur and does it pay? Native men, Turks, and other migrants in Germany. International Migration, 45(4), 71-100.

Crenshaw, K. (1991). Mapping the margins: Intersectionality, identity politics, and violence against women of color. Stanford law review, 1241-1299.

Der Spiegel (2012, January 17). "Döner-Morde" ist Unwort des Jahres. Der Spiegel.

Fekete, L. (2014). Anti-fascism or anti-extremism?. Race & Class, 55(4), 29-39.

Frisch, M. Überfremdung 1 (1965). ders.: Gesammelte Werke, 5, 2.

Gaedt, T. & Schmid, P. (2011, October 6). Hat der unheimliche Döner-Killer wieder zugeschlagen?. Bild-Zeitung.

Grassmann, P. & Käppner, J. (2010, May 17). Tod am Dönerstand. Süddeutsche Zeitung.

Göktürk, D., Gramling, D., & Kaes, A. (Eds.). (2007). Germany in transit: Nation and migration, 1955-2005 (Vol. 40). Univ of California Press.

Herrera, G. (2013). Gender and International Migration: Contributions and Cross-Fertilizations. Annual Review of Sociology, 39, 471-489.

Hürriyet (2006, April 18). Almanya'daki 'Kebap Cinayetleri'nde Nazi şüphesi.

Kaya, A. (2005). Citizenship and the hyphenated Germans: German-Turks. Keyman, E. F. and İçduygu A. (eds.) Citizenship in a Global World: European Questions and Turkish Experiences. London and New York: Routledge.

Kaya, A., & Kentel, F. (2005). Euro-Turks: A Bridge or a Breach between Turkey and the European Union? A Comparative Study of French-Turks and German-Turks. CEPS EU-Turkey Working Papers No 14, 1 January 2005

Luft, S. (2002). Mechanismen, Manipulation, Mißbrauch: Ausländerpolitik und Ausländerintegration in Deutschland (Vol. 63). Wissenschaft und Politik.

Neumann, C. Röbe, S. & Ulrich, A. (2009, December 12). Mysteriöse Erschießungen: Spur der Döner-Mörder führt zur Wettmafia, Der Spiegel.

Prantl, Heribert (2012, January 17). Unwort, Untat, Ungeist. Süddeutsche Zeitung.

Puar, J. (2007). Terrorist assemblages: Homonationalism in queer times. Duke University Press.

Sarrazin, T. Frank Berberich (2009, Fall). Thilo Sarrazin im Gespräch: Klasse Statt Masse. Lettre International, pp. 197- 201.

TAVAK. Türk-Alman Eğitim ve Bilimsel Araştırmalar Vakfı (2012). Türk Girisimciler Raporu. Retrieved from http://goo.gl/fhOU2E on 25.10.2014.

Virchow, F., Thomas, T., & Grittmann, E. (2014). Das Unwort erklärt die Untat. Retrieved from http://goo.gl/o9IQxA on 20.04.2015.

Yükçü,O & Onay, B. (2013, May 12). Dönerci Cinayetleri, Radikal.

The notion of integration and economic aspects in the German discourse of a culturally sensitive eldery care

Nevin Altıntop[173]

Introduction

The subject of health care for elderly migrants in Germany, especially the subject of culturally sensitive health care solutions, has received certain attention over the past decade. My investigation of the discourse finds that the topic of health care for migrants is predominantly strained between two poles: integration (or inclusion) on the one side and economy on the other side, however both are well linked to politics. The connections in the discourse of health care for elderly migrants to aspects of integration as well as of economy are content of this manuscript and will be discussed in more detail below. Sociological or health care theoretical discourses are less well established on this topic, despite some existing educational and training activities for employees in the health care sector. In earlier publications I have already shed a light on the political process of Intercultural Opening in Germany with respect to elderly care for migrants (Altıntop 2014a, 2014b). Here, I will point out the strong connection between the established discourse of a culturally sensitive elderly care and integration policies on the one and economy on the other side.

Method

Data was gathered by field research. The field research covered 1) observations from site visits in different German cities, mainly Berlin, Hamburg and Munich where home care, daily care, assisted living facilities, and stationary health care options were inspected, 2) participation in conferences and workshops about culturally sensitive elderly care, and 3) interviews with scientists, employees of welfare organisations and elderly care facilities, patients in culturally sensitive elderly care facilities and their relatives, employers of culturally sensitive elderly care facilities and staff members, and politicians. These primary sources were saved as digital recordings and as written field notes in several note books. For data analysis, a German wide e-mail and telephonic correspondence with experts in the field of elderly and social care helped to clarify many details. In addition to the field notes and the research data, a progressive analysis of media (print media, government reports, audio-visual media from internet or broadcast, research papers, etc.) available to the topic of culturally specific health care was undertaken in order to follow the discourse. Because of the vast activities in the field and because of my language skills I focused on Turkish migrants. They also represent the largest group among elderly migrants in Germany. In the following I will speak of 'migrants', although my investigations but and also the public discourse has a strong focus on Turkish migrants. I also will not discriminate between culturally sensitive, transcultural, intercultural, etc. health care because this theoretical

---

[173] Nevin Altıntop is PhD candidate at the Department of Social and Cultural Anthropology, University of Vienna, Universitätsstraße 7, 1010 Vienna, Austria. E-mail: vienna-dok2013@gmx.at.

discussion is not of concern here. However, I will write culturally specific health care, whenever I speak about ethnic specific health care options and whenever it also concerns the discourse (Altıntop 2014a, 2014b). In my analysis I followed a Grounded Theory categorisation scheme as proposed in the earliest version of Glaser's & Strauss' seminal work (Glaser & Strauss 1967).

Results and discussion

The development of the discourse in brief

The German discourse of health care for migrants is buttressed by the paradigm of Intercultural Opening. Rooting in education of and streetwork with teenager migrants the core idea of Intercultural Opening is the identification and the removal of access barriers to public institutions or the labour market that exclude specific members of the society (Filsinger 2002). The demand for an intercultural opening process intrinsically criticised institutions and social services for their institutional discrimination. Historically, the counselling of recruited labour migrants was split among different social welfare organisations based on the migrants' ethnic/religious origin in newly established offices. For Turkish labour migrants these offices provided by the Workers' Welfare Association (Arbeiterwohlfahrt) were called 'Türk Danış', literally meaning something like 'Turk, ask for advice!', or short for 'Türkçe danışma bürosu' (Turkish consulting office). Their number of tasks and field of responsibilities steadily grew and, in retrospect, these structures not only lead to an extra in administration but also to social segregation. Indeed, Germany's social welfare organisations were harshly criticised therefore and they were even blamed for impeding integration of migrants when providing specific social services separated from service units for the German-speaking population (Puskeppeleit & Thränhardt 1990).

Concerning an aging population and the fact of a statistically growing number of former labour migrants entering the retirement age the scheme of Intercultural Opening was cloned for the health care sector at the end of the 1990s, however with a less academic tribute from health care science. Possibly this is why the discourse about a culturally sensitive health care for elderly migrants itself contains many blurred and vague contents. It inevitably relates to concepts such as 'culture' or 'integration' that are multidimensional in themselves. Because of missing definitions the discourse can be seen as a bunch of different descriptions and opinions, not necessarily constant with the years. A more theoretical orientation is hardly found, the existing forums on the topic or the mainstream of articles in media generally do not refer to preceding debates in education and pedagogics as mentioned above or to sociological and philosophical investigations, as given exemplarily by the concept of 'transculturality' of the German intellectual Welsch (Welsch 1999).

The discourse itself is pronounced promotion- and campaign oriented. The accent lies on recurring invocations and claims of intercultural actions but it must be noted that finally concrete implementations of culturally sensitive or specific health care, the 'how' to do it, is less clear and, therefore, lacks regulation. In addition, there seems to be only small progress: there is a repetition in statements that gives an impression that all preceding campaigns and workshops have had little impact on improving the situation for elderly migrants. The remarkable quick rise of so-called 'intercultural experts' fits also into this context. In this sense we have a quite paradox situation of Babel-like language chaos, the obvious ineffectiveness of the discourse on the one side and the emergence and flourishing of intercultural trainers and coaches on the other side.

This lack of conceptualisation within the discourse is problematic and can also lead to disadvantages, for example in the case when Article 1 of volume XI of the Social Insurance Code states that 'the health care insurance should consider culturally sensitive care as far as possible' without providing a proper definition as if everybody uses the term 'cultural sensitivity' identically and is able to estimate how far is 'far as possible' (SGB XI 2008). The lack of a definition in the law signals that there should not result any mandatory claim from receiving or not receiving 'culturally sensitive health care' – in contrast to other in detail defined terms such as 'in need of care' and 'disabled'. Thus, culturally sensitive health care is not really taken as a serious health care option by lawmakers. It is characteristic for the discourse to frequently operate with loosely made associations.

Another problem of the discourse is the systematic concealment of real actual problems. Culturally sensitive health care should be presented as model of success. This strategy is, probably, believed to raise chances of further or future project support and financial funding. One of the problems pointed out in a previous publication: for providers of elderly care 'culturally sensitive or culturally specific can often mean anything but are certainly used in order to signalize the aim of acquiring migrant customers' (Alnntop 2015). To be more concrete, especially private providers promise much in the advertisement of their service in order to acquire migrant customers. They are easily tempted to sign the contract with the agency because of a real lack of experience with mobile home care providers in general.

The following statements of former employees of different private culturally specific home care services should serve as examples: Around five years ago respective agencies for home care have boasted about their fantastic employees who work even extra time hours – without giving here the impression that this extra time is paid. Speaking the same language and having the same cultural background made it easy for elderly Turkish patients to build up a too close relationship with the caregivers. The younger caregiver was quickly regarded as family member and, consequently, treated as such, including that it was also expected from him/her to behave as a family member. This is not always comfortable. Familiarity, in some cases the loss of privacy, and the extra working time involved were at the expense of the young caregiver who stated later: 'I hate it to call the clients uncle or aunt. This exceeds [a limit]' (Interviews Berlin 2014, translated by the author).

The situation is not better for an assisted living community in Berlin that is bluntly controlled by a private home care service. The effective control of patients in an assisted living setting, also described as 'assisted living community within the regime of a health care service' (Klie 2006, translated by the author), is obviously the complete inversion of what was anticipated by legislation, i.e. the strengthening of patient autonomy. In fact we encounter the unrestricted autonomy of the private health care service and a former employee states about the alleged leisure activities of the patients: 'They [i.e. the health care provider] say: we make this and that. That's all lies. Isn't done." (Interviews Berlin 2014, translated by the author)

There exist many more examples about serious problems in and with culturally sensitive elderly care in Germany that are not addressed by the actual dialogue, but which does not mean that participants of this dialogue would not be aware of them. There are cases of striking evidence in culturally specific health care that both, employees and clients are exploited, which does not quite fit to a role model of success. In the following two sections I will discuss the subject pair to which the topic of elderly care for migrants is strongly subordinated: 1) The term 'integration', that bears the expression of an ethical obligation of the German society but also a confession that integration measures for labour migrants were completely neglected in the decades before. Furthermore, 'integration' is a mission statement of German government, thus it is a highly politically loaded term. 2) Economy is the other sector that plays the decisive role for the motivation and the implementation of culturally sensitive or specific health care facilities. It is also a control element. Profit-oriented motifs can be identified not only for private investors but also for those participants of the discourse who hope for a personal career within the network fed by government or social welfare organisations.

Health Care and Integration

In my progressive analysis of significance of health care for migrants and its discourse it is observed that the subject of health care for elderly migrants is strongly superordinated by the topic of integration. In principle, the core position of the discourse participants regularly affirms the importance of integration of elderly migrants in the health care sector and the strengthening of assistance measures. In general, it supports culturally sensitive and specific solutions or at least prefers one, culturally sensitive (transcultural, etc.) or culturally specific.

When culturally sensitive health care is connected with integration then basically as recognition and acceptance of difference: elderly migrants should receive a health care option that meets their needs. Culturally sensitive health care is also seen as an expression of 'equality' (interview Barth 2011). The term 'integration', often enriched with more recent concepts such as 'inclusion', acts here as some sort of ethical code and social conscience. The motif of integration amalgamates with ethical values. For the already second annual meeting of the German Ethics Council in 2010 the topic 'Migration and Health' was chosen (Deutscher Ethikrat 2010)

Politically, the general subject of integration of migrants is addressed in Germany by some structural developments such as the National Integration Summit (Integrationsgipfel), since 2006, or the Federal Advisory Committee for Integration (Bundesbeirat für Integration), since 2011. It is interesting to note when the topic of health care for elderly migrants entered more concretely the scene. The National Action Plan for Integration from 2011 (NAP) that should replace the former National Integration Plan (NIP), contains for the first time the subject of healthcare – 'particularly with regard to the aging population with immigrant backgrounds' (The Federal Commissioner for Migration, Refugees and Integration 2011). For the preparation of the NAP so-called Dialogue Forums were established in early 2011, one of them by the Ministry of Health. The elaborated 'benchmarks' and if achieved should be evaluated by the end of 2014. An actual evaluation for measures on Intercultural Opening, as stated in the NAP e.g. the improvement of intercultural knowledge, the reduction of language barriers, the continuation of the work group on 'Migration and Public Health', (Bundesregierung 2011) etc., was not yet given.

A lot of brain storming, workshop discussions, project models and project money were put up to now into the field of culturally sensitive elderly care without much successful impact after more than a decade, if impact is in first instance measured as number of elderly migrants in a health care facility provided by private investors or a social welfare organisation. It is evident that there still exist access barriers in respective services and their elimination is not pushed forward on the one hand (Khan-Zvorničanin 2009), on the other hand, a series of articles in print media and the report from Transparency Germany about the cases of corruption by a large number of culturally specific private home care services also demonstrates, unfortunately, the power of nearly unpunished fraud: customer's loyality is often rewarded financially – less with an exceptional quality of care – a welcome income for many patients. Fraudulent bills to the care insurance fund in turn are expected to be on the daily agenda (Stolterfoht & Martiny 2013). It can be already seen that the conflicts behind this discussion which is always reduced to 'integration' are found in the economic sector. Integration unavoidable is running into a problem when it is defined as acceptance of particular services only, or defined in an economic sense as particular consumption pattern.

Health Care and Economical Aspects

The often encountered statement that a 'culturally sensitive health care' means 'individual health care', a holistically oriented care that recognizes the individual biography of each patient, creates expectations that are utopian. The biographical aspect is mostly limited to filling out a sheet of paper with biographical entries when being admitted to a stationary health care facility. Sharply said, the nursing staff has neither time nor is paid of singing every patient's favourite song from childhood. The health care options provided by welfare or public institutions and private services are all specific ones, not individual ones. This does not change when the patients are migrants.

The term Intercultural Opening was already equipped with competitiveness with respect to 'new demands' by society (Hinz-Rommel 2000). Later, adopted for elderly care the term was filled with new content and the desire not only for a better quality of care but also for personal participation and benefit. It is also characteristic for the discourse that it is carried out by a few circles with a small amount of members who want to make their way in the rare job positions or projects provided by welfare organisations, scientific or government institutions in this field. In addition, providers of elderly care – welfare institutions on the one hand and private investors on the other hand – launched a race about the growing but finite amount of migrants who need and who also decide to receive health care by professionals.

This competition between different health care services (in fact services provided by social welfare organizations and those provided by private investors) is reflected since ever in the discourse about a culturally sensitive care. A statement from 2002 already explicitly mentions economic competition and, in addition, opposes 'good' versus 'bad' health care providers: 'In future it must be made clear to operators of health care services that only a culturally sensitive health care concept in the business concept is successful in the acquisition of migrant costumers.' and it is pointed out that 'a pure instrumentalisation of migrants in the sense of a short-term economic success' would not be helpful for 'culturally sensitive health care' and furthermore 'can lead to economic failures' (Dibelius 2002, translated by the author).

These statements above contain much content for analysis. They give possibly insight in some personal expectations of a nursing scientist but certainly cannot base on empirical observations. Even today, more than ten years later, the statements cannot be confirmed. Culturally sensitive health care concepts in the business plan do not guarantee a higher request by migrant customers, which was also recognized by a more recent publication (Protschka 2012). From the context – the speech was given in June 2002 at the German Federal Ministry for Work and Social Order in the official presentation of the Memorandum (Forum für eine kultursensible Altenhilfe 2009) to officials of government and social welfare organisations – it is a straightforward evidence what representatives of social welfare want to hear and representatives of government should hear: culturally sensitive elderly care should be competitive and attractive for migrants, a praising hymn for the Memorandum, and the promotion for funding culturally sensitive activies by the public sector. It is the invitation for the government and for the social welfare organisations to congratulate each other. In the last years also private providers of culturally specific elderly care have found their communication level with government representatives and sell their services as good-practice examples. The interconnections are quite complex, and cannot be discussed in detail here, but the general trend as observed is the reduction of elderly migrants to a source of capital in case of nursing care. Culturally sensitive health care obviously has lost its ethical standards.

Conclusion

To conclude, the discourse of health care for elderly migrants is strongly oriented on integration policies on the one hand and also strongly determined by economical decisions on the other hand. The notion of 'integration' transports an ethical conscience of society, and the aim to control social cohesion. However, economical aspects do play a decisive role in the promotion and establishment of elderly care facilities, in the funding of culturally sensitive elderly care projects and in the acquisition of customers for home care services.

References

Altıntop, N. (2014a). Health Policies and Cultural Sensitivity in the Care for Elder Turkish Migrants in Austria and Germany and the Role of Turkish Migrants. In: İlkılıç İlhan; Ertin, Hakan; Brömer, Rainer and Zeeb, Hajo (eds.) (2014) Health, Culture and the Human Body, Conference Proceedings, BETİM, p.127

Altıntop, N. (2014b). Barriers versus promotion: Culturally sensitive health care for elderly Turkish migrants in Austria and Germany. Border Crossing: Transnational Working Papers, No. 1404, p.41 available at http://www.tplondon.com/journal/index.php/bc

Altıntop, N. (2015). Elderly Care for Migrants: Between Marginalization and Sensitive Inclusion. In: Pamukkale Üniversitesi (ed.) Conference Proceedings of the 8th Ulusal Yaşlılık Kongresi, 16-18 Nisan. p.409

Bundesregierung. Die Beauftragte der Bundesregierung für Migration, Flüchtlinge und Integration (ed.) (2011). Nationaler Aktionsplan. Zusammenhalt stärken – Teilhabe verwirklichen. p.192 (in German)

Deutscher E. (ed.) (2010). Tagungsdokumentation Migration und Gesundheit. Kulturelle Vielfalt als Herausforderung für die medizinische Versorgung. Vorträge der Jahrestagung des Deutschen Ethikrates 2010. available at http://www.ethikrat.org/ (in German)

Dibelius, O. (2002). Stellungnahme zur „Handreichung für eine kultursensible Altenpflege" aus Sicht der Pflege. In: Arbeitskreis Charta für eine kultursensible Altenpflege, Kuratorium Deutsche Altershilfe, Beauftragte der Bundesregierung für Ausländerfragen (ed.) (2002). Dokumentation der Präsentation Für eine kultursensible Altenhilfe! Memorandum und Handreichung. Ein Beitrag zur interkulturellen Öffnung. p.8 (in German)

The Federal Commissioner for Migration, Refugees and Integration (ed.) (2011). Flyer: National Action Plan on Integration. available at:
http://www.bundesregierung.de/Webs/Breg/DE/Bundesregierung/BeauftragtefuerIntegratio n/nap/integrationsgipfel/integrationsgipfel5/_node.html;jsessionid=743A27557C0428A82202 4FFA21D31410.s4t2

Filsinger, D. (2002). Zusammenfassung der Expertise: Interkulturelle Öffnung Sozialer Dienste. Paper presented at E&C Fachforum: Miteinander – Nebeneinander – Gegeneinander? Integration junger Zuwanderinnen und Zuwanderer in E&C-Gebieten. November 6-7, 2002. available at: http://www.eundc.de/pdf/63003.pdf (in German)

Forum für eine kultursensible Altenhilfe. (ed.) (2009). Memorandum für eine kultursensible Altenhilfe. Ein Beitrag zur Interkulturellen Öffnung am Beispiel der Altenpflege. 2nd edition available at www.bagso.de/fileadmin/Aktuell/Themen/Pflege/memorandum2002.pdf (in German)

Glaser, B., & Strauss, A. (1967). The discovery of grounded theory. Chicago: Aldine

Hinz-Rommel, W. (2000). Interkulturelle Öffnung als Innovation. Erfahrungen für die Praxis. Blätter der Wohlfahrtspflege 7-8, p.154 (in German)

Interviews Berlin (2014). Interview with former employees of specific elderly care services, anonymised. (unpublished)

Interview Barth (2011). Interview with Wolfgang Barth, AWO Bundesverband, Blücherstr. 62/63 10961 Berlin, Germany (unpublished)

Khan-Zvorničanin, M. (2009). Geschlossene Gesellschaft. Altenhilfen tun sich schwer, zugewanderte Ältere zu integrieren. WZB-Mitteilungen 126, p.25 (in German)

Klie, T. (2006). Ambulante Wohngruppen im Schatten des Rechts. Häusliche Pflege 12, p.38 (in German)

Protschka, J. (2012). Deutsches Ärzteblatt vol. 109, issue 27, p.A1426 (in German)

Puskeppeleit, Jürgen and Thränhardt, Dietrich (1990). Vom betreuten Ausländer zum gleichberechtigten Bürger. Lambertus, p.45 (in German)

Stolterfoht, B. and Martiny, A. (2013). Transparenzmängel, Betrug und Korruption im Bereich der Pflege und Betreuung. Schwachstellenanalyse von Transparency Deutschland. 3rd edition, available at http://www.transparency.de/

Sozialgesetzbuch, SGB XI §1(4a) available at http://dejure.org

Welsch, W. (1999). Transculturality – the Puzzling Form of Cultures Today. In: Featherstone, Mike & Scott, Lash: Spaces if Culture: City, Nation, World. London: Sage, p.194 available at http://www2.uni-jena.de/welsch/Papers/transcultSociety.html

Turks in German political life:
Effects of Turkish origin politicians to integration

Tolga Sakman[†]

Historical perspective

Turks started to voice their requests through associations that founded at beginning of 1960s and 1970s. In the 1970s, associations and federations that works as a part of political parties in Turkey entered to the life of Turks in Germany. At the same time, concepts that advocated in Turkey became popular among Turks in Germany.

Sevim Çelebi was a member of Alternative List for Democracy and Environmental Protection[174] (which then united with Green Party). She became first Turkish-origin Member of Parliament when she elected to West Berlin Parliament in 1987 local elections. (Bundeszentrale für Politische Bildung, 2011)

In 1990s with effect of West Germany and East Germany unification and increasing crisis in economy, which was not performing well already, unemployment rate has increased. German society put blame on immigrants on this case. Some political parties, especially Christian Democrats, have noticed that this understanding on immigrants contributes to gain votes and they started use anti-immigration discourses as a political tool. This political and social campaign that started to immigrants connected Turks to each other. In this process Turks, who both German and non-German citizens, became more interested with politics and especially young people in second generation started work either in local elections or in young branches of SPD or Green Party.

At the same time, integration of immigrants became as an issue among German political parties. German Turkish Forum that founded under CDU (Deutsch Türkisches Forum in der CDU – DTF) and Turkish German Liberals Association (Die Liberale Türkisch-Deutsche Vereinigung – LTD) that is connected with Free Democrat Part (FDP) are main platforms to pull Turks to their sides. The Turks who are members of such initiatives were also participating in meetings, being involved in the management and also shared the ideas that emerged in those meetings with other Turks. These examples of political participation are very important for Turks to get used to or even participate to active political life. Cem Özdemir was one of the two Turkish MPs that elected to Bundestag in 1994 elections. However he was unsuccessful at first because of charges in intra-party local organizations during intra-party elections about being a "Turkish intelligent agent", failure to adopt to party policies or just being a Turk (Özdemir, 1999, p.118).

[†] Tolga Sakman is Specialist on European Studies in Turkish Asian Center for Strategic Studies (TASAM), Eski Ali Pasa Cad, No.20, Fatih, Istanbul, 34091,Turkey and PhD Candidate in Political Science and International Relations Department, Istanbul University, Beyazit/Fatih, Istanbul, 34452, Turkey. E-mail: sakmantolga@gmail.com, tolgasakman@tasam.org

[174] The Green Party was started its political life in West Germany in 1980, then the Party came together with East Germany origin "Alliance 90 (Bündnis 90)" in 1993. Officially the Party is living with the name of "Alliance 90/Greens Party" but generally recognized only "Greens" (Eroğul, 2006, p. 237-238).

Graphic 1: Number of Turkish-origin Voters in Germany per Election Years

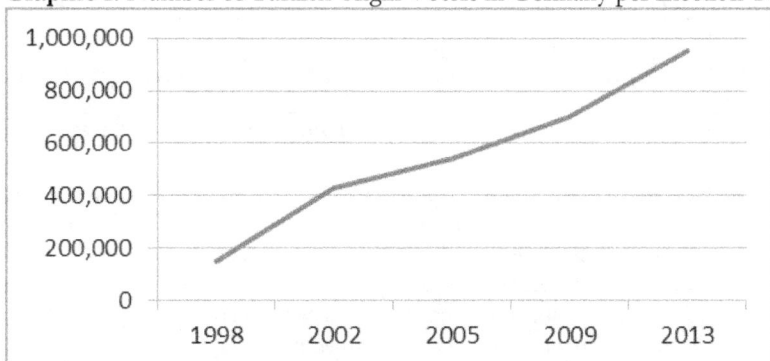

Sources: Acar, M. (2011, Mayıs). Almanya'da Türk Kökenli Seçmenlerin Seçmen Davranışı. 21. Yüzyıl (29), 49-53; Erdoğan, Murat. "Türkiye Kökenli Alman Vatandaşlarının Almanya Federal Meclisi (Bundestag) Seçimlerinde Siyasal Davranışları", HÜGO, Eylül 2013

In 2009 elections, number of Turkish voter reached to 700.000. It is important to note that there were Turkish MP's in every party, with the exception of CDU after this elections. The other notable thing is that a Turkish MP elected from FDP, a liberal right wing party which most distant party for Turks.

After all these attempts in politics, Turks started to establish political party. Unity Party for Justice and Innovation (BIG-Partei) that established in 2010 joined to North Rhine-Westphalia elections but could not get the number of vote to enter to parliament. (Apin, 2011)

The Prime Minister of Lower Saxony State, Christian Wulff, from CDU, appointed Turkish-origin Aygül Özkan as Women, Family, Health and Integration Minister in 2010. It was the first time a Turk became a minister. In 2011 the second Turkish-origin minister, Bilkay Öney from SPD appointed as Integration Minister in Baden-Württemberg State.

Table 1: Proportional Divisions of Turkish Origin Votes per Parties

%	SPD	CDU	Greens	FDP	Left Party
2002	60	12	17	5	5
2005	77	4,8	9,2	1,2	7,8
2009	55,5	10,1	23,3	0,9	9,4
2013	*64*	*7*	*12*	*-*	*12*

Source: Acar, M. (2011). Almanya'da Türk Kökenli Seçmenlerin Seçmen Davranışı. 21. Yüzyıl (29), 49-53; Erdoğan, M. (2013) "Türkiye Kökenli Alman Vatandaşlarının Almanya Federal Meclisi (Bundestag) Seçimlerinde Siyasal Davranışları", HÜGO.

Table 2: Number of Tukish Origin MPs in Bundestag per Period

	SPD	CDU	Greens	FDP	Left Party	TOTAL
1994-1998	1	-	1	-	-	2

1998-2002	1	-	2	-	-	3
2002-2005	1	-	2 (-1)[175]	-	-	2
2005-2009	1	-	1	-	3	5
2009-2013	1	-	2	1	1	5
2013-	5	1	3	-	2	11

Source: Official Web Site of German Federal Parliament Bundestag

However, there were several problems between her and Turkish community in Germany. His discourses which cannot link with integration such as being against removal of visa requirements for Turks, her objections to non-EU citizen's right to vote in local elections, although it was given in states' government protocol, took reaction specifically from Turkish associations and other Turkish-origin MP's and also from many others (Danışman, 2011).

Turks started to take management roles in political parties alongside governments at the same time. In 2008, Cem Özdemir became Co-chair of the Green Party and shared the office with Clauida Roth. In SPD plenary session in 2010 federal MP Aydan Özoğuz became vice-chair of the party. Through the end of the 2012, also CDU did an evolution. In the 25th plenary session, three Turkish-origin politicians entered to CDU administration.

2013 German federal elections and Turks

After last elections, 11 Turkish-origin MP's elected to Federal Parliament. When we analyzed proportionally, number of Turkish voter in Germany, which has 61.9 million voter in total, is equal to %1.5 of the voters and elected 11 MPs is equal to %1.7 of parliament which has 631 MP's in total. This proportional equality occurred first time in German politics. (Erdoğan, 2013)

Cemile Yusuf (Giousouf) can be considered as most notable Turkish-origin MP among others after the elections. The reasons for this are; first, she was the first Muslim MP that elected from CDU, second, because she is a Western Thrace Turk, she also represents multiculturalism in Turkish community. She is a Muslim-Turkish origin German with a Greek identity. She advocates that CDU is a conservative party but it should not link with only Christianity. She claims it is a party that a religious Muslim should also vote for conservative parties and she indicates "Positive developments can be happen for integration when politics made on similarities not on differences" (Sabah Gazetesi, 2013).

The other notable Turkish-origin MP after the elections is Aydan Özoğuz from SPD. She joined to elections as vice-chair and also participated in coalition negotiations and made a change happen on citizenship law. When coalition formed she has appointed as Commissioner for Immigration, Refugees and Integration. Thus, a Turkish-origin politician became a member of cabinet council in German politics first time.

Mahmut Özdemir was the youngest MP, he was 26 when he got elected from SPD to Bundestag. Özdemir is can be seen as a symbol of Turks interest in

---

[175] Cem Özdemir was elected but resigned immediately after the election.

politics. He is in politics since he was 14 and it shows that young Turks capabilities to gain achievements when they are interested in politics.

In CDU-SPD government that formed after 2013, there are five Turkish-origin MP's in the parties in power and it shows that Turks moved forward one more step on influencing the power.

Political interest and problems of Turks in Germany

It is known that political issues on the agenda in Turkey exist on the agenda of Turkish community in Germany. For this reason, Turkish origin MPs give attention to some issues from Turkey during the election and holding office period. But taking statement from Turkish origin MPs as representative of these issues whenever opened, is in past! According to a Turkish origin German MP, the attention of the Turkish community is still direct in Turkey but now they begin to see themselves as German, albeit slowly. Also he emphasized the result of fully integrated society and MPs for these issues with talking as "these issues are perceived as a foreign policy issue with this way" (Sakman, 2015, p.156).

Graphic 2: Rates of Interest in Politics for Turkey and for Germany of Turkish Community.

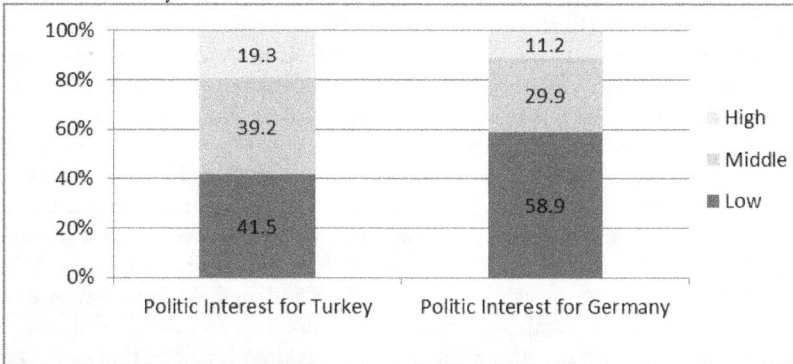

Source: Sauer, M. (2009). Teilhabe und Orientierungen türkeistämmiger Migrantinnen und Migranten in Nordrhein-Westfalen. Essen: Stiftung Zentrum für Türkeistudien (ZfTI).

According to the study of ZfTI, as seen in the above graph, generally there is a lack of interest but more than half of Turkish origins (58.9%) were distant from German politics.

The other study shows nearly same conclusion. 32.6% of the surveyed Turkish origins in this study is completely uninterested in politics. The rate of interested in politics in Germany is %9.1 and in Turkey is %18.7 (Şahin, 2010, p.183). So it means less than a half.

If Turkish community ask from Turkish origin politicians to work as MPs of the Turks, the success of them and contribute to the integration are affected in a negative way. The opinion with the stereotype as "MPs of the Turks think benefits of the Turkish community" is so wrong and actually needs them to act on behalf of all society including the Turkish community. Thus it can be seen by all sections, by everybody, that the Turks are part of the society which they live in. Their best thing to do for them is speak as *"1 minute! I am not a Turkish MP. They are in Ankara. I am a Turk but I am an MP for all German society and represent in German parliament."*[176] We know that this belief is now accepted among these MPs.

Some initiatives that are being done in order to prevent assimilation of community also delay or complicate the integration of other part of the community. Several actions that Turks took at the beginning such as refusal, not learning the language, not being a citizen, minimum communication with the state, watching Turkish TV channels etc. restricted their existence in German politics and prevented the emergence of conditions that is needed for integration.

Conclusion

As the conclusion, Turkish-origin MP's are both an accelerator and result of the integration. If we consider that diasporas are participated to politics only when they feel comfortable in the places they live, MP's are responsible to provide that environment and they are also stronger when it provided. Also, an invitation from Turkish-origin candidates to Turkish society to vote might be more effective. Naturally, they encourage Turkish-origin voters to meet minimum requirements. These minimum requirements are common denominator of the host country, which is Germany. Furthermore, participation of voters and candidates gives them a chance to stand against prejudices about them. According to this, being in a position which influence politics rather than being a material to political strives gives confidence. With that confidence they will start to conceive and act for region they live or Germany in general.

Turks in Germany could be MP in Federal and State Parliaments, Head of Political Parties and Ministers. But when we look to last half century, it is clear that they progress quite slowly. There are some discourses that it should be prepared to the prime ministry of a Turkish origin politicians in the lobbies. However, it is more realistic opinion in the short and medium term that an attempt which will make political participation of Turks more active as shaping the political life of Germany or playing a role in making decisions that could create large effects is not happened. Indeed, ideas sourced from be immigrant of Turkish origin politicians continues to be a barrier to them even if they enter to parliaments. This also causes to questions about the direction of integration.

Increase on the number of Turkish-origin MP's and importance of roles that they took was parallel to increasing existence of Turkish society in politics and Turkish-origin MP's, who have these roles, illustrated that they work for integration of the Turkish society.

References

Apin, N. (2011). Islamische BIG-Partei: Angst vor Schwulkindern. Received from http://www.taz.de/!76635/ available on: 05.06.2015

---

[176] It was inspired from the interview of Tunahan Kuzu (MP in the Netherland) in the book (Sakman, 2015, p.161).

Bundeszentrale für Politische Bildung (2011). 50 Jahre Anwerbeabkommen - Sevim Celebi-Gottschlich. Received from http://www.bpb.de/geschichte/deutsche-geschichte/anwerbeabkommen/43199/sevim-celebi-gottschlich available on: 05.06.2015

Danışman, J. (2011). Türk Kökenli Bakana Tepki. Received from http://www.dw.de/t%C3%BCrk-k%C3%B6kenli-bakana-tepki/a-15342077 avaliable on: 05.06.2015

Erdoğan, M. (2013). Rapor: Türkiye Kökenli Alman Vatandaşlarının Almanya Federal Meclisi (Bundestag) Seçimlerinde Siyasal Davranışları [Report: Political Behaviors of the Turkish Origin German Citizens in German Federal Election (Bundestag)]. Hacettepe Üniversitesi Göç ve Siyaset Araştırmaları Merkezi (HÜGO). (in Turkish)

Eroğul, C. (2006). Çağdaş Devlet Düzenleri. Kırlangıç Yayınevi.

Özdemir, C. (1999). Ben Almanyalıyım. İletişim Yayınları.

Sabah Gazetesi. (2013, September 24). Merkel'in Türk Prensesi.

Sakman, T. (2015). Türk Diasporası'nın Avrupa Siyasal Sistemine Katılımı. Çizgi Kitapevi.

Şahin, B. (2010). Almanya'daki Türkler. Phoenix Yayınevi.

The integration of immigrants in rural communities: an example of city council's approach towards Turks in France

Markéta Seidlová[177]

Introduction

France has among the European countries one of the longest tradition of receiving immigrants (Freeman, 1994) and was considered for long time as one of the model countries of incorporation of immigrants. France has represented the model called "assimilation", i.e. the attitude that gives to immigrants all the civic rights very quickly, but in exchange it's expected that they will give up their cultural particularities and that they will in some sort "forget" from where they come (Seidlová, 2008).

In 1999[178], 4.3 milions persons born outside France lived in this country, making thus 7.4 % of population (INSEE, 2011a). From them, 37 % lived in the region of Paris (Île-de-France). The uneven distribution of immigrants within the French territory can be seen clearly from the figure 1, where we can also easily identify the second and the third most attractive regions for immigrants: Rhône-Alpes (11 %) and Provence-Alpes-Côte d'Azur (10 %). All this means that in only three regions lived almost two thirds (58 %) of all immigrants in France. The regions at the opposite end of the spectrum in what concerns the overall presence of immigrants were Corsica (only 0.6 % of all immigrants living in France), Limousin (0.6 %) and Basse-Normandie (0.7 %) (INSEE, 2006). The vast majority of immigrants were then living in big cities (2 of 3 immigrants lived in the city with more than 200 thousands of inhabitants) and urban areas, and only 3 % of them lived in rural areas (Boëldieu et al., 2000).

Also the spatial distribution of particular and most represented groups of immigrants was quite uneven, as we can see also from fig. 1. The Turks, making in 2012 4.4 % from all immigrants in France (INSEE, 2015) (compared to 4.0 % in 1999) were extremely concentrated in three departments[179]: Orne in the Basse-Normandie region (1,749 persons, i.e. 17.0 % of all immigratnts in this department), Jura in the Franche-Comté region (2,488 persons, i.e. 16.9 %) and in Bas-Rhin in the Alsace region (18,464 persons, i.e. 16.5 %).

---

[177] Markéta Seidlová is postdoctoral researcher at Geographic Migration Center – GEOMIGRACE, Department of Social Geography and Regional Development, Faculty of Science, Charles University in Prague, Albertov 6, 128 43 Prague, Czech Republic, e-mail: mseidlova@seznam.cz
[178] Given the fact that the main research was conducted between the years 2007 and 2011, the input data were those from the census of 1999, last available at the beginning of research (INSEE, 2011a). However, they were updated in the time of preparation of this article in order to see the evolution. So, for example, in 2012, 5.6 milions persons born outside France lived in this country, making thus 8.8 % of population (INSEE, 2015).
[179] We verified that the spatial distribution of Turks didn't change significantly between the years 1999 and 2012.

Figure 1: Spatial distribution of immigrants in France in 1999

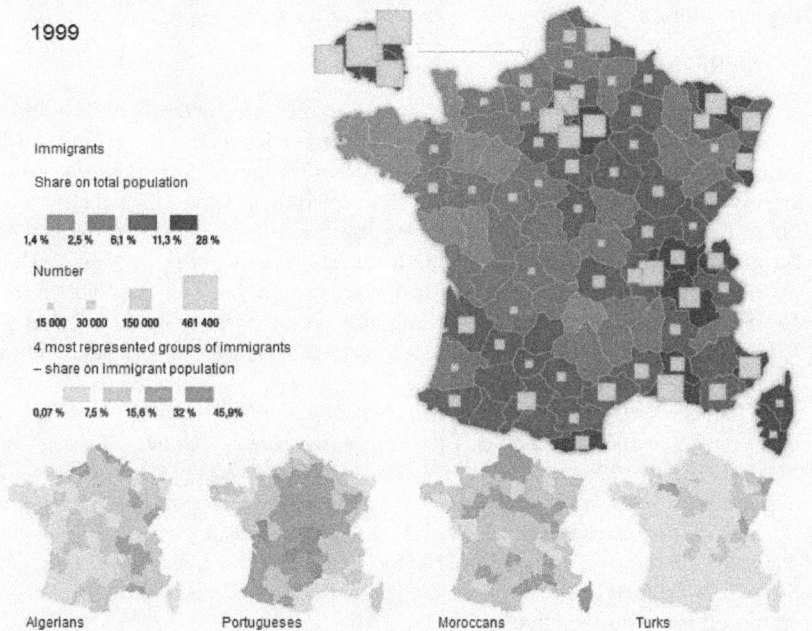

NB: *The Algerians represented 13.3 % of all immigrants in France in 1999; the Portugueses 13.3 %; the Moroccans 12.1 % and the Turks 4.0 %.*
Source: Sciences Po, 2007

Local dimension of immigration

The process of integration of immigrants into the host society always has a strong local (and especially urban) dimension. From the point of view of history, the biggest experience with integrating diverse and culturally enriching populations had big cities with strong economies (Borkert et al., 2007), serving as "machines of integration". Therefore, "the integration of immigrants takes place at the local level" (Bosswick, Heckmann, 2006, p. 17). The city administrations may then act as "only" implementing national integration policy or, on the contrary, they may have considerable autonomy and independence in both finance and opinion (Borkert et al., 2007). The processes and the structures working on place are, of course, heavily influenced by the policy of higher levels, i.e. counties/regions, states or even by supranational organizations such as European Union (OECD, 2006). However, the everyday practice in implementation of laws and regulations at the local level always provides some space for own reading by municipalities. As result, the attitudes and everyday practices of municipal councils and of their administrations are the most important ones because they have significant influence on the results of the process of integration of immigrants into host society. The type of migration coming to city defines the attitude of municipality to the integration policy and lists the integration as a key or marginal priority within the issues solved (Bosswick, Heckmann, 2006).

Methodology

All the over mentioned inspired our research, conducted between 2007 and 2011 (Seidlová, 2012). This research compared in particular the attitude of local councils towards the immigrants in Paris and in the cities of the Basse-Normandie region. The unattended finding from this research was that in of the researched cities, Flers, the Turks were representing about a half of all its immigrants – 41 %. So in fact, when speaking about the local integration policy in Flers, we speak about the policy towards Turks. Moreover, due to the fact that Turks are the fourth most represented group of immigrants in the Basse-Normandie region (see below), we can presume that they benefit in particular from this policy. The tested hypothesis was then as follows:

"The way of implementation of national integration policy by local councils varies depending on the context in which they act: the bigger share of immigrants in the total population of their city, the bigger awareness of the need to deal with immigrant integration. Better knowledge of local conditions allows local governments to better formulate specific projects which aims to promote the integration of immigrants into the host society. The tools and measures used by local governments in rural and metropolitan areas are quite similar; the only difference is the extent."
So the city council of the city with bigger share of immigrants on its population is supposed to be more active.

Figure 2: The composition of immigrant population in the cities of the Basse-Normandie region (1999)

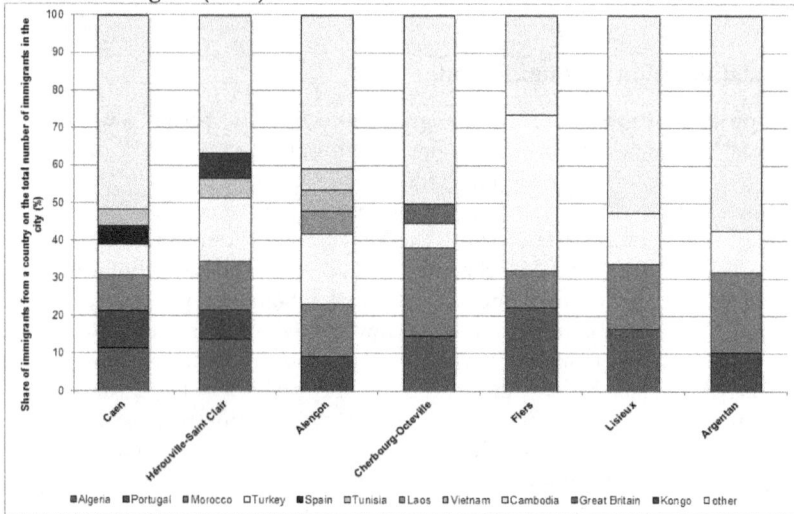

Source: Blazevic, 2005; Seidlová, 2012

Besides the analysis of secondary data and participative observation, the method of semi-structured interviews was used. In the region of Basse-Normandie, we interviewed 16 representatives of cities and of NGOs on 22 questions, divided into three main areas: *Relationship to national immigration policy, Migration situation in the municipality* and *Role of municipal government in the integration of immigrants.*

The friendliness of every researched town hall to immigrants – as well as the comparison between themselves – was then evaluated with the help of our own four step methodology as invented in Seidlová (2012).

Immigration in the basse-normandie region

In the studied region of Basse-Normandie, situated in the northwest of France, lived in 1999 a total of 28,146 immigrants, making thus 1.98 % of all inhabitants of the region. Immigrants who were also foreigners born abroad were 17,387, making 1.22 % of all inhabitants of the region[180]. More than half of the immigrants lived in the department of Calvados (52.5 %; i.e. 14,774 persons), the second half was distributed quite evenly into two others departments of the region (Orne: 26.9 %, i.e. 7,579 persons; Manche: 20.6 %, i.e. 5,793 persons). Almost half of immigrants (41.0 %) lived in seven cities: Caen, Hérouville-Saint-Clair, Cherbourg-Octeville, Flers, Alençon, Argentan and Lisieux (see fig. 2). The most important in number was the immigrant population in Caen, the administrative centre of the region (4,727 persons, i.e. 16.8 % of immigrants in the region), then in Hérouville-Saint-Clair (1,892 persons, i.e. 6.7 %) and in Alençon (1,648 persons, i.e. 5.9 %). The largest share of immigrant on the population of the whole city had the immigrants in Hérouville-Saint-Clair (7.9 % of total population), Flers (6.2 %) and Alençon (5.7 %). Almost half (45.3 %) of immigrants in the region came from five countries: Morocco (10.0 %), Portugal (9.6 %), Turkey (8.9 %), Great Britain (8.5 %) and Algeria (8.3 %) (INSEE, 2006; Seidlová, 2012). Due to the concentration of immigrants into the above mentioned cities, these cities were selected as our cities of interest.

Tools and measures used by local integration policies

To show in detail the practice in all seven studied cities would be above the extent of this article. So the obtained findings were summarized and divided into three major groups, according to the target population. The presented tools and measures are the ones which are really and actively in use by local councils.

The first group of tools and measures are the ones who *target primarily immigrant population,* ranked from the most commonly used ones to less used ones in surveyed cities:

- *Public declaration of support to diversity* or, in other words, the statement of the city leaders about fostering open and multicultural society. This openness is then translated in the number of activities that city does for its immigrants;

---

[180] In French statistics the most important is the division of inhabitants according to their citizenship. The French citizens (French) and citizens of another state (foreigners) are distinguished. An immigrant is then a person born outside of France with another than French citizenship and living currently in France.

- *Advisory Body of the City composed of representatives of immigrants from third countries* (i.e. non-EU countries) which allows immigrants to express their points of view, wishes and requirements to the town hall of their city;
- *Promoting the right to vote of foreigners in local elections* motivates the foreigners to participate actively in public life;
- *Support for non-profit organizations (NGOs) which helps to immigrants* could be financial or material or in the form of help with organisation of multicultural events;
- *Language courses (French), Literacy courses* and *Courses of "everyday life";*
- *Preparatory classes in schools for children of immigrants* work for example in Flers: their aim is to teach French to children of immigrants, and mainly to those of Turkish origin (90 % of participants in these classes);
- *"Parenthood" of foreigners including the interventions at the prefecture* means that the elected members of municipal councils can intervene in prefectures in favour of an immigrant using letters, personal meetings or by accompanying him to a meeting;
- *Ceremonies to celebrate the gain of French citizenship* at the town hall;
- *Advisory places targeting their activity on traditionally marginalized groups of immigrants:* for example two *"Clue for women"* were working in the city of Cherbourg-Octeville. They were opened daily and they were designed especially for women from Turkey and Morocco as a place where women could come and learn French or ask for a French speaking assistant who then helped them in dealing with everyday issues in the town (doctor, post office, school, etc.).

The second group of tools, *targeting primarily on the major society*, is not so large in its number, but it is the most visible for all, as these tools are *supporting the projects that increase the awareness of the majority about the diversity of cultures present in the town.* These may be of two types:
- *Multicultural festivals* that shows the details of other cultures to city's inhabitants, quite often by performances of traditional music groups or by tasting typical food;
- *Lectures, conferences, exhibitions, theatre and film performances* showing the country of origin of immigrants, their life in France or the life of immigrants in general.

Last but not least come the third group of tools and measures *targeting to all city residents* and *promoting social cohesion of the city.* These tools help all disadvantaged groups of inhabitants or promote the active participation of citizens in public life (Seidlová, 2012).

From the very concrete tools we can mention for example:
- *Partnerships and cooperation with cities abroad* which can be either more formal (signed partnership) or more friendly and project cooperation, giving real results;

- *Special section in the local magazine* which presents two successful people who grew up in the city and at least one of them is of immigrant origin;
- *Teams for school success for children from disadvantaged backgrounds* help all disadvantaged families dealing with problems in school attendance (tutoring), family relationships, culture and health;
- Formulation of own *city policy of social cohesion*;
- *Advisory Body of the City Council intended for all inhabitants* of the city;
- *Financial and material support for NGOs* that provide legal and social assistance for free to all citizens (Seidlová, 2012).

When listing these measures, we can conclude that our research confirmed the validity of the above defined hypotheses, i.e. that *the tools and measures used by local governments in rural and metropolitan areas are quite similar; the only difference is the extent.* However, as we have seen while acquiring the data for this list, the level of activity of local councils and the level of their friendliness towards immigrants was very different in the researched cities. So the question which becomes obvious is: which factors caused this difference?

Factors influencing the helpfulness and friendliness of local integration policy

The presumed relationship between the share of immigrants on the total population and the quality of implemented policy was confirmed only in two cases: in Hérouville-Saint-Clair and in Lisieux (see tab. 1). The cities of Caen and of Cherbourg-Octeville performed in fact relatively "better" policy than the one they should do according to the share of immigrants on the total population of these cities. On the other hand, the towns of Flers, Alençon and Argentan implemented "worse" policy. These differences may be explained mostly by other considered factors, such as political affiliation of mayors; possible migrant origin of members of the city council; presence and activities of nongovernmental organizations (NGOs) in the fields of human or migrant's rights or humanitarian aid; or promotion of culture of foreign communities etc.

Testing by Spearman's rank correlation coefficient, searching for correlation between the final ranking of a city in the region of Basse-Normandie according to the policy implemented in reality and all other rankings one by one[181] showed positive correlation[182] in two cases at chosen significance level (0.05): with the number of immigrants living the city and with the number of NGOs with local scope founded by immigrants.

It can be therefore concluded that in rural region the activity and the initiatives of immigrants themselves are most important factors for implementation of

---

[181] I.e. ranking according to the criteria: Share of immigrants on the total population of the city; Number of immigrants living in the city; Political affiliation of mayor; Possible migrant origin of mayor; Number of members of the city council – from them of possible migrant origin (% of total); Deputy mayor in charge of integration of immigrants; NGOs with national scope – number of branches; NGOs with local scope in the fields of human or migrant's rights or humanitarian aid – number; NGOs with local scope – founded by immigrants – number.

[182] The value of $r_{sp} = 0.821$ were only in these two cases of all detected values greater than the critical value of r_{sp} for chosen significance level and number of monitored subjects, i.e. 0.745 (Tvrdík, 2008).

migrant-friendly policies, while the activity and the initiatives of immigrants are likely to be higher when more immigrants live in the city. The dependence on other observed factors probably also exists even if these other factors may not play such important role as the two above mentioned; however, due to the small number of studied cities it was not possible to prove it statistically.

Table. Ranking of cities in the region of Basse-Normandie according to the input assumptions about nature of implemented local integration policy and by its real form

Town	The ranking of the city in region by the share of immigrants on the total population of the city	The ranking of the city in region by other prerequisites for the implementation of integration-friendly policy*	The ranking of the city in region by policy implemented in reality**
Hérouville-Saint-Clair	1	1	1
Flers	2	6	3
Alençon	3	4	5
Caen	4	3	2
Argentan	5	5	7
Lisieux	6	7	6
Cherbourg-Octeville	7	2	4

NB: * *according to the sum of ranking according to the criteria: Political affiliation of mayor; Possible migrant origin of mayor; Number of members of the city council – from them of possible migrant origin (% of total); Deputy mayor in charge of integration of immigrants; NGOs with national scope – number of branches; NGOs with local scope in the fields of human or migrant's rights or humanitarian aid – number; NGOs with local scope – founded by immigrants – number. ** i.e. according to the resulting classification according to Alexander (2007), where ad hoc policy was considered as the least friendly and the multicultural policy as most helpful and friendly; then the cities were lined up by the number of tools and measures used.*
Source: own survey, 2008, as in Seidlová, 2012

Conclusion

We have seen that not all surveyed cities use the tools and the measures that can help immigrants with their integration into major society with the same intensity. In some cases we found even inverse relationship between the share of immigrants on the total population of studied city and the number of tools used by local governments. In the rural region of Basse-Normandie, the most important factors for performing "immigrant-friendly" policy were the activity and the initiatives of immigrants themselves. At the same time, these activities and initiatives are likely to be higher if there is higher number of immigrants living in the city. Other observed factors could also interfere in the nature of adopted policy, but they are likely not playing such important role as the two above mentioned factors, even if – due to the small number of studied cities – we cannot prove it statistically (Seidlová, 2012).

The results of the undertaken analysis of attitude of French cities towards immigrants can be used as inspiration for concrete and specific tools of local integration policies in cities and towns in other countries of world. Even if the current composition of immigrant population in every country is the result of specific migration history of each country, the basic principles of successful integration of immigrants into major society remains the same. However, every city council should still bear in mind also the needs of the people from major population, in order to prevent their feeling that the city council is so immersed in combating discrimination and promoting diversity issues that it forgets the needs of other disadvantaged populations of its city.

References

Alexander, M. (2007): Cities And Labour Immigration. Comparing Policy Responses In Amsterdam, Paris, Rome And Tel Aviv. Asghate, Hamsphire, 242 P.

Blazevic, B. (2005): Les Populations Immigrées En Basse-Normandie. Insee, Paris, 28 P.

Boëldieu, J., Borrel, C. (2000): La proportion d'immigrés est stable depuis 25 ans. In: INSEE Première, 748, pp. 1-4.

Borkert, M., Bosswick, W., Heckmann, F., Lüken-Klaßen, D. (2007): Local integration policies for migrants in Europe. European Foundation for the Improvement of Living and Working Conditions, Dublin, 69 p.

Bosswick, W., Heckmann, F. (2006): Integration of migrants: Contribution of local and regional authorities. European Foundation for the Improvement of Living and Working Conditions, Dublin, 45 p. In: http://www.eurofound.europa.eu/pubdocs/2006/22/en/1/ef0622en.pdf

Freeman, G. P. (1994): Can Liberal States Control Unwanted Migration? Annals of the American Academy of Political and Social Science, vol. 534, Strategies for Immigration Control: An International Comparison, p. 17-30.

INSEE (Institut National de la Statistique et des Études Économiques) (2006; 2011a; 2015): Résultats du recensement de la population – 1999; 2008; 2012. In: http://www.recensement.insee.fr/home.action (30. 7. 2015)

OECD (2006): From Immigration to Integration. Local solutions to a global challenge. OECD Publishing, Paris, 326 p.

SCIENCES PO (2007): Migrants – Installation en France – 1891; 1931; 1975; 1999. In: http://cartographie.sciences-po.fr/en/cartotheque (14. 11. 2011)

Seidlová, M. (2008): The French Immigration Policy: what do we learn? In: GeoScape, 3, pp. 60 – 67. ISSN: 1802-1115.

Seidlová, M. (2012): Imigrační a integrační politika Francie – v nadnárodní, národní a lokální rovině. Disertační práce. Praha, Univerzita Karlova, Přírodovědecká fakulta, 233 p.

Tvrdík, J. (2008): Analýza dat. 2. upravené vydání. Učební texty Ostravské univerzity, Přírodovědecká fakulta, Ostravská univerzita v Ostravě, Ostrava, 83 p.

Londra'da Çalışan Türkiyeli Göçmenlerin Çalışma Süreleri ve Sosyal İlişkileri[183]

Mehmet Rauf Kesici[184]

Giriş

Göç konusu, ulaşım olanaklarının artması, ucuz işgücü gibi kapitalist/ekonomik gereklilikler, baskıcı rejimlerden kaçan muhalifler vb. vesilelerin yanı sıra farklı farklı yollarla Avrupa'ya ulaşmaya çalışan göçmenlerin yaşadıkları olumsuzlukların daha görünür olmasıyla kamuoyunun ve akademinin dikkatini çekmeye başlamıştır.

Göç, göçmenler, emek piyasaları ve çalışma koşullarına dair, bu konuları ayrı ayrı ele alan yaygın bir literatür olmasına rağmen, birbiriyle ilişkilendirerek ele alan, etkileşimleri anlamaya ve açıklamaya çalışan az sayıda çalışmanın olduğu ifade edilebilir. Sosyal ve ekonomik değişmelerden dolayı göç hareketleri dinamik bir alanda cereyan etmektedir ve bu alanda yeni çalışmalara ihtiyaç duyulmaktadır. Bu veriden hareketle ilk dipnotta ifade edilen alan araştırmasından elde edilen bulgulara dayalı olarak, bir mikro çalışmayla literatüre katkı sağlanması amaçlanmaktadır. Bu çalışmada özetle, Londra'da Türkiyeli etnik ekonomisinde çalışmış ya da çalışmakta olan Kürt, Türk ve Kıbrıslı Türklerin çalışma süreleriyle sosyal ilişkileri arasında nasıl etkileşimlerin söz konusu olduğu araştırılmakta ve sosyal entegrasyona ilişkin bulgular tartışılmaktadır.

Londra'da çalışan Türkiyeli göçmenlerin çalışma sürelerinin ve günlerinin, bu göçmen topluluğun sosyal ilişkilerinde nasıl sonuçlar yarattığını irdelemek araştırmanın temel sorusunu oluşturmaktadır.

İlgili göçmenler arasında çalışma koşulları, çalışma süreleri ve günlerinin günlük yaşamda nasıl etkiler yarattığı, sosyal ilişkileri ve sosyal entegrasyonu ne yönde etkilediğinin araştırılması en önemli hedef olarak ortaya konulabilir.

Bu çalışmada Türkiyeliler olarak ifade edilen göçmen toplulukları etnik, dini, politik vb. bakımlardan heterojen bir yapı arz etmektedir. Buna göre Türkiyeliler, etnik olarak Kürt, Türk, Kıbrıslı Türk, British, Kürt-Türk vd. kimliklere sahip olduklarını; dini olarak Alevi, Ateist, Sünni-Müslüman, agnostik vd. olduklarını; politik bakımdan sosyalist, özgürlükçü, demokrat, liberal, Labour[185], muhafazakâr, sağcı vb. sıfatlarla kendilerini tarif ettiklerini belirtmişlerdir. Dolayısıyla çalışma boyunca Türkiye'den ve Kıbrıs'tan Britanya'ya göç eden Kürt, Türk ve Kıbrıslı Türkleri nitelemek için Türkiyeli ifadesi kullanılmıştır ancak bu toplulukların ortak özellikleri kadar etnik, linguistik, dini, politik ve ideolojik farklılıklarının söz konusu olduğu ve bu ifadenin de geneli nitelemek için yeterli olmadığı göz önünde

[183] Bu çalışma, "Londra'da Yaşayan Türkiyeli Göçmenlerin Emek Piyasalarındaki Konumlarının Belirleyicileri" başlıklı, Regent's University London, Regent's Centre for Transnational Studies'da yürütülen, TÜBİTAK, **2219**-Yurt Dışı Doktora Sonrası Burs Programı tarafından desteklenen, 12 ay süreli doktora sonrası araştırma projesi kapsamında yapılmıştır.
[184] Kocaeli Üniversitesi, Öğretim Üyesi (mehmet.rauf@kocaeli.edu.tr), Regent's University London, Regent's Centre for Transnational Studies (RCTS), Posdoctoral Visiting Fellow (kesicim@regents.ac.uk).
[185] Bazı görüşmeciler, Britanya'daki İşçi Partisi'ne atıfla kendilerinin politik yönelimini ifade etmek için bu nitelemeyi kullanmaktadırlar.

bulundurulmalıdır.

Yöntem

Kalitatif özellikli bu çalışma Britanya, Londra'da Eylül 2014 – Eylül 2015 tarihleri arasında yapılan 12 aylık alan araştırması üzerine kurgulanmıştır. Çalışmanın hazırlık döneminde Türkiyeli topluluğa dair mümkün mertebe fazla ve derinlemesine bilgilere ulaşmak amacıyla ilgili bilimsel yayınlar, araştırmalar taranmış, dernekler, kahveler, işyerleri ve evler ziyaret edilmiş ve enformel görüşmeler yapılmıştır. Bu çerçevede Londra'da yaşayan Türkiyelilerin Enfield, Haringey, Hackney ve Islington ilçelerinde yoğunlaştığı tespit edilmiş ve araştırma ağırlıklı olarak Kuzey Londra'nın bu ilçelerinde yoğunlaştırılmıştır[186].

Ön hazırlık aşamasında yapılan bilimsel araştırma ve alana ilişkin gözlemlerin ışığında 20'si Kürt, 20'si Türk ve 20'si de Kıbrıslı Türk göçmenlerle olmak üzere 60 görüşme yapılmıştır[187]. Katılımcılarla yarı-yapılandırılmış mülakat formları kullanılarak derinlemesine görüşme ve gözlem yapılan bu araştırma işçi, işveren, kendi hesabına çalışan, işsiz, emekli vd. Türkiyelilerle ve bunlardan etnik ekonomi ve topluluk örgütleriyle ilgili olanlarla yürütülmüştür. Görüşmeciler, ilgili dernek, işyeri ve topluluğa dair bilgi sahibi olan kişilerden önerilerle ve kartopu tekniği kullanılarak bulunmuş ve kendilerine bu proje için hazırlanmış özel bir taahhütname imzalanarak verilmiştir.

Mülakat formu göçmenlerin demografik özelliklerini, sosyal ilişkilerini, geçmiş çalışma deneyimlerini ve emek piyasalarındaki mevcut durumlarını anlamaya, soruşturmaya çalışan bir form olarak tasarlanmış ve görüşmeler esnasında görüşmecilerin ifade etmek istedikleri tüm ayrıntıları ve farklı durumları açıklamalarına olanak tanınmıştır. Görüşmeler esnasında da kişisel bilgilerle birlikte mümkün mertebe kişinin ilişki ağları ve topluluğa dair bilgilerini sergileyecek mülakatlar gerçekleştirilmeye çalışılmıştır. Buna rağmen fenomonolojik özellikleri baskın bu tarz çalışmalardan bütünlüklü bir biçimde geneli yansıtması beklenmemekte, genele dair fikir edinilmesi hedeflenmektedir.

İngiltere'de Çalışma Süreleri[188]

İrlanda'da bazı farklı düzenlemeler olmak kaydıyla Britanya'da çalışma süreleri, iç hukuk ve Avrupa Birliği (AB) direktiflerine göre düzenlenmektedir. Bu çerçevede kural olarak Londra'da çalışan herhangi bir işçi, yazılı ve imzalı bir anlaşmayla bu hakkından vazgeçmiş değilse, haftalık, ortalama 48 saatten fazla çalıştırılamaz. Bu ortalama, 17 haftalık referans döneminde belirlenir. 16-17 yaşındaki işçiler ise günde 8 saatten ve haftada 40 saatten fazla çalıştırılamaz. Burada tam zamanlı çalışma haftada 36-40 saat arası çalışmayı ifade ederken kısmi süreli çalışma haftada 35 saat ve altındaki çalışmayı ifade eder.

Normal çalışma süresi iş sözleşmesiyle belirlenir ve fazla çalışma süresi, belirlenen normal çalışma sürelerinin üzerindeki çalışma sürelerini ifade eder ve işveren, işçinin ortalama ücreti asgari ücretin altında değilse, fazla çalışma süreleri için normal çalışma süresi dışında ek bir ödeme yapmak zorunda değildir. İş

---

[186] Bkz. London Datastore, London Borough Profiles, (http://data.london.gov.uk/dataset/london-borough-profiles, 14/06/2015).

[187] Sirkeci ve Esipova (2013: 6-7), Britanya'da 200-250 bin arası Türkiye'den Kürt ve Türk ile Kıbrıs'tan Türkün yaşadığını ve bu üç gurubun nüfus olarak birbirine yakın olduğunu ifade etmektedir.

[188] Bkz. GOV.UK, (2015), Working, jobs and pensions, (https://www.gov.uk/browse/working/contract-working-hours, 15/06/2015).

sözleşmesi çoğunlukla fazla çalışma sürelerine dair nasıl çalışılacağı, ne kadar ödeneceği gibi detayları içerir ve sözleşmede ifade edilmişse çalışan, fazla sürelerde çalışmak zorundadır. Bu noktada "zero-hours contract" olarak ifade edilen oldukça esnek bir iş sözleşmesi biçiminin de söz konusu olduğunu ifade etmek gerekmektedir. Zira bu sözleşmeye göre işveren, iş garantisi vermeksizin, yani ne zaman ihtiyaç duyarsa, o zaman ilgili işçiyi çalıştırabilir. İşçi saat başına ücretlendirilir. Çoğunlukla hastalık ödemesi söz konusu değilken, çalışma süresi düzenlemeleri uyarınca tatil ödemesi olmalıdır[189]:

Çalışma saatleri hala köle düzeni. Sabah 8, akşam 5. Normalde 8-5 günlük ama dediğim gibi as required [gerektiği gibi], zero hours contract, liberal ekonomi diyelim (Görüşme 18).

Gece çalışması normal koşullarda gece 11:00 ile sabah 6:00 saatleri arasında yapılır ancak işçi ve işveren yazılı anlaşarak bunu, gece yarısıyla sabah 5:00 saatleri arasında olmak koşuluyla, esnetebilirler.

On sekiz yaşının üzerindeki işçi günde 6 saatten fazla çalışıyorsa çalışma süresi içinde kesintisiz en az 20 dakika ara dinlenmesi hakkına sahiptir. İşçinin iş günleri arasında en az 11 saat dinlenme hakkı vardır. Ayrıca işçinin haftada kesintisiz en az 24 saat dinlenme hakkı söz konusudur.

On sekiz yaşından küçük işçi ise günde 4.5 saatten fazla çalışıyorsa çalışma süresi içinde kesintisiz en az 30 dakika ara dinlenmesi hakkına sahiptir. Bu işçinin iş günleri arasında en az 12 saat dinlenme hakkı vardır ve haftada kesintisiz en az 48 saat dinlenme hakkı söz konusudur.

Londra'da Yaşayan Türkiyeli Göçmenlerin Etnik Ekonomisi

Bir göçmen grubun üyelerinin sahip olduğu ve işlettiği işyerlerini ifade eden etnik girişimcilik, göçmenlerin ekonomik adaptasyonunun bir türüdür (Dedeoğlu, 2014). Etnik ekonominin temel taşı olan göçmen girişimciliğinin çeşitli veçheleri söz konusudur. Büyük ölçüde toptancılık, perakendecilik, restorancılık gibi işlerden müteşekkil etnik ekonomiye girişin önündeki engeller görece azdır zira bu işler yüksek sermaye gerektiren işler değildir ve emek gücü gereksinimi etnik ağ ve aile/akraba üyeleri havuzundan karşılanabilmektedir (Ojo vd., 2013: 592).

Chrysostome ve Lin (2010: 78) göçmen girişimciliğinin ekonomik etkilerinin yanı sıra etnik toplulukların dinamizminin gelişmesi, sosyal entegrasyon ve göçmenlerin tanınması, girişimcilik ruhunun beslenmesi ve göçmenler için rol modeli sağlama gibi çeşitli etkileri olduğunu ifade etmektedir. Bu etkilere haiz göçmen girişimciliğinin temel formunun küçük işletmeler ve kendi hesabına çalışma (self-employed) biçiminde tezahür ettiğini ifade etmek gerekmektedir. Dolayısıyla ekonomik değişim ABD ve Britanya gibi göç alan ülkelerde göçmenleri küçük işletmeler kurmaya itmekte ve kendi hesabına çalışma formuna çekmektedir (İbrahim & Galt, 2011: 608). Bu göçmen grupları içinde Türkiye'den Almanya ve İngiltere başta olmak üzere çeşitli ülkelere göç eden insanlar da genel özellikleriyle etnik ekonominin bu çizilen çerçevesi içinde yer almaktadır.

Genel olarak, Türkiye'den Avrupa'ya 1970'li yılların ilk yarısına kadar göç eden insanlar, çoğunun böyle bir formasyonu olmamasına rağmen, imalat sanayisinde endüstri işçisi olarak çalışmaya başlamışlardır. Dünya çapında etkileri söz konusu olan 1973 krizi ve daha sonra uygulamaya konulan neoliberal politikalar birçok

---

[189] Bkz. Department for Business Inovation & Skills, (2013), Zero Hours Employment Contract, (https://www.gov.uk/government/uploads/system/uploads/attachment_data/file/267634/bis-13-1275-zero-hours-employment-contracts-FINAL.pdf, 14/06/2015).

göçmen işçinin işsiz kalmasına yol açmış ve böylece etnik ekonomi olarak nitelendirilen, kendi işini kurma ve istihdam yaratma süreci başlamıştır. Bu çerçevede, başlarda göçmenlerin ihtiyaç duyduğu yoğurt, döner, kebap gibi etnik yiyecekleri sağlama hizmetleri, zamanla büyüyerek yaygınlaşmıştır. Kimi kaynaklarda (Panayiotopoulos, 2010) "döner-kebap devrimi" olarak da nitelendirilen bu süreç Almanya, Berlin'de doğmuş ve gelişmiştir. Şöyle ki Avrupa Birliği'nde (AB) kendi hesabına çalışan Türkiyelilerin tahminen %70'i Almanya'da çalışmaktadır ve bu küçük girişimcilik yerel yönetimlerin politika ve önlemleriyle desteklenmektedir (Constant vd., 2007). Bu kendi hesabına çalışılan döner-kebap sipariş işyerlerinin başını çektiği, restoranlar, kafeler, içki dükkânları, marketler gibi etnik ekonomiyi oluşturan işyerleri, zamanla diğer Avrupa ülkelerine ve Britanya'ya da yayılmıştır (Dedeoğlu, 2014: 42, 46).

Britanya'da bulunan Türkiyeli göçmenlerin yarattığı etnik ekonominin tarihi de, ortaya konulan bu genel çerçeve içinde yer almaktadır. Fordist fabrikalarda, özellikle tekstil/hazır giyim sektöründe çalışan Türkiyeliler bu sürecin sona ermeye başladığı dönemden itibaren küçük girişimciliğe dayalı bir etnik ekonomi yaratmaya başlamıştır:

13 sene bir fabrikada çalıştım, 7 sene başka bir fabrikada managerlik [ustabaşı] *yaptım, 35 tane makineciye bakıyordum... Bir ara fabrikalar kapandı, tekstil Romanya'ya, oralara taşındı. Ondan sonra da, kapandıktan sonra da biz burayı (Kafe/ restoran) açtık. İşte... 12 senedir de buradayım*[190] *(Görüşme 15).*

Bu durum birçok sanayi işçisini işsiz bırakan neoliberal yeniden yapılanmaya Türkiyeli topluluğun verdiği bir cevap ve etnik azınlıklar için emek piyasalarında istihdam fırsatlarının az olmasına bir reaksiyon olarak da ifade edilebilir (Dedeoğlu, 2014: 43).

Bu reaksiyonun yaşandığı metropollerden biri de Londra'dır. Bu başkent göçmenlerin sayı olarak ana nüfus grubu olarak tariflenen ve beyaz Britanyalı (White[191]) olarak ifade edilen nüfustan daha fazla olduğu bir kenttir (Sirkeci ve Açık, 2015: 143-144). Londra, Britanya'da yaşayan Türkiyelilerin de hem nüfus bakımından hem de etnik ekonomi bağlamında başkenti olarak nitelendirilebilir. Büyük ölçüde fabrika işçiliği döneminde sağlanan küçük birikimlerle (sermaye birikimiyle) yaratılan Londra'daki Türkiyeli etnik ekonomisi bazı kendine özgü karakteristiklere sahiptir. Etnik ekonomide yer alan kafe, restoran, döner/kebap sipariş işyeri, market, içki dükkânı, taksicilik, ithalat-ihracat şirketi gibi küçük iş ve işyerleri, aile/akraba işletmesi özelliği gösteren, işyeri sahibinin de aktif olarak çalıştığı işlerdir:

Türkiyeliler genelde inşaat, kebap, dükkân, shop işi gibi işlerdeler... birçoğunun da kendi işi var aslında (Görüşme 2).

Etnik ekonomilerde piyasaya giriş engelleri görece düşük olduğu için rekabet, kaliteden ziyade fiyat rekabeti biçiminde tezahür etmekte, bu da iç sömürüye yol açan önemli etmenlerden biri olmaktadır (Rath & Kloosterman, 2000). Örneğin Aldrich (1977) Londra'da Asyalı göçmenlerin etnik ekonomisinde, Dedeoğlu (2014: 62) ise Türkiyelilerin etnik ekonomisinde çalışanların, iş sahibi ve ailesinin

---

[190] Görüşmeci, eşiyle sahibi oldukları ve birlikte çalıştıkları (kendi hesabına çalışma) restoran/kafeden bahsediyor.
[191] Ulusal İstatistik Ofisi (The Office for National Istatistic) de "Etnik Azınlıklar" grubunun dışında kalanları "White" olarak sınıflamakta/nitelemektedir.

emek gücünün sömürülmesi biçiminde, uzun çalışma saatleri, düşük ücretler gibi unsurlara dayalı yoğun bir içi sömürünün bulunduğunu ve bu sömürünün yoğun rekabet ortamında ilgili işletmelerin ayakta kalma yöntemlerinden biri olduğunu ifade etmektedirler. Bu çalışma kapsamında ilgili iddianın doğruluğunu teyit edecek bazı bilgilere ulaşılmıştır. Şöyle ki kendi hesabına çalışılan işyerlerinde iş sahibinin en az işçiler kadar hatta bazen işçilerden daha uzun sürelerle çalıştığı görüşmeciler tarafından ifade edilmiştir:

9, 5:30 benden hariç [gülüyor], *elemanların yani. Benim 6 ya da 7 gün, saat 7:30'dan 7'ye kadar. Offf, gün içindeki iş yoğunluğu çok yani hiç durmuyor. Bayağı yoğun. Çalışanlar tamamdır, onlar tamamdır. 1 saat öğlen dinlenmesi var, 1 – 2 saatleri arasında herkes yemeğe çıkar (Görüşme 53).*

Gün içinde 15-16 saat çalışırdım. Tabi dükkân senin olunca bitmeyen iş varsa çalışırdık içeride. Haftada 7 gün çalışırdık. Pazar çalışmazdık bazen temizlik yapmaya giderdik (Görüşme 54).

... zor şartlarda yürütüyorsun, tamam belki işverensin ama işveren de zor şartlarda, yani gitse bir dert gitmese ayrı bir dert. İşverenle işçi arasında fark yok aslında İngiltere'de, biri biraz daha fazla kazanıyor, biri az kazanıyor, biri tam sömürülüyor diyeyim de biri de... (Görüşme 49).

Öte yandan birkaç kişinin çalıştığı bu küçük işletmelerde genellikle iş sahibi ya eşiyle ya kardeş(ler)iyle ya akrabasıyla ya da köylüsü/hemşerisiyle birlikte çalışmakta, eskiler yeni gelenlere "yol/yordam" öğretmekte ve aile/akraba/hemşeri ilişkileri çoğu durumda iç sömürüye dayanak oluşturmaktadır:

Kendi köylümüzün yanında, burada başladım. Herkes 500 lira alırken bana 150 lira verdi. İngilizce bilmediğimiz için, yol/yordam bilmediğimiz için (Görüşme 4).

Etnik ekonomi kadın emeği açısından değerlendirildiğinde önceki Fordist döneme göre belirgin farklılıklar ihtiva ettiği görülmektedir. Kadınların görece erkeklere yakın koşullarda istihdam ve ücret fırsatı buldukları Fordist üretim dönemine nazaran etnik ekonomi döneminde genel olarak kadınlar için ücretli istihdam olanakları azalmış ve kadınların çoğu geleneksel, patriarkal, toplumsal cinsiyet ilişkilerinin bir yansıması olarak eş, anne, gelin vd. rollerle birlikte ücretsiz aile işçisi konumuna doğru geri itilmiştir[192].

Türkiyeli Göçmenlerin Çalışma Süreleri ve Günleri

Tarihsel olarak çalışma süreleri ve çalışma koşulları emek piyasaları konusunda temel tartışma alanlarının başında gelmektedir. 1800'lü yılların sonlarından 1900'lü yılların sonlarına kadar olan dönemde ABD, Britanya, Japonya gibi sanayileşmiş ülkelerde çalışma süreleri neredeyse yarı yarıya azalmıştır (Bosch ve Lehndorff, 2001: 214-215). Eurostat verilerine göre Avrupa ülkeleri genel olarak değerlendirildiğinde 2000'li yıllarda bu azalış trendi azalarak da olsa devam etmiştir. Britanya da bu ülkelerden biridir zira 1956 yılında 48,3 saat olan tam zamanlı çalışan için haftalık ortalama çalışma süresi (Lee vd., 2007: 26) 2003 yılında 43,7 saate düşmüş ve süreç içinde düşük bir oranda azalarak 2014 yılında 42,9 saat olarak gerçekleşmiştir.

Britanya'nın geneliyle karşılaştırıldığında, alan çalışması kapsamında görüşme

---

[192] Bu konuda kapsamlı ve nitelikli bir çalışma için bkz. Saniye Dedeoğlu, (2014). *Migrants, Work and Social Integration / Women's Labour in Turkish Ethnic Economy*, London: Palgrave-Macmillan.

yapılan göçmenlerin beyanlarına göre, genel olarak etnik ekonomideki çalışma süreleri ise çok uzun ve çalışma koşulları zordur[193]:

Genelde 9 sabah, akşam 7-8'e kadar normal bazen daha fazla olabilir. Hafta sonları ara sıra en az bir günüm işe gider. Toplantı olabilir, işte yetiştirmediğim işleri yapmam gerekir (Görüşme 58).

Market dediğimiz işte en az 60 saat çalışırdık (Görüşme 51).

Çalışma saatlerimiz en az 10 saat. 10 saatten aşağı kimse çalışmıyor yani. Ben de günde 11 saat çalışıyorum. Haftanın, şu an 7 günü, ama normalde 6 günü çalışıyorum (Görüşme 43).

Ben daha Türklerin yanında çalışıp da 8 saat çalışanı görmedim. 12 saatten az çalışanı göremiyorum ben burada. Çünkü genellikle Türklerin işyerlerinde çalışıyorlar ve hep 12 saat. Genellikle 6 gün çalışılıyor (Görüşme 1).

... danışmanlık yaptığım zaman müşterilerimin çoğu Türk'tü ... onlar her zaman asgari ücretin altında alırlardı ve 40 saat, 50 saat çalışırlardı. Yani çok ezilirlerdi ve birçok Türk şirketinde böyle olduğuna inanıyorum (Görüşme 58).

Lee vd. (2007: 37, 120-123) ücretler ve çalışma zamanı arasında bir etkileşimin söz konusu olduğuna işaret etmektedir. Şöyle ki özellikle saat ücreti düşük olduğu zaman çoğunlukla uzun çalışma süreleriyle karşılaşılmaktadır. Örneğin Filipinler'de 48 saatten daha fazla çalışan işçilerin %90'ından fazlası daha yüksek kazanç elde edebilmek için bunu yaptığını ifade etmektedir (Mehran, 2005: 4). Messenger (2011: 303) ve Toksöz (2008: 36) ise fiili çalışma süresinin çok uzun olduğu Türkiye'de, bu durumun en önemli nedenlerinden biri olarak, düşük ücretler ile uzun çalışma saatleri arasındaki bağlantıya dikkat çekmektedirler. Genellenirse özellikle az gelişmiş ülkelerde düşük ücretlerin telafi edilmesi ve verimlilik düzeyinin artırılması için uzun çalışma sürelerinin söz konusu olduğu görülmektedir.

Bununla birlikte ekonomilerin içinde de sektörden sektöre çalışma sürelerinde farklılıkların olduğunu ifade etmek gerekmektedir. Örneğin AB ülkeleri birlikte değerlendirildiğinde en uzun çalışma sürelerinin tarım, inşaat, otel ve restoran sektörlerinde olduğu görülmektedir (Parent-Thirion vd., 2007: 19). Bu sektörler ise göçmenlerin görece daha fazla sayıda çalıştığı sektörlerdir. Londra'da Türkiyeli göçmenlerin ağırlıklı olarak hizmet sektöründe çalıştığı ve alan çalışmasında bazı göçmenlerin düşük ücretler ile uzun çalışma süreleri bağlantısına işaret eden beyanlarda bulundukları görülmektedir:

İhtiyacın var 10 saat çalışırsın, yarın ihtiyacın yok 5 saat çalışırsın (Görüşme 33).

Türkiyelilerin çok zor tabi ki, çok uzun saatler çalışıp çok az para alıyorlar. O yüzden ben Türkiyeli bir yere gittiğim zaman kapanış saatiyse hemen çıkarım, yani biliyorum çünkü o işleri, o işlerde çalıştığım için, çok zor onların işleri (Görüşme 24).

Ayrıca hizmet sektörü işlerinde uzun çalışma sürelerinin açık işler ile işsiz nitelikleri arasındaki uyumsuzluktan dolayı diğer sektörlerde ve/veya etnik ekonomi dışında çalışma olanaklarının kısıtlılığıyla ve görece daha yüksek işsizlik oranlarıyla da bağlantısı vardır.

İşsizlik oranları Londra'da, nüfusun azınlıklar dışındaki grubuna (White) nazaran, göçmenler arasında daha yüksektir. Örneğin Eylül 2014 itibarıyla

---

[193] Bu noktada Kıbrıslı Türk göçmenlerin Kürt ve Türklere nazaran, çalışma koşulları bakımından, biraz daha müspet koşullarda oldukları ifade edilebilir zira 20 numaralı görüşmede, görüşmeci; *"Kıbrıs'ın AB'ye girdikten sonra, çalışma koşulları Kıbrıslılar için önemli ölçüde değişti. İyileşti. Çünkü serbest olarak gelip çalışabiliyoruz, iş kurabiliyoruz, oturabiliyoruz"* diyerek bu durumu örneklemektedir.

Londra'da White olarak nitelendirilen grupta işsizlik oranı %5,0 iken Etnik Azınlıklar grubunda % 10,9 düzeyindedir (ONS, 2015). Bunun yanı sıra Sirkeci ve Açık (2015: 156), göçmenler arasında ekonomik olarak aktif olmama durumunun beyaz Britanyalılara göre daha yüksek olduğunu ifade etmektedir. Genel olarak bu durumların Türkiyeli göçmenler açısından da geçerli olduğu söylenebilir. Ancak bu verilere mesafeli yaklaşmayı gerektiren unsurlar da söz konusudur. Şöyle ki alan çalışması esnasında kaçak çalıştığını/çalıştırdığını, Ankara Anlaşması kapsamında gelenlerden ilgili resmi kuruma bildirdiği işin dışında bir iş yaptığını ya da başka bir işte çalıştığını[194], bir, hatta bazen iki işte çalıştığını ancak sosyal yardımları kesilmesin diye çalışmayı resmi olarak göstermediğini ya da sadece kısmi zamanlı çalışma olarak gösterdiğini ifade eden görüşmecilerin olduğu ifade edilmelidir:

Bizde çalışanların çoğu, mesela 2-3 tane kaçak var. Bakıyoruz adama, cash veriyoruz burada, itiraz edecek hali mi var. Değil mi? Yine içeride 2-3 adam var, part-time gösteriyor kendini, devletten yardımını alıyor ayrıca, şimdi bu adamın itiraz edecek hali mi var (Görüşme 18).

Çünkü part-time çalışıyor gözüküyoruz. Çünkü öyle göstermezsek yaşanmaz bu ülkede. Çünkü kiralar yüksek, giderler fazla, mecbur öyle gösteriyoruz (Görüşme 1).

Ayrıca bazı görüşmeciler topluluk içinde bunun yaygın bir davranış biçimi olduğunu ifade etmektedirler:

Zaten biliyorsunuz birçok insan çalıştığını göstermiyor. Devletin yanında çalışmıyor gözüküyor, adam devlet yardımı alıyor. Bundan ziyade gidip çalışıyor. Çalışınca ne oluyor? Zaten devletin haberi yok. Adamın da işine geliyor (Görüşme 1).

Yüksek işsizlik oranı, hukuksal ve siyasal yapının el vermesi, etnik ekonomi dışındaki işler için yeterli niteliklere sahip olmama, Britanya toplumuna entegrasyonda inişli/çıkışlı seyir, geri dönmenin ekonomik olabilirliğini sağlama çabası gibi faktörler uzun çalışma sürelerine yol açan etmenler arasında öne çıkmaktadır.

Sosyal İlişkiler Bağlamında Türkiyeli Göçmenlerin Çalışma Süreleri ve Koşulları

Göç ve göçmenlerin sosyal ilişkileri/entegrasyonu konuları kuramsal olarak Ravenstein'ın göç kanunlarını ortaya koyduğu 1800'lü yılların sonlarından itibaren çalışılmaktadır (Kaygalak, 2009: 13). Böylece literatürde göçmenlerin sosyal entegrasyonuna dair çeşitli yaklaşımların geliştirildiği görülmekte, bu durum ise üzerinde uzlaşı sağlanan bir tanımın bulunmamasına yol açmaktadır. Örneğin Dedeoğlu (2014: 32) göç bağlamında çeşitli veçheleri olan entegrasyonu genel olarak göçmenlerin o ülkede yaşayan topluluğun bir parçası olma süreci olarak ifade etmektedir. Bu çalışma çerçevesinde ise sosyal entegrasyona dair Birleşmiş Milletler Mülteciler Yüksek Komiserliği'nin, göçmenin kendi kimliğinden vazgeçmeden topluma uyumlaştığı (adaptation) ve toplumun ve kamu kurumlarının da göçmenleri kabul ederek ihtiyaçlarını karşıladığı (welcome) çift taraflı bir süreç olarak ifade eden, yaklaşımı benimsenmektedir[195]. Bu çerçevede Türkiyeli göçmenlerin sosyal ve ekonomik ilişkileri, topluluk içi sosyoekonomik ilişkiler ve Britanya toplumuna sosyal entegrasyon bağlamında ele alınabilir.

Sosyal ilişkiler ve sosyal entegrasyon açısından değerlendirildiğinde Türkiyeli

---

[194] 1993 Tarihli Ankara Anlaşması ve Katma Protokol
[195] Bkz. UNHCR. (2013). *A New Beginning Refugee Integration in Europe,* (http://www.unhcr.org/52403d389.html, 13/06/2015).

göçmenler arasında Britanya'ya göç tarihi Kürt ve Türklere nazaran daha eski olan, adadaki eski İngiliz varlığı hasebiyle İngilizce yeterliği daha fazla olan, AB pasaportuyla Britanya'ya vizesiz gelebilen ve kültürel uyum konusunda görece daha az sorun yaşayan Kıbrıslı Türkleri, Kürt ve Türklere göre Britanya toplumuna daha adapte topluluk olarak nitelemek yanlış olmayacaktır:

Kıbrıs pasaportu tuttuğumuz için o Kıbrıs pasaportu Avrupa Birliği pasaportudur, AB tarafından koşulsuz ve şartsız olarak %100 kabul edilir. Her türlü şartta kabul edilen bir pasaport olduğu için gelip burada oturma ve çalışma hakkına sahip olabiliyor. Ama Türkiyelilerin burada aynı koşullarda değil, çalışma ve oturma şeyleri (Görüşme 20).

...sanırım, Kıbrıslılara daha fazla sıcak bakılıyor. Çünkü Kıbrıslılar daha fazla tanıdıklar diyelim ve Kıbrıslılar genelde İngilizlere daha kolay adapte olabileceği için... (Görüşme 35).

Kıbrıslı Türklerden farklı olarak çoğu Kürt ve Türk göçmen, Britanya vatandaşlığına geçme sürecinde mevcut prosedürü, hukuksal yapıyı bilmemek, dil yeterliği olmamak gibi durumlardan dolayı Halkevi, Kurdish Community Centre, Cemevi, Day-Mer gibi derneklerle ilişki kurup bu derneklerin "danışmanlık" hizmetlerinden yararlanmaktadır. Ayrıca Londra'da kamuyla ilişkilerde ve Britanya toplumuyla ilişkilerde de ilgili derneklerin yardımına başvurulmaktadır. Örneğin bu derneklerden birinin lokalinde, dernekte danışmanlık hizmeti veren bir avukat ile görüşme yaparken; Türkiye'den gelmiş bir Britanya vatandaşı Kürt'ün, kendisini arayan ve İngilizce konuşan ev sahibinin ne söylediğini öğrenmek için telefonu danışmana verdiğine ve danışmanın da son derece akıcı bir İngilizce ile görüşmeyi yaparak; kiracıya, ev sahibinin, ev sahibine de, kiracının söylediklerini aktardığına şahit olunmuştur. Bu ve benzeri durumlar, Britanya toplumuyla Türkiyeli topluluk arasında bireysel, zorunlu iletişimin üretebileceği sosyal ilişkilerin eksik kalmasına yol açmaktadır.

İngilizce öğrenememek, Britanya'daki hukuksal yapıyı, kamu ile ilişkilerin nasıl kurulacağını, yürütüleceğini öğrenememek gibi sosyal ilişkileri noksan bırakan, sosyal entegrasyonun yavaşlamasına yol açan "eksiklerin" en önemli nedenlerinden biri, iş gününün yoğunluğu ve çalışma sürelerinin uzunluğudur:

Hiç katılmadım. Doğrusunu söylersek, imkânım, zamanım olmuyor. Öyle bir alana gidip zaman ayırma durumum hiç olmuyor... Yani burada biraz apolitiklik geliştiriliyor. Uzun süre çalışmaktan dolayı sosyal alanın bitiyor. Yani ekonomizm insanları vuruyor (Görüşme 7).

Bana göre, kimisi erkenden açılan, kimisi 24 saat açık olan Türkiyelilerin restoranları ve içki dükkânı gibi dükkânlarında, çalışma saatleri çok aşırı fazladır. Şef olan babam bazen haftada 52-54 saat çalışır. Ve bu normal değil, zira makine/araç değilsiniz. Bence Türkiyeli insanlar, gün boyu, 24 saat açık olan, Türkiyelilerin restoranlarında çok aşırı bir biçimde çalışıyor (Görüşme 46).

Buradaki toplum yabancılara açılmamış, İngilizlere açılmamış. Toplum birbirlerinden alışveriş, iş birbirlerinden, her şey birbirlerinden. O zaman ne oluyor, ee dil de öğrenemiyorsun (Görüşme 1).

Bununla birlikte uzun çalışma sürelerinin ve zorlu çalışma koşullarının söz konusu olduğu etnik ekonomi üzerinden geliştirilen, sosyal entegrasyonun sağlanmasında katkı sağlaması olası, sosyal ilişkiler de söz konusudur. Örneğin haftanın 7 günü, günde (gece çalışması biçiminde) 10-12 saat arası çalışan, içki dükkânı sahibinin, kasa başındayken ödeme yapmaya gelen müşterilerinin büyük bir kısmıyla ayaküstü sohbet ettiği, Britanya'daki genel seçimlere[196] dair fikir aldığı, görüş beyan ettiği görülmüştür. Müşterilerin yanı sıra toptancılar, nakliyatçılar, belediye görevlileri, komşular vb. ile etnik ekonomi üzerinden kurulan ilişkiler söz konusudur:

Yabancılarla da olabildiğince var yani müşterilerimle sürekli her şeyi konuşurum. Siyaseti konuşurum, ticareti konuşurum, aileyi konuşurum... (Görüşme 7).

Benim toptancılarım, Türkiyeli de var, Pakistanlı da var ama genelde Pakistanlılar. Bizim Türk toplumunun gittiği toptancıların %90'ı Pakistanlı (Görüşme 49).

Topluluk içi sosyal ilişkiler bakımından da çalışma sürelerinin uzunluğu ve yoğun çalışma koşulları çeşitli etkiler yaratmaktadır. Bu noktada topluluk içindeki ilişkilerin azalması, eşler arasında, ebeveynlerle çocuklar arasında, akraba, hemşeri ve komşular arasında iletişim, dayanışma, sosyalleşme vb. ilişkilerin zayıflaması gibi unsurlar öne çıkmaktadır:

Türkiyelilerin çalışma saatleri çok uzun... özellikle erkeklerin. Ailesiyle sosyal aktiviteleri yok, uzun çalışma saatlerini biraz da ben kendilerinin yarattığını düşünüyorum. Çünkü şunu yapalım, şu şunu aldı, şu ev aldı, şu araba aldı diye biraz da parayı sevme, parayı önemseme olduğunu görüyorum. Günün sonunda çocukları, işte ya aileden kopuyor ya çok farklı bir kişilik oluyor. İstediğin tarzda çocuk yetiştiremiyor. Ailesini bir arada tutamıyor, ben de bir örnek olarak bölünmüş bir aileyim (Görüşme 14).

Geçmişe göre daha da zorlaşıyor. Tekstil işinde taşeronluktu ama bir nevi şimdiki işçiliğe göre biraz daha iyiydi. Çünkü hafta sonları zamanın oluyordu, community çevrenle, komşunla veya şunla bunla bir pikniğe bir şeye gidebiliyordun. Ama şimdi yok, müthiş koptu, öyle bir koptu ki, bildiğin gibi değil, toplum tam koptu birbirinden yani (Görüşme 49).

Ya işten dolayı katılmıyorum açıkçası pek. Ama katılmak istiyorum aynı zamanda. Burada iş hayatım biraz yoğun tempo ile geçtiği için zaman olmuyor açıkçası (Görüşme 48).

Kadın göçmenler açısından etnik ekonomiye geçiş ve çalışma sürelerinin sosyal ilişkiler ve entegrasyon konularında yarattığı sonuçlar topluluğun genel durumuna önemli etkiler yapmaktadır. Şöyle ki tekstil, hazır giyim imalathanelerinin kapanmaya başlaması ve yerini etnik ekonomiye bırakmasıyla kadın göçmenlerin ekonomik ve sosyal fonksiyonları da değişmeye başlamıştır. Bunula birlikte topluluk içinde ikinci jenerasyonun okul başarısızlığı, şiddet eğilimi gibi menfi sonuçlar kadınlara, kadınların çalışmasına yüklenmekte, ailevi meselelerde ayıplanarak toplumsal baskı altına alınmakta ve nihayet toplum ve etnik ekonomi içinde, patriarkal rollerinin altı çizilmektedir. Böylece genel olarak ücretli işçilikten, ev işleri, çocuk bakımı, ücretsiz aile işçiliği gibi "geleneksel işleri"ne doğru geri itilen kadınların etnik ekonomi üzerinden sosyal ilişkiler kurma ve Britanya toplumuna sosyal entegrasyon konularında fonksiyonları farklılaşmıştır:

Ev ve çocuk bakımı işleri çok yorucu, genelde çocuklarımla ilgilenmeyi tercih ediyorum. Evet, onlar uyduktan sonra da ev işlerimi yapıyorum. Yani, yoğun geçiyor günümüz diyelim (Görüşme 50).

Genellikle Türkiyeli ev kadınları çalışmak istiyorlar çünkü artık ev hayatı insanı yoruyor. Belirli bir şeyden sonra, sabah kalk, çocuğu hazırla, okula götür, eve gel, temizlik, yemek, misafir... hep aynı işler olduğu için insan bunalıyor. Sıkılıyor ve bu defa çalışmak istiyor (Görüşme 10).

Bunula birlikte ailenin/evin kamuyla ilişkilerini düzenlemek, çocuklar

---

[196] 7 Mayıs 2015 tarihinde yapılan genel seçimler.

üzerinden kamu kurumları, göçmen nüfus ve Britanya toplumuyla ilişkilenmek yollarıyla kadın göçmenler için yeni fonksiyonların söz konusu olabileceği görülmektedir:

... iş teklifleri geliyor, ama ben şey yapmıyorum pek, yani yoğun olduğumuz için, ondan her halde. Aslında istiyorum çalışmayı da, bir kendimi düzene koyayım diyorum. Ev işi, çocukların kursları, onların arkasından koşturmam çok, ... gerçekten de 5 günüm dolu, onu oraya, onu oraya götür, hepsine koşturuyorsun. Gündüz okuldalar, akşam ise kimisini saza götürüyorum, kızımı dansa, müzik-dramaya götürüyorum İngiliz yerine, öbür oğlum futbola gidiyor, piyanoya gidiyor. Yani hep böyle koşturuyorum. (Görüşme 12).

Örneğin 50 numaralı görüşmede ücretli bir işte çalışmayan kadın göçmene *"Evin kamuyla, belediyeyle ilgili işlerinde siz mi varsınız, eşiniz mi var?"* sorusu sorulmuş ve *"Ben varım."* yanıtı alınmıştır.

Ücretli veya kendi hesabına istihdam olanağı bulan kadınların ise "geleneksel işleri"nden dolayı daha yoğun sömürüye maruz kaldıkları ve sosyal ilişkilerin üretilebileceği etkinliklere katılamadıkları ifade edilebilir:

Çalışıyorum ya hiç öyle bir şeye zamanım olmuyor. Haftanın 7 günü buradayım, bir de buradan çıkıyorum koşa koşa eve gidiyorum, Hakan gelmeden, Rahime gelmeden yemek yapmam lazım. Ev işleri var, çamaşır, bulaşık, ütü... yani öyle şeylere zamanım olmadı. Zamanım olsa belki katılırım (Görüşme 15).

Bu çalışma kapsamında, kadınların sosyal ilişkiler ve sosyal entegrasyon konusundaki fonksiyonlarında meydana gelen değişmelere dair, elde edilen sonuçlara benzer sonuçları ifade eden Dedeoğlu (2014: 146-169), kadınların Türkiyeli topluluğun Britanya toplumuyla sosyal ilişkileri ve bu topluma sosyal entegrasyonu noktasındaki fonksiyonlarını, müspet ve menfi öğeleri iç içe barındıran dinamik bir süreç olarak değerlendirmekte ve zikzaklı (inişli-çıkışlı) bir sosyal entegrasyon patikası olarak nitelemektedir.

Kadınların yaklaşık yarısını oluşturduğu Türkiyeli topluluğun sosyal ilişkiler ve sosyal entegrasyonu konusunda, bu noktada, topluluğun geneli için de sosyal entegrasyonu sağlama anlamında *müspet* ve sosyal entegrasyonun sağlanmasını yavaşlatma anlamında *menfi* öğelerin iç içe olduğunu ifade etmek gerekmektedir. Diğer bir deyişle sosyal entegrasyonunu hızlandıran ve yavaşlatan öğelerin iç içe olduğu dinamik bir süreç anlamında zikzaklı sosyal entegrasyon patikasının topluluğun geneli için de geçerli olduğu söylenebilir. Bununla birlikte bu zikzaklı ve dinamik sürece göz atıldığında, sosyal entegrasyonu yavaşlatan (içinde yoğun çalışma koşulları ve uzun çalışma sürelerinin önemli bir yer tuttuğu) öğelerin sosyal entegrasyonu hızlandıran öğelere baskın olduğu görülmektedir.

Sonuç

Londra'da yaşayan Türkiyeli göçmenlerin etnik ekonomi ve emek piyasalarındaki konumları, çalışma koşulları ve çalışma süreleri, ekonomik ve sosyal açıdan çeşitli sonuçlar doğurmaktadır. Özellikle çalışma koşulları ve sürelerinin sosyal ilişkiler ve sosyal uyum çerçevesinde yarattığı sonuçlar, bu konularda mevcut sorunların çözümü için uygulanacak politika ve programlara ışık tutacaktır.

Çalışma sürelerinin iç hukuk ve AB direktiflerine göre düzenlendiği Britanya'da, uzun çalışma sürelerine el verecek, esnek bir çalışma rejiminin söz konusu olduğu ifade edilebilir. İlgili hukuksal çerçevenin de gelişimine yol verdiği, hizmet sektöründe yoğunlaşan Türkiyeli etnik ekonomisi, kendi hesabına çalışılan döner-kebap sipariş işyerlerinin başını çektiği, restoranlar, kafeler, içki dükkânları, marketler gibi işyerlerinden müteşekkildir. Bu işyerlerinin çoğunluğunda çalışanların, iş sahibi ve ailesinin emek gücünün sömürüsüne yol açan düşük ücretler ve uzun çalışma saatleri söz konusudur. Bunun yoğun rekabet ortamında ilgili işletmelerin ayakta kalma yöntemlerinden biri olduğunu gösteren emarelerden biri, iş sahibinin en az işçiler kadar hatta bazen işçilerden daha uzun sürelerle çalışmasıdır. Bu etnik ekonomide ücretli istihdam olanakları az olan kadınlar ise geleneksel, patriarkal, toplumsal cinsiyet ilişkilerinin bir yansıması olarak eş, anne, gelin gibi rollerle birlikte ücretsiz aile işçisi durumundadırlar.

Türkiyeli etnik ekonomisinin belirgin özelliklerinden biri uzun çalışma süreleri ve zorlu çalışma koşullarıdır. Şöyle ki Britanya'nın geneliyle karşılaştırıldığında, göçmenlere dair bilimsel yayınlara göre ve bu alan çalışması kapsamında görüşme yapılan göçmenlerin beyanları esas alındığında, genel olarak etnik ekonomideki çalışma süreleri çok uzun ve çalışma koşulları zordur. Bu duruma yol açan etmenler göçmenlerin yoğunlukla çalıştığı hizmet sektörünün emek çalışmaya uygun olması, göçmenler arasında işsizliğin yüksek olması, ücretlerin düşük olması, geri dönmenin ekonomik olabilirliğini sağlama çabası, göçmenlerin dil yeterliğinin az olması ve diğer sektörlerde iş bulma olanaklarının zayıf olması olarak sıralanabilir.

Kıbrıslı Türklere nazaran çoğu Kürt ve Türk göçmen, Britanya vatandaşlığına geçme sürecinde mevcut prosedürü, hukuksal yapıyı bilmemekte, dil yeterliği de olmadığı için ilgili derneklerden yardım almaktadır. Bu "eksikler"in giderilmesinin önündeki temel engellerden biri zorlu çalışma koşulları ve çok uzun çalışma sürelerinin göçmenlere bu işlere ayıracak zaman ve enerji bırakmamasıdır. Diğer bir deyişle İngilizce yeterliğini geliştirememek, Britanya'daki hukuksal yapıyı, kamu ile ilişkilerin nasıl kurulacağını ve yürütüleceğini öğrenememek gibi sosyal ilişkileri noksan bırakan, sosyal entegrasyonun yavaşlamasına yol açan eksiklerin temel nedenlerden biri, iş gününün yoğunluğu ve çalışma sürelerinin uzunluğudur.

Topluluk içi sosyal ilişkiler bakımından çalışma sürelerinin uzunluğu ve yoğun çalışma koşulları topluluk içindeki ilişkilerin azalması, eşler arasında, ebeveynlerle çocuklar arasında, akraba, hemşeri ve komşular arasında iletişim, dayanışma, sosyalleşme gibi ilişkilerin zayıflaması gibi sonuçlara yol açmaktadır.

Öte yandan uzun çalışma sürelerinin ve zorlu çalışma koşullarının söz konusu olduğu etnik ekonomi üzerinden geliştirilen, sosyal entegrasyonun sağlanmasında katkı sağlaması olası, müşteriler, toptancılar, nakliyatçılar, kamu kurumları vb. ile kurulan sosyal ilişkiler de söz konusudur.

Kadın göçmenler açısından etnik ekonomiye geçiş süreci ve uzun çalışma süreleri kadın göçmenlerin ekonomik ve sosyal fonksiyonlarının değişmesine yol açmakta ve bu durum da topluluğun sosyal ilişkilerine ve Britanya toplumuyla entegrasyonuna çeşitli etkiler yapmaktadır.

Şöyle ki etnik ekonomiye geçiş sürecinde genel olarak ücretli işçilikten, ev işleri, çocuk bakımı, ücretsiz aile işçiliği gibi patriarkal/geleneksel işlerine doğru geri itilen kadınların etnik ekonomi üzerinden sosyal ilişkiler ve Britanya toplumuna sosyal entegrasyon konularında fonksiyonları farklılaşmıştır. Burada etnik ekonomi üzerinden kurulması muhtemel sosyal ilişkiler bakımından fonksiyonu azalan kadınların ailenin/evin kamuyla ilişkilerini düzenlemek, çocuklar üzerinden kamu kurumları, göçmen nüfus ve Britanya toplumuyla ilişkilenmek yollarıyla yeni fonksiyonlarının söz konusu olabileceği görülmektedir.

Nihayet sosyal entegrasyonu hızlandıran *müspet* ve yavaşlatan *menfi* öğeleri iç içe barındıran dinamik bir süreç anlamında zikzaklı sosyal entegrasyon patikasının topluluğun geneli için de söz konusu olduğu söylenebilir.

Bununla birlikte bu dinamik süreç çalışma koşulları ve çalışma süreleri açısından değerlendirildiğinde sosyal entegrasyonu yavaşlatan öğelerin, sosyal entegrasyonu hızlandıran öğelere baskın olduğu ve sosyal entegrasyonun yavaş ilerlediği görülmektedir.

Kaynakça

Aldrich, H. (1977). Testing the Middleman Minority Model of Asian Entrepreneurial Behavior: Preliminary Results from Wandsworth, England. Chicago: Paper presented at *the Annual Meetings of American Sociology Association*.

Bosch, G. & Lehndorff, S. (2001). Workink-time reduction and employment: experiences in Europe and economic policy recommendations. *Cambridge Journal of Economics*, 25, 209-243.

Chrysostome, E. & Lin, X. (2010). Immigrant entrepreneurship: Scrutinizing a promising type of business venture. *Thunderbird International Business Review*, 52(2), 77-83. doi: 10.1002/tie.20315

Constant, A., Shachmurove, Y. & Zimmermann, K. (2007). What makes an entrepreneur and does it pay? Native men, Turks, and other migrants in Germany, *International Migration*, 45(4), 71-100.

Dedeoğlu, S. (2014). *Migrants, Work and Social Integration / Women's Labour in Turkish Ethnic Economy*, London: Palgrave-Macmillan.

Department for Business Inovation & Skills. (2013). *Zero Hours Employment Contract*, (https://www.gov.uk/government/uploads/system/uploads/attachment_data/file/267634/bis-13-1275-zero-hours-employment-contracts-FINAL.pdf, 14/06/2015).

GOV.UK. (2015). *Working, jobs and pensions*, (https://www.gov.uk/browse/working/contract-working-hours, 15/06/2015).

İbrahim, G. & Galt, V. (2011). Explaining ethnic entrepreneurship: An evolutionary economics approach, *International Business Review*, 20, 607-613. doi: 10.1016/j.ibusrev.2011.02.010

Kaygalak, S. (2009). *Kentin Mültecileri*, Ankara: Dipnot Yayını.

Lee, S., McCann, D. & Messenger, J. C. (2007). *Working Time Around the World: Trends in Working Hours, Laws and Policies in a Global Comparative Perspective*. Geneva and New York: ILO and Routledge.

London Datastore, *London Borough Profiles*, (http://data.london.gov.uk/dataset/london-borough-profiles, 14/06/2015).

Mehran, F. (2005). *Measuring excessive hours of work, low hourly pay, and informal employment through a Labour Force Survey: a pilot survey in the Philippines*, Geneva: UNECE/ILO/Eurostat Seminar on the Quality of Work.

Messenger, J. C. (2011). Working time trends and developments in Europe. *Cambridge Journal of Economics*, 35, 295-316.

Ojo, S., Nwankwo, S. ve Gbadamosi, A. (2013). Ethnic entrepreneurship: the myths of informal and illegal enterprises in the UK, *Entrepreneurship & Regional Development*, 25(7-8), 587-611. http://dx.doi.org/10.1080/08985626.2013.814717

ONS (The Office for National Statistics). (2015). *Unemployment Rate, Region*, http://data.london.gov.uk/dataset/unemployment-rate-region

Panayiotopoulos, P. (2010). *Ethnicity, Migration and Enterprise*, London: Palgrave-Macmillan.

Parent-Thirion, A., vd. (2007). *European Foundation for the Improvement of Living and Working Conditions 'Fourth European Working Conditions Survey 2005'*, Luxembourg: Office for

Official Publications of the European Communities.

Rath, J., & Kloosterman, R. (2000). Outsiders Business, Research of Immigrant Entrepreneurship in the Netherlands. *International Migration Review*, 34 (3), 656–680.

Sirkeci, İ. & Açık, N. (2015). İngiltere'de Göçmenlerin Ekonomik Uyumu ve İşgücü Piyasasında Azınlıklar, *Göç ve Uyum*, Derleyenler: Şeker, B., Sirkeci, İ. & Yüceşahin, M. M., London: Transnational Press, 143-164.

Sirkeci, İ., Cohen, J. H. & Yazgan, P. (2012). Turkish culture of migration: Flows between Turkey and Germany, socio-economic development and conflict, *Migration Letters*, 9(1), 33-46.

Sirkeci, İ. & Esipova, N. (2013). Turkish migration in Europe and desire to migrate to and from Turkey, *Border Crossing: Transnational Working Papers*, No: 1303.

Toksöz, G. (2008). *Decent Work Country Report – Turkey*. ILO EUROPE Regional Office.

UNHCR (United Nations High Commissioner for Refugees). (2013). *A New Beginning Refugee Integration in Europe*, (http://www.unhcr.org/52403d389.html, 13/06/2015).

Sharing bread in the local Brussels vicinity[197]

J.M.L. Kint[198]

Introduction

Globalisation creates new horizons. The Norwegian anthropologist Fredrik Barth speaks of the way the global, with its transnationalism and transnational social movements, becomes the site of the beginning of 'in between' trans-border median spaces (Barth, 1994, p.11-32). Barth proposed to distinguish three levels of processes that evolve by themselves: a micro (or personal) level, a macro level (of 'state policies'), and a median level, where processes 'create collectivityand mobilize groups for diverse purposes by diverse means' (Barth 1994 cited in Leman et al., 2014).

Looking at European continental countries, Habermas describes modern societies as 'post-secular'. He refers to a change in the public-private consciousness (Habermas, 2008). The implication of newcomer's beliefs and their visibility is, according to Habermas, challenging the modus vivendi in continental Europe that exists between citizenship and cultural- particular difference. This modus vivendi has been drastically questioned in recent years (Habermas 2008 cited in Leman et al., 2014).

According to Baumann, 'multiculturalism is not a patchwork of five or ten fixed cultural identities, but an elastic web of crosscutting and always mutually situational, identifications' (Baumann 1999, p.118). Johan Leman and all put it: 'Immigration and mobility are giving rise to the possibility that individuals will exchange one identity for another, even though the boundary between two groups is maintained in terms of cultural difference. Crossing borders, real or imaginary, is part of an disincorporation and displacement of the identity issue. The borders may be rigid or fluid, but they are always changing, transforming and challenging the existence of fixed identities. The variety of ethnic-religious communities poses some challenges, such as adaptation to new cultures, loyalty to the practices of parents' (Leman 2014, p.12).

We also subscribe to Brubakers point of view that 'what cognitive perspectives suggest in short, is that race, ethnicity, and nation are not entities in the world but ways of seeing the world' (Brubaker 2004 cited in Leman et al., p. 2014). As such, the coexistence of several identities of the migrant communities maintains a new hybrid identity. Ethnic identities are sustained by what Fredrik Barth called the maintenance of 'boundaries' or lines, which mark off one group from the other. These lines are not drawn by simple cultural difference but by social behaviour, which is relevant to the recognition of membership. Language is described as one major cultural marker. In this paper we focus our attention on food, and bread in particular, as relevant ethnic-cultural marker, besides dress, house-form or general style of life, amongst others (Barth, 1969, p. 14).

[197] *Sharing bread* receives financial support from the Impulse Fund for Migration Policy, Brussels.
[198] Johanna Kint is researcher, coach & lecturer at the University of Technology Eindhoven, Netherlands & LUCA School of Arts, Brussels, Belgium. E-mail: *J.M.L.Kint@tue.nl*, Johanna.Kint@luca-arts.be

Food and culture

Eating and cooking are activities that are very much embedded in culture (Mennell, Murcott & Van Otterloo, 1992; Bruns et al, 2012). Culture is perhaps the most obvious influence on food preferences and choice as 'food-related attitudes, behaviours, and habits are deeply rooted in our culture and are an integral part of our identity' (Rajagopal & Hamouz, 2009). It has strong historical antecedents, embedded in unique combinations of environment, e.g. in the Mediterranean climate the presence of olive trees favours the use of olive oil versus the use of butter in northern European countries due to the large availability of pastures. Secondly, it addresses rituals and belief systems, e.g. the catholic opposition towards Jewish and Islamic religion in the early renaissance Spain increased the consumption of various types of cured pork meat. Thirdly, the community and family structure, human endeavour, mobility, are of relevance e.g. in Spain, which was conquered by the Northern-African Muslims in the 8th century, the Islamic influence can still be observed in the variety of sweets combining honey and almonds, traditionally eaten during Christmas time. Finally, one may consider the economic and political systems, which are integrated in different cuisines (Furst, Connors, Bisogni, Sobal & Winter Falk, 1996).

Research on food and meals focused on dealing with preparation, cooking and eating, both from historical and current viewpoints (Gustafsson, 2004). Food is a major source of pleasure for almost all humans (Rozin, 1998 cited in Pettinger, Holdsworth & Gerber, 2006) and is known to play an essential role in strengthening social ties in Southern Europe (Volatier, 1995 cited in Pettinger et al., 2006). But, while in France the kitchen has been described as a room where everyone meets and lives together (Volatier, 1995 cited in Pettinger et al., 2006), in England, many may just regard food as a necessity (Wright, Nancarrow, Kwok, 2001; Burnett, 1989). Douglas (cited in Gustafsson, 2004) thinks that food and eating are symbolical parts of a social system and she has studied a British meal in detail, focusing on its structure and composition. Traditional dishes may have special functions and symbolical meanings in certain rituals. Culture also has a major role in determining where and how foods are consumed (Fischler, 1998; Mela, 1999) and food is a way of expressing sociability and hospitality (Fieldhouse, 1996), as mealtimes bring groups together, both physically and symbolically (Mennell, Murcott, van Otterloo, 1992; Marshall, 1995).

The brabantwijk as ethnic and cultural melting pot

The project started with the 'Urban Rituals' workshop, which took place in the Brabantwijk, location of LUCA School of Arts, Brussels. According to Brabantwijk specialist Tim Cassiers, researcher at Cosmopolis Free University of Brussels (VUB) and Earth and Environmental Sciences at the Catholic University of Leuven (KUL), it is a highly neglected neighbourhood and one of the poorer areas of Brussels. A multitude of groups and functions are concentrated here. The population is mainly Turkish and Moroccan in origin, but also many newcomers find their first residency here such as Roma gypsies and people from the Balkan area. These people live together in this poor area of transition. They tend to stick to their (small) community, often without making an effort to communicate or integrate with other people in the neighbourhood. The area has a high population turnover.

Aside from the residential function, the Brabantwijk also has a number of supra-local functions, such as ethnic trade and window prostitution, besides colleges and offices. Not until the late nineties did this area become an item on the political agenda. After years of depravation the required budget was available to renovate the public space. But this didn't solve all the problems in the area. 'The social problems remain considerable: educational disadvantages, unemployment, poverty haven't disappeared, no more than social cohesion has become a fact.' Therefore it is, according to Cassiers, necessary to invest in this area. He mentions: 'the area has a multitude of functions (shopping, schooling, living, leisure, prostitution, working...) that capture flows from a multitude of scales and is therefore used by a huge variety of people. All these persons (groups or individuals) have their own, proper way of living, using, exploring or just passing through the neighborhood, their own agendas and time schedules, their own interests and passions as well as fears and prejudices' (Kint, 2013, p. 152).

Figure 1. In the metropolis we are all strangers. Brabantwijk graffiti.
Source: Photo by I. Ferwerda.

The Brabantwijk is a melting pot of residential multiculturalism. This multiculturalism provides great and -more often- small frictions, which remain hidden but sometimes become visible through urban messages from graffiti (Figure 1) or huge amounts of waste, thrown daily onto the streets on purpose (Figure 2).

Figure 2. Typical local shops in the Brabantwijk alterate with loads of waste and cardboard boxes, left in the streets.

Source: Photo by I. Ferwerda.

Urban rituals

How do young designers / artists / filmmakers / photographers alleviate the small frictions in this multicultural community and society? How do they ideate and give shape to new rituals, embedded in the urban context? With these specific questions in mind, we developed the workshop 'Urban Rituals'. We invited social design students from Brussels and industrial design students from the University of Technology Eindhoven to start practice-based investigation in the neighbourhood. We asked them to map and document urban frictions that they discovered in the streets with photographs and movies of different situations that caught their attention. We asked them to start from everyday reality, look for interaction with the vicinity, research existing phenomena of rituals and what new rituals might be developed to alleviate frictions.

Rituals relate to important moments in our life. They mark forgiveness, reconciliation, or transitions to adulthood, married life, divorce, healing from sickness, and death. General research into this field has been developed by Bell on ritual theory and practice (Bell, 1992), by Rappaport on ritual and religion in the making of humanity (Rappaport, 1999) and many others. We estimate that rituals also relate to small, everyday life activities such as greeting, talking, smoking, drinking coffee or tea, playing with beads, and many more. We asked our students to consider what these rituals do uphold? What function do they serve? What social structures do they maintain? How do we understand them? How and in what way do they 'move' across cultures? How do we re-interpret them trans-culturally? Can we learn to talk the same language through the medium of ritual?

Sub-questions within the workshop were: what do rituals mean for us (from a Western perspective)? Which rituals do we still perform? Which rituals are lost? How and why they are lost? Are they superseded with new rituals? What rituals do the different cultures living in this vicinity perform? In what way do they differ from ours? Context and relevance are important by means of looking for interaction with the people living in the Brussels community.

From trash to bread

Carolyn Steel is an architect, lecturer and writer. In Hungry City she describes how, despite its obsession with 'efficiency', everything about our modern food industry is precisely the opposite. Of all forms of waste involved in modern food production, none is more damaging than that of food itself because, according to Steel, 'it contains all the others put together. When we waste food, we waste all the effort, labour, water, sunshine, fossil fuels - even life itself- that went into making it' (Steel, 2009, p. 261). The reasons why we waste food all boil down to the same thing: our disconnected food culture. 'In our post-modern, clinical, hygiene-obsessed world, food makes us fearful (...)' (Steel, 2009, p. 262). In her 1966 book Purity and Danger, anthropologist Mary Douglas analysed how rejected food comes to be classified as 'dirty'. There is no such thing as dirt in nature. It is our habit of separating and categorising objects that creates it. Douglas contrasts the way in which 'dirt' in primitive cultures is often adopted as part of a sacred structure, whereas in the West it is almost entirely a matter of 'hygiene or aesthetics' (Douglas, 1966 cited in Steel, 2009, p. 263).

How would it be if one tried to describe a city through food? What about the idea of using food as a common mediator within urban life? Sitopia or small answers is Steel's reply to this question (Steel, 2009, p.xi-xii, p. 320). Small answers were also looked after and provided during the 'Urban Rituals' workshop. One group or multicultural mix of Dutch, Flemish and Turkish students, focused on the Brabantwijk ritual of sharing leftover bread with people who are in need of it. This is a phenomenon these students occasionally came across with and started to closely observe during their fieldwork in the quartier. Instead of throwing bread into the trash, in some streets of the Brabantwijk it is put aside in separate bags, next to trees and trash. The students were impressed by the discrete presence of this sense of social care within a district that is known for its frictions, dirt and poverty. Their observation of the bread bags and the image it created brought them to the conclusion that this sharing ritual did not look appealing at all, amidst all the other trash.

Currently it seemed as if this phenomenon was more randomly happening by several households. This observation inspired the students to explore whether the restaurants were doing something similar. After visiting several markets, bakers and restaurants it was found out that only a few of them were giving away the bread leftovers. One of them gave it away to a mosque. Another one had a few people in need that received the bread for free.

Within the current situation the people who give the bread have the sole task of putting the bread outside. Within the household areas it was difficult to find out what happened to the bread if it was not taken by anyone. The students learned that one of the snack bars that put bread outside is cleaning it up afterwards. The other bakers, grocery shops and snack bars did not have a specific plan for the leftover bread.

Since the bread ritual already existed it was not necessary to design something that would change the behavior of people. The focus went to a support for their activity. The students came up with the simple idea to design something that could transfer the message 'this is old bread in a bag rescued from the trash' to 'here is bread for you'. A few rules had to be taken into account. It was their initial idea that the people who put the bread were also responsible for throwing it eventually away. The action had to be easy and efficient. It was necessary to have clear who would be responsible for taking out the too old bread, as it otherwise would appear as a trash again.

How would the deposit look like? Where could it be placed? Who would be involved and how could the concept be implemented in context? The students wanted to create a service through which to enhance this beautiful gesture or ritual and make it better known in the Brabantwijk. They focused on the conceptualising of bread deposit boxes through which people can leave bread in the street, without plastic bag. (Figure 3) As such, the target group can be divided in the takers and givers. The so-called givers are mainly merchants and owners of different snack bars and local shops. They also could eventually be inhabitants who like to share their old bread with others. The takers are especially inhabitants who are financially unstable and could use a little help.

Figure 3. From trash to deposit. Film Still from the 'Urban Rituals' workshop movie. Source: Movie (2013)

Next step to this project is the elaboration of the system as to make the container, in collaboration with the inhabitants, attractive, efficient, user friendly and with no extra responsibility of taking the bread out of the deposit. The ambassador idea also has to be realized, besides having permission from the municipality for the placement of breadboxes.

Conclusion

Along with Leman and all, we argue that the 'public sphere should be adapted, where needed and where it may be positively embedded in view of a realistic and positive pluralism. (...) We need a reformulation of multiculturalism which does not have an anti-religious secularist bias and is open to intercultural dialogue that brings differences together' (Leman, 2014, p. 25). Working out different perspectives linked to the meaning, usage and consumption of bread as intercultural marker, we hope to bring together people in the Brabantwijk - be they merchants, inhabitants, or even daily commuters and students. Steel mentions that food is all about networks. The global food system is a network in which we are all complicit. 'Man and corn- it all comes back to that. Cultivation and civilisation, city and country, paradise and hell: food has always shaped our lives, and it always will' (Steel, 2009, p. 324).

We approach and work in first instance with the local Muslim merchants and inhabitants of the Brabantwijk. We invite everyone to join this unobtrusive ethnographic and design related project and participate. Through this approachable project, initiated by the local community, we want to shed a positive light upon the Brabantwijk. We want to argue that local, ethnic-cultural markers are not to be underestimated or neglected. Once highlighted and integrated into the existing socio-cultural network, these markers eventually enhance solidarity and connection, not only of the communities among themselves, but also within the multicultural modus vivendi of European cities.

References

Barth, F. (1969). Ethnic groups and boundaries. The social organization of cultural difference. Oslo: Universitatsforlaget.

Barth, F. (1994). Enduring and emerging issues in the analysis of ethnicity', Vermeulen, H. & Govers, C. (Eds.). The Anthropology of Ethnicity: Beyond 'Ethnic groups and boundaries'. Amsterdam: Het Spinhuis. pp. 11-32.

Baumann, G. (1999). The multicultural riddle: Rethinking national, ethnic, and religiuos identities. London: Routledge.

Bell, C. (1992). Ritual Theory. Ritual Practice, New York, Oxford: Oxford University Press.

Brubaker, R. (2004). Ethnicity without groups. Harvard University Press.

Bruns, M., Tomico, O. & Kint, J.M.L. (2012). Applying intercultural markers obtained from cooking in the design process. International Conference on Designing Food and Designing for Food. Londen. June 28-29.

Clifford, J. (1994). 'Diasporas'. Cultural Anthropology. 9(3). 302-338.

Furst, T., Connors, M., Bisogni C.A., Sobal, J. & Winter Falk, L. (1996). 'Food choice: a conceptual model of the process'. Appetite 26. pp. 247-266.

Gustafsson, I.B. (2004). 'Culinary arts and meal science – a new scientific research discipline'. Food Service Technology. 4. 9-20.

Habermas, J. (2008). Notes on a post-secular society, Received from in http://www.signandsight.com/ features/1714.html available on: 24.04.2015

Kint, J.M.L., Tomico, O. & Ferwerda, I. (2013). NextDoor/Quartier. Improving social cohesion in a Brussels neighborhood through research and design in interaction. Koegeler-Abdi, M. and Parncutt, R. (Eds.). Interculturality: Practice meets Research. Cambridge scholars Publishing. pp. 149- 164.

Leman, J., Toguslu, E. & Mesut Sezgin, I. (2014). The manifestation of Identities in a Plural Post-Secular Europe. Toguslu, E. (Eds.). New Multicultural Identities in Europe. Religion and Ethnicity in Secular Societies. Leuven: Leuven University Press. pp. 9-34.

Mennell, S.J. Murcott, A. & Van Otterloo, A.H. (1992). Sociology of food: eating, diet and culture. London: Sage Publications.

Pettinger, C, Holdsworth, M. & Gerber, M. (2006). 'Meal patterns and cooking practices in Southern France and Central England'. Public Health Nutrition 9(8). 1020-1026.

Rappaport, R.A. (1999). Ritual and Religion in the Making of Humanity, Cambridge University Press, Cambridge Mass.

Rajagopal, L. & Hamouz, F.L. (2009). 'Use of food attitudes and behaviors in determination of the personality characteristic of openness: A pilot study'. International Journal of Intercultural Relations. 33(3). 254-258.

Steel, C. (2009). Hungry City. How Food Shapes Our Lives. London: Vintage Books.

The Controversy Surrounding the Construction of Mosques by Turkish-Muslim Organizations in Austria: A Multidimensional Analytical Framework

Ernst Fürlinger[199]

Introduction

The controversy surrounding the construction of mosques has been part of Europe's political landscape during the past forty years, and it has reached a new level of intensity since the beginning of the new century. The controversy crystallizes public debate and struggle over Islam, migration, and European identity. It's about more than architecture, the height of minarets or the number of parking places around a mosque. The heated debates surrounding the development of Muslim infrastructure are public forums where societies negotiate questions of belonging or exclusion of the Muslim minority in the national state. In my paper, I will propose a multi-dimensional framework for the analysis of these controversies. This paper is based on empirical research on opposition to mosque construction in Austria, which I conducted between 2009 and 2012 (Fürlinger 2013)..

Overview

In Austria, social and political conflicts regarding the development of Muslim infrastructure, especially in the form of community centers with social and religious functions, are not a new phenomenon. In the 1980s, we see sporadic local discussions regarding the establishment of mosques. In 1993, there is the beginning of political instrumentalization of the 'mosque'-topic by the FPÖ, with the case of a plan by a local association of labor migrants from Turkey to establish the first representative mosque in Salzburg. In 2005, public debates and protests regarding the construction of mosques and minarets intensified, and reached national politics, with the construction of the first minaret in Tyrol, by the local Turkish mosque association in Telfs. In Vienna, between 2007 and 2010, the enlargement of an existing mosque center of a Turkish-Muslim association was a main focus of intense ethno-political mobilization by the FPÖ, for example with two large demonstrations against the construction project. In spring 2008, the legislative assemblies of the federal states of Carinthia and of Vorarlberg adopted amendments to the building regulations with the explicit intention of preventing the construction of representative mosques.

These are only a few examples of the manifold faces of the controversies surround mosque construction in Austria. How can we explain these conflicts? My hypothesis is that any analysis of these processes which focuses only on a certain set of factors (e.g. the local level) is not sufficient to grasp the complexity of intertwined elements and levels of conflict. Therefore, I put forward a multi-dimensional analytical framework which combines different conflict systems and

---

[199] Ernst Fürlinger is Head of the Center for Religion and Globalization, Danube University Krems, Dr. Karl-Dorrek-Str. 30, 3500 Krems, Austria. E-mail: ernst.fuerlinger@donau-uni.ac.at.

factors at the macro-level, meso-level and micro-level. These levels are interconnected and influence conflicts over mosque constructions at a given site. I will mention selected aspects at the different levels.

Multi-dimensional Analytical Framework

Conflict Systems At The Macro-Level

The 1970s saw the rise of political Islam in different parts of the Islamic world, peaking with the Islamic Revolution in Iran in 1979. In the 1990s, we also saw the emergence of radical Islamist groups who use violent means to achieve their objectives (key-word al-Qaida). In the west, the public perception of Islam became dominated by these political developments, with the result that the concepts of Islam and Muslims became primarily associated with violence, fanaticism and militancy. The extremely negative perception of Islam in general and the "clash of civilizations" (Huntington 1997) as an interpretative framework was further reinforced by the political and military events in Iraq, with the rapid advance of the so-called "Islamic State" in Iraq and Syria in summer of 2014, as well as the terrorist attacks in Europe related to global jihadism.

As in other European countries, local mosque construction projects in Austria by associations of former guest workers of Turkish origin and Islamic affiliation are directly affected and impacted by these wars and conflict systems at the global level. In many cases, these local Muslim communities are perceived in the context of the negative image of Islam, and are seen as part of a constructed Islamic 'block'. This imaginary Islam is projected on the local reality of Muslim citizens. Local administrations and governments dealing with a construction project end up not only discussing questions concerning regional building regulations and urban planning, but also the topic of radical Islamism. For right-wing populist or radical parties, it is relatively easy to cultivate a "politics of fear" (Nussbaum 2012) by spreading rumors, strengthening existing suspicions and fears towards Muslim organizations and Islam in general and by initiating political campaigns against the building of new mosques.

These processes are a concrete example of the close entanglement and interconnectedness of the global and the local, of "glocalisation" (Roland Robertson) in a global age. That which is local is far from being the opposite of that which is global: rather, it becomes an aspect of the overall globalization process (Robertson 1995; Robertson/ White 2003). In our case, the global conflict systems become an element of local conflicts, and local conflicts are part of a global conflict system, including their common interpretation along the line of a dominant 'clash of civilizations' model.

Conflict Systems at The Meso-Level

Another conflict system is related to the two republics of Austria and Turkey and involves the 'guest workers' from Turkey who were recruited in the 1960s. Massive migration processes can generate 'de-territorialized nations', as in the case of the Turkish state, which has some 4 million of its citizens living in Western European countries. The Turkish state sees them as belonging to the Turkish nation and emphasizes its responsibility for the 'Turkish community' abroad, even when this consists partly of expatriates who have obtained the citizenship of their host country.[200] On the other hand, the government of the host country considers these sustained and permanent transnational relations of migrants to their country of origin to be a hindrance to their integration in their 'new' country. In Austria, there is intense critical debate regarding aspects of Turkish *diaspora* politics. One such occasion was the participation of approximately 8000 people of Turkish origin in a pro-Erdogan demonstration in Vienna in June 2013, in the context of the Gezi Park-protests in Istanbul, organized by the "Union of European-Turkish Democrats" (UETD) in Austria.

Local mosque construction projects become part of these tense relations and fierce public debates, since the major player behind most of the projects is the umbrella organization ATIB, which is directly connected to the General Directorate of Foreign Relations of the Presidency of Religious Affairs (*Diyanet*) in Ankara, and thus to the Turkish government. In recent years, the recruitment of Diyanet-employed *imams* for the 64 ATIB mosques in Austria has developed into one of the major issues of Austrian integration politics. Areas of dispute include the *imams'* lack of knowledge about Austrian society, a lack of proficiency in German and their limited stay in Austria, all of which are seen as contributing to the social isolation and insufficient integration of Muslims of Turkish origin in Austria. In 2008, the Austrian foreign ministry and the *Diyanet* set up a joint course for ATIB *imams* learn about the Austrian and European legal and political systems, and the school system and professional education in Austria. The *Diyanet*, for its part, changed its policy by introducing an obligation for *imams* to attend German courses before they are sent from Turkey to mosque associations in German speaking countries. In general, ATIB imams are considered to be theologically moderate and well-trained.

For years now, the *FPÖ* has been campaigning against the ATIB Union. As the major entity involved with the construction of representative mosques and minarets in Austria, the ATIB Union has become the *FPÖ's* main target among the Austrian Muslim organizations. One example is a press release by the head of the *FPÖ* Club in the municipal government of Vienna in June 2013, referring to the Gezi-park-protests, their violent abolition by the AKP government and the pro-Erdogan demonstrations in Vienna. He called the ATIB Union "an extension of Erdogan's arm in Vienna", claimed that the ATIB was under "strong suspicion of having radical Islamist tendencies" and expressed the conviction that "ATIB is under orders to deliberately undermine our western democratic society and to spread the backward-looking ideas of the autocratic head of state Erdogan."[201] The rhetorical and ideological strategy consists in directly linking authoritarian measures of the AKP government in Ankara against the Gezi-Park protestors with the umbrella organization of mosque associations ATIB in Austria, using the metaphor of a battalion of radical Islamists within Austria

[200] See the website Republic of Turkey, Ministry of Foreign Affairs, Foreign Policy, 'Turkish Citizens Living Abroad'. Websource: http://www.mfa.gov.tr/the-expatriate-turkish-citizens.en.mfa - 8 June, 2015.

[201] Source: OTS, press release, "FP-Gudenus: Verfassungsschutz muss Türken-Verein ATIB überprüfen!", 25 June, 2013.

commanded by Erdogan. This strategy of paranoia leaves little space for a careful analysis and consideration of the complex relations between the Turkish government and the Presidency of Religious Affairs (Sunier, Landman, van der Linden et al. 2011).

It seems that years of political debates about ATIB *imams* and right-wing smear campaigns, aimed at ATIB Union in particular, paved the way for one of the most disputed regulations in the new Islam Law (30 March, 2015). The Law includes a restriction on foreign financing for Islamic organizations in Austria (§ 6 para. 2). This new regulation was proposed by the Minister for Integration and the Federal Chancellery responsible for religious communities, with the explicit intention of abolishing the system of Diyanet-funded *imams* in Austria.

These new regulations fit into the general picture of the politics of integration of the Muslim minorities in Western European countries in recent years, where 'double-edged' policies combine measures of inclusion and the expansion of religious freedom with restrictive measures and a greater control of Muslim religious practice by the state (Laurence 2012).

Conflict Factors At The Micro-Level

My hypothesis is that the conflicts and struggles surrounding the construction of mosques and minarets in Austria today are long-term consequences of the special 'guest worker' migration regime established in the 1960s by the Austrian state. It is a state migration system characterized by strict limitation on the stay of labor migrants, very restrictive regulations regarding naturalization, and strict limitation of access to the labor market and to social and political rights. Labor migrants were seen as 'temporary guests', and not as future citizens. The whole rotation system was orientated towards preventing the permanent settlement and integration of the migrants. The failure of the 'guest worker' system resulted finally in the uncontrolled, chaotic and unwanted settlement of labor migrants from Turkey and former Yugoslavia. Large-scale immigration occurred in a host country which didn't see itself as a 'country of immigration'.

In this context, the construction of new and representative mosques becomes the clear, physical expression of the fact that the former migrants and 'guests' have become new citizens who will stay and establish permanent religious infrastructure. It destroys the illusion that the changes – the ethnic and religious pluralization of the nation – are just temporary. It is possible that the sites of mosque and minaret constructions become public forums and outlets for the majority to communicate not only about the concrete building projects but also about the social changes produced by migration and globalization in general. In this perspective, mosque conflicts could be seen as expressions of a "society of fear" (Bude 2014) and insecurity, where it is permissible to express anxieties and anger, and to direct these towards the Turkish-Muslim minority.

In this way, these conflicts strengthen the demarcation between majority and minority, the construction of the minority as the exceptional 'other', and at the same time re-fresh, actualize and stabilize the imagination of the national community.

References

Bude, H. (2014). *Gesellschaft der Angst.* Hamburg: Hamburger Edition.

Castles, S. & Miller M.J. (2009). The Age of Migration: International Population Movements in the Modern World. New York: Palgrave, 4th edition.

Fürlinger, E. (2010). The politics of non-recognition: mosque construction in Austria. Allievi, S. (Ed.) Mosques in Europe. Why a solution has become a problem. London: Alliance Publishing Trust, 183 – 216.

Fürlinger, E. (2013). *Moscheebaukonflikte in Österreich. Nationale Politik des religiösen Raums im globalen Zeitalter* (Wiener Forum für Theologie und Religionswissenschaft; 7). Göttingen: v & r unipress.

Hafez, F. & Potz, R. (2009). Moschee- und Minarettbauverbote in Kärnten und Vorarlberg. Bunzl, J. & Hafez, F. (Eds.) Islamophobie in Österreich. Innsbruck/ Wien: Studienverlag, 144–156.

Huntington, S. (1997). The Clash of Civilizations and the Remaking of World Order. London: Simon & Schuster.

Kübel, J., Pfeffer D., Stöbich, K. (2008). "Ka Moschee wär schee". Ein Fall aus dem 20. Wiener Gemeindebezirk zum Thema „Islam und Öffentlichkeit". Österreichische Zeitschrift für Politikwissenschaft 37 (4), 471 –487.

Kübel, J. (2008): »moschee ade oder moschee.at?« Eine Konfliktanalyse zu der Frage, inwiefern oder ob Islamophobie in Österreich tatsächlich existiert. Unpublished diploma thesis, University of Vienna.

Laurence, J. (2012). *The Emancipation of Europe's Muslims* (Princeton Studies in Muslim Politics), Princeton: Princeton University Press.

Nussbaum, M. C. (2012). The New Religious Intolerance: Overcoming the Politics of Fear in an Anxious Age. Cambridge: Belknap Press.

Öktem, K. & Abou-el-Fadl, R. (Eds.) (2009). Mutual Misunderstanding. Muslims and Islam in the European Media, Europe in the media of Muslim majority countries. Oxford: European Studies Centre.

Poole, E. & Richardson, J. E. (Eds.) (2006). *Muslims and the News Media.* London/ New York: I.B. Tauris.

Robertson, R. (1995). Glocalization: Time-space and homogeneity-homogeneity. Featherstone, M., Lash, S. & Robertson, R. (Eds.) Global Modernities. London: Sage, 25–44.

Robertson, R. & White, K.E. (2003). Globalization: An overview. Robertson, R. & White, K.E. (Eds.) Globalization: Critical Concepts in Sociology. Vol. 1: Analytical Perspectives. London: Routledge, 1–44.

Sunier, T., Landman, N., van der Linden, H., Bilgili, N., Bilgili, A. (2011). *Diyanet: The Turkish Directorate for Religious Affairs in a changing environment.* Amsterdam: VU University Amsterdam.

Turkish Mosques in Britain as a Religious Socialisation Agent

Yakup Costu* and Elif Büşra Kocalan**

Introduction

A mosque, as a religious place, is one of the constituent institutions of social structure of Muslim society. It is not only a place where religious practices are carried out by participants, but it also has a significant role in the formation of their Islamic identity, and in creation and preservation of sacred memory of the community.

It is known that Turkish Muslim immigrants living in various European countries have established mosques/religious places. These places have many different social functions besides being houses of worship. In this regard, religious institutions represent a space where culture and values from the homeland are shared, where courses and educational activities are carried out, possible problems that are experienced in the host countries can be solved and religious and cultural differences towards host countries are symbolized.

In this paper, we will focus on the mosques established by Turkish Muslim immigrants in Britain. In this context, the paper will try to search for answers to the following questions: What kind of Islamic discourse Turkish mosques in Britain have? What types of activities are carried out by mosques? Are there any differences among their religious, social and cultural activities? What is the role of mosques in the Turkish Muslim immigrants' religious socialisation processes? This research is methodologically based on empirical evidence. To answer the abovementioned questions, observations which were obtained from on-going field researches, over a long period of time about these issues, will be used.

Turkish mosques in Britain

Starting with the migration of Cypriot Turks in the 1920s, growing with Turkish immigrants from Turkey in the 1970s, and also the Kurdish immigrants from Turkey in the 1990s, nowadays Britain has a significant number of Cypriot Turks, Turkish and Kurdish people from Turkey (see. Ladbury, 1977; Robins and Aksoy, 2001; Mehmet Ali, 2001; Issa, 2005). Aforementioned 'Turkish speaking communities'[202] do not have a homogeneous pattern due to the differences of their life styles, experiences, thoughts, feelings, hopes and expectations. Therefore, it has been observed that Turkish immigrants live in different ethnic, ideological, cultural and religious groups (see. Costu, 2013a).

* Dr. Yakup Costu is Associate Professor in Sociology of Religion Department, Faculty of Divinity Hitit University, Corum, Turkey. E-mail: yakupcostu@hitit.edu.tr
** Elif Busra Kocalan is Ph.D. candidate in Sociology of Religion Department, Social Science Institute, Hitit University, Corum, Turkey. E-mail: ebusrakocalan@hitit.edu.tr
202 This definition is used for Cypriot Turks, Turkish and Kurdish people from Turkey living in Britain in academic literature (see. Mehmet Ali, 2001; Issa, 2005; Atay, 2006).

Mosques are not only places that religious practices are performed in, but they also have a significant role in the formation of Muslim identity. This identity, in addition to possible social, political and cultural aspects, can also have aspects that depend on language, attitude, living place and favourite activities. In this sense, mosques function as a demonstration of cultural, religious and ethnic aspects of Muslim identity (see. Isgandarova, 2009; Kucukcan, 2009).

The first attempt of Turks living in Britain towards being organised as a religious sphere was in the beginning of the 1970s. However in these years, religious life for the Turkish society was only on a personal scale. The religious life of first generation immigrants was limited in practising some basic religious duties. Small spaces were hired or bought to practise these duties. When these people realised that it was impossible for them to return to their homeland, and when the second and third generations arrived, these places started to be insufficient. Moreover, needs of the society had increased and differentiated; therefore there was a need for an institutionalised and systematic organisation. In this sense, organisations in which national, religious and cultural values would be transmitted to future generations, and immigrants would build their own semantic world had started to be established. (see. Atay 1994; Kucukcan, 1996; 1999). Mosques and religious and cultural establishments around the mosques have an important place among the organisations based on social, political and economic reasons.

Islamic Discourse of Turkish Mosques in Britain

It has been understood that in the establishment of Turkish religious organisations, or in another words these religious support networks, migration reasons, inhabiting patterns, the identity focuses of lower class immigrant citizens, also political, ideological and religious structures in Turkey and North Cyprus had important roles. (see. Kucukcan, 1999; Costu, 2013a). A significant amount of foundations and unions within Britain that provide religious services for Turks are only footprints of religious groups, sects and movements within Turkey and North Cyprus. The content of discourse and the ideological standpoints of religious group in Britain, as similar the groups in continental Europe especially in Germany, follow the agenda of their homeland (See. Persembe, 2005; Adiguzel, 2011).

In field research done by Costu, ten (10) religious organisations established by Turkish and Cypriot immigrants were identified (Costu, 2013a, p.97-98; 2013b, p.496). Within the limits of legal legitimacy provided by the host country, they carry out cultural, religious and educational activities for their participants. As far as we detected, the content of religious discourse of these places established by Turkish immigrant in Britain can be classified into four main categories; (Costu, 2013a, p.97; 2013b, p.495):

1. Religious discourse inspired by the Sufi movements in Turkey and North Cyprus[203],

---

[203] Sufi organizations; the followers of Sheikh M. Nazim Kibris, the followers of Mahmut Ustaosmanoglu, the followers Muhammed Rasit Erol/Menzil (See for further information Costu, 2013a, 2013b).

2. Religious discourse inspired by the religious movements in Turkey[204],

3. Religious discourse inspired by the religious-politic movements in Turkey[205],

4. Mosques/mosque unions affiliated with the official religious discourse in Turkey[206].

It is seen that the Turkish speaking communities are heavily concentrated in the Greater London region (DCLG, 2009). Due to the fact that most of the Turkish immigrants live in Central London, the head offices of Turkish religious organizations are located in London (Costu, 2013a).

Activities in Mosques

Unions and foundations which belong to Turks and conduct religious activities were mostly organised around mosques. In field research done by Costu, there are a total of 27 active religious prayer places (mosque, prayer room) across Britain (Costu, 2013a, p.144-145; 2013b, p.498). It can be observed that, these religious places, teaming up with other organisations around them, have differentiated from the roles they were given in the homeland and transformed into social spaces which have social, cultural and educational services alongside religious ones.

Taking immigrants' expectations into consideration, various services are provided in these social-religious places. These services can be categorised such as; (see. Kucukcan, 1996; 1999; Costu, 2013a):

i) Religious services: Support and assistance are given to immigrants with regard to the performances of religious practices.

ii) Educational services: Various educational activities are arranged for children, young-adult and adult immigrants.

iii) Socio-cultural services: Cultural activities, health, sports, accommodation services, legal and economic support, and supports and assistances in any other troublesome situations are arranged.

We tried to arrange service areas of religious based civil organisations in three main categories, but with every passing day they diversify, parallel with the needs and expectations of immigrants. Furthermore, in parallel with the increase in population, the number of religious places and civil organisations also increase. It can also be observed that this increase brings a differentiation within service forms and types of social solidarity networks of the Turkish immigrants in religious, cultural, political and economic spheres.

Religious places that belong to Turks in Britain have a great variety of religious and social functions. However, it has been observed that service fields of these organisations differentiate due to some religious and social variables. According to this:

---

[204] Religious movement organizations; the followers of Suleyman Hilmi Tunahan/Suleymancis, the followers of Fetullah Gulen/Hizmet, and Alevis (See for further information Costu, 2013a, 2013b).
[205] Religio-political movement organizations National Vision/Milli Gorus and Milliyetciler/Nationalists (See for further information Costu, 2013a, 2013b).
[206] Official religious organization; Turkish Religious Foundation of the UK/Diyanet (See for further information Costu, 2013a, 2013b).

The number of mosques that belong to Turks in Britain increases each passing day. This increase brings along a rivalry in the religious service area. The rivalry is thought to cause an authority controversy via religion within the society.[207] In order to hold on among immigrants, the religious organisations diversify their service areas and aim to increase the number of followers. Moreover, there is a great effort in establishing new religious places, and with this, it is aimed to strengthen the institutional structure.

Another reason for differentiation of service areas of religious unions and foundations is diversified interpretations of "religious identity". For example, identifying the religious identity according to conservatism, nationalism, modernity, ethnic diversity, and political position transform religious support networks into a heterogeneous structure. Each group that try to determine their socialisation style and to form their religious attitude and behaviour based on criteria used to identify religious identity tend towards different fields of activity and try to serve in these fields.

Another differentiation can be observed in between areas significantly populated by Turks and areas that Turks are minority. Religious places positioned in the areas significantly populated by Turks, as a result of the law of supply and demand and to strengthen the institutional structure, might seek to serve in a large variety of areas. In addition to differentiation by population density, heavily Turkish populated areas also have segregation in itself. It can be observed that different religious groups that build new mosques around currently available mosques aim new service styles in order to appeal to the Turkish and Muslim population around those mosques.[208]

Mosques; as a Religious Socialisation Agent

Mosques are institutions that establish a social structure, alongside family, economy, education, politics and law. Due to this aspect, it has a continuous relationship with other institutions. Hence, as a social institution, mosque cannot be understood if it is separated from the society that it is involved with. The social organization of a mosque show parallelism with the social patterns of the society which the mosque is located in, and these patterns present a context to understand the role and importance of the mosque. In a society that Muslims are a majority, generally the mosque is only a prayer place, however in a society that Muslims are a minority or immigrant, the mosque also has the role of being a place of refuge which has social, cultural and educational functions. In this respect, as far as we can determine, the socializing functions of Turkish mosques in Britain can be expressed as follows:

It serves as a place for socialisation: Mosques have significance among Turkish Muslim immigrants as places of religious and social activities performed within.

---

[207] In the interview made on 05/08/2013 with Prof. Dr. Seyfettin Erşahin who is a consultant for England Religious Services and the head of England Turkish Religious Foundation this subject was significantly pointed out.
[208] As an example, it can be mentioned that in the month of Ramadan in 2012, one of the Turkish mosques performed tarawih prayer as eight-rakat. There is no doubt the main aim behind this implementation is to encourage individuals to pray. However, we also think increasing the number of attendees of the mosque was also another aim behind this implementation.

In these places, on one hand religious practices are being performed and on the other hand Muslim immigrants who live as minorities have a chance to socialise. At the same time, aforementioned religious places function as places to share knowledge, to establish social networks and as shelters for immigrants. (See. Aktay and Subası, 2006).

It creates a specific religiosity as a typology: Every Turkish religious organisation in Britain has been built around certain religious places (mosque) and organised in a distinctive congregational structure. From the content of their religious discourse to conducted activities each organisation has a specific religious outlook (see. Sahin, 2012).

It provides an important contribution to the integration process: It is thought that with these services for immigrants carried out by aforementioned socio-religious places, religious and national identity is being protected, internal solidarity is increased, and moreover some contributions are being made on the integration process to the host country. Besides it is also observed, due to the reason that effects of assimilation, hidden or explicit, which second and third generations are faced with are being minimised by these services, sensitive parents regard these places as natural and matchless shelters (see. Cilingir, 2010)

It provides preservation of cultural and religious identity: It is observed that immigrants who stay close or attend activities of these religious places protect their cultural and religious identities. It is also witnessed that the ones who are not connected with these places or prefer secular lifestyles lose their religious identities in the process over time and are clearly assimilated culturally and linguistically (see. Kucukcan, 1998)

It provides preservation of native language: It is seen that in the religious places built by Turks, during religious practices (sermon, khutbah, etc.) sometimes Turkish, sometimes English, and sometimes both languages are being used (especially in Friday prayer). Considering each religious organisation conducts their religious services with a purpose in mind, it can be thought that the preferred language has a common side with this purpose. Hence, it can be said that the preferred language during religious ceremonies has a significant impact on language socialisation.

It triggers competition and tension among community: Due to the reason that unions and foundations were established by members or sympathisers of religious groups, sects and movements in Turkey and Northern Cyprus and in parallel with religious, political and ideological discourse within the motherland, some differentiations occur. These differentiations can form a basis for rivalry, conflict and segregation in between organisations. This situation is believed to be a major obstacle in front of social unison of immigrants (see Kucukcan, 1996; 1999). In some respect, it was observed that this subject was strongly emphasized in the interviews made with religious leaders.

Additionally, the efforts of each religious organisation to protect their distinctive congregation and to strengthen their institutional entity among Turkish immigrant society might cause rivalry and sometimes tension in between organisations. These tensions based on intellectual, social and economic reasons can provoke segregation among immigrants and have a damaging role on cultural integrity. It can be said that this situation might have negative effects on the religious socialisation processes of immigrants.

Conclusion

There are many organisations and mosques, established by Turks living in Britain, carrying out cultural and religious activities towards specifically Turkish immigrants and generally other Muslim communities. These organisations which were founded on elements such as their identity, ideological standpoint and religious view, with taking immigrants expectations into consideration, tend towards various service fields. As a result of this, it can be observed that the mosques founded by Turks living in Britain, teaming up with other organisations around them, have differentiated from the roles they were given in the homeland and transformed into social spaces which have social, cultural and educational services alongside religious ones.

For Turkish Muslim immigrants, the mosques are important spaces that carry out religious and social activities. On one hand religious practices are being performed; on the other hand Muslim immigrants living as minority find an opportunity for religious socialising. Also at the same time mosques are institutions where knowledge is shared, social networks are established, and immigrants find shelter for themselves.

References

Adiguzel, Y. (2011). Yeni Vatanda Dini İdeolojik Yapılanma Almanya'daki Türk Kuruluşları (Religious And Ideological Structure In New Homeland; Turkish Organizations In Germany), İstanbul: Şehir Yayınları. (In Turkish).

Aktay, Y. And N. Subasi (Project Coordinators). (2006). Referans Grupları, Avrupa'da Türkler, Dinsel Organizasyonları Söylem Ve Tasavvurları (Reference Groups, Turks In Europe, Their Religious Organizations, Imagination And Discourses), Konya-Muğla: T.C. Diyanet İşleri Başkanlığı Dış İlişkiler Daire Başkanlığı Proje Raporu. (In Turkish)

Atay, T. (1994). Naqshbandi Sufis In A Western Setting. Unpublished Ph.D. Dissertation, School Of Oriental And African Studies, University Of London, London

Atay, T. (2006). Türkler, Kürtler, Kıbrıslılar İngiltere'de Türkçe Yaşamak (Turks, Kurds, Turkish Cypriots;The Turk Living In The Uk) . Ankara: Dipnot Yayınları. (In Turkish).

Cilingir, S. (2010). "Identity And Integration Among Turkish Sunni Muslims In Britain", Insight Turkey, Vol. 12, No.1, Ss.103-122.

Costu, Y. (2013a). İngiltere'deki Türk-Müslüman Gocmenler; Dini Organizasyonlar. (Turkish Muslim Immigrants In The Uk; Religious Organizations). Çorum: Lider Matbaası. (In Turkish).

Costu, Y. (2013b). "Turkish Muslim Immigrants in Britain; Religious Life and Religious Organizations", Sociology Study, Volume: 3, Number: 7, pp. 493-501.

DCLG. (2009). The Turkish and Turkish Cypriot Muslim Community in England; Understanding Muslim Ethnic Communities, London: Queen's Printer and Controller of Her Majesty's Stationery Office.

Isgandarova, N. (2009). "Mosques As Communities Of Memories Vis-A-Vis Muslim Identity And Integration In The European Union", European Journal Of Economic And Political Studies, 2/2, Ss. 61-70.

Issa, T. (2005). Talking Turkey: The Language, Culture And Identity Of Turkish Speaking Children In Britain. Staffordshire: Trentham Books.

Kucukcan, T. (1996). The Politics Of Ethnicity, Identity And Religion Among Turks In London, (The Degree Of Doctor Of Philosophy), Warwick: Centre For Research In Ethnic Relations, University Of Warwick.

Kucukcan, T. (1998). "Community, Identity And Institutionalisation Of Islamic Education: The Case Of Ikra Primary School In North London", British Journal Of Religious Education, Vol. 21, No. 1, Ss. 32-43.

Kucukcan, T. (1999). Politics Of Ethnicity, Identity And Religion Turkish Muslims In Britain. Aldershot: Ashgate.

Kucukcan, T. (2009). "Turks In Britain: Religion And Identity", Turks In Europe, Culture, Identity, Integration, Ed. T. Kucukcan, V. Gungor, Amsterdam: Turkevi Research Centre, Ss. 79-102.

Ladbury, S. (1977). "The Turkish Cypriots: Ethnic Relations In London And Cyprus". Watson, J. L. (Ed.), Between Two Cultures: Migrants And Minorities In Britain. Oxford: Blackwell, Pp. 301-331.

Mehmet Ali, A. (2001). Turkish Speaking Communities And Education -No Delight. London: Fatal Publication.

Persembe, E. (2005). Almanya'da Türk Kimliği Din Ve Entegrasyon (Turkish Identity In Germany; Religion And Integration), Ankara: Araştırma Yayınları. (In Turkish).

Robins, K. And A. Aksoy. (2001). "From Spaces Of Identity To Mental Spaces: Lessons From Turkish-Cypriot Cultural Experience In Britain". Journal Of Ethnic And Migration Studies. 27(4), Pp. 685-711.

Sahin, I. (2012). "From Tradition To Religion: Organisational Transformation Of The London Turkish Migrant Community", Zeitschrift Für Die Welt Der Türken (Journal Of World Of Turks), Vol. 4, No. 2, Ss. 53-78.

Psychological Processes of Acculturation of Turkish/Muslims in Germany

Hacı Halil Uslucan[209]

Introduction

One of the very stable social myths in the public discourse in Germany is that the process of social integration of Turks as an ethnic group and Moslems as a religious group has failed. Problems with head scarf, honour murderings, juvenile violence acts, higher unemployment rates or lack of german language competencies are even shown as valide indicators for this assumption.

Especially after the debate, which was in September 2010 triggered by the book of Thilo Sarrazin (*Deutschland schafft sich ab*) and some followers in media blogs, these topics was a matter of both intensive discussion in the public media as well as social scientific literature. The main points were, in how far Moslems and Turks, which sometimes used as synonymous, represent a threat for the German society, in how far Islamic religiosity blocks social integration processes, in how far Muslims or an Anatolian Turk can be loyal to democratic values etc.

Beyond this apocalyptic and group-focused devaluing rhetorics, the question is, in how far these supposed threats are based on empirical facts. What are the magnitudes we speak about? The number of people with an Islamic background varies in Germany between 3.8 and 4.3 millions. With a population rate of nearly 5%, Islam is after Christianity the second greatest religious denomination (Haug et al., 2009). Nearly half of them (45%), round about two millions, are German citizens. The religion of Islam is no more an alien element, but an essential part of German and European culture. Multicultural and multi-religious society is already a social fact with a lot of challenges as well as chances. The number of people with Turkish origin is nearly 2.9 Millions; nearly 1.2 Millions of them are now German citizens. In the last years, the number of emigration rates from Turks from Germany to Turkey is greater than the immigration rates from Turkey to Germany.

In this article, I will at first sketch the psychological process of acculturation, focusing on the topic of managing cultural and religious diversity on the individual level. In the next step, the question of measuring and quantifying of acculturation processes will be examined.

At least, some own empirical results about Muslim pupil and their parents concerning their acculturative strategies/orientations in Germany are presented. The article ends with some suggestions how to overcome hindrances for a better social integration of this group.

Acculturation process of Turkish Muslims in Germany

We are focusing on Turkish Muslims, because nearly two third of the Muslims in Germany have a Turkish origin and represents the largest group. Islam in

---

[209] Prof. Dr. Haci Halil Uslucan, University of Duisburg-Essen/Germany, Faculty of Humanities, Institute for Turkistik

Germany is widely influenced by the Turkish version of Islam. Many of them are second or already the third generation whose parents came as guest workers since 1961 to Germany. Beside that, this group is the best researched group. The second greatest group represents Muslims from South East European Countries (Bosnia, Albania, former Yugoslavia etc.) with a population number between 500.000 and 600.000, the third largest group are Muslims from near East with numbers between 260.000 and 300.000 (Haug et al. 2009). The most of the Muslims in Germany belongs to the Sunni tradition (nearly 74%), followed by the Alewi (nearly 13%) and Shia (7%). In how far Alewis are to assign as Muslims is even both in science as well as amongst Alewis still disputed.

Looking on longitudinal studies about Muslim migrants in Germany, the findings elucidate a surprising intergenerational stability of religiosity (between first and second generation of Turkish migrants) and further, that religiosity is neither a compensation for a lack of social status nor that it does become gradually just symbolic in character (Diehl & Koenig, 2009).

Direct comparisons between German and Turkish migrants show in general a higher religiosity of Turkish migrants, especially concerning the indicators faith, religious practice, believing in the existence of God etc. The "Bertelsmann-Religionsmonitor" for instances identified the proportion of Muslims with a "high-religiosity" as nearly by 41 %, whereas the rate of "high-religiosity" in the German population lay by nearly 18% (Mirbach, 2013).

Studies with European Muslims show that they are more socially conservative than the general European population; on issues like authoritarian parenting styles, abortion, homosexuality or other sexual taboos their values are closer to the agenda of the Roman Catholic Church (Soper & Fetzer, 2007). Insofar, their acculturation problems are not even and not in every case genuine problems of Muslims, but sometimes problems of a traditional world view in modernity. From a psychological point of view, it is to point out that religiosity can represent an important source of emotional security and sense in life, especially in situations of strangeness, isolation and social withdrawal; insofar, it can facilitate the acculturation process and can compensate experienced devaluations.

Measuring and quantifying acculturation

What does acculturation means? Acculturation in the broadest sense of the notion means the process of cultural encounter and the gaining of a new balance between the individual and his environment in a new cultural context after a process of acculturation, that means after an acquisition and internalisation of basic cultural standards of the first culture during the socialisation. In this sense, acculturation refers to changes that take place when two cultural or ethnic groups come into continuous contact with each other.

Intercultural encounters bears even for everyone some kinds of stress and changes; but the requirements for migrants involves more challenges than for autochthonous population.

For a better understanding of processes of acculturation, stress-theoretical approaches seem to be the most appropriate ones: In general, rapid cultural and social changes lead individuals to stress, destabilization and excessive demands. The consequences of these changes affect especially migrants from Turkey very hard. In their everyday-life, Turkish migrants are – in comparison to natives - clearly more confronted with situations of intransparency and ambiguity; situations, in which habitualised routines break down (Uslucan, 2005).

This discrepancy between own competencies and the requirements are usually felt as individual stress. That means that the feeling of challenge to master the own life in a new country is replaced by the feeling of overwhelming. Lazarus and Folkman (1987) postulated that stress evolves from situations in which people have not enough resources to master the demands of personally relevant domains like school, education, job or social relations. Stress raises the susceptibility to diseases and weakens the immune system.

Social and personal resources may influence the effects of stress-inducing strains (Schwarzer & Jerusalem, 1994). Personal resources are aspects like individual coping behavior, self efficacy and higher education. On the other side, networks like familial relationships or friendships – in case of migrants also people of the same region, the same religion etc. - pose as social resources, on which people can refer in situations of misery and privation.

For the experience of acculturative stress and destabilization the degree of voluntariness of the migration is another determining factor; if migration is forced through external conditions and pressures, people will undergo more stress. It is well known, for example, that both refugees and their children experience more acculturative stress than voluntary migrants (Garcia Coll & Magnusson, 1997).

Furthermore, the question of how appropriate people cope with strains of a removal is depending on their migration motives, on their expectancies and anxieties, which were associated with a migration and which kind of preparations they had already in their home country (Berry, 1997). Beyond that, the influence of the familial status and the availability of supporting social networks are essential: being involved in a tight social network seems to buffer stressful situations (Schwarzer & Leppin, 1989).

Studies in Netherlands could find that Turkish migrants tend to more strongly identify themselves with their own ethnic group than other migrant groups (Fassaert, et. al, 2011). In the long-run this can hinder their social integration.

On an individual level, people with few language competencies are more exposed to acculturative stress; in addition, people with inflexible personality, who feel themselves highly dependent from changes of their social contexts, experiences high acculturative stress. Concerning the Muslim group, often women experiences more stress than men, because women mostly live stronger forms of traditionalism, which bears more tensions and frictions in modern societies and is also associated with more social defeat and stigmatisation in every-day encounters (Fassaert et al., 2011).

Nevertheless, in the process of acculturation, migrants and families are always involved in a double social network of references. They have to form an idiosyncratic relationship to the own ethnic group on the one hand, and to the receiving country, respectively members of the new society, at the other hand.

How can we measure and quantify acculturation processes? What are the indicators of a successful or failed integration?

Especially in the psychological literature, there exists a broad variety of measuring acculturation or integration processes of migrants. The most of them are inclined to the Berry model and contains items on these three major categories:

Linguistic oriented items (language preference, proficiency, fluency etc.). Example: In my leisure time I speak the language of my home country/new home.

Psychological oriented items (ethnic identity, attitudes, values etc.) Example: I feel myself more Turkish than German etc.

Sociocultural oriented items (preferences in domains like family-life, friendship, customs, traditions, cuisines etc.) Example: I live strongly according traditions of my home country/my new home (Olmedo, 1979).

These items focus more on the individual level. On a group level, we can differentiate between three types of measuring integration processes:

The comparison of migrants vs. host population (attitudes, values, preferences, competencies etc.)

These measurements can also be focused on religious groups, e.g. differences between Muslims and Christians.

The comparison of migrants in region 1 vs. migrants in region 2 or with the average nationwide index (e.g. how successful is a specific commune in comparison to the average or a country in comparison to another country?)

The longitudinal analysis: The comparison of migrant group X at t 1 vs. migrant group X at t 2. This question focus on how integration processes progress over time and what kind of generational effects are to expect (Olmedo, 1979).

We should be aware that integration processes are differential and segmented in social spheres: Success in one area does not imply success in another area (e.g. sports/economy/social integration, neighbourhoods, friendship, partners etc.). Sometimes, young Turkish migrants are very well integrated in their social context, having German friends, partnerships etc., but have not equal access to job or education market. Religiosity seems especially for Muslim women (with a headscarf) an obstacle for good job-market integration: In direct comparison with non-Muslim women their embedding in the job market was significantly lower, which sometimes were due to discriminatory practices (Stichs & Müssig, 2013).

We can at least underline that processes of social integration can only be understood as an interaction of individual readiness and disposition on the one side, and the openness of social institutions and structures for participation of migrants on the other side. Human behaviour is even to understand as a function of respectively interdependence of personal factors and environmental restrictions and opportunities. But integration-shortcomings especially of Muslims/Turks are often viewed as their individual faults and unwillingness; the structural and everyday discriminations of Muslims – for instances if visible aspects of Islamic identity (like the headscarf) identify them - are hardly taken into account, when explaining hesitances to accept German norms or the dominant life style. Under these circumstances, religiosity is cause for disadvantages, strangeness and stigmatisation with negative effects on further motivation to participate and struggle for social upward mobility.

Some studies on acculturation show that religious aspects of everyday life and feelings of religious belonging loose their impact with the stay in the host society, for example for Turks in France and the Netherlands (Diehl & Koenig, 2009), but this seems not to be true for Turks in Germany.

In addition it is to mention that in opposition to other secular migrants or Christian migrants Muslims are faced with specific challenges: They have to work out a balance with a migrant friendly policy of the left wing parties, which favour at the same time anticlerical attitudes, and with a conservative and pro-clerical right wing parties, who have on the other side more hesitances against Islam and migrants. So Muslims have to defend their social and political position in a cross-fire; both political groups in Germany cultivate a sceptical view on Muslims. Besides them, as Dirk Halm noted, especially Muslim organisations in Germany have to justify their activities not only to their members, but also to social actors and institutions of their country of origin as well as the receiving country (Halm, 2013).

Empirical results of Acculturation of Muslims from Turkey

Empirical research could demonstrate very clearly that the Muslim population in Germany is severely underprivileged in the fields of education, in their employment status (their unemployment rates are significantly higher) and by the income indicators. Inequality and discrimination in these structural dimensions are greater than for some specific indicators of social integration, like e.g. contact to the receiving society. Further, in the last years rising anti-Muslim attitudes could be validated by a lot of empirical studies (Heitmeyer, 2012).

In Germany, the Country of Lower Saxony started a model project in 2003 by enabling Muslim pupil religious Islamic education. The language of the instruction was German; the teacher was former Turkish or mother-tongue teacher, who get advanced trainings in Islam and religious education. We had the chance to evaluate this model project in a longitudinal study with focus on integrative effects and contentment with the program and the curriculum.

In the following I will just draft the results concerning integration respectively acculturative strategies of a Muslim population in Hanover/Germany (see Uslucan, 2011).

Acculturation orientations of Muslim pupil

As summarised in the table, the results show that the favourite orientations in the examined group were integration (the higher the values, the higher the specific orientations); that means here, that the Muslim pupil were interested to stay in a close distance to the values and orientations of their culture of origin (Turkish language, Turkish family life, Turkish friends etc.), but they also were interested to learn and use the German language, keeping friendship with German and adopting German family life in their everyday life. The second rank was the orientations towards ethnic closeness (separation), the wish to stay closer to the values of the culture of origin and refuse German values.

Table 1: Values of acculturation orientations (pupil)

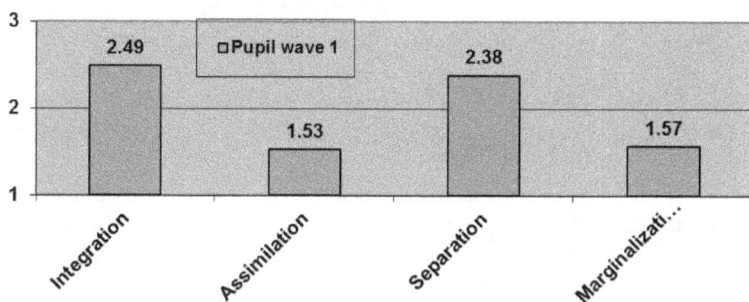

However, assimilation as well as marginalization was refused remarkably. Now, it is interesting to regard in how far this attitudes change over time and which effects the implementation of the Islamic education displays:

Figure 2: Acculturation orientations over time (pupil)

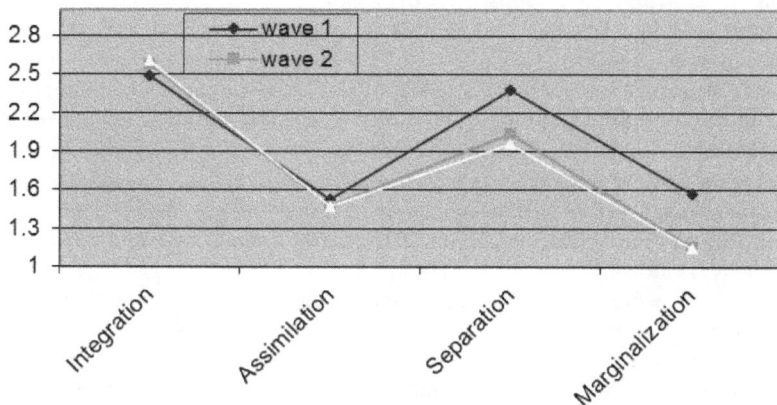

Regarding the results over time, we could identify that integrative orientations rises from the first wave to the second; although the values was on a high level, small gains could also identified at the third wave. Assimilative orientations were even low and changed hardly. Further, a small decline of the values of separation was observable. Marginalization was to every measurement point the least favourite orientation of the Muslim pupil.

These results have throughout a positive message: The fear that by an implementation of a religious education at elementary schools the anti-integrative and separationist orientations of this group would be enhanced, seems to be completely unjustified. In connection with Islamic education at the school, the separationist dispositions declined, the integrative rose.

On the other side we should not overstretch the effects and empirical findings and should be very cautious by their interpretation: pupils at the age of 9 or 10 years are very flexible in their development. The effects of two hours Islamic education in the week can not influence human actions, cognitions and traits so vividly.

Conclusions and implications

How can a successful integration – especially of Muslim population - be happen?

The main aspect of a successful social integration is to guarantee the equal access and equal chances in every branches of society, especially with regard to the job market, residential market, education, policy, art, sports etc. It is unquestionable that Muslim migrants also have to do their homework, for example learning the German language, supporting the school careers of their children (main problems in schools are often the participation of young girls in sports[210], or biology, etc.), but in the most cases, integration shortcomings are not only an individual or a motivational problem.

The claim, that migrants refuse every kind of integration is very seldom: In the data of the ZfTI (2009) just 2% of the administered Turkish migrants in North Rhine Westphalia. The reasons are in most cases more structural nature, especially in form of invisible, glassy hindrances in institutions, which lead migrants to resignation and separation.

For example, the rate of Muslims in official departments and administrations is at most 2.5%; but their rate in the society is double. This discrepancy refers to impermeable structures in filling representative jobs and professions. Discourses, in which the demand for reciprocity is claimed with an absolute power, that means that the right to practice their religion is connected to the freedom of religious minorities in the countries of origin of the Muslim migrants, hampers the social and political life.

Further, generalised speaking about Muslim migrants refers often to a constructed and imagined community. Muslims are not always migrants: nearly two million of the Muslims in Germany are German citizens, and Muslims live not in one, but several diverse communities simultaneously and have in the most cases multiple identities; they share characteristics and problems in everyday life with other groups or with the autochthonous, because they are liable to the same economical, educational or psychological strains.

Focusing on faith by constructing identities neglects the impact of the social life conditions. Muslims are not only and exclusively Muslims; their identity and their life conditions are also shaped by aspects like gender, ethnic and economic factors, social capital and Zeitgeist, which are contingent and beyond individual availabilities.

It is to underline that effective social integration is not an effort to bring just only by Turkish or Muslim migrants, and it is indisputable that a successful integration can principally avoid social conflicts and isolation. But not just from a moral point of view, also regarding the genuine own interests, a reflective society should not urge to homogeneity, but enhance more the ethno-cultural and

---

[210]   The rate of Muslim pupil at the age of 6 to 22, who refuse to take part at sport education or swim courses vary between 2 and 7 percent (Foroutan, 2012).

religious diversity and should try to benefit from the opportunities of alternative life-styles (see Schönpflug & Phalet, 2007).

References:

Berry, J. (1997). Immigration, acculturation and adaptation. Applied Psychology: An International Review, 46, 5-34.

Diehl, C. & Koenig, M. (2009). Religiosität türkischer Migranten im Generationenverlauf: ein Befund und einige Erklärungsversuche. Zeitschrift für Soziologie, 38 (4), 300-319.

Fassaert et al. (2009). Acculturation and psychological distress among non-Western Muslim migrants--a population-based survey. International Journal of Social Psychiatry, 19, 132-143.

Foroutan, N. (2012). Muslimbilder in Deutschland. Wahrnehmungen und Ausgrenzungen in der Integrationsdebatte. Friedrich-Ebert-Stiftung: Berlin.

Haug, S. / Müssig, S. & Stichs, A. (2009). Muslimisches Leben in Deutschland. Im Auftrag der Deutschen Islam Konferenz. Berlin.

Garcia Coll, C. & Magnusson, K. (1997). The psychological experience of immigration: A developmental perspective. In A. Booth, A. C. Crouter & N. Landale (Eds.), Immigration and the family (pp. 91-132). Mahwah, N J: Erlbaum.

Halm, D. (2013). Muslim Organizations and Intergenerational Change in Germany. The International Spectator, 48-57.

Heitmeyer, W. (2012). Deutsche Zustände: Folge 10. Berlin: Suhrkamp Verlag.

Lazarus, R. S. & Folkman, S. (1987). Transactional theory and research on emotions and coping. European Journal of Personality, 1, 141-169.

Mirbach, F. (2013). Das religiöse Leben von Muslimen in Deutschland. Ergebnisse des Religionsmonitors. In D. Halm & H. Meyer (Hg.), Islam und die deutsche Gesellschaft (S. 21-47). Wiesbaden: Springer VS

Olmedo, E. L. (1979). Acculturation: A psychometric perspective. American Psychologist, Vol. 34 (11), 1061-1070.

Sarrazin, T. (2010). Deutschland schafft sich ab: Wie wir unser Land aufs Spiel setzen. München: Deutsche Verlags-Anstalt.

Schönpflug, U. & Phalet, K. (2007). Migration und Akkulturation. In G. Trommsdorf & H.-J. Kornadt (Eds.), Anwendungsfelder der kulturvergleichenden Psychologie (pp. 1-48). Sonderdruck aus Enzyklopädie der Psychologie. Hogrefe: Göttingen.

Schwarzer, R. & Leppin, A. (1989). Sozialer Rückhalt und Gesundheit. Göttingen: Hogrefe.

Schwarzer, R. & Jerusalem, M. (1994) (Eds.). Gesellschaftlicher Umbruch als kritisches Lebensereignis. Weinheim: Juventa.

Soper, J. C. & Fetzer, J. (2007). Religious Institutions, Church-State History and Muslim. Mobilization in Britain, France, and Germany. Journal of Ethics and Migration Studies, 33 (6): 933-944.

Stichs, A. & Müssig, S. (2013). Muslime in Deutschland und die Rolle der Religion für die Arbeitsmarktintegration. In D. Halm & H. Meyer (Hg.), Islam und die deutsche Gesellschaft (S. 49-85). Wiesbaden: Springer VS.

Uslucan, H.- H. (2005). Ankommen in der neuen Heimat: Akkulturationsbelastungen von Migranten. In R. Golz & R. Kollmorgen (Hg.), Internalization, Cultural Difference and Migration (pp. 201-225). Münster: LIT Verlag.

Uslucan, H.- H. (2011). Integration durch islamischen Religionsunterricht? In H. Meyer & K. Schubert (Hg.), Politik und Islam (S. 145-167). Wiesbaden: VS-Verlag für Sozialwissenschaften.

ZfTI (2009): Download: http://www.deutsch.zfti.de/downloads/downmehrthemenbefragung2009.pdf.

Embodiment of Recognizing Differences: Alevis in Germany

Deniz Coşan Eke[211]

Introduction

Recognition is a form of respecting or valuing another (human) being (the different meanings of recognition are described in Inwood, 1992: 245-47; and Margalit, 2001: 128-129)[212]. Perhaps the most influential formulation of this concept is Hegel's "struggle for recognition" argument. Hegel discusses as Inwood (1992) states, recognition in mainly three implications which are identification, detecting and honouring the status of others in order to gain 'self-consciousness or self-knowledge'. Generally, we can argue that recognition is also one of the most complicated topics because it involves political results and legal effects.

Taylor (1994: 32)[213] reminds us about the connection between recognition and identity in terms of the "fundamentally dialogical character" of the human life. Ideally speaking, recognizing differences is the first step to ensure the inclusion of a plurality of voices in a society's major institutions because recognition is related with belonging. The reality, however, is that distinct ethnic, religious or cultural groups are more likely to suffer exclusion and subordination within the social hierarchy. Social exclusion can be defined as a social context in which certain ethnic groups have fewer participatory rights in a society due to lack of their economic, political, social and/or cultural influences. De Haan (2001)[214] defines the political dimension of social exclusion by using the aspect of rights, freedom of association and citizenship statuses. Generally, as he asserts, social exclusion can be defined as the rupture of solidarity between the individual and society. As a consequence, cultural and religious minorities and their differences in one country may face varying modes of social, economic, and cultural exclusion. Yet the political struggle for recognition raises its own issues which must be examined on the specific merits of each individual group (Kymlicka 1995: 19)[215]. In the light of above content, the Alevi community will serve as the focus of the current study in order to specify the struggle of recognition, which includes a multi-dimensional discussion in terms of migration, identity transnationalism, diaspora and collective action.

Alevism is the second largest branch of Islam in Turkey after Sunni Islam and is mostly defined as a heterodox and syncretic belief system associated with Anatolian folk culture. Alevi beliefs are mainly based on oral history to teach their principles, which are experienced differently at the local, regional and national level in Turkey. This is mainly due to the absence of central authority and

---

[211] Deniz Coşan Eke, Phd. Student in Ludwig-Maximilians-Universität München, Germany.
[212] Inwood, Micheal. 1992. A Hegel Dictionary. Oxford: Blackwell
[213] Taylor, Charles. 1994. "The Politics of Recognition." In *Multiculturalism: Examining the Politics of Recognition*, Amy Gutmann (ed.).Princeton: Princeton University Press
[214] De Haan, Arjan. 2001. "Social Exclusion: Enriching the Understanding of Deprivation". *World Development Report*
[215] Kymlicka, Will. 1995. Multicultural Citizenship: A liberal Theory of Minority Rights, Oxford: Clarendon Press

protection against the persecution or the *taqiya* which is a religious dissimulation. The increase of migration has also influenced and transformed Alevism and the Alevi community at both the national and the transnational level. Alevism has no longer been kept as a secret since the beginning of the 1980s thanks to the strengthening of the Alevi organizations in different countries.

In the current study, the Alevi community chosen as an example case has had their differences officially recognized as a separate belief system in Islam by some Federal States of Germany. This article focuses on these achievements of Alevis in Germany to reach many of their demands through the Alevi organizations and on the meanings of recognition of the Alevi identity in Germany. Mainly, the aim of this article advocates providing some opportunities for identities to be able to be renewed by recognition of the differences. In that point, it is important to find a response to the main question why the renewed identitary revival should be supported by recognition of the differences.

Connected to this first line of inquiry, two research questions will be explored. The first is related to the kinds of achievements the Alevi community in Germany gained when it is recognized with its cultural and religious differences. The second question asks what it actually means to have differences for Alevis in Germany officially recognized. The main research tool used for the current research is participant observation of Alevi Associations in Munich, Hamburg and Stuttgart from 2011 to 2013. Also the ethnographic experience has been proceeded as the part of a larger research about Alevis in Germany and Turkey. During this research, numerous *cem* gatherings in *cemevi*s have been attended, unofficial or formal interviews have been conducted with many Alevis in all three locations, and discourses in debates surrounding Alevism in media channels and newspapers have been observed in Turkey and in Germany.

A Brief Overview of Alevi Migration Phases in Germany

The largest Alevi migration in the history is a part of the common migration from Turkey to Germany after the Bilateral Recruitment Agreement in 1961. Like other Turkish immigrants, the Alevi community first came to Germany as `*Gastarbeiter*´ or guest workers who were expected to eventually return to their homeland after a short stay. But it has been shown that this expectation was incorrect because the size of Alevi immigrant population from Turkey continued to grow. The peak of labour migration was the year of 1968 because of the nation-wide polarization in Turkey with the influence of events of the 1960's and 1970

Furthermore, the 1973 recession following the oil shock changed labour conditions in Germany and led to the labour recruitment stop (*Anwerbestopp*) in 1973 (Friedman, 2010: 2)[216]. The immigrant situation in the 1970s in Germany can be summarized with the statements of Faruk Şen, "the year 1973 was a milestone with regard to the historical development and changes which have occurred in the social structure of Turkish migrants" due to the implementation of non-recruitment policy and family reunification (2003: 214)[217]. In fact, with the impact

---

[216] Friedman, G. 2010. Germany and the Failure of Multiculturalism. *Stratfor*. <http://www.stratfor.com > (Retrieved at 20.04.2015)
[217] Şen, Faruk. 2003. "The Historical Situation of Turkish Migrants in Germany". Immigrants & Minorities, 22(2/3), 208-227.

of family unification, most of the Alevis chose to settle down in Germany. In addition to this, economic and political instability in Turkey have made for difficulty returning to the home country. Also, the military regime between 1980 and 1983 led to an increase in the number of Turkish refugee and asylum seekers in Germany and forced many of Alevis to stay in Germany because of their political leftist ideology. The military coup of the 1980 tried to end relations between the political left and Alevis in Turkey. However, this attempt at a split was not totally successful since old leftists have taken more active roles in the Alevi associations not only in Germany, but also in Turkey and the other European countries.

Even though the revival of Alevi identity started after the 1980s, the organization process of Alevis was to remain low until the Sivas Massacre of 2 July 1993[218]. The violence of 2 July 1993, however, had a large effect on Turkey's Alevi community and also created tremendous international support for Alevis. After the Sivas Massacre, it has reanimated a greater sense of awareness for Alevis about their identity and saw a rise in the number of Alevi organizations (Kaleli,1995:46)[219]. The solidarity-based Alevi associations attempted to protect the Alevi community against the risk of a future reoccurrence of a similar massacre. Therefore, the Sivas Massacre can be seen to have provided a catalyst for the flourishing of Alevi organizations in Turkey and in the European countries, especially in Germany.

After the 1990s, there has been a growing interest in Alevi-related issues due to increased social and political mobilization which is based on ethnic and religious identities. The first visible signs of this process in the public domain is the tackling of Alevism as a subject of the books and articles in Turkey and Germany. Besides many academic works, internet sites, festivals and social activities started to offer information about Alevi culture and religious practices in both social and political fields. Alevis have started to perform their ceremonies in public places in order to make an attempt to show case of their differences. As David Shankland put it "A rural, remote, diverse, private, largely oral Islamic society (Alevism) has become urban, public, active, secular, and to a great extent, begun the express process of codification of its previously diverse largely unrecorded culture within the modern city setting"(Shankland 2003:13)220. Following these developments, the first Alevi organization were established with the Alevi name in Hamburg (Hamburg Alevi Culture Center) in 1989 and also the same year, the first Alevi manifesto was issued by mostly Alevi and some Sunni intellectuals in Germany. This manifesto221 included the recognition of Alevism as a different faith and culture, the equal representation and opportunity in education and in the media, and the proportional assistance in religious

---

[218] In 1993 in Sivas, an extreme-radical Sunni group set fire to a hotel full of Alevis attending a festival. Unfortunately, the attack killed 37 people.
[219] Kaleli,Lütfü. 1995. "Kosulları bilmek", *Nefes* 2:18 (Apr.)
[220] Shankland, David. 2003. The Alevis in Turkey: The Emergence of a Secular Islamic Tradition. London: Routledge Curzon.
[221] The same manifesto was published in Turkey in 1990, but the same demands has been still asked for the Turkish state but some of the German states have started to accept these demands since 2002.

services.222 In 1993, after the Alevi Manifesto was published, Alevis organized across Europe under the umbrella organization of the European Alevi Unions Federation (AABF) in Cologne. Now, members in the AABF, the biggest Alevi federation in Europe, number almost 100,000 Alevis. AABF is not only the umbrella organization of Alevis, with 147 local organizations throughout Germany, but also is one of the transnational migration organizations in Europe with the European Confederation of Alevi Communities (Avrupa Alevi Birlikleri Konfederasyonu), founded in 2002, which represents more than 250 Alevi Cultural Centres. The Confederation is organized in 12 European countries which are Austria, Belgium, Denmark, Germany, France, the Netherlands, Romania, England, Norway, Sweden, Italy and Switzerland (more details about these federations, see Coşan-Eke, 2014)[223].

Recognition Processes for Alevi community in Germany

As far as the recognition process in Germany is concerned, the institutions such as *Deutsch-Auslaendische Begegnungsstaetten* (German-Foreign Meeting Center) in Hamburg were established in order to deal with the problems of immigrants and promote their integration to the German society as a result of the requirements of multicultural policies (Sökefeld and Schwalgin, 2000)[224]. Via the activities of this institution, as Sökefeld and Schwalgin (2000: 15) claimed, Alevis gained an awareness of their peculiar culture and identity. According to Kaya (1999)[225], Alevis negotiated with the German society to frame their distinctiveness mainly in terms of a culture because, up until that point, no migrant group had ever been recognized as a religious group. However, in February 2000 the Islamic Federation of Berlin (IFB) was officially recognized as a religious community. After this event, the Anatolian Alevis' Cultural Center in Berlin (BAAKM) applied for the same status and activists in this Center began to frame Alevism as a religion and demanded equal rights like Sunnis in order to be able to teach Alevism in public schools. Finally, in 2002, the BAAKM obtained the same status as a religious community (Sökefeld, 2008: 192-193)[226]. This new framing seems to be goal-oriented since it is developed to use legal conditions and to provide resources. But Sökefeld (2008a: 288) points out that "it is difficult to explain to German authorities why Alevis should need religious classes separate from Muslim if Alevism is a part of Islam. Therefore, this discursive commitment

---

[222] The Alevi Manifesto can be found in Zelyut, Riza. 1990. *Öz Kaynaklarina Göre Alevilik*. Istanbul: Anadolu Kültür Yayınları.
[223] Coşan-Eke, Deniz. 2014."Transnational Communities: Alevi Immigrants in Europa". Forschungszeitschrift über das Alevientum und das Bektaschitentum- Internationale Forschungszeitschrift (6 monatlich). Heft : 10/Winter. Pp: 167-194.
[224] Sökefeld, Martin &Schwalgin, Susanne. 2000. "Institutions and their Agents in Diaspora:A Comparison of Armenians in Athens and Alevis in Germany", the 6th European Association of Social Anthropologists Conference, Krakau, 26-29 July 2000. http://www.transcomm.ox.ac.uk/working%20papers/schwal.pdf <Retrieved at 25.04.2015>
[225] Kaya, Ayhan. 1999. "Türk Diyasporasında Etnik Stratejiler ve 'Çok-Kültürlülük' İdeolojisi: Berlin Türkleri", *Toplum ve Bilim*, 82 (Güz):23-57
[226] Sökefeld, Martin. 2008. "Difficult Identifications: The Debate on Alevism and Islam in Germany", Ala Al Hamarneh &Jörn Thielmann (ed.) *Islam and Muslims in Germany*. Nederlands: Brill

clearly favours a perspective that explicitly categorizes Alevism as a separate religion".

After the recognition of the BAAKM as a belief community at the local level, the Federation of Alevi Communities in Germany (AABF) attempted to generalize this recognition at the national level as the umbrella organizations of Alevis. The federation of Alevi Communities applied for the recognition in all states in Germany, where Alevis have settled. Finally, five states which are Berlin, North Rhine Westphalia (NRW), Hessen, Baden Württemberg and Bayern accepted their applications by activists and institutions.

These processes led to change the status of Alevi organizations in conformity with the arrangements about religious organizations in Germany. From 1993 until 2002, the status of the AABF denotes itself as a democratic mass organization, but after 2002, AABF is registered as a religious organization in Germany. That is why German authorities have declared that specific type of religious education course can be taken by Islamic religious organization. Via the AABF, Alevis are legally recognized as a separate belief from Sunni Muslims and their activities have more often focused on their religious objectives than before.

The Acquisitions of Alevis´ Rights in Germany

Germany as a Federation of States does not have one arrangement dealing with the religious communities. Instead, they vary from state to state. The recognized differences of Alevis in Germany may be explained with two important arrangements in the some states: `Alevism courses´ in the school and ´Equality of Rights Agreement´.

Alevism Courses in the school

The first Alevi courses began in Hamburg in 1999 as a pilot study and the course began with an official in Berlin in 2002 after BAAKM was recognized as a religious organization. In 2006, Bavaria, Baden-Württemberg, North-Rhine Westphalia and Hessen states explained a co-decision to allow teaching of Alevism in their public schools and until 2008 all the states mentioned above had permitted a course of Alevism in schools. In 2009, Lower Saxony also began to allow Alevism to be taught in schools.

A course of Alevism can be taken between the 1st and the 10th German classes and involves two hours per week and electives. As part of the requirements of the course, students must pass an examination. It is not required to be Alevi to take this course. The teachers of Alevism courses have been educated in Germany and they should work on the permanent staff in schools because the salaries of teachers are paid by each States´ Ministry of Education.

The reason why the Alevism courses started in particular states is that the Alevi community there was well-organized. On the other hand, in many states in Germany, such as Berlin and Bremen, state religious education in public schools can be taken as optional elective courses. Another reason is that religion courses in some states in Germany, such as Hamburg, aim to provide interreligious dialogue and so religious course includes comparative religion in order to increase religious knowledge and beliefs. Therefore, each recognized religious group in

Germany can formally demand to be taught their faith except in addition to the general religious instruction (Noormann, 2000)227.

Equality of Rights Agreement

Alevis in Hamburg (2012), Lower Saxony (2013) and Bremen (2014) have signed an "Equality of Rights Agreement" with these state governments that grant Alevis important rights and give legal status to the Alevi community in Germany. Alevis in these states are defined as "a liberal Islamic religious community" and have gained an equal legal status as Christians and Jews after signing an official contract. According to the headmaster of AABK Turgut Öker (2014)228 "These rights are granted to all institutions that fit in and support Germany's legal structure and social life. We have gained the first results of our efforts by giving Alevism classes at schools for 12 years and such agreements allow religious beliefs to come under the state's protection and grant them legal rights."

One of the most important rights is teaching Alevism in school, and the agreement includes officially celebration of religious holidays, maintenance of cultural facilities, exemption from compulsory religion classes at schools, construction of Alevi worship places (cemevis), observance of funerals according to religious rules, provision of religious services at hospitals and prisons, representation at the state media council, education of clerics and the creation of Alevism chairs at Universities229. In fact, the first Department of Alevism was opened at the University of Hamburg Academy of World Religions. Department of the Alevism Presidency of the Ethnologist Dr. Handan Aksünger states in the official ceremony that "Alevi oral histories will be investigated together with the date of writing. This is being done will be given a theological religion to teachers lecture".230

Besides the aforementioned states, eight other states in Germany (Berlin, North Rhine Westphalia (NRW), Hessen, Baden Württemberg and Bayern) have not yet signed Equal Right Agreements with Alevi community in their states at the time of this writing, but they have accepted, as mentioned above, the procurement of the right to hold religious classes in schools, recognize religious holiday, and foster religious tuition in schools231.

---

[227] More information about this issue, please look at: Noormann, Harry, (2000). *Almanya'da Hristiyan Din Dersinin Hukuksal Çerçeve Koşulları ve Türkiye ve Almanya'da İslâm Din Dersi Tartışmaları* . Ankara: CÜ İlâhiyat Fakültesi ve Konrad Adenauer Vakfı Yayını & http://www.alevi.org/cms25/images/ARU1/Lehrplan_Grundschule_auf_Tu%C3%AArkisch.pdf < Retrieved at 25.04.2015>

[228] http://www.hurriyetdailynews.com/alevis-in-germanys-bremen-win-equal-status-as-other-religious-communities.aspx?pageID=238&nID=73141&NewsCatID=351

[229] Bu anlaşmanın ayrıntıları için lütfen bakınız: http://alevi.com/TR/hamburg-eyaleti-fhh-ve-almanya-alevi-birlikleri-federasyonu-aabf-arasinda-anlasma/ <Retrieved at 19.04.2015>

[230]http://alevi.com/de/eroffnung-der-weltweit-ersten-juniorprofessur-fur-alevitentum-an-der-universitat-hamburg/<Retrieved at 29.04.2015>

[231] Coşan-Eke, Deniz. 2014. "Transnational Communities: Alevi Immigrants in Europe". *Forschungszeitschrift über das Alevitentum und das Bektaschitentum(6 monatlich)*. Heft : 10/Winter. Pp: 167-194.

Conclusion

The international migration of Alevis from Turkey to Germany, which was mostly based on economic concerns and the social and political dislocations in Turkey, has led to the emergence of an Alevi movement in Germany. By the end of 1980s, Alevis started to arouse their traditional and cultural values by means of Alevi organizations in Turkey and Germany. As a result of the legal and political arrangements for Alevi immigrants in Germany throughout the last decades, several states in Germany have legally recognized them and guaranteed the right to perform their religious and cultural rituals.

In conclusion, a few points should be emphasized: First of all, the Alevi associations in Germany had, at first, been largely motivated by Turkish politics to partially or completely oppose Turkish government policies about Alevism. This original purpose has continued, however, as many of Alevis and their descendants feel that they belong to Germany. Most identify themselves by their family's country of origin, i.e. Turkey, but have not pursued emigration to their home-country because later generations with immigrants background from Turkey identify with more than one identity, with many of them naming Germany as their new "home country".

Secondly, after more than 50 years, the migration experience from the first Alevi generation to third Alevi generation in Germany, the AABF defines their main goal as serving Alevi immigrants in Germany even though they have continued to support their connections with Alevis in Turkey by means of remittances transfer and by attracting attention to remedy their disadvantaged position in Turkey on an international scale. Therefore, it can be stated that AABF supports achieving strong transnational networks among Alevis but, at the same time, promotes Germany as the most important transnational space for the Alevi community.

Thirdly, the increase of organizational structure among Alevis has demonstrated that Alevis are not only defined as religious and cultural groups, but can now be redefined as a transnational political organization and a kind of new social movement which has gained increasing strength while struggling for their acquired rights. As explained above, it is possible to cite two important achievements of Alevis in Germany as a result of their struggle for recognition: The Alevism course and the Equal Rights Agreements.

The teaching of Alevism as a separate belief from other Islamic faith supports the process of institutionalization of Alevism because Alevism is being taught in one syllabus at school and at the University apart from *dedes'* conversation in the *cem* rituals. Therefore, the teaching of Alevism at school shows us a kind of transformation or change in Alevism as a result of the Alevis' migration to Germany. This change influences also the construction of the Alevi identity. Also, Alevis are legally recognized as a religious community (*Religionsgemeinschaft*) and they have achieved the status of public legal personality under public law (*Körperschaft des öffentlichen Rechts*) in some states of Germany resulting from the

Equal Rights Agreements232. It is assumed that this process will contribute not only to perpetuate and protect the differences of Alevism, but also to decrease the prejudices against their religious and cultural diversity.

To summarize, it is important to find a general response to the main question why recognition is important for Alevis as a separate belief system from the other Islamic groups in Germany. Basically, official recognition of distinctness of the Alevi community is one way to access material resources, as well as legal rights and political power. Therefore, Alevis have made their political demands on the basis of recognition of religious difference and changed their organizational structure from cultural to religious organizations in Germany after 2002 because Alevi community has been motivated by the present political and legal context in Germany. In that point, it may be stated that the Alevi identity in Germany has been renewed and reformed not only by the immigrants´ experiences which have been gained in Germany, but also by the historical and structural opportunities and limitations that the immigrants are provided in one country.

In contrast to the German example, the struggle of Alevis in Turkey has not gained the same pace up to date. Alevi identity shows variability in accordance with socio-political context, so the achievements of Alevis developed in the German context have proved not easily transferable to the Turkish context. Identity with a flexible and dynamic character is not only the self-production and is built by others (Mead, 1973)233. That is why the recognition especially in political, legal and cultural levels is so important. Hence, it can be assumed that the people who have socio-cultural or religious differences in one society can be adapted to system of values and norms even if they are very divergent from their own ones (Özyürek,2010)234. Indeed, the Alevi movement with the struggle for recognition of their differences continues to gain ground by transforming the Alevi identity through transnational networks which play a crucial role in the formation of a better adaptation to different socio-cultural environments.

---

232 Coşan-Eke Deniz & Özkan T.ürkan. 2014. "Transformation of the Alevi Movement in Diaspora: A Case Study in Munich", Vol. III, Issue 5, pp.55-66, Centre for Policy and Research on Turkey (ResearchTurkey), London, Research Turkey. (http://researchturkey.org/?p=6253).
233 Mead, H:George. 1973. Geist, Identität und Gesellschaft aus der Sicht des Sozialbehaviorismus. Frankfurt/m.: Suhrkamp Verlag
234 Özyürek, Esra. 2008. "Beyond Integration and Recognition: Diasporic Constructions of Alevi Muslim Identity between Germany and Turkey."In *Transnational Trascendence*, edited by Tom Csordas. Berkeley: University of California Press.

A transnational actor: "Monsieur imam"

Evren Irmak[235]

The ideal that determines the French model of a nation, elaborated in "One and indivisible Republic" and "lacité"; is accompanied by the emergence of "segmented society" (Maurin, 2004) fostered by the immigrants, now sheds light on the transformation which gives possibility for the co-existence of "unity" and "differentiation" in France. This transformation, substantially is prone to immigration patterns, would stress on the negotiations of identities and in the context of Muslim migrants in France, puts religion to the forefront (Kastoryano, 2012). Concurrently, identity politics concerning Turkish migrants started to cyristallize on account of the legislation in 1961 in Turkey, permitting the movement of Turkish citizens to Western Europe as "guest workers". France, comes second after Germany, has the most Turkish migrant population, firstly was addressed by the "Five Year Development Plan" in Turkey which covered the constitution of bilateral agreements between Turkey and Western European countries[236] in order to respond the excessive demand of labour from these countries which bestowed to the economic expansion after the second World War (Danış, Üstel, 2008:14) These agreements stipulated temporary stay of Turkish citizens/workers, referred as "rotation" , notifying their return to their home countries. However, the outbreak of economic crisis in 1973, resulted in high level of unemployment further invigorated the "rotation" policy in ideal terms, which bore repercussions. In the first place, the "cheap" labour force was needed due to the fulfillment of specific jobs, that were not desired by the indigeneous workers. These were the jobs referred as 3D- dirty, dangerous and demeaning (Connell, 1993) corresponded the positions substantially in the automative, manufacturing and constructing industries that at the same time, were the driving forces behind the economic growth. Therefore, the rotation policy in ideal was not reciprocated practically as a matter of its imbuement to the persistance of economic structure in France and led the implementation/ modification of new regulations that granted permanent residence as well as family reunification; coupled with a possibility for double citizenship. This very transformation re-defined primarily economic and social spheres of the host country- France vis-á-vis the demographic characteristics of the migrants. During the first decade of the migration from Turkey to France, migrant population had a gendered pattern, predominantly men, working in construction, automative and metal industries. After the legislation on permanent residency that allowed family reunification; the single male profile altered to a certain extent. However, relevant cultural and social characteristics of the migrant population remained intact; the overall profile depicted a picture where migrants, coming mainly from the Black Sea, Central Anatolia, Eastern and Southeastern Anatolia of Turkey; they were under or semi skilled workers associated with the increasing demands of French companies for

[235] Middle East Technical University, Ankara, Turkey.
[236] The bilateral agreements are constituted, firstly with Germany in 1963 and secondly with France in 1966.

low skilled workers having basic vocational competence (Autant-Dorier, 2008:191), with an average of 5 years of education and had a rather isolated life without any intention for integration. They were living in ghetto like units-*bidonvilles* with other migrants, having no or little interest neither in learning the language of the host country nor vocational training (Abadan-Unat, 1976:12) ; they were driven solely by pecuniary interests that granted them a degree of subsistence.

As Dubet (1989a:59, cited by Silverman, 1992:13) puts forward that immigrants are torn between two cultural and social worlds in which they want to be a part of the new world without losing their identities, and also transform themselves. Herein, integration as a social problem couples with the socio-economic structure of the Turkish migrants, in question meets the process of "isolation" which is equated with their inclination to non-integration, provided a ground for *communautarisme* in relation to other migrant groups. However, this would further lead to accentuation on " permanent differences" (Kastoryano, 2000:136) of migrants in the host countries and in Turkish migrant case, it is ensured through either or both their Turkish and Muslim identities. Berger (2010) suggests that migrant workers rather than being politically conscious, their thoughts are mainly traditional. His argument becomes evident when the first generation of Turkish migrants are taken into consideration, also sheds light on the tendency of Turkish migrants to set up a substructure based on their religious affiliations. In relation with the conflicts due to the industrial change which shifted the demand for unskilled to speacialized workers for the progress of automation system, it necessitated the replacement of Fordism (Leveau, Hunter, 2002:18) that signalled the migrant workers to be pushed outside of the employment pattern. Migrants who were not supported neither by the political parties nor the unions because the migrants relations with France were not regarded as permanent, pointing out that they could not involve in any voting practices so that political parties could not benefit by prioritizing their situation. As the "work" itself was the fundamental anchor that allowed workers to remain in the country, the conflict emerged as traumatic and as the conflict was surpassed to a certain extent, according to Leveau and Hunter (2002:19):

"The more difficult periods in terms of loss of jobs became less violent than earlier ones, when badly organized and badly informed workers who had been traumatized by changes tended to adopt more uncomprising and unrealistic stands. It appeared that the assertion of a religious identity had helped to create some form of communication, solved some problems, and had made the acceptance of an inevitable evolution more palatable"

In this respect, Kepel and Leveau (1987) argues that religion was rationally instrumentalized by the managers of these highly-migrant populated factories due to the reason that would curtail migrants' engagement in political activities (in terms of unionization of the workers) which eventually could risk the economic outcome. The attempts made for the Muslim migrants to claim their religious identities, firtstly emerged within the the factories as a request for a room to perform their religious practices, particularly for friday prayers. Then, they addressed their requests in the foyers that they lived and by negotiating with the residents, the areas at the basement of each or assigned foyer transformed as "salle(s) de prière" (praying room). By the time family reunification was legalized as the numbers grew, the praying rooms became insuffcent so the search for larger spaces and the tendency of Muslim migrants to differentiate oneselves from the other Muslim migrants, was firstly responded by the mosque, appropriated by "Milli Görüş" (National Vision) Hareketi. While, having both political and economic engagement with the home country- they were the international segments of the youth branch of National Vision in Turkey- , this movement could be regarded as one of the examples of recreated transnational organizations as Levitt (2004) suggests, which is now also stood as "one of the leading Turkish diaspora organizations in Turkey" (Çarkoğlu, Rubin, 2006:64). On the other hand, this engagement had repercussions on the people who came to mosque for perform his religious practices without any need to manifest his political affiliation. The ones who did not share the same political vision with this movement, wanted a ideologically free place to perform their religious practices, started to detach themselves from there and searched for alternatives. Herein, they had a consensus to pursue the idea of form an association that would be a departing point to build a mosque as well as the naissance of DITIB France (Diyanet İşleri Türk İslam Birliği- Turkish Islamic Union for Religious Affairs) in Paris. A background story on the search of Turkish Muslim migrants , interpreted by Mehmet T., a religious official who was assigned by the Presidency of Religious Affairs in Turkey, spent his four years, from 2007 to 2011, working for the association of "Amicale de Franco-Turque" (French-Turkish Association- Türkiye Fransız Dostluk Derneği) in Carrières sous Poissy, Paris. Through the viewpoint of Mehmet T, a study based on oral history which would aim to contribute to the dialogue of empirical and theoretical framework to further illustrate the significance and the ways of functioning of a transnational organization by instrumentalizing a micro-perspective embodied in a transnational actor- a religious official, assigned by the Presidency of Religious Affairs in Turkey to conduct religious service to Turkish-Muslim migrants in Paris for four years, between 2007-2011.

Born in 1976 in Konya, Mehmet T. , since his senior year in the Faculty of Theology/ Religious Studies (İlahiyat Fakültesi) at Gazi University in 2001, has been working as a religious official, affiliated to the Presidency of Religious Affairs in Turkey. Respectively, as an imam in Çorum, a preacher in Emirgazi, Konya and now, as a senior preacher, he works and lives in Konya. Never thought of being a religious official, however, the insists of his father was responded by Mehmet T and after successing the national examination for public officials (DMS-Devlet Memuru Sınavı), he was assigned to his fourth (last) choice, as an imam to a Alevi populated small town, named Hamdiköy in Çorum. Later, as a part of his training as a religious official, he went to Erzurum where he stayed for 30 months. His training in Erzurum is significant since during his time in there, he applies for the serving as a religious official abroad which the Presidency of Religious Affairs calls for applications, annually. He did not intend to apply fort his post, nevertheless, was moved by the turn of phrase of his colleague :" Did not Mehmet T , apply for the position abroad? Well, sure he did not. It is a matter of knowledge; one who cannot rely on his knowledge, cannot apply" (Tabii bu bilgi meselesi, bilgisine güvenmeyen başvuramaz) Being among the two persons, his colleague and himself who met the requirements for this post, which entails certain level of higher education and experience as a religious official, he was invited to Antalya, for the first sitting of examinations, total of three. The first one was a written exam, comprised the questions on basic Islamology, legislations of the Religious Affairs in Turkey and general knowledge. Among 5000 candidates who took the first examination, they were reduced to 2000 for the second sitting, a proficiency exam on reading of Quran, recitation and meaning (Kuran meali). It was then followed by a third stage; last sitting referred as an examination held by the Commission of Culture. The commission comprises of four judges, from the Ministry of Foreign Affairs, Ministry of National Education, Ministry of Culture and Tourism and Presidency of Religious Affairs. As an oral exam, there are not any set of questions that would be addressed to the candidate, yet, questions ranging from "Who is Ahmet Kabaklı, and what are his works?" to " What is your opinion about the Turkish migrants in Europe?" could be among some examples. A highly selective tripartite examination has an aim to assign competent officials who are capable to enhance the *cultural* and *religious* affiliations of the Turkish Muslim migrants abroad to Turkey without propogating any *ideological* indoctrination. It is significant to highlight that, religious officials have a mission to help the migrants to conserve their both Turkish and Muslim identities. After the results have announced at Kocatepe Cami in Ankara, among the most successful 26 candidates, he was assigned to a position in France (where the exact location of his field of work, to be announced later during his language course programme as, Carrière sous Poissy, situated in the suburbs of Paris). Then, all 26 officials enrolled to 3 month intensive French course at the French Institute in Ankara, followed by 1 month of "orientation programme", 4 days in a week, which offers several courses and conferences on the current situaiton of the Turkish migrants abroad, their family patterns, issues on fıqh that are likely to be addressed along with courses on counselling (rehberlik) and conferences on the experiences of former officials who were assigned abroad. The wide scope of courses are intended to prepare the officials for their future position. However, as Mehmet T. argues, these courses would not delineate the specific issues relevant to each country, he tells: " They (the instructors) are talking like as if the conditions are the same in every country, as well for the associations, as if all Turkish migrants abroad has the same experiences, problems" The "associations" are the constutive elements that lead the way for the establishment of DITIB in France. After the breakaway of some Turkish migrants from the mosque of National Vision, they intended to form an associatio because without through the formation of associations, a right granted to the immigrants by Autain's Law in 1981, they had no other chance apart from the associations to be able to manifest their religious identities, collectively. On the other hand, by the virtue of the tradition of laicité, as the fundamental tenet of France, associations would not be allowed to be formed under any kind of "religious" umbrella; as a consequence; Turkish migrants associations, named under "cultural", "solidarity" or "friendship" not only in Paris but also in several cities as Nantes, Lyon and Strasbourg.

As they were "legal" before the law, it was not difficult for the associations to claim a space to base their operations. As a result, they rented a mansion near

Carrière sous Poissy which would be renovated as a mosque. A duplex mansion, while the first floor was transformed to space for the 5 time prayers, the second floor was reserved for the women Turkish Muslim immigrants. However, there was a major problem: they did not have a religious official, an imam to deliver the prayers. They contacted to Counselor of Religious Affairs (Din Hizmetleri Müşaviri) who functions within the Turkish Consulate in Paris, delivered this demand to the Presidency of Religious Affairs in Ankara, were responded positively and later created the need for an umbrella organization, that would represent all the associations in France under the direction of Turkish Presidency of Religious Affairs. Hereby, DITIB (Diyanet İşleri Türk İslam Birliği- Turkish Islamic Union for Religious Affairs) France was established in 1986 in Paris. As an umbrella organization of the associations, they maintain a bilateral relation with them. The associations are responsible for consigning a place (i.e. rent or buy a place with their own resources) to be renovated as a mosque so that DITIB assigns a religious officials from Turkey to carry out their duties. Even though these associations are formed as a matter of religious affiliations of Turkish migrants, the mosques are only the part of the associations, not the founding elements which again has the motivation to comply with the principle of laïcité in France.

None the less, DITIB, now as the dominant umbrella organization which represents % 58 (126 associations in total) of the Turkish Muslim associations in France while National Vision respresents % 28 (61 associations) (Akgönül, 2008:102) where Bowen (2010:60) argues that both live in a tacit arrangement of "live and let live" , corresponding detachment from each other's territories. However, Mehmet T while confirming such a situation that predominantly occured in 80s; now, there is a certain level of integration between these two, when to take community members in Amicale Franco Turque into account; a member both participates the prayer in one of the mosques of National Vision while sending his son to the courses of Quran in the mosque of DITIB happens to be the case. In addition, Mehmet T participates the prayers and organizations for the Ramadan and Eid-Al Ahda, held by the members of the mosques of the National Vision Movement. The reason of his participation has dual characteristics. On the one hand, it is an act of recognition of National Vision as well as an act of goodwill in order to form a dialogue, on the other hand, Mehmet T. asserts that " I regard DITIB as an organization, above National Vision and other religious groupings. I am in Paris as a member of the Presidency of Religious Affairs in Turkey and DITIB in France, therefore, it makes me being the sole representative of the state, assigns me a supra-identity (üst kimlik)"

Whether for a year or four, the officials have the liberty to determine their duration of work abroad, however, their work areas are assigned by the Presidency of Religious Affaires in Turkey. Formed as an association in 1989 and became a member of the DITIB Paris in 1991, Mehmet T. is the third religious official assigned to "Amicale Franco-Turque". A hierarchical classification refers that religious officials are at the bottom; DITIB has a top-down structure, positions the Counselor of Religious Affairs in the Turkish Consulate in Paris- the representative of the Presidency of Religious Affairs in Turkey, who is also the President of DITIB Paris on the top and followed by the Attaché of the Religious Affairs and the Coordinator of religious officials, respectively. In Paris, recently there are total of 150 religious officials, assigned in various associations. The number has grown by 40 when compared to 2007, and Mehmet T. puts forward that " diplomacy becomes determinant, as the visit of the Prime Minister and/or President of Turkey is well received, it directly affects our presence and puissance in here"

Even though Mehmet T. is assigned as a "religious official" by the Presidency of Religious Affairs in Turkey, in France he is entitled as "a social assistant (assistant de service social) " who also works as a "family counsel (accueil familial)" tells that " I have multiple responsibilities, which in Turkey, each of them is delivered by one religious official but in here, it is different. I am an imam, muezzin, preacher, instructor of Quran and a counsellor" , however, the function of the association is rather restricted. He continues:

'The sole function of the association has been to collect membership fees as well run the Turkish market and the café (lokal) , raise money for the fund of association, nothing more. When I came here, I wanted to organize events in 23 Nisan, Aşure Ayı, Şeb-i Aruz and Çanakkale Şehitlerini Anma Günü, I could only manage to do it thrice, nobody is interested. When I attempt to organize these events, the community starts complaining as "Turkey did not send him here to organize such events, Turkey sent him to France to make prayers with us" But, for me, religious officials who are assigned by The Presidency of Religious Affairs in Turkey, means everything in here. These people have no other source to contact which reciprocate their religious needs. On the other hand, how could you possibly expect them to understand and reform the association; it has been founded by the first generation of Turkish Muslim migrants, lack of education, lack of knowledge about their surroundings, lack of religious training; they are the ones who comply with " volk Islam" and advised in Turkey not to consume anything except of bread and pasta in France, conceive God as an instrument of "threat", even thinking that visiting a Church makes them Christian. As for the third generation, they do not even come to mosque, they are "invisible" and they see me as "invisible", they conceive "Allah" in abstract terms, detached from them, they live like French people. Only when they are around with their Muslim friends, be that Algerians or Tunusians, they come to think that whether they are consuming halal food or not. "

DITIB France, helps the members of the association of "Amicale Franco Turque"to be recognize both in France and Turkey. The official correspondances are responded effectively, when they are addressed by DITIB to the statesmen in France. Moreover, DITIB fulfills several functions to foster them to maintain their ties with Turkish and Muslim identities. The main functions of DITIB in that sense, comprises the employment of religious officials who help Turkish Muslim migrants for their integration to France- through the officials by counselling the significance of their status in France, and responding the demands of the associations for Turkish courses. DITIB accentuates the importance of the integration of migrants by being true to themselves, without being assimilated but conserving their "Turkish" and "Muslim" identities. As Mehmet T. delivers, people in the community within the association have very weak relations to Turkey. Even though, the first and second generations can speak Turkish, the third generation has difficulties in Turkish. Turkey, for them, represents a destination for vacation where once his/her grandparents lived even though in the discursive level they identify themselves as Turkish instead of French. Overall, DITIB, according to Mehmet T. is a "lifesaver" for the migrants, both help them to maintain their ties with Turkey and encourage them to take part in the public sphere in France.

Conclusion

When two former officials who served for the association in Carrières sous Poissy, told Mehmet T. before his journey to France as he was going to his honeymoon for 4 years, Mehmet T. felt reassured. However, by the time the plane landed at Orly Airport in Paris, "disillusion" started to take over. When he met Turkish- Muslim migrants in his community, he realized that migrants' problems were not uniform as he was instructed back in the orientation course in Ankara. At the same time, Mehmet T. had the impression that, their lifestyle was the backdrop of a life in Turkey in 1970s and 80s. Concurrently, *fiqh of reality* (Moussa, 2004; cited by Bowen, 2006:888) emerges as a crucial factor that Turkish migrants have such conflicts to reconcile their everyday life with the Islamic codes. Having such matters, Mehmet T also contacts the intelligence of France government and officers of the Ministry of Finance in a meeting, held once in a month to exchange information about the functioning of the association where Mehmet T. claims that the intelligence wants to *keep them under control.* During these meetings, he is referred as "Monsieur Imam" while Mehmet T. is preoccupied with many other tasks as well. An imam who wants to fulfill more than both the Presidency of Religious Affairs in Turkey and the Counselor of Religious Affairs in Paris guide them to do: he is not just an actor of this transnational process, he also advances himself to be transnational, too.

References

Abadan-Unat, N. (2002). Bitmeyen Göç: Konuk İşçilikten Ulus-Ötesi Yurttaşlığa. İstanbul: İstanbul Bilgi Üniversitesi Yayınları

Akgönül, S. (2008). Din, Çok Bağımlılık ve Kimlik Korkusu Ekseninde Fransa Türkleri. Danış, D. , İrtiş, V. (Ed.) , Entegrasyonun Ötesinde: Türkiye'den Fransa'ya Göç ve Göçmenlik Halleri. İstanbul: İstanbul Bilgi Üniversitesi Yayınları

Autant-Dorier, C. (2008). Bilmemekten Tanımaya: Fransa'daki Türkiye Kökenli Göçmenler. Danış, D. , İrtiş, V. (Ed.), Entegrasyonun Ötesinde: Türkiye'den Fransa'ya Göç ve Göçmenlik Halleri. İstanbul: İstanbul Bilgi Üniversitesi Yayınları

Berger, J. (2010). A Seventh Man: A Book of Images and Words About the Experience of Migrant Workers in Europe. London, New York: Verso

Bowen, J. R. (2004), "Beyond Migration: Islam as a Transnational Public Space," Journal of Ethnic and Migration Studies, Vol. 30, No. 5, pp. 879-894.

Bowen, J.R. (2010). Can Islam be French? Princeton and Oxford: Princeton University Press

Çarkoğlu, A. , Rubin, B. (2006). Religion and Politic in Turkey. New York: Routledge

Connell, J. (1993). Kitanai, Kitsui and Kiken: The Rise of Labour Migration to Japan. Economic and Regional Restructuring Research Unit: University of Sydney

Danış, D. , Üstel, F. (2008). Türkiye'den Fransa'ya Göçün Toplumsal ve Tarihsel Boyutları. Danış, D. , İrtiş, V. (Ed.), Entegrasyonun Ötesinde: Türkiye'den Fransa'ya Göç ve Göçmenlik Halleri. İstanbul: İstanbul Bilgi Üniversitesi Yayınları

Kastoryano, R. (2000). Kimlik Pazarlığı: Fransa ve Almanya'da Devlet ve Göçmen İlişkileri. İstanbul: İletişim Yayınları

Leveau, R. , Hunter, S.t. (2002). Islam in France. Hunter, S. T (Ed.) Islam, Europe's Second Religion: The New Social, Cultural and Political Landscape. Connecticut: Praeger Publishers

Leveau, R. C. W. de Wenden, G. Kepel. (1987). Les Musulmans en France. Revue Française de Science Politique, Vol. 37 (6)

Levitt, P. (2004), "Redefining the Boundaries of Belonging: The Institutional Character of
    Transnational Religious Life," Sociology of Religion, Vol. 65, No. 1, pp. 1-18.
Maurin, E. (2004). Le Ghetto Français: La République des Idées. Paris:Seuil
Silverman, M. (1992). Deconstructing The Nation: Immigration, Racism and Citizenship in Modern
    France. London, New York: Routledge

Greek migrants in Istanbul: "home-leaving" or "home-coming"?

Georgia Mavrodi[237]

Introduction

Most migration scholars treat Turkey as a country of emigration, a transit route, and a country of immigration for migrants and refugees from Eastern Europe, the Middle East and Africa (Erzan & Kirişci 2008; Içduygu & Kirişci 2009) or a country of settlement of co-ethnic, second generation immigrants from western European countries. By contrast, the movement and settlement of EU nationals of non-Turkish descent has attracted attention only recently (Içduygu *et al* 2013: 3; OECD 2014), although the phenomenon lies at the intersection of key political, economic and institutional developments both in the EU and in Turkey itself (Tolay 2012; Linden *et al* 2012). Obviously, one of the crucial dimensions is the processes of political and institutional reforms in Turkey upon its preparation for EU membership and the impact of such changes on the rights, preferences and migration strategies of foreign nationals in general and EU citizens in particular (Içduygu *et al* 2013: 6-16). Furthermore, the migration of EU citizens to Turkey offers an alternative and yet undiscovered angle to view the recent rise of identity and ethnicity politics in the EU member-states (Hsu 2010), the fluid and variable geometry of European borders and identities (Del Sarto 2010), and the resulting formation of conceptions of "the other", both in the EU and in Turkey.

The above considerations notwithstanding, the presence of Greek migrants in Turkey goes both beyond and deeper than the mere debates about the intertwining economic, political, and cultural relations between Turkey and Europe. *Beyond*, because it relates to additional dimensions such as the historically charged, sensitive, and conflicting bilateral relations between Turkey and Greece, and the recent efforts for their *"rapprochement"* within the wider European context. And *deeper*, as it touches on fairly recent historical legacies and traumatic memories of nation-building processes in the 19th and 20th centuries, and on the very understandings of inclusion and exclusion that lie at the core of national identity in both countries.

In this paper we examine the reasons Istanbul has become an appealing destination for Greeks since the year 1990. Who are these people and why do they choose to settle there? What are their motives, expectations and experiences prior to their migration and settlement in the Turkish metropolis? Moreover, we attempt to integrate the movements of today into a wider historical framework: how can we conceptualise these migrants in the light of past Greek migrations and diasporic communities? Are recent and current Greek migrants in Istanbul connected to Turkey through ancestry, family ties and/or past migratory experiences? In this context, are they "home-comers" to the city or land of their

[237] Georgia Mavrodi is post-doctoral academic assistant at COSMOS – Center of Social Movement Studies, Robert Schuman Center for Advanced Studies, European University Institute, Via Delle Pallazzine 17-19, San Domenico di Fiesole, 50014, Italy. E-mail: Georgia.mavrodi@eui.eu.

ancestors or rather "home-leavers", migrants leaving Greece in search of better opportunities and choosing Istanbul among a variety of other possible destinations on the basis of their life and career aspirations?

This paper is based on original empirical work. An anonymous online survey named *POLIIS* and containing 90 questions was open for respondents to fill out from October 2013 until July 2014. The questionnaire was addressed to adults of Greek origin (derived from at least one of their parents), irrespective of their citizenship, who were born in any country apart from Turkey and who have stayed, studied and/or worked in Istanbul for a period of at least nine (9) consecutive months since the year 1990. The survey was advertised in a number of new media (websites, blogs, as well as Facebook pages). To promote it further, personal and professional networks as well as contacting people who had already attracted Greek media attention due to their migration to Istanbul were also utilised. A total of 84 persons chose to engage with the questionnaire, most of them during October 2013 and January 2014. Of those, 69 persons submitted it complete, and analysis in this paper is based on their responses. The majority of respondents declared their willingness to participate in personal in-depth interviews at a later point in time.

In what follows, I will first provide preliminary accounts and estimates on the recent phenomenon of Greeks migrating to Istanbul, based on the available sources. Then I will provide the historical background related to the existence of Greek Diaspora communities in the eastern Mediterranean and the related creation of common cultural spaces, embedded migratory traditions and identities. Finally, I will present and discuss the preliminary findings of the *POLIIS* survey in relation to the initial questions presented in this paper.

Greeks mirgating to Istanbul: recent accounts and estimates

In 2009, EU citizens settled in Turkey – both professionals and retirees - were estimated at about 100,000 – 120,000, living mainly in Istanbul and on the Turkish Mediterranean coast (Içduygu & Sert 2009a: 6). In the meantime, Turkish newspapers have reported estimates of about 200,000 EU-citizens employed in Turkey in 2011 (*Zaman* 12/06/2011). Against this background, in 2011 Greece appeared to be the 10th most significant country of origin of non-nationals issued with a residence permit in Turkey (Içduygu *et al* 2013: 4).

The first Greek media coverage of the phenomenon of emigrating young Greek citizens to Turkey - specifically to Istanbul - coincided with the outbreak of the crisis (Massavetas 2009). Although the beginnings of the phenomenon had clearly preceded Greece's economic collapse, in the last couple of years it has acquired new meaning and attracted media attention in the context of economic developments. Web-based sources run by members of the *Rum* community in Istanbul claim that the Greek population in the Turkish metropolis has increased in recent years due to the arrival of Greeks from Greece proper who aim at middle- or long-term settlement, currently reaching just over 5,000 people.[238] According to the German broadcasting service *Deutsche Welle* there are currently

---

[238]http://www.omogeneia-konstantinoupoli.com/id/omogeneia-turkey.html <accessed 24 March 2012>

"some thousands" of Greek "labor migrants" ("Gastarbeiter") in Turkey, mainly in Istanbul and active in several professional sectors.[239]

The issue has also been covered by Turkish media, particularly newspapers (such as the daily *Hürriyet*). Sometimes, interviews are conducted not only with "fresh" Greek migrants who arrive in Turkey for the first time with the intention of employment and settlement, but also with former *Istanbulu* or their descendants who refer to the past difficult migratory experience of their families and their recent decision to "return".[240] Another category of Greek citizens in Istanbul that has received some attention by Turkish media are Greek young University students and their growing numbers in Turkish Universities, who are now contemplating to stay in Turkey and seek employment following the end of their studies. In 2010, it was reported that Turkey was on the rise in the preferences of Greek students abroad, attracting almost 2,5% among the latter, particularly post-graduate students who may also envisage a professional career in Turkey.[241] More recently, the settlement and professional activities of "new" Greeks in Istanbul have been highlighted in Greek TV programs, too (Alpha TV 2014; MegaTV 2014), and they are often portrayed as a "return of Greeks to Istanbul".

Apparently, the size of recent Greek immigration in Turkey is negligible when compared to other nationalities. Yet such a movement - however small in numbers - would have been unthinkable or impossible for most people up until the early 2000s. In addition, the case of Istanbul merits particular attention. This is not only because the Turkish metropolis is a major economic, educational and cultural center in Turkey and in the eastern-Mediterranean. It is also because Istanbul attracts many foreign immigrants, either in transit or aiming at mid- or long-term settlement.[242] Even if the estimates about the 5,000 or "some thousands" of Greek migrants currently present in the city are inflated, there were about 1800 *Rum* living in Istanbul in the mid-2000s (Örs 2007: 83). Such a small number of people easily renders any increase in hundreds as qualitatively significant for the Greek-speaking population in the city. In 2011, Massavetas estimated the number of these "new Greek Istanbulites" ("Νεο-Πολίτες") at about 200 people (Massavetas 2011: 456, 460). Here, the issue at stake is that Turkey has become a country of choice and destination for *some* Greeks at the turn of the new century, and that this choice deserves attention owing to particular historical (and political) legacies as well as broader processes of European migration(s) to Turkey. In this paper, we are interested in the degree to which this movement is related to past migratory trajectories and can be understood within the context of the latter.

---

239 Undated. "Viele Griechen wollen auswandern – in die Türkei", http://www.dw.de/popups/popup_single_mediaplayer/0,,6712271_type_video_struct_0_contentId_15726331,00.html <accessed 24 March 2012>

240"Jobseekers from Greece try chances in Istanbul", http://www.hurriyetdailynews.com/jobseekers-from-greece-try-chances-in-istanbul.aspx?pageID=238&nID=11009&NewsCatID=347 <accessed 24 March 2012>

241"Interest grows among Greek youth for Turkish universities", http://www.hurriyetdailynews.com/interest-grows-among-greek-youth-for-turkish-universities.aspx?pageID=438&n=interest-grows-among-greek-youth-for-turkish-universities-2010-10-10 <accessed 24 March 2012>

242For the case of Afghan, African, Iranian, Iraqi, Maghrebi & Moldovan immigrants in Istanbul see Daniş, Taraghi & Pérouse (2009); Brewer & Yükserer (2009); Kaşka (2009).

The poliis survey: preliminary findings

The *POLIIS* online survey included 90 questions concerning basic information (age, sex, place of birth, level of education achieved, occupation, etc.) as well as more detailed accounts of the respondents' family status, migratory experiences, family roots as well as migratory decisions, strategies and practices. Only the data derived from fully completed and promptly submitted questionnaires (a total of 69 respondents) will be discussed here. There has been an equal distribution of respondents according to gender, with most of them being between 26 and 45 years of age.

The vast majority of respondents was born and grew up in Greece, mainly in the regions of Attica and Thessaloniki, followed by those coming from northern Greece (Macedonia and Thrace) and Crete; a few of them were born abroad. One of the completed questionnaires concerns a male who was born in Istanbul but actually grew up in N. America. For that reason, it was decided to include his responses in the analysis. Out of 69 respondents, 41 were actually living in Istanbul at the time of the survey while 1 respondent had changed place of residence within Turkey. Out of the remaining 27 people who had already left Turkey, 20 resided in Greece; 4 moved to other EU countries (Cyprus, France, the Netherlands, and Spain); and 2 resided in the U.S.A.

Most participants in the survey are economically active. Employees in education and research are the most prominent group (20 respondents,[243] followed by those employed in tourism and catering (5 respondents) and music-related professions (5 respondents). Other occupational sectors mapped out by the survey included Art and Archaeology, International Organisations, Banking and Insurance, Journalism, Culture, Marketing, Constructions, Mechanical Engineering, Industry, Shipping, Transport, Trade, Medical specialization, IT and employment in Non-Governmental Organisations. Most of these people are high-skilled, holding a degree in higher education, including Master's degrees and doctoral titles. Our findings agree with Massavetas (2011: 456), himself a member of the Greek migrant community in Istanbul for a number of years, who identified it as "professionals – journalists, artists, musicians, white-collar employees, businessmen – and students (…) of young age, highly skilled, in their vast majority having post-graduate degrees".

Migratory trajectories should not be taken as linear and settlement decisions should not be regarded as "given" and "granted". Rather, they can be treated as episodes in a dynamic and volatile pathway that may well change or reverse itself in space and time. Indeed, many of our respondents had studied in at least one foreign country other than Greece – mostly in the United Kingdom - before deciding to settle in Istanbul. A number of respondents made the first step towards settling in Istanbul by pursuing studies at an educational institution in the city and choosing to stay after completion. Yet another sub-group chose to leave the city after a first period of settlement and come back again later on. This dynamism and volatility may well be connected to the impressive degree of international mobility of our respondents: 48 out of 69 people declared having

---

[243] This piece of information should not be taken at face value, as it may reflect a selection bias due to our facilitated access to academics and researchers during the dissemination face of the survey.

lived in a country other than their country of birth prior to their settlement in Istanbul. For most of them, though, living outside of their country of birth did not include parts of Turkey other than Istanbul, as only 12 respondents declared having done so for any period of time. Thus, for many among the Greek newcomers to the city, Istanbul is the metropolis, the gateway, a "global" city which may be, at the same time, a confined space of life and work: an enclave within Turkey.

Concerning the choices to move to and settle in Istanbul, as well as the primary motives and migratory patterns, our respondents chose Istanbul as their place of settlement primarily in search for better opportunities. Out of 69 people, 50 declared that their main motivation behind their movement was career-related: 25 respondents were searching for employment or had already found a job in the city (most of them had previously looked for work elsewhere - primarily in Greece but some had also done so abroad) while another group of 25 people wanted to pursue studies or research or vocational training. A smaller group chose to settle in Istanbul for personal reasons, either because they followed their spouse or partner or because they wanted to spend part of their life in Istanbul out of personal interest for the city or for Turkey more generally. Only 4 respondents mentioned their wish to discover their family roots as their primary motivation. However, most respondents had some degree of contact with people related to Istanbul / Turkey prior to settling there, either on personal or professional grounds (friends, former colleagues, acquaintances, etc.). Moreover, Istanbul has kept newcomers for longer periods than what they had initially planned for: the vast majority had envisioned a shorter period of stay, which was eventually prolonged and even led to long-term or quasi permanent settlement in some cases. When it comes to the geographical distribution of the newcomers within the city, Beyoglu is by far the most popular choice (half of our respondents chose to live there at least for some time when they first settled in the city). Finally, in most cases their move invited further visits of people belonging to their personal or professional circles, including people who have also moved to Istanbul in the meantime or are currently contemplating of doing so.

On the basis of our findings, then, recent and current Greek migrants in Istanbul are a young, dynamic, highly-skilled, internationally-oriented and career-motivated group of Greek citizens, attracted to the opportunities a global city like Istanbul has to offer. As such, their movement can be well understood in the context of international mobility of the highly-skilled and the migratory patterns observed in the centers of international economic and cultural activity. But how do the primary motivations for moving to Istanbul and the places of settlement within the city relate to the family migratory histories of our respondents? Is the search for better career opportunities unrelated to past migratory experiences of their ancestors?

It is difficult to see the recent and current move of Greek migrants to Istanbul as a clear return to an ancestral "home". Having family roots in the city concerns only a tiny minority among our respondents. By contrast, more than half of them (37 out of 69 people) do not have family roots in Turkey in general or in Istanbul in particular. However, if we take into account family origins in other parts of the former Ottoman Empire (including the Balkans and Egypt but also the parts of

Greece that had stayed under Ottoman rule after the establishment of the Kingdom of Greece in 1830) or the Mediterranean (Italy, France) and Black Sea (Russia), the picture differs: 43 out of 69 respondents have ancestors that lived in what is today's Turkey (western coast, Izmir, Istanbul, Cappadocia, Adrianople, Bursa, Paphlagonia, Konya, Caesarea), in Egypt (especially in Alexandria and Cairo), Romania and Moldova, tsarist Russia, Armenia, the Kingdom of Serbia, France (Marseille), Italy, western Thrace, Macedonia, Crete, and the Aegean islands. For these people, it seems that Istanbul is part of a wider region characterised by intense economic relations and periodic population movements in the last centuries, familiar to them due to past family migrations and proximity. The latter may be understood both as "real" (while geographic), or "imaginary" (in cultural and historical terms).

Thus, movement and settlement in Istanbul is primarily connected to "home leaving" for a global city, the Mediterranean metropolis, the big economic and cultural center and a gateway to better opportunities for career and personal advancement, than with "home-coming". Yet, the particular choice of migratory destination is not unrelated with ancestral migratory trajectories and the Greek Diaspora communities of the past. That leaves us still with a quite important group of "home-leavers" with no family roots in any of these places. The overwhelmingly "migrant" character of the newcomers from Greece (Ελλαδίτες) (as opposed to that of real or imagined "returnees") resonates well with the observed indifference or even hostility displayed by the Rum (Ρωμιοί) towards them. Along with differences in mentality, customs and morals between the two groups, it has been noted that the newcomers from Greece are often reminded that they are "foreign and unwanted", despite their wish to integrate themselves in the life of the Rum community (Massavetas 2011: 456). Yet, there may be elements of a "symbolic return" through the choices these new migrants make concerning their places of settlement within the city and the way their arrival is understood by the Turkish society. In this context, the choice to settle primarily in the districts where Greek communities flourished in the past (such as Beyoglu, Cihangir, etc.) may be related to recent conscious efforts to revive the old European quarters through architectural projects of gentrification and the revisiting of the city's past through the lens of a now cherished but lost "multiculturalism".

Concluding remarks

In this paper we sought to map out recent and current migration and settlement of Greeks in Istanbul and to examine the reasons the Turkish metropolis has become an appealing destination for them. Their numbers may be negligible when compared to those of other nationalities but their migration is qualitatively significant. Current Greek migrants to Istanbul are often portrayed as "returnees" or "home-comers" in the Greek media, a statement that we preferred considering as a hypothesis rather than as a given fact and sought to examine on the basis of the experiences, motivations and family histories of our respondents.

The data we collected in the POLIIS survey does not support the above hypothesis. New Greek migrants in Istanbul are not actually "going back" to the city or homeland of their ancestors, - not in the strict sense. Out of 69 respondents, only 4 declared their wish to discover their family roots as the main motivation for moving to and settling in Istanbul. On the contrary, the vast majority chose to settle in the city in search of better opportunities in their studies and employment while a few have had personal considerations in mind – living with their spouse or partner or pursuing personal interests. When the educational level and personal migratory background of our respondents is taken into account, it becomes obvious that this is a group of young and highly skilled people, dynamic and mobile, who are able to explore career opportunities offered in a globalised world in general and in global cities, such as Istanbul, in particular.

However, a look at the family migratory background of these people reveals that the historical context is still relevant. The majority of our respondents possess the skills to choose from among a variety of destinations to pursue their personal goals. Yet, they chose to move within a familiar geographical space where strong cultural affinities are still present and many Greek-speaking urban communities flourished in the past. For the majority of our respondents, these affinities include the migratory histories of their families and their origin in geographical areas of today´s Greece that have been fully integrated in trade and cultural roots in the Mediterranean or even remained under Ottoman rule until the early 20th century. The ancestors of many of our respondents came to Greece from Asia Minor, the Black Sea, and eastern Thrace, and some of them from Istanbul proper. Still others do not derive their origin from the lands of today´s Turkey but their ancestors were present in other urban centers of the Mediterranean (Alexandria and Marseille being two examples) as well as parts of Greece proper with strong historical ties to these areas. In this broader sense, recent and current Greek migrants in Istanbul may be continuing on a similar path as their predecessors of the 18th and 19th centuries. In much lower numbers, and following several decades of hostility between the two countries, they have started anew on old roots of population movements in the region. As such, they constitute an interesting case for European migration scholarship, one that illuminates some factors currently making Turkey an appealing migration destination while taking into account regional migration systems and their significance across space and time.

References

Alpha TV (2014). 360 Μοίρες – Έλληνες μετανάστες στην Κωνσταντινούπολη, 13 February 2014, http://www.alphatv.gr/shows/informative/360moires/webtv/360-moires-ellines-metanastes-stin-konstantinoypoli (accessed 31 May 2015)

Brewer, K. T. & D. Yükserer (2009). "A Survey on African Migrants and Asylum Seekers in Istanbul", in Ahmet Içduygu & Kemal Kirişci (Eds.), Land of Diverse Migrations. Challenges of Emigration and Immigration in Turkey, Istanbul: Bilgi University Press (pp. 637-718)

Daniş, D.; Cherie T. & J.-F. Pérouse (2009). " 'Integration in Limbo': Iraqi, Afghan, Maghrebi and Iranian Migrants in Istanbul", in Ahmet Içduygu & Kemal Kirişci (Eds.), Land of Diverse Migrations. Challenges of Emigration and Immigration in Turkey, Istanbul: Bilgi University Press (pp. 443-636)

Del Sarto, R. A. (2010). "Borderlands: The Middle East and North Africa as the EU's Southern Buffer Zone", in Dimitar Bechev & Calypso Nicolaidis (Eds.), Mediterranean Frontiers. Borders, Conflict and Memory in a Transnational World, London & New York: Tauris (pp. 149-165)

Hsu, R. (Ed.) (2010). Ethnic Europe. Mobility, Identity, and Conflict in a Globalized World, Stanford: Stanford University Press

Içduygu, A. & K. Kirişci (Eds.) (2009). Land of Diverse Migrations. Challenges of Emigration and Immigration in Turkey, Istanbul: Bilgi University Press

Içduygu, A. & D. Sert (2009a). "Country Profile Turkey", Focus Migration No. 5, April 2009, http://focus-migration.hwwi.de/Turkey-Update-04-20.6026.0.html?&L=1 <accessed 27 March 2012>

Içduygu, A. & D. Sert (2009b). "Immigration and Integration Policy", Dossier Migration, Bundeszentrale für Politische Bildung, Country Profile 5, 1 April 2009, http://www.bpb.de/wissen/ZZCD8A <accessed 27 March 2012>

Içduygu, A.0; Z. Gülru Göker; L. Bertan Tokuzlu & S. P. Elitok (2013). MPC Migration Profile: Turkey, Florence: Migration Policy Center, European University Institute, http://www.migrationpolicycentre.eu/docs/migration_profiles/Turkey.pdf (accessed 3 May 2015)

Kaşka, S. (2009). "The New International Migration and Migrant Women in Turkey: The Case of Moldovan Domestic Workers", in Ahmet Içduygu & Kemal Kirişci (Eds.), Land of Diverse Migrations. Challenges of Emigration and Immigration in Turkey, Istanbul: Bilgi University Press (pp. 725-804)

Linden, R. H.; A. O. Evin; K. Kirişci; T. Straubhaar; N. Tocci; J. Tolay & J. W. Walker, Turkey and Its Neighbors. Foreign Relations in Transition, Boulder & London: Lynne Rienner Publishers

Massavetas, A. (2009). "Νέοι Ελλαδίτες της Κωνσταντινούπολης", Κ – Καθημερινή, Vol. 312, 24 May 2009 (pp. 38-50)

Massavetas, A. (2011). Κωνσταντινούπολη. Η Πόλη των Απόντων, Athens: Pataki

MegaTV (2014). Οι Έλληνες επιστρέφουν στην Πόλη, 14 December 2014, http://www.megatv.com/megagegonota/summary.asp?catid=27383&subid=2&pubid=32640 311 (accessed 3 June 2015)

OECD (2014). "Turkey", in International Migration Outlook 2014, Paris: OECD Publishing, http://www.oecd-ilibrary.org/turkey_5jxswc7jhhs5.pdf;jsessionid=1d03ipnk8cvko.x-oecd-live-03?contentType=&itemId=%2fcontent%2fchapter%2fmigr_outlook-2014-42-en&mimeType=application%2fpdf&containerItemId=%2fcontent%2fserial%2f1999124x&accessItemIds=%2c%2fcontent%2fserial%2f20746873%2fcontent%2fserial%2f20746873%2c%2fcontent%2fbook%2fmigr_outlook-2014-en (accessed 3 May 2015)

Örs, I. R. (2007). "Beyond the Greek and Turkish Dichotomy: The Rum Polites of Istanbul and Athens", in Dimitrios Theodossopoulos (Ed.), When Greeks Think About Turks. The view from Anthropology, London & New York: Routledge (pp. 79 – 94)

Südwestliche Rundfunk - SWR (2012). "Immer mehr Hellenen wandern aus", 16 January 2012, http://www.swr.de/international/de/-/id=233334/nid=233334/did=9147724/1jzq244/ <accessed 24 March 2012>

Tolay, J. (2012). "Coming and Going: Migration and Changes in Turkish Foreign Policy", in Ronald H. Linden; Ahmet O. Evin; Kemal Kirişci; Thomas Straubhaar; Nathalie Tocci; Juliette Tolay & Joshua W. Walker, Turkey and Its Neighbors. Foreign Relations in Transition, Boulder & London: Lynne Rienner Publishers (pp. 119-143)

Delineating the geographical mobility of African immigrants towards Greece: Between transnationalism and integration

Apostolos G. Papadopoulos[244] and **Loukia-Maria Fratsea**[245]

Introduction

Currently migration in the Mediterranean Sea has risen to the top of the policy agenda. The press and the media of the EU countries are full of images of sub-Saharan African (SSA) migrants attempting to land to the EU soil. These images often focus at the end of "boat peoples" journey to Europe and more particularly at the events referring to the crossing of the land and sea borders of Turkey to Greece or Lambedusa and Italy.

African migrants on route to Europe travel through the Canary Isles, the Spanish areas of Melilla and Ceuta or through Malta and the Italian islands of Pantelleria, Lambedusa and Sicily in the Mediterranean (de Haas 2007). Since 2011 the number of irregular African migrants increased tremendously in the Central Mediterranean due to the overturn of migration control mechanisms caused by "Arab spring". In 2011, it was reported that at least 1,500 people are known to have lost their lives attempting to cross the Mediterranean (Strik 2012: 3) while in 2014 this figure increased to 3,072 people (Brian and Laczko 2014, p. 20). In response to the human tragedy in the whole of the Mediterranean, a "10 point plan" of the immediate actions to be taken in response to the crisis situation in the Mediterranean Sea was presented by the European Commission, calling for consensus and rapid action to save lives and to step up a joint EU action (European Commission 2015).

Migration flows towards Greece have changed significantly. While in 1990s migrants originated from Balkans and Central and Eastern European (CEE) countries, by 2014 the majority of migrant flows are from the Middle East (45 percent), Asia (24 percent) and Balkans and CEE countries (24 percent) and Africa (8 percent). In other words, the geographical proximity with sending countries (e.g. Albania, Bulgaria) is replaced by geographic accessibility for shaping migration patterns in Greece. This transition is related to the pressure exerted by FRONTEX missions on the West and Central Mediterranean sea border as well as the bilateral agreements signed between the South European and the North African countries led to changing directions of irregular migrant flows to Greece (Bredeloup and Pliez 2011). The attempt of the EU to externalize its migration policy beyond its south Mediterranean Sea borders led to the shift of migration flows to the east Mediterranean, where borders have higher porosity due to the policies adopted by Turkey.

In more detail, during the last couple of decades Turkey has become an important country of immigration (Sirkeci 2005). Three factors seem to be shaping migratory movements to Turkey. First, the ongoing political turmoil and

[244] Professor, Department of Geography, Harokopio University of Athens, Greece. Email: apospapa@hua.gr
[245] Ph.D. Candidate, Department of Geography, Harokopio University of Athens, Greece. Email: fratsea@hua.gr

clashes occurring in neighbouring areas have pushed people from their homelands in the hope of a better life, security and protection from persecution. Second, Turkey's geographical location between East and West, and South and North, has made the country a suitable transit zone for those intending to reach western and northern countries. Finally, the policies of 'Fortress Europe', applying very restrictive admission procedures and increasing immigration controls, have diverted immigration flows targeting Europe to Turkey. More recently, there is complex and detailed discussion about Turkey as a 'migration hub' for irregular migrants from Africa and the Middle East, heading towards the EU (İçduygu 2007; Elitok and Straubhaar 2011; Ozcurumez and Senses 2011).

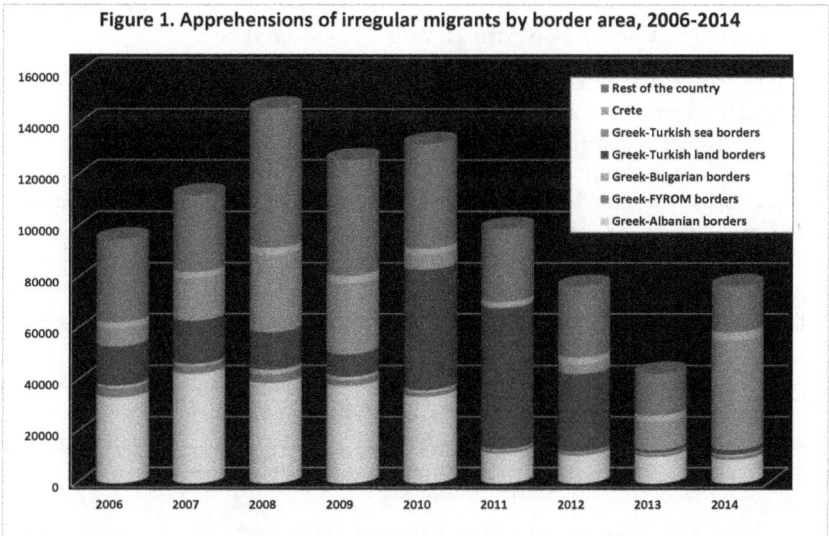

Figure 1. Apprehensions of irregular migrants by border area, 2006-2014

Source: Greek Ministry for the protection of the citizen, 2006-2014. Note: The processing of the data has been done by the authors.

The latest FRONTEX report stresses that "an increasing number of migrants from North Africa and the Middle East are expected to transit to Turkey via the air border, before attempting to cross illegally the border to the EU, also by using forged document. Istanbul airport (IST) is an important hub for irregular migrants travelling by air to several Member States, with continuous in-crease in passenger flows for the past several years and Turkish Airlines' expansion strategy towards Africa and the Middle East. Turkish airports are thus likely to remain common embarkation points for irregular migrants arriving in the EU" (FRONTEX 2015, p.48)

Migratory flows towards Turkey seem to play an important role for migration in Greece. Taking into account the apprehensions data of irregular migrants in Greece, it is evident that the composition of the migrant flows by border gate has significantly changed during the last years. By 2011, the arrests at the Albanian border have gradually diminished and then the Turkish land border became the main border gate to the country (2010-2012), but later lost its significance due to the building of a security fence along the Evros River. By 2013, the irregular crossings via the land border virtually stopped and the apprehensions at the sea border rose again (until 2015) (Figure 1).

The aim of the present paper is to map out the migration process of African immigrants towards Greece as well as to investigate the various dimensions of their geographical trajectories. Looking at seven Sub-Saharan African nationalities, we examine the 'journey' of African migrants through Turkey to Greece, the routes they followed and their integration prospects into Greek society. The distinction between different 'types' of African mobility shed light to the migratory strategies of African immigrants, which interact with structural and institutional factors.

Research findings on African migrants in Greece

The data presented in this paper have been collected during an empirical research which was carried out in the Athens area during the period June-July 2011. In total 532 semi-structured questionnaires were completed using face to face interviews. Aiming at interviewing both migrants with regular and irregular legal status; the snowball sampling was followed by using multiple contacts and different types of places and networks (e.g. migrant associations, NGOs, acquaintances, friends, relatives, public places, migrant's shops etc.). Seven SSA nationalities were selected; representing the more populous SSA nationalities living in Greece and illustrating older and more recent migration histories: Nigeria, Ethiopia, Ghana, Somalia, Congo (former Zaire), Senegal and Guinea.

In addition to the quantitative research, over fifty qualitative interviews were conducted during 2011-2013 with African immigrants, several state institutions and civil society. Those interviews shed light to migrants' experiences during the migration journey and their aspirations and integration prospects into receiving society.

The majority of respondents are males (76 percent) and one quarter is female (24 percent). Gender distribution differs between the seven nationalities. Women represent the two thirds of Ethiopian respondents, one quarter of Nigerians, one fifth of the Somalis, one sixth of the Ghanaians and one tenth of the Congolese.

Regarding the age of African migrants, they are usually in their 30s (average age 33.7 years - median 32 years old), although there are significant gender and nationality differences. Specifically, one fifth of the respondents is younger than 25 years old, one fifth belongs to the age bracket from 26 to 30 years old, 23 percent are from 31 to 35 years old, one fourth belongs to the age bracket from 36 to 45 years old and a little over one tenth is over 46 years old. On average women are older than men (average age 35.5 years old against 33.2 years old; median 34 years old against 32 years old).

Contrary to the popular view in which African migrants in their majority are uneducated and unskilled, a large share of the respondents (29 percent) has attained tertiary education, in most cases in their sending countries. Additionally, a remarkable proportion of the respondents - among those with tertiary education - have proceeded to postgraduate studies (4 percent). While it is worth mentioning that a significant proportion has pursued technical education (12 percent). Including also those respondents who are currently university students (in Greek

Universities), we realize then that four out of ten respondents (42 percent) have obtained post-secondary education, a fact which classifies SSA migrants, on average, among the most educated migrants in the country. Only a small share of the respondents has primary education (8 percent) or no education (8 percent). This is mainly due to the Somalis, who have very low education and the Senegalese who have followed only religious primary schools.

In terms of family situation the sample is divided equally between unmarried and married respondents (44 percent respectively), 8 percent are divorced or separated and just over 5 percent they have not been married but they have children. Of interest is that one sixth of married respondents are married with Greek or EU citizens. The majority of female respondents are married (47 percent), while the figure for male respondents drops to 43 percent. Furthermore, for the majority of respondents their family lives in the country of origin, just over one third live with his/her family in Greece. For the remaining 2/3 their family is divided between the country of origin and/or other countries and Greece.

Taking into account the length of residence in Greece we can distinguish two basic groups of African nationalities. One group consists mainly of nationalities with significant proportion of migrants who arrived relatively early in Greece (i.e. 7-10 years on average). This first group includes many Ethiopians, Nigerians, Ghanaians and Congolese. The second group consists of these nationalities that came recently to Greece (i.e. less than 3 years on average). This second group includes the vast majority of Guineans, the Senegalese and the Somalis. Moreover, there is a significant difference among males and females due to the fact that the large majority of the newcomer nationalities are males. Moreover, those who live for many years in Greece tend to be married, while those who came recently are in their majority unmarried.

In terms of labor market participation the majority were unemployed during the time of the survey. In particular, more than half of the respondents (52 percent) did not work, some do not belong to the active force (5 percent), while the rest (43 percent) were employed. The majority of the respondents (61 percent) has worked sometime during their residence in Greece, while the rest 39 percent has never worked in Greece. Among those who never worked, the vast majority (88 percent) are men who arrived recently in the country and failed or did not even attempt to find employment. As a result, 45 percent of men and 20 percent of women have never worked in Greece.

The main nationalities of those who have never worked in Greece are the Somalis (92 percent), the Guineans (86 percent) and the Congolese (57 percent). The majority of those who haven't found employment in Greece are these who arrived to Greece two to three years before the survey took place (i.e. by 2008 or 2009) (78 percent). At the other end of the spectrum, all Ethiopians and Senegalese have worked in Greece. In the middle of the spectrum, one may find the Nigerians and Ghanaians of which only 25 percent have never worked in Greece.

Mapping the SSA Migration Process

The relevant literature emphasizes that migration is hardly a simplified physical movement from one place to another (King and Skeldon 2010, Cohen and Sirkeci

2011, Schapendonk and Steel 2014). Almost 70 percent of the respondents migrated to other country/ countries before arriving to Greece. More precisely, with the exception of half the respondents from Ethiopia who arrived directly from Ethiopia to Greece, the majority of Somalis (99 percent), Guineans (98 percent), Senegalese (90 percent), Ghanaians (68 percent), Congolese (62 percent) and Nigerians (57 percent) migrated to other countries during their journey to Greece.

Those migrants who came more recently (i.e. during the last 2-3 years) in the country, when they are compared to earlier migration flows, are considered as 'more mobile' due to their tendency to migrate to other country/ countries before arriving to Greece, (Figure 2). The increased mobility of current migrant flows may be seen as a way of them adapting to the changing geopolitical and economic environment against the legal constraints/ barriers that migrants face during their migratory journey in order to reach a destination country.

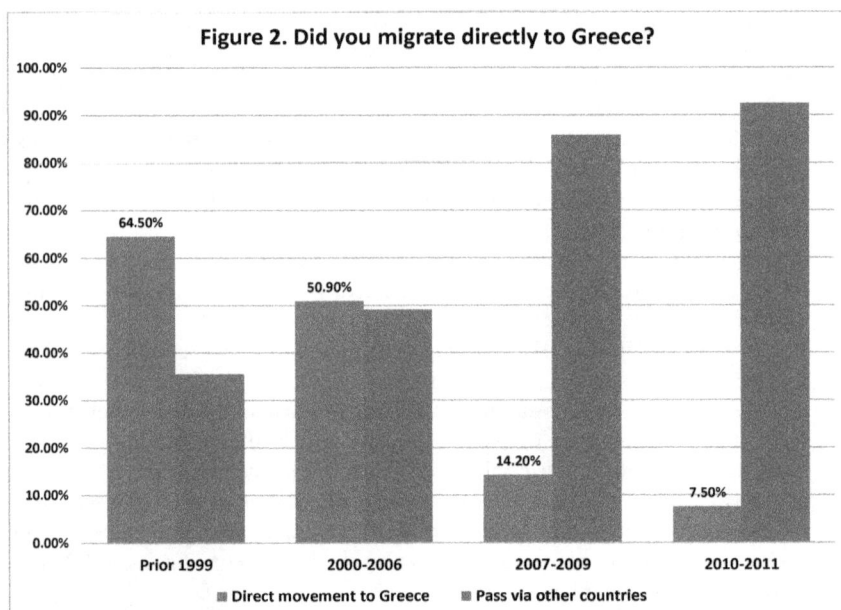

Figure 2. Did you migrate directly to Greece?

Source: Empirical research data gathered June-July 2011.

Sub - Saharan migrants follow a number of multiple and complex trajectories till they reach the European shore. Following the SSA's trajectories the Middle East countries (i.e. Lebanon, Syria, Yemen, Saudi Arabia and Turkey) and North Africa countries (i.e. Libya and Egypt) are among the initial destinations. It became evident from the fieldwork that for a number of SSA migrants, some of these countries were considered as transit countries; where migrants could take some rest in their long migratory journey and could also plan their next movement. Other countries are presented more like 'stepping stones'; where migrants work, collect information and money so they can 'fund' their migration journey. Those who originate from West African Countries used to pass through northern Africa (i.e. Libya or Algeria) to their way to Europe.

The complexity of SSA migratory journey is reinforced when adding the time spent in each country before arriving to Greece. Indeed, some SSA migrated in just one country for a long or short time before arriving to Greece; while others migrated into several countries. The migratory journey itself may last from approximately one month up to 17.5 years. More particularly, nearly one third of the respondents arrived directly to Greece from their country of origin; over a quarter followed a short time route through other countries (less than one month) before arriving to Greece; less than one quarter extended their stay in other countries to a period of a year; and the remaining one tenth spent in other countries over a year before arriving to Greece. The duration of the migratory journey shows that there are various migrant groups, which should not be aggregated according to their nationality but they could rather be utilized to discern the dynamics of migrant integration processes and strategies in host country.

Table 1. Average period in Turkey and duration of journey by time period of entry to Greece (time is measured in months)

Time period of entry	Average period of journey within Turkey	Average total duration of journey	Number of respondents
Prior 1999	9.07	17.50	15
2000-2006	6.90	16.97	34
2007-2009	3.19	12.28	97
2010-2011	2.60	10.43	161
Total	3.58	12.09	307

Source: Empirical research data gathered June-July 2011. Note: The calculations refer to the respondents who passed through Turkey during their migratory journey.

An important finding is that nearly 80 percent of all those SSA migrants who cross another country before entering Greece have passed through Turkey. This is a major empirical finding which corresponds with the wider picture offered by the recent official data (Greek Ministry for the protection of the citizen) presented in the previous section. Furthermore, when examining the duration of stay in Turkey, it is evident that SSA migrants do not only cross Turkey on their way to Greece, but they also spent much of their time there before taking their decision to migrate or until they organize their movement to/through Greece (Table 1), although there are significant differentiations depending on the time period of entry. In more detail, the average period of stay in Turkey seems to be reduced recently compared to previous years. Additionally, the average stay in Turkey is 3.6 months, which represents on average 30 percent of the time spent in the migration journey towards Greece.

Conclusions

Immigration to Greece has kept changing due to the wider changes in the economies and politics of countries in Asia, Middle East and Africa in recent years. Especially for SSA migrants their flows to Greece peaked by 2011, while in the last couple of years there are decreasing numbers entering Greece.

Migratory flows towards Turkey seem to play an important role for migration in Greece and in the EU. Indeed, Turkey remains a 'migration hub' to the EU and more particularly to Greece, while there are recent modifications in the types and intensity of migrant crossings.

The empirical data illustrate that SSA migrants to Greece are a mixture of 'old' and 'newcomer' flows (e.g. Congolese, Nigerians, Ghanaians, Ethiopians), while some others consist mainly of 'newcomer' flows (e.g. Guineans, Somali, Senegalese). The recent flows appear to be more 'mobile' as they tend to migrate or sojourn from country to country when they are compared to earlier flows. This pattern of mobility is an indication of the changing geopolitical environment in Northern Africa and Middle East (de Haas 2006), and of the tightening migration policies and controls by the EU.

By analyzing the time period that migrants spent in other countries in the course of their migratory journey we may come up with a number of migrant groups, which should not be aggregated by nationality, and therefore discern the dynamics of migrant integration processes and strategies in Greece.

References

Bredeloup, S. and Pliez, O. (2011). The Libyan Migration Corridor, Research Report Case Study, EU-US Immigration Systems 2011/03, European University Institute.

Brian, T. and Laczko F. (2014). Fatal Journeys Tracking Lives Lost during Migration. Switzerland, International Organization for Migration.

Cohen, J. H., and Sirkeci, I. (2011). Cultures of Migration: The Global Nature of Contemporary Mobility. Austin: The University of Texas Press.

de Haas, H. (2007). Irregular migration from Africa to Europe: Questioning the transit hypothesis. Oxford: International Migration Institute.

de Haas, H. (2006). Trans-saharan Migration to North Africa and the EU: Historical roots and current trends, Migration Information Source, November 1st.

Elitok, S. P., and Straubhaar, T. (2011). Turkey as a Migration Hub in the Middle East. Insight Turkey, 13(2), 107-128.

European Commission (2015). Joint Foreign and Home Affairs Council: Ten point action plan on migration. Press release, 20 April 2015. Luxembourg. Available from <http://europa.eu/rapid/press-release_IP-15-4813_el.htm>.

FRONTEX (2015). Annual Risk Analysis 2015. European Agency for the Management of Operational Cooperation at the :External Borders of the Member States of the European Union, Warsaw, Poland.

Içduygu, A. (2007). The Politics of Irregular Migratory Flows in the Mediterranean Basin: Economy, Mobility and 'Illegality'. Mediterranean Politics, 12(2), 357-367.

King R. and Skeldon R. (2010). "Mind the Gap!" Integrating Approaches to Internal and International Migration. Journal of Ethnic and Migration Studies, 36(10), 1619-1646.

Ozcurumez, S., and Şenses, N. (2011). Europeanization and Turkey: studying irregular migration policy. Journal of Balkan and Near Eastern Studies, 13(2), 233-248. doi: 10.1080/19448953.2011.578867.

Schapendonk J. and Steel G. (2014). Following Migrant Trajectories: The Im/Mobility of Sub-Saharan Africans en Route to the European Union, Annals of the Association of American Geographers, 104(2), 262–270.

Sirkeci, I., & Martin, P. L. (2014). Sources of Irregularity and Managing Migration: The Case of Turkey. *Border Crossing: Transnational Working Papers*, 2014(1401), 1-16. http://tplondon.com/journal/index.php/bc/article/viewFile/373/294

Strik, Y. (2012). Lives lost in the Mediterranean Sea: Who is responsible? Report from the Committee on Migration, Refugees and Displaced Persons, Doc. 12895, Parliamentary Assembly, Council of Europe.

Tracing Deep Scars of 1915 in Art and Literature

Esin Gülsen[246], Erdem Çolak[247] and Selen Yamak[248]

Introduction

Regardless of whether we call it genocide, massacre, exile or deportation, events experienced in Ottoman lands in 1915 cost countless lives, forced millions of Armenian people to leave their lands and left deep marks on next generations. In the 100th anniversary of 1915 events, it is impossible to say that Turkey has made a considerable way in terms of coming to terms with 1915 events.

We can argue that there is a bilateral relation with Armenian culture following the genocide. On one hand, songs, stories etc. of this culture have been translated into Turkish and made a part of "our national culture"; on the other hand, most of them were caused to be forgotten, ignored or to say the least, they were presented as foreign cultures as if there was nothing common with cultures of other communities living on the same lands. So, as result of these cultural policies, works of art bearing signs of pains of Armenians who were killed or exiled and creators of them are mostly unknown by people living in Turkey. The fact that millions of Armenian people lived in Anatolia before 1915 and they left many important cultural artifacts behind them has been erased from collective memory of people who lived with Armenian people[249]. It is necessary to emphasize that Armenian genocide is definitely related with construction of Turkish national identity. Turkish national identity both rejects existence of different ethnical groups and at the same time, it is based on expropriation of cultural, social and economic heritages of these communities (Bilal, 2014, p. 239-240).

Art and literature are critical tools to trace events and to come to terms with the past by people who continue to live on lands left behind by people killed or sent into exile. In this term, we can mention mainly two roles of art and literature. First of all, collective memory that is shared by communities which lived together in the past may be preserved through art and literature. Secondly, these have an important curative role in terms of curing deep psychological scars, traumas both for the people experiencing genocide and exile and next generations. So, they are irrevocable both for individual and collective healing.

---

[246] Esin Gülsen is research assistant and Phd student at Department of Political Science, Middle East Technical University. Esatoğlu Mah. Başak Sok. No: 16/16 Küçükesat Çankaya/Ankara Turkey. E-mail: esingulsenn@gmail.com

[247] Erdem Çolak is joint Phd student at Department of Political Science, Ankara University. İncesu Mah. 9 Eylül Sok. No: 50/9 Çankaya/ Ankara – Turkey. E-mail: erdemcolak42@gmail.com

[248] Selen Yamak is graduate student at Department of Political Science, Middle East Technical University. Uğur Mumcu Mahallesi, Başkent Bulvarı, 184 Evler, E Blok, No: 76, Yenimahalle/ Ankara – Turkey. E-mail: selenyamak@hotmail.com

[249]According to conceptualization of Barış Ünlü, the effort to erase culture- and even names- of Armenians from Anatolia originates from "Turkishness Agreement". In accordance with this abstract agreement, real or potential opportunities of being Turk would be benefited as long as what is done to non-Muslims (and especially Armenians) is not talked or written about (Ünlü, 2014).

Collective memory and hegemony

Halbwachs, in his work titled *On Collective Memory,* states that collective memory reestablishes past images under impact of dominant social thoughts (Halbwachs, 1992, p.40). This collective memory is continuously destroyed and reconstructed in respect to changing balance of power in the society. It means that memory is not simply based on a chronological ordering of past events; on the contrary, it is collected partially in a way to legitimize a certain power relation of the past and integrated. Memory is not a mirror; it is an area where the past is reconstructed (Sancar, 2014, p.43). Collective memory appears as a political narrative in this context. This political narrative indicates not only what we are to remember, but also what we are to forget. Therefore, studies oriented at formation of memory have importance in the process of coming to terms with the past (Sancar, 2014, p.46).

Connerton argues that Halbwachs did not differentiate between questions of 'how does the individual preserve and rediscover his memories?' and 'how do societies preserve and rediscover their memories?' and he explicitly showed that individual memory could not exist as separated from collective memory in this way (Connerton, 1999, p.62). Thus, selected fragments released by socially-determined collective memory through various means establish memory of the individual. That is the reason why official history theses are attached such importance and people who do not believe in official history or go beyond it are easily described as "betrayer". These ever-changing fragments create images oriented at memory of friend-enemy differentiation that is considered as possibility of politics by Carl Schmitt (Schmitt, 2006, p.46-56). In that way, the nation gets collective friends and collective enemies and people out of the narrative are also tried to get out of the life.

It is certain that memory is not a collective action form which only dominant powers and classes of the society can establish. If we think the memory within the framework of hegemony theory of Gramsci, memory appears as an area of struggle. We may determine two poles of this hegemonic struggle area as the official wing that uses the narrative for maintenance of power relations and validates its own position through the other and the second wing which struggles against this and aims at constructing a new common narrative as to the future by coming to terms with the past. This struggle should not be thought as a simple projection of individual remembering practices. Remembering also assumes to undertake the responsibility of the past and compensate the events both in material and spiritual terms. However, official narrative always fictionalizes the concept of coming to terms with the past as an attack to national unity.

Gomez-Barris indicates that construction of memory excludes something while including other things during examining role of memory symbols in national identification. Stating that freezing memory with reports, commissions, monuments and following the way of "remembering by forgetting" would cause reestablishment of state hegemony, Gomez-Barris expresses that it is necessary to put alternative memory symbols against that and we should not forget that it is a complex and unending process to establish memory (Gomez-Barris, 2009, p.4-6).

Svetlana Boym addresses the dual character of remembering as a struggle through the concept of nostalgia. Boym, divides nostalgia into two forms in her study titled *The Future of Nostalgia*: reconstructive nostalgia and ideational nostalgia. She concentrates on how the first official discourse is constructed with reconstructive nostalgia and how objections that can be opposed to this discourse are eliminated. Ideational nostalgia consists of fragments on individual and collective memory. While reconstructive nostalgia, namely *nostos*, provides fiction of returning home ignoring all changes, ideational nostalgia, namely *algia*, has a view attaching importance to being on the road more than returning home based on longing and loss (Boym, 2009, p.76). What is to be thought as a political area beyond these two concepts is breaking up *nostos* by *algia* collectively and reconstruct it again collectively. It means that, we need a capacity to create a unity in a way to allow both coming to terms with the past and mourning without ignoring pains. When we think about potential of the art for establishing empathy, thinking, feeling and changing, it is seen that it has a very important possibility to establish alternative memory symbols to construct a course from *algia* to *nostos*. As Iwona Irwin-Zarecka states, collective memory as a unity of thoughts, images and feelings as to the past nests at means and possibilities that people share, not in their individual memory (quoted by Gómez-Barris, 2009, p.7).

"The Fish Separated from its Water"[250]: Arshile Gorky

Paul Klee compares the artist to body of a tree that provides passage between roots and branches. According to Klee, the artist that is fed with its roots in the depth only makes transfer and he cannot determine how colorful and beautiful his branches are to be in this transfer process. He says "Juice sap flows to the artist from the root, it flows to eyes of the artists from inside" (Klee, 2013, p.13). No matter it is conscious or unconscious, continuous feeding of the artist appears in his works of art in any way. Trauma and reflection of pain both allows the artist to heal and they function as "remembering moments" or "mirrors" in transformation of the society in the form of objects of art that are always faced within the life.

Since the juice sap coming from roots of Arshile Gorky includes tragedy and trauma, it is critical to think about his works of art. Being one of the leading names of expressionism, Arshile Gorky –or with his real name, Manug (Vosdan) Adoyan– was born in Horkom Village of Van in 1902. He assisted in city defense during the rebellion in Van after starting of deportation. Matossian states that struggle of Armenians from Van would lead the way for coming to terms with the depression by Gorky in the future even it was a complex process (Matossian, 2011, p.98). After death of his mother due to hunger in 1919 following the genocide, Manug migrated to the USA in 1920 with scars which would not be closed during his life. He introduced himself as Russian by taking the name of Maksim Gorky whom he admired very much and he started his career as painter. It is sure that his wish to maintain his career was effective while he introduced himself as Russian because the German painter from whom he got painting classes had told him only German or Russian painters could use their own names; however, another reason was the

---

[250] Matossian, 2011, p.458.

hope to escape from the events he experienced (Matossian, 2011, p.160). He maintained his profession which lasted in financial difficulty during his life mainly in non-figurative form. Although he was affected by surrealism and cubism much, he resisted on abstract painting that was not valid much in that period and he became one of the founder figures of abstract expressionism. The effort of Gorky to hide his identity as Armenian got him closer to being an Armenian. Thus, he started to think about "old country" more due to turning to earth and nature towards the end of his life. Gorky remembers especially images as to his childhood, Akhtamar Island, Van Lake and nature, his mother as the lost and long-awaited things. So, we can say that Gorky is interested in *algia*, he is busy with rust of the past, not returning home.

Assmann states that cultural memory is oriented at certain points of the past. The past is concentrated on symbolic figures rather than being preserved as the same in cultural memory. Story of the father, exile or passing over desert are such remembering figures (Assmann, 2001, p.55). The main mark observed in works of art of Gorky associated with this aspect of cultural memory is his famous painting named *The Artist and His Mother*. His desire to make his mother who is founding figure of his own past and leaving her hands unfinished in the painting reflect traumatic duality of Gorky. His mother has an image but does not have hands to keep just as the old country. Other works of art of Gorky also wander this loss sometimes with their form and sometimes their names: "Nighttime, Enigma and Nostalgia" serial, "They Will Take My Island", "How My Mother's Embroidered Apron Unfolds" etc. Since this loss also presents a modern representation of events experienced and marks left by them, Gorky prevents oblivion of Armenian art and tragedy by carrying them to American art (Balakian, 1988, p.126). What is to be done after now is to open the way for this modern representation to spring to life on its own lands.

William Saroyan and Live Armenians

It is sure that one of the important means to tell what Armenians experienced after 1915 is literature. Works of art of many authors are full of stories arising from this tragedy; however tragedy has also triggered creativity:

"There are many themes in these stories, but they ultimately return to the Aghed (Catastrophe) itself and revolve around the key issue of how the children and grandchildren of genocide survivors have assimilated the trauma of their forebears in a creative manner. Thus, the writers have bridged the chasm from catastrophe to creativity by unleashing their creative efforts and by the act of writing" (Mugrdechian, 2008: p.65).

William Saroyan is one of these authors. He was born in the USA in 1908 since his family migrated there before genocide but he introduced himself as "An Armenian author from the USA and Bitlis". His father was a revolutionary Armenian and he had to migrate to the USA as Saroyan tells: "Unfortunately, he was also a revolutionist, as all good Armenians are. He wanted the handful of people of his race to be free…Finally it got so bad that if he did not leave the old country, he would kill and be killed." (Saroyan, 1997, p.60).

Dedicating himself to writing about the human during his life, Saroyan has a style called as "Saroyanesque" due to his specific plain expression. His stories are about life struggles, feelings, contradictions, bothers, traumas and happiness of

Armenian migrants living in the USA especially after the genocide. As Güler states, Saroyan "teaches us that the smallest thing is the most important thing" (Güler, 2002, p.116). He is interested in living people rather than getting a keen political position and establishing big narratives as to that: "There is only one class of Armenians in Armenia, Fresno, the world. That is live Armenian. The upper, middle, lower. These are nonsense. We have two classes: who are dead and who are alive" (Saroyan, 2004, p.85).

Coding the different one as a unity and forcing it to be the "other" is deemed as a way of drawing own borders and establishing own unity (Tuğal, 2012, p.141). Despite the fact that both Turks and Armenians may perform this as an official policy and they may maintain the duality of guilty/innocent, many stories of Saroyan concentrates on lives and feelings of people beyond official narratives and he does not place the Armenian people against the Turkish people. He emphasizes that Turks also suffer as the Armenian and hating from the Turkish people is equal to hating from the Armenian people in his story named Antranik of Armenia (Saroyan, 2004, p.69)

In contrast to a generalized point of view, Saroyan uses a language to embrace the whole Anatolia, however he was not known and remembered by many people although some of his books were published in Turkish. He travelled to Bitlis in 1964 to find remaining Armenians there and he had a very pleasant time with some artists in Turkey such as Yaşar Kemal, Fikret Otyam, Gülten Akın and Fakir Baykurt. He did not write anything about this voyage for a long time since Bitlis was far away from his dreams. Saroyan is exiled into silence on these lands such as other Armenian artists. If we will be able to read his stories in literature books in high schools with Turkish authors, it will be an important step in terms of reconstruction of collective memory.

Gomidas: Memory of Voices

Gomidas, whose original name is Soğomon Soğomonyan, was born in Kütahya in 1869. Before he was one year old, he lost his mother and when he was eleven he lost his father, too. In 1881, under favor of his impressive and strong voice, he had a chance to get education in Etchmiadzin which is the center of Armenian Church. When he was considered worthy to be "Vartabed" degree as a priest in 1985, he had also a good grasp of Hampartsumyan musical notation and all Armenian chants. Moreover, he had borne down on collecting and recording Turkish, Kurdish, Arabic, Syriac, Farsi and especially Armenian songs. With the well-known Armenian linguist Manuk Apeğyan, they collected around 3-4 thousand songs (Gomidas Bu Toprağın Sesi, 2010, p.18). Gomidas wanted to improve himself on music more. After a six-month music classes in Tbilisi, he went to Berlin and studied music at the Frederick William University between 1896 and 1899. As a result of his success and his great knowledge about Armenian music, he became the only student who was accepted to International Music Society as a founder member. While his conferences on Armenian music disturbed Armenian clergy, these conferences and Gomidas's music performances impressed musicians in Europe and introduced Armenian music to them. Moreover, as a result of Gomidas's great effort to organize full chorus in different parts of the world such as Tbilisi, Baku, İstanbul, İzmir, Alexandria, Cairo, Paris,

Lausanne and Geneva, the influence of Armenian music reached most of the Europe (Kuyumjian, 2010, p.15). Actually great effect of his work was on the Armenian society itself. It may be said that the Armenian music, which Gomidas pried out and shined, created a connection between many young Armenians in different regions and made them aware of their cultural heritages (Kuyumjian, 2010, p.15).

5 years after moving to İstanbul, he became one of the 235 people taken from their houses during the arrestments in the night of 24 April 1915 which may be regarded as the first wave of İstanbul Armenian arrestments. This group of people consisted of different occupational groups including doctors, journalists, artists, lawyers. Most of them were taken and brought to İstanbul central jail with a fake kindness that did not reveal the real purpose (Andonyan, 2012, p.22). After staying there for 24 hours, they were entrained in Haydarpaşa Railway Station in order to be deported to Ayaş- Çankırı and Deir ez-Zor direction. Some of these people were called back with the help of some people having power and few of them could get out alive as a result of coincidences. Aram Andonyan, who was an Armenian writer, journalist writes that the people got out alive from this train, as himself, could not escape from the effects of this cruelty (Andonyan, 2012, p. 20). Gomidas was one of the people that would feel these effects worst during the rest of his life.

After being kept in prison for 13 days, Gomidas was discharged with his seven friends from the camp in Çankırı. However, this relatively short exile changed Gomidas's life so much. While in the first days of his imprisonment he was the one that did not lose his hope and was supportive to others, after a while he could not deal with what they were supposed to (Gomidas: Bu Toprağın Sesi, 2010, p.39). He started to experience a mental breakdown after the first days of his imprisonment. What happens to him is now called as Posttraumatic Stress Disorder (PTSD) (Kuyumjian, 2010, p.132). Rest of his life was under the shadow and fear of his memories from his exile days.

In contrast to Saroyan and Gorky, there is no work left from Gomidas after 1915. However, the rest of Gomidas's life itself may be regarded as an indicator of the disaster that he faced. His silence was the disaster itself. In his book *Writers of Disaster*, Nichanian writes as "what is the loss of the survivor is the loss of the capacity to talk about what was lost" (Nichanian, 2011, p.88). When Gomidas died in a nuthouse in Paris in 1935, he had not composed, sang or played any piece of music and talked with anyone except several people in his last 18 years. In Turkey, even there is no single museum, monument or conservatoire established in the name of Gomidas.

Conclusion

In the hundredth anniversary of 1915 genocide, it is important for us to turn our faces to Archile Gorky, Gomidas Vartabed, William Saroyan and many other Armenian artists and authors whose names we even do not known both to come to terms with the past and heal our scars. It is very critical to open our eyes, ears and hearts to voices, colors and words coming from the past. It is our responsibility to learn, remember, remind and preserve art and culture of people who or whose relatives had lived on these lands in the past. The road to coming to terms with the past may be opened if arts of work of Gorky, Saroyan, Gomidas and others are included in alternative memory symbols. No work of art of Gorky has been exhibited in Museums or Exhibitions in Turkey. Only one play of Saroyan was staged by State Theaters. There has been no official organization for memorizing these artists. In last years, there are some good efforts to remind these people such as the night for respect to Gomidas that was organized in 2010 and Saroyan Library opened by Bitlis Municipality in 2015. However, we have a long way and many things to do to understand, remember and remind this tragedy. Not forgetting that collective memory is an ongoing struggle area which is continuously restructured and reconstructed, we may use art and literature as great means to reconstruct an alternative collective memory and heal scars of the past.

References

Andonyan, A. (2012). *Gomidas Vartabed ile Çankırı Yollarında*. Belge Yayınları.
Assmann, J. (2001). *Kültürel Bellek*. Ayrıntı Yayınları.
Balakian, P. (1988). Arshile Gorky's Embroidered Apron. *Agni*. No. 26, Mentors and Tormentors, 123-126.
Bilal, M. (2014). Türkiyeli Ermenileri Hatırlamak. Laçiner, Ö. (eds.) *Bir Zamanlar Ermeniler Vardı. Birikim Yayınları*.
Boym, S. (2009). *Nostaljinin Geleceği*. Metis Yayınları.
Connerton, P. (1999). *Toplumlar Nasıl Anımsar?*. Ayrıntı Yayınları.
Gómez-Barris, M. (2009) *Where Memory Dwells: Culture and Violence in Chile*. University of California Press.
Gomidas Bu Toprağın Sesi, Doğumunu 140. ve Ölümünün 75. Yılı Anısına (2010), İstanbul Avrupa Kültür Başkenti Ajansı.
Güler, A. (2002). *Yeryüzünde Yedi İz*. Yapı Kredi Yayınları.
Halbwachs, M. (1992). *On Collective Memory*. The University of Chicago Press.
Klee, P. (2013). *Modern Sanat Üzerine*. Altıkırkbeş Yayınları.
Kuyumjian, R. S. (2010). Deliliğin Arkeolojisi: Gomidas: Bir Ermeni İkonun Portresi. Birzamanlar Yayıncılık.
Matossian, N. (2011) *Arshile Gorky – Kara Melek*. Aras Yayıncılık.
Mugrdechian, B. D. (2008), Across the Chasm: From Catastrophe to Creativity. Hovannisian, R. (eds.) *The Armenian Genocide. Transaction Publishers*
Nichanian, M. (2011) *Edebiyat ve Felaket*. İletişim Yayınları.
Sancar, M. (2014) *Geçmişle Hesaplaşma*. İletişim Yayınları.
Saroyan, W. (1997). *The Daring Young Man on the Flying Trapeze*, New Directions Book.
Saroyan, W. (2004). *Yetmiş Bin Süryani*. Aras Yayıncılık.
Schmitt, C. (2006). *Siyasal Kavramı*, Metis Yayınları.
Tuğal, C. (2012). 1915 Hatıraları ve Ermeni Kimliğinin İnşası. Özyürek, E. (eds.) *Hatırladıklarıyla ve Unuttuklarıyla Türkiye'nin Toplumsal Hafızası*. İletişim Yayınları.
Ünlü, B. (2014). Türklük Sözleşmesi'nin İmzalanışı (1915-1925). *Mülkiye Dergisi*. 38(3), 47-81.
http://arshilegorkyfoundation.org/research-resources/exhibition-history. avaliable on: 24.01.2015.

Community Building in Diaspora through Political Engagement Forms: Case of Kurds from Turkey in Marseille, France

Zuhal Karagöz[251]

Introduction

The Kurdish diaspora's configuration and mobilization strategies provide excellent ground in understanding plural dynamics of diasporization as it is built on experiences and memories of oppression and exile, forced displacement, labor migration, and insecure environment. Following this socio-constructionist approach that examines diasporas as being imagined transnational communities (Sökefeld, 2006)[252], in this paper, the diaspora politics formation is conceived through a specific mobilization process that leads to the politicization[253] of the Kurdish migratory space. The political engagement serves as an instrument of community building within the Kurdish Diaspora and is conceived as the core of the diasporic identity (Adamson, 2008; Baser, 2013).

In this perspective, all members of the immigrant population are not automatically or originally conceived as a part of the diaspora. Even if the survival of the community and the construction of a specific identity are conceived as the Leitmotiv of the diaspora by its political entrepreneurs, the scientific use of these terms is still to be nuanced. The community is not considered as a pre-established entity. It is socially constructed and symbolized by institutions, representatives, myths and symbols and founded on a subjective belief of affiliation to the same group, on a basis of similar customs and memories (Simmel, 1999). Using the term "community building", involving both communalization [*Vergemeinschaftung*] and the societization [Vergesellschaftung] forms as theorized by Weber, allows us to emphasize the processual dimension and to draw attention to the continuous and strategic renegotiation of the community by its members. Similarly, identities are discursively constructed and constantly renegotiated.Therefore, the intention of the actors must be taken into account to understand how some identification mechanisms are used and promoted by individuals/groups while building diasporic projects. Even though the PKK[254] has a centralized ideology at a European scale and intends to homogenize the mobilization forms (Rigoni, 1998), this paper argues that the identity and community formation is an interactive

---

[251] Zuhal Karagöz is PhD candidate in CNRS, Mediterranean Laboratory of Sociology, Aix-Marseille University. 5 rue du *Château* de l'*Horloge*, BP 647 13094 Aix-en-Provence cedex 2. France. E-mail: zuhal.karagoz@yahoo.com

[252] Based on Anderson's theorization of nation as an imagined community (1983), Sökefeld argues that imagined communities are not strictly fictional as they are imagined as being real and these imaginations have real impacts on social life.

[253] Kastoryano (2002) conceives politicization as a border-defining factor for a group.

[254] *Partiya Karkerên Kurdistan*, Kurdistan Workers' Party is considered here as a macro level of analysis regarding to its transnational organization that implies a structural modal of Kurdish people, living within the territories of Kurdistan and the host territories where Kurdish immigrants are settled. This organization dominates the Kurdish movement since its foundation in 1978, not only in Turkey but also in diaspora.

process that depends on local, national, and transnational frameworks. Local and national social and political environments and the socio-demographic composition of the immigrant group as well as the interaction of immigrants with local actors of the host society all affect the evolution of mobilization forms.

Case study[255] and research strategies

Little is known about diasporas having a social movement dimension[256], and the effects of their homeland oriented politics on immigrants' interaction with the host society in France. The republican system in France is still strong, with a citizenship model based on nationality and limited political opportunities for foreigners and immigrants, despite a *de facto* recognition of cultural diversity in the 2000s. Besides,   The homeland orientation in political transnational activities is perceived negatively in the integration discourse of the French state because of the apprehension of the foreigners' and immigrants' non-identification with the national community (Kastoryano, 1997) The Kurdish Institute of Paris estimates that the Kurdish population in France is between 200,000-220,000, which makes France the second largest receiving country of Kurds in Europe after Germany[257]. Marseille, the city where this field study was conducted, is the second largest city of France after Paris, with a population around 850,000. Historically built on immigration flows, this city is being stigmatized within the national context by politics and media with an image of insecurity , focusing on its immigrant populations, drug trafficking, and problematic urban zones.

Kurdish immigrants in Marseille represent a small group; there are around 6,000 individuals according to the Cultural Center of Mesopotamia. Despite the small size of the population, Marseille is an important area for the Kurdish diaspora in France in terms of political mobilization. An annual monitoring report delivered in 2012 by an executive of the PKK's European organization during the annual congress of the popular assembly[258] of Marseille praised the dynamism of the Kurdish diaspora in Marseille in protesting capacity, compared to other cities in France.[259] It is also an important city for long-distance citizenship practices, for instance in case of vote catching strategies of pro-Kurdish parties in Turkey[260]. Still, Khayati (2008) argues that Kurds in Marseille remain weaker than Kurds in

---

[255] The fieldwork conducted between April 2011 and September 2014 is a part of my ongoing PhD research in sociology.

[256] Besides researches on the Kurdish Diaspora (Bozarslan, 1997; Bozarslan and Mohseni, 2004; Rigoni; 1998, 2005; Mohseni, 2002; Khayati, 2008; Grojean, 2008) see Goreau-Ponceaud (2008) and Dequirez (2009) for pro-Tamil mobilization.

[257] Similar to most of the other host countries, French state categorizes Kurds as nationals of Iraq, Iran, Syria or Turkey. Only asylum seekers are registered with their Kurdish ethnic identity, by the institutions responsible for the asylum request process.

[258] The popular assembly of Kurdistan is the supreme legislative organism of *Koma Civakên Kurdistan*, Union of Communities of Kurdistan, founded in 2005.

[259] The observations of political demonstrations and, the Press and Media Committee's archives and pro-Kurdish newspapers all confirm the high frequency of contentious actions. For example, 59 protest events between 19 January, 2013 and 3 December, 2014 were noted as in a search on the website of the newspaper *Yeni Özgür Politika*.

[260] In 2015's parliamentary elections in Turkey, Marseille is the zone where the vote pro-HDP has the highest ratio in regard with the general vote. And it is the third city, after Paris and Strasbourg where pro-HDP votes are most numerous in France.

Stockholm in trans border citizenship and long-distance nationalism practices due to their limited political and cultural diversity, and due to the French context restraining the scope of diasporic projects. Nevertheless, increasing recognition and legitimization of the Kurdish movement at the international level could change this marginal position of Kurds in the eyes of both politicians and social scientists.

The methodology chosen to understand community building dynamics in diaspora was a long-term ethnographic fieldwork. Simple or multiple taped semi-directive interviews were realized with 50 individuals in addition to informal conversations. The sample composed of employers and employees in the food-service and construction industries, members of Kurdish and Alevi[261] associations (employed staff, members), non-adherent visitors of associations, and participants of political demonstrations regardless of their gender and age. The legal status of the interlocutors varied from political refugees and asylum seekers to foreign workers and irregular immigrants to. In addition, I spent several periods of participant observation in workplaces (except construction sites), associations, political meetings, and different types of political activism such as marches, rallies, and sit-ins. Repeated interactions and interviews with the same interlocutors, by the presence *in situ*, brought them to trust the researcher, a sort of intruder in their group, in the long term. The data collected from the press and media, and the Kurdish association's archives provided secondary elements of the analysis.

Building an imagined community: regulation and mobilization strategies

The Kurdish association, founded in 1992 and initially called the House of the Kurdish People, took the name the Cultural Center of Mesopotamia (CCM) in 2009. Kurdish cultural associations established in Europe on behalf of PKK's ideology since the latter is considered as a terrorist organization by European Council. In fact, the association is one of the committees of the Kurdish popular assembly in the Marseille area[262]. It has a valid legal status in France as it depends on the French 1901 association law. However, because of the criminalization of the association and its workers due to their relation with PKK, the cooperation between the association and the local authorities are limited[263]. In the absence of other Kurdish organizations with different ideologies and objectives in the area, the CCM became the dominant structure. This monopoly is strengthened by the insufficiency of institutions offering services to immigrants in Marseille[264].

---

[261] The Alevi Cultural Center of Marseille operates as an association and a place of worship.

[262] Women's Committee, Organization Committee, Cultural Committee, Peace and Negotiation Committee, Education Committee, External Relations Committee, Social Relations Committee, Media and Press Committee, Faith Committee.

[263] The House of Kurdish People was dissolved after a trial's verdict in December 2013. Ten workers of the association were sentenced from six months to three years in prison because of financial support to the PKK via the associative structure. It was the second Kurdish association dissolved in France, after the dissolution of the Cultural Center of Ahmet Kaya in Paris, in 2011.

[264] There are few establishments of this kind, except the reception centers for asylum seekers, an office of CIMADE *(Comité Inter-Mouvements Auprès Des Evacués)* which offer an ecumenical service of solidarity specialized in immigrants' and refugees' rights, and a couple of translation/interpreting offices.

The association combines "hot nationalism" practices such as demonstrations, rallies, etc. with "banal nationalism" (Billig, 1995) through daily use of the association premises. It also serves as a gathering place, where sociability helps to strengthen the comrade links among immigrants with different degrees of political engagement. Still, the association has different symbolic meanings for the individuals depending on their activist capital, their social trajectories, and the importance of political engagement in their migratory "*career*" (Martiniello and Rea, 2011)[265]. Individuals who do not have political reasons for migration can also participate, temporarily, to the social field of mobilizations in some cases: if they were already sensible to the claims conveyed by the political network, or if they have been sensibilized following some "*bifurcations*" (Bessin et al., 2010) such as violent actions on Kurds in Kurdistan(s) and in the diaspora. This is where the articulation of sensibilization and coercion mechanisms (Grojean, 2015) within the same institution comes into play. These mechanisms are shaped around the victimhood and patriotism discourses built on their exile, oppression and resistance stories. They are mobilized in order to strengthen the internalization of the constructed Kurdish identity - its values, social roles, and practices.

The sensibilization mechanism operates, on a practical scale, through different forms of contentious mobilizations of such as marches, rallies, information stands, occupations of public spaces, and sit-ins. These extra-parliamentary forms of political participation represent the core of the Kurdish diaspora's collective action. Similar to other Kurdish diaspora cities, these demonstrations might be regular (for Newroz or the anniversary of the foundation of PKK for instance) or *ad hoc,* following critical events in the homeland or diaspora (like the murder of three Kurdish woman activists in Paris, in January 2013). They correspond to the strong moments of the community building process, including both the reinforcement of the allegiance to the diasporic community and the efforts of raising awareness among the host society. But how is the link to the politically engaged community is constructed for a Kurdish immigrant?

Built upon 'patriotism'[266] the political engagement shapes the social position of Kurdish immigrants within the diasporic community. Political engagement practices depend on the social trajectories of immigrants and their affiliations to networks. Networks can not only facilitate the financial flows and diffusion of information necessary as material support, but they are also vital to the construction of common values and a cohesive identity. Resorting to inter-acquaintance groups allows the political organization to reach a larger public, composed of people tangled up by obligation links forged by mutual acquaintances (Massicard, 2009). Nonetheless, the anterior affiliations reproduced in diaspora and the acquisition of new capitals, are also capable of renegotiating the mobilization interpretations of political entrepreneurs.

---

[265] The migratory career approach enables one to grasp the uncertainties of the migration experience, the evolution of the project over time and the ongoing adaptation of immigrants to the situations they encounter.

[266] A term used by activists, to point out Kurdish people supporting the Kurdish cause in many ways like participating in the political activities, visiting the association center, supporting the Kurdish storekeepers, etc.

Firstly, kinship networks that run across *hemşehri* (in Turkish, from the same city) links maintain their primary role in the arrival and settlement processes. In Marseille, there are two dominant localities of origin: Erzurum and Muş – two cities connoted with Sunni Muslim allegiances. The political entrepreneurs perceive these confessional allegiances as too traditionalist, if not feudal, thus as a barrier to an effective political mobilization. Although they are often from these cities themselves, their spokesperson position distinguishes them by attributing social roles related to their specific objectives and perspectives.

Considering the kinship affiliations, the role of social trajectories and transnational family links should not be neglected given the fact that political and economic motives are entangled. Majority of interviewees has a family member who was or still is in the guerilla. Interviewees often referred to transnational links and/or collective memory while they were explaining their motivations to participate – as active members or just temporary participants – to the mobilizations in the host land. Words like, *conscience, duty, and responsibility* were used frequently, which illustrates the weight of internalization as a result of the raising responsibilities discourse. These were also mentioned by employers to explain their financial support, but one should note that they also benefit from such engagement in terms of professional networking during the political and cultural events organized by the CCM.

Yet, the accumulation of capitals derived from economic success, from affiliation to a solid kinship network, and from possessing activist knowledge can produce conflict: the increasing number of *Erzurumlu* (person from Erzurum) within the political network, which leads to a consolidation of their group as a lobbying resource that can compete the political network's core. Hence, although the Kurdish identity via political engagement is built and communicated as a unity, it gives rise to power and exclusion circumstances.

Besides being a strategic resource or a challenging instrument, these small interaction groups, strengthened by tight kinship affiliations, make the engagement more constraining and facilitate the social control. The politicization is employed by the political entrepreneurs as the key instrument to avoid the assimilation or the anomy in the host land.

Finally, in regard with the confessional affiliations, one could notice that the political entrepreneurs try to manage both Sunni and Alevi allegiances of Kurdish population. On one hand, they mobilize the sensibilization mechanism that gives birth to ritualized forms of communitarian allegiances among Sunni Kurds. For instance, the Faith Committee settles the commemoration events organized under the roof of the CCM, accompanied by a pray session called *Mevlit,* for the Kurdish guerilla martyrs. It represents a pragmatic maneuver to re-adapt the repertoire of contention (Gürbüz, 2014). On the other hand, the political entrepreneurs expand their activist agenda to a larger public: the Alevist activist group including both Kurds and Turks organized under the roof of the Alevi Cultural Center. The annual Kurdish popular assembly's congress in 2012 has settled new committee in order to reinforce their bounds with the Alevi Kurds and increase awareness on the Kurdish cause.

Consequently, political entrepreneurs have to deal with their field having complex identification systems of the community members. As argued by

Adamson (2012, p. 32), diasporas are built "by political entrepreneurs who are acting rationally and strategically through the strategic deployment of identity frames and categories".

Beyond the community: political engagement as self-validation and societization instrument

At a collective scale, political engagement helps not only to keep the communitarian link alive but also to distinguish Kurdish diaspora from other immigrant groups like Maghrebis who represent the largest and most stigmatized immigrant population in Marseille. It also allows interaction with non-Kurdish activist groups and political networks such as the French communist party, which became nearly a traditional partner of Kurdish activism. The field study showed that new forms of contentious performances are born from the increasing interactions between some Kurdish activists and actors from other activist and/or cultural networks in Marseille, such as the anti-fascist activist network or feminist groups. A recent cooperation of this kind is the emergence of "Collective Rojava-Marseille" founded by both Kurdish and non-Kurdish anarchist activists in Marseille. In the absence of formalized collective projects with state subvention, the CCM adopts a strategy of consolidation of such *"weak ties"* (Granovetter, 1973). These activists are at the same time members of popular assembly's committees, such as the External Relations or the Cultural Committee. One should note that the Kurdish actors in consideration are mostly young people, fluent in French, with more heterogeneous networking capacities and socialization spheres. The bifurcation impact of resistance in Kobane multiplied extra-community collaborations, since this specific incidence has increased the mediatization and legitimation of Kurdish movement, which was longtime associated with terrorist acts.

In concordance with the new extra-community links, *"innovations"* (Tilly, 2008) among the contentious performances are staged, such as the introduction of the Kurdish traditional music into the activist sphere in Marseille with the QWX group[267]. Founded in 2010 by three musicians all of whom political refugees, the main aim of QWX is to convey their political views about the Kurdish issue. The former absence of Kurdish artistic projects in Marseille provided them with an opportunity to be the main cultural representative of the Kurdish community, while the political engagement distinguishes them, in their words, from *"wedding musicians"*; that is to say, from Kurdish popular culture[268].

The music is already used as a mode of mobilization in accordance with PKK's evolution in the homeland[269], where the prohibition of singing in Kurdish consolidated the use of Kurdish music as an instrument of identity claims. However, QWX's interaction with non-Kurdish artistic and activist networks helps them to stand as locally oriented artist-activists than 'party's [PKK] official

---

[267] For an analysis on cultural disembeddedness through activist music, see: Karagöz, Z. (2013) QWX: Les immigrants kurdes sur la scene marseillaise, *Faire savoirs*, 10, 103-111.
[268] A kind of stigma's reversal, the music contributes to the self-decovery process in relation with others.
[269] Culture and art are considered by Abdullah Öcalan as key instruments for the Kurdish identity's reconstitution See : Öcalan, A. (2008) *Kültür ve Sanat Devrimi Üzerine*, Istanbul, Aram.

artists'. Therefore, this new form of engagement through music contributes to an emergence of a hybrid field of contention between political and cultural fields. Within the context of normalization of the Kurdish identity by the diaspora elite, *"the hybrid strategy or discourse opens up a space of negotiation"* (Bhabha, 1996, p. 58), although the political network can partly control the artists as they are cultural committee members.

Conclusion

This paper aimed to explore the community and identity building strategies through a politicization perspective employed by the political entrepreneurs in Kurdish diaspora in Marseille. Findings showed that a centralized regulative modal is applied to the local context of immigration via the regulation and mobilization dispositive. The diaspora elite adopt a homogeneous discourse of Kurdish community and identity. The sensibilization mechanism, articulated to some latent coercion, is the main instrument of this community and identity formation, especially in a context of limited political participation opportunities, fragmented integration, and criminalization of the Kurdish movement that hindered its legitimacy. In return, the multiple identifications – confessional, kinship, and regional solidarity – and different social trajectories of immigrants produce a heterogeneous interpretation of this imagined community. Also, the increasing links built with external actors contribute to gain recognition and legitimacy in the eyes of the host society while transforming the traditional forms of contentious action. As shown in the case of Marseille, the homogeneous, unique, and solid forms of community and identity definitions are evolving to more heterogeneous, diverse and, fluid ones. This transformation would give rise to a more porous political network, while challenging its monopolistic position. Hybrid spaces of contention nourished by increasing weak ties within the activist field of Marseille, could contribute to the sustainability and the effectiveness of Kurdish mobilization in a national framework with limited political participation opportunities.

References

Başer, B. (2014). Diaspora'da Türk Kürt Sorunu. Almanya ve İsveç'teki İkinci Kuşak Göçmenler, İstanbul: İletişim

Adamson, F. (2012) Constructing the diaspora: diaspora identity politics and transnational social movements, In Lyons, T. & Mandaville, P. (eds.) Politics from Afar: Transnational Diasporas and Networks, New York: Columbia University Press, 25-45.

Bessin et al. (2010). Bifurcations. Les sciences sociales face aux ruptures et à l'événement, Paris : Découverte.

Bhabha, H. (1996). Cultures in-between. In: In: Hall, S. & Du Gay, P. (eds) Questions of cultural identity, London-California-New Delhi: Sage, 53-61.

Billig, M. (1995) Banal nationalism, London: Sage.

Granovettter, M. (1973). The Strength of Weak Ties, American Journal of Sociology, 78(6), 1360-1380.

Gürbüz, M. (2014) Ideology in Action: Symbolic Localization of Kurdistan Workers' Party, [Electronic version] Turkey Sociological Inquiry, 85(1), February 2015, 1-27, DOI: 10.1111/soin.12066

Kastoryano, R. (1997). La France, l'Allemagne et ses immigrés, Paris : Armand Colin.

Martiniello, M. & Rea, A. (2011). Des flux migratoires aux carrières migratoires, SociologieS [Electronic version] http://sociologies.revues.org/3694 Khayati, K. (2008). From Victim

Diaspora To Transborder Citizenship? Diaspora formation and transnational relations among Kurds in France and Sweden, PhD dissertation [Electronic version] Retrieved from : http://www.diva-portal.org/smash/get/diva2:18336/FULLTEXT01.pdf

Massicard, E. (2009). Gerer les fragmentations identitaires dans les mobilisations de Turquie. In: Sala Pala, V. et al. (eds.), L'action collective face à l'imbrication des rapports sociaux, Paris: L'Harmattan, 119-139.

Rigoni, I. (1998). Les mobilisations des Kurdes en Europe, Revue européenne des migrations internationales. 14 (3), 203-223. Doi : 10.3406/remi.1998.1654

Tilly, C., & Violencia política. (2008). Contentious performances. Cambridge: Cambridge University Press.

Weber, M. [1922] (1995). Economie et société / 1. Les categories de la sociologie, Paris: Pocket

The Kurdish Community in the Czech Republic and Its Transnational Practices

Michael Murad[270]

Introduction

The fairly sizable Kurdish community in Western Europe, particularly in Germany, has been a focus of scholarly interest for some time now. But Kurds are also present in other parts of Europe, where they have received much less attention. One such community has settled in the Czech Republic. Small in size, it has nevertheless taken an organized approach to promoting its interests in the public sphere and is connected, to some extent, with the broader diaspora of Kurdish nationals in other countries, and with the homeland(s). Particularly in recent decades, globalization and its attendant phenomena have made it easier to pursue domestic politics while abroad. Before the 1989 revolution, the former Czechoslovakia (CSSR) supported various Middle Eastern associations — some terrorist in nature — whose members often resided in Czechoslovakia. Many Middle Eastern communities became established, as well, including the Kurdish community.

This essay describes and analyses the Kurdish diaspora, in the Czech Republic, detailing its transnational practices. It elucidates the way in which Kurds have promoted their (political) interests in the Czech Republic, describes the nature of their connections to other Kurds living abroad, and sheds light on the nature of their activities and the degree to which these have become institutionalized. The text is built upon the conceptual scheme of transnationalism. It was constructed on the basis of semi-structured interviews with representatives of the Kurdish community living in the Czech Republic, complemented by an analysis of primary and secondary data. The chief sources of primary data were the documents of the Kurdish Civic Society (Kurdské Občanské Sdružení: KOS) and archived documents. Research was also undertaken at events organized by the Kurdish community.

Transnationalism

The research undertaken here into the Czech Republic's Kurdish community was set within the transnationalism conceptual framework. Political activities by members of a diaspora are nothing new. They became quite common with the establishment of the European national states in the nineteenth century and the resistance from colonies which followed. To cross-border processes and cross-border social formations refer terms diaspora, transnationalism, or transnational communities (see among others Bauböck & Faist 2010; Østergaard-Nielsen 2003a, Sirkeci 2003 and Mügge 2010). As formulated by Faist: (…) term "diaspora" always refers to a community or group and has been heavily used in history and literacy studies, concepts such as transnationalism (…) refers to processes that transcend international borders and therefore appear to describe more abstract phenomena in a social science language (Faist 2010, p.13).

During the 1990s, the transnationalism concept became a favored theoretical framework in migration studies for explaining the ties between migrants and their homelands. Host countries consider activities by migrants transnational if they evince evident ties to the homeland, in other words if they show evidence migrants are directly or indirectly getting involved in issues in their countries of origin. These transnational activities may be classified as economic, sociocultural, and political, and may be further differentiated by whether they take place in the host country of the diaspora or its country

[270] Michael Murad is Ph.D. candidate at the Department of Political Science, Faculty of Social Studies, Masaryk University, Joštova 10, 602 00 Brno, Czech Republic. E-mail: m.murad@mail.muni.cz

of origin (Mügge, 2010, p. 36). Transnational political activities are defined by Østergaard-Nielsen as: "various forms of direct cross-border participation in the politics of their country of origin by both migrants and refugees (such as voting and other support to political parties, participating in debates in the press), as well as their indirect participation via the political institutions of the host country (or international organizations)" (2003b, p.762)

It should be noted that a neat breakdown into economic, sociocultural, and political activities is possible only on the analytical level. In practice, these areas overlap.

The stability of transnational activities depends upon the degree to which they have become institutionalized. They do so at the moment they have become predictable, constant, and structured. A high level of institutionalization is present in activities which are carefully planned on a regular schedule, including festivals, congresses, and regular discussion meetings that follow designated rules. Transnational activities may also be classified on the basis of the level at which they are initiated (and institutionalized) (Mügge, 2010, p. 36; Van Amersfoort, 2004, p. 367; Mareš & Murad, 2015).

The Kurdish Diaspora in Europe

The Kurdish people associate their efforts to exercise their rights to Kurdistan. But because of the massive emigration from the country, these efforts have become internationalized. Kurds have been leaving their homeland for Europe since roughly the mid-twentieth century, an exodus which saw the emigration of both workers and students. The greatest number left Turkey to go to Germany, but they also emigrated to work in the Benelux countries, in Switzerland, and in France. This established the basis for a continued migration making use of these ties (Wahlbeck, 1999, p. 50). With the outbreak of armed conflict with the central government of Iraq, Kurds left Iraqi Kurdistan, and another substantial migration wave from Turkey took place in the 1980s (Mareš & Murad, 2015).

Kurds in The Czech Republic

The Kurdish community in the Czech Republic is not particularly large. Based upon the Kurds' own estimates and on the size of the Kurdish Civic Association, there are approximately 250 - 300 Kurds in the country. Great number of these people came to the Czech Republic or to Czechoslovakia to study and stayed on for various reasons, or returned to this country after spending some time in their homeland. But some Kurds in the Czech Republic consist of successful applicants for international protection.

Starting in the 1960s, Kurdish students came to Western Europe, and to Czechoslovakia, as well. The country's communist government maintained special relationships with socialist countries in the Middle East, and this extended to cultural collaboration. That brought in a relatively high number of students from the region for study at Czechoslovak universities (Murad, 2009, p.13). Kurds were among them. In fact, similar as with Western Europe, the majority of Kurds studying in Czechoslovakia were Iraqi. The second most frequently represented group consisted of courage from Syria and Iran, followed by smaller groups from Turkey (Respondent 5, personal communication, May 16, 2011).

Organisation of the Kurds after 1989

After the events of 1989 in Czechoslovakia, later the Czech Republic, the number of students from the formerly 'friendly' Arabic countries dropped off in the Union of Kurdish Students in the CSSR (that was formed before) for all practical purposes ceased to exist. Some Kurds left for Western Europe, some returned to their homelands. A significant but gradual shift occurred in the composition of Kurdish people living in the Czech Republic — Kurds from Turkey are now present in greater numbers than Kurds from Iraq.

Only in 2003, and only after several attempts, did the Kurdish Civic Association come into being. It was founded upon the basis of the Union of Kurdish Students and is the only Kurdish organization in the Czech Republic. But the Kurdish community in the

---

Czech Republic is not as large as it once was. Even during the interim period in which there was no such organization for Kurds in the CR, they organized themselves in some fashion, particularly before the Newroz celebration. In this interim period, though, the events organized were private in nature with no public aspect (Respondent 8, personal communication, November 24, 2014).

Currently the Kurdish Civic Association has approximately 150 members, all of whom are Kurds. The association is also open to Czech friends of Kurds. The association's statutes state its objectives as 'associating persons living in the Czech Republic who have a relationship to the Kurdish nation and its culture.' The association wishes to 'strengthen friendly relations by organizing cultural, sporting and other social activities' and to 'inform citizens about the cultural traditions and contemporary culture of the Kurdish nation through lectures' (Kurdské občanské sdružení, 2003b). Iraqi Kurds are mostly also members of the Iraqi Forum, which brings together Iraqis in the Czech Republic. The relationships between the Iraqi Kurds and other Iraqis (Arabs, Assyrians, and Turkmens living in Iraq) may be evaluated as excellent and friendly (Respondent 3, personal communication, May 15, 2011).

The association's annual budget is fairly meagre at around €700, which limits the potential activities the association can organize. These usually depend upon the personal commitment and enthusiasm of individuals. The association has no employees, not even part-time.

Comprising Kurdish people originally from Syria, Turkey, Iraq, and Iran, regardless of political orientation, makes the association unusual in comparison to the Western European model. This inclusiveness does, of course, introduce certain complications into the practical operations of the association. It should be noted that the current situation in the individual countries in which Kurds live differs widely. In Iraqi Kurdistan, for example, there is a significant level of autonomy even in terms of foreign policy, and Iraqi Kurds have a substantial influence on national politics in the country. The Kurdish language is in fact the country's second official tongue. Thus the issues Kurds deal with in relation to their homelands and the relatives who live there also differ markedly. To this add the fact that Kurds differ in their political orientations. Issues arise in coming to a consensus on how to present the association and the Kurdish community because of the changing composition of the community in the Czech Republic. Previously, the association had been dominated by Iraqi and Syrian Kurds, but today they have been supplanted by Kurds whose roots are in Turkey (Respondent 3, personal communication, May 15, 2011). Despite this, they are able to agree on key issues, but the process of arriving at a consensus has become ever more difficult.

One thing Kurds living in the Czech Republic do agree on is that they welcome the extensive autonomy enjoyed by Iraqi Kurdistan. Those who come from other countries hope for similar developments in their homelands. Some wish for a unified Kurdistan uniting all Kurds. The association's activity has significantly influenced the situation in Syria, where a conflict broke out in 2011. From the start, association members organized demonstrations in the Czech Republic against the regime and have been playing an active role in them since. The strengthening of the Democratic Union Party (PYD) in Syrian Kurdistan has been reflected in the direction and public presentations of the association in the Czech Republic, under the influence of party members (Mareš & Murad, 2015). KOS members did not agree on the role political parties should play in the operation of the association and the presentation of parties and individual figures in Kurdish politics and events it organizes. But the crisis precipitated by the rise of the Islamic State has united Kurds in the Czech Republic and it does not at this juncture appear that independent organizations of, e.g., Turkish Kurds, will be formed, although this had been contemplated (Respondent 9, personal communication, November 28, 2014).

There is regular criticism that the association functions purely as a formal platform, registered but lacking any overall concept or means to be able to attract people who would work with full commitment. Because Kurds committed to the association have their own jobs, they have limited time for association activities. The fact that, with few exceptions, women do not participate in the association's activities is not surprising, given that most members are men under forty-five years of age. Women take part frequently in the Newroz celebration (Pettrichová, 2011, p. 78).

Ties abroad are essentially not institutionalized. Particularly in the past, Kurds living abroad have come to Prague to celebrate Newroz but even this was not a frequent occurrence. But those Kurds living within the Czech Republic definitely have ties to other Kurds abroad, whether they have ties of friendship or family. They see each other, and communicate by phone or over the internet. But the great majority of events in the Czech Republic are not coordinated, and there are no frequent official meetings between representatives of the Kurdish Civic Association and representatives of foreign organizations. Similarly, the Kurds living in the Czech Republic keep in touch with the Kurds in their "homelands". They actively follow the current situation in the countries of their origin and follow the new from both Kurdish and Arabic satellite TV stations. The current situation in the region is a dominant topic of discussion among the community members (Respondent 2, personal communication, May 28, 2014).

The Sociocultural Activities of the Kurds in the Czech Republic

Within the Kurdish community, even events which would at first sight appear cultural take on a political character. This is because even at these events, Kurds present information on their situation and on the political attitudes of some members of the Kurdish community to their host countries. The differing status of Kurds in contemporary Iraq, Turkey, and other countries motivates differences in the opinions of association members on the focus of his presentations at cultural events the association organizes. At 2011 celebration of Newroz, long the most significant regular event for Kurds living in the Czech Republic, a photograph was displayed of Abdullah Öcalan, founder of the Kurdistan Workers' Party, greatly popular among Kurds. But some members, particularly those from Syria and Iraq, did not agree. Any display of symbols associated with the PKK has consequences. In the past it was relatively common for representatives of the countries from which Kurds hail to take part in the Newroz celebration, particularly Iraq after 2003, and four members of Parliament of the Czech Republic to do so, but this is no longer the case. In 2008, approximately 400 people took part in the celebration, including the Iraqi ambassador to the Czech Republic and representatives from the Czech Ministry of Foreign Affairs. Recently, some Kurds have themselves opted not to come to the event, which they think should be purely cultural and not the site of political presentations. The last large-scale Newroz celebration was in Prague on 26 March 2011. In 2012, it did not take place at all, due to the happenings in Syria. Continuous fighting resulting in many casualties influences the atmosphere in the local Kurdish community. Partially because so many Kurds had come from Syria, it was decided not to celebrate the holiday that year. In 2013 and 2014, Newroz festivities were resumed, but without as many participants as before. Short-term conflicts within the Kurdish Civic Association on the presentation of individual political parties resulted in Iraqi Kurds organizing independence celebrations.

The KOS also took part in an exhibition presenting Kurdish culture in Vlastivědné Muzeum ve Slaném (the Slany Homeland Museum) called Wild Kurdistan in 2011. It targeted Czech museumgoers, attempting to acquaint them with Kurds and their issues. The same objective is also true for Newroz, but to a great extent, it also targets the Kurdish community itself. The association also participates in organizing evening social affairs related to charity. In January 2014, Kurds took part in organizing a visit by Haitham Hussein, a Kurdish writer from Syria who writes in Arabic (Mareš & Murad, 2015).

Political Activities of Kurds in the Czech Republic

The Kurdish diaspora in the Czech Republic is not large, but its purely political transnational activities clearly make an impact. They currently placed a special focus on Syria and Turkey, because of the substantial share of Kurds in the Czech Republic for whom these countries are home and where their rights are suppressed. It is less common than it has been in the past for Kurds to get involved in the political parties in their countries of origin, although some are still members. Typologically, their politics is oriented towards that of the homeland and the diaspora.

In 2008, KOS sent an open letter to the Turkish ambassador to the CR condemning border operations by the Turkish army in Iraqi Kurdistan and military operations within Turkey itself. In a letter which was more an appeal to the Turkish government than a call for terminating the violence and arriving at peaceful resolution for the situation. In addressing the Turkish ambassador, KOS represents itself as 'an organization associating members of Kurdish nationality in the Czech Republic' (Kubálek, 2008).

Members of the Kurdish diaspora in the Czech Republic frequently organize demonstrations and petitions targeting both their homelands and the Czech Republic. The Kurds stood behind asylum seekers in the Czech Republic (mostly Kurds from Syria): in December 2010, as part of International Human Rights Day, about forty refugees – mostly Kurds – protested conditions in a refugee camp and criticized the lengthy asylum procedure.

Since 2011, KOS activities, especially those engaged in by members originally from Syria, have focused on protests against the Syrian Baasist regime of President Asad, particularly against the violence committed by his security forces. The association, concretely Rachid Khalil, its former chairman and Syrian Kurd, working together with other Syrians and Kurds, organized demonstrations in Prague in which dozens of people participated. These demonstrations took place outside the Embassy of the Syrian Arab Republic in Prague and, in some cases, also in Wenceslas Square and in front of the building housing the Government of the CR.

The role played by Kurds in these protests is important. They frequently organize them and account for most of the participants and speakers, gradually joined by other Syrians. In some cases, Kurds from other European countries also arrive to take part in the protest and the course of individual events is also consulted with organizations directly inside Syria. Especially at the beginning, protesting Syrians received support from the local Amnesty International office or a Czech civic association organized the protests. Initially, Kurdish flags appeared at demonstrations whose participants organized via Facebook; gradually they were replaced by the Syrian 'opposition' flag. Chants for a free Syria are heard as well as for the unity of the Syrian people, whether Arab or Kurd. These demonstrations are usually calm, the greatest "outburst" has been to throw eggs on the Syrian Embassy building. In autumn 2014, the Kurdish Civic Association took part in organizing three demonstrations in Prague, reacting to the crises related to the seizure of territory by the Islamic State in Syria. Attention was drawn particularly to the town of Kobane, as with other demonstrations in Europe. The demonstrations particularly criticized the Turkish attitude to the crisis – two demonstrations took place directly outside the Turkish Embassy — and frequently featured photographs of Abdullah Öcalan and the flag of the Syrian PYD.

Another example of political engagement is the criticism expressed by Kurds in the Czech Republic (specifically Khalil) for the visit of Jiri Paroubek, the former chairman of the Czech Social Democratic Party, to Syria. An example of direct transnational participation in the politics in the countries of their origin is the participation of Iraqi Kurds in the elections: starting in 2005, Iraq established polling places in 14 selected countries for Iraqis living outside their homeland, so that they could go vote in the elections for the national parliament. The procedure was similar also during the 2010 and

2014 elections. Iraqis (including Kurds) from the Czech Republic could go to these polling places on their own or make use of bus transportation (Mareš & Murad, 2015).

Economic Activities of Kurds in the Czech Republic

Transnational economic activities have a very low level of institutionalization. They comprise mostly informal business dealings between people in the Czech Republic and Kurdistan, particularly Iraqi Kurdistan, or the sending of payments from Kurds living in the Czech Republic to their families at home. With the developments in Syria, smaller amounts have been sent more frequently to those in need of them, identified by the relatives of Kurds in the Czech Republic living directly in Syria. Occasionally, Kurds living in the Czech Republic are asked by Czech businesses to mediate contacts with someone in Kurdistan. This is part of the business activity of Khalil, who also works as an interpreter in the Kurdish and Arabic languages. Kurdish entities occasionally express interest in particular Czech products, but all of these business dealings are in relatively small numbers. One example of a significant business exchange, realized primarily by individuals in the Kurdish community in the Czech Republic, is the success of the Skoda automobile dealership in Iraqi Kurdistan. Another is the planned construction of a gas power plant near Erbil, the capital of Kurdistan in the Iraqi autonomous region, by Czech and Turkish companies (Mareš & Murad, 2015).

Conclusion

Kurdish people have created an ethnic-state diaspora in the Czech Republic. It originated as the result of forced migration from Turkey, Syria, Iran, and Iraq. The first Kurds arrived in the Czech Republic in the 1960s, mostly as students. Some subsequently remained in the Czech Republic. This generation founded the first Kurdish organization — the Union of Kurdish Students in the CSSR — and was behind the establishment of the contemporary Kurdish Civic Association. Over time, they have been supplanted by a younger generation of Kurds. Kurdish people from Iraq, originally the most numerous, have been replaced by Kurds from Syria and Turkey, substantially influencing the Kurdish community's orientation towards events taking place in Turkey and, most recently, in Syria, as well. They have organized frequent protests against the Syrian Baas party.

In contrast to other European countries, the Kurds are associated in a single umbrella organization in the Czech Republic. Their numbers are small, especially compared to Kurdish communities in neighbouring Germany and Austria. But the Kurdish community possesses the elements of an independent, politically and culturally active, multigenerational organization interconnected to Kurdish organizations in other countries that are similarly oriented. The community is thus transnational not only by virtue of its orientation, but also because its members are tied to the diaspora abroad. Some of the activities it engages in are institutionalized and therefore predictable, such as Newroz. The dominant association in the Kurdish community at the present time in the CR is a grassroots organization, established 'bottom-up' by members of the Kurdish community to promote their interests. A framework has been created for the political and cultural development of Kurds in the CR, and for their further population growth, framework which will be influenced by processes at the European and global levels, and particularly by current affairs in the Kurds' homelands of Turkey, Iraq, Iran, and especially Syria.

References

Van Amersfoort, H. (2004). Gabriel Sheffer and the Diaspora Experience. Diaspora: A Journal of Transnational Studies, XXIII (2/3), 359–373. doi: 10.1353/dsp.2008.0009

Bauböck, R. & Faist, T. (Eds.). (2010). Diaspora and Transnationalism: Concepts, Theories and Methods. Amsterdam: Amsterdam University Press.

Kubálek, P. (2008, March 1). Otevřený dopis velvyslanci Turecké republiky [Open letter to ambassador of Turkey]. Message posted to http://kurdove.ecn.cz/clanky.shtml?x=2079383 (in Czech).

Mareš, M. & Murad, M. (2015): Kurská komunita v České republice [Kurdish Community in the Czech Republic]. Český lid. Etnologický časopis, 102 (2), 75-96 (in Czech).

Mügge, L.(2010). Beyond Dutch Borders. Transnational Politics among Colonial Migrants, Guest Workers and the Second Generation. Amsterdam: Amsterdam University Press.

Murad, M. (2009). Bezpečnostní aspekty irácké imigrace do České republiky [Security features of Iraqi immigration into the Czech Republic]. Defence & Strategy. 9 (2), 5-23. doi:10.3849/1802-7199.09.2009.02.005-023 (in Czech).

Østergaard-Nielsen, E. (2003a). Transnational Politics - Turks and Kurds in Germany. London, New York: Routledge.

Østergaard-Nielsen, E. (2003b). The Politics of Migrants' Transnational Political Practices, International Migration Review, 37(3), 760-789.

Pettrichová, D. (2011). Role Kurdského občanského sdružení v procesu integrace Kurdů do české společnosti [Role of Kurdish association in the process of integration of Kurds into the Czech society]. Thesis. Prague: Faculty of Humanities, Charles University (in Czech).

Sirkeci, I. (2003). Migration, Ethnicity and Conflict. The Environment of Insecurity and Turkish Kurdish International Migration. Doctoral dissertation, University of Sheffield.

Wahlbeck, Ö. (1999). Kurdish Diasporas. A Comparative Study of Kurdish Refugee Communities. London, New York: MacMillan Press, St. Martin´s Press.

Transnational Spaces between Dersim and Vienna

Maria Six-Hohenbalken[271]

Introduction and the context

In this contribution, I will address a few of the multiple layers of interconnectedness between environmental issues, village reconstruction, and memory processes settled in the transnational community of people from the province of Dersim/Tunceli. In the last decade, community development projects as realized by the succeeding generation have been part of a common environmental consciousness and reflect how they deal with the fate of their ancestors, untold family histories, and the orally transmitted knowledge of persecution their parents and grandparents had to experience in the eve of WWII. Their way of dealing with the past in relation to or through environmental issues shapes a very specific space. Strasser and Akçınar (2014) elaborated on the level of community building processes in the Dersim transnation as well as the political context in Turkey and showed the multiplexity of remittances and the meaning of 'political remittances' in the Dersim case.

In general, only a few empirical works and theoretical approaches have been dedicated to the atrocious living conditions as well as long-term effects of persecution of a civil population or civil war. This development can be attributed to epistemological concerns and the Culture/Nature divide. In this regard, I will follow the outlines of Alex Hinton (2002) and Andre Gingrich (2014). Gingrich generally proposes to elaborate on a 'third space' (referring to Homi Bhabha's approach of 1994) outside the great divide, in which anthropological debates may offer valuable contributions. Alex Hinton, a pioneer in the anthropology of violence, stressed the necessity of studying not only human suffering but also material devastation and social implications (Hinton 2002: 12). Past contributions mainly focused on recent violent events and their effects on socio-economic developments. Nevertheless, we still have only little information on the long-term effects and the nature/culture interplay. Therefore, focusing on a 'third space', the interplay of human suffering, material devastation and social implications, and how the next generation remembers and deals with all of that, can be a tool to address long-term effects and consequences. As my presentation is a work in process, based on problem-centered and narrative interviewings with activists in Vienna's Dersim community conducted in the last three years as well as the findings of my project collaborator, Dr. Özlem Göner, collected in Dersim in the last year. The methods of analysis of this anthropological approach are qualitative data analysis and case-by-case analysis. Eastern provinces have been in a state of emergency, some over decades, due to the Kurdish resistance movement in Turkey since the 1960s. Migration to Central Europe, either in the context of bilateral guest worker contracts or chain migration, presented an opportunity to flee from the extreme political situation at home. Kurds from Dersim had a

---

[271] Maria Six-Hohenbalken is a researcher at the Institute for Social Anthropology, Austrian Academy of Sciences, Vienna, Apostelgasse 23, 1030 Vienna. E-mail. Maria.six-hohenbalken@oeaw.ac.at

difficult stand within the community building processes of the highly diverse Kurdish diaspora. In Vienna, two umbrella organizations emerged in the 1980s (one organized by Kurds from Turkey close to PKK politics, one by Kurds from Iraq and Iran) with hardly any interaction at the beginning. In Austria, the 'political opportunity structure' (Østergaard-Nielsen 2001: 14 ff.) was marked by exclusion and the outsourcing of both adaptation and integration work (e.g. language courses, social work) to the respective hometown associations of the migrant and exiled population. Although today the two umbrella organizations run offices, publish irregularly, organize festivals and exhibitions, and are engaged in social work, the Dersim 1937/38 case or the Zaza language/dialect issue has become an issue mainly in the last decade. New communication and transportation facilities – beginning with the first European-based Kurdish satellite TV station in the 1990s and various follow-up projects – allowed for the development of new dynamics marked by extension and contraction, thus intra-ethnic diversification, and new national ideologies also encompassing nation-state boundaries. Alevi and Yezidi organizations built up their networks, while linguistic initiatives promoted the Zaza language, which went hand in hand with various other cultural and environmental initiatives. In 1994 the first Dersim association was found in Berlin and the umbrella organisation *Avrupa Dersim Dernekleri Federasyonu* was established in 2006 (Strasser, Akçınar 2014: 212).

In Austria and here mainly in Vienna, newspapers and journals supported the use of Kurmancî. Only in the last decade, their support was extended to Zazakî which was mainly used as an oral language with limited sources of printed materials. Examples include *Kurdî*, a multilingual journal published between 2009 and 2010 by independent, leftist activists using Kurmancî, Zazakî and German to write about political, social and environmental issues in Dersim. A well-established project founded in 2000 is the independent Kurdish both classic and online radio *Radio Dersim*, transmitting two to three programs a week in Kurmancî, Zazakî and Soranî. As it was founded when there was hardly any formal education in their mother tongue(s), one of its main tasks is to support the young generation in speaking Kurmancî und Zazakî. One of the protagonists in terms of language maintenance has even established a program in Zazakî as a form of online TV program *SoBe* (at *Okto TV*, a free TV station). The program presents ethnographic documentation, oral tradition, interviews with activists (writers e.g. Aslan (2009), artists, musicians) or reports from meetings, and discusses environmental issues in Zazakî, Kurmancî and German, all with subtitles. The protagonists are committed in various fields to further develop Zazakî and Kurmancî – such as language courses for adult education or voluntary mother-tongue instruction at elementary school. Moreover, there were various high-pressure projects organized by Alevi communities in Austria (of Turkish and Kurdish descent), when one such branch managed to have Alevism officially recognized as a religious confession in Austria in May 2013. Many Zazakî and Kurmancî-speaking Alevi Kurds separated from them due to political and religious reasons. While the acknowledged community emphasized its ties to Islam, those of Kurdish decent labeled 'Old Alevis' minimized their connection to Islamic traditions and focused their specific Alevi Kurdish revival (Çelik, 2003). Even in the late 1990s, France-based scholar Hamit Bozarslan questioned the existence of one Kurdish diaspora and argued that we could only speak of at least several Kurdish diasporas in terms of heterogeneity. At the same time that this high level of diversification was reinforced, activists worked on their connections and networking using a comprehensive narrative of the Kurdish past. This religious and linguistic context seems to be essential for understanding further initiatives and the shaping of different narratives addressing a violent and revolutionary past in the various Kurdish homelands.

The fateful history

On the eve of WWII, Dersim's Kurdish Alevi population was confronted with policies of mass deportation, closed provincial borders, and rigid language laws in later decades. In the 1930s, Turkey was officially divided into four zones, each with a specific population policy *(İskan Kanunu)*. One intention was to completely evacuate Dersim (Kendal 1986). In 1937, military operations began attacking Alevi leaders. Heads of tribes were killed without any sort of trial. In 1938, planned and coordinated massacres killed thousands of villagers with forced expulsions taking effect one year later. It is estimated that between 25,000 and 100,000 people were killed in these events – the same that were denied and silenced in Turkey until the last few years. In the 1990s, scientists like Ismail Beşikçi who tried to scrutinize the historic developments and shed a light on the issue were still arrested because of their work. Various political initiatives in Turkey and conferences on EU-level in Turkey in the years before, enforced the Turkish government in 2011 to officially apologize for massacres in which about 13,800 (first official numbers) lost their lives. Depending on the political orientation of their parents, their violent experiences and family narrations, members of the second generation sometimes learned what had happened to their parents and grandparents only in the last one or two decades. They knew that 'something' terrible had happened but could not find out what in the context of Turkish history because it was officially denied and they had never learnt about it in school. As both Kurdish identity and history were underplayed or silenced, Turkish leftist groups and parties, which were very strong in Dersim in the 1970s and 1980s, also hampered to bring the topic up, as Kurdish identity and history were underplayed or silenced. It was only when the Kurdish movement became stronger, the PKK more successful, and Anfal was internationally discussed and studied as genocide in Kurdistan Iraq that Kurds in the diaspora began addressing the issue of Dersim. In my interviews with children of those who had survived persecution in Dersim, they argued that they had learnt early on in school that they were different, were often laughed at and excluded – due to language and religion. In contrast, they learned very late – in a Turkish prison or the diaspora in Vienna – how the fear of their parents had shaped the assimilation process, the denial of their Kurdish identity, and their own unawareness of the painful past. Only in recent years, the 1937/38 massacres of Dersim have also been included in the (semi-) official diaspora discourse but not only within Dersim groups and networks but increasingly also in wider Kurdish diasporic networks.

The (im)possibility of coming to terms

Victims of genocide and other crimes against humanity as well as their descendants not only have to cope with such tremendously cruel deeds but must also face the perpetrators' denial of culpability and responsibility (Robben 2011: 268, see also Cohen 2001) as well as the manipulation of historical developments, moral constraints, testimonies of bystanders, and media coverage. Since the 1960s, the socio-economic and political developments in Dersim have not allowed coming to terms with the past. The province experienced several emigration waves to western Turkey and Europe due to conditions similar to civil war between the Turkish military, Kurdish supporters, and PKK guerillas. This semi-continuous warfare caused the depopulation of various areas and barred the civil population from even more regions. Some of the remaining villages do not even have an economically active population anymore due to economic underdevelopment and out-migration. In the late 1990s, it was often possible to find 200 or more inhabitants from the same village in Vienna or larger German cities. The members of the first generation already retired and either remigrated to Dersim or keep travelling between Dersim and Vienna. While the villagers founded social networks and hometown organizations, the younger generation established cultural and environmental initiatives in the past two decades (e.g. 'Natur- und Kulturschutzverein' Dersim-Tunceli in Vienna, 'Initiative Munzur' or 'Föderation der Dersim-Gemeinden in Deutschland') in which they worked together with International Non-Governmental Organisations and showed the collaboration of the Turkish government with European companies to construct huge dam-projects.

Environmental issues

Both external and internal factors, the improved political situation in the course of the last decade, and the generation being in its 40s and 50s made it possible to engage in reconstruction work, infrastructure projects, environmental issues, and culture work. In 2005, Marie Le Ray outlined the deep emotional connection of people from Dersim who migrated to Istanbul in the 1970s to their hometown. In this context, the key contributing factors are private and political ties, such as family graveyards, agriculture, fruit cultivation, and the environment, e.g. the river Munzur, as she mentioned one statement of a person in Istanbul 'Le Munzur est présent dans tous mes rêves (2005: 57). Gabriel Ignatow focused on transnational environmentalism in a comparative perspective and showed the connection between identity constructions, discourses on cultural heritage, and environmental issues in Lithuania and Dersim. He analyzed the activism of various environmental groups (above all of projects against the dam project of Munzur) and elaborated on the interconnectedness of environmentalist ideals and cultural heritage (2008: 858). In one of his interviews, an Alevi dede explained how environmentalism was an intrinsic value in the Alevi religion. "Our ancestors planted a tree wherever they saw water. The importance of trees has come down to us. When we were young, our elders used to say 'Plant trees as long as you live. Even if you yourself cannot benefit, other living things such as birds and wolves can benefit', and they planted a love of nature in us. But over time, the slaughter of nature increased" (Ignatow 2008: 858). Concerning the obligation to keep discretion about the religious beliefs over centuries - a measurement of the persecuted Alevi communities to protect themselves - , we have only limited knowledge of Alevi creeds and traditions in Dersim. Referring to Andranig (1900), Martin van Bruinessen (1997) emphasized the tradition of nature worshipping and the sacredness of certain places in the environment (water, rocks, trees). When the government planned to build several dams and power plants, various environmental initiatives were founded both in Dersim and the transnational community. These plans were opposed regionally, nationally and also transnationally by *hemşire* (hometown) organizations, branches of environmental groups in Turkey (Ignatow 2008), self-organized initiatives in Vienna, and European networks like the 'Free Munzur initiative'. Moreover, the Munzur environmental initiatives took legal steps against these project plans including dams and hydroelectric power plants in the heart of Turkey's largest nature reserve. In October 2014, the third administrative court in Ankara canceled these plans because the mandatory environmental impact assessment report (ÇED) was against the law.[272] Not only transnational resistance movements but also huge culture festivals in Dersim demonstrated the deep connection between environmental initiatives, remembering the fateful past, and endangered cultural heritage. It seems that environmental projects and environmentalism itself provide a platform for addressing silenced topics from the past.

Memoryscapes in the transnation

It was up to the young generation to foster remembrance through semi-official narratives and to hand down their parents' and grandparents' experiences of violence, of which they had only learnt through family narratives themselves, based on oral history, musical performances and recitations from the *dengbej*, the traditional singers in the village. Depending how the family or the villagers were able to deal with such 'public secrets', others only learned of those incidents their parents and grandparents had avoided to remember very late. Young people told me that the first time they had heard of the 1937 persecutions in Dersim was in Vienna. This encouraged them to find out more about such secrets and family histories. Today, the accounts of the next generation are very emotional: including how their parents had survived often due to a fortunate coincidence, the pain of waiting so long for their parents to be able to share their experiences, how they had come up with these secrets, and certain grey zones of collaboration. Only in recent years, some of my interview partners had the opportunity to finally visit the *village* they had been displaced from several years or decades ago. These first visits of former villagers to their abandoned agricultural land and deteriorated houses are sometimes documented on film and then put online. Some of this new information on the villages' past is either connected to the rather recent political resettlement policy or to past developments in 1937/38 where some of these regions had become forbidden zones. These abandoned and deteriorated villages

---

[272]http://www.hurriyetdailynews.com/landmark-victory-for-ecologists-as-court-aborts-fourth-energy-project-in-eastern-turkish-valley.aspx?pageID=238&nID=73847&NewsCatID=340[accessed: 15.03.2015]

are now the *lieu de memoire* of 1937/38. Specific places of massacres, such as certain gorges or valleys, are often reminded in songs and unofficial narrations (only recently memorials were erected in Dersim). After one of my informants, a descendant of Seyid Riza, the assassinated leader of the Alevi Kurds 1937/38, had been able to visit his old village, he developed a plan to rebuild the houses and infrastructure. He also mentioned the example of Seyid Riza's granddaughter who has begun living in her grandfather's abandoned village during the summer months. In the last few decades, the landscape and specific places were muted signs closely connected to the persecution. In the last few years, however, a certain kind of political tourism has emerged that is much more than environmental tourism; travelers are also visiting the historic sites and places of, for example, recently found mass graves. Dersim Kurds of Austrian citizenship have also begun showing great interest in their regions of origin and initiated small-scale community projects to rebuild villages, lay water lines, build roads, restore homes, or reforest the area. Aside from such infrastructure projects and trying to find alternative ways of sustainable development, several of my informants mentioned planting fruit trees, e.g. nuts, that are less labor-intensive and provide additional income. Such village initiatives pursue the goal of getting together during the summer months and bringing members of the transnational community from all over Europe and their children closer to village culture. In addition, Dersim Kurds in Vienna seek to establish connections between the 'villagers' in Europe by organizing village Facebook sites or homepage. These projects seem to be the archives of a transnational community. They provide the opportunity of storing family histories, local traditions, and the songs of the *dengbej* (local reciter/singer/musician), while informing about the villages' more recent past and holy places. Moreover, they not only refer to Armenians who had settled there or sought refuge until 1917 but also function as the book of condolences in case a villager passed away.[273] Some of these projects already started a decade ago, when people individually organized village documentation projects to save their mostly orally handed down memories. In 2010 the *Avrupa Dersim Dernekleri Federasyonu*, started a Germany based project to collect the Oral History of Dersim and are seen as a form of political remittances by Strasser/ Akçınar (2014: 213). Today the villagers are often spread all over Turkey and several European countries. Some started moving to cities in western or central Anatolia very early on. In consequence, some of my interview partners have only spent a few years in 'their' villages so far. The village homepages or Facebook sites link people and include stories on the founding history of the lineage and connections, e.g. to Xorasan and the experiences of villagers in 1937/38. They provide information on the first satellite villages in the Turkish metropolis and their glocal engagements. Some of these homepages are multilingual and connected to further 'village cyber sites'. Crucial in remembering Dersim's fateful history are singers, musicians, and their songs, especially about the Dersim rivers and places in the Munzur valley, e.g. Derê Laç where one of the massacres of 1937/38 took place. Talking about these songs, one of my informants explained the political suppression in terms of the language ban and assimilation by saying, "they could take our language but they

---

[273]http://www.conag.org/tr/kigida_eski_demografik_yapi_tr.html.[accessed: 15.03.2015]

couldn't take our melodies." Before the Internet, people usually recorded the traditional singers and copied their songs using their private tape decks. One of my informants in Vienna documented a recitation of the dengbejs in his village in 1992 and provided these recordings to Metin & Kemal Kahraman, two famous musicians in the transnational Dersim community, who used his material in their work on traditional Dersim music. The song 'Derê Laç', for example, is widely known across all generations and has been interpreted various times, e.g. by Mikail Aslan, a musician from Dersim living in Germany, who also initiated a documentation project on the Armenian culture and musical traditions in Dersim. In WWI, several Armenians found refuge in the Dersim villages where Kurds of Alevi and Sunni denomination lived together with Armenians. The Armenian population was persecuted just as well in 1937/38; a fact that has become part of the current discourse linking the Armenian genocide and Dersim 1937/38 in various ways. Törne (2015) has critically examined several layers of this discourse and explained the strategies of several memory projects. She concludes that these projects do not address the involvement of Kurds in the Armenian genocide. In general, it can be said that the responsibility of some Kurdish tribes has not been sufficiently analyzed yet. Törne stresses that in spite of using such empowerment strategies to interlink Dersim 1937/38 with the Armenian genocide, "As a consequence, these 1938 commemorations and memoralisation projects ultimately fail to counter the dominant denialist discourse" (2015: 17). In Vienna, my interview partners mentioned contrasting individual narratives and memories, e.g. the heterogeneity in Dersim (Kurmancî speaker with Sunni denomination, Kurmancî speaker with Alevi denomination, Zaza speaker with Alevi denomination), the collaboration of certain tribes with the Turkish military during 1937/38, and the Armenian roots in their own families. Therefore, critical issues and grey areas are not easy to question in the semi-official narratives of the diasporic public but are addressed in individual narratives and smaller group interviews. Although rejection and exclusion may be found in semi-official narratives, such essential topics are always present on the individual level.

Referring to the 'third space' discussed initially, environmental and cultural preservation projects show various interconnections of (counter) discourses including political and social initiatives leading to restoration projects and transnational entanglements. They show the long-term effects and interplay of human suffering, environmental devastation and social implications and how this interplay is remembered in the Dersim transnation. Projects for the preservation of nature go hand in hand with the development of counter-narratives to official historiography. Planned dams do not only harm or destroy the environment and living conditions but are closely connected to the *lieu de mémoire* and Alevi beliefs. At the same time, the transnational commitment organized by the next generations coincides with a revival of Alevi identity, traditions in Dersim, and the shaping of narratives of a violent past.

References

Aslan, K. (2009). Fremdes Schicksal – Yabanci Kader. Unbekannte Lebensgeschichten der Frauen aus Anatolien. Deutsch/Türkisch. Istanbul: Veng.

Çelik, A. B. (2003). 'Alevis, Kurds & hemsehris: Alevi Kurdish revival in the nineties'. In: White, P. J. and Jongerden, J. (eds.), Turkey's Alevi Enigma. Leiden: Brill, 24-40.

Gingrich, A. (2014). Establishing a 'Third Space'? Anthropology and the Potentials of Transcending a Great Divide. In: Hastrup, K.(Ed.), Anthropology and Nature. New York: Routledge Studies in Anthropology, 108 – 124.

Göner, Ö. (2005). The transformation of the Alevi collective identity. Cultural Dynamics July 2005 vol. 17 no. 2 107-134

Hinton, A. L. (2002). Introduction: genocide and anthropology. In: Hinton, A.L. (Ed.): Genocide: An Anthropological Reader. Malden, Oxford: Blackwell, 1-23.

Ignatow, G. (2008). Transnational Environmentalism at Europe's Boundaries: Identity Movements in Lithuania and Turkey, Current Sociology (56) 845-864.

Le Ray, M. (2005). 'Associations de pays et production de locality: La "Campagne Munzur" contre les barrages', European Journal of Turkish Studies (2),   HometownOrganisations in Turkey'; at:www.ejts.org/document370.html

Nezan, K. (1986). Kurdistan und die Kurden. Türkei und Irak, Band 2. Göttingen, Wien: Pogrom Reihe bedrohte Völker.

Østergaard-Nielsen, E. K. (2001). The Politics of Migrants' Transnational Political Practices. Working papers of Transnational communities. WPTC-01-22
    http://www.transcomm.ox.ac.uk/working%20papers/WPTC-01-22%20Ostergaard.doc.pdf [accessed 12.02.2014]

Robben, A.C.G.M Silence (2011). Denial and Confession about State Terror by the Argentine Military. In: M. Six-Hohenbalken; N. Weiß (eds.),Violence Expressed. London: Ashgate, 169-186.

Strasser, S.; M. Akçinar (2014). Dersim Dernekleri: transnationale Betrachtungen 'politischer Flüsse' zwischen Europa und der Provinz Tunceli/Dersim in der Türkei. In: Ilker Ataç et al. (eds.) Migration und Entwicklung. Neue Perspektiven. Historische Sozialkunde/Internationale Entwicklung 32. Wien: Promedia, 207-223.

Törne, A. (2015). "On the grounds where they will walk in a hundred years' time"- Struggling with the heritage of violent past in post-genocidal Tunceli. European Journal of Turkish Studies (20).

Van Bruinessen, M. (1997).' "Aslını inkar eden haramzadedir!"': The debate on the ethnic identity of the Kurdish Alevis'. In: K. Kehl-Bodrogi, B. Kellner-Heinkele and A. Otter-Beaujean (eds.), Syncretistic religious communities in the Near East. Leiden: Brill, 1-23.

Van Bruinessen, Martin (2008). 'Religious practices in the Turco-Iranian world: continuity and change'. In: M.-R. Djalili, A.Monsutti, and A. Neubauer (eds.), Le monde turco-iranien en question. Geneva: The Graduate Institute / Paris: Karthala, 123-142.

Spatial Segregation and Politics of Equilibrium in Mersin: Unintended Consequences of Forced Migration

Bediz Yılmaz[274]

Introduction

More than twenty years after the peak of forced migration process, we have an important bulk of knowledge related to this phenomenon thanks to many academic works conducted on its political as well as social aspects. We know that, being an involuntary form of migration, it differs considerably from the economic (i.e. voluntary) waves of migration both quantitatively and qualitatively: it is massive, unprepared neither in material nor immaterial terms, it leaves the migrants deprived of supporting resources from the village, the hostile environment in the urban setting marked by a stigmatising discourse. Thus, the consequences related to the integration-adaptation-survival of the forced migrants in the cities are also different.

One of the first researchers to note these differences, Erder qualifies this migration as "migration of the villagers without a village" referring to the destruction of the villages as a measure by the Turkish army to cut-off the local support to the Kurdish revolters; other researchers underlined the impoverishing dimension (Kaygalak, 2001; Doğan, 2002; Buğra and Keyder, 2003); others identified a poverty-in-turns mechanism that summarised the whole migration history of Turkey in which the forced migration of the Kurdish population during the 90's meant the introduction of a new poor segment at the very lowest level of the economy who will not be as lucky as the previous ones (Işık and Pınarcıoğlu, 2001); Keyder and Yenal (2013) have analysed this phenomenon under the title of "semi-proletarianisation by forced dispossession" in the agricultural sector which would turn them into an underclass. Similar observations have been made by myself some 10 years ago, i.e. a decade after the massive migratory flows related to the low-density war in the South-eastern provinces of Turkey. Based on a fieldwork conducted in the Tarlabaşı neighbourhood situated in the inner-city of Istanbul, I have argued that the Kurdish involuntary migrants were subjected to risk of becoming an underclass, and their situation could be analysed by a multidimensional exclusion approach; I have concluded that they presented a new condition that could be identified as perpetual poverty" (Yılmaz, 2008). Rightful criticisms to these analyses have been made by the following generation of researchers: Kanzık (on Yenibosna) and Kılıçaslan (on Kanarya) made observations showing that the Kurdish migrants' occupation of the lowest ranks of the labour market indicated their integration as cheap labour and not their exclusion.

Resting on the assumption that confrontations do matter among different ethnic groups, Duman (2013) asks the question of "which encounters stimulate ethnic conscious/conflict and which of them produce solidarities that discourage

---

[274] Bediz Yılmaz is Assistant Professor in Mersin University Department of Public Administration, Mersin,Turkey. E-mail: bedizyilmaz@yahoo.com.

and substitute ethnic identities   " in metropolitan cities that attracted great deal of ethnic migration. It is found that the presence or absence of economic competition among ethnic groups and the quality of that competition can produce ethnic competition/conflict which can further articulate into political competition when it combines with the power-threat perception. Furthermore, Saraçoğlu's (2011) "exclusion by recognition" conceptualisation on İzmir needs to be tested in other contexts where ethnic competition/conflict have other forms of relationship.

In this present paper, I would like to ask the following question which follows the same axis of observation: is it now possible, 20 years after the peak of forced migration practices, to approach the issue in a similar manner, or can we, at least concerning some specific localities, produce other analyses other than exclusion or underclass? Quite rapid change have been observed between the first and second decades following the mass migration that started -roughly speaking- in the mid-90s. Concerning the city of Mersin where I did my observations, three major factors contributed to this change:

1. eviction/ displacement which is not accompanied with a planned, directed, calculated resettlement scheme, marking a shift from the previous displacement practices of the state

- spatial outcome of this practice: spatial concentration of the displaced Kurds leading to a high level of spatial segregation within the city

2. the particular social history of Mersin city as an ever-cosmopolitan city formed by migrations + spatially segregated pattern of the city

3. the habitus of the migrants, a powerful agency that can be observed in the survival strategies + political militancy

In this paper, I will only be discussing the first factor: privileging a spatial approach, arguing that the latest of the forced migratory practices -i.e. that applied roughly through the 90's is an "eviction" (*tehcir*) process that is not accompanied by a "settlement" (*iskân*) and in that sense it differs considerably from the previous ones -i.e. especially those applied during the first decades of the Republican Turkey- which are clearly organised according to a resettlement approach. This paper will mainly discuss the spatial outcomes of these differentiated policies and argue that the latest forced migration has, unlike the previous ones, provoked an unintended consequence: spatial concentration of the migrant population. Hence, I argue that this latest forced migration process had been realised in such a way that, paradoxically, exclusion is not a sufficient conceptual framework to grasp the social reality.

Forced migration in the republican turkey: a history of displacements and (re)settlements

Forced migration is a widespread state practice that has its origins in the Ottoman Empire and that continued through the Republican period. In a sense, state intervention to the distribution of the population over land has been a major concern for the Ottoman urban policy and economic purposes, to the extent that "the population has been conceived as a mobile resource that can be carried and shaped according to the economies of the localities from which the population departs and to which it settles" (Barkan quoted by Erder, 1978: 46). In a report on the migratory policies of Turkey, Erder who wrote the chapter concerning the question of settlement from Ottoman to Republican period, states that population movements in the Ottoman Empire have essentially been "forced movements" which took divergent forms such as exile (sürgün), re-populating (şenlendirme) and settlement (iskân) as a result of divergent causes such as disasters, revolts, wars, famines and labour force needs; and she suggests that the forced and controlled population movements shifted from a policy oriented to "mix in order to govern" to a policy oriented to "segregate to govern" following the periods in which the needs and emergencies of the administration changed (for instance, migration practices of a territorial expansion period is inevitably different from those of a period in which the territory shrunk) (İçduygu et al., 2014: 96ff). Especially during the period of the dismantling of the Empire, the population movements have become a greater concern for the administrators; the State, at that time, had to deal with the revolting minorities on the one hand, and with the massive immigration of Muslim populations (Babuş, 2006: 36).

The argument of this paper is that the forced displacement that took place during the 90's was an eviction process which lacked the resettlement dimension. In other terms, as a deep-rooted practice of the state, forced displacement had two dimensions: first dimension is eviction, and second, settlement. Starting as early as the initial geographical expansion of the Ottoman Empire through conquests, the state has been in the position of defining minutely the following: which social group would be displaced, which portion of this group would be settled to where, which economic activities they would engage in, whether land would be attributed to them or not, etc. These issues were planned and decided before the displacement, and settlement was being conducted in a precise manner with a cooperation between different state agencies. In other terms, population movements were well beyond mere security arrangements and engaged various societal measures. That's why, in the year of 1923 when the Law of Resettlement was legislated, the Ministry of Exchange, Construction and Settlement has been established to organise the movements of population in all its dimensions, and social measures accompanied the military measures in every single case.

Tekeli (1990) analyses the population transfer from the 16th century to the 70s, emphasizing the ways in which the state legitimizes these practices and the development of relations between the state and the individual. There are six periods of forced displacement and "through time, with changes in the character of the state, the bases of legitimacy of displacement and content of human rights are also changing, and in connection with this, the institutionalization and forms of forced displacement of the population are renewed" (Tekeli, 1990: 68).

The author first analyzes how forced displacement has been carried out in the classical Ottoman era in the 16th century where the logic was based on three factors: first, the fact that the Empire has continually expanded on the principle of *gaza* (conquest) and had to reinstall some of the Anatolian Muslim population in the newly conquered territories; secondly, the use of the mobility of the workforce to balance the redistribution of resources; thirdly, the maintenance of order and security within the Empire (ibid, 51).

The second period covers the 17th and 18th centuries when the enlargement of the Empire was stopped and people from the villages in the plains fled to face Celali revolts. In these conditions, the displacement and resettlement aimed restocking villages in the plains to ensure the continuity of crops through the forced settlement of nomadic tribes of Yörük, Turkmen and Kurds to go from west to east and Arabs in the south (ibid, 53).

The third period includes the 19th century is marked by narrowing of the territories of the Empire and the establishment of nation-states in the Balkans that put pressure on the Muslim population and cause a large movement of flight. During the same period, the Tanzimat reforms profoundly altered the relationship between the state and the individual as the absolute sovereignty of the Sultan began to be restricted by the recognition of certain rights to individuals, including the right to property established in 1858. Another important factor is the opening of the Ottoman Empire to capitalist relations with the internal operation caused voluntary movements of people that were beyond state control. Large Muslim populations waves of migration took place from the Caucasus, the Crimea and the Balkans during this period, putting heavy resettlement issues and changing the balance of rural and urban populations (ibid, 54-55).

The fourth period is the decade of wars between 1912-1922; it includes the large movements that occurred during and after the wars. This period corresponds to the gradual transition from a multiethnic empire to a nation-state. Efforts to institutionalize the resettlement of immigrants during the Balkan War were interrupted by the First World War broke out, during which a large deportation of Armenians living in the eastern Anatolian took place (1915). This deportation resulted in massacres and large-scale losses. After the defeat of the Empire in this war, its dismantling has been anticipated by the Treaty of Sèvres (1920); but it never entered into force because the War of Independence which allowed the founding of the Turkish Republic is declared and won in 1923. The striking result of this war is the reduction of the Greek population, not only during the war, which was primarily a Greek-Turkish war, but following the Treaty of Lausanne (1923), which stipulates the exchange of populations between Greece and Turkey (ibid, 59-61).

The next period, between 1923-1950, was marked primarily by continued resettlement efforts of the people of the Balkans who continued to immigrate though not forced to do so. This period saw the enactment in 1934 of Law of Resettlement No. 2510. Quite decisive for the creation of "one nation, one people, one homeland" this law will be discussed below in length.

The last period of analysis of Tekeli extends from 1950 to the late 70s; it was marked by a relative democratization process despite the *coups d'Etat* and the development of the welfare state. The acceleration of urbanization is also a major factor in this period. Problems related to resettlement were threefold: the arrival of the Turks outside Turkey who continued since the 19th century (including Bulgarian Turks), forced displacement of populations due to economic decisions or related to development (dams), and finally, movement undertaken as a preventive measure against natural hazards (Tekeli, 1990: 65-68).

I will now try to make a comparison between the population displacement practices of the State in the 1930s by using the Law of Resettlement as the main instrument and the practices during and after the 90s in order to be able to discuss their differing spatial outcomes.

According to Tekeli, the Law of Resettlement no. 2510 applies not only to the resettlement of immigrants from other countries, but also to people displaced within Turkey himself: "Behind the articles on the internal resettlement, there is the influence of Kurdish uprisings Sheik Said in 1925, Ağrı in 1930 and Dersim in 1937" (ibid, 63). Indeed, after the uprising of Sheik Said, a law called the "Law on the transfer of a few people from the eastern region to the western provinces" in 1927, and the 1934 law strengthened the powers of the State in this area. It provided a program of "correcting the territorial distribution of the population by the affiliation to the Turkish culture" that was prepared by the government and implemented by the Ministry of Interior (Ibid.). In his book of the "forced resettlement of the Kurds" İsmail Beşikçi (1977) longly discusses on each article of this law, arguing that this is the main legal text which demonstrates the assimilatory aims and practices of the State over the Kurds. Jongerden, in contrast, argues that this law aims not only a repression -and assimilation of Kurds- but it is also part of a greater target, that of creating a homeland for the Turks (2008: 250) notably in an era of nation-building and where thousands of immigrants needed to be settled, resettled and integrated.

In this Law, Turkey is divided into three zones [mıntıka] according to the criteria of attachment to Turkish culture and resettlement policy is designed accordingly (article 2):

- the first zone consists of the areas where an increase in the density of population with Turkish culture is aimed: these are the areas of eastern Anatolia and Southeast inhabited by people whose mother tongue is Kurdish. In these areas Turkish immigrants who came or come from the former provinces of the Ottoman Empire but did not get the relocation assistance will be resettled,

- the second includes regions where the groups that are needed to be adopted to the Turkish culture are resettled,

- the third zone comprises those regions which should be depopulated and prohibited for the installation for health, economic, security, cultural and military reasons. It is planned to resettle the population in the areas in the first or second type regions according to their affiliation to the Turkish culture.

The aim of assimilation is clear in the law and the tools for its realisation are spatial:

- in Article 9, it is stipulated that those [unsettled vanderers] with Turhish nationality who were not attached to the Turkish culture would be "scattered" among the Turkish towns and villages located in zone 2, paying attention that they do not constitute a community (Beşikçi, 1977: 138)

- Article 11 stipulates that those whose mother tongue is not Turkish are not allowed to constitute a collective village or neighbourhood, nor an artisanal cluster, nor to monopolise a village, a neighbourhood, a profession or an art, this, according to Beşikçi, is one of the most important articles to reveal the spirit of the Law no. 2510 (1977: 142)

The concern for a spatial concentration of the migrant/minority populations can be also seen in the laws rationale: "The autocracy based its own existence upon the coexistence of elements that could not get along with each other and on their uncompromise and their non-cohesion. That's why the aim of assimilating migrant elements by distributing and melting them household by household in

Turkish towns and villages could never be realised. The population which arrived at divers provinces would settle among the local Turks by establishing their independant villages and towns as a block. These remained for many years as speaking their languages. For all the Ottoman rule they could not adopt the Turkish as their mother tongue."

This policy of resettlement was a direct continuation of the last decades of the Ottoman rule during which nationalistic ideas were decisive. Dündar notes that the Kurds who fled away from the East or who were subjected to resettlement by the Ottoman administration have been split into groups of no more than 300 persons and they have been resettled in regions where they would form no more than 5 % of the population; moreover, their leaders were resettled elsewhere (2001: 247). Jongerden qualifies that the resettlement policies have been organised as assimilationist practices as part of the nation-building process (2008: 257).

Tekeli notes that with the implementation of this law, 5,074 households in the provinces of Tunceli, Erzincan, Bitlis, Siirt, Van, Bingöl, Diyarbakır, Ağrı, Muş, Erzurum, Elazığ, Kars, Malatya, Mardin and Çoruh, or 25,831 persons are transferred to the west (ibid, 64). According to Yeğen, Resettlement Act can be understood as "a manifesto of centralist unification" because it "recognizes the government the power to organize and 'fix' the demographic composition of the country as it is defined by the political needs" (1999: 137).

Tekeli's paper, written in the 90s naturally does not include the latest -to date- of forced displacements, that lasted throughout the 90s and that is of a different vein. Of course, it should first be made clear that by "forced" displacement, I do not *only* mean the evictions or village evacuations, but also the circumstances in which it was made for the local people to continue living in their villages, because of armed fights, banned economic activities such as farming or animal husbandry etc. For this reason, I claim that even voluntary migrations are partly involuntary because of reasons beyond the control and will of people are the determining factors most of the time. But for the sake of this paper's argument, I will be taking into account solely the forced displacement practices *strictu sensu*.

Preliminary conclusion: a new form of displacement practice: eviction *without* resettlement

In the 90s, the Turkish army started a series of military measures which resulted in a deprivation of the rural population from their ancestral settlements: village evacuations, embargoes, banishments, evictions were among these measures and their common feature is that none of them is complemented with a complementary measure envisioning the settlement dimension of the displacement. Hence, the population movement remained a military practice; it is neither accompanied with Ministry of Interior measures that defined and regulated where and how would the evicted would go to their new settlement places, nor with Settlement and Social Assistance Ministry measures that undertook the procedure of settlement, economic activity planning, land distribution or that eased the passage for them.[275]

Jongerden (2008) qualifies this last wave of displacement as a "non-schemed" but "tracked" displacement. He says that "the evacuation of villages was organized in the form of what may be termed 'rural-to-urban resettlement tracks'—in essence, the various routes from rural to urban settlement entities along which people were forced to move, without support or assistance from the authorities" and that "in contrast to a scheme, tracked resettlement is little more than a collection of local and regional routes from hamlet and village to town and city. The evacuation and destruction of villages was haphazard but orchestrated. The concern of the military was to clear the villages. They were not concerned with what happened to the people after eviction, and in the towns and cities the hundreds of thousands and more of the displaced were just left to their own devices." (Jongerden, 2013: 382) In his deep and detailed analysis of the resettlement policies concerning the Kurds, Jongerden draws attention to the contradiction between the spatial policies of the military and governments, because of this incompatibility, a real plan of resettlement could not come to life though some considerable initiatives have been taken (such as *city-village* and *central village* schemes). According to Jongerden (2008: 88), the uncertainty as a *fait accompli* was a victory in terms of a military strategy, but it implied a *de facto* resettlement pattern. This pattern, for Mersin and for other cities, has been the formation of new neighbourhoods with a high level of concentration of Kurdish inhabitants.

The forced displacement of the 90s is an eviction procedure decided, planned and realised by the Turkish military forces which is not accompanied by a planned and controlled resettlement procedure. This practice contradicts or differs sharply from the previous state practices concerning the population displacement. Yeğen writes about the population movements of the first decades of the Republican period that "the political needs of the day was clear: assimilate Kurds who resisted the social unification project [which was] centralist and nationalist of the new regime in order to break their resistance; indeed, the reason for the law was defined as that of deciding 'how to prevent concentrations of people whose mother tongue is not Turkish and redistributing'"(1999: 138). However, for the 90s, the projects of resettlement and village return which have been made public by the authorities remained mostly unrealised, according to Jongerden, the reason behind this is clear: the political situation in Turkey recognizes an important right to the army about the resettlement of the displaced population to the Region, and for the military reason, this practice is not acceptable nor applicable (2008: 308).

The direct consequence of this "uncontrolled" population movement is that these internally displaced persons have, similar to the previous voluntary migrations, settled in places with which they have previous contacts in economic or social terms (having a relative who settled, periodically going there as seasonal workers etc.). What this movement has in particular is that the recent one is massive, unpredicted, unprepared and unsupported in comparison to the

---

[275] The Project for Village Return and Rehabilitation inaugurated in 1999 and the Law on Compensation for Losses Resulting from Terrorism and the Fight against Terrorism (Law no. 5233, 2004) can be cited as the only examples of action beyond security measures.

voluntary (i.e. economically motivated) migrations and that the newcomers have confronted an exclusionary discourse, making an identification "between being Kurdish" with "being a terrorist".

Briefly, I argue that, contrary to the understanding of the displacement practice after the 90s as a direct continuation of the assimilationist state policies, we should note the difference between them: in terms of their consequences, the displacement practices of 90s differs from those of the 30s, that they have only been organised by the military (and paramilitary) forces, and they have neither predicted nor regulated the socio-spatial outcomes, and 20 years after, the outcomes include many unintended elements which can be summarised around two domains that I would just mention in this paper: *(1)* spatial concentration / demographic density, and *(2)* socio-political and economic power. Further analysis would complement these arguments.

References

Aker, T., Çelik, B., Kurban, D., Ünalan, T. & Yükseker, D. (2005) Türkiye'de ülke içinde yerinden edilme sorunu. Tespitler ve çözüm önerileri, Istanbul, TESEV.
Ataç, E. & Oğuz, I. (2013) "'Büyük Dönüşüm' öncesi Türkiye kentlerinde ayrışma ve siyaset", *Toplum ve Bilim*, 127, 229-247.
Babuş, F. (2006) Osmanlı'dan Günümüze Etnik-Sosyal Politikalar Çerçevesinde Göç ve İskan Siyaseti ve Uygulamaları, İstanbul: Ozan Yayıncılık.
Beşikçi, İ. (1977) Bilim Yöntemi Türkiye'deki Uygulama 1, Kürtlerin 'Mecburi İskan'ı, Komal Yayınları.
Doğan, A.E. & Yılmaz, B. (2011), "Ethnicity, social tensions and production of space in forced migration neighbourhoods of Mersin: comparing the case of the Demirtaş neighbourhood with newly established ones", *Journal of Balkan and Near Eastern Studies*, 13 (4), 475-494.
Duman, B. & Alacahan, O. (2012) "Getto Tartışmasına Bir Metropolden Bakmak", *International Journal of Social Science*, 5 (2), 55-74.
Duman, B. (2013) "Yoğun Göç Almış Metropollerde Etniklik ve Öteki ile İlişki", *Sosyoloji Dergisi*, 3. Dizi, 27. Sayı, 2013/2, 1-24.
Dündar, F. (2001) İttihat ve Terakki'nin Müslümanları İskan Politikası (1913-1918), İstanbul: İletişim.
Erder, L. (1978) "Türkiye'de Uygulanan Yerleşme Politikaları" *in* Tekeli İ. & Erder L., *Yerleşme Yapısının Uyum Süreci Olarak İç Göçler*, Ankara: Hacettepe Üniversitesi, 45-56.
Erder, S. (1998) "Köysüz 'köylü' göçü", *Görüş*, 34, March, 24-26.
Gambetti, Z. & Jongerden, J. (2011) "The spatial (re)production of the Kurdish issue: multiple and contradicting trajectories -introduction", *Journal of Balkan and Near Eastern Studies*, 13(4), 375-388.
İçduygu, A., Erder, S. & Gençkaya, Ö.F. (2014) *Türkiye'nin Uluslararası Göç Politikaları, 1923-2023: Ulus-devlet Oluşumundan Ulus-Ötesi Dönüşümlere*, MiReKoc Araştırma Raporları 1/2014, TÜBİTAK 106K291, Sept. 2009, İstanbul.
Jongerden, J. (2008) Türkiye'de İskan Sorunu ve Kürtler - Modernite, Savaş ve Mekân Politikaları Üzerine Bir Çözümleme, İstanbul: Vate.
Jongerden, J. (2013) "New perspectives on Forced Migration and Return to Village in Kurdistan-Turkey", *2. Uluslararası Dersim Sempozyumu*.
Kanzık, A. (2010) The Kurdish Migrants in Yenibosna: "Social Exclusion", Class, Politics", unpublished MA thesis, Boğaziçi University.
Kaya, A. (Yay. haz.) (2009) Türkiye'de İç Göçler: Bütünleşme mi, Geri Dönüş mü? İstanbul Diyarbakır Mersin, İstanbul Bilgi Üni. Yay.
Kaygalak, S. (2001) "Yeni kentsel yoksulluk, göç ve yoksulluğun mekânsal yoğunlaşması: Mersin/Demirtaş örneği", *Praksis*, 2, Spring, 124-172.
Kılıçaslan, G. (2015) "Generational differences in political mobilization among Kurdish forced migrants: the case of Istanbul's Kanarya Mahallesi", in Gambetti Z. & Jongerden J. (eds.) *The Kurdish Issue in Turkey: A Spatial Perspective*, New York: Routledge, 157-184.

Saraçoğlu, C. (2011) Şehir, Orta Sınıf ve Kürtler: İnkârdan "Tanıyarak Dışlama"ya, İstanbul: İletişim.
Tekeli, İ. (1990) "Osmanlı İmparatorluğu'ndan günümüze nüfusun zorunlu yer değiştirmesi ve iskan sorunu", *Toplum ve Bilim*, 50, Summer, 49-71.
Yeğen, M. (1999) *Devlet Söyleminde Kürt Sorunu*, Istanbul: Iletişim

Internal migration: socio-economic and spatial perspectives

Murat Öztürk, Besir Topaloğlu and Joost Jongerden

Introduction

The changing character of villages in Turkey within the context of migration studies is a topical issue (Öztürk et al. 2014). Looking at the main tendencies in migration in Turkey since the 1980s, some of the main developments are the following:

i) During the period 1923–2011, the share of Turkey's rural population fell from three quarters of the total population to one quarter. This relative decline took off after 1950, with, among other things, the modernization (including mechanization) of agriculture. Though the relative share of the rural population decreased after 1950, generalized population increase meant that the number of people living in the countryside still rose until 1980, when over 25 million people were recorded as living in villages (non-urban administrative areas). After 1980, however, when the then rural population share stood at 56%, the absolute number of villagers started to decline, falling by 2011 by nearly a third, to a recorded 17 million people, or 23% of the total population (Öztürk 2012).

ii) The received wisdom is that people move from the countryside to cities, since the labor demand in agriculture is reducing and job opportunities in the city increasing. However, statistics also reveal a steady migration from the city to the countryside, even outweighing urban migration in particular periods (Öztürk et al. 2014).

iii) The main form of migration is not between countryside and city, but between towns and cities (urban-urban migration).

iv) One result of the decline in village population is to leave whole villages abandoned. This represents a forced migration by economic means.

v) Government strategy (to reduce the primary sector employment proportion) and internationally supported and required programs (by the IMF and EU) leading to specific agro-economic policies contributed significantly to a decline in farming income, which led again to a search for alternative income sources. This resulted in a new demographic of people who live in both rural and urban settings, or live on the countryside but work in non-agricultural jobs—in fact, non-farm employment in rural areas reached 37.6% of the total rural employment (TUIK 2011a: 8).

vi) A decline of the younger population in rural indicates that birth rate and population will reduce in the future. Not only is the village population aging, moreover, but the rate of people who are out of employment, ill or disabled is also going up (Relatively share of rural population of this group of people is high than cities) . These populations survive through (kinship) solidarity, charity, and state support.

vii) The poverty rate in rural areas is much higher than in urban areas.[276] In the cities, the second biggest group of the poor after homeless children are the newly arrived from the countryside (SAM 2004).

The objective of this article is to understand the socio-spatial strategies of migrants from a socio-economic perspective: how people move between the rural and the urban for reasons of income. Data has been collected through analysis of the state (TUIK)[277] and other statistics on population and settlements combined with original field-work. For the former, the population data of 35,000 villages between 1965 and 2008 was analyzed. For the latter, qualitative and quantitative research was carried out. In total, 25 focus groups were organized in 25 villages in 19 different provinces. This was followed by face-to-face interviews with 436 members of family households in 74 different villages in 23 provinces. Also, 410 face-to-face interviews were conducted with people who live in cities and had migrated during the last twenty years. All unreferenced figures/numbers given here refer to the latter, the original research project.

Backgrounds

As stated, the number of people living in the countryside has been falling for some time now, both in relative and absolute terms (Table 1). Turkey thus stands as a rather striking case of rapid urbanization combined with rural depopulation. There are, of course, a wide range of factors involved in this twin process, among which have been developments related to agriculture.

First, the mechanization of agriculture played an important role in reducing labor needs. In 1928, for example, there were about 1,200 tractors in the country, a number that had only reached 1,750, twenty years later, in 1948.[278] Upon the introduction of the Marshall plan for Turkey, however, this all changed, and by early 1952 the number of tractors had increased to 26,000 (Machado 2007). In other words, the relative decrease in the rural population from the 1950s was concomitant with the introduction of machines on the land. We still witness an absolute increase of the rural population to the 1980s, however, since the introduction of machinery was used not only to save labor, but also to increase the area under cultivation, and productivity also rose with the use of fertilizers and pesticides. Next, from around 2000, came the implementation of neo-liberal policies in the agricultural sector. It is no coincidence that the rapid fall in rural population commenced when state supports to farming were largely withdrawn, agricultural industries denationalized, and protective import duties abandoned

---

[276] In 2009, poverty rates (including food and non-food) were over fours times higher in rural than in urban areas, at 38.7% as compared to 8.9%. (TUIK http://www.tuik.gov.tr/UstMenu.do?metod=temelisti visited 14 May 2015).

Yoksulluk (gıda+gıda dışı) - Complete poverty (food+nonfood)

	2002	2003	2004	2005	2006	2007(3)	2008	2009
Urban	21,95	22,30	16,57	12,83	9,31	10,36	9,38	8,86
Rural	34,48	37,13	39,97	32,95	31,98	34,80	34,62	38,69

[277] *Türkiye İstatistik Kurumu* (Turkish Statisical Institute), ADNKS, Adress Based Population Counting System

[278] With iron wheels and limited traction power, these vehicles were hard to operate on stony and hard ground (Toprak 1988: 33–4)

(Öztürk 2012). The mid and end (twentieth) century points thus mark major transformations in the economics of farming that were closely linked to the restructuring of rural demographics.

Table 1. Population, villages and hamlets in Turkey, 1927–2011

Year	Population (million)	Rural population (million)	Rural population (%)	Number of villages	Number of hamlets	Total no. of rural settlements	Total no. of settlements
1927	14	10	76				
1940	18	13	76				
1950	19	14	73	34,063	30,198	64,261	64,825
1970	36	22	62	35,400	38,600	74,000	74,934
1980	45	25	56	36,076			
1985	51	24	47	36,155	52,398	88,553	89,076
2000	67	23	35	35,427	37,573	72,990	75,860
2011	75	17	23	34,438	47,000	81,438	82,576

Sources: Tütengil 1975; Güzelsu 1983; Dülger 1984; Doğanay 1993; DPT 2000, DIE 2000; TÜİK 2011, TKİB 2011; Öztürk 2012: 140)[279]

Migration and Employment

There has been a significant change in employment at the countryside. Whereas agriculture used to dominate, almost totally, now some 38% of rural households have individuals employed in non-agricultural jobs. Some of these people are full-time, but many of them continue to work their land, as part-time farmers. What transpires from this research is that households with relatively low incomes supplement this through employment in non-agricultural jobs for subsistence reasons. Households with relatively high incomes also have members in non-agricultural work, for additional income and savings.

Concerning the gender dimension of rural employment, although the employment level of women in villages is low (33,8%), it is higher than in cities (27,4%) (TUIK). Among women living in rural areas, we found that some 36% of women work at household farm activities, 32% are employed in agricultural jobs, and some 10% in non-agricultural jobs (the remaining 22% being mostly young [at school], or aged [retired/incapacitated]). Mechanization—releasing people from the land—is a major reason for the transition of women from non-waged household labor to wage-labor in agricultural and/or non-agricultural jobs (i.e., their entry onto the job market).

The main reason for migrating from rural areas to urban areas is to find opportunities for regular work and relatively high income, followed by a socially better environment and education. The rural perception of high income, however, varies considerably. For example, we found that income from labor is similarly regarded as both high income (by 18%) and low (19%). Perception of high income

---

[279] This table is composed of figures from different sources, and therefore may be based on different ways of counting; the patterns are consistent, however, and the authors believe they reflect the general trends.

work is clearly very subjective; it depends on the individual situation and the comparison made with other people's situation in the same environment. Only if there is a job opportunity supported by sufficient capital does this alone direct people's behavior.

When look at income perception in cities, wage labor appears to be less highly valued. Only 5% of city workers regarded their job as "high income" – entrepreneurs (20%) and civil servants (18%) are mentioned more often as high level income earners. Focusing on the employment situation of recent/first generation urban migrants (those who migrated in the last twenty years), some 30% of households include unemployed people, 60% have people in wage labor, 27% in self-employment and 34% in temporary work.[280] Some 39% of employed people work outside the social security system and go unrecorded for tax purposes. Officially employed people are found in 76% of families. It can be seen from these numbers that a major group comprises wage laborers in temporary jobs and unrecorded work; they live in conditions determined by precarious labor. The overall outcome is clear: the majority of people who have migrated to the city for work over the past two decades have not been able to reach their aims.

More specifically, as a result of this urban migration that may be classified unsuccessful in terms of employment, the following conclusions may be drawn:

i. Some people cannot really survive in the city; indeed, going back— village return—becomes a valid option, observed, for example, especially during economic crisis, such as in 2001 (when there was an economic crisis in Turkey), or downturns, such as after 2007 (when Turkey was impacted by the crises in the world economy).

ii. Some people manage to get by, one way or another; they do not return, yet neither are they able to properly integrate into the city and take their place in urban life.

iii. These people constitute an important part of urban poverty; this applies in all its aspects, in terms of population numbers, for example, since the (urban) migrant proportions of city populations are high, and in terms of area or territory, since the incomers tend to cluster in specific parts of a city.

iv. After urban migration, partial return migration is one of reasons for the development of dual- and multi-place living strategies; this involves movement back to the village and/or between village and city (e.g., by part of the family, such as older people to retire or men to tend the land, and/or for some of the time, such as on a seasonal basis, for farming or holidays, involving more than one urban center, such as nearby provincial as well as metropolitan cities, etc.).

Summarizing, although one of the main reasons for urban migration is to find a regular job with high income and social security, in actual fact, only a rather small proportion of those leaving their villages are able to succeed in this. Therefore, important rate of every migration has a potential for return migration and a dual life. Along with other factors, such as emotional attachment to the homeland (*memleket*), this probability contributes to families deciding to not to sell up and instead maintaining their properties in villages.

---

[280] Combinations of these figures do not total 100% since households may have more than one member counted.

The migration process

Most (74%) urban migrations these days are undertaken as a family. This constitutes a major sociological shift, since in the past men would migrate first, followed by (often new) wives and other family members. Age remains, as ever, an important factor in migration dynamics. The average age of urban immigrants (i.e. when they leave the village) is rather low at 27. The relatively high number of young people moving to the city contributes to both rural population decrease and average rural age increase, since fewer children live in the villages (shown by the mass closure of village schools). It also leads, therefore, indirectly as well as directly, to a decline in rural labor power. Much of this is offset by mechanization (a reason for the decline in the first place), but it also causes some agricultural land to become uncultivated and some agricultural activities to end.

A major cause of the migration is financial difficulties: only 20% of recently migrated people reported having enough land and animals with which to secure to sufficient means for subsistence. Nevertheless, given that work is not a particularly successful outcome of urban migration, one may wonder why it has continued in such high volumes—and notwithstanding the obvious push from (neoliberal) economic necessitates. Indeed, there are other motivations. Hope (for high level income jobs) remains an important motivating factor, but so do the general desire for a better social environment and specific wish to live with family. Other main reasons for migration are for health (older people), marriage (women) and education (youngsters). These obviously factor into return migration in various ways. For example, we found that one in five rural families have at least one member who had come back after going to the city for (school and/or university) education.

The most important preparation for migration is finding a job, and secondly, housing. Some migrants sell their own properties in the village to pay for migration expenses and to survive for a period after migration, or to purchase a property in the city, or for/towards start-up capital for entrepreneurship (setting up a small, typically retail business). Some 46% of recently migrated people still have land kept for agricultural reasons, with a tractor, animals, vegetable plot, and/or vineyard. The remaining 54% had either never had property or sold their own properties after migration. The agricultural properties of migrants are typically cultivated by their remaining family members in the village to enable them to continue to hold the rural assets. Other reasons for the relatively high level of continued landownership are poor land prices (especially dry land) and traditional values (indeed, families do not take kindly to selling land instead of giving it to a family member). Most migrants who do sell make the transaction before and/or soon after migration, this also indicating that property sale is used to finance to the migration process.

Family and kinship solidarity for and among migrants is strong for those arriving in the city. We found 19% of villages to have a fellow countryman association in cities and that 57% of these associations help migrants. Rural support continues, meanwhile, which becomes extended to mutual support. Overall, rural-to-urban solidarity comes mostly in the form of food and necessities for life, while urban-rural solidarity is mostly in form of remittances. Despite or alongside this support, however, migrants do not necessarily see themselves as permanent migrants.

One underlying basis of the return movement is psychological: 45% of migrants self-identify as belonging to their villages. Some 29% of rural-to-urban migrants imagine returning to the village at some point in the future. The largest group of these likely or potential returnees is that of retirees, while the second comprises those who have earned enough (so they are thinking of retiring from urban-based employment and, generally, returning to farm).

Putting down roots after migration

When migrants cannot find a suitable job they look for other alternatives to survive. One these is through increased their labor value on the market. We found 30% of all migrant households to have one member who had developed a profession after migration. Education and achieving a professional qualification (diploma) is the usual method for this. Although impressive, however, this remains a minority option and poverty much more widespread.

If assume to a daily income of $4.3 as the poverty criterion, then, calculating from the family income reported in interviews, 41% of recent migrant families are poor. In these families, according to our data, the average per capita income is 60% of the nationwide average. If a family cannot escape poverty, the children will not get adequate education and the family will not benefit from social resources beyond basic aid for survival. A third of the families who migrated in the last twenty years, receive at least one item and an average of 1.7 items of social aid. The main aid type is for health (a Green Card, which gains them access to free health services), followed by heating and then food aid (in the form of reimbursements for bills paid, organized donation schemes, etc.). In these families in receipt of social aid, the average number of working people number is 1.1—indicating that these people work but cannot enough money and/or work out of the main social security system. Poverty amongst the employed thus extends to migrant families. If income and aid are not sufficient to survive, families borrow. Some 27% of migrant families survive through the use of credit, the interest payments on which bring further hardships, of course. Eventually, if things become too difficult and they cannot survive in the city, they have the alternative of rural return. We found over half (56%) of those migrants considering going back were doing so because of their difficult situation, and almost a half (44%) of them had their own house to go back to.

After migration: rural-urban relations, return migration and dual life

Although there are many combinations of multi-place living, these can be characterized for convenience in terms of the rural-urban binary as "dual life." This represents a different situation from that of traditional migration. Essentially, the locus of the rural family lies in both rural and urban environments. The largest category of people leading the dual life is the retired who live in the city in the winter and live in go back to the village for the summer (with spring and fall variable, largely depending on the climate/weather). People in the higher income group are similar to the retired in this sense of seasonally based residence, although the rural movement may be not to a village of origin but to the location of a second home. Among rural families, we found that of the 11% that have at least one flat/house in the city, most (88%) are leading a seasonally defined dual life. This indicates that this group of the dual lifers are relatively wealthy. Overall, the rising number of retired people (as a function of population increase and longer life expectancy) combined with higher income levels and the difficulties of urban life (as discussed) are the primary reasons for the rising prevalence of this dual life style.

As noted, a significant proportion of migrants maintain their rural ties, which render reciprocal and continuity of rural-urban relations. According to our research, 58% of migrant households have family members in the village, and 39% have property (dwelling and/or land). In addition to the reasons given (above), they maintain these assets as an option for when life in the city becomes difficult in cities; as a facility to use during the summer (a place to stay/live); or else as a source of income (either through renting or cultivating the land, or a combined crop-share agreement). The people who live in a town or city and do farming may be placed in a specific category. These are urban migrants who hold their rural assets specifically for agricultural purposes. Some 7% of all urban migrant households continue to farm in the village; for 2% agriculture is their main occupation, while for the other 5% the village farm provides a supplementary income source.

Rural land is not just maintained by urban dwellers: another urban-to-rural movement is that of capital investment as urban migrants purchase land for others, mostly family members, (who may or may not themselves be urban migrants). We found that 5% of migrant households had bought land and/or buildings in the village. Parallel to the expectations of villagers, also, approximately one of four of the recent migrants plan to go back to their former village or homeland. Of course many will not—just as some will who do not plan to—but this potential rural-to-urban movement can certainly be expected to continue, with ongoing implications for rural life and agriculture, and also for urban populations and problems. Elderly people and retires have the idea of going back to villages more than younger people and those still in employment, but plans to return migrate are not differentiated by income level. On the other hand, different income groups do have different reasons to live in summer or fall down the job.

One of the best known material relations between rural and urban is that of food flow, mainly in solidarity or kinship relations. This flow is not so extensive, however, and the main reasons for it, in fact, are healthy nutrition, so that people can consume their own (family) produce and maintain their dietary habits, rather than economic. Some 7% of migrants receive traditional food from the village, 2% of them make it at home and 89% buy their food (the remainder subsist by other means, such as support from family in the city and food aid). Against this, however, traditional food-making in villages is also declining as the market penetrates this area of life in parallel with increasing rural incomes.

Table 2. Village number, population and average village size changes (1965–2008)

		1965 -1970	1970 -1975	1975 -1980	1980 -1985	1985 -1990	1990 - 2000	2000 - 2008	1965 -2008
Village Number Changes	No.	352	88	28	-93	148	1,193	-1,273	443
	%	1.0%	0.2%	0.1%	-0.3%	0.4%	3.3%	-3.4%	1.2%
Village Population Changes	No.	-231	1,584	1,316	-978	-636	703	-6,062	-4,304
	%	-1.0%	7.2%	5.6%	-3.9%	-2.7%	3.0%	-25.2%	-19.3%
Average Village Size Changes	No.	-13	43	36	-25	-20	-2	-146	-127
	%	-2.0%	6.9%	5.5%	-3.7%	-3.1%	-0.3%	-22.6%	-20.3%

Source: Calculated from TUIK 1965–2008 population censuses and address-based population data

Migration and villages

Because of the urban migration of younger people and the return migration of older people, the village population is reducing in young age and number. According to TUIK data, the populations of 70% of villages is decreasing, 20%

staying at the same level, and 10% rising. Because of the population loss, the average village population size is decreasing and number of small villages rising (Table 2).

Middle-size villages are losing population the most, while growing villages are becoming urbanized through rural investment or integrated into expanding cities, which becomes another source of rural population loss. The rise in numbers of small villages can be seen all regions of the country, but as occurring at varying rates. In three regions (Mediterranean [in the south], Middle Anatolia and Southeast Anatolia) population loss declined after 2000 (in the Southeast due to specific circumstances related to the Kurdish conflict), and the population is actually higher than it was in 1965. The reasons for this are the introduction of year-round agriculture (with market entry, irrigation projects, etc.), tourism (national and international) and also high birth rates.

Finally, it is important to note that the largest proportion of internal migration is not urban but intercity. Although this does not necessarily impact greatly on demographics, it is obviously a major element of the social experience. One of distinctive characteristics of this migration is that of public employees (e.g. all newly qualified state health-workers—doctors and nurses—are posted, mostly in other cities from those in which they have trained). Clearly, this group of migrants is distinguished from rural migrants by employment and other (class, etc.) considerations.

Conclusion

According to the classical migration perspective, people permanently move from one place to another. Nowadays, however, movement may be realized in other ways. There may be more than a single movement involving more than one place and including return to the starting place. One type of living form involves seasonal migration, living in one place for a part of year and another for the rest of year. This involves a repeated rather than single return migration, and there may also be geographically and temporally more complex patterns, repeated or unique, especially if the unit of analysis is taken to be a group (e.g., family) rather than individual (which is certainly warranted to the extent that members share resources and in other ways show solidarity). Therefore, in order to understand these multi-place, multi occupation, multi-directional living forms, the concept of *movement* is more suitable than that of migration.

Although there are many reasons for an urban migration, the main one is to find a job, in another words, this is an economic movement. People go to another place (a city) since they need or desire a higher income. In this regard, in order to balance population distributions or find permanent solutions to urban migration-related problems, we have look to the employment problem. In the city, the inability of migrants to find jobs and gain sufficient income contributes to urban poverty. Almost all the poor only survive with aid, but this also helps to masks the problem, insofar as poverty aid reduces poverty numbers in statistics but does not and cannot solve poverty itself. Therefore, a proper livelihood policy approach (e.g., involving minimum crop price guarantees) should be to ensure opportunities for regular income and social security and pension rights. Currently, the number of the unemployed, poor and needy working for low wages is accumulating in urban environments, creating a rise in the army of reserve workers. This, of course, constitutes a pressure on wage levels, leading, in turn, to condition of permanent poverty. Indeed, our research has shown significant numbers of urban migrants who are both employed and also poor.

Today in Turkey, some rural settlements are growing while many are declining; this process signals both the development and disappearance of villages. To follow village (and hamlet) population changes carefully, further study of official statistics is required. This implies a stronger rural database, including old and new settlement names to better follow changes in time. Very generally, elderly and retired people exhibit a desire to move to rural areas, be it back to their homeland or to a new place (often as a development over time of a holiday home). This tendency needs more detailed research. On the one hand it promotes quality of life, with a natural life in a healthy and intrinsically sustainable environment; on the other hand, it increases the aged rural population, contributing to various economic and social issues.

Understanding empowering effects of the Kurdish Diaspora on women's agency in Sweden: An ontological paradox

Berivan Erbil[281]

Introduction

There is considerable literature pointing out the male-dominated structure of Kurdish society in which women's problems have never been prioritized (Mojab 2001, Bruinessen 2001, Alinia 2004, Gambetti 2005); yet there is still limited number of research on Kurdish women's problems. The existing studies focus on the ostensible (de jure) empowerment they gained, particularly among immigrant/diasporic Kurds. However, the lack of empowerment in practice generally sustains even if they acquire immigrant status or formal citizenship status in the West.

The concept of diaspora is intertwined with both homeland and host society's politics (Nielsen 2001). The disadvantaged members (i.e., women, LGBTs) of the Middle Eastern diasporas are generally assumed to be the ones who take the most benefit of the migrant transnational political orientation which provides them a platform to raise their voices for the first time (Nielsen 2003). However, previous research in Sweden demonstrates that their voice does not always raise significantly (Mojab 2001 & Alinia 2004). Referring to James Clifford's "diasporas think globally, live locally" approach (Clifford 1994, in Anthias 1998: 566), this article attempts to demonstrate that Kurdish Diaspora in Sweden both thinks and lives locally (namely 'patriarchally') in the context of women's agency. In the first part, based on the data obtained by five semi-structured, face-to-face in-depth interviews with Kurdish women from different backgrounds and direct observations in Diyarbakir, Turkey-where Kurdish population is quite high-the author analyzes patriarchal relations in the homeland. The second part reviews the recent studies on Kurdish women's (dis)empowerment within the diaspora, indicating the social, financial and political (dis)empowerment they gain particularly in Sweden. In the last part, the article examines how patriarchy is enacted and resisted by Kurdish women comparing their experiences at the homeland and the host land.

A Brief Overview of Women's (Dis)Empowerment at Homeland

In the literature, the Kurdish community is depicted as a patriarchal society (Mojab 2001 & Bruinessen 2001). Yet, the present studies also show that Kurdish movements(s) tend to give place to the feminist agenda more and more (Alinia 2004 & Tekin 2014). The question is whether this place is capable of generating Kurdish women's emancipation or not. Not only five Kurdish female interviewees, but random ten students, living in Diyarbakir with whom the author had informal conversations, also think that Kurdish movement in Turkey has not managed to liberate Kurdish women yet. They all agree on the idea that women

---

[281] Berivan Erbil is a master's degree student in the School of Global Studies in University of Gothenburg, Sweden. Email: erbil.berivan@gmail.com

are able to act freely compared to the previous years, but according to them, it cannot be called as the freedom but only progress:

"We do not claim that Kurdish movement have liberated us. Yes, the situation is better. However, it is not enough. In this system, women's empowerment is impossible. We have to change the system." (Deniz282, 46, teacher)

Regarding the views of the interviewees, the priority of nationalist ends over the gender issues underlies a major problem:

"Gender issues come before the problem of nationality. However, Kurdish men still have the difficulty to understand this." (Fatma, 48, sociologist)

Even though there is an increasing number of Kurdish activists and politicians who focus on varieties of the domestic violence against women, it seems that some women have already become the agents of patriarchy:

"We always listen our husbands. That is how we were raised. It is a matter of 'namus' (honor). We do not raise our voices even if we are oppressed. It is about our culture." (Arjin, 34, cleaning worker)

All of the interviewees stated that they had difficulties to communicate with men in their families including their fathers and husbands. What they mean by lack of communication is that their words are not respected. Furthermore, they always felt that they had to fight for what they wanted to be. In other words, they were not allowed to raise their voices, they knew that it was against 'the rules' (i.e. patriarchal rules). The story of Meryem, a 38-year-old woman of Kurdish origin constitutes one of the typical examples in the region. She was threatened to be reported due to her nationalist activities by her father when she refused to get married with a guy she did not like. After she got married, she was forced to have children, to stay at home and not to attend the school. She had to secretly study for the university entrance exam. When she wanted to have a voice regarding her sexuality; when she refused to sleep with her ex-husband, she was exposed to mental violence:

"When I refused to sleep with my ex-husband, he was not giving money even for a bread, he was leaving my children hungry. In a way, he was punishing us and I had no choice but to accept this situation." (Meryem, 38, working in Baglar Country Municipality)

Although this sample is quite small to bring about general results; considering the existing literature, it is detailed enough to demonstrate that despite the recent activities of the women organizations, most of the Kurdish women are still discouraged for empowerment before they go to abroad. Regarding the maintenance of patriarchal relations in different ways at the host society-which will be discussed in the next section-, it is important to mention that the subjugation of Kurdish women still exists at their home society and it is not easy to rupture those deep-rooted patriarchal relations even in a country which is famous for gender equality as Sweden.

---

[282] Fictive names are used in the article. Each interview lasted for about three hours.

The Home/Host Dichotomy in Swedish Context

The term of diaspora is "often limited to population categories that have experienced 'forceful or violent expulsion' processes (classically used about the Jews)" (Anthias 1998: 560). However, that kind of definition obscures transnational and heterogenous dimensions of diasporas. Similar to other social movements, diasporas are not homogenous as they are seen. Anthias argues that "The diaspora is constituted as much in difference and division as it is in commonality and solidarity" (1998: 564). Accordingly, Kurdish diaspora is not an exception. The reasons and results of internal divisions are especially important to understand the patriarchal aspects of Kurdish diaspora since women may experience two types of subordination at the same time: the one related to their class and to their ethnic group in the host society (Anthias 1998). Therefore, it is argued that internal divisions within Kurdish community may become strikingly visible particularly at the transnational level.

Swedish citizenship provides foreigners to have equal rights with Swedish people no matter which ethnic/religious background they originally have (Alinia 2004). However, de facto representation of Kurdish women in Sweden is greatly affected by the cultural essentialist discourses embedded in the institutions and Eurocentric tendencies of the society (Kaplan 1999). Seeing an educated-independent Kurdish woman can easily be newsworthy since the public opinion already has a tendency to 'help' and 'rescue' those 'needy' women (Akpinar 2003). It is generally envisaged by the orientalist attitudes, particularly towards immigrants with low-income level (Kaplan 1999). As women mostly constitute low-level job groups such as cleaning or factory laborers, they are the ones being exposed to this kind of discrimination the most (Mojab & Gorman 2007). Consequently, before enjoying the equal rights with Swedish citizens they firstly need to overcome the above-mentioned stereotypes.

On the other hand, it is true that transnational environment provides a more objective platform for the expression of Kurdish diaspora women's problems (Mojab & Gorman 2007). Additionally, most of them are already politicized when they migrate due to their nationalist struggles in Turkey. Hence, despite the above-mentioned difficulties, some of them achieve to be organized against the racist and sexist types of discrimination independently of male-dominated Kurdish associations. Yet, due to the lack of recognition and access to international projects, they face problems to receive funding or support from the NGOs (Mojab 2001).

Besides, it should also be noted that no matter how much they seek to integrate, the level of their 'public acclaim' depends mainly on the degree of inclusion of the migrants through integration policies at the host society. The exclusionary attitudes of the receiving countries sometimes overwhelm the inclusionary ones. Furthermore, as Yural-Davis (1997) reminds that "multiculturalist integration policies simultaneously include and exclude immigrants and/or minorities by "locating them in marginal spaces and secondary markets, while reifying their boundaries"' (In Akpinar 2003: 17). This mostly results in the polarization between 'immigrant' and 'host' cultures or even explicit cultural fundamentalism in the eyes of Western host societies such as Sweden.

The more they integrate, the more their cultural difference is visible and discriminated. Eventually, they turn into 'symbolic foreigners' with judgmental eyes staring at them rather than citizens with equal rights.

Three Pillars of the Alleged (Dis)Empowerment in Sweden

The idea of women empowerment (or emancipation) is simply related to the re-allocation of power in the society by enabling the oppressed (i.e women) against the oppressor (i.e men). In this article, women's empowerment is defined in terms of the (re)creation of organized women's power including opposition and defense against the gender inequality in every sphere of the society. Therefore, it is directly related to the concept of consciousness. What is meant by consciousness here is that a woman is aware of her self-conception; her social, economic and political rights and capacity to achieve her goals if she has any. As noted above, de jure improvements do not automatically translate into de facto changes. Hence, in the case of Kurdish diaspora women, empowerment refers to the acknowledgement of women's capacity to become active agents not only in their nationalist struggle but also in their private spheres (Gokalp 2010: 563) by challenging the patriarchal relations both in their ethnic community and the receiving country.

In the literature, the scope of women's empowerment in Kurdish diaspora is primarily analyzed in terms of the financial means. The relative attainment of financial success of Kurdish women in the host land is generally regarded as the evidence to claim their emancipation (Cakmak 2010, Alinia 2004, Akpinar 2003). Although economic independence or the rise of economic power might bring about social improvements, recent studies demonstrate that they do not always walk together (Akpinar 2003); money does not necessarily bring empowerment at home (Akpinar 2003). Since the patriarchal relations remain almost the same in the house, it would be too optimistic to assume that financial gains at the outside provide the freedom at home. Moreover, in most cases women are not well aware that they have the capacity to take the advantage of their emergent economic independence mostly because they tend to underestimate their own labor-value. According to Cakmak (2010), the majority of the women undervalue the importance of their jobs (such as cleaning or babysitting) for several reasons. Firstly, they have always been performing those actions without receiving a salary resulting in the internalization of their 'inferior' labour force. Secondly, 'their men' often attempt to prevent them from expressing the question of equality, which can easily be a byproduct of the financial empowerment, at the house. Thirdly, women can be even more under control of the male family members due to these men's desire to substitute increased suppression of women's acts for the diminution of their pre-existing financial power (particularly if they experience a loss of status). In one way or another, socioeconomic gains of Kurdish diaspora women at the public sphere is likely to remain invisible at their domestic realm.

Political empowerment which may be defined as increased access to the political decision-making processes in the civil society (Gokalp 2010) is another matter of debate. It is assumed that the war between Kurdish guerrilla groups and the Turkish army has already led to the acquirement of rights-based and/or justice-based consciousness for Kurdish women, particularly in the southeastern part of Turkey (Gokalp 2010). Although it is an important gain as a part of women's emancipation, that kind of mentioned awareness does not necessarily pave the way for political empowerment. The degree of their politicization is limited considering the ongoing domination of male-leading figures in their mobilization (Mojab & Gorman 2007). It should also be indicated that not all conflict-affected Kurdish women have turned into political activists. The increased political awareness of Kurdish women often refers to the rhetoric that 'their men' (i.e., son, husband, brother) fight for their liberation (Gokalp 2010).

Yet, due to the liberal means of the Kurdish diasporic context, not only the Kurdish nationalist movement has contributed to the development of their ethnic identity but Western feminist movements have also affected the reconstruction of their gender identity (Mojab & Gorman 2007). But is the existence of a few leading women enough to claim a crack in the male political monopoly in the Kurdish society? Even though they often obtain vast opportunities for education and work in the receiving country resulting in somewhat of an acceleration in their political empowerment, they are still more respected as family members (mothers, wives) rather than 'individuals' (Mojab 2001). Their entrance into the politics mostly initially confronts their (future) husbands and fathers. In return, as in the example of Sweden, Kurdish women tend to gather under the name of 'immigrant women' instead of 'Kurdish' (Mojab 2001). However, this 'temporal' solution creates a vicious cycle on diasporic women's side since it does nothing but forms a delay to unveil their unique problems at the transnational level.

Social empowerment is seen as the last component of the women's empowerment. On the one hand, the ability that the Kurdish feminist agenda has acquired to position itself among Western women organizations and challenge the transnational space in which it takes place, demonstrates that there is a sort of organized women's power to alter the hegemonic relations such as the International Kurdish Women's Studies Network or Radio Dengi Jinan (Women's Voice Radio) based in Stockholm (Mojab & Gorman 2007). Yet, apart from these international examples, women are either explicitly or implicitly regarded as 'the outsiders' in their own translocal organizations (i.e. Kurdish diasporic associations). To put it simply, while men can easily feel at home and socialize in the associations, women do not feel that confident due to the loss of their original social networks.

Although the argument can be made that men also suffer because of such deprivation, it should also be noted that the expenses of losing status are not the same for Kurdish women and men. As noted before, existing gender inequality in the society can become aggravated due to the potential status loss of men (Alinia 2004, Mojab 2001). Furthermore, the administration of many diasporic associations is already dominated by men (Gill & Begikhani &Hague 2012). Women's contributions are either underestimated or ignored by the leading male figures of such associations. One example can be in the fact that few men have shown up in the first anniversary celebration of Radio Dengi Jinan in Stockholm in 2002 (Mojab & Gorman 2007).

Quadruple Oppression

Considering the historicity of the subjugation of Kurdish women, the author argues that the experiences of Kurdish diaspora women can be described as the quadruple oppression. As Yuksel (2006) indicates, when Kurdish women migrated to Europe from Turkey, their double marginalized position accompanied them on the journey. They were not Turkish citizens but 'the other' in Turkey and this otherness has constituted the first degree of marginalization. Furthermore, Kurdish resistance movement also considered their works through sexist perspectives. In other words, they were not properly welcomed either by the feminist movement or by the Kurdish movement. Following their migration process, this time Kurdish women have started to cope with orientalist and racist stereotypical notion of Middle Eastern women (Alinia 2004) paving the way for the third and fourth level of patriarchal oppression they have been exposed to.

"They deal with their non-state status, the politics of state-seeking projects and immigration as well as settlement projects of the host-land:each of these reproduce the patriarchy in different ways."(Mojab & Gorman 2007: 77)

This is best exemplified with a case study conducted in Sweden. According to recent findings, there are "two different types of oppression that Kurdish women have to face with: being a Kurdish migrant and being a female Kurdish migrant" (Alinia 2004: 120). It is understood that their previous dilemma has become even more complicated: in addition to their initial problems, intertwined orientalist and sexist approaches have formed their new transnational stigmatization.Before becoming a diaspora member, they were only 'local aliens' in Turkey; after their status changed in Sweden they have now become 'transnational aliens'.

Preventive formal policies against segregation of immigrants do not guarantee their integration in the society. As nationalism and masculinity intersect and affect each other (Bourdieu 2001), the reflections of long-lasting orientalist and sexist stereotypes matter in practice. Furthermore, gossip and stigma in immigrant neighborhoods have substantial effects on the perpetuation of the feeling of 'otherness'. As in the cases of 'honor' killing, women who attempt to act freely, i.e. arriving home late may easily become victims of slander (Akpinar 2003). Consequently, many of them prefer to 'accept' their so-called traditional position and even start to control each other by promoting honour/shame codes in their community to 'empower' themselves. For instance, those who work outside of home may see no harm in the fact that when both they and their husbands return home, women are the ones who do the domestic work (Alinia 2004).Therefore, some of them internalize the discursive perceptions (re)produced by their own community and the host community in order to avoid stigmatization in the public sphere.

In Bourdieuian terms, this internalization can be defined as the following: "the habitus cognitively replicates a field of objects that preexists and structures the habitus itself" (Samuel 2013: 400). In other words, 'the oppressed' accepts the stabilization of power relations for the sake of her/his own ontological and physical security. Accordingly, Kurdish diaspora women may paradoxically become the agents of the patriarchal oppression through which they are subordinated. However, such attitude inherently obscures the achievement of resistance and hence indirectly disempower them preventing their emancipation and creating self-imprisoning identities.

Conclusion

This article has not intended to underestimate the existing progress on behalf of Kurdish women's empowerment. However, the author aimed at pointing out the inconsistencies and deficiencies of the Western and Kurdish perspectives underlying Kurdish diaspora women's disempowerment by reviewing the patriarchal relations in Turkey and Sweden.

Despite the significant improvements in the gender issues, the patriarchal nature of Kurdish nationalism keeps its chair stonewalling the achievement of women's empowerment in the Kurdish community. Women's emancipation has been mostly seen as the byproduct, not the goal in itself (Gambetti 2005). In other words, the unmasking and transformation of the patriarchal structures have denoted that nationalist ends have had higher priority than those 'secondary problems'. And the consequences of this patriarchal domination on women's empowerment are still effective at the host societies such as Sweden.

References

Alinia, M. (2004). Spaces of Diasporas: Kurdish identities, experiences of otherness and politics of belonging, Unpublished doctoral dissertation, Department of Sociology Göteborg University

Akpinar, A. (2003). The Honour/Shame Complex Revisited: Violence Against Women in the Migration Context, Women's Studies International Forum, 26 (5): 425-442

Anthias, F. (1998). Evaluating 'Diaspora': Beyond Ethnicity?, Sociology, 32(3): 557-580

Bourdieu, Pierre (2001). Masculine Domination, Cambridge: Polity Press

Bruinessen, M. V. (2001). "From Adela Khanum to Leyla Zana: Women as Political Leaders in Kurdish History", in Mojab, S. (eds) (2001) Women of A Non-State Nation: The Kurds, California: Mazda Publishers

Cakmak, S. (2010). Değişen Hayatların Görünmez Sahipleri: Göçmen Kadınlar (Invisible Owners of the Changing Lives: Migrant Women), Fe Dergi, 2(2): 50-64 (in Turkish)

Gambetti, Z. (2005). The conflictual (trans)formation of the public sphere in urban space: the case of Diyarbakir.New Perspectives on Turkey 32: 43–71.

Gill, A. K., Begikhani, N. and Hague, G. (2012) 'Honour'-based violence in Kurdish communities, Women's Studies International forum 35: 75-85

Gokalp, D. (2010). A gendered analysis of violence, justice and citizenship: Kurdish women facing war and displacement in Turkey, Women's Studies International Forum (33): 561-569

Kaplan, C., Alarcon, N. and Moallem, M. (1999) Between Woman and Nation: Nationalisms, Transnational Feminisms, and the State, Durham and London: Duke University Press

Mojab, S. (2001). (eds) Women of a Non-State Nation: The Kurds: Mazda Publishers

Mojab, S. and Gorman, R. (2007). Dispersed Nationalism: War, Diaspora and Kurdish Women's Organizing, Journal of Middle Eastern Women's Studies, 3 (1): 58-85

Nielsen- Eva K. (2001). Transnational political practices and the receiving state: Turks and Kurds in Germany and the Netherlands, Global Networks, 1(3): 261-281

Nielsen- Eva K. (2003). The Politics of Migrants' Transnational Political Practices, International Migration Review, 37 (3): 760-786

Samuel, C. (2013). Symbolic Violence and Collective Identity: Pierre Bourdieu and the Ethics of Resistance, Social Movement Studies: Journal of Social, Cultural and Political Protest, 12 (4): 397-413

Tekin, G. (2014). Özgürleşen Ruhlar: Kürt Gerilla Hareketi (The Liberatory Spirits: Kurdish Guerilla Movement), Istanbul: Belge Press (in Turkish)

Yuval-Davis, N. (1997). Women, Citizenship and Difference, Feminist Review, No.57, Citizenship: Pushing the Boundaries: 4-27

Yuksel, M. (2006). The Encounter of Kurdish Women with Nationalism in Turkey, Middle Eastern Studies, Vol. 42, No.5: 777-802.

Contributor or Barrier: Role of the Kurdish Diaspora in Turkey's European Union Accession Process[283]

Şevin Gülfer Sağnıç[284]

Introduction

"The momentous events around the world increasingly involve international migration" (Castles & Miller, 1998, p. 5).Stephen Castles and Mark J. Miller explain the character of the international as a part of a "transnational revolution that is reshaping societies and politics around the globe" (Castles & Miller, 1998, p. 5). Diaspora communities which form as the direct result of the international migration process constitute a driving force for restructuring world politics. Trans-national activities of diaspora members change the meaning of local and global; and conflicts no longer stay in their national border but reach the international arena.

One of the frequently studied diaspora communities is the Kurdish diaspora in Europe, mainly comprised of guest workers and political refugees from Turkey. The Kurdish diaspora's activities in Europe were instrumental to Kurdish identity formation: television channels served as tool for national awareness, non-political Kurds in Europe were politicised and the relatively liberal conditions in Europe compare to those in Turkey had been used to improve the Kurdish literature and history writing. Arrival of Kurdish migrants also brought the Kurdish question into Europe. The Kurdish question which arose due to mass killings, forced evacuations and displacement of Kurds in Turkey was no longer limited to the domestic politics of Turkey. Kurdish diaspora organizations, through violent and non-violent means, promoted their cause in Europe and forced European governments and the European Union (EU) to become a party in this conflict. Meanwhile, Turkey is trying to become a member of the EU. The negotiations for accession took longer than expected. After 40 years of efforts, in 2004, Turkey finally achieved candidacy status. However, the accession process in open-ended with many barriers such as the Kurdish issue. In the annual progress reports of the EU on Turkey's improvement in the accession path, the volume and emphasis on the Kurdish issue are increasing by time as a function of the diaspora activities in Europe.

The main question of this paper is "what is the role of diaspora activities in considering Turkey's accession to the EU?" The answer to this question is very important for general international migration research by aiding scholars to grasp the changes in world politics due to international migration. Secondly, as indicated by Wahlbeck (2002, p.221), diaspora studies are helpful for closing the gap

[283] I am sincerely grateful to Dr. Amanda Klekowski von Koppenfels for her aspiring guidance and constructive comments and to Dr. Elise Féron for her support and enlightining comments.

[284] Şevin Gülfer Sağnıç is a M.A. candidate in Bogazici University Political Science and International Relations Department, Istanbul; and has a M.A. degree from University of Kent International Migration programme, Brussels-Belgium. Postal address: Oguzhan Cad. Mimoza Sok. No: 3-14 34843 Adatepe- Maltepe, Istanbul, Turkey. E-mail: gssagnic@gmail.com

between before and after migration analysis and understanding the transnational reality in which refugees live and thus showing the continuity in the migration phenomenon . Thirdly, it is important to understand the abilities of the refugees in their host communities. While the Kurdish diaspora in Europe has been studied sociologically and politically, there is lack of study to investigate the relationship between the transnational sources and actors of the Kurdish question in Turkey and the effect on the Turkey's EU accession process.

This study argues that the Kurdish diaspora in Europe utilized Turkey's EU accession process to gain more democratic rights in Turkey, which has had a negative influence on Turkey's chances for joining the EU. The diaspora is both a barrier and a contributor for the accession process; it wants Turkey to join the EU and spends effort on the continuation of the process but it does not want to Turkey to join without solving the Kurdish question in a democratic way and so barriers the process in terms of enforcing the EU to not to accept the Turkey's membership without a peaceful solution to the Kurdish question. The paper aims to analyse the role of the Kurdish diaspora and its activities in Turkey's European Union accession process through focusing on the importation of the Kurdish question into Europe through Kurdish migration. The main objective is revealing the consequences of the diaspora activities in this context.

The correlation between the changes in the attitude of the EU and the advancement of the diaspora constitutes the main pillar of the argument. The increasing influential capacity, and change in the means and opportunities exposes the advancement of the Kurdish diaspora in the transnational political strategies. In order to study this correlation the Human Rights and Protection of Minorities chapters in the progress reports before (1998, 1999, 2000) and after (2011, 2012, 2013) the advancement of the Kurdish diaspora will be analysed. The correlation between changes and improvements in the reports and the diaspora activities constitute an important indicator for the influential strength, consequently the discussions will demonstrate how the process had been effected by the diaspora activities. Interviews with the representatives of the Brussels Kurdish Institute, The Kurdish Bureau and the Nûçe TV will be used to analyse the motivations and expectations of the Kurdish diaspora organizations.

The evolution of the diaspora activities and its advancement

The Kurdish diaspora is not homogenous; different political, economic and sociological conditions created different migration waves and thus different profiles within the diaspora. The character of the diaspora activities also changed by time and so its effectiveness.

After the 1980 military coup in Turkey political refugees arrived to Europe and brought the conflict with them; in the other words the Kurdish issue had been exported to Europe. Political activities that led to domestic disruption and violence between Turkish and Kurdish communities in the Kurdish diaspora subsequently forced the EU to take a position (Barkey & Fuller, 1998, p. 165); the Kurdish question became a domestic issue for the European states.

Despite the fact that there are different Kurdish organizations in Europe, such as Rizgari or Kawa, PKK was the major organization that shaped the diaspora (Başer, 2011, p. 15). In the 1980s and 1990s the PKK's ideology consisted of a combination of Marxism and Kurdish nationalism. The PKK defined as a militarist separatist group by European states (Eccarius-Kelly, 2014, p. 65). Its activities in Europe by the exiled cadres were in line with its ideology and tactics in Turkey (Eccarius-Kelly, 2014, p. 65). The PKK conducted activities as organising petitions and campaigns, violent and non-violent mass demonstrations and protests, sit-ins, highway blockades, hunger strikes and self-immolation (Başer, 2011, p. 15). But the violent activities were placed on the front burner. In the late 1980s in the Western Europe, twenty people died due to the conflict among Turkish-born Kurds; according to the police the PKK was responsible for these deaths (Gunter, 1991, p. 13). Because of the killings in Sweden between 1984 and 1985, nine Kurds were held under "commune arrest" for several years (Gunter, 1991, p. 13). Consequently, the PKK was added to the terrorist organization list in Sweden in 1984 and the PKK leader Abduallah Öcalan's entry into the country was refused (Gunter, 1991, p. 13). When Swedish Prime Minister Olof Palme was assassinated on 28 February 1986, officials including Stockholm Chief of Police Hans Holmer were convinced that the PKK was responsible for the murder (Gunter, 1991, p. 13). The police forces were breaking into every Kurdish apartment, not only in Sweden but in all of Europe (Lelyveld, 1986). Another assassination in 1988 led once again to accusations against the PKK. Siegfried Wielsputz, the West German consular affairs attaché was killed in Paris. For a long time these violent activities associated with the PKK barriered the diaspora's ability to make the EU take a stance against Turkey on the Kurdish issue. Even it made a reverse effect.

When the Kurdish question became a domestic problem in the Europe, European countries offered financial aid and political asylum in exchange pacification of the PKK (Gunter, 1991, p. 16). As a reaction to Europe's negative attitude, and pacification attempts towards PKK the Kurdish movement adopted a more hostile attitude. Öcalan argued that European countries are no different from the Turkish state, both of whom try to assimilate Kurds and corrupt the PKK; the "Brussels circle", by which he means the institutions and members of the EU, was fellow NATO member and its aim was protecting Turkish territorial integrity. Kurds should have had party and military training in the "war zone" and struggle against Turkey in order to avoid from European trap (Gunter, 1991, p. 16).

In the meantime, Kurdish intellectuals continued to mobilize the Kurdish migrants; get institutionalized; and politicize the guest worker organizations. The Paris Kurdish Institute, the Kurdish Parliament in Exile (*Parlamana Kurdîstane Lî Derveyî Welat-* PKDW); the Kurdistan National Congress (*Kongreya Neteweyî ya Kurdistanê-* KNK); and the television channel MED TV can be listed as the main bodies created by the diaspora in this migration period.

The arrest of the PKK leader Abdullah Öcalan in February 1999 became a turning point for Kurds. In his defence, Öcalan explained the PKK's objective as obtaining political and cultural rights for Kurds instead of an independent Kurdish state (Turkey vs. Abdullah Öcalan, 1999). It was an ideological shift for the PKK. The new political reality made structural and strategic adjustments unavoidable. The European diaspora was affected deeply by the ideological shift; subsequently they started to adopt the discourse of national minority rights instead of independence (Khayati, 2008, p. 87). Eccarius-Kelly explains the new agenda of the Kurds in Europe as: "Diaspora Kurdish protesters shifted away from separatist articulations to more culturally based grievances such as the right to study and speak their ethnic language, to select Kurdish names for their children, to operate Kurdish TV and radio programs, and to openly perform regional cultural practices" (Eccarius-Kelly, 2014, p. 7). The change in the agenda resulted in the transformation of the structure of the diaspora political organizations in favour of transnational social movement organizations (Eccarius-Kelly, 2014, p. 8). The aggressive protests were mostly replaced by non-violent social movement activities. In terms of considering themselves legitimate representatives of the Kurds, publicly presenting a unified front, pushing for the recognition of their agenda, developing connections with allied actors and seeking new political opportunities for achieving acceptance, the Kurdish diaspora assumed the role of a typical transnational social movement (Khayati, 2008, p. 87). The early claims of the Kurdish diaspora, such as independence and socialism, had low receptivity at the EU level. Negative attitudes towards Europe as well as legitimacy problems for its institutions and violent activities were the main internal propensities that decreased the diaspora's access to the EU institutions. The changes in ideology and activities of the Kurdish intellectuals increased its access the EU institutions mainly by defending human rights in Turkey, an issue that has very high receptivity in the EU. The Kurdish approach renounced violence and embraced peaceful activities, resulting in increased legitimacy, power and effectiveness. Slowly after this consolidation the diaspora's effect became visible in the EU- Turkey relations. But before moving to its effects the current position of the diaspora should discussed.

The Kurdish movement is generally regarded as a trap for Turkey's EU accession process. Yet the reality is far from this belief. Instead of putting an end to Turkey's integration dream, the Kurdish movements generally approach this process as an opportunity for democratization in Turkey. In other words, they are instrumentalizing the process in order to empower their struggle for more rights. Additionally, Kurds generally see Europe as the third party responsible for the conflict. Derviş Ferho, the head of the Brussels Kurdish Institute, says "it is the European states who drew borders in the middle of the Kurdistan" (Ferho, 2014). Amed Dicle, a well-known journalist from the Kurdish television channel Nûçe, adds "the current situation of Kurdistan is the result of European policies. This is the main reason that the powerful decision-making mechanisms in Europe refuse to do anything to change the status-quo" (Dicle, 2014). The founder of the Brussels-based organization the Kurdish Bureau for Liaison and Information (*Buroya Kurdî*), Pervîn Jamîl says, "I want Turkey to be member of the EU because it will mean that Turkey has fulfilled the criteria, and then by being a part of the Union it will be have to protect democracy" (Jamîl, 2014). If Turkey enters the EU without solving the Kurdish problem, it will also use European power to supress Kurds, and actually this is what Turkey hopes" (Dicle, 2014). This concern explains the Kurdish desire to put the Kurdish issue on the top of the accession agenda. These motivations do not stay on the discursive level. In 2004 a leading Kurdish diaspora organization, The Paris Kurdish Institute prepared an announcement which was signed by 200 Kurdish intellectuals living in Europe and Turkey just before the EU summit in which they explained their support and expectations from the process (BIA News Center, 2004). As addition to this letter, Leyla Zana's letter to EU officials such as then President of the EC Romano Prodi and the EU term president Anders Rasmussen to demand a negotiation calendar for Turkey proves that the support of the Kurds for the process is not only theoretical but also active.

The Kurdish organizations desire Turkish membership once Turkey meets the criteria. In sum, currently Kurds do not want to halt the accession process; instead they want it to continue. But they want to reach their objectives at the end of the process, and in order to do so they are trying to be an actor in the EU-Turkey negotiations. They also see Europe as a natural actor in the Kurdish issue, so they want European governments to pay more attention to the region. The activities of the Kurdish diaspora should be analysed from this angle.

Progress reports and the Kurdish issue

Progress reports constitute the main documents about the accession process. They also provide a good illustration of the EU's stance on particular issues such as the Kurdish issue. In the first report in 1998 there was limited reference to the Kurdish issue and Kurds; the Kurdish issue was seen to be bounded with terrorism and the PKK. EU support for Turkey in combating terrorism was underlined several times. The report criticizes regular disappearances, torture and extra-judicial executions, but also states that these abuses, mostly, had occurred in the army's and government's reactions to the problems in the southeast. Despite the EU's sensitivity on human rights, this emphasis gives the impression that the EU followed a state security-centred approach. After this empowering period of the Kurdish diaspora in Europe we observe drastic change in the EU's attitude towards the Kurdish issue in the progress reports.

The report in 1999 has a special importance due to the capture of Öcalan on February 15th 1999. Widespread Kurdish protests took place in more than 20 European and Western cities including, featuring self-immolation and hostage taking (Claffey, Bugua, & Sisk, 1999). Such events brought the Kurdish issue into European agenda. The following progress report in 2000 again dealt with the Kurdish issue under the general evaluation of rights. The decreased tension between PKK and Turkey, due to postponing the death sentence of Öcalan and PKK's declaration of ceasefire.

Nevertheless when we come to the 2011 there was a specific part in the progress report for the Kurdish issue called "the situation in the east and the south-east". It should also be noted that the scope of analysis also included the eastern provinces which are relatively less problematic as compared to the south-east. Another symbolic change had been made to the part about *Newroz*; it had been written in Kurdish. (The European Commission, 2011, p. 27). This was important because when the commission published this report, the letters "q, x, w" were forbidden in Turkey to eliminate writing in Kurdish.

Additionally, the focus on the problems regarding the Kurdish issue shifted away from state security concerns due to terrorist activities, and towards the practice of democratic rights by the Kurdish population. However, the EU continued to condemn the PKK's activities in the region. The human rights violations had not been seen as unintended but rather avoidable consequences as they started to be analysed to understand the essence of the Kurdish issue. Police and security forces' attitudes towards demonstrators and legal proceedings on charges of terrorist propaganda were criticized; protests and protestors began to be seen as related to the civil society and human rights instead of the PKK (The European Commission, 2011, p. 27).

One of the most important points of the reports in 2011, 2012, and 2013 was the more overtly pursued stance towards arrest due to the PKK/KCK membership. The report defined the arrested people as journalists, academicians, students, and human rights defenders (The European Commission, 2013, p. 15) rather than members of an armed group.[285] The last reports offered some solutions for local governance, education in the mother tongue, the KCK arrests, and the concept of citizenship. These issues actually constitute the main demands of the Kurds in Turkey (Al Jazeera, 2013). The indirect general recommendations were replaced by direct criticisms, and solutions were recommended in the latest reports right after the Kurdish diaspora settled its institutions and activities. Some Turkish commentators and think tanks such as Bilgesam pointed to alternative information sources of the commission as the main reason of this pro-Kurdish attitude, claiming that the EU was not being informed objectively (Dede & Kaya, 2013). Similarly, in his press release on the 2013 progress report, the minister of EU affairs, Mevlüt Çavuşoğlu, stated that there are efforts to instrumentalise the EU-Turkey relations and that the EU was supporting these efforts (Çavuşoğlu, 2014). Casier says that without the activities of the Kurdish diaspora there would not have been such an emphasis on the Kurdish issue (Casier, 2011, p. 11).

The emphasis on the Kurdish issue increased by time and the attitude of the EU towards the issue changed. Özsöz states that in the first reports the Kurdish issue was seen as more politically related with the terror and explained within the armed conflict framework, but in the following years the Kurdish issue's economic, social and cultural aspects had been analysed also (Özsöz, 2012, p. 11). As it is shown in this part, the Kurdish issue was separated from terrorism context, the Kurdish issue had been included into different chapters, the definition of the Kurdish issue had been introduced separately from terrorism, and Kurdish words had been included into the report. The demands of the Kurdish movement were proposed as a solution to the Kurdish question. All these changes, including the evolution and the consolidation of the Kurdish diaspora, took place within this short time frame between 2000 and 2012.

Conclusion

This study set out to explore the role of the diaspora activities in transnational politics with the example of the Kurdish diaspora in Turkey's EU accession process. The discussion showed that Kurds are instrumentalizing the process instead of being against the Turkey's accession and the diaspora shapes its activities in this regard. The changes in the means that it employs and the discursive change turned the Kurdish diaspora into an insider group in the EU.

---

[285] These arrested people charged as the members of an armed group, on the base of the Turkish Criminal Code Article 314 (European Commission, 2013, p.15).

The Kurdish diaspora in Europe transformed from a separatist terrorist organization to a social movement. The human rights discourse empowered its institutions. Activities and the scope of these activities widened and broadened; they publish reports, prepare monthly newsletters, organize conferences in the EU parliament, and do lobbying. As it is shown in this paper there is also a shift in the EU's approach towards the Kurdish issue. This study does not ignore other elements (newly opening chapters, increasing relations between Turkey and the EU, beginning the accession negotiations since 2005, and the steady increase in the scope and page amounts of the reports) that co-created the increase in reference to the Kurds. Nevertheless, the analysis in this paper showed that there was an increase in the emphasis on the Kurdish issue together with a change in mentality, and these positive changes for Kurds occurred in parallel with the diaspora's improvement and in the line of the diaspora's objectives.

"Diasporas powerfully embody broader trends in the changing nature of nation-states" says Steven Vertovec (2005). Indeed, diasporas are creating new political realities and they are among the most influential actors in these realities. This also what the Kurdish diaspora did in the European context.

References

Al Jazeera. (2013, December 26). *Kürtlerin ana talepleri* [The main demands of Kurds]. Retrieved July 26, 2014, from Al Jazeera: http://www.aljazeera.com.tr/dosya/kurtlerin-ana-talepleri

Başer, B. (2011). *Kurdish Political Activism in Europe with a Particular Focus on Great Britain.* Berlin: Berghof Peace Support and Centre for Just Peace and Democracy.

BBC News. (1999, February 17). *Kurds protests sweep Europe.* Retrieved June 22, 2014, from BBC News: http://news.bbc.co.uk/2/hi/europe/280355.stm#top

Casier, M. (2011). The Politics of Solidarity: The kurdish Question in the European Parliament. In M. Casier, & J. Jongerden, *Nationalisms and Politics in Turkey. Political Islam, Kemalism* (pp. 197-217). New York: Routledge.

Castles, S., & Miller, M. J. (1998). *The Age of Migration.* New York: The Guilford Press.

Claffey, M., Bugua, M. M., & Sisk, R. (1999, February 17). *Kurds protests capture with violence, threats.* Retrieved June 22, 2014, from New York Daily News: http://www.nydailynews.com/archives/news/kurds-protest-capture-violence-threats-article-1.825808

CNN. (1999, February 17). *Kurds seize embassies, wage violent protests across Europe.* Retrieved June 22, 2014, from CNN: http://edition.cnn.com/WORLD/europe/9902/17/ocalan.protest.01/

Çavuşoğlu, M. (2014, March 13). *Statement by Mevlüt Çavuşoğlu on the European Parliament Resolution on Turkey 2013 Progress Report.* Retrieved from Republic of Turkey, Ministry for EU Affairs: http://www.ab.gov.tr/index.php?p=49475&l=2

Dede, O., & Kaya, E. (2013, October 31). *AB'nin 2013 İlerleme Raporu Üzerine Bir Değerlendirme* [An evaluation on the EU's 2013 Progress Report]. Retrieved June 28, 2014, from Bilgesam: http://www.bilgesam.org/incele/737/-ab%E2%80%99nin-2013-turkiye-ilerleme-raporu-uzerine-bir-degerlendirme/

Dicle, A. (2014, July 19). (Ş. G. Sağnıç, Interviewer)

Eccarius-Kelly, V. (2014). The Kurdish Conundrum in Europe: Political Opportunities and Transnational Activism. In W. Pojman, *Migration and Activism in Europe Since 1945* (pp. 57-80). New York: Palgrave Macmillan.

Ferho, D. (2014, July 16). (Ş. G. Sağnıç, Interviewer)

Gunter, M. M. (1991). Transnational Sources of Support for the Kurdish Insurgency in Turkey. *Conlict Quarterly,* 7-30.

Khayati, K. (2008). *From Victim Diaspora to Transborder Citizenship?* Linköping: Linköping Studies in Arts and Science 435.

Lelyveld, J. (1986, March 2). *The Swedish Officials Pursue 2 Theories in Palme Slaying.* Retrieved July 7, 2014, from The New York Times: http://www.nytimes.com/1986/03/02/world/swedish-officials-pursue-2-theories-in-palme-slaying.html?pagewanted=1

Özsöz, M. (2012). *İlerlemenin Matematiği* [The mathematics of the progress]. Brussels: İktisadi Kalkınma Vakfı.

The European Commission. (2011). *Turkey 2011 Progress Report.* Brussels.

The European Commission. (2013). *Turkey 2013 Progress Report.* Brussels.

The European Union Commission. (1998). *Regular Report: Progress Towards Accession.* Brussels.

The European Union Commission. (1999). *Regular Report: Progress Towards Accession.* Brussels.

The European Union Commission. (2000). *The Regular Report: Progress Towards Accession.* Brussels.

Tilly, C. (2002). *Stories, Identities, and Political Change.* Maryland: Rowman& Littlefield.

Turkey vs. Abdullah Öcalan, 1999/21 (Ankara Second State Security Court June 06, 1999). Retrieved June 24, 2014, from http://dosyalar.hurriyet.com.tr/hur/turk/99/06/08/sondakikaozel.htm

Vertovec, S. (2005). *The Political Importance of Diasporas.* Oxford: Centre on Migration, Policy and Society. Retrieved July 26, 2014, from https://www.compas.ox.ac.uk/fileadmin/files/Publications/working_papers/WP_2005/Steve%20Vertovec%20WP0513.pdf

Construction of ethnic identity among young Kurdish voluntary migrants in Istanbul[286]

Karol Kaczorowski

The aim of the article is to present partial results of ongoing research project devoted to examining social construction of ethnic identity of young Kurdish voluntary migrants in Istanbul. In the first part of the paper theoretical context of the study is shortly explained, with emphasis on: importance of Istanbul for Kurdish culture, conceptualization of identity and migration. The second part depicts preliminary results of interviews with migrants. It presents respondents' attitudes towards Istanbul, perceived qualities and flaws of conditions that it provides, and potential relation of metropolis to Kurdish culture.

Significance of Istanbul for Kurdish culture and society

The largest part (often referred to as *Northern*) of geographical and cultural region treated by Kurds as their homeland - Kurdistan is located within the borders of modern Turkey. The estimations of Kurdish population in Turkey vary between 14 and 20 million (ref. CIA 2008)[287]. The population of Istanbul, the biggest city in Turkey, is of more than 14 million. Headquarters of Turkish corporations and national media are located in this great metropolis (see Karpat 2004; Ciplak 2012).

Istanbul bears a great significance for the Kurdish culture as many Kurdish organizations were active in the city over the 19th and 20th century (see Alakom 2011, p. 19-21; Pirbal 2008). The largest Kurdish community in the world lives in Istanbul (The Economist 2005). The metropolis has been for years called as "the biggest Kurdish city" (see Alakom 2011, p. 9-19). Research carried out by Rüstem Erkan in 2009 demonstrated that over 5 million of Turkish Kurds live outside the eastern regions of the country (which are named by the Kurds as the Northern Kurdistan). The highest percentage of this group lives in Istanbul (TimeTurk 2010). The city of Istanbul is also special due to domination of Turkish culture. Here, cultural dominance is understood not only as majority of citizens of Istanbul of Turkish descent, but also as cultural phenomenons which show their hidden diameter at both symbolic and societal level, i.e. interactive level (Mucha 1999: 27-31).

Theorizing identity and ethnicity

Identity - as theoretical notion and a subject of social studies has gained popularity in last decades of the twentieth century. Some social psychologists and

---

[286] The article was written in the scope of project financed by Polish National Science Center by the decision number DEC-2013/09/N/HS3/02014.
[287] Both global and Turkish populations of Kurds are hard to estimate. Resettlement and assimilation processes forced by inhabited states are obstacles in this matter. Some estimation from the first decade of 21st century implicate that there are 30-38 millions of Kurds worldwide and 12-20 million live in Turkey (see. Yıldız 2005: 6). Therefore it can be assumed that probably Turkish Kurds are half of world's Kurdish population.

micro-sociologist tend to put more emphasis on individual self and even state that such thing as *collective identity* is non-existent. Other scholars - often macro-oriented sociologists and historians study only dominant traits of large groups (usually nations, societies). There are however also contemporary social scientists who suggest that studies of individual and collective identity should be connected with themselves (e.g. Jenkins 2004, p. 15-18).

Ethnic identity is often regarded as one of the key components of individual identity, as the ethnic group is one of the main reference groups. Belonging to a particular ethnic group in the eyes of society and the state can influence one's economic, legal and political situation: hence there is a need to negotiate ethnic identity. (Fenton 2010, p. 190-213). In the foreword to *Ethnic Groups and Boundaries* Frederik Barth (1969) stated that despite earlier theories of ethnicity in social anthropology, its' constitutive features are largely not objective and not biological. Barth did not, however, overestimate the cultural interpretation of ethnicity, noting that in conducting research anthropologist has access only to socially effective traits of ethnicity, and in practice cultural values are often used instrumentally by ethnic groups (e.g. for gaining political or economic support). In presented study, ethnic identity is treated as connected with cultural identity (e.g. Steve Hall 2006; Comaroff i Comaroff 2009), subject to changes in time and socially constructed.

Frederik Barth (1969: 12-13) underlined the importance of consideration of ecological factors in studying ethnicity as people who identify themselves as members of the same ethnic group can practice their ethnic identity completely differently in different environments. Urban environment can be crucial to the construction and negotiation of all elements of identity (Mach 1989: 153-193). Antagonistic relations between metropolises (treated as place of exile) and villages in Kurdistan (treated as homeland) are also often depicted in Kurdish literature (see. Bocheńska 2011; van Bruinessen 2013).

Kurds and internal migration flows in Turkey

One of most important theoretical and analytic divisions in migration studies concerns forced and voluntary migration. Janet Abu-Lunghod (1988, p. 61-62) notes that there is still an enormous difference between situation when a migrant is pulled by needs and an exile when he is pushed from his homeland. Drawing from these differences, in presented study, a spatial mobility undertaken after own decision is treated as voluntary migration. In the situation of Kurds in Turkey such migration contrasts with forced resettlement led by state in country's South-East especially from 1980's until the beginning of twenty-first century (see Jongerden 2007).

Voluntary migration is usually theorized with focus on (more or less) rational calculation of potential loss and gain analyzing migration. Scholars often enumerate push and pull factors for migration while putting emphasis on different dimensions of decision making. Frequently cited push factors for internal migration in Turkey are: lack of services, inadequacy or low standard of infrastructure and insecurity. According to Ayşe Gedik (1997) who analyzed internal migration in Turkey (in years: 1970, 1980, 1985) pull factors to the same extent influence potential migrant during the decision making. These would be:

existing social networks in the migration area, job-opportunities,communication and transportation facilities. Psychological distance may be more important than physical one as proximity of a destination place seems to be irrelevant if only family members, neighbors or friend reside there.

Apart from pull factors that are most frequently enumerated by scholars of migration, important might be also less evident factors of cultural and social advantages in cities that provide wider range of free time activities and social atmosphere allowing migrant to partake in them. International Organization for Migration (2003) have noticed while studying international migrants from Kurdistan Autonomous Region in Iraq (Southern Kurdistan) to United Kingdom, that general atmosphere of freedom (including leisure activities) played a substantial role in respondents decision and evaluation of migration.

It is important to note that contrary to theories of internal migration in developing countries it is not rural to urban but urban to urban which is the most popular type of migration within Turkey. Analysis by Gedik (1997) proved that migration from city to a city (even in the least urbanized provinces), since 1970's have become a most frequent type of migration. The road to a new home for many forced migrants in 1990's was multi-step (from the South-East to some city closer to the region but situated usually in more western part of country, and from that city to other urban area located in a further distance, often Istanbul). Kurds who migrate contemporary may also do it in a multi-step manner - one can study (or complete a part of their studies e.g. undergraduate) in one city and then move to another (as was the case with some of my respondents).

Waves of internal migration in Turkey can be divided between pre-1960's era, rapid industrialization and urbanization of 1960's and 1970's, dominance of forced migration due to military fight of state with PKK and resettlement policy in 1980's and 1990's (especially in the latter decade) and potential new wave of voluntary migration connected with economic growth in the beginning of twenty-first century. Kurds that migrated voluntary could rely on social networks constituted people coming from the same village, city or region of Turkey (hemşehri). Those who migrated for economic reasons before mass resettlement, would easier integrate and cope economically while internally displaced people have problems with speaking proper , official Turkish language, lacked recognition and support from state until the beginning of twenty-first century (see: Betül Çelik 2012). Considering that Turkish state eventually abstained from policy of resettlement in the break of the centuries, while migration-rate still grew in first decade of twenty-first century, we can argue that a new wave of Kurdish migration would be voluntary one, basing mostly on economic and educational needs.

Characteristics of studied group

Preliminary research results presented below base on 22 semi-structured in-depth interviews with Young Kurdish migrants from different districts of Istanbul, and one group interview with 6 conservative Kurdish women (among whom two were migrated to Istanbul). Selection for the interviews was based on snow-ball effect. Interviews were made in Turkish language in August and September 2014. Interview questions were concentrated on three broad topics: history of migration, (taking into consideration changes in habits that have taken place after arriving to Istanbul), social construction of Kurdish identity (it's understanding and perceived every day and festive practices which maintain this identity) and attitudes towards Istanbul (advantages and disadvantages of the city and places especially connected with the Kurdish culture) Below are mentioned general characteristics of interviewed people.

From 22 in-depth interviews, 6 were done with women. Almost all of respondents were Sunni Muslim (there were 2 Alevi women) and kurmanci dialect speakers (one respondent's native language was zazaki). The youngest respondent was a 19 years old student, the oldest were 35. Majority of the respondents were students or graduates of one of the universities in Istanbul, two of them were studying in other cities but stated Istanbul as their residence. Among graduates were: beginner advocates, high school teachers, physiotherapists, one entrepreneur and one unemployed person. Most of respondents of in-depth interviews were also leftist Kurds, although not all of them were voters of Kurdish *Peoples Democracy Party* (Turkish shortcut *HDP*) and one respondent described himself as former AKP voter.

Young migrant's attitudes towards the city of Istanbul

Majority of the respondents have migrated to Istanbul in order to study in one of the universities functioning in the city. Its multiculturalism, educational prestige, economic situation and availability of rare majors were cited as reasons for choosing studying in the city. Some of respondents have completed part of their higher education in other Turkish city and moved to Istanbul for graduate studies, studying second major or to pursue a career. Almost all of interviewed migrants at first sight of Istanbul felt overwhelmed by its enormous size and crowded nature. Respondents underlined the difference between their homeland and Istanbul citing direct contacts with almost every one living in the district of their origin. Close relations were contrasted with thousands of anonymous people passing by themselves in Istanbul – *very crowded, very hectic, everyone was in hurry ...* (third respondent from Mardin on his first impression of the city). *I came to university, in our place people talk with themselves while walking, here they talk very rarely, no one looks the other in the face...*(respondent from Bitlis). Reaction to vastness of cities' landscape was described a few times as experiencing fear of being lost.

Narrations on relation between Istanbul and Kurdish culture differed depending on one's general attitude to the city. While enumerating discussing Kurdish population in Istanbul, respondents would often point out that many Kurdish migrants are getting assimilated to Turkish culture in the city – *For Kurdish culture Istanbul is disadvantageous... people living in metropolis became similar to each other (...)* (respondent from Bitlis) . Some respondents pointed out that Istanbul is not a Kurdish homeland in a way cities of Kurdistan are - *Istanbul is important for Kurdish culture...but more for Turks... as for lives of Kurds... Diyarbakır, Erbil, Mohabad, Qmişlo, Kobane, Efrin...* (respondent from Batman). Some underlined that Kurdish traditions cannot be cultivated there. Many respondents stated that the city has a place in Kurdish history as it was a home for living for Bedirxan and is a destination of Kurdish migration. Many respondents accented that the city was a place of cross-cultural exchange – *Istanbul is important for every culture* (respondent from Şırnak). This difference in views on the city was mirrored also in varying emphasis on its advantages and disadvantages. Most of respondents pointed to availability of employment and variety of possible activities that one can find in the city as its main qualities – *You can find everything that you want* (respondent from Konya). *If you want to work in Istanbul you can find the job* (second respondent from Mardin). *It was like going to Disneyland, it was a city like Disneyand, everything looked great* (respondent from Batman on his first impression of Istanbul). *In our place, in the evening, everybody altogether stop for the call for prayers - ezan - and life ends. Here it's not like this, in Taksim, in Kadikoy, at night at any hour you can sit with your friends* (respondent from Bitlis) At the same time majority of interviewees have found living there difficult and working conditions hard. One of the respondents noted that Istanbul is great city for the rich ones while there is a widespread economic exploitation and exclusion of many Kurdish migrants - *In other Kurdish districts if you live with Kurds there (...) they are poor...they are oppressed...* (second respondent from Mardin). Overpopulation, pollution, traffic and more indirect inter-personal relations were also cited as disadvantages of living in the city.

Maintaining Kurdish identity in Istanbul

Being Kurdish as being born from Kurds appears to be a part of common-sense among respondents (and probably among most of Istanbul residents basing on observations and conversation made during the fieldwork). This does not however mean that every person who was raised in Kurdish family would in every situation publicly and openly admit that he or she is a Kurd. Some people think of their ethnicity as just simple fact (e.g. Seeing more value in religious affiliation and community) - while other underline it consciously and often politically in order to be identified as opposed to those who discriminate Kurds in Turkey. It is however important to note that majority of respondents when asked what is in their opinion the meaning of being Kurdish and how Kurds differ from other groups would start they answer with emphasis on statement that one's ethnicity does not matter much to them and people of various origins have similarities (implying at the same time that they are not nationalists and Kurds are not fundamentally different from other cultures, ethnic groups and nations) – *Being Kurdish.. so...normally... if it's necessary to express than...It's nothing. Being Turkish does not matter, being English does not matter, being German, being French does not matter...* (respondent from Batman). Many of my interviewee's have stated that if they would have to describe in some way Kurdishness they would refer to resistance, oppression and discrimination, thus referring to difficult history of Kurds and their homeland – *Being Kurd in this country means death, means pain, means tears* (respondent from Van). Many of them have also pointed to having darker skin color than Turks and being generally warm in social relations (phrase used was - *sıcak kanlı* – literary having warm blood) and hospitable as Kurdish characteristics. These latter two can be associated more personally than general values and ideas symbolizing Kurdish identity enumerated before.

Maintaining Kurdish identity in respondents narrations was usually connected with using Kurdish dialect (most of respondents spoke kurmanci), collective commemorations like participating in *Newroz* celebrations and knowing Kurdish history. Although respondents did not name the latter in a straightforward manner, preserving collective Kurdish memory was often important to them as during the interview many of them would mention important Kurdish characters and tragic events that Kurds experienced (e.g. Halabja genocide or killing of Kurdish smugglers in Roboski). Some respondents were also active members in youth of Kurdish leftist People's Democratic Party (*Halkların Demokratik Partisi*) or other leftist parties close to it (e.g. Socialist Party of Opressed - *Ezilenlerin Sosyalist Partisi*). Most of respondents could name some Kurdish institutions functioning in Istanbul. Apart from most frequently cited were: Mesopotamia Cultural Center (Turkish: *Mezopotamya Kültür Merkezi*) and Kurdish Institute of Istanbul (Kurdish name - *Enstîtuya Kurdî Ya Stenbolê*). Some of them took part or were involved in organization of activities provided by those institutions (e.g. one of the respondents was teaching Kurdish language in Kurdish Institute) but many of my interlocutors would admit that they do not recall the addresses of these organizations nor that they regularly participate in events organized there.

Although majority of respondents would think mainly about Kurdish traditions and high culture when asked about cultivating customs, after I have pointed to possibility of individual cultivation of Kurdish habits, for example in leisure activities and food preferences they would admit that they do preserve them for example by drinking ceylon tea (the so-called smuggled tea – *kaçak çay* as it used to be smuggled to Northern Kurdistan from Arab countries) instead of Turkish tea from black sea or eating specially prepared cheese with herbs (which is typical for Şırnak province). Many respondents stated that they listen to Kurdish music most notably to Şivan Perwer, Ciwan Haco and Ahmet Kaya.

Various ways of preserving ethnic identity enumerated by respondents does not however mean that they could do it completely freely. Policy of state was almost invariable states as the greatest obstacle on maintaining Kurdish identity in Istanbul. Examples of perceived discrimination and descriptions of situations when they preferred to hide their ethnicity point to the need of negotiation of public display of Kurdish identity. It is however important to note that in respondents narrations Istanbul was viewed generally as a multicultural city with better atmosphere for exercising identities other thank Turkish than other cities in the country (e.g. Izmir or Adana). Interviews have proved also that it is not necessarily a demonstration of distinctive identity that draws discrimination from others in Istanbul but sole admission of province when they come from. Many respondents have pointed that they could not find apartments for rent when they would reply for a question about homeland with a name of city, village or region that was from South-East –I came to Istanbul, *I was a student, I was supposed to find home, I searched for home, but I couldn't find it. In most places they asked me where are you from, what is your homeland, Hakkari I would say, we do not give it (for rent) they would say* (respondent from Hakkari).

Conclusion

With growing migration rate in the beginning of twenty-first century, after Turkish state withdrew from the policy of resettlement, it appears that new wave of internal migration emerged in the country. As Istanbul is the city gathering largest Kurdish group in the country, there is a need to study new Kurdish voluntary migration – their ways of preserving identity and coping with space and conditions provided by metropolis. Preliminary results of in-depth interviews with young migrants from different districts of the city show that Istanbul is not necessarily treated by migrants as city connected with Kurdish culture – as tradition is associated more with collective life in Northern Kurdistan – but more as a place with wider social freedoms and enabling activity of Kurdish organizations. The metropolis can be treated by migrants as endless source of possibilities – a *Disneyland* but also as an urban space of hard work necessary for economic support but empowering assimilation – a place of an exile.

Preserving Kurdish habits in Istanbul is mirrored not only in publicly visible, collective actions but also in everyday activities done by young migrants. The latter may be maintained not consciously as Kurdish cultural traits but rather as something obvious for people brought up in Northern Kurdistan. Multiculturalism and job availability pose as qualities which make Istanbul better than other Turkish cities in the eyes of migrants. It is however important to note that this atmosphere of openness does not mean that there are no perceived obstacles in maintaining Kurdish identity in Istanbul. Lack of legal recognition as separate group and cases of discrimination are examples of the necessity for social negotiation of one's identity. District, city or village of the origin of family remains a strong marker of identification. Ties with people from the same place can help migrants accommodate but at the same time the sole admission of being born in place inhabited by Kurds can cause adverse reactions from some Turkish inhabitants of the city.

References

Abu-Lunghold J. L. (1988), "Palestinians: Exiles at Home and Abroad", Current Sociology 36 (2), pp. 61-69.

Alakom R. (1998). Eski İstanbul Kürtleri, Istanbul: Avesta Basın Yayın.

Barth F. (1969). Ethnic Groups and Boundaries in: idem, Ethnic Groups and Boundaries: The Social Organization of Culture Difference, London: Allen and Unwin, p. 9-37.

Berger P. L. and T. Luckmann. (1991 [1966]). The Social Construction of Reality - A Treatise in the Sociology of Knowledge, London: Penguin Books.

Bocheńska J. (2011). Między ciemnością i światłem. O kurdyjskiej tożsamości i literaturze. Kraków: Księgarnia Akademicka.

van Bruinessen M. (2013). Kurds and the City, in: Hamit Bozarslan and Clémence Scalbert- Yücel (eds.), Joyce Blau, l'éternelle chez les Kurdes, Paris: Institut Kurde de Paris, pp. 273-95.

CIA Central Intelligence Agency. (2008). The World Factbook – Turkey: People and Society, online: https://www.cia.gov/library/publications/the-world factbook/geos/tu.html#People [02.02.2015].

Ciplak B. (2012). The Relationship between migration and crime in Istanbul, Turkey - and social support in practice, ISZU Sosyal Bilimler Dergisi online http://www.academia. edu/3052392/Migration-Crime_Relations_in_Istanbul_Turkey [23.05.2013].

Comaroff J. and J. Comaroff. (2009). Ethnicity Inc. Chicago and London: University of Chicago Press.

Çelik A. B. (2012). State, Non-Governmental and International Organizations in the Possible Peace Process in Turkey's Conflict-Induced Displacement, Journal of Refugee Studies Vol. 26, No. 1.

The Economist. (2005). Can't they get along anymore? online: http://www.economist.com/node/4389654 (8/9/2005) [06.08.2012]

Fenton S. (2010). Ethnicity (2nd edition, revised and updated), Cambridge: Polity Press.

Gedik, A. (1996). Internal Migration in Turkey, 1965-1985: Test of Some Conflicting Findings in the Literature. ANU Working Papers in Demography, 66.

Hall S. (2006). Cultural Identity and Diaspora in: Jana Evans Braziel and Anita Mannur (eds.) Theorizing Diaspora, Malden, MA: Blackwell, pp. 233-246.

IOM International Organization for Migration. (2013). Perspectives On Migration From Iraq
- A Survey of Migrants and Potential Migrants in Iraq and the UK 2013, online:
http://iomiraq.net/file/152/download?token=NB2ev20y [18.02.2015].

Jenkins R. (1996). Social Identity, London and New York: Routledge.

Jongerden J. (2007). The Settlement Issue in Turkey and the Kurds. An Analysis of   Spatial
Policies,Modernity and War, Social, Economic and Political Studies of the Middle East and
Asia vol. 102,Leiden, Boston: Brill.

Karpat K. (2004). The Genesis of the Gecekondu: Rural Migration and Urbanization (1976),
European Journal of Turkish Studies.

Mach Z. (1989). Symbols, Conflict and Identity, Kraków: WUJ.

Mucha J. (1999). Dominant Culture as a Foreign Culture. Dominant Groups In the   Eyes of
Cultural Minorities. Introduction, in: idem (Ed.), Dominant Culture as a   Foreign Culture.
Dominant Groups in the Eyes of Minorities, New York: Columbia   University Press
and East European Monographs, pp. 7-23.

Pirbal F. (2008). The Apostrophe: Istanbul: the Capital city of Kurdish Literature, The
Kurdish Globe online: http://www.thefreelibrary.com/The+Apostrophe%3A+Istanbul
%3A+ the +Capital+city+ of+Kurdish +Literature%3A...-a0180426162 [06.08.2012].

Sirkeci, I. (2006). The Environment of Insecurity in Turkey and the Emigration of   Turkish
Kurds to Germany. New York: Edwin Mellen Press.

TimeTurk. (2010). En büyük Kürt şehri, Istanbul online:
http://www.timeturk.com/tr/2010/03/25/en-buyuk-kurt-sehri-istanbul.html
[06.08.2012].

Todaro M. (1969), A Model of Labor Migration and Urban Unemployment in Less Developed
Countries. American Economic Review, 59, pp. 138-148.

Yıldız K. (2005). The Kruds in Turkey. EU accession and Human Rights, London: Pluto Press.

Westin C. (1983). Self-reference, Consciousness and Time, in: Anita Jacobson-Widding   (ed.),
Identity: Personal and Social-Cultural. A Symposium. Uppsala, pp. 93-110.

Language Trouble within Ethnic Households: "Never Speak Their Mother Tongue Near Children!"

Yaprak H. Civelek*

Introduction

In ethnic households, concern for children is the leading factor pushing parents to speak the official language to ensure their children's success in public schools, especially with the thought, *"we never wish them to go through what we went through in the past."* In the official discourses, *Turkishness* has been superior over other ethnic identities since the 1920s: the language rights of the Jewish, Greeks, and Armenians living in Turkey have been guaranteed by the 1923 Treaty of Lausanne; however, the government recognizes only these three non-Muslim groups as minorities. Tevhid i Tedrisat Kanunu (the Law of Unification of Education) implemented in March 1924 is also part of the strategy for achieving national unity and integrity by Turkifying all ethnic groups in Anatolia. In 1934, İskân Kanunu (The Settlement Law) was supposedly passed to address new arrangements for migration and population issues; however, these "arrangements" were obviously reflecting a monolingualistic approach, and the Law directly targeted assimilating the Kurds and their language (Beşikçi, 1991). The last Constitution (1982, Code 42) commands: *"No language other than Turkish shall be taught as a mother tongue to Turkish citizens at any institutions of training or education...."*Today, language shift has been kept fortified by the education system, including Turkish-medium public schools and private universities in accordance with monolingualism, which aims to make Turkish the primary language among the members of all ethnic groups, mostly the Kurds (Smits & Gündüz-Hoşgör, 2003; Zeyneloğlu at all.,. 2011). Nowadays, for instance, the frequency of using Kurdish has decreased expressively among Kurds with higher educational attainment. *Higher the educational attainment, the lower the use of Kurdish language as it declines from over 96% among uneducated to 74% among secondary school graduates* (Zeyneloğlu at all., 2015: 4).

However, this article does not aim to seek out historical exposures of the Turkish government to ethnic groups or language politics directly: it assumes ethnic households as the smallest units of four major consecutive processes: migration, settling, livelihood, and language preferences. It gets into the ethnic households in a given territory, Zeytinburnu, in order to research the effects of the political-linguistic exposures to the mother tongue, which, at the same time, requires a decision and/or strategy mechanism. To be precise, it argues about lingual inclinations that put the parents into an in-between position with regard to either speaking the official language *"for saving the future,"* which precisely means constructing a decent life for the new generation, or, speaking our mother tongue

* Yaprak H. Civelek is Assist. Proffessor in Sociology Department. Faculty of Arts and Letters, Istanbul Arel University. Tepekent Campus, Buyukcekmece-Istanbul , Turkey E-mail: hyaprak.civelek@gmail.com

"for protecting the culture." Therefore, more than language socialization and/or language acquisition concepts, which mainly recognize caregiver-child interactions in which the children acquire linguistic and social skills and embrace cultural aspects. The focus is on language shift, which is one of the particularities of language socialization taking place in a culturally heterogeneous setting.

In fact, both language acquisition as a learning process that is based on how to use language in socially appropriate ways to build durable relationships with others in social and cultural activity areas (Garrett & Baquedano-Lopez, 2002) and language shift as a process that boosts cultural interaction, sociocultural reproduction, and transformation are naturally and logically political. In other words, the efforts to establish the official language, Turkish, as the principle everyday language and assigning the mother tongue a "minor" status (secondary language) denotes a pre-described political desire and cultural position. The first location where the dominant language or everyday language interferes with the secondary one, in a way retarding distinction (Loo, 1985), is in the household.

As Cohen & Sirkeci (2011) suggest, while considering their well-being and security, individuals who are members of cultural groups and societies desire to live well by taking into account cultural, economic, and social security in their decisions and come to their decisions after discussion with other members of their households. The interviews with ethnic households put forth that the decision to migrate and settle in a safe place mostly relies on communal traditions, customs, rural community practices such as birth, festivals, or funeral rituals, and national expectations in order to survive and keep their culture alive. Likewise, resistances or adoptions to language shift ought to be understood as the outcomes of a sort of decision-making process related to the ideals of "protecting the culture" and "having a good future," in particular for the prospective group members.

During the field survey, just as McKenon (1994:22) mentions in *"Language, culture and schooling"* for immigrant groups, education has appeared as a vital investment because it is embraced as the key to advancement. As Loo researched, the advancement is connected to take the opportunity of socioeconomic mobility that is always available, which is completely affected by majority-language speaking ability. So, adult minorities, when practicing the dominant language as a second language, are similar to children—dependent on others for reproducing and transforming social relations (Loo, 1985); then, they guide the younger members. The children who are taught to comply with the school's rules for getting better at social relations, activities and success remain in-between. They have been exposed to two cultural frames of reference—that of the home and of the school. Thus, for the parents, language shift at home appears as a requirement facilitating their adaptions to the school, the dominant language, and culture.

Based on the arguments above, while the first chapter presents the methodological details of the field study, the second chapter, by putting forward schooling as a contributing factor, creates a theoretical-critical debate on communal ideals and language preferences reflected from the in-depth interviews.

Method

Verkuyten (2006) suggests that the location that an ethnic identity provides is both situational and historical; therefore, the group narrative about the group's history or genealogical characteristics put forth a particular understanding of ethnic identity. Each ethnic group has its own story and intergroup relations and this explains why each group has a different response to the same circumstances. Ethnic households, just like the dominant ones, may have either "nuclear" or "extended" structures or just be single-headed, but in any case, they represent a history, cultural values, norms, and ideals. *The common thread that links households is their purpose and role* (Cohen & Sirkeci, 2011: 28-29). But the mother tongue, providing uninterruptable interaction in the language at home is the major preserver of the cultural network among ethnic group members.

In such a case, when multilingual matters in the multiethnic societies are framed by a critical-qualitative perspective, what we expect is to observe some ideological impacts on the link between mother tongues, the dominant language, and a strong pragmatic government. Household or family as one of the most effective "state apparatus" undertakes political constructions of the subject. Ethnic households are the units where "other" subjects are transformed into "normal" or "desirable" political subjects by way of "being included" and exposed to external institutional and relational effects.

Zeytinburnu, the location of the ethnic households I interviewed, according to the archives of the municipality information center, was initially part of the district of Bakırköy when the Republic was proclaimed. Zeytinburnu was growing very fast because of the industrial facilities developing progressively, and it became a district in 1957. In 1969, Hart and Saran published "Zeytinburnu: Gecekondu Bölgesi," explaining that 52 percent of the population was born abroad: Most of the inhabitants were from Bulgaria, Yugoslavia, Greece, and Romania. However, at that time, the rest of the population was indeed coming from various regions of Turkey such as the Black Sea, East Anatolia, and Central Anatolia. After the tanneries, the places where the people living in the East and South East Regions had been employed, were closed in turn, the number of immigrants in Zeytinburnu doubled. Also, movements of the Kazakhs, Kyrgyzs, Uighurs, Turkistan, West Thracian Turks, and ethnic Turks living in Afghanistan and Bulgaria to the district have never stopped since the 1960s. There is no reliable data or a map providing a good ethnic profile. Today, the population of the district is 284,814. Mostly low-income and middle-income households have been encountered.

My study, entitled *"Perception of mother tongue among the ethnic households in Zeytinburnu,"* was conducted in the spring of 2014, with a visit to 42 households, and in 2015, an additional 15 households were added to this study in order to enlarge the sample of those who have children attending primary and secondary schools.

Basic characteristics of the field-study are listed below:

a) The purposive sampling technique, also called *subjective* sampling, is used.

b) First criterion for being interviewee—a minimum of ten years had to be spent in Zeytinburnu.

c) With the help of key contacts, such as mukhtars, high school teachers, and students, 57 households in total were visited in Zeytinburnu and there was an interview with one person who was 25 or above for each household having at least one child attending primary or secondary school.

d) 20 Kurdish, 15 Arabian, 8 Armenian, 8 Kazakhs, 4 Georgian, 2 Greek households have opened their doors.

e) Voluntary participation was an ethical requirement. Some Kurdish families who had welcomed me into their homes were more perturbed, but never refused to talk about their ethnic identity and language practices. This is because, in my opinion, their interests in talking about their mother tongue might have been another way of declaring their ethnic existence. Most of the Armenians refused to participate in the study. Some Armenians who participated demanded a document authorized by the Patriarchate in Istanbul; therefore, only Armenians who felt unrestricted about sharing were interviewed. The Greeks were also another group who mostly refused to participate and questioned the study. Those who agreed to talk to me felt so uncomfortable that they kept their answers quite short. The Arabic-Sunni, Arabic-Alawites, and Kazakh households invited me without questioning.

f) Also, it was notable that the persons who were eligible to talk to us were sending the old members of the household away from the room where we interviewed; most of them could speak very little or no Turkish.

The main limitation of the study relates to the questions due to a political fear of being interrogated by the state forces, with queries such as *"Why are they interested in our ethnicity and language practices?" "Is this kind of a governmental operation to open a file on me?"* These demonstrate how past experiences and memory constantly reproduce their pressures on citizens from different ethnic identities, and we will continue to be aware of them while reading the following chapter.

Transcription of language trouble: interplay of schoolyard and houshold

Sustam's story about what his mother advised right after he was registered for the primary school is noteworthy: *"Son, you must think twice from now on."* It is because he is Kurdish, also Alawite, and he continued, *"They were speaking Turkish at home to get us become more adapted to the school and the language"(2014)*. Most of the narratives, like Sustam's, make it possible to argue about the relationship between political ideals and language trouble to which ethnic household members have been exposed. For this reason, this paper concentrates on the discourse-parents-school relationship. Ethnic parents, for Smits & Gündüz-Hoşgör (2003), by speaking the country's official language at home, aim to teach their children this language and guarantee their upward social mobility chances, which allow a member of the ethnic minority to become part of the *core* ethnicity of a nation (Smith, 1986: 76).

[We, Kazakh families want our children to be successful in schools and most of the parents must speak Turkish in the houses for their future. Kazakh, 42, Kazakh]

[New generation must learn Turkish very well, you see; their future, just like ours, has been shaped by the Turkish-medium schools. Kurd, 37, Kurdish]

[Every Armenian cares about his/her identity and language. I went to Armenian schools too. But, I say official language is the mother tongue, my perception is so. Same thing for my seven years old boy… he is attending Armenian schools… But… Turkish should be his main language throughout his life. Armenian, 37, Turkish]

If the subjects' choices and ideological practices in a minority household have been voluntarily adjusted to each other and transformed into a politically "desired outcome" by means of not speaking the mother tongue, this situation becomes part of an ideological project that makes the government both cause and effect. As a matter of fact, Tollefson (1989, 2012) claims that changes in the social or political role of language are identified with social, economic, and political aims. During a language planning process, bases of the transformation are developed by taking the interests of the dominant class into account. Most of the minorities living in Turkey are bilingual; an ethnic individual can easily speak Turkish as his/her main medium of expression during early adulthood and drop his/her mother tongue to second position even if that was the language she first learned from her parents (Smits & Gündüz-Hoşgör, 2003; Zeyneloğlu et al., 2014).

However, the parents are totally aware of the burden of becoming the "minority" or "other"; therefore, they know they need to watch their children's psychological states, which sometimes oscillate.

[Children can easily learn their mother tongue before starting their school life. However, after they become students, they notice that their language begins to make them different, I mean, other and, this teaches them otherization. Kurdish, 45, Kurdish]

[It is definitely a self-division! My daughter attending secondary school reacts when I speak Kurdish now. The perception of being Kurdish is not normal at the school and in the public area. She thinks that Kurdish makes her an inadequate person. Kurd, 45, Kurdish]

[She was crying when she came back home because other children at school made fun of her, saying Arabian girl, Arabian girl! She barely know Arabian culture, can't speak Arabic, even one word. It was so difficult to explain what actually happened to her. Arabian, 37, Arabian]

Demirtaş, the current Kurdish leader of a political party, mentions that *"Our parents taught us Turkish as a favor to us, not to let us bear the heavy burden of Kurdishness. So, that we succeed in this state, so that we can achieve a good position, succeed in education."*

[A child wants to be socialized at school, but you know, Arabic doesn't let him/her to do this. I want my child to have self-confidence and be happy among his peers, so I never force him to learn Arabic. Arab, 45, Arabian].

[Shapes of his eyes already give him away… other children keep him asking if he is Japanese or Chinese though he keeps saying he is Turkish, too. He speaks Turkish fluently in order to socialize, also to save his confidence. Kyrgyz, 37, Kirghiz].

Another point here is that the linguistic assimilation process refers to an internalization process, which Bourdieu's habitus totally points out: *what is possible and what is not possible for one's life*, and how one develops objectives and practices in full awareness (Dumais, 2002:46). Furthermore, the relationship between the context of linguistic market which entails the ability to speak clear, in a manner that fits the situations, conditions and objectives and discourse can be associated with grammar; *"The market plays a part in shaping not only the symbolic value, but also the meaning of discourse* (Bourdieu, 2012:38). A linguistic habitus has socially constructed dispositions, which entail a certain propensity to speak and to express certain interests, a certain capacity to speak which involves grammatical principles, and a social capacity to use this competence in certain situations. So, the linguistic market, which has rules (grammar, pronunciation, etc.) and inwardly imposes a system of censorships is, in fact, in cooperation with the linguistic habitus and they offer their products. However, Portes & Rumbaut (2001) argued that if an economic motivation appears for maintaining the mother tongue, which mostly comes out within the ethnic economic enclave model maintenance and transmission of the mother tongue across the generations appears as a challenge, and then is fortified. Also, they point out that bilingualism may be related to educational achievement and *cognitive* advantages, which provide superiority over those who are monolinguals. The remarkable result of Alba et al's study (2002) shows that for the children of third and later generations, the pressures to speak the dominant language exclusively are so strong that parental endogamy, by itself, is not enough to maintain the mother tongue, and living in ethnic neighborhoods serving the emergence of biethnic cultural bilingualism is significantly widespread (like Cuban children growing up in Miami, Mexican children growing up near the US-Mexican border). So, the communal context is important: For the crowded and segregated groups, the mother tongue is more likely to be spoken on every occasion, and maintaining it is an intense desire, which makes the linguistic assimilation process slower. So, the linguistic habitus, in fact, has been fed by the decisive role of the educational system; first of all, the primary school teacher *fixes* children's language *to build common consciousness of the nation* (Bourdieu, 2012:49) and could be traumatic for a child asking himself, *"Who am I?"* as a child that has been ignored by school schedules and mostly by teachers—in fact, by discourse itself.

[Our children's trouble with their identity starts with a school registration. Kurd, 29, Kurdish]

[She attended Armenian schools since she was 11. When she wanted to go to Anadolu high school, I felt comfortable since she spoke Armenian very well. But, later... I understood how speaking Turkish would change her life; she needs it to survive! Also, she was noticing strongly that ever before that she is different... also painful. Armenian, 60, Armenian]

[In Mardin, we were learning that our friends we had played in the playgrounds with were actually Armenians, when they did not join the religion class... I also first tasted otherization in the schoolyards, which is a situation my children will go through, too. Kurd, 24, Kurdish]

Ethnic students feel as strongly as the lower-class students that the school environment is different from their home because of lower cultural capital, which consists of poor linguistic and cultural competence (McKenon, 1994). For this reason, the coworkers of the teachers and the school programs generally are parents supporting their children in practicing the official language at home.

[Sure, they can speak Kazakh, we have grandparents in the house. But, actually, I and their father prefer to speak Turkish near them, because they might feel confused about words in school Kazakh, 50, Kazakh]

In a Foucauldian sense, dominant institutions attaching importance to the historical and cultural capitals construct people's lives, and the parents, as the experienced individuals or subjects who are aware of the objective of the official relationship between language and education, have to follow the scheduled pedagogic system as carefully as the teachers: The objective of the power is to find out and understand the nature of children attending schools, who are part of "a multiple network of diverse elements"—walls space, institutions, rules, discourse—and then, develop their faculties who are *discursively positioned as both "modern" and "moral"* (Ball, 2013:41). Thus, schooling, or, in general, literacy, as an activity cannot be associated with the language in use, which is neither one's nor the other's mother tongue, and it refers to the language that is commonly used, and mainly political and biased.

[...we all have learned Turkish in schools. May be, on the streets, too...my daughter must speak it as good as her mother tongue, because, look back! If you're not Turkish, you have to be well-educated; otherwise, you cannot understand what's going on around your identity. Alawite-Arab, 37, Arabian]

[1960s! My father had attended Armenian secondary school in Üsküdar. Just like me, and my children are going to also attend such schools. But, we should accept that Turkish is our mother tongue, Armenian is the second language, spoken among friends sometimes and in the churches customarily. Armenian,37, Turkish]

Bernstein suggests that language unifies discourse and activity; therefore, the language spoken in school and home are not necessarily the same for those who are minorities (Yıldırım, 2011). Thus, considering the teaching system as an ideological instrument for arranging the interchange among economics, politics, ethnic households, and the decision-making process that is based on which language one will be able to use within the house, choices of habitus are accomplished without consciousness and constraint, and definitely, product of social determinism. In addition, what Bourdieu said about recognizing them as responsibilities, not "causes," makes it impossible to understand the *intimidation, a symbolic violence* (Bourdieu, 2012:51).

[What a sh...t! The history taught in the schools affects your conscious and social relations. Education system, official registrations, heroism...every trouble with the identity and language is because of the government. How can you throw your child right into a chaos by forcing him/her to speak the mother tongue? Kurd, 27, Kurdish]

[Turkish is the government's language, Arabic is our privacy. Arab, 42, Arabian]

However, accomplishment of choices of habitus without consciousness is not at all in progress for most ethnic households. Most of the narratives indeed call attention to having a loyalty to the strong tie between identity and mother tongue. While discussing their children's language troubles, they have never ignored the elements defining their identity and culture. McKenon (1994:22) suggests that such attitudes verify that ethnic families do not embrace cultural beliefs and practices of the dominant group; they are just led to develop survival strategies to cope with the conditions and these strategies might be unharmonious with what is required for school success; they just see the conflict and simply prefer to experience two different cultural frames. Then, however, the dilemma for such ethnic students is that they encounter two competing cultural structures and they have to be both "a good student "and "a good member of the ethnic group."

[My children and grandchildren must know my father's and mother's language. Even when they want a glass of tea, they may say -Tu dikari avé bide min?- It is not a shame to speak their mother tongue, it is part of their beings. However, language taught in the schools is the official one: Turkish saves their lives, Kurdish protects their Kurdishness. Kurd, 37, Kurdish]

[Turkish is official, Arabic is more sincere. The official language is spoken everywhere, even in your house… for your family's good. Of course, you have to make a decision… and you finally choose your family's comfort, especially your children's success. Mother tongue is necessary to protect your identity, your tradition, but Turkish guarantees you a life. Arabic, 41, Arabian]

The tendency to develop survival strategies instead of adopting the dominant group's values is based on the past experiences, which are based on cultural memory, and some ethnicity-related events remembered in a chronological order. Their togetherness refers to a long-term challenge against the attitudes that deeply discrediting both identity and the mother tongue. For Assmann (1988), cultural memory's horizon does not change with the passing of time, and language-based memory is maintained by keeping the tie between culture and mother tongue strongly alive. Thus, constant confirmation of an identity is possible, which reflects an awareness of group unity and peculiarity.

[My elder brothers were telling that our parents did not allow them to speak Arabian in 1960s because learning Turkish very well at schools meant protecting yourself and your child's future. I have done the same thing; my two children can speak their mother tongue, but not as fluent as Turkish. See, nothing has changed. Arabic, 42, Arabian]

However, Aleida Assman's words define another point I want to get at: *One group remembers the past in fear of deviating from its model, the next for fear of repeating the past* (Assmann, 1988:133). The narratives include both groups and viewpoints. The fear of repeating the past is associated with all the reinforcements to guarantee a generation's success, socialization, economic indecency in the future, and correspondence of their language practices at home and school. In addition, it also brings about a self-defensive approach and challenges against the political, financial and institutional enforcements with the aim of not deviating from peculiarities of the model.

[*In our time, there was Martial Law and speaking Kurdish was forbidden. We abandoned our hometown and never taught Kurdish to our children since we were afraid. However, we always know that they both will be strong individuals and they will fight for their culture, identity, and mother tongue, when they are adults. Kurd, 42, Kurdish*]

[*As Kazakhs, we must keep our traditions alive. Yes, we speak Turkish in the house or outside. But we have associations teaching our language, music, and traditions. All the celebrations, like weddings, birthdays, and funerals, are always held in the Association of Kazakhs. A Kazakh child must learn his/her mother tongue and counts at least seven of his/her family ancestors. Kazakh, 47, Kazakh*]

Nevertheless—also by the ethnic persons—adaptation to the dominant language seems like abandoning their own identity by weakening the mother tongue's power, which the government has already targeted. The fear and the perception in Goffman's literature, in fact, as results of stigma and violence addressed to ethnic groups in the past, are the signs of discretion? (Goffman, 1986). It is part of a *discrimination through which we effectively, if often unthinkingly, reduce a person's life chances* (1986:10). Language politics have made it sustainable and pushed the group members who are devoted to their social and cultural values and ethnic identity to perform their *existence* as a reaction to the discretion?of *normal* ones. Besides, what narratives also put forth typically is that ethnic parents try hard to show that their difference does not prevent them from being successful in society; they believe and make believe their children that it is possible to excel in society (at school, work etc.) to achieve something that is hard even for the *normal* ones (Goffman, 1986).

[*Perception of being Kurdish is not normal at school and in public area. The question "Are you Kurdish?" creates perception of an "other" immediately and the outside is dominant. My child knows that Turkish let her to be successful at school and to be loved by other children and her teachers. All I know is I must be supportive. She will understand what Kurds have gone through for years, sooner or later. Kurd, 42, Kurdish*]

Language planning as a piece of discursive politics puts the education system in charge of discrediting minority languages. But, remarkably, most of the ethnic parents I interviewed are quite sure their little children will be the strong defenders of their culture and mother tongues when they are grown-ups.

When we linked the results and discussions so far to Deleuze and Guattari's approach, unity of language appears as a political demand and grammar represents power relations that subjugate people by way of forcing them to speak in a corresponding manner. What he called "self-closure of language" signifies a sense of representation, which leads to a limitation by the translation of the known world into the unknown. As long as every statement meets an action, the language, beyond being a mean of transmitting information, will impose order-words, which actually are employed for rearranging the world (questions, explanations, threats, desires, demands, requests, and, maybe, expectations). Every statement and action that brings about a social responsibility is dominated by order-words. Education as a discipline represents language of the "orders," but effective use of the order-words—in other words, the process of "self-closure of the language"—starts with the doors of a household opening to the outside world. The more ethnic households speak the official language, the more the government reproduces itself. (Çalcı, 2012). Elements of the mother tongue (accent, words, grammar, etc.) have been confronted with various, strange, more "governing" elements of a language; thus, as suggested in "What is a Minor Literature?", *"the primary characteristic of a minor literature involves all the ways in which the language is effected by a strong efficient of deterritorialization" (1993:16)* Besides, everything in them is political and everything has a collective value.

A high-school teacher I talked to during the field study had this to say:

[I wanted my students to write their utopia as homework. Each brought two or three pages of homework except a Kurdish one, who is really hardworking and well-behaved. After I asked why, he told me that "I have a utopia, but every detail in it is Kurdish, and so hard translating it it into Turkish, so hard picturing it in Turkish... sorry..."]

For Baudrillard, *there is always a desire not to be produced, not be interpreted and expressed in terms that an interpretation employs...interpreter is an agent of dominant social code* and its main objective is to transform things by means of interpreting – decoding or deterritorializing them, which is very crucial for minorities attempting to remain minorities (cited by Deleuze at all. 1983:13). The government's language includes grammar and order-words, and tries hard for achieving deterritorialization of the ethnic languages, or, in other words, re-interpreting them in correspondence with the discourse's. As other institutions, schools, books, and teachers are the interpreters serving assimilative or transformative purposes of the discourse of the outside world.

However, the ethnic parents whom I interviewed in Zeytinburnu create various settings to speak the mother tongue and the official language are aware of "interpellation" in an Althusserian sense, or, of "power" that forces them to transform their identities and languages in a Foucauldian sense, so, they precisely have known that Turkish-medium schools force monolingualism in a nationalist manner. However, most of them, especially Kurdish parents who "believe in the Kurdish case," encourage their children to learn and speak Turkish and believe that when their children become grown-ups, they will know much more about the Kurdish problem and "Kurdish's sad story," so, they will fight for their identity, culture, and language in the future.

Ball (1990) suggests that *meanings...arise not from language but institutional practices* and schools are the places where "other" texts, "other" voices, "other" words and concepts are forced to change their meanings of the discourses'. Ethnic households are always the objects of political-institutional expectations and those who have student members attending primary and secondary schools just do the necessary by making a decision in favor of the official language. But, such a decision should not be assumed as an achievement for a perfect assimilation or full-deterritorialization because those who believe that their identity and culture have never disappeared have also developed survival strategies for keeping their cultural values alive, especially their mother tongues.

Conclusion

Ian Chalmers claims that language constitutes people's *sense of identity, place and belonging* and they experience *violence of alterity, of other worlds, languages, identities* and constantly face other histories, places and people (1993: 4,5). Therefore, the final point that they reach is "their world" acquiring a shape in dialogues. Based on the narratives pointing out that mother tongue is home, tradition and identity, I believe, members of the ethnic households constitute "their world" and this world does not refer to "full-adoptions", it is full of strategies that also yield a constant confirmation for their cultural-symbolic elements, essentially their mother tongues.

The narratives derived from ethnic households settled in Zeytinburnu commonly reproduce a logic that confirms the idea above and also Smith's definition of ethnic group (1991): they all make a reference to cultural collectivity by associating it with certain historical memories, cultural values, customs, and importance of mother tongue. They show that ethnicity is consciousness of difference (Eller, 1997) and acts of ethnic subjects have been arranged by discursive construction of identities. Also, apparently, when you talk about language of ethnicity or minority, you mean language of kinship (Horowitz, 1985). Therefore, when it comes to learning the official language, it reflects a decision-making process coercing intrafamilial interaction.

The report prepared by Ball for UNESCO (2010) points out that ethnic parents' perception about the value of learning a different language, in other words, choosing to conduct the intrafamilial interaction over the official language, is crucial for their children because parents are the bridge between advocating mother tongue preservation and school education and success. Ball mentions that parents in bilingual homes frequently construct *context-specific communication systems* to speak different languages, *including a one parent-one language practice, using a particular language in particular settings, or at particular times or occasions* (Ball, 2010: 39).

As reflected by the narratives, such a context-specific communication system cannot be taught apart from ideological state apparatuses to which ethnic households have commonly and constantly been subjected. Language shift, for instance, as a part of educational requirements, focuses on their domestic lives and is one of them.

Pease-Alvarez & Vasquez (1994) suggest that different cultural and linguistic practices of minority children are generally wasted at schools and this process may either increase the conflict between household and school, thus *threatening children's ability to interact and learn from one another*, or, *by acknowledging and building upon the meanings and experiences that students bring to school*, parents, teachers, students, all together can be in cooperation (p.94).

Most of the interviews put forth that ethnic parents are totally conscious of monolingualistic-educational expectations and in favor of being in cooperation. But this does not reflect a perfect solidarity; they just have developed some survival strategies, mainly three: a) being aware of the nationalist perspective, but not refusing institutional norms totally; b) supporting children for gaining healthy socialization skills and guaranteeing their success in life by allowing the official language to get into the house in a very active way; however, c) never giving up mentioning and teaching ethnic-cultural characteristics, especially the mother tongue and historical prices of being different or defined as the "other." In view of that, a call, like "never speak their mother tongue near children" is a reality; but, it does not refer to a complete language shift.

References

Alba, R. Logan, J. Lutz, A. & Stults, B. (2002). Only English by the third generation? Loss and preservation of the mother tongue among the grand children of contemporary immigrants. *Demography*, 39(3), 467-484.

Assmann, J. (1988). Collective memory and cultural identity. *Kultur und Gedächtnis*, Jan Assmann and Tonio Hölscher (eds.). Suhrkamp, Frankfurt/Main, pp.9-19

Ball, S. J. (1990). Politics and policy making in education: Explorations in policy sociology. Routledge, London.

Ball, S. J. (2013). *Foucault, power, and education*, Routletge. New York.

Ball, J. (2010). Enhancing learning of children from diverse language backgrounds: Mother tongue based bilingual or multilingual education in the early years *Presentation to UNESCO International Symposium: Translation and Cultural Mediation*, Paris: UNESCO, 22/23 February 2010, on the occasion of the 11th International Mother Language Day in collaboration with the International Association for Translation and Intercultural Studies, 2010 International Year for the Rapprochement of Cultures.

Ball, J. (2011). Enhancing learning of children from diverse language backgrounds: Mother tongue based bilingual or multilingual education in the early years. United Nations Educational, Scientific and Cultural Organization (UNESCO), Paris.

Beşikçi, İ. (1991). *Kürtlerin mecburi iskanı*, Yurt Yayınları, Ankara. (In Turkish)

Bourdieu, P. (2012). *Language and symbolic power.*.John B. Thompson. (Ed.) Gino Raymond and Matthew Adamson. (Trans.) Polity Press, Edition,14, Cambridge.

Chalmers I. (1994). *Migrancy, culture, identity*. Routledge. London and New York.

Cohen J. H. & Sirkeci İ. (2011). *Cultures of migration. The global nature of contemporary mobility*. University of Texas Press. Austin, Texas.

Çalcı, S. (2012). Deleuze ve Guattari'de dilin yersiz yurtsuzlaştırılması: Emir sözcüklerden tercihler mantığına. *Posseible Düşünce Dergisi*, 2 (15), 6-27 (In Turkish)

Deleuze, G., Guattari, F. and Brinkley, R. (1983). What is a minor literature? *Mississipi Review*, 11(3), 13-33.

Dumais, S. (2002). Cultural capital, gender, and school success: The role of habitus. *Sociology of Education*, 75, January, 44-68.

Eller, J. D. (1997). Ethnicity, culture and "the past". *Michigan Quarterly Review*, 36, Received from: Issue 4. http://quod.lib.umich.edu/cgi/t/text/text-idx?cc=mqr;c=mqr;c=mqrarchive;idno=act2080.0036.411;view=text;rgn=main;xc=1;g=mqrg

Hart, W. M. C., Saran N. (1969). *Zeytinburnu: Gecekondu bölgesi*, Ticaret Odası. Istanbul.

Horowitz, D. (1985). *Ethnic groups in conflict* , University of California Press. Berkeley, CA.

Garrett, P. B. & Baquedano-Lopez, Patricia (2001). Language socialization: Reproduction and continuity, transformation and change. *Annual Review of Anthropology*, 31, 339-361

Goffman, E. (1986) Stigma: Notes on management of spoiled identity. Simon & Schuster, Inc. N.Y.

Loo, C., M. (1985). The 'billaterate' ballot controversy: Language acquisition and cultural shift among immigrants. *International Migration Review*, 19(3), 493-515.

McKenon D. (1994). Language, culture and schooling. Fred Genesee (Ed.), Educating second language children, the whole child, the whole curriculum, the whole community. Cambridge Language Education Series. Cambridge University Press. pp.15-55.

Pease-Alvarez L. & Vasquez O. (1994) Language socialization in ethnic minority Communities Fred Genesee (Ed.), Educating second language children, the whole child, the whole curriculum, the whole community. Cambridge Language Education Series. Cambridge University Press. pp. 82-102.

Portes, A. & Rumbaut R. (2001). *Legacies: The story of the immigrant second generation*. University of California Press, Berkeley.

Smith, A. D. (1986). *The Ethnic origins of nations*, Blackwell, Oxford.

Smith, A. D. (1991). *National identity*. University of Nevada Press, Reno.

Smits, J. & Gündüz-Hoşgör,A. (2003) Linguistic capital: Language as a socio-economic resource among Kurdish and Arabic women in Turkey. *Ethnic and Racial Studies* 26(5), 829-53.

Tollefson, J. (1989). Language policy and social theory. In V. Gjurin (Ed.), *Festschrift for Jakob Rigle,r* Slavic Society of Slovenia, Ljubljana, pp. 309-318.

Tollefson, J. W. (2012). *Language policies in education: Critical issues.* (2nd edition). Routledge, New York.

Verkuyten, M., (2006). The social psychology of ethnic identity: European monographs in social psychology. Psychology Press. Taylor & Francis Group. Hove & N.Y.

Yıldırım, A. (2011). Eleştirel pedagoji: Paulo Freire ve Ivan Illich'in eğitim anlayışı üzerine. Anı Yayınları, Ankara. (In Turkish)

Zeyneloğlu, S., Civelek, Y. H. & Coşkun, Y. (2011). Kürt sorununda antropolojik ve demografik boyut: Sayım ve araştırma verilerinden elde edilen bulgular" *Uluslararası İnsan Bilimleri Dergisi,* 8(1), 335-384. (In Turkish)

Zeyneloğlu, S, Sirkeci, İ. & Civelek, Y. (2014) Simultaneous divergence & convergence: Transitive ethnicity in the Turkish-Kurdish context", *BSPS Annual Conference*, 8-9 September, Winchester, UK.

Interregional migration and language shift among Turkey's ethnic Kurds[Υ]

Sinan Zeyneloğlu[*], Ibrahim Sirkeci[♦], Yaprak Civelek[♥]

Introduction

Analysing population patterns and behaviour of ethnic groups in Turkey is a challenge due to paucity of reliable data drawn upon representative samples as well as overall very sensitive political context. However, the ethnic differences in Turkey's demography are significant as in many other multi-ethnic countries. Due to rapid urbanisation and violent ethnic conflict in the second half of the 20th century, Turkey has seen a major geographic shift of population which has also resulted in changes in ethnic mix of populations across regions. In this study, we aimed at mapping out these shifts. Nevertheless, finding the appropriate proxy to measure ethnic patterns is difficult as there has been no census or major survey data detailing language use published since the 1965 Turkish census while ethnic identity, as such, has been never been openly asked for in any census or major survey. Historically, mother tongue in surveys and censuses have been used as a proxy of ethnicity. However, we have first analysed a relatively recent survey data to raise concerns about the use of language as ethnic marker. Hence, we opted to utilise second language use as well as parental language besides birth-region as ethnic markers instead of mother tongue/main language as over the years Turkish has become the most commonly used language among the Kurds in Turkey.

Alba (2005) argued that blurred boundaries –which we often see in migration literature on second generations- can be associated with "the prospects and processes of assimilation and exclusion". Alba et al (2002) pointed that languages spoken at home by third-generation immigrant children are most affected by factors including intermarriage. These arguments are not exclusive to international migration context and thus well be relevant to internal migration of ethnic groups such as Kurds from east to the west of Turkey. Considering language shift as well as widespread bilingualism among the Kurds (Zeyneloğlu et.al. 2014), we reject the approach equating mother tongue to ethnicity in censuses and surveys in Turkey.

Our analysis of the TDHS data in regards to parents' language and educational attainment shows that more than 3% of children whose both parents speak Kurdish as main language are reported not to be Kurdish speaking. At the same time, Kurdish speakers are almost non-existent among the children of those who do not speak Kurdish at all. Furthermore, Kurdish is only the second language

[Υ] We would like to thank Turkish Statistics Office for permission to analyse the 2000 Census data; Hacettepe Institute of Population Studies and Macro Inc. for the dataset of TDHS 2003.

[*] Assistant Professor at the Department of City and Regional Planning, Gaziantep University, Gaziantep, Turkey and Affiliate Member of the Regent's Centre for Transnational Studies, Regent's University London, UK.

[♦] Professor and Director at Regent's Centre for Transnational Studies, Faculty of Business and Management, Regent's University London, United Kingdom.

[♥] Assistant Professor at the Department of Sociology, Istanbul Arel University, Istanbul, Turkey.

among about 5% of children whose both parents speak Kurdish as main language. This figure declines below 2% among the children of persons whose main language is not Kurdish. It appears that some of the children of Kurdish parents have been raised in Turkish or have adopted that language as their main medium of expression at a later time.

Table 1 Cross-tabulation of parents' language versus respondent's language[a]

	Parents' language		
	Both parents speak Kurdish as main language	Only one parent speaks Kurdish as main language	Neither parent speaks Kurdish as main language
Respondent's own languages	Column %	Column %	Column %
Main language Kurdish, does not speak Turkish as second language	21.3	3.8	0.0
Main language Kurdish, does speak Turkish as second language	70.0	25.7	0.1
Main language not Kurdish, but does speak Kurdish as second language	5.4	26.3	1.5
Does not speak Kurdish at all	3.3	44.1	98.4
Total	100.0	100.0	100.0
N	1,203	62	6,805

[a] Ever married women aged 15-49
Source: TDHS 2003 data

Education seemingly plays a role in language shift. We found that higher the educational attainment the lower the use of Kurdish language as it declines from over 99% among the uneducated to 87% among secondary school (including middle school) or above graduates. Kurdish is not even a second language for 13% of secondary school graduates. As Smits and Gündüz-Hoşgör (2003) have noted, there appears to be a *strong relationship between going to school and speaking Turkish* among Kurds. It appears that there is no bijective link between mother tongue/main language and ethnicity in the Turkish context.

The main focus of this paper is to explore internal migration of Kurds in Turkey and whether migration affects language shift besides education. We argue that overt questions on ethnic identity are needed to properly identify ethnic groups. Due to missing information on ethnicity as such, we employ 'birth region' as a proxy for ethnic origin, establishing that persons born in the predominantly Kurdish-speaking provinces are 'mostly' of Kurdish origin. Further, we make use of second language as well as parental mother tongue to locate ethnic Kurds within the data besides childhood region. First, we explain our methodology before analysing the internal migration of the Kurds in Turkey. Finally language shift is examined by migration patterns.

Data and methods

We have used tabulations from the 2000 Census full data, which is the latest available[288]. Considering the significance of intermarriage in language shift, we have focused on those aged 25 to 64 and thus avoided the institutional population and retired persons. The census 2000 data contains 29,801,881 persons aged 25-64. When persons born abroad as well as those whose birth place is unknown are excluded 29,083,058 persons remain. Persons living outside their birth region are classified as interregional movers in this study. Details of the choice for birthregion instead of language are explained in another study (See Zeyneloglu, Sirkeci, Civelek, forthcoming).

Table 2 Distribution of population born in regions according to region of residence and age groups (column % within each region of birth)

Region of birth	Region of residence in 2000[a]		Age group							
			55-64		45-54		35-44		25-34	
			Male	Female	Male	Female	Male	Female	Male	Female
MAR	Mar		90.3	89.9	91.4	90.1	91.8	90.7	90.7	90.1
AEG		Mar	4.7	4.9	5.5	5.9	5.3	5.7	5.7	5.8
	Aeg		92.6	92.3	91.1	90.4	90.5	90.0	87.2	87.8
MED		Mar	3.8	3.4	4.6	4.0	4.7	4.1	5.6	4.5
	Med		89.6	90.4	87.9	88.9	87.1	88.7	82.6	86.2
CEN		Mar	10.5	9.7	13.4	12.4	14.6	13.7	15.8	14.7
	Aeg		5.3	4.4	6.0	5.2	5.9	5.4	5.4	5.2
	Cen		80.2	82.6	75.8	78.0	74.1	76.0	71.4	74.1
WBS		Mar	20.0	19.9	26.6	26.2	30.6	29.9	33.4	32.1
	Cen		4.4	4.7	5.1	5.3	5.5	5.3	5.8	5.4
	WBS		72.6	72.6	64.6	64.9	59.7	60.8	55.0	57.7
EBS		Mar	24.0	22.5	31.3	29.7	34.9	34.7	36.0	35.5
	WBS		7.1	7.3	6.7	6.9	5.7	6.6	4.3	5.2
	EBS		61.6	63.9	53.3	55.8	50.3	50.4	49.7	50.8
ESA		Mar	18.9	18.3	21.7	20.2	23.3	21.9	23.1	21.2
	Aeg		5.6	4.9	6.1	5.5	5.8	5.7	5.3	5.1
	Med		5.8	5.2	6.8	6.2	6.5	6.4	5.8	5.9
	Cen		5.6	5.6	6.0	5.9	5.9	5.7	5.3	5.0
	ESA		62.4	64.3	57.3	60.3	56.3	58.3	57.6	60.7
KSR		Mar	12.3	11.9	15.0	13.6	16.4	14.4	18.1	14.6
	Aeg		7.6	7.0	8.8	7.9	9.1	8.3	8.7	8.0
	Med		7.3	6.8	8.1	7.5	8.0	7.8	7.5	7.3
	KSR		66.1	67.9	60.1	64.1	58.3	62.3	57.4	63.6

[a] Only those regions of residence with a share of over 5% in any age or gender group are indicated.
Source: Census 2000 data

Turkish censuses publicly reported the language questions until 1965. Kurds have been largely concentrated in 10 eastern provinces (Ağrı, Tunceli, Bingöl, Muş, Bitlis, Van, Diyarbakır, Mardin, Siirt and Hakkâri). Based on the 1945 Census results, we classified these as the KSR (Kurdish speaking region). Majority of people born in the KSR is expected to be of Kurdish origin. There are socio-

---

[288] Until the year 2000 Turkey conducted de facto censuses and moved onto an address based population record system in 2007. The '2011 Housing and Population Census' is an 11% sample survey of the population.

economic development level differences between regions (Dinçer et al., 2003) and therefore out-migration propensities differ too (Sirkeci et al., 2012). The eastern and south eastern provinces we divide into two regions: the predominantly Kurdish speaking region (KSR) and the rest of Eastern and South Eastern Anatolia (ESA). Persons born outside ESA and KSR at ages 25-64 according to census 2000 are assumed to be of non-Kurdish origin.

Almost 80% of persons living in West and South who spent their childhood in KSR have a connection with the Kurdish language either as main, second or parents' language. Most of the remaining 20% we assume being Kurdish. In the less-than-primary education category only 4% have no connection to the Kurdish language which roughly equal to the Arabic speaking KSR population. Among primary school graduates this proportion rises to 30% while more than 59% of KSR-origin dwellers at secondary or above level in western regions have not expressed personal or parental usage of Kurdish.

Inter-regional Kurdish movers in Turkey

Interregional human mobility in Turkey has risen dramatically in the second half of the 20th century: While among the 55-64 year olds less than a quarter of couples had either wife and/or husband living outside their birth region, this figure rises to 39% among the 25-34 year olds.

Some regions have retained their native born populations. For example, 90% of population in all analysed cohorts and each gender born in Marmara region continues to live there. Similarly, around 90% of population born in Aegean region remained in that region with a small decline among younger age groups. In Eastern and Southeastern Anatolia regions, the percentage of those remaining in their birth region is very low. The percentage of KSR-born population still living in their birth region ranges from 57% to 68%. The out-migrating population from Eastern and Southeastern Anatolia is destined to several regions. While 18% of men and 15% of women at ages 25-34 born in KSR live in Marmara region, 9% of males and 8% of females do so in the Aegean (AEG). A further 8% of KSR-born males and 7% of females in that age group live in the Mediterranean (MED).

An interesting difference between age groups has to be noted for KSR. While in the groups above age 35 regardless of gender more than 95% of the population has been born in that region, among 25-34 males this percentage drops to 87% for males whilst measured as 92% among females in the same age group.

Migration and language shift

We found that monoglot Turkish speakers share in the KSR resident female population increases as educational attainment level rises. Unsurprisingly bilingualism increases sharply with education. We see similar pattern among Kurdish women resident in the Western parts of the country but with higher monoglot Turkish speakers and much higher levels of bilingualism irrespective of educational attainment levels.

Conclusion and suggestions for further analysis

In this paper, we have analysed interregional migration among the Kurds and language shift. Sizeable Kurdish populations have emerged in three regions, namely Marmara, Aegean and the Mediterranean. Language shift has blurred the relationship between Kurdish language and the Kurdish ethnie so that mother tongue alone is declining in value as an appropriate ethnic marker in contemporary Turkey. Our analysis, using census 2000 data as well as TDHS 2003 data, provides an example of how and under which assumptions birth region together with second language as well as parental language use can be employed as an ethnic marker, though this method will probably be inappropriate with more recent data considering children of Kurdish migrants born in the western regions in the last few decades. Some of these offspring will adhere to the Turkish identity but some might retain their Kurdishness even with high levels of educational attainment. The time has come for ethnicity, as such, to be openly asked and recorded in Turkish surveys and censuses. Until then, most researchers including the authors of this article will have to utilize proxies as substitute.

References

Alba, R., Logan, J., Lutz, A., & Stults, B. (2002). Only English by the third generation? Loss and preservation of the mother tongue among the grandchildren of contemporary immigrants. *Demography*, 39(3), 467-484.

Alba, R. (2005). Bright vs. blurred boundaries: Second-generation assimilation and exclusion in France, Germany, and the United States. *Ethnic and Racial Studies*, 28(1), 20-49.

DPT (1982). Türkiye'de Yerleşme Merkezlerinin Kademelenmesi: Ülke Yerleşme Merkezleri Sistemi. Ankara: DPT Kalkınmada Öncelikli Yöreler Başkanlığı.

Gündüz-Hoşgör, A. and Smits, J. (2002). "Intermarriage between Turks and Kurds in Contemporary Turkey." *European Sociological Review* 18(4): 417-32.

Koç, İ., Hancıoğlu, A. and Çavlin, A. (2008). "Demographic Differentials and Demographic Integration of Turkish and Kurdish Populations in Turkey." *Population Research and Policy Review* 27 (2008): 447-57.

Mutlu, S. (1996). "Ethnic Kurds in Turkey: A Demographic Study." *International Journal of Middle Eastern Studies* 28: 517-41.

Mutlu, S. (1989). "Population and Agglomeration Trends in the Turkish Settlement System: an Empirical Analysis and some of its Applications." *METU Studies in Development* 16: 99-125.

Smith, A. D. (1986). *The Ethnic Origins of Nations*, Oxford: Blackwell.

Smits, J. and Gündüz-Hoşgör, A. (2003). "Linguistic capital: Language as a socio-economic resource among Kurdish and Arabic women in Turkey." *Ethnic and Racial Studies* 26(5): 829-53.

SIS. (2003). 2000 Census of Population, Social and Economic Characteristics of Population.

SIS. (1969). 1965 Census of Population, Social and Economic Characteristics of Population.

SIS. (1950). Recensement Général de la Population du 1945, Population de la Turquie.

Sirkeci, I. (2003). Migration, ethnicity and conflict: the environment of insecurity and Turkish Kurdish international migration (Doctoral dissertation, University of Sheffield).

Zeyneloğlu, S., Sirkeci, I., Civelek, Y. (2014). "Simultaneous divergence & convergence: Transitive ethnicity in the Turkish-Kurdish context", *BSPS Annual Conference*, 8-9 September 2014, Winchester, UK.

The Event of Bulgaria Migration and the Discourses of Nationalism and Gender in Ahmet Er's Theaters

Başak Akar[289], Özge Öz Döm[290], Melike Güngör[291]

Introduction

Migration mainly refers to the "permanent movement of persons over significant distance" (Sills and others, 1968, p.286). In addition, another typology of forced migration is defined as migration is a result of coercion and crisis. The definition provided by the International Association for the Study of Forced Migration, is the movements of refugees and internally displaced people (those displaced by conflicts) as well as people displaced by natural or environmental disasters, chemical or nuclear disasters, famine, or development projects (IASFM, 2015). Not only are the reasons for the migration important but so are the crises behind these migrations (Kuhlman, 2000, pp.4-5). So, the agents of forced migration can be the state, terrorist groups, commercial entities, and natural disasters; however mainly violence and persecution are the main reasons behind it (Kuhlman, 2000, p.5). These forced and involuntary migrations can be categorized into three subcategories. The first one is ethnic dilution, the second one is ethnic consolidation and the third category is ethnic cleansing defined as forcing undesired population to flee from that specific area (Bookman, 1997, pp. 122-125). The methods of ethnic cleansing are "…coerced departures, harassment to induce departure, cultural cleansing, payment for expulsion and genocide" (Bookman, 1997, pp.133 – 137).

In the specific case of migration of Turkish population from Bulgaria in 1950-1951, this study uses the definition of forced migration from Kuhlman (2000) and categorization of Bookman while making an analysis. The case of migration of the Turks from Bulgaria shows the characteristics of forced migration of specific ethnic (or national) group with the aim of cleansing of this population from Bulgaria.

This study understands the migration from Bulgaria not only to be a transfer of population from one country to another, but also it is a matter of transition from one culture to another, one political system to another and escape from oppression. The study investigates the construction of the identity by the help of nationalism where the rise of the gender discourse goes hand in hand with nationalism during the migration. Our study focuses on nationalism discourse related to the migration phenomenon in a theater script where many authors preferred conducting their research either on the official ideology discourse and state in theater (Başbuğ, 2013), genesis and identity discourses in a wide range of literature (Belge, 2008), modernity and national identity construction in

[289]Başak AKAR is PhD Candidate and Research Assistant at Yıldırım Beyazıt University Faculty of Political Sciences Public Administration, Ankara, Turkey. E-mail: akar_b@hotmail.com
[290] Özge ÖZ DÖM is Research Assistant at Yıldırım Beyazıt University Faculty of Political Sciences Public Administration, Ankara, Turkey
[291] Melike GÜNGÖR is Research Assistant at Yıldırım Beyazıt University Faculty of Political Sciences Public Administration, Ankara, Turkey

architecture (Bozdoğan, 2002) or the relationship between the language and the identities in migration (Cengiz, 2010).

Migration, Nationalism and Gender, Migration of Turkish population from Bulgaria in 1950-1952

More than 150,000 Turks had migrated between the years of 1950 and 1952until an agreement was signed in 1968. The 1968 agreement led the way to the migration of more than 100,000 Turks aimed at uniting the members of dispersed families (Parla, 2007, p.159). The Turkish population migrated in 1950 and 1951 to Turkey had been faced with many obstacles, according to a survey depending on the responses of 9446 migrants among heads of the family, 74% of the immigrants stated that they have been treated badly and 85.3% of them thought that it was impossible to live in Bulgaria under those conditions (Çolak, 2013, p.121). Therefore, the movement of Turkish people from the lands in which they called "home"- "homeland" so many years include many experiences and such a movement had an impact on so many lives that touches the lives of many people even today. So, it is crucial to understand the underlying reasons behind this forced migration to evaluate the experiences of people who were forced to migrate and how they constructed their identities on nationalism afterwards.

There are two prominent reasons for Bulgaria's policies aiming the Turkish population migrate from Bulgaria. One of the reasons is the economic concerns. When collectivization was introduced in 1950s Bulgaria, minorities were forced to leave their homes and migrate to urban centers of the country in order to search for new jobs and better economic conditions since government charged them with heavy taxes and forced them to hand over most of their products to the government (Çolak, 2013, p.119). Deducing the fact that the minorities were forced to leave the country to provide the Bulgarian population economic advantages and opportunities (Şentürk, 2010, p.16-17) where the main objective of Sovietization was to provide the settlement of the class mentality and equality caused neglecting ethnies (Jennison, 1975). The main problem in terms of Soviet Union, with Marxist ideals, was to combine nationalism question with socialism's ideals referring National Delimitation Policies as a step for Soviet identity.

The second and the most important reason were the nationalist projects of the Bulgarian government. Benedict Anderson states that "nation is an imagined community", as the members never see the homeland and experience directly the shared feelings of the others, but feel as if it was that way. However, some other scholars such as Ernest Renan defines it as "culmination of a long past of sacrifice and devotion" (Zuelow, 2010) yet he signifies an oblivion and remembrance. This study refers to an adoption of these two definitions of nationalism, where the study investigates a narration of identity through the migration including nationalism and gender discourse. The migration from Bulgaria can be explained with this desire of Bulgarian state to create a homogenized nation. The identity, ethnic and religious sense of belonging of the Turkish people had been seen as a threat to the Bulgarian nation-state. As a consequence, the Bulgarian government forced its Turkish population to migrate to Turkey. In the 1950s, with the effect of Communist Party's being in power in 1942, the assimilation of the Turkish people and institutions had begun with the aim of cultural and economic homogenization of Bulgaria, as any other minorities in Bulgaria, with Party's aim of "creating one united nation" (Çolak, 2013, p.19). At this point, the Bulgarian government denied the ethnic origin of Turkish population and stated that Turks had originally come from Bulgarian descent, and they have been assimilated and Islamized by Ottoman Empire. This statement gave the government the opportunity to justify the policies implemented in the name of uniting the Bulgarian nation. Turks in Bulgaria were forced to take Bulgarian names, Muslim practices were curbed and the right to get an education in the Turkish language in schools was terminated. The Bulgarian government aimed to secure its territorial unity and internal stability by suppressing the Turkish population. There are always "them" and "us" in the minds of people depending on the nationalist discourse they grow in, and this creates a vicious circle to construct the "us" and "them". When "we" stand for "our" ethnic identities, this paves the way to "them" to hold on what they are told to be have had in their ethnic identity. So one nationalist spark can turn into many and in the case of Turkish population in Bulgaria, they started to glorify Turkey and its land as a worshipful entity. Turkish population developed a sense of Turkish nationalism and started to think Turkey as a place of salvation (Şentürk, 2010, p.8).

The themes regarding national identity, are "samehood- selfhood" (Cillia et al, 2013). Selfhood and Samehood is the coherence of an identity with symbols and its construction before the "other" identities. Since a nation would identify itself on the reverse reflection (Cillia et al. 1999; Wodak, 2009). "The Us" is always constructed on positive manners while "The other" always have negative aspects. The features that are referred throughout the theater screenplay. Political consciousnes arises as victimhood (Jacoby, 2015) during the immigration as well as history glorification including oblivion and remembrance (Renan, 1882), homeland as motherland (Najmabadi, 1997), cultural and religious dedication. The themes regarding gender in nationalism are patriarchy with "braveness" (Nagel, 1998) and women's fragility.

However, when gender appears as an important categorical analysis on migration phenomenon becomes more complicated. When nation-states have already categorized immigrants with their detailed criterions gender exists as a discriminative cosmos which all these categories stand upon. Yuval-Davis (2010) mentions that processes such as foundation or reforms, revisions are so significant for how different citizenship roles for women and men are constructed. These processes make patriarchal oppression more powerful and by this way actually try to define women and draw lines to their positions. Nationalists generally tend to re-traditionalize society and count traditions as the legacy resources of nation and cultural renewal. These real or invented traditions are generally patriarchal and strictly involved with the relation between nationalism and masculinity (Nagel,1998, p.83). On the other hand the politically powerful resemblance between nation and family also discerns successful discourse which could perceive people to this strict relation. In this manner, when family are forced to migrate these gender roles become more apparent with the effect of a reactionist nationalism. In addition to that, the political elites were used by the Soviets as a tool to spread ethnic particularistic nationalism instead of civic universalist nationalism in the region (Morawska, 2000). Gender is a concept which includes social meanings of men's and women's behavior. Moreover most of the writers in literature emphasize that gender got involved in discussion recently. Yet it is significant that by immigration roles are redefined towards gender (Schrover&Moloney, 2014, p.256) and when we think forced migration with ethnic conflict nationalism in relation with gender appear as the other significant category of our study.

Methods and findings

Narrative identity and national identity are observable throughout the texts as we follow Genette's (1980) narrative discourse theory and Wodak's (2009) point of view on discursive construction of national identities. While examining the fiction of "the other" and "the us" in the text throughout the basic themes, we also look at the scene, whether there is a clue for decoration and scene; a way to criticize the literature, who is the target reader or implied author. Also the narrative discourse examines whether the narration is a whole in the text. Moreover, there is preface, notes in the text, stage instructions and narration of the author to be analysed, too.

The space of the theater play is Bulgaria and the story is told in a small Turkish border village in the Balkans. The space has a feeling of lack of belonging. There are two basic themes: political borders (in preface) and the wistful for the motherland in the space in the script. The script was published by the New Prison Press for the first time 1951, which gives us a clue on the timing of the text. The play was probably written in the context of the Turkish immigration after World War II under Sovietization of the land. The preface calls the period "under the Red Imperialism". Later on, the second edition which we analyse has been published in 1980; during the days of the coup.

The Immigrant is a "national screenplay" written by a Turkish nationalist. "The other" identity of the "The Immigrant" is basically the Bulgarians. However, in the dialogues we meet more than one "other"s including the "Russians" and "Chinese"."The Immigrant" shows a clear pathway for the construction of a "selfhood" and "samehood" of a nationalistic identity. The certain circumstances of the Cold War, post World War 2 and the Migration puts it more apparently."Us" fiction is based on coreligionists and kinship that were perceived as hostages. Although the land used to be owned by the Muslim population, they feel as if they were captives and in dilemma of either leaving or staying in their villages. As the no name preface writer, who edited the script, claims that the immigration from the Balkans were forced migrations with atrocity.The author, Ahmet Er is a gendermary officer. The editors think that this officer finds the "other" (probably Western) screenplays are somewhat unable to fit "our" traditions.

The theme "Turkish history" goes hand in hand with the feelings regarding respect. The theme refers to the Battle of Dardanelles in the Great War at first, and then to the sorrow and success during the war. Those memories remind national traumas and pride of the success towards the "West". The theme often represents Central Asia where the "first homeland" of the Turks were. The reason why the Turks left their first homeland is again forced migration, though the forcing power is nature rather than a concrete enemy. So the author creates "the other" in the body of the Chinese, where he also builds the myth of born as a member of a "militarist tribe" in the name of brave Gokturks.We observe that the militarist tribe and the religious themes move together usually (Er, 1980, p.107). The glorious Turkish history has been represented by Mehmet the Second who was a symbolic figure of the conquering of a Christian land and made Istanbul the second homeland of the Turks.

The peoples who the Turks brough civilization, justice and light as positive manners were originally Christian according to the script. Therefore, the author assumes that they were uncivilized and unwarranted. Also the second "other" Russians embrace injustice in the land where the Muslim Turkish were expecting for justice and righteousness (Er, 1980, p.118). We can easily understand why the author calls non Muslims "gavur"s, which is directly translated as "non believers", yet, it is an insulting word. The author also makes the dialogues more sensitive while imagining the clashing scenes on Friday, that is the sacred day for the Muslims. "Gavur" is repeated for the non-Muslim kids who gave a start to the fight between the brave Turkish kid "Bahadır", where Bahadır symbolizes the brave youth of the Turkish population. His name is intentionally chosen because of its meaning: brave-hero. He is the hero of a brave defense during the atrocity and immigration.

"Love of the motherland" theme integrates those when the Turks crave their motherland while they are martyrised with hearts full of love of Turk and motherland (Er, 1980, p.108-109). The discourse has been constructed on the traditional values and essence which were archaic and deep rooted. The motherland is sacred and something to die for.The heroism regarding victimhood, emerges. Another theme can be covered under "obedience". There is an emphasis on a feature of the Turkish people who never "takes order", even if they were young students in a classroom. "Turkish nationalism" theme is often apparent in the classroom, where the identity is mostly rationalized and institutionalized. The slogan of "God Almighty save the Turk!"is often used (Er, 1980, pp. 111,115,117) which was also Nihal Atsız's slogan for the Turkish nationalists in Turkey. It refers to the roots of Turkish nationalism and National Movement Party. The children of the class were perceived as the future of the population; they are Turkish blooded and homeland scented (Er, 1980, p. 119).

When we read the script in the light of these concepts, being Turkish exists with masculinity and some conflicting tensions are seen as opportunities to expose the heroism of manhood. The Turkish women characters in the script are very passive and like objects inside due storyline. There are only a few woman characters and they are all children. The text puts an emphasis on dramatic and tragic assaults of the Turks by the Bulgarians. In many scenes, these girls are used merely as reporters. They are demonstrated as too delicate for the harshness of wars. Girls generally ask questions to men to let them tell the story to audience.

When the family decides to immigrate to the "motherland", all characters feel both happy and upset. The family is seen as lucky that they could reach their homeland but also they couldn't accept easily to leave lands they rooted. When Bahadır and Ayşe say goodbye to Yeşim a drama rises to try to enhance the glory of the motherland Turkey. Moreover Yeşim is appreciated Bahadır for protecting herself from 'outlanders'. When we analyze this position of women with reference to Najmabadi (1997) forced immigration enable interpreting these roles in different way. Najmabadi asks that how men could die for and kill someone for a homeland; how homeland becomes a political power which gathers men around the same goal. Consequently the homeland appears more than a land and it is not non-sexual. Actually the homeland is something had to be protected from enemies' bad intentions, harassment and rapes. (Najmabadi, 1997) This position is inevitably supported by nationalist feelings which charges men as protectors especially of women. At this point homeland emerges as erotic objects in the eye of men (actually they are potential soldiers) and it is something more than metaphorical. Because these metaphors become apparent in wars and sharpen the differences of gender roles with regards to the homeland. Similarly characters in the script frequently mention the difficulties of being away from the homeland in dramatic and romantic way. Homeland secondly arises as mother. Thus homesickness away from 'motherland' is something like rupture from mother's body. And also returning to homeland is interpreted like returning to uterus (Najmabadi, 1997). So that in the play the writer describes forced immigration to Turkey actually with feelings for completion of all characters. In fact being away from homeland is described as awful enough for everybody. Indeed during the play they try to reach homeland with exceeding outlanders' obstacles. Actually being immigrant means close to others assaults that this kind of foreignness could disappear only in homeland. The "victims" of the forced migration do not feel at home in their dwellings anymore but they bear longing for the new homeland. The reality perceptions of the forced immigrants are dynamic in terms of their cultural identities and socio-cultural realities (Öner, 2012).

Consequently, when the family in the play, try to reach their homeland, Bahadır gets shot by a Bulgarian soldier. But the rest of the family hurry to cross the border and with a deepened sorrow of leaving Bahadır's body out of Turkey's borders. In fact, Bahadır couldn't reach his homeland despite his struggle, but he is still proud of himself that he reads a poem: "We ran to the moon and the star with blue wings; the beautiful homeland: Turkey here we are back!" Also Bahadır consoles his crying father with being back to the homeland that he mentions that there is no need to cry in the homeland. This tirade is full of patriotic metaphors and rhapsodies dedicated to Turkey as the motherland.

Discussion and conclusion

Converting the regional identity into a national identity, finally led the immigrants to be aware of their nationalities. They somehow caught on it to reflect their discontent to the regime. To assimilate all the nations, promoting their national identities could be seen as irrevelant but, Soviet regime had its logic to save the ethnic groups from subnational identities. However, this logical move, from the perspective Soviet Union, led these people see ethnic conflicts more important than the class conflict and wounded upon the regime's main goal. Ultimately, we see representations of nationalism and gender discourse in Ahmet Er's theater script as a reflection of those conversion and identity perception.

The support for "Homeland"as the motherland provides a reason for the forced immigrants, and the ideal of returning back. Parallel to the alienation, their longing for the homeland which is defined as "motherland" keeps growing.

Theater playscript reflects this feeling among the dialogues. Dedication to the traditions and Turkish identity arises; accordingly, nationalism, which empowers patriarchial social discourse, rises in Turkish immigrant population in accordance with the rise of nationalist feelings. Therefore, inequality reflected by the script demonstrate the deepening of gender inequality. Although we are not able to classify the "Göçmen" script as a part of the immigration literature eventually, we observe that literature has been used for populist objectives, where rise of the nationalism has been a fact in certain years in Turkey.

References

Belge, M. (2008). Genesis "Büyük Ulusal Anlatı" ve Türklerin Kökeni, 2nd ed., İletişim, İstanbul

Bookman, M.Z. (1997). The Demographic Struggle for Power the Political Economyof Demographic Engineering in the Modern World. Frank Cass & Co. Ltd.: London

Bozdoğan S. (2002). Modernizm ve Ulusun İnşası: Erken Cumhuriyet Türkiyesi'nde Mimari Kültür, Metis, İstanbul.

Cengiz, S, (2010), Göç, Kimlik ve Edebiyat, Zeitschrifft für die Welt Türken Journal of World of Turks, 2 (3), 85-193.

Cillia, R., Reisigl, M., & Wodak, R. (1999). The Discursive Construction of National Identitites, Discourse&Society (10)2, 149-17.

Çolak, F. (2013). Bulgaristan Türklerinin Türkiye'ye Göç Hareketi (1950-1951). In The History School 14. Retrieved January 24, 2015 from http://dergipark.ulakbim. gov.tr/usakjhs/article/viewFile/5000039651/5000038537

Başbuğ E. D. (2013). Resmi İdeoloji Sahnede, İletişim, İstanbul.

Er A. (1980). Göçmen, Hürriyet Yağmuru ve Göçmen, 2nd ed., Derya Dağıtım A.Ş, İstanbul

Genette G. (1980). Narrative discourse: an essay in method. Cornell University Press, New York.

Sills, D. & Others (1968). International Encyclopedia of the Social Sciences (10) New York: Macmillan

IASFM (2015). What is Forced Migration? Received from http://www.forcedmigration.org/whatisfm.htm, available on: 13.03. 2015

Jacoby, T. A., (2015) A Theory of Victimhood: Politics, Conflict and the Construction of Victim-based Identity, Millenium: Journal of International Studies, 43 (2), 511-530, doi: 10.1177/0305829814550258.

Jennison, E. W., (1975) The Neglected "Ethnics" in Russian History Surveys, The History Teacher, 8(3), 437-451.

Kuhlman, T. (2000). 'Forced Migration: An Economist's' Serie Research memoranda, Vrije Universiteit Amsterdam. Faculteit der Economische Wetenschappen en Econometrie

Nagel, J. (1998). Masculinity and Nationalism: Gender and Sexuality in the Making of Nations. Ethnic and Racial Studies, 21(2), 242-269

Najmabadi, A. (1997). The Erotic Vatan (Homeland) as Beloved and Mother: To Love, To Possess and To Protect, Comparative Studies in Society and History, 39(4), 442-467

Öner A. Ş. (2012). "Son mu, Başlangıç mı? Göç Çalışmalarında Sosyal Bir Olgu Olarak Geri Dönüş", Ihlamur-Öner S.G and Öner N. A. Ş. (eds) Küreselleşme Çağında Göç Kavramlar, Tartışmalar, İletişim, İstanbul, 263-286

Parla, A. (2007). Irregular Workers or Ethnic Kin. International Migration, 45 (3), 157-181

Renan E. (1882). "What is a Nation?" in Becoming National: A Reader, New York and Oxford: Oxford University Press, 1996: 41-55.

Schrover, M.,& Moloney, D. M. (2013). Making a Difference, Schrover, Marlou; Moloney, Deidre M. (eds) Gender, Migration and Categorisation: Making Distinctions Between Migrants in Western Countries 1945-2010, Amsterdam University Press, Amsterdam.

Şentürk, H. (2010). The 1989 Migration from Bulgaria to Turkey: Nationalism and Identity among the Migrants, Boğaziçi University Press, İstanbul.

Yuval-Davis, N. (2010). Cinsiyet ve Millet, İletişim Yayınları, İstanbul

Wodak R. (2009.) Discursive Construction of National Identity, 2nd ed., Edinburgh University Press

Zuelow, E. G., The Nationalism Project: What is Nationalism? Nationalism Studies Information Clearinghouse Received from http://www.nationalismproject.org/what.htm available on 29.11. 2010.

Language and Identity Perception in Nazım Hikmet's Poetry during Exile Years

Hülya Bayrak Akyıldız*

Introduction

In this paper, Nazım Hikmet's poetry in exile years, from 1951 to his death in 1963, is examined in terms of identity projection and the role of language in this.

Nazım Hikmet is one of the greatest poets of our age. His greatness lies in his ability to meet universality and the search of novelty with the contemporary and universal interpretations of the conventional. His poetry, meeting futuristic effects with socialist realistic, Marxist art and then with the voice of folk poems, gets the final touch by the poet's distinctive sensitivity. This is why "earth", "land" and "Turkish" are the key concepts in Nazım Hikmet. Before examining his language and identity perception, let's take a global look on the relation between language and indentity /culture.

Kramsch defines communities of language users and how the use of language affects viewing the world and thus identity:

People who identify themselves as members of a social group (family, neighborhood, professional or ethnic affiliation, nation) acquire common ways of viewing the world through their interactions with other members of the same group. These views are reinforced through institutions like the family, the school, the workplace, the church, the government and other sites of socialization throughout their lives. Common attitudes, beliefs and values are reflected in the way members of the group use language – for example, what they choose to say or not to say and how they say it. (2009:6)

Kramsch defines a speech community as a community of people who use the same linguistic code and a discourse community to refer to the common ways in which members of a social group use language to meet their social needs. This is a view of culture that focuses on the ways of thinking, behaving, and valuing currently shared by members of the same discours community.

Another view with more historical perspective lets us see cultural ways that have evolved and become solidified over time. They have sedimented in the memories of group members who have experienced them first hand or merely heard about them, and who have passed them on in a speech or writing from one generation to the next. The culture of everyday practices draws on the culture of shared history and traditions. (Kramsch, 2009, p. 7)

Language is not a culture-free code, distinct from the way people think or behave, but rather it plays a major role in the perpetuation of culture, particularly in its printed form, Kramsch argues. (2009:8) So language is not only a group of symbols to express what we see or feel, but a system that affects to the core our understandings and perceptions of the world.

Language is a symbolic expression of ways of thinking of a culture. Ways of thinking of each culture is determined by centuries of formation process of that culture. Titiz states that, languages are not only different in terms of vocabulary but also these formation processes and thus ways of thinking. (1998:307)

* Assist. Prof. Dr. at Anadolu University, Department of Turkish Language and Literature. E-mail. hbayrak@anadolu.edu.tr

Akarsu states that language is a system that forms our mental patterns. A human being is born into a language as in a culture. Ways of thinking is shaped by language. (1998:85)

According to linguist W. von Humbolt, one can go down to a nations's culture and world view from that nation's language. Language is the appearence of a nation's soul. (in Akarsu, 1998, p. 62)

Each language contains a tissue of concepts and is a reflection of a part of humanity's way of projection, Akarsu argues (1998: 62-63). She adds that each language is an echo of a world view.

So language is a system that is closely connected to identity. It's by language that we define ourselves, constructing values and norms through our use of language and interactions with other members of our speech community. The effect is even more obvious for a poet whose work is not only done by language but also is the languge itself. It is the atmosphere where he breathes and lives in. In Nazım's case, he does speak another language fluently but it's not the language that shaped him as a person in the earlier years of his life. That's why Turkish language was the passport to Nazım Hikmet when he actually never had one.

Kramsch argues that, to identify themselves as members of the community, people have to define themselves jointly as insiders against others, whom they thereby define as outsiders. (2009, p. 8) This idea is also found in Said who points out the role of negation in construction of identity. Said's ideas on the construction of identity make it easier for us to understand why Nazım's already present ties with his language and country becomes more accentuated in the exile years:

> To a certain extent modern and primitive societies seem to derive a sense of their identities negatively. A fifth-century Athenian was very likely to feel himself to be nonbarbarian as much as he positively felt himself to be Athenian. The geographic boundaries accompany the social, ethnic, and cultural ones in expected ways. Yet often the sense in which someone feels himself to be not-foreign is based on a very unrigorous idea of what is "out there", beyond one's own territory. All Kinds of suppositions, associations, and fictions appear to crowd the unfamiliar space outside one's own (Said, 1994: 54).

Be the suppositions about the others fictious or true, Nazım found himself in exile in a foreign surrounding, where he continued to write in and only in Turkish, recreating an aura of belonging. It's being in a different speech community and people of a different culture from that point on, that made him accentuate his ties with his original country and culture more and more.

Nazim Hikmet's exile years

For Nazım Hikmet, who had not written a single verse other than in Turkish, not being able to speak his own language was the biggest exiles of all. Doğan writes that he would search for the Turks first in the cities he visited; he was a motormouth in Turkish over the phone; he would carry around the books of Orhan Veli, Melih Cevdet and Oktay Rıfat whom he calls "the best poets of Turkish" in his suitcase during his travels. All these facts are indicators of his solitude (1994). For him, Turkish language and poems in Turkish was the water that he lived and breathed in.

In his short writing, titled "Sürgündeki Dil" (Language in Exile), Doğan asks:

> Braudel, the historian says that "language = identity". A person who loses his language, or is driven away from the speech community, finds himself in identity troubles.

In old ages, and later in Rome, sometimes the death sentence would be turned into exile and the murderer would be given a chance to be sent into exile instead of being exucuted. Can we think that the underlying thought here is derived from such identity troubles? (1994).

If we ask this question, focusing on the exile of a poet whose work is the language itself, rather than an ordinary person who is exiled from the community he/she identifies with, we may get to see how the first case can lead to more severe and multi layered identity troubles. In Pırağ'da Vakitler (Times in Prague)(1956), he says: *Ah my rose, being an immigrant is worse than death.* Being exiled from the language that he lives in and writes with, forces the poet to reevaluate his identity projection while it leads to a kind of romanticism that makes it very hard for him to do this objectively: the romanticism of being away from his homeland.

When Nazım got out of prison and fled to Russia, he didn't know that he would find a different country and a political milieu than his years of pupillage. He was followed by the secret service like all the other foreigners. He neither had a citizenship nor a passport. Finally, he was given a Polish passport due to his Polish roots.

In Nazım's poetry during exile years, we see the same convinced communist, but a romantic attachment to his roots can be observed as well. His language becomes more lyric and romantic in this era.

In Russia, he had his comrades that surrounded him, his poetry was largely recognized, he had internationalist views that made him write verses like *The country that I like most is the earth* ("Dörtlük", 1959). All these must have had a relieving effect on him. We see his internationalist views in his poem, "Gelmiş Dünyanın Dört Bir Ucundan": *We've come from the four sides of the World / We speak different languages and understand each other / We are green branches from the world tree / There's a nation called youth, we are from it.* (1956)

But being abroad, away from his homeland affects his identity projection, the internationalist views melts into homesickness. This amalgam changes the themes in his poems, the vocabulary, the meanings attributed to the language and the land. His poetics become gradually romantic.

In "Memet'e Son Mektubumdur" (My Last Letter to Memet), the verses below is an example of the two conflicting concepts: his nostalgia for his roots and internationalist views:

Memet,/ I'll die far from my language and my songs, / my salt and bread,/ homesick for you and your mother, / my friends and my people, / but not in exile, / not in some foreign land / I will die in the country of my dreams / in the white city of my best days (Moscow, 1955)

Turkish, with all its feeling and perception, is fundamental in Nazım's sensitivity. We hear the voices of Yunus Emre and Fuzulî in "Kerem Gibi", a poem which is a turning point in his poetry and avant-garde and revolutionary in Turkish poetry. We see Kerem as a modern hero, ripped off from its original context and reinterpreted. Bu still the sensitivity that lies beneath the original story is present in the poem. The expressions like "O diyor ki bana"("He says to me"), "Ben diyorum ki ona" ("I say to him"), are different versions of minstrels' "Aldı aşık" ("the minstrel took the word") expression. (Gürsel, 2001: 45)

I say to him: / - Let me burn / let me become ash / like Kerem. / If I do not burn / if you do not burn / if we do not burn / how will dark-ness/ ever turn into / light...

As we see in "Kerem Gibi", Nazım profites from the traditional poetry but transforms it into an avant-garde, contemporary poetry. He modernizes the traditional and makes it meet with the universal. He is a world poet while he stays true to his roots.

His "Rubai" is a sign of his perception of language and identity: *Utterance rot in emptiness / If it does not come from earth / If it does not plunge into earth / If it does not put down roots to earth.*

Earth symbolizes a culture area, a cultural accumulation that covers this area (Gürsel, 2001, p. 19). We can observe that Nazım uses the notion of putting down roots and describes his identity based on these cultural roots, from the early times of his poetry.

For Nazım Hikmet, language is the most important constituent of identity. In one of his writings in 1934, he writes:

"The words of my language are like precious stones. Precious stones: red, green, yellow, white, of different sizes; they lay in front of my eyes. They sparkle. My eyes are dazzled. I grisp them. They fall through my fingers, brilliant, like water with sun! I am a jeweler's apprentice. I want to crash these stones into one another and make voices that are unheard of. I want to align them in a way so that my eyes are like listening to the best song ever." *(in Gürsel, 2001: 23)*

In one of his letters, Nazım says that Turkish is one of the most beautiful languages in the world, and adds: "I love Turkish language in the way a peasant loves his land, a carpenter loves his wood and grater. " (in Gürsel, 2001: 24)

As a poet who spent a great deal of his life in exile, in a different surrounding of language and culture, he never fails to protect his ties with his language. In 1961, he writes: *My books are printed in thirty or forty languages / But in my own Turkish, in my own Turkey / I am banned.* ("Autobiography", 1961, Berlin)

During his exile, he visits many European cities towards the end of 50's: Prague, Sophia, Varna, Paris... During these visits he becomes more nostalgic. He complains about getting old, his health condition, being away from his homeland. In Varna, homesickness becomes unbearable:

It's not a heart, but a rawhide sandal, made of buffalo leather
hoofs the rocky roads constantly
but does not get torn apart
A steamer passes by Varna,
Oh the silver strings of Blacksea,
A steamer passes towards Bosphorus
Nâzım caresses the steamer quietly,
His hands get burned. ("The Steamer",1957, Varna)

A few days after this poem, he writes the one below:
The opposite shore is homeland, /I call out from Varna, /Do you hear it? / Memet! Memet! ("Memet", 1957, Varna)

Another example of elements and traces of his culture capturing him from the heart:

This Varna has driven me mad / has driven me crazy. / tomatoes, green peppers, fried turbot on the dining table, / A Blacksea air, "Ha uşaklar!" on the radio / rakı in the glass, lion's milk, anise, / oh the smell of anise! / My language, spoken friendly, brotherly. ("Sofra" 1957, Varna)

He finds a brief relief at Varna, feeling like home with the memory of the food of his homeland:

Cucumber soup in a blue bowl. / they brought a cheese pita / -it's as if I'm in Istanbul- / they brought a cheese pita / with sesame seeds, soft and steaming.../ This summer day in Varna, / all big talk aside, / even for a very sick, very exiled poet / this happiness to be alive. ("The Balcony", 1957, Varna)

In "Gözlerin" (Your Eyes) (1956), he likens the eyes of the beloved to, "the crops in Antalya towards the end of May", to "the chestnut trees of Bursa in fall" and then to "İstanbul in every season and every hour". Again in 1956, in "Karlı Kayın Ormanı" (Snowy Night Woods) he turns his homeland and youth into a distant dream with the verses: *Is my country the farthest away, or my youth or the stars?*

He gets depressed and loses hope from time to time:

Great days in the future / They won't see me / At least let them send me regards / I'm dying of sorrow. ("Days", 1958, Warsaw)

He smittens with the idea of having lost every material thing of his homeland:

My country, my home, my homeland,
Nothing you made remains in my possession,
not a cloth cap
or a pair of shoes that once trod your roads.
Your last shirt wore down long ago to bare threads on my back;
        It was homespun cotton.
Now you live only in the white of my hair,
        the failing of my heart,
        the lines of my forehead,
my country,
my home,
my homeland... (Prague, 1958)

He has nothing material left from his homeland, but his homeland is now engraved in his body and soul.

Nazım also wrote propagandist poems in those years. In those poems we see a communist and internationalist, quiet sure of himself. He is the part of peace movement against nuclear weapons, he writes about radioactivity, post war polarizations, Turkey becoming a colony of the United States, etc. But frequently, some disturbed feeling finds its way to daylight and makes him suffer. In "About the Sea", he says: *I thought of Engels. / How beautiful to have your ashes scattered at sea! / But me, I want to be laid in a pine box / and buried on the Anatolian plateau.* (1954, Tbilisi-Moscow)

He sees almost everything connected to his homeland. Even the expected socialist revolution in Turkey, is a way back home. Wherever he goes, he writes verses that reflect his longing to find a way back home. Turkish and soil nest in his poetry, they transform into one another and becomes the past that is now a distant dream. Nazım defines himself with that longing to go back:

No clouds in the sky
The willows are rainy
 I've ran into Danube
 Flowing muddy
 Hey Hikmet's son, Hikmet's son
 If only you were the water of Danube
 If only you came from the Blackwoods
 If only you flew into Blacksea
If only you became blue, and blue and blue
If only you pass from the Bosphorus
The air of İstanbul over your head
If only you beat the Kadıköy pier
If only you beat and flutter
When Memet and his mother gets on the steamer. ("On Danube River",1958)

He watches his son grow in photographs:
 My heart writhes with the pain of a branch whose fruit has been plucked, / the image of the road that goes down to the Golden Horn never leaves my eyes, / a pair of knives stuck right into my heart: / yearning form my child and nostalgia for İstanbul. ("My Son is Growing up in Photographs", 1954)

In the first verse, we see an image of separation from an Anatolian folk song: "Ham meyvayı kopardılar dalından /Beni ayırdılar nazlı yârimden." (They have plucked the green fruit from its branch / They have separated me from my beloved). The voice of folk songs that often melts into Nazım's voice, is used here to describe separation from his son and from İstanbul.

Conclusion

I write poems / they don't get published / but they will ("Optimism", Leipzig, 1957), says Nâzım Hikmet. And they are now. He missed seeing his poems published in Turkish by two years. But he is now the first name to come to mind in Turkish Poetry. His belated recognition is closely connected with the epic way of him narrating Turkey and its people.

He feels like he gets his swerve on in a balcony in Üsküdar against the sunset while sitting in a tramway station in Leipzig ("Kederleniyorum", 1958). On the road to Stockholm from Leningrad, he looks out of the port hole and sees the white sea, he remembers İstanbul's warm sea, then looks at this rigid, white sea with absolute grief (1959). Near Vienna, he wishes to become a river, pass by Bosphorus and reach and touch the steamer his wife and son gets on. He gets worn out of calling out to his wife from Paris ("Sensiz Paris", 1957). In Prague, he suddenly realizes he has no material left from his homeland and he grieves ("Yine Memleketim Üzerine Söylenmiştir", 1958). In Varna, he gets excited sitting by a dining table full of food and beverage that reminds him of İstanbul. He sometimes loses hope and tells the captain to not wait for him anymore, as he cannot take him to that blue port with plane trees and a dome ("Mavi Liman", 1957). Sometimes he is so puckish and becomes the walnut tree in Gülhane Park, where nobody –including the police- notices him: *My leaves flutter like silk handkerchiefs. / Break one off, my darling, and wipe your tears*("Ceviz Ağacı", 1957). He is mostly not bitter. But one can understand how being in exile affected him as a person and a poet judging by things he and his poetry has gone through.

His last will is to be buried in a village cemetery in Anatolia, which is a striking sign of his idea of belonging: *Comrades, if I die before that day, I mean, / -and it's looking more and more likely- / bury me in a village cemetery in Anatolia, / and if there's one handy, / a plane tree could stand at my head, / I wouldn't need a stone or anything* ("Vasiyet", 1953)

References

Akarsu, B. (1998). *Dil-Kültür Bağlantısı*. İnkılap Yayınları. İstanbul.
Doğan, M. (1994) Sürgündeki Dil. *Varlık*. S. 1039.
Fuat, M. (2001). *Nâzım Hikmet*. Adam yayınları. İstanbul.
Göksu, S.; Timms, E. (1999). Romantic Communist, The Life and Work of Nazım Hikmet. Hurst &Co.. London.
Gürsel, N. (2001). *Dünya Şairi Nazım Hikmet*, Can Yayınları. İstanbul.
Hikmet, N. (2002). *Beyond the Walls, Selected Poems*. Anvil & YKY. London.
            (2002) *Yeni Şiirler*. YKY, İstanbul.
            (2002) *Son Şiirleri*, YKY, İstanbul
Kramsch, C. (2009). *Language and Culture*. Oxford University Press. Oxford.
Said, E. (1994). *Orientalism*. Vintage Books Edition. New York.
Titiz, T., (1997). Süper Türkçe, *Dil Dergisi*, S. 60.

What Exile Brings Along: Signs of Migration and Exile in the Novels *Yezidin Kızı, Sürgün* and *Nilgün*

Yakup Çelik [292]

Introduction

Migration and exile are human tragedies that cannot be characterized. Since the beginning of time, the world is the scene of these tragedies. Migration is a mostly conscious, sometimes forced movement to a new life which aims to have better life conditions and styles. However exile is leaving a habitual, accepted life style usually under pressure and being sent away by force.

Migration sometimes involves free will and desire; people are ready to a transition. However in exile, enforcement stands in the forefront; everything happens out of free will. In migration, there is a target to a better life or at least there is hope. On the other hand in exile, there is moving away of experiences, there is hopelessness and resentment.

In author's life, there were two exile periods after 1910. The first one was between 1913-1918 The second period was between 1922-1938. (For further info, see: Aktaş, 2014). The novels telling the tragedies of young girls are the products of the second period.

The Beauty in the Middle of the Desert: Zeliha

After writing *İstanbul'un İç Yüzü* (1918), Refik Halid Karay didn't write anything could be named as "novel" for about 20 years. A short while later returning to Turkey, *Yezidin Kızı* first was serialized in a journal called Tan; then, it is published as a novel in 1939. In this novel, the story of a young Yezîdî woman, whose life is full of migration and exile experiences, is narrated. A life in confinement; being watched closely, being interrogated because of every single behaviour.

Yezidin Kızı states the dedication of a young woman to her origins and also emphasizes the emergence of a spontaneous impossible love. The novel starts with the desciption of the moment in which Hikmet Ali, the narrator travelling to his village in Suriye and a young and beautiful woman talking in Kurdish meet. This young woman introducing herself as an Argentinian Miss Zeli della Yezdi, was born in 1910 in the city Mendoza in Argentina. She was from Sincar area, she was a Yezîdî. Her ancestors ran away from racist attacks during the period of Ottomans and settle down in Argentina. In the novel, she defines herself as in the following lines:

> "*We are the people who lived on the east coast of Caspian Sea; maybe our people cannot be considered as Iranian, Turkish or Kurdish for now but the fact is that we have been the children of oil territory, so we have been fire worshippers. We went to the South because of the shaking occupation; but we came to such an area of oil again that*

---

[292] Yakup Çelik is Professor of Turkish Language and Literature Department of Yıldız Technical University, Faculty of Arts and Science, Davutpaşa Campus, 34220, Esenler-İstanbul. E-mail: yacelik@yildiz.edu.tr

strenghtens the idea 'the fire had led us under the soil on our way'." (Karay, *Yezidin Kızı*, 1972, p.60).

Zeliha informs Hikmet Ali (the narrator) about misconception of the beliefs of Yezîdî people like 'they don't believe in God', even 'they are satanists'. She has never broken the ties of love between her and her ancestors, her homeland. Her ultimate purpose of being in Syria is to be able to rescue her relatives and to establish a free community. She defines herself as the daughter of Yezid, therefore she is idealist. Because of this idealism, she goes to Sincar Mountains with Hikmet Ali, to see relics which has been left by grand Yezid.

In the novel, the love of Zeliha and Hikmet Ali approaches to a tragedy of people in exile. Control and political context of that territory prevents this love to be revealed but keeps it at an emotional level. Both Hikmet Ali and Zeliha are aware of this impossibility.

In this novel, a young woman is devoid of love and living in a tragedy because of her ethnicity. Being nonresident and living in different regions become destiny for her. It is observed that the narrator Hikmet Ali experiences a similar one to her. We can easily say that *Yezidin Kızı* generates the basis of *Nilgün* which is written in 1950's in terms of themes and fiction. Apart from the situations of young women, themes and properties of fiction are almost the same.

Seher - The Daughter of Exiled Father: Sitti Nevber

The novel starts with the arrival of Hilmi Efendi to Beirut. A nebulous life is waiting for him. He will live in the lost territory of Ottoman Empire. The real tragedy is not about Hilmi Efendi himself but about the family of him destroyed after exile and also about his daughter Seher. In the novel, besides experiences of Hilmi Efendi, the main focus is the tragedy of Seher.

Seher seems to be vengeful because of the bad things have been done to her father during the exile period. She chooses a meaningless life far from feelings as if she is taking revenge of her suffering. Her behaviour becomes to tire İrfan who is in love with her and others. She becomes a famous "club girl".

Hilmi Efendi is forced to live among people whose language he cannot speak, whose national history he doesn't share. Thus, he feels rootless and disidentificated. The only thing helps him to survive, seems to be hankering for his family. He is with people like "Çopur Apti", "Şair Kenan", "Nuri Hoca" and "Daim Bey" who have different personalities and beliefs. This is a kind of consolation for him.

The encounter at the end of the novel is tragic:

> *"Hilmi Efendi turned his eyes to the stage. His sight was clear. A half naked woman, back facing, moving her round shaped hips... She was standing on the stairs and talking to the musicians. Her face couldn't be seen yet. Who was this playful girl whom İrfan had fallen in love with? She should be an attractive, tricky, despotic, unreliable slut.*
>
> *This slut turned her face to the audience wheezing and gabbling since she showed up. She stopped for a while and then laughed brassily. Hilmi Efendi couldn't believe in his eyes; he stood up. He saw the girl bending over the audience and saying:*

"Will you want 'Hoples' again? We got tired of it!" imprudently. When he heard the voice of Seher, he didn't doubt. His glass fell of his hand and he tried to hold the table in order not to slide into the smoky gap opened in front of him." (Karay, *Sürgün*, 2009, p. 219).

This scene all about the death of Hilmi Efendi. He is in the center of this novel and his experiences are the reasons for Seher's plight. He lives away from his city, his homeland, the society that he belongs to, even his family. He doesn't feel like a part of the whole. He lives as a stranger sliding through time. This situation of Hilmi Efendi in exile leads his daughter to become a "club-girl"; this is a self-evident fact.

After having an affair with an actor called Kani, Seher is drifted. She becomes unreliable and uses a nickname "Nevber Sitti". She is unaware of her father's death. Her preceding speech with İrfan is like a confession about her sorrow, her drifted life and her mask.

"Please don't use this false name, call me Seher... My real name is Seher, my mother used to call me like this, my father use to fondle me calling this name." (Karay, *Sürgün*, 2009, p.160).

These words conduce İrfan to understand that she is the daughter of his friend Hilmi Efendi. He wants to save both Seher and Hilmi Efendi from this torture; but Seher prefers to stay with paradoxes. On one hand, she thinks that details of her life can kill her father immediately; but on the other hand, she does what a club girl should do.

"He shouldn't see me, he shoudn't learn about my situation, I should go away immediately. It's impossile for me to confront him; this shame kills both of us.' said Seher and then she begged as if she decided to go away and to leave the very next day: 'There should be my pictures on leaflets, please gather them all, put them away, when I come back, I don't want to see them. And also let's stop by the photo shop on Hendek Street and ask the photographer to remove my big photo from the shop window.'" (Karay, *Sürgün*, 2009, p.161).

These words reveal the features of the relationship between her and her father and also her nurture. But exile causes a big change in her personality. Thus İrfan observes the same disengagement:

"When it was getting dark, he entered the garden; he thought that Seher or before her Kani would come in a hurry and talk to him about the 'going away issue'; but he couldn't see what he expected. He was shocked: The girl was sitting with very noble people, talking in a usual, frivolous manner; doing her job in a usual, fake impression." (Karay, *Sürgün, 2009*, p.164).

Kani is a man who shapes his attitudes according to his benefits. His contribution to the big change of Seher should also be taken into consideration. So, Seher is also decieved and desperate.

After exile, İrfan can be seen as the only common point between the father and daughter; and his decision forms the turning point of the plot:

"Seher wouldn't get better. She was a miserable, ordinary, awful, harmful being; she was a slut in the strict sense; she was living what she had deserved. The only thing he would do was to keep Hilmi Efendi away from Halep. He would write to him that the farm business had been spoiled and he was returning back to İstanbul. That was it!" (Karay, *Sürgün, 2009*, p.166)

Traces of Exile Far Away and a Princess: Nilgün

Refik Halid Karay sets the fiction of his novel *Nilgün* around the experinces of an Ottoman princess after exile. *"Nilgün is a novel shaped by a writer who listened to a story of a friend, and had known Middle East well and combined the story with his imagination and novel technique."* (Aktaş, 2014, p.90). But we should also say that there are many traces of Refik Halid Karay's life in the novel. For instance, the group of 150's is usually mentioned; the name of Nilgün's son is Ömer; and the narrator resembles to the writer in many ways.

The novel starts with an encounter which makes the reader think of the victimization and poverty of the Ottoman noble family exposed to exile. Nilgün is the daughter of the Sultan's son, deceased Rüknettin Efendi. So when she wants to meet the narrator, he gets suspicious; and this detail is significant.

"The first idea occured in my mind was this: They are in trouble, they will ask for help. Then, I thought. 'Where are they going?" (Karay, *Nilgün*, 2009, p.10)

Nilgün has a ticket for travelling in the third section of the ship; but with the hope of meeting a rich man, she gives all her money and travels in a luxurious cabin during half of the journey. The narrator is interested in this situation. His comment is a brief summary of the argument of the novel.

" 'Vah vah! A sultan from Ottoman noble family is a kind of a prisoner in this ship. She cannot go wherever she wants. She is deprived of the right to move closer to rich people just because she has no money. It shouldn't be like this. They should have left the children alone; or maybe they should destrain the wealth of the noble family and send the income to the children monthly. Most of them are miserable.' " (Karay, *Nilgün*, 2009 p.12)

The tragedy in the novel is first seen at the level of materiality and then love. The relationship narrated in the novel starts with a meeting in 1936 and lasts till 1950. Initially something is unnamed between Nilgün and the narrator, which then turns into love. At the end it grows up stronger as a result of world politics and war.

Nilgün is a kind of woman who cannot make a clean breast of herself. She is obliged to leave herself to time and the material issues because of the exile conditions. In fact, Nilgün doesn't know what she is looking for and even why. When she goes to the narrator, she listens to her heart; but when she goes to King of Mapa Ahmet, she listens to her mind guarding her benefits by being with the powerful. She gets confused between high values and material values; and she is inclined to choose material values in the atmosphere of exile. These give an opportunity to have a prestigious, luxurious life far away from poverty; opportunity to be safe due to money and power. The reason of the marriage of Nilgün and the King is the trauma caused by exile.

Nilgün becomes the Queen of Mapa and the narrator's comment about this is essential:

"Being the Queen of Mapa is not raising her honour, but insulting her. I observed and I am still observing. New apellations for our princesses – despite all the faults of the Ottoman nobel family – are so weak in comparison with "Sultan!" (Karay, *Nilgün*, 2009, p.364).

This comment points out victimization and desperation of Nilgün and the Ottoman nobel family; and also it establishes their lost magnificence and power.

A young woman's dilemma of life conditions and love... This novel indicates the extent of influences of social and political conditions on people's feelings and livings. Besides, in this novel; the group of 150's, political developments in Turkey and in the World, effects of II. World War are indirectly mentioned.

Conclusion

In the three novels of Refik Halid Karay (*Yezidin Kızı, Sürgün and Nilgün*) reflecting the impressions of the second exile period of his life (1922-1939); political events turning into tragedies of young women are indicated. On one hand, there is the choice of living the beauty of life along with emotions; and on the other hand there is the obligation of dealing with material and political problems caused by migration and exile. This stream causes young women to fall apart themselves, their own personalities and feelings. In *Yezidin Kızı*, Zeliha is a woman who becomes insensitive and unfamiliar to her own personality due to migration and exile, based on the religion of her family. Finally, she goes mad. In *Nilgün*, because of the exodus of Ottoman noble family, Nilgün slides into darkness. First she fails to choose material power, magnificence or love; but then she chooses power because of her trauma caused by exile. In *Sürgün*, Seher becomes lonely because of the exile of his father; and she has nobody to trust. Desolation makes her a wealth hunter; and also a man hunter.

All young women mentioned in this study become "the missing" instead of making decisions, taking steady positions against migration and exile.

References

Aktaş, Ş. (2014), *Refik Halid Karay*, Turkish Language Association Press, Ankara.

Karay, R. H. (2009), *Nilgün*, İnkılap – Aka Press, İstanbul.

Karay, R. H. (2009), *Sürgün*, İnkılap – Aka Press, İstanbul.

Karay, R. H.(1972), *Yezidin Kızı*, İnkılap – Aka Press, İstanbul.

TÜRK GÖÇ KONFERANSI 2015
TÜRKÇE BİLDİRİLER

"Zorunluluk mu?", "Gönüllü mü?" Türkiye'den Britanya'ya Yeni Göç Dalgası: Ankara Anlaşması

Tuncay Bilecen

Giriş

Bu makale, Ankara Anlaşması olarak bilinen Avrupa Topluluğu Ortaklık Anlaşması'dan (European Community Association Agreement -ECAA) Britanya'da yararlanan kişilerle yapılan görüşmeler neticesinde şekillendirilmiştir. Ankara Anlaşması yoluyla oturum almanın, göçün değişen karakteri ve göç etmeyi zorlaştıran düzenlemeler bağlamında "yeni bir göç yolu" olduğu makalenin iddialarından birisidir. Makalede üzerinde durulacak bir başka husus ise, göçe sebep olan çatışmaların göçten sonra da başka şekillerde devam ettiği ve bunun da insan hareketliliğini artırdığı görüşüdür.

Ankara Anlaşması ile oturum alan göçmenler eğitim, meslek, dil yeterliliği gibi bir takım özellikler bakımından Britanya'da yerleşik olan birinci kuşak göçmenlerden ayrışmaktadırlar. Bu yeni göç akımını ele alırken, göç etme sebepleri (ekonomik, politik, kültürel, ailevi sebepler, akraba ilişkisi vs.) ve göç edilen ülkedeki uyum süreçleri çatışma modeli dolayımında yorumlanacaktır. Bu bakımdan çatışma kavramı; şiddeti değil gönderen, transit ve göç alan devletler arasında göç politikaları bakımından yaşanan gerilimleri, göç eden ve etmeyen haneler arasındaki ilişkileri, göçte cinsiyet rolünün etkisini, göç kararı almada ve yerleşilen yerde yaşanan tüm çatışmaları içerisine alan geniş bir anlam zenginliğini ihtiva etmektedir. Bu bağlamda göç kültürü, göçmenlerin akraba, sosyal bağlantı, deneyim aktarımı vs. ilişkileri kullanarak güvenli yerlere doğru hareket etmelerini ifade etmektedir.

Veri ve Yöntem:

Çalışmada, nitel araştırma yöntemlerinden yarı yapılandırılmış mülakat tekniği kullanılmıştır. Yirmi kişilik örneklem grubu Londra'da yapılan üç aylık saha çalışmasının ardından basit rastgele yöntemle belirlenmiştir. Saha çalışması sırasında Türkiyeli göçmenlerin sosyalleştikleri mekânlar (hemşehri dernekleri, toplum merkezleri, kültür merkezleri, restaurant, cafe, bar, üniversite kantinleri vs.) ziyaret edilmiş, buralarda kurulan ilişkiler neticesinde örneklem oluşturulmuştur. Ayrıca göçmenlerin çalıştıkları işyerlerine ziyaretler gerçekleştirilmiş, böylece çalıştıkları koşullar hakkında bilgi sahibi olunmuştur. Anlaşmaya ilişkin hukuksal ve mali sürece ilişkin bilgi almak amacıyla bu konuda bilgi ve deneyim sahibi iki avukat ve bir muhasebeci ile kayıt cihazı kullanmadan görüşmeler yapılmıştır.

15 Şubat- 15 Mayıs 2015 tarihleri arasında Londra'daki çeşitli mekânlarda gerçekleştirilen görüşmelerin her biri yarım saat ile bir saat yirmi dakika arasında sürmüştür. Görüşülen kişilerin adı soyadı alınmamış, her birine, birden yirmiye kadar numara verilmiştir.

Görüşme soruları dört başlıkta toplanmıştır. Birinci kısımda görüşmecilere ilişkin demografik bilgilere ulaşmak hedeflenmiştir. İkinci kısımda kişilerin göç etme nedenleri, başvuru sırasında yaşadıkları sorunlar, üçüncü kısımda uyum süreçleri ve bu bağlamda Türkiyeli toplumla ve diğer topluluklarla kurdukları ilişkiler, dördüncü kısımda ise yaşadıkları psikolojik çatışmalar ve geleceğe beklentilerine ilişkin sorular yer almıştır. Araştırmaya ilişkin diğer veriler Home Office'in Ankara Anlaşması'na ilişkin yayınlarından ve çeşitli gazete ve dergilerde çıkan yazılardan derlenmiştir. Örneklemin sayısı ve seçim yöntemi; özellikle sosyal uyum süreçlerinin analiz edilmesi noktasında bu araştırmanın sınırlılığı olarak göz önünde bulundurulabilir.

Britanya'daki Türkiyeli Göçmen Varlığı

Türkiye'den yurtdışına düzenli emek göçleri 1960'lı yıllarda çeşitli ülkelerle yapılan ikili anlaşmalar yoluyla başlamıştır. Britanya ile de bu çerçevede 1961 yılında ikili anlaşma imzalanmıştır. Ne ki, Britanya'ya emek göçü Almanya, Hollanda, Fransa ile kıyaslandığında son derece düşük seviyelerde kalmıştır.

1960'lı yıllarda Türkiyeli misafir işçiler açısından Almanya kadar cazip bir ülke olmayan Britanya, 1970'li ve 1980'li yılların ardından başlayan politik göçlerin merkezlerinden birisi haline gelmiştir. Göç açısından Britanya'yı özgün kılan özelliklerden biri de politik sığınmacıların toplam Türkiyeli göçmen nüfusu içerisindeki oranının yüksek olmasıdır. Özellikle Kürt bölgesindeki iç savaş ortamı 1990'lı yıllardan itibaren Kürt nüfusun yoğun olarak Britanya'ya göç etmesine neden olmuştur (Kirişçi, 2003: 83; Sirkeci, Erdoğan 2012). 23 Haziran 1989'dan itibaren Türkiye vatandaşlarının Britanya'ya girişinde vize uygulamasına başlanması bu ülkeye girişlerde yeni bir dönemi başlatmıştır.

1990'lı yılların başında düzensiz göç ile gelen çoğunluğu Kürt/ Alevi toplumlarından oluşan göçmenler Londra'nın Enfield, Hacney, Haringey ve Islington ilçelerine yerleşmişlerdir. 2011 nüfus sayımına göre Britanya'da Türkiye doğumlu 91 bin kişi bulunmaktadır. Sirkeci ve Açık'a göre (2015: 144) bu konudaki spekülasyonların aksine ikinci ve üçüncü kuşak ve Kıbrıs Türkleri ile birlikte Britanya'daki Türkiyeli nüfusu 200-250 bin kişi civarındadır.

Politik sığınmacı akınının durmasının ardından göç bir müddet aile birleşmeleri ve kaçak yollarla girişlerle devam etmiştir. Göçmen kabul kurallarının, vize ve sınır kontrol politikalarının değişmesinin ardından Ankara Anlaşması'ndan yararlanarak Britanya'ya göç etmek, oturum almanın en uygun yollarından biri haline gelmiştir. Dolayısıyla; eğitim, dil öğrenmek, çocuk bakmak amacıyla Britanya'ya giriş yapanların bir kısmı bu ülkede kalıcı olmak için anlaşmadan yararlanma yoluna gitmişlerdir. Aynı şekilde ekonomik, politik, kültürel vs. çeşitli sebeplerle Türkiye'yi terk etmek isteyenler için de Ankara Anlaşması en uygun göç yollarından birisi haline gelmiştir.

Ankara Anlaşması

Ankara Anlaşması, Türkiye ile Avrupa Topluluğu arasında 1963'te Ankara'da imzalanan, taraflar arasında ekonomik ve ardından da siyasal bütünleşmeyi sağlanmayı hedefleyen, bu süreci de hazırlık, geçiş ve son dönem olmak üzere üç aşamadan ibaret sayan temel anlaşmadır. İngiltere 1973'te Avrupa Topluluğu'nun üyesi olduğunda anlaşma bu ülkede de geçerli olmuştur. "AB'nin İşleyişine İlişkin Anlaşma"da işçilerin serbest dolaşımına ilişkin hükümler, "Hizmetlerin ve Sermayenin Serbest Dolaşımı" başlığıyla İşçiler başlıklı ilk kısmında 45, 46, 47 ve 48. maddelerde düzenlenmiştir, daha sonra serbest dolaşıma ilişkin mevzuat çeşitli

(Katma Protokol, Ortaklık Konseyi Kararı vs.) düzenlemelerle yeniden yorumlanmıştır (Sevimli, Reçber, 2014). Ankara Anlaşması'ndan yararlanarak oturum alma başvurusunun bir tek Britanya'da yapıldığına ilişkin bir yanlış kanı olsa da Türkiye Cumhuriyeti vatandaşları AB üyesi bütün ülkelerde anlaşmadan yararlanmak için başvuruda bulunabilmektedir.

İngiltere Avrupa Topluluğu Ortaklık Anlaşması'na 1973 yılında imza atmış olsa da, anlaşmadan Türkiye vatandaşlarının yararlanma süreci Mehmet Darı davasıyla başlamıştır. İngiltere'ye yasadışı yollardan girerek kendi işini açıp başarılı olan Mehmet Darı'nın anlaşma başvurusunun reddedilmesin ardından Avrupa İnsan Hakları Mahkemesi'ne açtığı davayı kazanması üzerine Türkiye'den Britanya'ya göçlerde Ankara Anlaşması yaygın olarak kullanılmaya başlanmıştır (Sevimli, Reçber, 2014: 430).

Ankara Anlaşması'ndan Britanya'da iş kurmak veya bir şirket bünyesinde çalışmak isteyenler yararlanabilmektedirler. Britanya'da yaşayacağı süre boyunca geçimini sağlayacak kadar kazanç elde edeceğini belgelemek başvuru sahibinin sorumluluğundadır. Home Office'in başvuruyu kabul etmesi halinde, başvuru sahibine ilk etapta bir yıllık oturum verilmektedir (Gov.uk, 2015). Bir yılın sonunda kişinin oturumunu yenilemek için tekrar başvuru yapması ve Home Office'i işini yaptığına ve bu işten geçim sağladığına ikna etmesi gerekmektedir. Home Office, ilk yıllarda bir yılın sonundaki başvurularda üç yıllık oturum verirken, son zamanlarda oturumu sadece bir yıl daha yenilediği de görülmektedir. Bu süre sonraki süreçte verilen oturum süresine dahil edilmektedir. Dört yılın sonunda kişi Britanya'da dilediği alanda çalışma hakkını ve başka sosyal haklar elde ettiği süresiz oturum almakta, beş yılın sonunda ise vatandaşlık için başvurusu yapabilmektedir.

Ankara Anlaşması 2009 yılına kadar sadece Britanya'dan yapılırken Avrupa Adalet Divanı'na yapılan başvurunun Divan tarafından kabul edilmesinin ardından 7 Eylül 2009'dan itibaren Türkiye'den de başvuru yapılabilmektedir. (commonwealthcontractors, 2010).

Çatışma Modeli ve Yeni Göç Dalgası

Sirkeci'ye göre (2012) çatışma modeli, göç kuramlarındaki bazı sorunlardan kaçma olanağı sağlamaktadır. Böylece göçü çekici olan alana doğru kayış olarak gören itme-çekme modelinden, ağ modellerin doğrulama yanılgısından, uluslararası göçün bürokratik yaklaşımından (12 aydan kısa süreli ikameti göç kabul etmemesi gibi), ekonomik veya politik sebepli göç gibi ayrımlara gereksinim duymadan göç olgusuna bir başka gözle bakma imkanı bulabilmekteyiz. Bir başka deyişle bu modelde göç, göç kavramının içerisine hapsedilmeyecek kadar dinamik ve değişken bir süreç olarak değerlendirilmektedir. Bu noktada, insanları kısa ve uzun vadede mobilize olmaya iten saikler "çatışma" kavramının etrafında açıklanmaktadır (Sirkeci, Cohen, 2015).

Şekil 1: İnsani güvenlik ve çatışma eksenleri

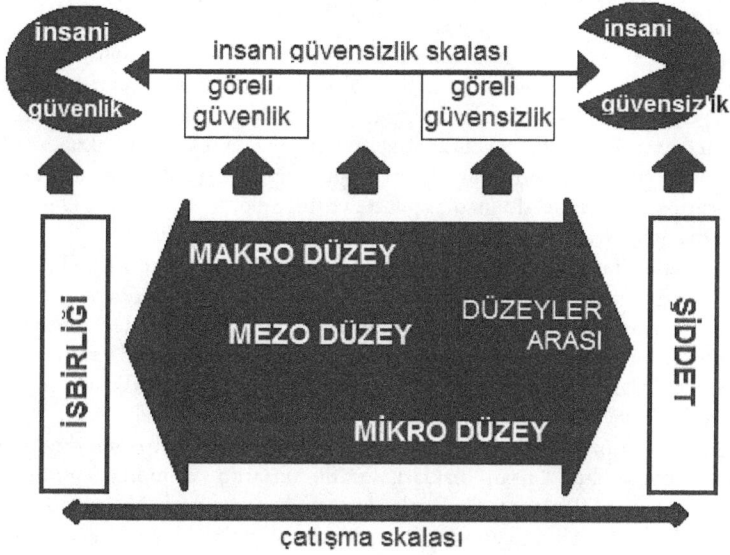

Kaynak: Sirkeci, 2012

Günümüzde göç, farklı yerellikleri birleştiren ulusötesi bir karakter kazanmıştır. Ryan ve Mulholland, 2014) 500 milyon nüfusu ile AB'nin ulusötesi göç bakımından çok iyi bir araştırma laboratuvarı olduğunu dile getirmektedir. Hareketlilik, dinamizm, esneklik göç yazınına yeni eklenen kavramlardır. Çatışma; sözünü ettiğimiz ulusötesi alanda ülkeler, devlet üstü kurum ve kuruluşlar, sınıflar, etnik veya dini gruplar, bireyler arasında vuku bulabilmektedir. (Sirkeci, 2012).

Çatışma modeli, karmaşık bir süreç olan göçü, çatışma ve güvenlik skalaları arasında bir etkileşim olarak kurgulamaktadır. Göç yazınında yer alan ekonomik, siyasi, kültürel faktörler burada çatışma skalası içerisinde konumlandırılır. Şekil 1'de, gönderen, transit ve göç alan ülkeler arasındaki çatışan siyasi tercihleri "makro", göç eden ve etmeyen hane halkları ve cinsiyet rollerinden kaynaklanan gerilimler "mezo", göçmenler ile göçmen olmayanlar arasında ve daha önce göç etmiş olanlar arasında yaşanan çatışma ise "mikro" düzeydeki çatışmalar olarak ifade edilmektedir. Söz konusu çatışmalar çapraz –yani düzeyler arasında da gerçekleşebilmektedir (Sirkeci: 2012: 359).

Katılımcılara İlişkin Sosyo-demokrafik Bilgiler

Çalışma kapsamında, Londra'da ikâmet etmekte olan 20 kişi ile yarı yapılandırılmış mülakat yapılmıştır. Görüşmelerin en kısası otuz dakika, en uzunu bir saat yirmi dakika sürmüştür.

Yirmi görüşmecinin, 8'i kadın, 12'si erkektir. Yaş ortalamaları 34,6, Britanya'ya geldikleri sıradaki yaş ortalamaları ise 29,8'dir. Görüşmecilerin 17'si bekâr, 3'ü evlidir. Eğitim durumlarına göre ise; 1'i ilkokul, 3'ü lise, geriye kalan 16 görüşmeci üniversite mezunudur. Bunlardan 4'ü yüksek lisans mezunudur. Etnik kökene göre görüşmecilerden 10'u kendisini Türk, 4'Kürt, 1'i Türkmen, 1'i Zaza, 1'i Hemşinli, 2'si de karışık olarak ifade etmiştir.

İngiltere, Avrupa Birliği üyesi olmasına rağmen kendi tercihiyle Schengen Bölgesi içerisinde yer almamaktadır. Son yıllarda sınır kontrollerinin artırılması ve değişen göçmen politikası nedeniyle İngiltere vizesi almak bir hayli zorlaştırılmıştır. Görüşmecilerin İngiltere'ye gelirken hangi yolla vize aldıklarına baktığımızda; dil eğitimi sebebiyle gelenlerin büyük bir çoğunluğu oluşturduğunu görmekteyiz. Yirmi görüşmeci içinde dokuzu İngiltere'ye bu şekilde gelmiştir. Diğerleri ise eğitim amacıyla ve turistik amaçlarla gelenlerden oluşmaktadır.

Anlaşmaya Türkiye'den başvuran dört görüşmeci bulunmaktadır. İlkokul mezunu Görüşmeci 5 müzisyen kimliği ile, hukukçu olan Görüşmeci 17 işlerini uluslararası alana taşıma isteğiyle, grafik tasarım bölümünden mezun olan Görüşmeci 13 askerlik yapmamak ve daha iyi koşullarda yaşamak için, akademisyen olan Görüşmeci 10 ise politik baskı ve toplum baskısından kaçmak amacıyla Türkiye'den başvuruda bulunmuştur.

İngiltere'den başvuruda bulunan; kuyumculuk, opera, radyo televizyon, sanat yönetimi, oyunculuk, insan hakları, grafik tasarım alanında eğitim gören görüşmeciler yine alanlarıyla ilgili işlerden oturum almışlar. Yaptıkları ihtisasın dışındaki alanlarda çalışan altı görüşmeci ise sırasıyla terzilik ve danışmanlık, satış elemanlığı, bisikletli yolcu taşımacılığı ve temizlik, pr şirketi, temizlikçilik ve muhasebecilik ve takı satıcılığı işlerinden başvuruda bulunmuşlar. Görüldüğü üzere vasıflı olmak başvuru sürecinde son derece önem taşımaktadır. Bu sebeple ihtisas yaptığı alan dışındaki işlerde çalışanların bir kısmı oturum almak amacıyla birden fazla iş için başvuruda bulunmaktadırlar. Bu işler arasında bisikletle yolcu taşımacılığı ve temizlikçilik gibi beden gücüyle yapılan işler de yer almaktadır.

Çoğu görüşmeci tam zamanlı olarak çalışmamakta, freelance diye tabir edilen, genellikle iş olduğu sürece/ iş çıktığı sürece çalışılan işler yapmaktadırlar. Kuyumculuk yapan, tv şirketinde çalışan ve hukuksal danışmanlık yapan görüşmeciler dışında tam zamanlı olarak mesai yapan görüşmeci bulunmamaktadır. Diğer bütün görüşmeciler part time veya esnek çalışma biçimleri ile yaşamlarını idame ettirmektedir. Bunda İngiltere'de esnek çalışma koşullarının yaygın olmasının da payı olduğu gibi opera sanatçılığı, tiyatro oyunculuğu, müzisyenlik, ressamlık gibi alanlarda çalışanlar işlerinin doğası gereği tam zamanlı çalışamamaktadırlar.

Britanya'ya Geliş Sebepleri

Sosyal Bağlantı

Göç edilecek yerin seçilmesinde etkili olan faktörlerden biri de bu ülkeye doğru bir "göç kültürünün" oluşmuş olmasıdır. Hızlı iletişim ve ulaşım olanakları, sözünü ettiğimiz ulusötesileşme döneminde göç yolları üzerinde karşılıklı ve sürekli nüfus hareketliliğine dönüşme eğilimi taşımaktadır (Zeyneloğlu, Sirkeci, 218: 2015). King ve Skeldon (2010) iç ve dış göçte sosyal bağlantının önemine dikkat çekmektedir. Şekil 3'te de görüleceği gibi A bölgesinden B bölgesine oluşan göç kültürü bir süre başka bir ülkedeki şehre, hatta oradan da başka bir şehre doğru uzanmaktadır. Oluşan göç kültürü sayesinde bu süreç daha sonra tersine de dönebilmektedir.

Görüşmecilerin nereli olduklarına ve nereden geldiklerine baktığımızda; büyük çoğunluğunun doğdukları şehirlerde değil büyük şehirlerde yaşadıklarını görmekteyiz. Beş görüşmeci hariç diğer bütün görüşmecilerin daha öncesinde Türkiye içinde bir göç geçmişi bulunmaktadır.Görüşmecilerden 10'u İstanbul'dan, 5'i Ankara'dan, 1'i İzmir'den, 1'i Bursa'dan, 1'i Gaziantep'ten, 1'i Antalya'dan, 1'i de Düzce'den geldiğini belirtmiştir. Nerelisiniz? sorusuna görüşmecilerden 3'ü Dersim, 2'si Maraş, 2'si İstanbul diğerleri ise Kayseri, Sivas, Denizli, İzmit, Mersin, Eskişehir, Muğla, İstanbul, Trabzon, Rize, Kastamonu, Antalya ve İzmir yanıtını vermektedir. Britanya'da yaşayan Türkiyeli göçmen varlığının önemli bir kesiminin Maraş, Tunceli, Kayseri ve Sivas illerinden göç ettikleri dikkate alınırsa Ankara Anlaşması'nda da sosyal bağlantının göç etme üzerinde etkili olduğunu söyleyebiliriz.

Şekil 2- Göç Kültürü- Göç Yolları

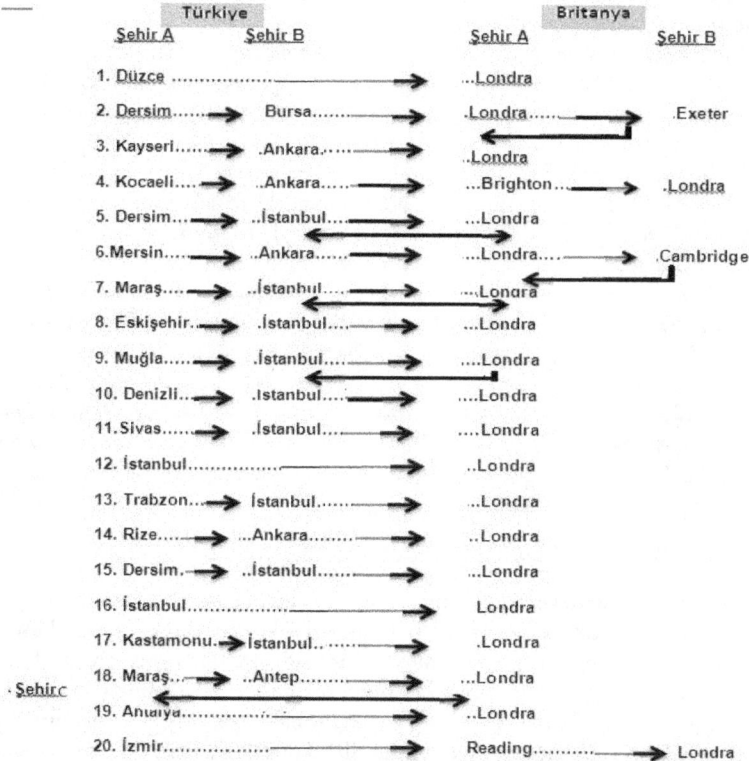

Türkiye — Britanya

Şehir A	Şehir B	Şehir A	Şehir B
1. Düzce		...Londra	
2. Dersim	Bursa	.Londra	.Exeter
3. Kayseri	.Ankara.	..Londra	
4. Kocaeli	...Ankara	...Brighton	.Londra
5. Dersim	..İstanbul	...Londra	
6.Mersin	.Ankara	...Londra	.Cambridge
7. Maraş	.İstanbul	...Londra	
8. Eskişehir	.İstanbul	...Londra	
9. Muğla	.İstanbul	....Londra	
10. Denizli	.İstanbul	....Londra	
11.Sivas	.İstanbul	....Londra	
12. İstanbul		..Londra	
13. Trabzon	İstanbul	...Londra	
14. Rize	...Ankara	.Londra	
15. Dersim	..İstanbul	...Londra	
16. İstanbul		Londra	
17. Kastamonu	İstanbul	.Londra	
18. Maraş	..Antep	...Londra	
Şehir c 19. Antalya		..Londra	
20. İzmir		Reading	Londra

Abim burada yaşıyordu. 1996'da gelmişti o. Ailesi var burada yaşıyor. Çocukları yaşıyor. Ablam var daha önce gelmişti. Teyzem var. Halam var. Bütün Maraşlılar gibi. Abimin yardımı oldu. (Görüşmeci 7, Erkek, 29 yaşında)

Sirkeci (2006) Türkiye'den Almanya'ya Kürt göçünü incelediği çalışmasında sosyal bağlantının göç üzerindeki etkisini, göçmenlerin aldığı riskleri en aza indirme davranışı olarak yorumlamaktadır. Diğer bir deyişle sosyal bağlantı güvenlik ihtiyacının bir tezahürüdür.

Görüşmecilerin bazılarının Londra'ya daha önce eğitim veya turistik ziyaret amacıyla gelmiş olmaları veya İngiltere'de akrabalarının yaşıyor olması yerleşme kararı almalarında etkili olmuştur. Yirmi görüşmeci içerisinde İngiltere'de herhangi bir sosyal bağlantısı olmayan sadece dört kişi bulunmakta, yedi görüşmecinin akrabaları İngiltere'de yaşamaktadır. Dokuz görüşmecinin ise İngiltere'de yaşayan ve göç esnasında küçük de olsa yardımda bulunan tanıdıkları bulunmaktadır. Bu bakımdan, Ankara Anlaşması yapan göçmenlerin bir kısmının daha önce açılmış olan göç yollarını takip ettiklerini belirtebiliriz. Örneğin, operacı olan görüşmeci ablasının İngiltere'de yaşıyor olmasının kalma kararında etkili olduğunu belirtmektedir.

Ablam buradaydı. Buranın vatandaşı idi. Yani ablamın yanında da olmak istedim. Yanında olmak derken, aynı evde değil. Çünkü o ailesiyle yaşıyor. En azından aynı şehirde ,yaşamanın verdiği psikolojik rahatlama oluyor. (Görüşmei 16, Erkek, 38 yaşında)

İngiltere'ye turist vizesi ile gelen Görüşmeci 20 de kalma kararını vermesinde kardeşinin rolüne değinmektedir.

Tatile gelmiştim, kardeşime (Reading şehrine), bir haftalığına ziyarete ondan sonra onlar kal dediler, ısrar ettiler sonra ben de kaldım ve o gün bugündür buradayım. Burada hayatımı kurdum bir daha geri dönmedim.Gezmeye geldim. Turist vizesi ile. Üç ay kadar orada kaldım sonra Londra'ya geldim. Reading'te idi. (Görüşmeci 20, Kadın, 31 yaşında)

Akraba ziyareti için Londra'ya giden Görüşmeci 1, niyetinin bir ay sonra Türkiye'ye geri dönmek olduğunu ama adeta akrabaları tarafından Londra'da alıkonulduğunu, Londra'ya yerleşme fikrinde kardeşinin ve burada yaşayan akrabalarının son derece etkin olduğunu söylemektedir.

Benim aslında niyetim bir ay sonra geri dönmekti ama planlar öyle olmadı. Altı aylık vize aldım ziyaret için gelmiştim. Ben geri dönmek istedim göndermediler beni. Bizim akrabalarımız da geniş. Onlar geldi, bunlar gitti, şuraya götürelim, buraya götürelim, zaman çabuk geçti. Anlamadım, Son iki ay kalmıştı vizemin bitmesine, ben dedim gitmek istiyorum, ondan sonra karar verdik. Kalsam daha iyi olur. Ailemizin zaten büyük çoğunluğu burada. Dayımlar burada, dayımların çocukları burada. Bir tek ben vardım Türkiye'de burada yaşamayan. Kardeşim de buraya benden dört beş sene önce gelmişti. O kendi isteğiyle, burada yaşamayı seçtiği için gelmişti. (Görüşmeci 1, Kadın, 27 yaşında)

Aile ve Toplum Baskısı, Politik Sebepler

Çalışmanın amaçlarından birisi de kişileri Ankara Anlaşması yaparak Türkiye'den göç etmeye iten psikolojik, sosyolojik, ekonomik, politik, kütürel vs. saiklerin neler olduğunu tespit etmekti. Yirmi kişilik dar örneklem grubununun çoğunluğunu üniversite mezunu ve kariyerli mesleklerini bırakıp gelenler veya Türkiye'de çalışsa beyaz yakalılar arasında çalışacak kişiler oluşturmaktaydı. Görüşmecilerin -en azından anlaşmanın ilk yıllarında- Türkiye'de görece daha iyi koşullarda yaşayacakken birçok güçlükle karşılaşmayı göze alarak neden göç ettiklerini anlamaya çalışmak çalışmanın bir başka amacıydı.

Kişinin ailesiyle ve sosyal çevresiyle yaşadığı çatışmalar zaman zaman göç etme isteğinde etkili olabilmektedir. Görüşmeci 19, üniversiteye giriş sistemi nedeniyle istemediği bir üniversiteye gitmek zorunda kaldığını ve aile ve akraba çevresinden gördüğü baskılar nedeniyle Türkiye'nin ona dar geldiğini ifade etmektedir.

Türkiye'yi terk etme isteğinde yaşadığı bu çatışmaların önemli bir etkisi olmuş. Bu sebeple dil okulu için başvuru yaptığını ailesinden saklamış ve banka kredisi çekerek İngiltere'ye gelmiş.

Türkiye bana dar geldi. Gerçekten öyleydi. Kendi hayatımla ilgili art arda gelen ters durumlardan geldim. Eğitim hayatımda istediğimi bulamadım. Kazandığım sevdiğim bir yer değildi. (...) Tek başıma başvurdum. Bankadan kredi çekerek geldim buraya. Ailemin bile haberi yoktu. (Görüşmeci 19, Kadın, 32 yaşında)

Görüşmeci 11 de üzerindeki aile baskısından söz ederken "ben yaşamak için kaçtım" demektedir. Onun da ailesiyle yaşadığı çatışmalar göç etme kararı vermesinde bir hayli etkili olmuş.

Bir aile baskısı her zaman. Bak o şunu yaptı, bak teyzenin oğlu şunu yaptı. Kendisi yaşamış mutsuz olmuş, erken yaşta evlenmiş, bir ekonomik kaygılar içine girmiş, şunu yapmam lazım, bunu yapmam lazım. Hani diyorlar ya, herkes doğar ama bazıları yaşar. Ama bizim ülkede kendi ailem de dahil, doğmuş ama yaşayamamışlar. Ben yaşamak için kaçtım. Yani yaşayabilmek için. Ben buraya geldiğimde ilk bir hafta yaşadığımı hissettim. (...) Evde aile ile yaşıyorsun, o şunu yaptı, bu bunu yaptı. Seni karanlığın içine çekiyorlar. Ve başarılı da oluyorlar maalesef. O cahil insanlar maalesef seni o çukura çekiyorlar bir şekilde. Bana ne oldu diyorsun ya seni kendi bulundukları ortama çekiyorlar. Biraz ondan kaçmak için geldim. (Görüşmeci 11, Erkek, 31 yaşında)

Bakewel'e göre (2010: 1705) klasik göç yazını "zorunlu" ve "gönüllü" göçü açıklamakta yetersiz kalmaktadır. Göçün zorunlu olması için göç etme ihtiyacı duyan kişinin mutlaka savaş, iç savaş mahalinde yaşıyor olması veya fiziksel şiddete uğraması gerekmemektedir. Çatışma modeli, uluslararası göçün zorunlu mu, gönüllü mü olmasından ziyade insani güvenlik arayışı olarak ya da başka bir ifadeyle güvensizlik ortamından kaçma isteği olarak değerlendirmektedir (Sirkeci, 2012: 356). Görüşmecilerin bir kısmı, göç etme kararı almalarında uğradıkları toplum baskısının ve Türkiye'nin gergin politik atmosferinin etkili olduğunu belirtmiştir. Örneğin Türkiye'den Ankara Anlaşması yaparak Londra'ya giden Görüşmeci 10, bir üniversitede öğretim elemanı iken politik koşullar nedeniyle işinden istifa ederek eşiyle birlikte göç etme kararı almış. Akademik kariyerini yarıda bırakarak Türkiye'den göç etme kararını şu şekilde açıklamaktadır:

Buraya gelmemin sebebi asıl son on senedir ivme kazanmış olan politik durum her şeyden önce. (...) Biz sadece gitmeyi düşünüyorduk. Tamamen bir yere gitmek üzere bir fikirdi. Çünkü İstanbul çok fazla bizi boğdu. Sıkıldık. (...) Türkiye'deki üniversitelerin durumu, politik durumu, sosyo politik durumun sokakta, gittiğim her yerde beni biraz sıkıştırdığını hissetmeye başladım. Eşim de aynı şekilde. Biz nereye gideriz'i son üç dört yıldır bayağı ciddi bir şekilde konuşmaya başlamıştık. (Görüşmeci 10, Erkek, 35 yaşında)

Görüşmecilerin iki ülkenin siyasal ve sosyal yapısını kıyaslayarak görece kendilerini daha güvende hissedecekleri yerde; Londra'da yaşamak istemeleri görüşmelerden çıkan bir başka sonuçtu.

Ne bileyim belli bir noktadan sonra, buradaki çok kültürlülüğü, çok renkliliği sevmeye başlıyorsun, aslında yapabilirsen çok güzel imkânların olduğunu falan... Türkiye'de problem olan şeyler burada oturmuş, konuşulmuyor. Onlar biraz kafamı şekillendirdi. Onların etkisiyle falan bu ülkede kalmaya karar verdim. (Görüşmeci 2, Erkek, 35 yaşında)

Görüşmeci 3, İngiltere'ye geldiği ilk yıllarda çok zorluk yaşamasına rağmen Türkiye'ye dönmek istememiş, bu kararında Türkiye'de iken özellikle iş hayatında etnik ve mezhepsel ayrımcılığa uğramasının önemli derecede etkili olduğunu düşünmekte. Türkiye'nin içinde bulunduğu politik koşulları gördükçe Londra'da yaşama kararı almakla ne kadar doğru yaptığını düşünmektedir.

Türkiye'de şimdi açıkçası iş anlamında çok parlak değildi. Yapmış olduğum iş bir dönem iyi olup başka bir dönem kötü olabiliyordu. Ya da ne bileyim, senin siyasi kişiliğin, etnik kökenin farklı bir yapıdaysa farklı kişi senin bu etnik kökenin ve siyasi kökeninle sana iş vermeyebiliyor. (...) Bu Türkiye'de büyük bir nasıl söyleyeyim bunu büyük bir sorun yani. Bizim gibi etnik kimlikte olanlar için. Burada hangi kültürden, hangi dinden, ideolojiden, inançtan olursan ol, adamlar buna bakmıyor, hatta seni teşvik ediyorlar, gel bu işi yap diye söylüyorlar sana ama Türkiye'de tam tersi. Senin önünü kesmeye çalışıyorlar. (...)Bir de Türkiye'deki son dönemdeki siyasi gelişmeleri görünce yani iyi ki de gelmişim diyorsun. (Görüşmeci 3, Erkek, 42 yaşında)

Memurluk görevini bırakarak Ankara Anlaşması ile Londra'da yaşamaya başlayan Görüşmeci 14, 'başarısız' adledilmek korkusuyla değil uğrayacağı toplum baskısı ve dışlanma nedeniyle, kendi istediği yaşamı sürdüremeyeceğini düşündüğü ve daha iyi bir iş bulamayacağı için Türkiye'ye dönmek istemediğini belirtmektedir.

Ben fena olmayan bir memurluk gibi bir işten vazgeçmişim. (...) Genel ortam, insanın insana davranışı... Mahalle baskısı... Kendin olamamak... Yargılanmak... Ne bileyim dini inancını özgürce söyleyememek, çalışma ortamında, arkadaş arasında. İş bunlardan daha önce değil. Sadece önce söyledim. (Görüşmeci 14, Erkek, 33 yaşında)

Ulusötesi göç açısından bir başka çatışma kaynağı da cinsiyet güvenliğidir. Kadın veya eşcinsel olmalarından dolayı kendilerini güvende hissetmeyen kişiler cinsel kimliklerini daha özgür biçimde yaşayabilecekleri yerlere doğru göç edebilmektedir. İngiltere'de yüksek lisans yaptıktan sonra bu ülkede yaşamaya karar veren Görüşmeci 4, cinsel yöneliminin kalma kararında etkili olduğunu ifade etmektedir.

Türkiye'de de dışarıdan çok belli olmadığım için öyle aman aman tacize uğramıyorum. Ama yine de burası biraz galiba Londra'nın 'gay capital' olması etkili olabilir birazcık. Biraz daha tanımak istiyorum Londra'nın gay life'ını. (...) Ha şeyi biliyorum, burada birisi bana homofobik bir harekette bulunursa, giderim polise, ağzına sıçılır onun. Onun güvencesi var. O güzel bir şey var. (...) Türkiye'deki bir gayin gözünden sen Londra'da yaşıyorsun. Bunun etiketi var yani anladın mı? Gay capital'desin. Ben de Türkiye'de yaşarken hayalim böyleydi. Brighton'u da biraz da bundan tercih ettim. O yüzden de cinsellik önemli ya insanın hayatında. Etkili oluyor yani. O fikir benim çok hoşuma gidiyor, dünyanın gay capitallerinden birindeyim şu anda ve bunu yaşamadan öldüm demeyeceğim. Bunu da görmüş oldum. Ne yaşıyorlar falan insanlar. Çünkü biz İstanbul'da, Ankara'da birçok şeyden mahrum yaşıyoruz. (Görüşmeci 4, Erkek, 30 yaşında)

Bir kadın görüşmeci Londra'ya geliş nedenini, artık Türkiye'de kendisini tarif edememesi ve güvende hissetmemesiyle açıklamaktadır.

Çünkü artık kendimi Türkiye'de tarifleyemiyordum. Hani bir sonraki aşamanın ne olacağının ne olduğunu bilmiyordum. Kendimi güvende hissetmiyordum. Belki biraz ara vermek belki de bir şeylere bakmak için aslında dil okuluna geldim. (Görüşmeci 6, Kadın, 44 yaşında)

Terapist olan görüşmeci ise, bir kadın olarak Türkiye'de kadına bakışın kendisini rahatsız ettiğini, Londra'da yaşama isteğinde bunun çok etkili olduğunu ifade etmiştir.

Hayatımı düşününce insanların kadınlara bakışı devamlı bir şekilde sinirimi bozuyor. Televizyon izlerken bile sinirimi bozuyor. Reklamları izlerken falan da sinirlerim bozuluyor o

yüzden böyle sürekli bir sinir bozukluğu içerisinde oluyorum tatile gittiğimde bile. Rahatsız hissediyorum kendimi o yüzden de dönmek istemiyorum. (Görüşmeci 12, Kadın, 29 yaşında)
Çatışma göç edildiğinde nihayete eren bir olgu değildir. Dolasıyla cinsiyet güvenliği veya cinsel yönelimi nedeniyle göç eden kişi bu çatışmaları yeni düzeylerde bireyler arasındaki ilişkilerde (mikro), aile ve toplum içinde (mezo) veya devletler arası (makro) veya düzeler arasında yaşamaya devam edebilir (Sirkeci, 2012: 356 ; Sirkeci, Cohen, 2015: 5).

Güvenlik ihtiyacı "çatışmaya" girmeme isteği şeklinde de tezahür edebilir. Bu da kişiyi daha güvenli alanlara doğru göç etmeye sevk edebilmektedir. Erkek görüşmecilerden ikisi ekonomik sebeplerin yanı sıra askerlik yapmak istememelerinin İngiltere'ye yerleşmelerinde etkili olduğunu söylemektedir. Bu da birey ve devlet arasındaki çatışmaya örnek olarak gösterilebilir.

Askerlik ve işsizlik beni buraya itti açıkçası. Türkiye dışında üç yıl yasal olarak bir ülkede çalışırsan, hiç askerlik yapmıyorsun sadece bedelli hakkın doğuyor. Onun da etkisiyle 2012'de buraya yerleşme kararı aldım. (Görüşmeci 7, Erkek, 29)

Askerlik yapmamak ve daha iyi imkânlarda çalışmak isteği ile yurtdışına çıkmak isteyen Görüşmeci 13, önce Berlin'de master yapmayı planlarken bir arkadaşının aracılığıyla Ankara Anlaşması'nı öğrenmiş ve Türkiye'den başvurarak anlaşmayı yapmaya karar vermiş.

Ekonomik Sebepler, Daha İyi Kariyer İmkânı

Dünyada her yıl 2,3 milyon insanın az gelişmiş ülkelerden gelişmiş ülkelere doğru göç ettiği tahmin edilmektedir (Hugo, 2014: 245). Bulundukları ülkedeki iş olanaklarının sınırlı olması, sosyo-ekonomik yoksulluk ve ücret farkları gibi nedenler şiddet içermeyen çatışma kaynakları olarak ifade edilebilir. Dolayısıyla, ekonomik sebeple göçte bir bakıma kişinin ekonomik anlamda kendisini ve ailesini güvenceye alma isteği olarak değerlendirilmektedir(Sirkeci, Cohen, 2015: 2).

Görüşmecilerin üzerinde en çok düşündükleri sorulardan biri de "Neden İngiltere'de yaşamaya karar verdiniz?" sorusu idi. Bu soruya verilen yanıtları, "Türkiye'de neden yaşamak istemiyorsunuz?" sorusuna verilen yanıtlarla birlikte ele aldığımızda göçmenlerin ruh halini daha iyi açıklayabiliriz. Dolayısıyla kişinin ekonomik anlamda kendisini daha güvencede hissedeceği yere doğru göç etmesinde sosyal, kültürel, politik faktörler de rol oynayabilmektedir. Görüşmeci 2, 2009 krizinde Türkiye'de sinema sektöründe işler kötüye gidince bir arkadaşının da etkisiyle İngiltere'ye gelmeye karar verdiğini belirtmekte ancak bu kararında kurduğu sosyal bağlantının etkili olduğunu söylemektedir.

Benim arkadaşım da benden önce buraya geldi. 2009 yılında sinema işinde çalışıyordum. İşler ekonomik sebeplerle durunca şeye karar verdim, o arkadaşın da etkisiyle bu tarafa gelmeye karar verdim. (Görüşmeci 2, Erkek, 35 yaşında)

Anlaşmadan yararlanmak için Türkiye'den başvuru yapan mesleği avukatlık olan Görüşmeci 17, işlerini daha iyi bir noktaya taşıma kararıyla yola koyulmuş, yaptığı ön araştırma sonrasında Almanya ve ABD gibi seçenekleri değerlendirmiş ve sonunda en elverişli yerin Londra olduğunda karar kılmış. Görüşmeci bu kararı almasını Londra'nın bir hukuk merkezi olmasına ve saat farkı olarak da dünyanın ortasında yer almasına bağlamaktadır.

Kendi işimi burada geliştirdim esasında. (...) İşimden dolayı burayı tercih ettim. Ankara Anlaşması'nı tercih etmemin sebebi de, ben zaten bu işi yapacaktım. Hangi ülkede yapacağımı kararlaştırmam gerekiyordu. Burası olunca dediler ki Ankara Anlaşması diye bir şey var, bunu kullanabilirsin. Burayı (Londra) seçtikten sonra Ankara Anlaşması'nı öğrendim. (Görüşmeci 17, Erkek, 45)

Mesleği sanatla ilgili olan kişiler, mesleklerini icra etme imkânlarının kısıtlı olması, yaşadıkları maddi sorunlar ve Türkiye'deki genel sanat politikasından veya politikanın sanat üzerindeki etkisinden rahatsız oldukları için Ankara Anlaşması yapma yoluna gittikleri görülmektedir. Sanat Yönetimi konusunda lisans eğitimi alan ve resim ve tasarım işleriyle geçimini sağlayan Görüşmeci 15, Türkiye'deki politik yapının mesleklerini ekonomik anlamda sürdürmelerini olanaksız kıldığını belirtmektedir.

Türkiye'deki yapacaklarınız bir yere kadar özellikle sanatla ilgileniyorsanız. Dolayısıyla kendi mesleğimde uzmanlaşmak, biraz daha ufkumu açmak için çok kültürlü bir yapıyı işime nasıl yansıtırım bunu görmek için geldim. Birinci nedenim buydu. İkincisi son on yılda Türkiye'deki hükümet nedeniyle sanat mesleğindeki insanların gelir düzeyinin korkunç derecede düşmesi nedeniyle. (...) On yıl önce aldığımız ücret aylık en az dört beş bin civarında idi. On yıl sonra bin beş yüzlere kadar düştü... (Görüşmeci 15, Kadın, 38 yaşında)

Görüşmeci 5'in dil yeterliliği bulunmuyor, ekonomik anlamda hayatımı idame ettirebilmek için Türkiyeli toplumla iç içe yaşamak durumunda. Geçimini düğünlerde, etkinliklerde saz çalıp türkü söyleyerek sağlıyor. Neden Ankara Anlaşması yaptınız sorusuna verdiği yanıtta mobilize olma isteğini, ekonomik ve politik nedenleri birarada bulmak mümkün.

Ben bir sanatçıyım... Benim kendimi tanıtmam gerekiyor. Sanatçılara Türkiye'nin biraz tolerans tanıması lazım. Uluslararası ülkelerle anlaşma yapması lazım. İşadamları nasıl çok rahat girip çıkabiliyorlarsa, sanatçılar da bu konuda serbest olmalı. (...) Ekonomik sebepler tabii ki vardır. Belki burada daha fazla kazanabilirsin. O doğrudur. Politik nedenler 2000'li yıllarda vardı. Bir de DGM'lik olduk yargılandık. Hatta bizim yerimize avukatlar gidiyordu. Albümlerimiz yasaklandı. Gazete reklamları veremiyorduk. Her yerde Kürtçe kendi ana dilimizde söyleyemiyorduk. (Görüşmeci 5, Erkek, 50 yaşında)

Opera sanatçısı olan görüşmeci Türkiye'deki sistemsizliğin ve adam kayırmacılığın mesleğini icra etmesinin önündeki en önemli engellerden birisi olarak görmekteydi. Görüşmecinin ilgili olduğu sanatı dünyanın neresinde icra edebilirse orada yaşamak istemesini belirtmesi de hareketliliğin bitimsiz bir süreç olduğunu göstermesi bakımından dikkate değerdi.

Açıkçası burayı gelmemdeki bir unsur da Türkiye'deki sistemsizlik. Mesleki açıdan da orada bir yere gelemeyeceğimin farkındaydım. Ahbap çavuş ilişkileri her sektörde olduğu gibi bizim sektörde de dönüyor. (...) Yani mesleki açıdan kendimi nerede rahat hissediyorsam. İdeallerimi nerede rahat gerçekleştireceksem oraya giderim. Şu anda Londra benim için en uygun yer. Yarın öbür gün başka bir yer çıkar oraya giderim. (Görüşmeci 16, Erkek, 38 yaşında)

Tiyatrocu olan Görüşmeci 9, sevgilisinden ayrıldığı için yaşadığı bunalımı seyahat ederek atlatmayı düşünmüş, turistik amaçla geldiği Londra'nın mesleği açısından potansiyel vaad ettiğini fark ederek burada yerleşmeye karar vermiş. Geldiği ilk dönemlerde vaktini Londra'daki çeşitli tiyatrolarda oyunlar izleyerek geçirmiş, Türkiyeli toplumda bu konuda gördüğü açık, kalma kararında etkili olmuş. Görüşmeci 9, süresiz oturumunu almasına birkaç ay kalmasına rağmen sinema filminde oynama teklifini kabul ederek Türkiye'ye dönme kararı aldı. Bu örnek, eğitimini aldıkları meslekleri yapma kararlığında bulunan göçmenlerin uygun çalışma ortamı yakaladıklarında yaşadıkları çevreyi değiştirebileceklerini göstermektedir. Uyum Sorunu ve Sosyo-Kültürel Çatışmalar bölümünde de yer vereceğimiz üzere Londra'da umduğunu bulamaması ve Türkiyeli toplumla yaşadığı çatışmalar da geri dönme kararında bir hayli etkili olmuş.

Eğitim Amacıyla Gelenler

Rizvi (2005: 179) "Globalleşme Döneminde Beyin Göçünü Yeniden Düşünmek" başlıklı makalesinde, ABD'de doktorasını yapan ülke dışından gelen öğrenciler arasında ABD'de yaşama isteyenleri ve bu niyetlerini gerçekleştirmek adına iş teklifi alanların oranlarına yer vermektedir. Bu çalışmada, ABD'de doktorasın yapan Türkiyeli öğrencilerin yarısının eğitimlerinden sonra ABD'de yaşama niyetinde oldukları, bunlardan yüzde 31'nin de iş teklifi aldıkları görülmektedir. Ulaşım ve iletişim teknolojisinde yaşanan gelişme içinde bulunduğumuz yüzyılda insan hareketliliğini bugüne değin hiç olmadığı kadar artırdı. Geleneksel göç yazınının yaklaşımı bu yaşanan hareketliliği analiz etmekte yetersiz kalmaktadır. Sirkeci ve Cohen (2015: 7) örneğin sınır boylarında yaşayıp başka ülkede çalışanların, sürekli hareket halinde olanların, öğrencilerin göçmen gruplarının geleneksel yaklaşımda göçmen grupları içinde zikredilmemelerini eleştirerek, göç kavramı yerine günümüzde "insan hareketliliği" (mobility) kavramının kullanılmasının daha uygun olacağını ifade etmektedir. Böylece düzensiz göç gibi konulara ilişkin belirsizlikler de ortadan kalkmış olacaktır. Britanya'ya eğitim amacıyla gelen ve vize sorunlarıyla karşılaşmamak için Ankara Anlaması yapan ve henüz hangi ülkede yaşayacağına karar vermemiş öğrencilerin durumu bunu örnek gösterilebilir.

Londra'da yayınlanan Olay Gazetesi'nin 1 Kasım 2013'te çıkan sayısında yer alan "Ankara Anlaşması'na en çok öğrenciler başvuruyor" başlıklı haberde bir hukuk danışmanlık firmasından alınan bilgiler doğrultusunda anlaşmaya en çok İngiltere'de eğitim gören öğrencilerin başvurduğu bilgisine yer verilmektedir (olay.co.uk, 2013).

Eğitim amacıyla Britanya'ya gelen üç görüşmeci daha sonra burada yaşamaya karar vermiş. Görüşmeci 12, Londra'da yaşamaya karar vermesini mesleki anlamda daha iyi kariyer fırsatı bulmamasına bağlalamaktadır. Öğrenciler birbirleriyle kurdukları iletişim ağı sayesinde Türkiye'ye dönen arkadaşlarının durumların haberdar olabilmektedir. Örneğin aynı görüşmeci daha iyi kariyer fırsatı yakalamış olmasının yanı sıra daha önce dönen arkadaşlarının mutsuz olduğunu bildiği ve Türkiye'deki hiyerarşik çalışma ilişkilerinden kaçmak için İngiltere'de kalmaya karar verdiğini dile getirmektedir.

Dönen bütün arkadaşlarım aşırı derecede mutsuzlar oradaki iş koşullarından. Aynı dönemde masteri yaptığım bir sürü insan vardı. Hepsi Türkiye'ye döndü ve hepsi çok mutsuz, kimisi hâlâ iş bulamadı. Bulanlar çok mutsuz geri gelmeye çalışıyorlar. Sakın gelme diyorlar. Gittiğimde mental olarak yoruluyorum. Sanki çok hırslı bir ortam var. Hiyerarşik bir şey de var işyerleri içerisinde. Öyle şeyler beni rahatsız ediyor. Orada özel terapi alanı için konuşursak o merkezlerde de bir patron var. Patron eziyor yani. Belli bir hiyerarşi var. Uzun saatler çalışman gerekiyor. Bayağı az para alabiliyorsun. Falan filan… (Görüşmeci 12, Kadın, 29 yaşında)

Mobilize Olma İsteği: British Pasaportuna Kavuşmak

Bir yere yerleşme isteği, sadece ekonomik olanaklar nedeniyle değil, sağlayacağı hareketlilik ve küresel dünya ile bütünleşme duygusuyla da gerçekleşebilmektedir (Rizvi, 2005: 188). Görüşmecilere önümüzdeki dönemde Türkiye'ye dönmeyi düşünüp düşünmediklerini ve bunun gerekçesini sorduğumuzda genel olarak göçmenlerin Türkiye'ye dönmek niyetinde olmadıkları sonucuna ulaştık. Ancak bu Londra'da hayatlarını devam ettirecekleri anlamına da gelmemektedir. Görüşmelerde çıkan ilginç sonuçlardan birisi de çoğu göçmenin British pasopurtu aldıktan sonra dünyanın başka ülkelerine gitme niyetinde olduklarıydı. Bu niyetin ne kadar gerçekleşeceği belli olmasa da, çeşitli nedenlerle göçmenlerin Türkiye'de yaşamaktansa Londra'da yaşamayı veya dünyanın başka bir yerinde yaşamayı tercih ettikleri görülmektedir. Bu durum, göçün dinamik ve bitimsiz bir süreç olduğu, kısa ve uzun dönemli insan hareketliliğinde sayısız yol ve mekanizmanın bulunduğuna ilişkin teorik yaklaşımımızı doğrular niteliktedir (Sirkeci, Cohen, 2015: 3). Örneğin Görüşmeci 4, Türkiye'ye döndüğü takdirde mobilize olma özelliğini yitireceğini düşündüğü için Londra'da yaşama fikrinin ona heyecan verdiğini ifade etmektedir.

Burası bana hâlâ 'challenging' geliyor, hâlâ yeni bir şeyler yaşarım gibime geliyor. Türkiye'ye gidersem Türkiyelilerle kendi mahallemde yaşıyor gibi hissedeceğim kendimi. Yine kapatacağım kendimi. Burada yabancı olma fikri bana bir alan açıyor sanki. (Görüşmeci 4, Erkek, 30 yaşında)

Bankacılık kariyerini yarıda bırakarak dil eğitimi için (bahanesiyle) İngiltere'ye giden Görüşmeci 18, yaşadığı bu deneyimi "kaçış" olarak nitelendiriyor. Londra'da bulunuduğu süre boyunca umduğunu bulamamış ve geri dönüp dönmemek arasında sürekli kendi içinde çatışmalar yaşamış ve sonra anlaşma sürecini yarıda bırakarak Türkiye'ye geri dönmüş fakat Türkiye'de de aradığını bulamayıncı tekrar Londra'ya gitme kararı almış. Görüşmeci 18, Londra'daki zor hayata British pasoportunu almak için katlandığını söylemektedir.

Şu süresiz oturumu alana kadar kalacağım burada. Çünkü Türkiye'de şunu düşündüm. Mesela dünyayı gezenleri tanıma şansım oldu. Ya bakıyorsun, abi senden hiçbir fazlaları yok. Hatta eksikleri var. Bakıyorsun sen ondan daha cesursun. O yapabiliyorsa, sen de yapabilirsin. Aslında çok sıradan bir insan. (...) Avrupalıların çok rahat gezmesi vize ve tamamen karar vermekle ilgili. Başka bir şeye gerek yok.Ben de dedim ki, dünyayı gezmek istiyorsan cebinde iyi bir pasaportun olmalı. (Pasaportu aldıktan sonra) İstediğim gibi, ister Türkiye'de kalırım, ister dünyayı gezerim. Buraya döndüğümde hiçbir sıkıntı olmaz, vizem var çünkü. Atıyorum Türkiye'ye döndüğünde pişman mı oldun, geç o zaman Londra'ya, ne bileyim... Mesela kendini mi arıyorsun, daha rahat arayabilirsin vizenden kaynaklı. (Görüşmeci 18, Kadın, 32 yaşında)

British pasaportunu elde etme dolayısıyla mobilize olma konusundaki güçlü istek Ankara Anlaşması'nın ilk yıllarında yaşanan güçlüklere göğüs germe konusunda kişilere irade kazandırmış gibi görünmektedir. Ankara Anlaşması'na Türkiye'den başvuran Görüşmeci 13, British pasoportu alana kadar anlaşma yapanların çektiği çileye değeceği görüşünde.

Yani ödülü büyük. Biliyorsun beşinci senenin sonunda vatandaşlık alıyorsun. Bir İngiliz pasaportu almak galiba bir Türkün rüyalarından biri olabilir. Artık vizesiz her yere gidebilmek. Ne bileyim... (Görüşmeci 13, Erkek, 28 yaşında)

British pasaportunu almak birçok görüşmeci için hem Türkiye'de yaşadıkları çatışmalardan uzak durmak hem de mobilize olabilmek anlamına gelmektedir. Görüşmeci 6, mevcut politik ortam içerisinde Türkiye'ye dönmeyi düşünmediğini British vatandaşlığının ona yaşayacağı ülkeyi seçme imkânı vereceğini yani hareket etme kolaylığı sağlayacağını söylemektedir.

Şu politik ortam içinde hayır düşünmüyorum ama başka bir ülke olabilir diyorum. Bütün hayatım boyunca bir sürü yeri gezip görmek o kültürlerin içinde yaşamak istedim. Birazcık vatandaşlığı beklememin nedeni de o. Vatandaşlığı almak için çabalamamın nedeni de o. Başka bir yere gidebilme olanağı buluyorum kendimde. Ekonomik anlamda bilmiyorum ne kadar gerçekleştirebilirim bunu. Avrupa ülkesi olabilir diye düşünüyorum. Bilmiyorum. Araştırmam gerekiyor. Hep kafamda Yunanistan vardı ama ayrı bir yer. Belki Afrika olur, Latin Amerika olur. (Görüşmeci 6, Kadın, 44 yaşında)

Göç sürecinin değerlendirilmesinde bireyin farklı gruplarla kurduğu temas sonucunda yaşadığı psikolojik ve kültürel değişimler "kültürleşme" kavramıyla ifade edilmektedir. Bu süreç içerisinde çatışmaları barındırdığı gibi uyumu da barındırmaktadır. Kültürler arası temasa bağlı olarak bireyin bu skaladaki konumu yaş, dil yeterliliği, kültürel yakınlık, eğitim gibi faktörlere bağlı olarak değişebilmektedir (Şeker, 2015: 20). Kültürleşme kavramı ile göç kültürünün oluşması arasındaki paralellik, kişinin hareket etme konusundaki bilgi ve tecrübesini artırmasıyla ilgilidir. Geleceğe ilişkin planları sorulduğunda birçok görüşmeci gelecekte Londra'da yaşayıp yaşamayacaklarını bilmediklerini, başka ülkelere giderek kendilerine yeni bir yaşam kurabileceklerini dile getirdiler.

Buranın vatandaşı olduktan sonra Almanya, İspanya veya Norveç, Amerika'ya, Kanada'ya giden var. O tarz bir şey düşünüyorum. (...) Türkiye'den farklı ülkelere gidebilirim. Ne bileyim, mesela Kanada olabilir. Ya da Avrupa ülkelerine... Arkadaşlar bazen diyorlar, başka ülkelere gidelim, başka ülkeler çok daha iyi. Pasaport alınca bakarsın gidebilirim. Bir araştırma yapmak için... Oradaki imkânlar varsa, orada da kalabilirim. (Görüşmeci 3, Erkek, 42 yaşında)

Amacım Avrupa'nın, dünyanın bana kapılarını açması. (...) Tek istediğim İngiliz pasaportu. (...) Benim şimdi tek istediğim bu. Sınırlar açılsın. (Görüşmeci 7, Erkek, 29 yaşında)

Bazı meslekleri icra edebilmek için kolay seyahat edebilmek son derece önemlidir. Türkiye yurttaşlarına çoğu ülkenin vize uygulaması çeşitli amaçlarla seyahat etmek isteyenlerin mobilizasyonunu zorlaştırıyor. Örneğin Türkiye'deki avukatlık bürosunda on beş çalışanı bulunan Görüşmeci 17, hem dünyaya açılmak hem de vize problemi olmadan daha rahat seyahat edebilmek için başvurmuş Ankara Anlaşması'na.

Valla hocam yaşım 45... Konforlu bir yirmi sene daha yaşarım. Konforu nerde bulursam... Burada da huzurluyum yani... İşimi de büyüttüm... Büyütmeye çalışıyorum. Dünyayı da gezmek istiyorum. İşlerimi dünyayı açarsam, dünyayla iş yapan bir adam olacağım. Türkiye'de yapacaklarımı yaptım zaten. (Görüşmeci 17, Erkek, 45 yaşında)

Opera sanatçısı olan görüşmeci de vize sorunu yaşamadan mesleğini icra etmek için Londra'ya geldiğini dile getirmektedir. Türkiye pasaportuna sahip olmak ona istediği zaman hareket etme olanağı tanımadığından British pasaportunu aldıktan sonra mesleğini dilediği ülkede icra edebileceğini düşünmektedir.

Niye Londra'ya geldim çünkü yine mesleki sebebi var. Önüme çok fazla fırsat çıkıyordu operayla ilgili, vizeyle uğraşmaktan çoğunu ya kaçırıyordum ya da psikolojik olarak kendini rahat hissetmediğin için iki ayağını bir papuca sokabiliyor. Bizim işimiz öyle bir şey ki, relaks olman gerekiyor. Sıkıntıyla, stresle iş yapamıyorsun çünkü konsantre olamıyorsun. O yüzden dedim geleyim, alayım burada pasaportu. Yarın bir gün önüme fırsatlar çıkınca hiç düşünmeden basar giderim yani. (Görüşmeci 16, Erkek, 38 yaşında)

Ankara Anlaşması: Mümkün Olan En Uygun Göç Yolu

'Makro çatışma' çatışma modeli içerisinde transit ve göç alan ülkeler arasıdaki birbiriyle çelişen farklı siyasal tercihleri ifade etmektedir. Göç alan ve göç veren ülke arasında değişen vize politikaları konusunda yaşanan gerilimler buna örnek gösterilebilir. 2000'li yıllardan sonra özellikle Avrupa'da dışarıdan göçün önüne geçecek birçok yasanın yürürlüğe girdiği görülmektedir (Hugo, 2014: 254; Salomoni, 2015; Faist, 2014, Kulu-Glasgow, Leerkes, 2013).

Britanya'nın 2000'li yıllardan sonra göçmen alımını sınırlandıran yasaları yürürlüğe sokması, politik iltica veya aile birleşmesi yoluyla göç etmenin zorlaştırılması ve sınır güvenliğinin artırılmasının ardından Ankara Anlaşması yaparak oturum almak göç etmenin en uygun yolu olarak karşımıza çıkmaktadır. Fakat bu konudaki devletler/ bireyler arasındaki çatışma devam etmektedir.

Ailesinin bir kısmı ve yakın akrabaları İngiltere'de yaşadığı için Londra'ya giden ve burada yaşama kararı alan Görüşmeci 1, Ankara Anlaşması'na başvurma sebebini şöyle açıklamaktadır:

Burada çok fazla seçeğenim yoktu kalabilmek için. Öğrenci vizesi alabilirdim ama ziyaretçi vizesi ile gelenlere öğrenci vizesi burada verilmiyordu. Buradan başvurabileceğim ya Ankara Anlaşması vardı ya da evlilik vizesi. Evlilik vizesine sıcak bakmadım. Aslında o zaman yasalar daha müsaitti. İki sene sonra oturum veriyorlardı. Çok sıkıntı yaşatmıyorlardı. Yasalar sonradan değişti. Evlilik mantıklı gelmedi bana. Ankara Anlaşması'na başvurdum. (Görüşmeci 1, Kadın, 27 yaşında)

Görüşmeci 9, Ankara Anlaşması ile Londra'da oturum alanların genellikle iyi eğitim almış olmak ve iyi mesleklere sahip olmak gibi benzer özellikler taşıdığına dikkat çekmekte ancak iltica ve evlilik gibi yolları deneyerek göç edememiş olanların da Ankara Anlaşması'nı deneyerek son çare olarak oturum almaya çalıştıklarını belirtmektedir.

Ankara Anlaşmalıların aşağı yukarı seviyeleri aynı gibi. Üniversite mezunu diye demiyorum ama öyle galiba. İyi meslekleri bırakmış gelmiş bazıları, bazıları da hiç değil. Evlilik yapmaya çalışmış olmamış, dükkân açmaya çalışmış olmamış, iltica etmeye çalışmış olmamış, Ankara Anlaşması son çare... Ama son dönem benim tanıştıklarım, ben geldikten sonra gelenler orada kariyer yapabilecekken, ya da yaparken bir şansını denemek için geliyor. (Görüşmeci 9, Kadın, 33 yaşında)

Ankara Anlaşması yapma sürecine ilişkin birey-devlet arasında yaşanan çatışmalara bir örnek olarak 20 kişilik örneklem grubu içinde tek ilkokul mezunu olan Görüşmeci 5'in tecrübesini örnek gösterebiliriz. 2001'de Newroz'da sahne almak için sadece 6 günlük vizeyle, 2006 yılında yine Newroz vesilesiyle bu sefer bir yıllık oturum alarak İngiltere'ye gitmiştir. Bir yılın sonunda vizesi uzatma talebi reddedildiği için Türkiye'ye dönen Görüşmeci 5, 2013'e kadar yaptığı vize başvurularından defalarca red cevabı almış ve en sonunda açtığı mahkemeyi kazanarak Londra'ya gitmiş ve burada kalıcı olmak amacıyla Ankara Anlaşması yapmıştır. Kanımızca, Görüşmeci 5'in red almasında eğitim seviyesinin, yaşının ve istenen nitelikte bir işte çalışmıyor oluşunun payı bulunmaktadır.

2007 ile 2013 arasında yaklaşık beş tane red verdiler bana. 2001 yılından sonra benim bu ülkeye giriş çıkışlarımda eğer insaflı davransaydılar benim Ankara Anlaşması yapmama gerek yoktu. Literatürde öyle bir şey de var. 2012'de biz başvurduğumuzda ben yine red aldım. Biz dava açtık. İtiraz hakkımızı kullandık. Mahkeme burada oluyor. Biz sadece yazışıyoruz benim aracı avukatla. Yazışınca davayı ben kazandım. Altı aylık vize. (...) Bir sene dava sürdü. Bir gün konsolosluktan beni aradılar, dediler gel pasaportunu al, davayı sen kazandın. Üç gün sonra vizemi aldım. Gelir gelmez de Ankara Anlaşması yaptım. Bir yılını aldım hiç sorunsuz. Bir yıl biter bitmez üç yıla başvurdum hiç tereddütsüz verdiler. (Görüşmeci 5, Erkek, 50 yaşında)

Şekil 3: Yıllara göre kabul ve ret sayıları (Home Office, 2015a)

YILLAR	KABUL EDİLEN	KABUL EDİLMEYEN RED ALAN	DİĞER	İŞLEMDE	TOPLAM
2002		*			*
2003		*			*
2004	5	10	5		15
2005	25	5	5		35
2006	55	20	10		85
2007	100	20	5		130
2008	265	20	10	*	300
2009	575	35	15		625
2010	815	35	25		875
2011	750	25	15		790
2012	625	20	10	25	680
2013	540	25	45	20 *	630
2014	480	10	5	5	25	530
2015	*		*		125	125
TOPLAM	4,240	230	55	135	155	4,820

Göçü düzenleyen birimlerle göç edenler arasındaki süreklilik arz eden çatışma, göç kurallarını ve kanunlarını değişime zorlamaktadır. Göçmen kabul kuralları zorlaştırıldığında bu değişime karşılık olarak ise göç eden bireyler ve gruplar kendi göç stratejilerini, göç yöntemlerini, göç rotalarını ve yollarını değiştirmektedir (Sirkeci, 2012: 359). Aksiyon dergisinde 8 Haziran 2015'te yayınlanan "İlticanın yerini Ankara Anlaşması aldı" başlıklı röportajda, İngiltere'de faaliyet yürüten bir hukuk firması yöneticisi Ankara Anlaması'nın günümüzde ilticanın yerini aldığını, Türkiye'deki politik atmosferden dolayı müvekkil sayılarının son bir iki yılda yüzde yüz arttığını ifade etmektedir (Aksiyon, 2015).

İngiltere'de 2010'da iktidara gelen Muhafazakar – Liberal koalisyonun imza attığı göçü zorlaştıran düzenlemeler Ankara Anlaşması'na ilişkin başvuruları da etkilemektedir. 4 Eylül 2014 tarihli Londra Gazetesi'nde "Ankara Anlaşması'na İlgi Azalıyor mu?" başlıklı haberde başvuruların 2004'ten itibaren 2010 yılına kadar katlanarak arttığını, 2011'den itibaren ise azaldığı ifade edilmektedir (Londra Gazetesi, 2014).

Nitekim Home Office (2015 a) verilerine baktığımızda; (Şekil 3) Ankara Anlaması'na ilişkin 2004'ten bu yana başvruların katlanarak arttığını, yapılan 4820 başvrunun 285'inin reddedildiği görülmektedir. 2012'den itibaren ilk defa bazı dosyaların değerlendirme sürecinin ardından reddedildiği bu tabloda ortaya çıkan bir başka sonuçtur. Bu da değerlendirme sürecinin daha titiz yapıldığının bir başka kanıtıdır.

Britanya hükümeti başvuruları sınırlı tutmak ve başvuralar arasında eleme yapmak amacıyla anlaşma yapmayı zorlaştıran çeşitli düzenlemeler yapma yoluna gitmektedir. Bu düzenlemelerin bazıları hali hazırda dava konusu oldukları için Türkiye ve Britanya göçmen kabul yasaları bakımından çatışmaya (makro) yol açmaktadır. Örneğin yapılan düzenleme ile İngiltere'de yaşayan Türkiyeli vatandaşların tüm aileye süresiz oturum (Indefinite) alabilmeleri için iki yıl önceden başvurmaları gerekmektedir (olaygazetesi.co.uk, 2015). Mayıs 2014'te çıkarılan göçmenlik kanunun Nisan 2015'te yürürlüğe girmesiyle ise Ankara Anlaşması'nda ret alan kişinin temyize başvuru hakkı kaldırılmış bunun yerine "idari inceleme" (administrative review) getirilmiştir (Home Office, 2015b). Bunun dışında Home Office'in son zamanlarda yapılan başvuruları anlaşma hükümlerini farklı şekillerde yorumlayarak reddettiği saha çalışması sırasında avukatlarla ve görüşmecilerle yapılan görüşmelerden ortaya çıkmaktadır.

Uyum Sorunu ve Sosyo-Kültürel Çatışmalar

Aidiyet duygusu, katılma ve yardımcı olma isteklerini de içine alan topluluklardaki bağlılık ve dayanışma ağlarını ifade eden uyum kavramının sosyal, kültürel, ekonomik ve politik boyutları bulunmaktadır. (Laurence, 2009: 522; Jacops, Phalet, 2007: 146). Dil becerisi, etnik/ dinsel/ mezhepsel köken, ev sahibi toplumla kurulan ilişki, emek piyasasındaki konum; yerleşilen toplumun etnik yapısı, sosyo politik durumu, ulusal politikaları, kültürel benzerlik ve farklılıklar, yaşanan ayrımcılık deneyimi de uyum süreçlerine etkide bulunmaktadır (Şeker, 2015: 23; Hugo, 2014: 257; Ensanıllı, Koopsman, 2011). Son yıllarda, özellikle aşırı sağın yükseldiği ülkelerde yabancı düşmanı politik söylem yaygınlık kazanmakta, göçmenler adeta ekonomik krizlerin günah keçisi ilan edilmektedir (Sönmez Efe, 2015: 63). Yabancı düşmanı politik söylem, göçmen karşıtı yasalar, kamusal alanda yapılan ayrımcı muamele göçmenlerin uyum süreçlerini olumsuz yönde etkilemektedir.

Yirmi görüşmecinin Londra'nın neresinde yaşadığına baktığımızda; 14 görüşmecinin Türkiyelilerin en çok yaşadığı Hackney (8 görüşmeci), Haringey (3 görüşmeci), Islington(2 görüşmeci) ve Enfield (1 görüşmeci) bölgelerinde yaşadıkları görülmektedir. Bu da örneklem grubu içerisinde yer alan Ankara Anlaşması yapan görüşmecilerin Türkiyelilerle yakın sosyal çevrelerde yaşadıklarını göstermektedir. Nitekim görüşmecilere Londra'daki sosyal çevrelerinin Türkiyelilerden mi oluştuğu sorulduğunda birçoğunun yanıtı "çoğunlukla Türkiyeliler" olmuştur. Yarıya yakın göçmen ise bu soruya diğer göçmen gruplarından da arkadaşlarının bulunduğunu ancak Türkiyeli arkadaşlarının da olduğu şeklinde cevap vermişlerdir. Sadece iki görüşmeci çevrelerinde hiç Türkiyeli bulunmadığını ifade etmiştir.

Görüşmelerde ve yapılan saha çalışmasında Türkiyelilerin düzenlediği sosyal etkinliklere katılım konusunda görüşmecilerin seçici oldukları gözlenmiştir. Dil sorunu yaşayanlar veya işleri gereği Türkiyeli göçmenlerle içiçe yaşamak durumunda olanların bu etkinliklere daha sık katıldıkları söylenebilir. Yaşanılan çevreye adapte olunmasının ve ekonomik olarak hayatın sürdürülebilirliğinin sağlanmasının ardından ise Türkiyelilerle kurulan ilişkide bir denge noktasına varılmakta, artık kişinin yavaş yavaş başka toplumlardan da arkadaş çevresi oluşmaktadır. Diğer bir deyişle, Ankara Anlaşması'nın bürokratik ve ekonomik sıkıntılarının nasıl üstesinden geleceğini öğrenmesi kişinin Türkiyeli toplumla ilişkisini kendi istediği biçimde düzenlemesine olanak sağlamaktadır.

Şekil 4: Londra ilçeleri ve görüşmeciler

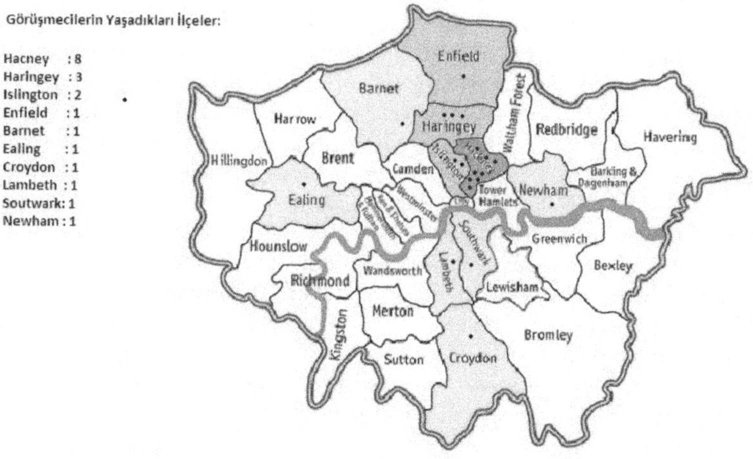
Görüşmecilerin Yaşadıkları İlçeler:
Hacney : 8
Haringey : 3
Islington : 2
Enfield : 1
Barnet : 1
Ealing : 1
Croydon : 1
Lambeth : 1
Soutwark: 1
Newham : 1
Enfield
Barnet
Harrow
Haringey
Waltham Forest
Redbridge
Havering
Hillingdon
Brent
Camden
Islington
Barking & Dagenham
Ealing
Tower Hamlets
Newham
Westminster
Greenwich
Hounslow
Southwark
Lambeth
Wandsworth
Bexley
Richmond
Lewisham
Merton
Kingston
Bromley
Sutton
Croydon

Görüşmecilerin Londra'daki sivil toplum örgütlerine üye olup olmadıkları sorulmuş, sadece üç görüşmecinin sivil toplum örgütlerine üye olduğu ortaya çıkmıştır. Üç görüşmeci ise üye olmadıkları halde belirli periyotlarla derneklere uğradıklarını ifade etmişlerdir. Türkiyeli topluluk dışında herhangi bir sivil toplum örgütüne üye olan ise sadece bir görüşmeci bulunmaktadır. Bu veriler de görüşmecilerin büyük oranda Türkiyeli topluluğun sosyal ve politik çevresi içerisinde sosyalleştiklerini göstermektedir.

2003 yapımı Lars von Trier'in yönettiği Dogville filmi 1930'ların Amerika'sında herkesin birbirini tanıdığı ücra bir kasabada geçer. Bir mafya hesaplaşmasından kaçarak Colorado'daki bu kasabaya sığınan Grace ilk başlada kasaba halkından ilgi ve iyilik görür. Fakat aradan zaman geçince Grace için işler günden güne zorlaşır ve bu küçük kasaba halkının diğer yüzüyle de tanışmaya başlar. Görüşmeci 9, Türkiyelilerle kurduğu ilişkiyi Dogville filmindeki atmosfere benzetiyordu. Tiyatro oyuncusu olması sebebiyle önce ilgi ve takdir gördüğünü, yaptığı başarılı işlerin ardından ise Türkiyeli toplum tarafından adeta aşağı çekilmek istendiğini düşünüyordu.

Londra bir Dogville'dir. Bunu daha önce de söylemiştim. (...) Burası küçücük bir köy. İnsanlar bir yerden sonra senin üzerinde söz hakkı kuruyorlar. (...) Neden bunu yaptıklarını anlamaya çalıştım bir süre. Sonra kendimce şöyle bir sonuca vardım yani, burası bir havuz ve bu havuzun içinde insanlar, tırmanma merdiveni yok. Bazıları ipe tırmanıp çıkarsa geri çekiyorlar. Çünkü burada kal istiyorlar. Konuşacak daha çok konu olsun, ya da daha çok malzememiz olsun. (Görüşmeci 9, Kadın, 33 yaşında)

"Çayda dem, askerlikte kıdem" ifadesini göçmen psikolojisini anlamak adına çayda dem, göçmenlikte kıdem şeklinde değiştirebiliriz. Göçmenler zaman içerisinde yaşadıkları sosyal ortama adapte olurken, nasıl ilk geldikleri sırada oraya son yerleşmiş olan göçmen grubu tarafından dışlanıyorlarsa, bulundukları yeri sahiplenme duygusuyla kendilerinden sonra gelen göçmen grubunu da dışlamaya başlıyorlar. Bu dışlama bazen değerler, tutum ve davranışlar üzerinden de tezahür edebilmektedir. Dil kursu için geldiği süreçte bir akrabasının yanında kalan görüşmeci, evini değiştirdikten sonra yanında kaldığı akrabalarıyla yaşadığı değer çatışmasını şöyle ifade etmektedir.

Mesela o zaman şöyle bir tepkiyle karşılaştım o benim çok tuhafıma gitti. Ben oda tuttum dedim Fransız bir kızla. Babam kızım iyi olmuş dedi. Aynı şeyi kuzenime (Londra'da yaşayan) anlattım. Kuzenim babamın yeğeni yani. Dedi ki kocama söyleme yabancı biriyle aynı odayı paylaşacağını. Ben böyle dondum kaldım. Belli bir kültürün insanıyız. Aynı yerden gelmişiz. Şey diyemem tabii ki Aleviler de bağnaz. Kendi toplumuma baktığımda biraz daha açıklar. Acayip şok oldum. Yirmi yıldır burada yaşıyor. Hâlâ yabancılar şey, oğlum evleneceği zaman Alevi olmalı. Düşünsene hâlâ bunu güden insanlarla karşılaştım. (Görüşmeci 18, Kadın, 32 yaşında)

Ankara Anlaşması yapanların yerleşik birinci kuşak göçmenlerle ilişki kurmak yerine birbirleriyle daha sıkı ilişki içerisinde olduklarını söylemek mümkün. Bunda farklı değerlere sahip olmalarının yanı sıra aralarında kurdukları dayanışma bağının da etkisi bulunmaktadır.

Evet. Yabancı arkadaş edinmek nasıl söyleyeyim, buradaki çevremiz Türkiye'den ama burada yerleşmiş Türkler'den değil. Çünkü onlar çok farklı. Onlarla uyum sağlayamıyoruz. Ancak bizler gibi sonradan gelen insanlarla...(Görüşmeci 19, Kadın, 32 yaşında)

Londra'ya dil eğitimi için gelen, bu süreçte abisinin yanında kalan Görüşmeci 7, Türkiyeli toplumun yaşadığı adaptasyon sorununu değişime kapalı olmalarına bağlamaktadır. Ankara Anlaşması ile göç eden kişilerin eğitimli ve sosyal entegrasyona açık olduğu görüşünde olan görüşmeci bu durumun bir yönüyle beyin göçü, bir yönüyle ise kaçış olarak değerlendirilebileceği görüşünde.

Görüyorum Ankara Anlaşması yapan insanları etrafımda gazeteci, müzisyen, sinemacı, fotoğrafçı Türkiye'de elle tutulan bir mesleği olan kalifiye insanlar bunlar... Kesinlikle Ankara Anlaşması'nı beyin göçü olarak kabul edebiliriz. Ama ne yazık ki o insanlar burada haketttiğini bulmuyor. Özellikle buraya ilk gelen Türkiyeliler karşısında haketttiğini bulmuyor. Çok arkadaşım var müzisyen, doktor, öğretmen... Şöyle bir söz var, buraya Ankara Anlaşması yapmaya gelip de off licence ya da bulaşıkçılıktan geçmeyen insan yoktur diye. Doktor arkadaşım var bulaşık yıkayan. Heykeltraş arkadaşım var bulaşıkçılık yapan restoranlarda. Öğretmen arkadaşım var Türk restoranlarında saati üç pounda bulaşık yıkıyor. Tam anlamında beyin göçü değil, kaçış gibi. Herkes o üç yılı, dört yılı atlatmanın derdinde. (Görüşmeci 7, Erkek, 29 yaşında)

Görüşmecilerden bazıları İngiltere'ye politik sığınmacı olarak gelen göçmenlerden ayrımcı muamele gördüklerini belirtmektedir. Görüşmeci 18, bunun bir ezen ezilen ilişkisi olduğunu, etnik ekonomiye sonradan dahil olan üniversite mezunlarının politik sığınmacılar kadar sıkıntı çekmedikleri için ayrımcılığa uğradığını düşünmektedir.

Ezen ezilen ilişkisi var. Adamlar şey ya, bana mesela şey dediklerine de şahit oldum, hepsi de aynı mantığa sahipler zaten. Şimdi sen Türkiye'de üniversite mi okudun, bankacıydın bir de Türkiye'de, ne işin var burada, şuna bak ya, ben köyden geldim, ilkokul mezunuyum, sen benim garsonum olarak çalışıyorsun. Yani benim altımsın. Benim işte arabam var, evim var, bilmem ne... Eee boşa okumuşsun sen. Adamın eline fırsat geçmiş. Ben ezildim diyor. Atıyorum seksenden, doksanda geldiğinde. Yine bizim insanımız ezmiş. Onlar kaçak yoldan geldiği için vize falan da yok. Bizim gibi değiller yani. Şartlar kötü kamplarda yaşamışlar. Mülteci kamplarında falan. Akla hayala gelmez sıkıntılar çekmişler. Bunu yüzdelik dilime vurursak yüzde sekseni böyle belki. Adam diyor ki, ben ezildim, sen de ezileceksin. Buna baştan inanamamıştım. Nasıl ya?! (Görüşmeci 18, Kadın, 32 yaşında)

Bazı görüşmeciler çatışmayı eğitimle ilişkilendirmektedir. Görüşmeci 6 ve 19'a göre, Türkiyeli göçmenlerin eğitim seviyelerinin düşük olması yaşadıkları çatışmanın en önemli sebepleinden birisi.

Bir de psikolojik olarak böyle üstünmüş gibi davranıyorlar. Bunun nedeni eğitimsiz olmaları. Bizim kuşak eğitimli, hatta bir kısmı İngilizce biliyor. Ezikliğini yaşıyor. Ezmeye çalışarak da tatmin oluyor. O üniversiteler bitirmiş ama benim verdiğim paraya muhtaç. (Görüşmeci 6, Kadın, 44 yaşında)

Benim diğer bir gözlemim Ankara Anlaşmalılara tavırla bakanlara ilişkin... Üniversite okudun da ne oldu böyle bir tavır var. Bak yine benim yanımda, bana hizmet ediyorsun tavrı var. (Görüşmeci 19, Kadın, 32 yaşında)

Yüksek lisans yaptıktan sonra Londra'da yaşamaya karar veren ve halihazırda terapistlik mesleğini ve doktora eğitimini aynı anda sürdüren Görüşmeci 12, Londra'ya politik sebeplerle iltica etmiş göçmenlerin kendilerini daha ayrıcalıklı gördüklerini, bunun da kendileri üzerinde psikolojik baskı oluşturduğunu ifade etmektedir.

Daha önce gelen kişilerden siz niçin çalışıyorsunuz lafını duydum mesela. Seni çok seviyorum. Çok iyi çalışıyorsunuz ama buradaki göçmenlerden buraya göç eden, iltica eden ailelerin çocuklarının işlerini çalıyorsunuz tarzında şeyler duydum. Buraya politik sebeplerden gelmek daha geçerli geliyor hani o insanlara. Ben gereksiz yere geldim ve yer kaplıyorum gibi geldiğini hissediyorum ben. (Görüşmeci 12, Kadın, 29 yaşında)

Sonuç olarak, Ankara Anlaşması yaparak oturum alan göçmenlerin önemli bir kısmı çeşitli nedenlerle Türkiyelilerle aynı sosyal çevrede yaşamalarına rağmen, aralarında akraba ilişkisi bulunanlar dahil olmak üzere birinci kuşak göçmenlerle çatışma içeresinde oldukları görülmektedir. Bu çatışmanın, sosyal, kültürel, politik, eğitim gibi boyutları bulunmaktadır.

Etnik Ekonomi İçindeki Çatışmalar

Türkiyeli göçmenlerle sosyal alanda yaşanan çatışmanın bir başka boyutu da ekonomik alanda yaşanmaktadır. Londra'daki Türkiyeli toplum genellikle kebap, off licence (içki ve sigara satan dükkânlara Britanya'da verilen isim) ve café shop gibi işleri yapmaktadır. İngiltere'deki en örgütsüz kesimi oluşturan[293] yiyecek servisi sektöründe eleman ihtiyacı genellikle etnik ekonomi içerisinden karşılanmaktadır. Etnik ekonominin genişlemesi bir bakıma yeni göçmen akımına bağlıdır. Çünkü bu göçmenler etnik ekonominin insan kaynağını oluşturmaktadır. Londra'ya yeni ulaşan göçmenler ve öğrencilerin emeği etnik ekonomi için ucuz

---

[293] 2013 verilerine göre yemek servisi sektöründe çalışanların sadece % 0,9'u sendikalıdır. https://www.gov.uk/government/uploads/system/uploads/attachment_data/file/313768/bis-14-p77-trade-union-membership-statistical-bulletin-2013.pdf

işgücü anlamına gelmektedir (Dedeoğlu, 2014: 53). Geçici süre ek işler yapma ihtiyacı duyan göçmenler bu ekonominin içerisine dahil olmakta, birinci kuşak girişimci göçmen grubuyla yaşanan çatışmanın ekonomik boyutu da bu noktada başlamaktadır.

Çalışma sınırlı bir örneklem grubuyla gerçekleştiği için görüşmecilerin çevrelerinde Ankara Anlaşması yapan kişilere karşı gözlemlerini almak da son derece önemliydi. Bu çerçevede her bir görüşmeciye "çevrenizde Ankara Anlaşması yapan kişiler var mı? Varsa bunlara ilişkin gözleminiz nedir?" sorusu soruldu. Bu soruya verilen yanıtlar Ankara Anlaşması yapanların yaşadıkları güçlükleri, çatışmaları ve Türkiyeli toplumla kuruldukları ekonomik ilişkileri daha iyi anlamamıza olanak sağlamaktadır. Örneğin kendisi de tezgâhtarlık yapan Görüşmeci 1, "Türkler asla para vermez" ifadesinin artık genel kabul gördüğünü söylemektedir.

Çok düşük ücretle çalıştırılıyorlar. Normal bir elemana mesela vermesi gereken ücretin belki yarısını veriyorlar. O büyük sıkıntı onlar için. Kaldı ki, evrakları tamam olsa da asla o parayı veremeyecek olan insanlardır bunlar. İşin tuhafı da budur. Mesela bir işi yapıyorsunuz mesela o işin haketiği 400'dür. Türkler asla para vermez insana. Bunu herkes bilir. Türkler asla para vermez. (Görüşmeci 1, Kadın,27 yaşında)

Ankara Anlaşması yaparak oturum alanlar ekonomik olarak hayatlarını devam ettirebilmek amacıyla çoğu zaman zorunlu olarak Türkiyeli göçmenlerle ilişki kurmak durumunda kalmaktadır. Daha önce dil yeterliliği konusunda belirtildiği üzere bu bazen gönülsüz bir ilişki biçimine de dönüşebilmektedir. Öte yandan sosyal bağlantılar, kültürel yakınlık, yapılan işin Türkiyeli topluluğa hitap etmesi (Türkiyeliler'e öğretmenlik yapan veya saz çalan görüşmeci) gibi sebeplerle de ekonomik ilişkiler kurulabilmektedir. İşte bu ilişkinin işçi/işveren, hizmet alan/hizmet veren ilişkisine dönüştüğü noktada da birtakım çatışmalar başgöstermektedir. Opera sanatçısı olan görüşmeci iş yaptığı kesimin Türkiyeli ya da diğer topluluktan olmasına göre aldığı paranın ve kendisine olan bakışın değiştiğini ifade etmektedir. Görüşmecinin, "Türkiyelilerle yaptığınız işlerden çok para kazandınız mı?" sorusuna verdiği yanıt şu şekildedir:

Çok değil hiç kazanamadım. Mesela bir yabancı toplumla iş yaparsanız yarım saatlik bir konsere bile adamlar minumum beş yüz pound veriyorlar ve bunu özür dileyerek veriyorlar. Bu sizin hakkınız değil diyerek. Ama ben bizim toplumumuzdan yarım saat için beş yüz pound istesem yaş odunla kovalarlar beni. Sen ne yaptın diye. Millet onu bir ayda zor alıyor. Sen dört beş şarkı söyleyeceksin o gözle bakıyorlar. Saat olarak bakıyorlar, senin aldığın eğitim, maddi manevi neler verdin, o işin kalitesi veya cvsi ona bakmaz... Dört çarpı on pound veya yol parası yeter gözüyle bakıyor. (Görüşmeci 16, Erkek, 38 yaşında)

Türkiyeli topluluk ile ekonomik ve sosyal ilişki kurmuş olan bütün görüşmecilerin hemen hemen üzerinde anlaştıkları nokta etnik ekonomi içerisinde ücretlerin asgari ücretten dahi düşük olduğu ve çalışanların zor koşullarda uzun süreli çalıştırıldığı yönünde. Ancak sözünü ettiğimiz bu koşullar sadece Ankara Anlaşması yapanlar için değil etnik ekonomi içindeki çoğu çalışan için geçerlidir.

Görüşmeci 14 de, etnik ekonomi içerisinde Ankara Anlaşmalı olanların diğer çalışanlardan çok farklı olmadıklarını, işletme sahiplerinin temel amacının maliyetleri düşürmek olduğunu söylemektedir. Öyleyse, British vatandaşlığını almış olan göçmenlerin neden asgari ücretin altındaki ücretlere razı olduklarını sorduğumuzda, görüşmecinin verdiği cevapla bir bakıma sahadaki gözlemimizi doğrulamış olmaktayız. Devletten sosyal yardım ve kira yardımı alan Türkiyeli göçmenlerin bir kısmı bu yardımların kesilmemesi için bazıları ise vasıflı olmadıkları için kayıtdışı, düşük ücretlerle çalışmaya rıza göstermektedirler. Dolayısıyla pratikte işveren Ankara Anlaşması yapan göçmenlere negatif ayrımcılık yapmasa da fiili olarak bu kişiler vatandaş olmamaktan kaynaklanan kayıpları nedeniyle dezavantajlı konumda yer almaktadırlar. Bu da yerleşik Türkiyeli göçmenlerle Ankara Anlaşması yaparak oturum alanların farkını ortaya koymaktadır.

Açıkçası, Ankara Anlaşması'nın ne olduğuna ilk başta pek de dikkat etmiyorlar. Sen onun için saati üç beş pounda çalışacak birisin. (etnik ekonomi içindeki işveren) (...) O da belki çalışır (yerleşik göçmen) ama o devletten aldığı çeşitli yardımlar, kira parası, hiçbir kira masrafı yoktur o insanın. Devletten kira yardımı, çocuk yardımı, sakatlık yardımı alıyordur. Üstüne saatini beş pounda çalışıp ek gelir elde ediyordur. Dolayısıyla o çalışabilir ama benim için olay farklı. Ben onunla kira vereceğim bilmem ne yani. (Görüşmeci 14, Erkek, 33 yaşında)

Psiko-sosyal Çatışmalar

Ankara Anlaşması'na başvuru yapıldıktan sonra British vatandaşlığının elde edilmesi ortalama beş - altı yıl civarında sürmektedir. Bu dönemde göçmenler sadece ekonomik ve sosyal anlamda değil psikolojik olarak da zorlu bir süreçten geçmektedirler. Home Office'e bildirilen işte çalışma zorunluğu, vize sürecinde ret alma korkusu, pasaport içerideyken seyahat edememek (veya bir yıl içinde belli bir süre seyahat edebilecek olmak) sosyal yardımlardan ve kira yardımından yararlanamıyor olmak, yerleşik göçmenlerle kurulan ilişkilerde yaşanan sorunlar Ankara Anlaşması yapanların psikolojisini olumsuz yönde etkileyen faktörler olarak sıralanabilir.

Göçmenlerin bulundukları ülkeye uyum sağlamalarında yaş, kültürel yatkınlığın yanı sıra dil yeterliliği de önemli bir rol oynamaktadır (Alexander vd., 2007: 784, Şeker, 2015: 20). Görüşmecilere dil yeterliliklerini sorduğumuzda; 6 görüşmecinin çok iyi, 6 görüşmecinin iyi, 6 görüşmecinin orta ve 2 görüşmecinin de kötü yanıtını verdiklerini görmekteyiz. Genel olarak İngiltere'de eğitim görenlerin dil sorunu bulunmamaktadır. Ancak dil kursu için gelip eğitimini yarıda bırakmış veya Ankara Anlaşması'nı henüz yapmış olanlar dil yetersizliğinden kaynaklanan çeşitli sorunlar yaşamaktadır. Bankadaki işini bırakarak dil kursu için İngiltere'ye giden Görüşmeci 18, yaşadığı dil ve adaptasyon sorunu nedeniyle kendisine olan inancını yitirdiğini belirtmektedir.

Dedim ki, ya dünyayı nasıl gezebilirim. İngilizce'yi öğrenmekle başlamalıyım bu işe, dedim. Ha geldim amacımdan tamamen saptım tabii ki, okulu bıraktım. İngilizce'yi öğrenmek için hiçbir çaba sarf etmedim falan filan. Ve amacımdan sapınca kendime olan inancımı da yitirdim. (Görüşmeci 18, Kadın, 32 yaşında)

Görüşmeci 1, ilk geldiği yıllarda dil yeterliliği olmadığı için ayrımcılığa uğradığını düşünmektedir.

Bir yere gittiğinizde, bir yerde oturduğunuzda ya da alışveriş yaparken, ya da resmi daireye giderken bir İngilizle göçmene davranış biçimleri çok farklı. Hele ki İngilizce seviyeniz çok iyi değilse... Ya da hani adaptasyon problemi yaşıyorsunuz kesinlikle çok problem yaşarsınız. (Görüşmeci 1, Kadın, 27 yaşında)

Ersanilli ve Koopmans (2011: 211) göçmenlerin ana dillerini kullanabilecekleri sosyal organizasyonların varlığını dili öğrenmeyi zorlaştıran bir faktör olarak zikretmektedir. Ankara Anlaşması yapanlarla Türkiyeli topluluk arasındaki sosyal ilişkiler ekonomik ilişkilerin paralelinde gelişmektedir. Özellikle dil sorunu olan göçmenler çalışmak için Türkiyeli toplulukla ilişki kurmak zorunluluğu hissetmektedir. Bu zorunluluğun ortaya çıkardığı paradoks ile göçmenler bir taraftan uyum sorunu yaşamaya devam ederken bir taraftan da dil öğrenme sürelerini uzatmaktadırlar.

Gelir gelmez bu topluluğun içine düştüm. Bu topluluğun içinden bir türlü çıkamadım yani açıkçası... (Görüşmeci 3, Erkek, 42 yaşında)

Hemen hemen hiç yabancı arkadaşım olmadı çünkü dilde problem yaşıyoruz. Arkadaşlarımız Türkiyeli ve Kürdistanlılar... (Görüşmeci 5, Erkek, 50 yaşında)

Göç etmekle doğru mu yaptım? sorusu özellikle göçün zorlu dönemlerinde göçmenlerin kafasını kurcalayan sorulardan bir tanesidir. Bu çatışma, uyum ve entegrasyon sorunu da beraberinde getirebilmektedir. Karşısına çıkan sorunlar nedeniyle kendisini yaşadığı yere tamamıyle ait hissetmeyen göçmen bu bocalama döneminde geri dönme kararı alabilmektedir. 20 görüşmecinin geldiği tarihteki yaş ortalamasının 29 olduğu göz önünde bulundurulursa, insanın ekonomik anlamda hayatını yoluna koymaya başladığı bir dönemde, başka bir ülkede sıfırdan bir mücadeleye atılmanın türlü zorluklarının olacağı bir gerçektir. Altı yıldan bu yana İngiltere'de yaşayan ama henüz hayatını yoluna koyamadığını söyleyen Görüşmeci 2, yaşadığı çelişkileri şu şekilde ifade etmektedir.

Şöyle bir şey var, ben buraya 2009'da geldim. Bakıp geriye mesela bu altı yıllık sürede ne yaptım diye düşünüyorsun, Yani gerçekten ortada bir şey yok. Ama ciddi anlamda çalışma ve stres var. Pozitif olarak sana getirdiği şeyler çok az. Diyorsun ki dil öğreneyim ama dil öğrenmek de kolay olmuyor. Çünkü ikinci üçüncü yıldan sonra tamam her şeyi daha rahat anlıyorsun ama yine konuşmada problemler yaşamaya başlıyorsun. Çünkü yabancı arkadaşlarla içiçe geçemiyorsun. Çünkü bunun için vakit lazım. Para lazım sosyalleşmen için. (Görüşmeci 2, Erkek, 35 yaşında)

Ekonomik, sosyal, kültürel çevresini değiştirmek isteyen, bu amaçla göç eden kişi uyum sürecinde çeşitli güçlüklerle karşılaşmaktadır. Dil sorununun aşılması, yaşanan çevreyle uyum sağlanması ve iş hayatında hedeflenen yere gelebilmek yıllar alabilmektedi. Bu periyotta göçmenler yaşadıkları psikolojik çatışmalar nedeniyle anlaşmayı yarıda bırakarak zaman zaman geri dönmeyi düşündüklerini belirtmektedir. Radyo, Televizyon ve Sinema bölümünden mezun olan, Londra'da Türkiyeli toplumun çıkardığı yerel bir gazetede fotoğrafçılık yapan Görüşmeci 7, geri dönüp dönmeme çatışmasını çok yaşadığını, defalarca geri dönmek için bilet aldığını, bu süreçte akrabalarından destek gördüğünü söylemektedir.

Daha birkaç ay öncesine kadar her hafta pes ediyordum. Bilet alıyordum. Vazgeçiyordum. Diyordum ki aylar kaldı. Biraz daha sabret biraz daha sabret. Amacım süresiz oturumu alıp direk rahatlamak değil. Sosyal yardıma başvurmak değil. (Görüşmeci 7, Erkek, 29 yaşında)

Görüşme yapılan göçmenlerin bir kısmı etraflarında koşullara dayanamayarak Türkiye'ye geri dönme kararı alan arkadaşları bulunduğunu ifade etmektedir. Görüşmeci 7, geri dönenlerin daha iyi koşullarda yaşayacaklarını ancak siyasi ortamın ve mahalle baskısının onlar için adaptasyon sorunu yaşatacağını düşünmektedir.

Pes edenler çok oldu. Etrafımda çok arkadaşım var bırakıp giden. Bırakıp gidip tekrar dönen çok arkadaşım var. (...) Türkiye'de bolluk içindesin. Yemek, çevre, arkadaşlar, sosyal ilişkiler kesinlikle buraya göre cennet. Ama Türkiye'de öyle bir siyasi ortam var ki, öyle bir mahalle baskısı var ki, buraya gelip burada bir iki yıl yaşayan insanlar tekrar Türkiye'ye döndüklerinde adapte olamıyorlar. (Görüşmeci 7, Erkek, 29 yaşında)

Görüşmecilerde baskın olan duygulardan birisi de anlaşmayı bırakıp dönerlerseTürkiye'de 'başarısız' olarak addedicelek olmalarıydı.

En kötü diyorduk, bir senenin sonunda döneriz, bir senelik bir macera... Bana en çok koyan o dönemde, dönme ihtimali idi yani. Dönseydim yani on senenin sonunda ya ben İngiltere'ye gittim, bir sene yaşadım demek falan istemiyordum yani. (...) Londra'yı sevdiğim halde burada kalamamak beni üzerdi. (Görüşmeci 13, Erkek, 28 yaşında)

Londra'da terapist olarak çalışan Görüşmeci 12; avukat, muhasebeci arasında koşturmanın, gereğinden fazla vergi ödemenin ve kötü koşullarda çalışma zorunluluğunun bir süre sonra ereceğini bu yüzden anlaşmayı yarıda bırakmanın zamanını boşa harcamak anlamına geleceğini dile getirmektedir.

Bu süreçte ne kadar yorulsak da insanın ne kadar dönesi gelse de, emek yani, avukata verilen para, muhasebeciye verilen para, vergiler, kötü şartlarda çalışmak, bunların hepsi dört yılda sona erecek o yüzden ondan vazgeçmek çok kolay değil. Bu çok önemli bir faktör...Boşa gitmesin yani...(Görüşmeci 12, Kadın, 29 yaşında)

Ankara Anlaşması yaparak oturum alanları bekleyen zorluklardan biri de seyahat engeli. Home Office'in oturum onaylarının son zamanlarda aylar sürmesi bu süre boyunca pasaportlara el konulması göçmenlerin İngiltere dışına çıkmasına mani olmaktadır. Öte yandan anlaşma yapanların ilk yıllarda hayata tutunmak için çok çalışmak zorunda olmaları ve maddi sıkıntılar çekmeleri de seyahatlerinin önündeki bir diğer engeldir.

Yirmi kişilik örneklem grubunun yaş ortalaması 34,6 olup üç görüşmeci evlidir. Medeni duruma ilişkin bu tabloda dikkat çekici unsur ise Ankara Anlaşması'nı İngiltere'de yapan hiçbir görüşmecinin evli olmamasıdır. Türkiye'den başvuru yapan dört görüşmeciden üçü evli iken, oturumlarını İngiltere'den başvurarak alan on altı kişinin tamamı bekârdır. Örneklemin rasgele seçildiği düşünülürse, medeni duruma ilişkin bu tablo göçmenlerin anlaşma süresi boyunca yaşadıkları güçlükleri ortaya koyan bir başka doğrulama kaynağı olarak ortaya çıkmaktadır. İngiltere'de özellikle kira ve ulaşım giderlerinin yüksek olması, avukat ve muhasebeci harcanan paralar, geçinecek düzeyde düzenli gelirin elde edilememesi veya zaman zaman bu gelirden yoksun olmak, etnik ekonomi içerisindeki düşük ücretler söz konusu durumun ekonomik nedenlerini oluştururken, göçmenlerin yaşadıkları uyum ve dil sorunu, birinci kuşak göçmenlerle kimi zaman zorunluluk temelinde kurulan ilişkilerin yıpratıcı etkisi ise sosyo psikolojik nedenini oluşturmaktadır.

Ankara Anlaşması ile oturum alanların şikayetçi oldukları konulardan birisi de sosyal hayatlarına zaman ayıramamaktı. Londra'da iş yaşamına ilişkin yoğun çalışma tempsu, ilk yıllarda maddi olarak kendilerini güvence altına almak için çok çalışmak zorunda olmaları göçmenlerin kendilerine zaman ayıramamalarına neden olmaktadır.

Yıllar geçtikçe şunu soruyorsun, biraz da idealist takılıyoruz, eğitimle ilgili bir iş yapalım diyoruz ama buna ne uygun zamanın oluyor ne de kafan sürekli bir şeylerle meşgul olduğu için boş otursan da evde oturup da iki üç sayfa kitap okuyamıyorsun. Gazete okuyorsun ama hangi verimi alabiliyorsun? (Görüşmeci 2, Erkek, 35 yaşında)

Türkiye'de beş sene önce ayda en az beş kitap okurken, beş yılda maksimum beş altı kitap okumuşumdur. Türkiye'ye tatile gidiyorum bir aylığına, her gittiğimde bir kitap bitiriyorum. Burada kaldığım on ay ya da on bir ay boyunca bir kitap bitiremiyorum. İnsanlarla konuştuğun zaman da herkes aynı şeyi söylüyor. Hiçbir şekilde nedenini bilmiyorum bunun. (Görüşmeci 7, Erkek, 29 yaşında)

Geriye düştüm. Türkiye'de yaşasaydım çok daha fazla beslenebilecektim. Oradaki entelektüel ortam farklıydı. Konuştuğun dil üzerinden okuduğun için çok daha tartışabiliyorsun. Buradaki politik ortam çok daha geri seviyede. Beni hiçbir zaman tatmin etmedi. Sosyal anlamda da öyle… Burada Türkiyelilerle girdiğim ilişkiler hiçbir zaman gelişmedi. Bu doğal olarak beni geriye götürdü. Bu mesela çok mutsuz edici bir şey. Ekonomik anlamda zaten doyurucu değil. (Görüşmeci 6, Kadın, 44 yaşında)

Bazı görüşmeciler ise Türkiye ile kıyasladıklarında Londra'da daha iyi bir hayat kurduklarını düşünüyorlardı. Örneğin grafik tasarım alanında işler yapan Görüşmeci 13, Türkiye'de kamusal alanda kendisini iyi hissetmediğini bu yüzden İngiltere'de hiç şikâyet etmediğini söylemektedir. Akademik kariyerini bırakarak Türkiye'den Ankara Anlaşması yapan ve eşiyle birlikte İngiltere'ye giden Görüşmeci 10, gelmeden önce Londra'ya ilişkin kapsamlı bir araştırma yapmış, böylece nelerle karşılaşabileceğini az çok hesaplamış. Hem mesleki kariyerinin geleceği bakımından hem de bulunduğu sosyal ortam itibariyle Londra'da kendisini çok daha rahat hissettiğini ifade etmektedir. Otuz sekiz yaşındaki ressam ve grafik tasarımcı Görüşmeci 15, Londra'ya geldiğinde eski alışkanlıklarını terk ettiğini yaşının gereği olarak yaşamını artık daha sakin sürdürdüğünü, Londra'nın buna imkân verdiğini söylemektedir. Dolayısıyla bazı görüşmelerde sözünü ettiğimiz sosyo-psikolojik çatışmaların çok daha az düzeyde yaşandığını söylemek mümkün.

Sonuç

Ankara Anlaşması ile oturum alan 20 göçmenin deneyimini incelediğimiz bu çalışmadan çıkan sonuçlar şu şekilde sıralanabilir:

Ankara Anlaşması ile Britanya'da oturum almak 2000'li yılların ortasından itibaren yaygınlık kazanmıştır. Bunda son on beş yılda (özellikle 2010'dan itibaren) Britanya'da göçmen politikasının değişmiş olmasının ve göçü sınırlandırmaya yönelik yapılan yasal düzenlemelerin etkisi bulunmaktadır.

Ankara Anlaşması gönderen ve göç alan üleler arasında çıkan çatışmaların uzlaşmaz tercihleri arasında yeni bir göç seçeneği olarak ortaya çıkmıştır. Nitekim Britanya'nın bu yeni göçü sınırlandırmaya yönelik yasal ve politik tutumu ve göçmenlerin de buna karşı hukuk mücadelesi devam etmektedir.

Kişileri Ankara Anlaşması yaparak Britanya'da oturum almaya iten sebeplere baktığımızda; aile baskısından politik baskılara, daha iyi bir sosyal çevrede yaşama isteğinden cinsiyet eşitsizliğine, askerlik yapmak istememeye kadar insani güvensizlik algısının çeşitli çatışma boyutlarıyla karşılaşmamız mümkündür.

Bu çatışmalar devletler arasında (göçmen politikaları), hane halkları arasında (aile baskısı), göç edilen yerdeki topluluklarla ve bireyler arasında ya da sözünü ettiğimiz düzeyler arasında tezahür etmektedir.

Ankara Anlaşması yaparak oturum alanları geldikleri sosyal çevre, aldıkları eğitim ve göç etme nedenleri bakımından tek bir kategoride toplamak mümkün değildir. Ancak ortalama eğitim durumu ve mesleki vasıf bakımından birinci kuşak Türkiyeli göçmenlerden daha iyi konumda oldukları söylenebilir.

Görüşmecilerin büyük bir çoğunluğunun Britanya'da yakın akraba, akraba ve tanıdıklarının bulunması göç kültürünün anlaşma yaparak oturum alanlarda da etkili olduğunu göstermektedir.

Görüşmelerden çıkan ortak noktalardan biri de görüşmecilerin mobilize olma yönündeki kararlılıklarıdır. Göçmenler British pasaportu almayı, yaklaşık beş yıl boyunca yaşadıkları zorlukların bir ödülü olarak görmektedirler. Vize sorunu olmadan seyahat etme ve yerleşme isteği birçok görüşmecide karşımıza çıkan çok temel bir istektir. Bu da bizi "göç" ve "insani hareketlilik" kavramlarını Ankara Anlaşması üzerinden bir kere daha tartışmaya sevk etmektedir.

Anlaşma yapan kişiler ilk yıllarda ekonomik, sosyal ve psikolojik olarak çeşitli zorluklarla karşı karşıya kalmaktadırlar. Bu çatışmaların üstesinden gelmede dil becerisi, eğitim, sosyal entegrasyon düzeyi, etnik ekonomiye bağımlılık gibi faktörler etkili olmaktadır.

Kaynakça

Alexander, C., Edwards, R., Temple, B. (2007). "Contesting Cultural Communities: Language, Ethnicity and Citizenship in Britain", Journal of Ethnic and Migration Studies, 33:5, Pp.783-800.

Bakewel, O. (2010). "Some Reflections on Structure and Agency in Migration Theory", Journal of Ethnic and Migration Studies, 36:10, Pp.1689-1708.

Dedeoğlu, S. (2014). Migrants, Work and Social Entegration, Women's Labuor in Turkish Ethnic Economy, Palgrave Macmillan.

Ersanıllı, E., Koopmans, R. (2011). "Do Immigrant Integration Policies Matter? A Three-Country Comparison among Turkish Immigrants", West European Politics, 34, 2, Pp208-234.

Faist, T. (2009). "Diversity – A New Mode of Incorporation?", Ethnic and racial studies, 32, 1, Pp.171-190.

Hugo, G. (2014). "Migrants in society: diversity and cohesion", Migration and Diversity, Ed. Stevin Vertovec, The International Library of Studies on Migration, An Elgar Research Collection, pp.243-294.

Jacops, D., Phalet, K. (2007). "Political Participation and Associational Life of Turkish Residents in the Capital of Europe", Turkish Studies, 7:1, Pp.145-161.

King R., Skeldon, R.. (2010). "'Mind the Gap!' Integrating Approaches to Internal and International Migration", Journal of Ethnic and Migration Studies, Journal of Ethnic and Migration Studies, 36,10, Pp. 1619-1646.

Kirişci, K. (2003). "The Question of Asylum and Illegal Migration in European Union-Turkish Relations,", Turkish Studies, 4, 1, 2003, pp. 79-106.

Kulu-Glasgow, I, Leerkes A. (2013). "Restricting Turkish marriage migration? National policy, couples' coping strategies and international obligations", Migration Letters, 10, 3, Pp. 369 – 382.

Laurence, J. (2009). "The Effect of Ethnic Diversity and Community Disadvantage on Social Cohesion: A Multi-Level Analysis of Social Capital and İnterethnic Relations in UK Communities, European Sociological Review, Pp.521-540.

Rizvi, F. (2005). "Rethiking 'Brain Drain' in the Era of Globalisation", Asia Pasific Journal of Education, 25: 2, Pp.175-192.

Ryan, L., Mulholland J. (2014). "Trading Places: French Highly Skilled Migrants Negotiating Mobility and Emplacement In London", Journal of Ethnic and Migration Studies, 40:4, Pp.584-600.

Salomoni, F. (2015). "Göçmenlerin İtalya'da Entegrasyonu", Göç ve Uyum, Turkish Migration Series, Transnational Press London, Pp.165-186.

Sevimli, K. A. S. Reçber. (2014). "Avrupa Birliği'nde İşçilerin Serbest Dolaşımı ve Türk İşçilerinin Serbest Dolaşım Hakkı", İstanbul Üniversitesi Hukuk Fakültesi Mecmuası, 76, 2, Pp. 391-440.

Sirkeci, İ.; Erdoğan, M. (2012). "Göç ve Türkiye", Migration Letters, 9, 4, pp. 297 – 302.

Sirkeci, İ. (2012). "Transnasyonal Mobilite ve Çatışma", Migration Letters, 9, 4, pp.353-363.

Sirkeci, İ.; Açık, N. (2015). "İngiltere'de Göçmenlerin Ekonomik Uyumu ve İşgücü Piyasasında Azınlıklar", Göç ve Uyum, Turkish Migration Series, Transnational Press London, Pp.143-164.

Sirkeci, İ. Cohen J.H. (2015). "Cultures of Migration and Conflict in Contemporary Human Mobility in Turkey", European Review, 22, 2 (forthcoming)

Sirkeci, İ. (2006). The Environment of Insecurity in Turkey and The Emigration of Turkish Kurds to Germany, The Edwin melen Press, Lewiston Queenston Lampeter.

Sönmez Efe, S. (2015). "To What Extent Are Migrant Workers' Rights Positioned within the Discourse of Human Rights?", Politics and Law in Turkish Migration, Ed. İbrahim Sirkeci vd., Pp. 53-70.

Şeker, B.D. (2015). "Göç ve Uyum Süreci: Sosyal Psikolojik Bir Değerlendirme", Göç ve Uyum, Turkish Migration Series, Transnational Press London, Pp.11-26.

Zeyneloğlu, S.; Sirkeci İ. (2015). "Türkiye'de Almanlar ve Almancılar", Göç ve Uyum, Turkish Migration Series, Transnational Press London,Pp.217-266.

İnternet Kaynakları

Home Office, (2015a), UK Visas and Imigration Costumer Service Depertmant 16, TURKEEL - Turkish Employed ECAA - LTR NB, Application number: 35837.

Home Office (2015b) ECAA Turkish employed applications (Erişim Adresi: https://www.gov.uk/government/uploads/system/uploads/attachment_data/file/421115/Turkish_ECAA_V9_0.pdf. Erişim tarihi 12 haziran 2015).

Gov.Uk., (2015), Turkish Businessperson visa, (Erişim Adresi: https://www.gov.uk/turkish-business-person/overview. Erişim tarihi 10 Haziran 2015).

Gov. Uk., (2011), "Turkish ECAA business EC applications – flowchart", (Erişim Adresi: https://www.gov.uk/government/uploads/system/uploads/attachment_data/file/265790/Turkish-EEA-business-chart.pdf. Erişim tarihi: 10 Haziran 2015).

Gov.Uk., (2014), Trade Union Membership Statistical Bulletin 2013. (Erişim adresi: https://www.gov.uk/government/uploads/system/uploads/attachment_data/file/313768/bis-14-p77-trade-union-membership-statistical-bulletin-2013.pdf, Erişim tarihi: 10 Haziran 2015).

Commonwealth Contractors, (2010), "Turkish ECAA Deadline Approaching", (Erişim adresi: http://www.commonwealthcontractors.com/tag/immigration/page/20/. Erişim tarihi 10 Haziran 2015).

Aksiyon, (2015), "İlticanın Yerine Ankara Anlaşması Aldı", (Erişim adresi: http://www.aksiyon.com.tr/roportaj/ilticanin-yerini-ankara-anlasmasi-aldi_551203. Erişim tarihi: 8 Haziran 2015).

Londra Gazetesi, (2014), "Ankara Anlaşması'na İlgi Azalıyor mu?", (Erişim adresi: http://www.londragazete.com/2014/09/04/ankara-anlasmasina-ilgimiz-azaliyor-mu/ Erişim tarihi 2015).

Olay Gazetesi, (2013) "Ankara Anlaşması'na En Çok Öğrenciler Başvuruyor", (Erişim adresi: http://olaygazetesi.co.uk/turk-toplumu/ankara-anlasmasina-en-cok-ogrenciler-basvuruyor.html , Erişim tarihi: 10 Haziran 2015).

Olay Gazetesi, (2015), "Ankara Anlaşması'na Sınırlama Getirildi"., Erişim adresi: http://olaygazetesi.co.uk/turk-toplumu/ankara-anlasmasina-sinirlama-getirildi.html 20, erişim adresi: 8 Haziran 2015).

Beş Sınır Kenti ve İşgücü Piyasalarında Değişim: 2011-2014

Kuvvet Lordoğlu[294]

Giriş

Bu çalışma esas olarak belirli bir bölgeyi içine alan göç hareketinin, o bölge içinde işgücü piyasalarını nasıl etkilemekte olduğunu kavramaya çalışmaktadır. Mevcut durumdan işgücü piyasalarının halen etkilenmekte oluşu ve ülke ölçeğinde geniş çaplı bir düzenlemenin yapılmamış olması son dönemde bu piyasaları etkileyen en önemli sorun alanlarından biri haline getirmiştir.bu çalışma söz konusu edilen beş ilde konu ile ilgili kişilerin kanaatleri ve yorumları dikkate alınarak ve sahadaki sınırlı veri kaynakları incelenerek tamamlanmıştır.[295]

Diğer taraftan bu çalışma, işgücü piyasalarında oluşan değişimi daha net olarak gözlemek ve etkilerini kısmen de olsa takip edebilmek için bir bölge ile sınırlandırılmıştır. Bu sınırlamayı ayrıca Suriyeli göçmenlerin[296] sayısal olarak en yoğun bulunduğu iller üzerinden yapmak iki önemli veri kaynağı oluşturmuştur. Bunlardan biri bölgedeki bu iller gelenlerin ülkelerine yakınlığı dolayısı ile tercih edildiği illerdir. Kamp dışındaki Suriyeliler tüm ülkeye yayılmış olsalar da büyük çoğunluğu Hatay, Kilis, Gaziantep, Şanlıurfa ve Mardin olmak üzere beş ilde yoğunlaşmaktadır (Kirişçi 2014: 17, Çağaptay 2014: ve Özerdem 2015:)[297]. Bu illerin bir diğer özelliği sınıra komşu olmaları ve sınırın öbür tarafındaki köy ve kasabalarla uzun yıllara dayalı akrabalık ve aşiret ilişkisinin bulunmasıdır. Bu özellik üstüne aynı dili konuşmak ve kültürel benzerlikler eklendiği zaman beş ilin Suriyeli göçmenlerin bir bölümü için diğer illere göre bir üstünlük sağladığı anlaşılmaktadır. Ayrıca bu bölgede çatışmaların durması halinde göç eden insanların bir bölümünün geri dönüşleri yakınlık nedeni ile onlara ciddi kolaylıklar sunmaktadır.

Beş İl Temelinde Suriyeli Göçmenlerin İşgücü Piyasalarına Etkileri

Hatay

Hatay, sınır kapıları ve geçiş imkânları nedeni ile Suriye iç savaşından en fazla etkilenen kentlerden biridir. Özellikle Suriye'deki iç savaşın vurucu etkisini Reyhanlı kentinde yaşanan bombalı saldırı ile en yüksek düzeyde hissedilmiştir. Yaklaşık 15 bini toplam beş kampta yaşayan Suriyeliler kamp dışındakilerle birlikte toplam sayıları 250 bin kişi civarında olduğu tahmin edilmektedir. Gerek kamplarda gerek kamp dışında kalanlar iş piyasalarına farklı biçimlerde

---

[294] Kocaeli University, Turkey.
[295] Bu bölgedeki beş il için Nisan 2015 tarihinde bölgedeki çeşitli kanaat önderleri ve STK temsilcileri ile iki araştırmacı toplam 36 derinlemesine görüşme yapmıştır. Toplanan bilgilerin bir bölümü bu görüşmecilerle yapılan mülakatlar sonucu elde edilmiştir. Sınırlı sayıda göçmen işçi ile görüşme yapılmıştır. Bazı görüşmecilerin isimleri istekleri doğrultusunda saklı tutulmuştur.
[296] Suriye'den gelenlerin literatürde farklı adlarla tanımlandığı görülmektedir. Mülteci, misafir, sığınmacı geçici koruma statüsü altındakiler vb. Bu metin içinde Suriye'den gelenleri genel bir tanım içinde "Göçmen" olarak adlandırmayı diğer kavramlara göre anlam açısından daha uygun bulduk.
[297] Bu beş il ayrıca çatışma bölgesine yakınlığı, bu nedenle göç etme maliyetlerinin düşüklüğü ve sınır kapıları dışında kolay geçiş imkânı sunulması nedeni ile göçmenlere kolaylık sağlamaktadır.

katılmaktadır. Hatay'ın işgücü piyasasına etkileri üç ana başlık altında toplamak mümkündür.

Suriyeli göçmenlerin bağımlı çalışmaları

Bu grupta çalışanların yoğunluğu nedeni ile tarım işçileri ve tarım dışı alanlarda işçiler olmak üzere iki gruba ayırmak mümkündür. Tarım alanı Suriyeli göçmenlerin çapalama, ekim, mevsimlik işçilik, ürün toplama gibi farklı iş gruplarını içermektedir. Bu işlerde çalışan göçmenler, genel olarak kendi ülkelerinde de çiftçi oldukları anlaşılmaktadır. Gündelik işçi olarak çalıştıkları tarımda ücretleri yerli işçiye göre daha düşük ve bu ücretten aracının payı önceden işvereni tarafından kesilmektedir. Tarım dışı alanlarda çalışan Suriyeli işçiler imalat sanayi, inşaat ve hizmet sektörlerinde çalışmaktadırlar. Yapılan işler bölgenin diğer illerinde olduğu gibi vasıf düzeyi düşük yerli işçiler tarafından yapılmak istenmeyen işler olmaktadır. Ücret düşüklüğü işverenler tarafından çoğu kez "bir yerli işçi yerine iki Suriyeli çalıştırmanın daha uygun" olacağı biçimde aktarılmaktadır. Bu tür işlerin başta inşaat olmak üzere mevsimlik tarım işçiliğinde yoğunlaşmaktadır. Hatay ilinin bütün ilçelerinde Suriyeli işçi bulunmasına rağmen en fazla yoğunluk, Cilvegözü sınır kapısına yakınlığı nedeni ile Reyhanlı ilçesinde toplanmıştır. Reyhanlı ve Antakya şehir merkezlerinde Suriyeli işçilerin toplandığı ve iş beklediği alanlar bulunmaktadır.

Suriyeli göçmenlerin bağımsız çalışmaları

Hatay ili içinde bulunan Suriyeli göçmenler küçük esnaf olarak işyeri açarak da faaliyette bulunuyorlar. Bu ticaretten yörede iş yapan küçük esnaf ve sanatkârın olumsuz etkilendiğine dair bilgiler vardır. Reyhanlı ilçesinde Suriyeli göçmenlerin yaygın olarak oturdukları yerlerdeki yerli esnafın mükellefiyetlerin belirli oranda azaldığı açıklanmıştır.[298] Ayrıca Hatay ekonomisinin önemli kaynaklarından biri olan sınır ticaretinin savaş nedeni ile durması 25 bin ailenin bu ticaret nedeni ile olumsuz olarak etkilendiğini belirten raporlar bulunmaktadır (Gaziantep-Hatay Raporu 2012: 58). Buna karşılık farklı yollarla yapılan ticaretin yön değiştirmesinden de söz etmek gerekir. Örneğin "2012 yılında Suriye ile olan sınırları kapattıktan sonra Türkiye'nin sınır ticaretinin çok düştüğü ancak Türk şirketlerin Suriye'deki STKlara yönelik mal ihracatına başlaması ve Suriyeli şirketlerin Türkiye'nin güney kentlerinde işyerleri açarak ticaret yapmasıyla birlikte" bu açığının kapandığı savunulmaktadır (Çağaptay 2014: 4). Nitekim Suriye'deki iç savaş nedeniyle pek çok Suriyeli işadamının Türkiye'ye sermaye taşıdığı ve bunun da ciddi bir dış sermaye girişi sağladığına dair yaygın iddialar da vardır (Erdoğan 2014: 17).

Hatay ve diğer illerde yoğun olarak şehirde yaşayan bir bölüm Suriyeli ailelerin çocuklarına Suriyeli öğretmenler tarafından eğitim verilmektedir. Bu öğretmenlerin Suriye'de izledikleri müfredatı takip ettikleri, dersleri Arapça verdikleri, aldıkları ücretin ortalama olarak değişmekle birlikte kamp içinde ise 170 USD kamp dışında ise 230 USD olduğu ve bu ücretin UNICEF tarafından ödendiği anlaşılmaktadır.[299]

---

[298] Hatay SMMMO başkanı Abdullah Korkmaz ile yapılan 11.04.2015 tarihli görüşme notları
[299] Gaziantep MEB şube müdürlüğünden 13.04.2015 tarihli bilgi notu

Gaziantep

Bölgedeki beş il arasında en fazla ekonomik gelişmeye sahip olanı ve ilginç bir olarak Suriye iç savaşından bu yana işsizlik oranı azalan, bu kentte hareketli ve canlı bir iş piyasası mevcuttur. Bu konuda çalışmaları olan Özerdem'e göre "Suriyeli göçmenler gelmeden önce Gaziantep iş piyasası, özellikle tarım ve inşaat sektörleri, vasıfsız işgücü bulmada zorlanıyordu. Türkiye'ye gelen Suriyeli göçmenler bu ihtiyacı karşılayarak Gaziantep özel sektör iş piyasasını olumlu yönde etkiledi. Buna karşın mülteciler yerli işçilerin aldığı ücretin dramatik bir şekilde düşmesine yol açtı" (Özerdem 2015: 1). Öte yandan Gaziantep en fazla nüfus artış oranına sahip olması yanı sıra, Suriye ile ticareti de çok büyük oranda artış gösteren bir ildir. 2012 yılına göre 2013 yılında Suriye için yapılan ihracatın yüzde 67 oranında, yani beş kata yakın bir düzeyde, artmıştır. İhracatın daha çok gıda ve çimento ürünlerini içermesi gerçekleşen ticaretin savaşın yıkımları ile yakından ilgili olduğunu göstermektedir.

Gaziantep kenti bölgenin önemli sanayi ve ticaret odağını oluşturduğu için, birçok küçük işyerinin Suriyeli göçmenler tarafından işletildiği görülmektedir. Küçük esnaflık olarak adlandırılan işyerleri arasında en yaygın olanı kahve (aromalı ve farklı türde kahvelerin bulunduğu) satış ve sunum işyerleri, lokantalar, ekmek imalat yerleri, turizm-seyahat acente işletmeciliği, yöresel ürünlerin satıldığı yerler olduğu görülmektedir. Ayrıca küçük sanayi içinde ve atölyelerde triko, kilim-savan, battaniye vb. küçük üretim yapılmaktadır.[300] Açılan bağımsız işyerlerinin belirgin biçimde bir tolerans ile karşılandığı daha önce Gelirler Kontrolörlüğü ilgili yazısı ile belirtilmişti. Benzer bir açıklama bu konuda yapılan bir görüşme esnasında da ortaya konmuştur. Görüştüğümüz kişi bu durumu şu şekilde açıkladı:[301]

> *"Suriye'den gelenlerin iş kurma taleplerindeki artış sonrasında Maliye Bakanlığı'ndan görüş istendi ve talep edilen evrak-belgelerin Suriyeliler tarafından temininde zorluk yaşandığının belirtilmesi üzerine, bakanlık bir yazı gönderdi. Gelen yazıda özetle "evrak-belge taleplerini oldukça azaltın, muadil belgeler ile işlemleri yürütün ve işlemleri kolaylaştırın" deniyor.*

Bölge illerinde çok sayıda yardım kuruluşu çalışmaktadır.[302] Bu kurumlardan alınan bazı bilgiler gelen Suriyeli göçmenlere ülkeye uyum, sağlık ve beslenme gibi konularda ilk ve acil yardım hizmetlerinin sağlandığı göstermektedir. Bu yardım kuruluşları dışında bölge illerinde faaliyet gösteren çok sayıda uluslararası kuruluşun bulunduğuna ve yardım sağladığına ilişkin bilgiler bulunmaktadır. Hatay ilinde yapılan bir görüşmede 28 yardım derneği bulunduğu bunlardan 14 tanesinin faal olduğu belirtilmiştir.[303]

---

[300] 23.4.2015 tarihli M.G ile yapılan görüşme notları

[301] 13.04. 2015 tarihli İ.D ile yapılan görüşme notları

[302] Bu Kurumların kayıtlara geçen ve resmi olarak belirlenenleri şunlardır. Refugee Education Trust (RET), Danish Refugee Cauncil (D.R.C), Concern Worldwide Turkey, Medecins Sans Frontieres (MSF), Norvegian Refugee Council (NRC), AAR JAPAN, Uluslararası Ortadoğu Barış ve Araştırma Merkezi (IMPR), UNHCR International Rescue Commettee (IRC), International Medical Corpd ,(IMC), Şanlıurfa STK'ları İnsani Yardım Platformu, Uluslararası Mavi Hilal İnsani Yardım ve Kalkınma Vakfı

[303] Bu derneklerden bazılarının ismi şöyle: Suriye Nur derneği, Suriye Türkleri Eğitim Derneği, Hayata Destek Derneği ve Keldani Asurî Derneği. M.B. ile yapılan 11.4.2015 tarihli görüşme notlarından

Kilis

Kilis ekonomik ve sosyal göstergeleri açısından oldukça küçük ve gelişme düzeyi sınırlı olan bir ildir (TÜİK Seçilmiş Göstergelerle Kilis 2013). Net göç hızı en yüksek olan illerden biridir. Sağlık göstergeleri açısından Türkiye genelinde bebek ölüm oranı en yüksek olan ildir. Aynı zamanda, kendi yerleşik nüfusundan daha fazla göçmen barındıran yerleşim yerlerinden biridir. Diğer bir deyişle Kilis'te Türk vatandaşlardan çok Suriyeli mülteciler bulunmaktadır (Özerdem 2015: 1) BM Mülteciler Yüksek Komiserliği 2014 verilerine göre Kilis ilinin nüfusunun % 59'unu Suriyeli mülteciler oluşturmaktadır (akt. Çağaptay 2014: 3). Konu ile ilgili Kilis'te görüştüğümüz kişiler sınıra ve Halep kentine yakınlığı nedeni ile çok sayıda Suriyeli göçmeni barındıran Kilis'in aslında bir transit merkezi olduğu, burada kayıt altına alınan Suriyeli göçmenlerin daha sonra farklı illere gittiklerini aktardılar. Aynı görüşmeciler gelen göçmenlerin tümünün savaş nedeni ile gelmedikleri, bir kısmının eğitim ve sağlık hizmetlerinden ücretsiz yararlanmak için geldikleri, hatta aralarında çok sayıda diyaliz hastası bulunduğunu da ifade ettiler. Öte yandan il içinde kalanların toplam geçiş yapanlara oranı % 20 civarında olduğu da tahmin edilmektedir. Diğer kentlerde olduğu gibi Kilis içinde göçmen işçilerin yaygın olarak inşaat ve tarım alanlarında çalıştıkları, ama kendi işyeri açanların da olduğu belirtilmektedir.

Kilis sınıra çok yakın olması ve sınırın her iki tarafındaki insanlar arasında var olan akrabalık bağları nedeniyle gelişen yardım mekanizmaları Suriyeli göçmenler için işletilmektedir. Kilis ili için Suriyeli göçmenlerin görünürlüğü sayıca fazlalıklarından kaynaklanmaktadır.[304] Burada görüşülen yardım yapan kuruluşların temsilcileri parasal yardım yapmak yerine göçmenlere üretime katılmayı özendirecek iş aletlerini sağladıklarını (bu amaçla örneğin dikiş makinesi, badana yapmak için boya veya fırça alınması, kadınlara da kuaför malzemesi verilmesi) belirttiler. Gelen göçmenlerden eğitimli olanların yardım kuruluşlarında günlük 50-60 TL ücretle Suriyeli aileler arasında değerlendirme anketi yaptıkları, yardım alacak olanları saptadıkları, sürekli çalışan Suriyelilerin ise kadrolu ve maaşlı olarak aylık 1000 dolar aldıkları, aynı görüşmeciler tarafından açıklandı.[305]

Kilis il sınırları içinde Suriye mültecilerin kaldığı iki konaklama merkezi bulunmaktadır. AFAD bilgilerine göre bu merkezlerde 2014 Kasım itibari ile 37 bini aşkın kişi kalmaktadır (AFAD brifing notları 2014). Bu kamplardan biri olan Öncüpınar yerleşim yeri Suriye sınırı ile tampon bölge arasında kalan arazide inşa edilmiştir. Bu kent içinde yaklaşık 20 bin kişi konaklamaktadır. Her aile için verilen alan yaklaşık 21 metrekaredir. Okul, sağlık ve alışveriş merkezinin bulunduğu kent içinde yaşamın temel ihtiyaçları karşılanmaya çalışılmaktadır. Buralarda konaklamanın esasları ve güvenliği Kilis Valiliği tarafından düzenlenmektedir.

Şanlıurfa

Gaziantep'ten sonra bölgenin en büyük ili Şanlıurfa'dır. Şanlıurfa büyük toprak mülkiyetinin hakim olduğu araziler üzerinde kuruludur. Yöredeki toplumsal ilişkiler büyük çapta ataerkil ve gelenekseldir. Bir sınır ili olan Şanlıurfa'nın nüfusu

---

[304] 14.4.2015 tarihli Y.F.A görüşme notları
[305] 14.4.2015 tarihli P.E görüşme notları

kırsal ağırlıklı olup kapsadığı alan çok geniştir. Bu ilde istihdam edilenlerin yaklaşık % 32'si tarım sektöründe çalışmaktadır (TÜİK 2014). Özellikle pamuk ve hububat bölgenin en önemli ürünlerini oluşturmaktadır.

Diğer yandan farklı etnik yapılardan oluşan Suriyeli göçmenleri en fazla barındıran Şanlıurfa ilidir. İl sınırları içindeki toplam 4 kampta 80 bini aşkın Suriyeli göçmen bulunmaktadır. AFAD verilerine göre Şanlıurfa'da kamplar dışında kalanlarla birlikte Suriyeli göçmenlerin toplam sayısı 350-400 bin civarında olduğu tahmin edilmektedir.

Makineli tarımın yaygınlaşması ile birlikte bir yandan civar illerden gelen mevsimlik tarım işçiliği azalırken diğer yandan Şanlıurfa'dan diğer illere mevsimlik tarım işçiliği göçü artmıştır. Mart-Kasım ayları arasında fındıktan soğana kadar birçok tarım ürününde çalışmak üzere, ilden mevsimlik tarım işçiliği göçü olmaktadır. Mevsimlik tarım işçiliği göçü Şanlıurfa dışında Mardin, Siirt, Diyarbakır ve Adıyaman gibi yörelerden de yoğun olarak olmaktadır (Aslan, 2013: 132). Şanlıurfa'ya dışarıdan gelen ve pamuk toplama işinde çalışan Suriyeli göçmenler yöredeki tarım işçiliğini daha da ucuzlatmaktadır. Ancak gündelik ücretin 20-30 TL olması tarla sahipleri açısından bir avantaj oluşturmaktadır.

Şanlıurfa'da hem Suriyeli hem yerli işgücü iki sektörde istihdam edilmektedir. Bunlardan biri ve en önemlisi inşaat diğeri ise toptan ve perakende ticarettir. Bu iki sektörün işyeri sayılarına göre oranı tüm işyerlerinin yüzde 48'idir (İŞKUR 2014: 11). Bu konuda bir görüşmeci şöyle bir değerlendirmede bulundu:[306]

"Denetlediğimiz inşaatlarda çalışan Suriyeli var. Bu sektörde yoğun olarak çalıştırılıyorlar. Örneğin denetlediğimiz 250 okul inşaatı bir yıl içinde bitirildi. Bu kadar işi sadece yerli iş gücünün çıkarması mümkün değil. Bu işlerin yapımında yerli işçiler yanında Suriyeliler de çalıştırıldı.

Nedeni Suriyeli işçilerin ucuz ücrete razı olmaları ve hiç bir talepte bulunmamasıdır. Örneğin ustalar düz işçi olarak çalışmaya razılar. Gerçi buraya gelen herkes kendini usta olarak tanıtıyor. İnşaat işine ilkin çok acemice başladılar. Ardından işi öğrendiler. Bazıları şantiyelerde yarı bitmiş dairelerde kalıyor. Onların varlığı genelde ücretlerin düşmesine neden oluyor. Ustalar günde 40 TL alıyor. Yerli ustalar ise 50-90 TL arası ücret alıyor. Suriyeli işçi 30 TL yerli 40-50 TL ücret alıyor."

İnşaat sektörü Suriyeli göçmen işçilerin ücretli olarak en yoğun çalıştıkları alanı oluşturmaktadır. Ancak bu sektörde yapılan bütün işler vasıfsız emek gerektirmediği için ince ve zor işlerin yapımı bu işçilere verilmediği görüşülen kişilerce ifade edilmektedir. Suriyeli inşaat işçisi ile yerli inşaat işçisi arasındaki farkın zor koşullarda çalışmayı kabullenmek olarak görülmektedir. Bu duruma karşılık usta ve vasıf gerektiren işlerde, örneğin taş işçiliğinde, Suriyeli ustaların gündelik ücretlerinin yerli işçiden farklı olmadığı belirtilmektedir.

Şanlıurfa'daki çalışma hayatında sadece bağımlı çalışan işçiler değil, bağımsız işyeri açan Suriyeli göçmenler de mevcuttur. Küçük esnaf olarak berberlik, bakkal işletmecisi, seyyar satıcılık, kuyumculuk yapan işyerlerine sahip Suriyeli göçmenler de bulunmaktadır. Burada dikkat çekici olan başka bir nokta söz konusu işyerlerin çoğunlukla Suriyeli göçmenlere hizmet vermesidir. Suriye'den getirilen çay, kahve ve benzeri temel ihtiyaç maddeleri bu dükkânlarda satılmaktadır. Hazırlanan ve bölge içinde satılan ekmekler yerine kendi üretimleri ekmekleri almak isteyen geniş

[306] 17.04.2015 İ.B. ile yapılan görüşme notları

bir Suriyeli topluluğu bulunmaktadır. Bu diğer gıda maddeleri gibi bu ekmekler de Suriyelilerin çalıştırdığı dükkânlardan temin edilmektedir.

Şanlıurfa'da Suriyeli göçmenlerin iş piyasalarına katılımlarına yardımcı olan bazı kurumlar da vardır.[307] Rızk Ofisi bunlardan bir tanesidir. Görüşülen yetkililerinden biri göçmen işçilere yönelik çalışmalar yapan ofisi şöyle tanımlamaktadır: *"İş arayanların mesleki yeterliliklerini geliştiren ve onlara iş fırsatları bulma amaçlı ve istihdama yönelik, kâr amacı gütmeyen bir kurum".* (www.rizkoffice.com) Kurum yetkilileri ile yapılan görüşmede Suriyeli göçmenlere iş konusunda yardım ettiklerini, Türkiye'nin her tarafından gelen iş taleplerini toplayıp bunları ilgili buldukları göçmenlere ilettiklerini, onların iş bulmaları dışında ücretlerini almamaları halinde destek olduklarını belirttiler. Kendilerine başvuran 13 bin Suriyeli göçmenden 3000 binden fazlasına bu şekilde bulduklarını aktardılar. Kurum yetkilileri Suriyeli göçmenlerin uzun çalışma saatlerine alışkın olmadıklarını, ama iş bulunmadığı için mecbur kaldıklarını, gelen göçmenlerin çoğunun eğitim düzeylerinin düşük olması nedeniyle iş bulmakta zorlandıklarını da açıkladılar.

Mardin

Mardin Suriyeli göçmenlerin en az ikamet ettiği sınır ilidir. Burada yaklaşık 70 bin civarında kayıtlı Suriyeli göçmen olduğu İçişleri Bakanlığı verilerinden anlaşılmaktadır (ORSAM 2015: 15). Kasım 2014 verilerine göre Mardin ili sınırları içinde bulunan 2 çadır kentte konaklayan göçmenlerin sayısı 2.881 olarak belirtilmektedir (AFAD brifingi).

Öte yandan Mardin iline ait işsizlik verileri 2011 sonrası yüzde 20 civarında seyretmektedir. Mardin'in ilk sıralarda yer almasına yol açan bu yüksek işsizlik oranı Türkiye ortalamasının çok üzerindedir.

Mardin'de iş piyasası hakkında bilgi veren iki görüşmeci ile yapılan mülakatta, aşağıdaki ifadelere rastlanmaktadır.[308]

"İşverenlerle yapılan işgücü anket çalışmaları sırasında çalıştırmak için elemana ihtiyaçlarının olmadığını ifade ettiler. Oysa Suriyeliler gelmeden önce işverenler bizden işçi talebinde bulunuyordu. Suriyeli mültecilerin gelmesiyle iş piyasası doygunluğa ulaştı, ama yerli işçilerin işsizlik oranında da artış oldu. Yaptığımız işgücü anketleri sonuçları bunu teyit etmektedir. Anket çalışması sırasında işverenlere kaç işçi çalıştırdıklarını sorduğumuzda bizi sigortalı mı sigortasız mı diye yanıtlıyorlar. İlkin cevap vermek istemiyorlar ama sonra detaylı bir şekilde anlatıyorlar. Bu durum organize sanayi bölgesinde açıkça gözlemlenebilmektedir. Suriyelilerin kaçak çalışmayı kabul etmeleri işverenlerin yerli işçilere karşı ellerini güçlendiriyor. Ama yerli işçiler İŞKUR'a tepki duyuyor. Suriyelilere karşı sadece, onlar geldi bizi işten çıkardılar şeklinde sitem ediyorlar. Ayrıca Suriye'de olup biteni yakından takip ettiklerinden ve buraya gelenlerin neler yaşadıklarını bildiklerinden Suriyelilere karşı fazla tepkili değiller. Bölgede kaçak çalışmaya bakış açısı daha esnek,

---

[307] Suriye Forumu adlı bu organizasyon, muhalif Suriyeli iş adamları tarafından maddi olarak desteklenen ve ÖSO ile ilişkili bir kurum niteliğindedir. Foruma bağlı olarak çalışan İhsan Yardım Derneği, Suriye Medya, İmran Stratejik Araştırmalar Merkezi, Pusula Eğitim Geliştirme Merkezleri bulunmaktadır. Bunların dışında Forumun stratejik ortaklarından biri de Rizik adlı Şanlıurfa'da 2014 yılında kurulmuş bir istihdam ofisidir.

[308] 6.04.2015 tarihli F.P ve B.B ile yapılan mülakat notları

göz yumuluyor. Kaçak işçi çalıştıran işyerlerine karşı toleranslı davranılıyor, para cezası kesilmiyor.

Yukarıda belirtilen çerçevede Suriyeli göçmenlerin vasıf düzeyi düşük işlerde ve yerli işçilerin yapmak istemedikleri işlerde istihdam edildiği anlaşılmaktadır. Bu işlerde güvencesiz çalışmanın en büyük riski iş kazasına uğranması halinde göçmen işçinin iş kazası sonrası bildirimde bulunamamasıdır. İş kazası geçiren işçinin hiç bir sosyal hakkı olmadığı gibi tedavi hizmetinden de yararlanması söz konusu değildir. Bir görüşmecinin bu konudaki ifadesi şu şekildedir:

"Diyelim işçi çalışırken bir parmağını makineye kaptırdı. Bu iş kazasını bildirip başına iş açacağına, kalan dokuz parmağıyla çalışıp ekmeğini kazanmayı tercih ediyor. Ayrıca iş kazasının bilinmesi ne işverenin ne de işçinin işine geliyor. Böyle bir durumda işveren kaçak işçi çalıştırmaktan para cezası alacak işçi de kaçak çalışma suçundan ceza alacak veya en azından sınır dışı edilme tehdidi ile karşı karşıya kalacaktır."

Mardin'de iş piyasasına dâhil olan göçmenlerin arasında vasıf düzeyi yüksek kişiler bulunmaktadır. Ancak bu kişilerin çalıştıkları işler onların vasıf düzeyi ile ilgili alanlar değildir. Bunun dışında az sayıda Suriyeli göçmen Mardin'de yatırım yapmaktadır. Örneğin Mardin'in Midyat ilçesinde kurulu bir hayvan çiftliği, Kızıltepe'de bazı küçük market ve lokanta türü işyerleri Suriyeli göçmenler tarafından yönetilmektedir.

İstihdam Piyasaları ve Suriyeli Göçmenlere İlişkin Bazı gözlemler ve Değerlendirme

Bu çalışma 2011 yılından bu yana sürmekte olan bir iç savaş ve neden olduğu sorunlarla bağlantılı olarak Türkiye'ye gelmek zorunda kalan Suriyeli göçmenlerin iş piyasaları üzerindeki muhtemel etkilerini kavramak üzerine kaleme alındı. Etki alanı ve yoğunluğu nedeni ile Suriye sınırında olan beş il bu çalışmanın alanını oluşturmuştur. Aşağıda belirlenen ana noktalar iş piyasalarına dönük olmakla birlikte kültürel ve toplumsal etkilerden ayrı ele alınmamalıdır.

Suriyeli göçmenlerin emek arzı açısından homojen bir grup oluşturmadıkları, kırsal kökenli ve vasıf düzeyi düşük göçmenler olduğu kadar kent kökenli ve belirli vasıflara sahip yüksek eğitimli olanları da bulunmaktadır. Bu itibarla Suriyeli göçmenlerin çalışma yaşamına katılımı sadece bulundukları yörenin ihtiyacı olan, yani yerli işçilerin yapmak istemedikleri işleri yapan işçiler olarak görmek hatalı olacaktır.

Suriyeli göçmenlerin Türkiye'ye düzensiz giriş ve çıkışlarından kaynaklı herhangi bir hak ve güvenceye sahip olamayışları onları özellikle inşaat ve tarım sektörlerinde ucuz işgücü kaynağı haline getirmektedir. Bölge içinde ucuz işgücü kaynağı oluşturmaları yerli işçilerle aralarındaki gerginlik ve çatışma riskini çok yükseltmektedir.

Türkiye'ye gelen Suriyeli göçmenlerin bulundukları veya ikamet ettikleri yerler onların sınıfsal ve ekonomik konumları ile yakından ilişkilidir. En alt gelir düzeyine sahip olan göçmenler kamplara yerleştirildikleri anlaşılmaktadır. Kamplara yerleşenler dışarıda ikamet edenlerin yaklaşık % 20si kadardır. İkinci alt grup kamplara çeşitli nedenlerle giremeyen ve kent varoşlarında veya kırsal kesimde kendi olanakları ile yaşamaya çalışanlardan oluşmaktadır. Bu iki grubun gelir düzeyleri arasında bir yakınlık bulunmaktadır. Üçüncü grup göçmen orta gelir seviyesine sahip olanlardan oluşmaktadır. Bu gruptakilerin kentlerde ikamet ettikleri, bazı apartmanları ortak olarak kullandıkları bilinmektedir. Dördüncü ve son grup göçmenin ise gelir düzeylerinin yüksekliği nedeni ile Batı ülkelerine göç ettiği veya etme hazırlığı içinde olduğunu varsaymak mümkündür.

Bu dört göçmen grup için ayrı çalışma ve istihdam koşulları düzenlenmelidir. Bu göçmenlerden vasıf düzeyleri yüksek olanların geri dönüş olasılığı diğer göçmenlere göre daha düşüktür. Vasıf düzeyleri düşük olanların da ancak bir bölümünün geri döneceğini düşünmek mümkündür. Nitekim sınır illerindeki üniversitelere devam eden Suriyeli göçmenlerin sayısında artış gözlemlenmektedir. Bunların dışında Türk dilini öğreten özel ve kamusal kurslardan yararlanan çok sayıda göçmen bulunmaktadır. Bu itibarla Suriyeli göçmenlerin geldikleri topluma entegrasyonu önem taşıyan bir unsur olarak görülmektedir.

Suriyeli Göçmenlerin geldikleri sınır illeri birbirlerinden farklı sosyo-ekonomik gelişmişlik düzeylerine sahiptir. Gaziantep ve Şanlıurfa bu anlamda bölgenin iki tipik kentidir. Gaziantep Suriyeli göçmenlere yaklaşımı oldukça faydacı bir metropol refleksi iken, Şanlıurfa göçmenlere "Ensar"[309] geleneği çerçevesinde yardımcı bir tarz da yaklaşmıştır. Bu geleneğe rağmen Suriyeli göçmenlerle yerli halk arasında zaman zaman çatışmalar yaşanmakta, ancak Gaziantep'te olduğu gibi göçmenlerin kamplara gönderilmesi söz konusu olmamaktadır.

Suriyeli göçmenlerin küçük bir bölümü ülkede ticari ve sınaî şirketler kurmuş ve çalışma izinleri almışlardır. Bu şirketlerin bir bölümünde Suriyeli göçmenler istihdam edilmektedir. Çalışma izinleri olan Suriyeli göçmen sayısı çok düşüktür. Yasalaşması beklenen yeni yabancılar çalışma yasası Suriyeli göçmenlerin çalışma izinlerinde kolaylaştırıcı unsurlar taşıması beklenmektedir. Ancak bu konuda belirli teşviklerin öngörülmesi gerekmektedir.

Suriyeli göçmenlerin önemli oranda kadın ve çocuklardan oluşan bir grup oluşturması iş piyasaları açısından diğer bir kırılganlık noktasıdır. Bu istismara konu olanların kentlerde dilencilik yapması, kadınların ikinci eş olarak evlendirilmesi, yeni dünyaya gelen çocukların "vatansız" olmaları ve eğitimleri konusunda ciddi sorunları barındırmaları bulundukları bölge içinde yeni sorunlar çıkarmaya hazır unsurlar haline getirmektedir.

Suriyeli göçmenlerin bir bölümü de bağımsız olarak çalıştıkları görülmektedir. Bunların daha çok küçük esnaf olarak faaliyet göstermeleri aynı alanda faaliyet gösteren yerli esnaf için ciddi bir rekabet sorunu oluşturmaktadır. Bu yeni göçmenlerin vergilenmeleri konusunda gösterilen hoşgörü gerginlik unsuru olmaya aday gözükmektedir. Bu işyerlerini işletenlerin dil bilgileri nedeni ile onlardan alışveriş yapanlar da kendi vatandaşları olmaktadır. Bu ve benzeri örnekler çoğu zaman Türkiye'den Almanya'ya giden işçi göçünü ve orada oluşturdukları ticari ağları akla getirmektedir.

Sonuç olarak, Türkiye'ye gelmek zorunda kalan Suriyeli göçmenlerin savaştan kaçma dışında insani yaşam koşullarının kaybolması nedeni ile burada olduklarını biliyoruz. Türkiye'nin son dönemde yönettiği dış politika bu ülkeden daha fazla göçmenin gelişinde tayin edici olmuştur. Bu göçmenlerin iş piyasalarına katılmalarının ortaya koyacağı başta gelir ve sosyal güvenlik ve insanca yaşam gibi hakların, merhamet cömertlik ve komşuya yardım çerçevesinde

---

[309] Ensar geleneği İslam peygamberine ve yakınlarına Medine kentinin yardımcı olması anlamında kullanılan bir hoşgörü anlayışıdır.

değerlendirilmemesi gerekir. Bu nedenle yapılacak düzenlemeler hak temelli olmalı ve Suriyeli göçmenlerin diğer yurttaşlarla eşit haklara kavuşturulması zorunluluğu ülke içinde muhtemel çatışma alanlarını azaltması için gerekli olacaktır.

Kaynakça

AFAD (2014). Brifing notları, Kasım 2014 Ankara.

AFAD (2013). Türkiye'deki Suriyeli Sığınmacılar Saha Araştırması Sonuçları.

Akdeniz E. (2014). Suriye savaşının gölgesinde Mülteci İşçiler, Evrensel Yayınları, İstanbul.

Aslan, M (2013). "Les Ouvriers Saisonniers kurdes travaillant a la cueillette des noisette en Turquie " Revue Hommes et Migrations 1301 Janvier, Fevriers Mars

Çağaptay, S. (2014). The Impact of Syrian Refugees on Southern Turkey, The Washington Institute for Near East Policy.

Çolak Y. (2015). Yeni Teşvik Sistemi ve Şanlıurfa "Karacadağ kalkınma Ajansı"

Erdoğan M. (2014). Türkiye'deki Suriyeliler: Toplumsal Kabul Ve Uyum Araştırması, Hacettepe Üniversitesi Göç ve Siyaset Araştırmaları Merkezi Raporu Ankara.

Gaziantep Sanayi Odası (2014). "Ekovizyon 2014", Gaziantep'in Ekonomik ve sosyal Göstergeleri.

İŞKUR (2014). Şanlıurfa İşgücü Piyasası Analiz Raporuö Ankara.

Kanat, K. Buğra ve Üstün K. (2015). Turkey's Syrian Refugees: Toward Integration SETAV, Ankara.

Kirişci, K. (2014). Misafirliğin ötesine geçerken: Türkiye'nin "Suriyeli Mülteciler" Sınavı, USAK (çev: S. Karaca).

ORSAM –TESEV (2015). Suriyeli Sığınmacıların Türkiye'ye Etkileri, Rapor No: 195.

TÜİK Nüfus ve Konut Araştırması (2011)..

Öngel, S. ve Tanyılmaz, K. (2013). Türkiye Ekonomisinde Küresel Kriz Karşısında Sermayenin Tepkisi: İşçilerin Artan Sömürüsü, DİSK-AR.

Özerdem, A. (2015). Turkey urgently needs to integrate its Syrian refugees. http://theconversation.com/turkey-urgently-needs-to-integrate-its-syrian-refugees-35984 erişim: 22/05/2015

SABR İstatistik Araştırmaları ve Kamu Politikaları Merkezi MDN (2015), Suriyeli Türk Uyumu.

TÜİK. İl bazında işgücü göstergeleri (2011, 2012, 2013 yılları)

TÜİK. Seçilmiş Göstergelerle Kilis 2013.

Uluslararası Ortadoğu Barış Araştırmaları Merkezi IMPR (2012), "Türkiye ile Suriye Arasındaki Krizin Hatay ve Gaziantep ekonomileri üzerine etkileri" Rapor no: 12

Suriye'den Türkiye'ye Göç ve Açığa Çıkan Temel Sorun Alanları

Fikret Elma* ve Ahmet Şahin**

Giriş

Türkiye kuruluşundan bugüne önemli ölçüde iç ve dış göç deneyimi yaşayan bir ülkedir. Geçmişte Türkiye açısından en büyük dış göç dalgaları olarak, özellikle Balkanlardan (Yunanistan, Bulgaristan ve Bosna gibi) Türkiye'ye gelen göçmenler ve Türkiye'den Avrupa ülkelerine yönelen işçi göçü ifade edilebilir. Dolayısıyla, dış göç çerçevesinde ülke farklı dönemlerde hem dış göç alan, hem de dış göç veren bir konumundadır. Ancak özellikle 1990'lı yıllardan itibaren küresel ve bölgesel gelişmeler bağlamında Türkiye'nin daha çok dış göç alan bir ülke haline geldiği dikkati çekmektedir. Bu süreçte ayrıca göçmenler ve mülteciler için Türkiye'nin güney-kuzey ve doğu-batı ekseninde transit geçiş ülkesi olma konumunun da giderek belirginleştiği görülmektedir.

1990'lar sonrasında Türkiye'ye yönelen dış göçü iki grupta toplamak mümkündür. Birincisi; yakın bölge ülkelerinden siyasal, ekonomik ve kültürel etmenler yanında savaş ve etnik çatışmalar gibi güvenlik nedeniyle yapılan göçler ve mülteci akını, ikincisi ise; büyük ölçüde Avrupa ülkelerinden özellikle Akdeniz ve Ege'deki sahil bölgelerine yönelen emekli akınıdır. Birinci grup bağlamında Bosna-Hersek, Rusya Federasyonu (özellikle çeçenler), Azerbaycan, Ermenistan, Gürcistan, Irak ve daha önceki dalgada İran, Bulgaristan ve Afganistan'dan Türkiye'ye gelen göçmen ve mülteciler söz konusudur. Türkiye'ye yönelen dış göçün son örneğini ise, Nisan 2011'den itibaren Suriye'den başlayan göç dalgası ve mülteci akını oluşturmaktadır.

Literatüre "Arap Baharı" olarak geçen ve öncelikle Tunus ve Mısır gibi Arap ülkelerinde gerçekleşen halk isyanları çerçevesinde Mart 2011'de komşu ülke Suriye'de başlayan olaylar kısa sürede büyük bir kaos ve iç savaşa dönüşmüştür. Suriye'deki iç savaş büyük bir insani trajedi, güvenlik sorunu ve komşu ülkelere kitlesel göç dalgasını beraberinde getirmiştir. Bu çerçevede, on milyona yakın Suriyeli iç ve dış göçe yönelmiştir. Bu bağlamda, insani kaygılar ve "açık kapı politikası" ile sığınma talebinde bulunan bütün Suriyelilere sınırlarını açan Türkiye hali hazırda iki milyon civarında Suriyeli mülteciye geçici sığınma hakkı vermiş bulunmaktadır. Bu çalışmada, Türkiye'deki Suriyeli sığınmacıların mevcut durumu ve temel sorunları incelenmektedir. Ayrıca çalışmanın sonuç kısmında sorunun Türkiye için taşıdığı mevcut ve muhtemel riskler değerlendirilmektedir.

Göç Olgusu ve Mülteci Sorunu

Göç olgunun özünde bireysel veya grup olarak insanların iç veya dış göç bağlamında yaşam yerlerini büyük ölçüde kalıcı olarak değiştirmeleri söz

---

* Department of Public Administration, Celal Bayar University, Turkey. E-mail: fikretelma@hotmail.com
** Department of Economics, Celal Bayar University, Turkey. E-mail ahmet.sahin@cbu.edu.tr

konusudur. Bu bağlamda göç olgusu Roberta Medda ve arkadaşlarının (Medda-Windischer vd, 2012: 194) da üzerinde durduğu gibi öncelikle bir coğrafi mobilite şeklidir. Bu mobilite aynı zamanda daha iyi veya daha kötü yaşam koşullarını gündeme getiren sosyo-ekonomik bir mobilizasyonu da mümkün kılmaktadır. Çünkü, göç sadece coğrafi ya da mekansal bir değişiklik değil. Göç neticesinde göçmenlerin yaşam biçimleri, koşulları ve sorunları da farklılaşmaktadır. Zamanla göç edilen alanlarda yeni durumlar, gerçekler ve sorunlar açığa çıkmaktadır. Bu nedenle, göçler hem göçmenlerin yaşamlarında, hem de göç edilen yerlerde kültürel, ekonomik, toplumsal ve politik farklılıklar nedeniyle bir değişime neden olmaktadır. Özetle, nedenleri ve açığa çıkardığı sonuçları bakımından göç; ekonomik, kültürel, sosyal, politik ve güvenlik etmenleri bakımından çok boyutlu bir olgu olarak karşımıza çıkmaktadır.

Göçle ilgili literatür incelendiğinde konuyla ilgili baskın tek bir kuram ya da yaklaşımdan bahsetmek mümkün değildir. Zaten çok boyutlu ve oldukça karmaşık bir sosyal olgunun tek bir yaklaşımla çözümlenmesi de mümkün değildir. Bununla birlikte, Ravenstein'in "Göç Kanunları" adlı çalışmasının konuyla ilgili önemli bir başlangıç oluşturduğu söylenebilir. Ravenstein, "Göç Kanunları" olarak adlandırdığı *göç ve basamakları, yayılma ve emme süreci, göç zincirleri, doğrudan göç, kır-kent yerleşimcileri farkı, kadın-erkek farkı* gibi kriterler çerçevesinde iç ve dış göç olgusunu esasen endüstrileşme, kentleşme ve ekonomik etkenler bağlamında ele alır. Ravenstein'in bu yaklaşımı göç olgusunu açıklamakta eksiksiz bir yaklaşım olmasa da ekonomik temelli göç teorilerine önemli bir alt yapı oluşturur (Vergil vd, 2014: 5-7). Bugün ekonomik etkenler, iç ve dış göç bağlamında hala büyük bir önem taşımaktadır. Çünkü Sirkeci ve Erdoğan'ın (Sirkeci&Erdoğan, 2012: 298) da vurguladığı gibi, "göçe etki eden dinamik faktörlerin başında çoğunlukla ülkeler, bölgeler ve gruplar arası ekonomik dengesizlikler... siyasetten kültüre çeşitli alanlarda ve düzeylerde karşılaşılan fırsat eşitsizlikleri" gelmektedir.

Göç konusundaki teoriler bugün genelde mikro ve makro yaklaşımlar bağlamında ele alınmakla birlikte, *klasik itme-çekme kuramı, ağ modelleri, transnasyonalizm* (ulusötesi) *ve çatışma* konusundaki yaklaşımların daha çok ön plana çıktığı ifade edilebilir. Konumuz açısından kuşkusuz dış göç bağlamında *transnasyonalizm* ve *çatışma* olgusu büyük önem taşımaktadır. *Transnasyonalizm,* köken ülke, göç edilen ülke, dinamizm, çok yönlülük ve üçüncü kuşak gibi konuları ön plana çıkarırken burada esas vurgu göçlerin yöneldiği transnasyonel topluma ya da coğrafyayadır (Sirkeci, 2012: 353). Bu çalışmada, Sirkeci'nin "çatışmayı transnasyonel göçü şekillendiren dinamik bir ana unsur olarak kabul eden" yaklaşımı esas alınmıştır. Sirkeci'ye göre çatışma olgusu, beraberinde insani güvensizliği, güvenlik sorununu, arayışını ve dolayısıyla ulusötesi insan mobilitesini açığa çıkaran temel etmenlerden bir tanesidir (Sirkeci, 2012: 354).

Gerçekten de *çatışma olgusu,* günümüzde örneğin "arap baharı" çerçevesinde kaynak ülkeden kaçışı, mülteci ve sığınmacı sorununu doğuran en temel etmen olarak karşımıza çıkmaktadır. Tablo 1'de görüldüğü gibi, çatışma süreci ve iç savaş öncesinde 2010 yılında Suriye en çok mülteci veren ülkeler sıralamasında yirminci sırada iken, çatışma sürecini takiben 2012 yılında ikinci sıraya, 2013 ve 2014 yıllarında ise listenin ilk sırasına yükseldiği görülmektedir. Suriye'nin yanı sıra Irak, Afganistan, Eritre gibi listenin üst basamaklarında yer alan hemen hemen bütün ülkelerin çatışma sürecinde olan ya da çatışma deneyimi yaşamış ülkeler olduğu gerçeği dikkati çekmektedir.

Bu çerçevede son dönemlerde ulusötesi göçün özel bir türü olan "mülteciler" ya da "sığınmacılar" konusunun giderek ciddi bir boyut kazanmakta olduğunu ve küresel çağın temel insani sorunlarından bir tanesi haline dönüştüğünü ifade edebiliriz. Özellikle 1980'li yılları takiben Balkanlar, Kafkasya, Orta Doğu ve Afrika coğrafyasında yaşanan sıcak çatışmalar mülteciler konusunu göç olgusu bağlamında ciddi bir noktaya taşımış bulunmaktadır. Öyle ki bugün, *Arap Baharı* sonrası Akdeniz mülteciler için bir ölüm denizi haline gelmiş bulunmaktadır. Neredeyse her hafta yüzlerce mülteci ya da kaçak göçmenin Akdeniz'de ölüm haberleri ajanslara düşmektedir. Buna rağmen, ölümüne yolculuklar ve kaçış çatışma coğrafyalarından devam etmektedir. Irak ve Suriye'deki kaosun Türkiye'ye yansımaları da bu bağlamda açığa çıkmış bulunmaktadır.

Tablo 1: 2010-2014 Döneminde Dünyada En Çok Mülteci Veren Ülkeler
Kaynak: UNHCR Asylum Trends (2014).

	2010	2011	2012	2013	2014
Syrian Arab Rep.	20	13	2	1	1
Iraq	4	3	7	3	2
Afghanistan	2	1	1	4	3
Serbia*	1	4	3	5	4
Eritrea	11	10	10	8	5
Pakistan	8	5	5	6	6
China	3	2	4	10	7
Nigeria	9	9	12	11	8
Islamic Rep. of Iran	7	6	8	9	9
Somalia	6	8	9	7	10
Russian Fed.	5	7	6	2	11
Albania	34	35	17	12	12
Stateless	24	36	28	13	13
Ukraine	57	58	53	52	14
Mexico	17	12	11	14	15

* Serbia and Kosovo (1999)

Suriyeli Sığınmacılar ve Türkiye'de Mevcut Durum

Türkiye gerek yakın tarihi açısından, gerekse Osmanlı'dan bugüne uzanan çizgide oldukça zengin göç kültürü olan bir ülkedir. Öyle ki, "iç göç, zorunlu göç, mübadele, sığınmacılar, dış göç ve benzeri her türlü insan hareketliliğinin yaşandığı Türkiye'deki sosyal, siyasal ve ekonomik yapının en önemli dinamiklerinden biri" göç olgusudur (Sirkeci&Erdoğan, 2012: 298). Bu bağlamda, Türkiye'nin göç hikayesindeki son halkayı Suriyeli göçmenler oluşturmaktadır.

Suriye'de 2011'den buyana yaşanan kaosun Türkiye'ye en önemli yansıması hiç kuşkusuz bugün sayıları iki milyona yaklaşan sığınmacı sorunudur. Tablo 2'de görüldüğü üzere Türkiye 2010 yılında en çok mülteci alan ülkeler sıralamasında ondördüncü sıradadır. Suriye'deki çatışma sürecini takiben 2014 yılında üçüncü sıraya yükseldiği görülmektedir. Üstelik, Türkiye'deki Suriyeli sığınmacılar bu listeye resmi mülteci sıfatı verilmediği için dahil edilmemiştir. Dolayısıyla gerçekte Türkiye 2012 yılından itibaren dünyanın en çok mülteci alan ülkesi konumundadır.

Tablo 2: 2010-2014 Yılları Arasında En çok Mülteci Alan Ülkeler Sıralaması

	2010	2011	2012	2013	2014
Germany	3	3	2	1	1
United States	1	1	1	2	2
Turkey	14	10	6	5	3
Sweden	4	5	4	4	4
Italy	13	4	11	7	5
France	2	2	3	3	6
Hungary	21	26	23	9	7
United Kingdom	6	7	5	6	8
Austria	11	11	10	10	9
Netherlands	9	12	14	11	10
Switzerland	8	9	7	8	11
Serbia*	26	19	19	20	12
Denmark	17	17	17	18	13
Belgium	7	6	9	14	14
Canada	5	8	8	16	15

* Serbia and Kosovo (1999)

Kaynak: UNHCR Asylum Trends (2014).

Çünkü listenin birinci sırasında yer alan Almanya'ya 2014 yılında yapılan sığınma başvurusu sayısı 173.100, ikinci sıradaki ABD'ye yapılan başvuru sayısı tahmini 121.200, sanayileşmiş ülkelerin tamamına ait rakam ise 866.000 olarak rapor edilmiştir. Bu sayı önceki yıllara göre büyük bir rekor olarak kabul edilmektedir (UNHCR, 2014: 3). 2014 yılına ait bu veriler Türkiye'de bulunan iki milyon civarındaki Suriyeli sığınmacı-mülteci yükünün ağırlığını net olarak ortaya koymaktadır. Konuyu en baştan ele almak gerekirse, Suriye'de Mart 2011'de başlayan halk hareketlerinin kısa sürede şehirlerin bombalandığı bir iç savaşa dönüşmesi Suriye'den Türkiye'ye kitlesel göç ve sığınmacı akınını başlatmış bulunmaktadır. Söz konusu sığınmacı ya da mülteci akınının temel nedeni, kuşkusuz çatışma ve iç savaş ortamından uzaklaşma ve hayatta kalma mücadelesidir. Türkiye Cumhuriyeti, bu kitlesel sığınmacı akını karşısında kısıtlayıcı bir politika oluşturmamış ve insani kaygılarla gelen bütün sığınmacılara kapılarını açmıştır. Böylece ülke ani, hazırlıksız, kontrolsüz, kapasite üstü ve ülke geneline yayılan bir sığınmacı sorunuyla bugün karşı karşıyadır.

Türkiye'deki Suriyeli Göçmenler ve Temel Sorunları

Türkiye'deki Suriyeli mültecilerin temel sorunlarını; statü, barınma, eğitim, sağlık ve istihdam bağlamında ele alıp incelemek mümkündür.

Statü Sorunu

Türkiye, 1951 tarihli Mültecilerin Hukuki Durumuna ilişkin Cenevre Sözleşmesi'ne taraf olmakla birlikte, Avrupa dışından gelenlere "coğrafi sınırlama" çekincesi koyduğu için "mülteci" statüsü tanımamakta, "geçici sığınma" sağlamaktadır. Bu çerçevede Türkiye'de Suriyeli sığınmacılar, İçişleri Bakanlığı'nın 1994 Yönetmeliği'nin 10. Maddesi gereğince 'geçici koruma statüsü'ne alınmış bulunmaktadır. 30 Mart 2012 tarihli Suriyelilerin durumuna ilişkin 62 sayılı hukuki düzenlemeyle de, "Türkiye'ye Toplu Sığınma Amacıyla Gelen Suriye Vatandaşlarının ve Suriye'de İkamet Eden Vatansız Kişilerin Kabulüne ve Barındırılmasına İlişkin Yönerge" çıkarılmıştır. Bu yönergeyle Suriyelilerin 'geçici koruma' altında oldukları hukuken kabul edilmiştir (ORSAM, 2014: 11). Başlangıçta belki de Suriye'deki iç savaşın uzun süreli olmayacağı varsayımından hareketle geçici koruma statüsünde kabul edilen Suriyeli göçmenler için statü konusu bugün iç savaşın uzamasıyla ciddi bir sorun haline gelmiş bulunmaktadır. Geçici-misafir statüsü sığınmacılar için iş, çalışma, sosyal güvenlik, eğitim, sağlık, entegrasyon ve daha pek çok konuda belirsizliği beslemektedir.

Barınma Sorunu

Türkiye'deki Suriyeli sığınmacıların en temel sorunlarından başında barınma konusu gelmektedir. Aşağıda Tablo 3'de de görüldüğü gibi AFAD'ın 2015 verilerine göre, Suriyeli sığınmacıların 260 bini Türkiye'nin güney ve güneydoğusundaki Suriye sınırına yakın 10 kentte bulunan 25 kampa yerleştirilmiştir. Geri kalanlar ise, ülke genelinde çeşitli kentlerde kamp dışında yaşamaktadır. Hatay, Gaziantep ve Şanlıurfa beşer kamp ile en çok kampın bulunduğu illerdir. Bu illeri üç kampla Mardin ve iki kampla Kilis takip etmektedir. Diğer şehirlerde birer kamp bulunmaktadır. Şanlıurfa, beş kampında 103 bin Suriyeli sığınmacı ile kamplarda yaşam bağlamında en çok Suriyeli sığınmacının bulunduğu kenttir (AFAD, 2015).

Türkiye'de kamp dışında yaşayan Suriyeli sığınmacıların 1 milyon 700 bin civarında olduğu tahmin edilmektedir. Sınıra yakın bölgelerde Gaziantep, Hatay, Şanlıurfa ve Kilis en fazla sığınmacının yaşadığı şehirlerin başında gelmektedir. Habertürk'te (Habertürk, 2014) kaleme alınan bir yazıya göre, Türkiye çapında 330 binin üzerinde bir rakamla en fazla sığınmacının İstanbul'da yaşadığı tahmin edilmektedir. İkinci sırada 200 bin civarında bir rakamla Gaziantep gelmektedir. Ancak bazı tahminlere göre de sadece Gaziantep'te 500 bin civarında Suriyeli yaşamaktadır.

Kamplarda Yaşam

AFAD (2013) ve ORSAM (2014)'ın raporlarına göre, yaşam ve sosyal imkanlar açısından kamplarda yaşayan Suriyelilerin durumu genel olarak kamp dışındakilere göre çok daha iyi durumdadır. Kamplar, sosyal alanlar, eğitim ve sağlık imkanları, güvenlik, gıda, beslenme ve hijyen gibi koşullar açısından diğer ülke örneklerinden çok daha iyi seviyededir. Konteyner kent ve çadır kentler arasında farklar olsa da genel olarak tüm kamplarda belli bir standardın yakalandığını söylemek mümkündür. Ulusal ve uluslararası medyada Türkiye'deki kampların diğer ülkelerdeki kamplara göre oldukça iyi organize edildiğine dikkat çekmektedir.

Mevcut kampların idaresinden sivil toplum ve yerinden yönetim kuruluşlarının da desteği ile esasen AFAD sorumludur.

Kaynak: AFAD (2015).

Tablo 3: Kamplar ve Kamplarda Yaşayan Suriyeli Sığınmacıların Kentlere Göre Dağılımı

Şehir	Kamp Sayısı	Sığınmacı Sayısı	Yüzdelik Dağılım
Şanlıurfa	5	103.352	39.6
Gaziantep	5	51.502	19.7
Hatay	5	15001	5.7
Mardin	3	15.647	6
Kilis	2	35.774	13.7
Kahramanmaraş	1	17.562	6.7
Adana	1	11.188	4.3
Adıyaman	1	9.374	3.6
Osmaniye	1	9.186	3.5
Malatya	1	7.621	2.9
TOPLAM	**25**	260.684	

Kamp Dışında Yaşam

Türkiye'deki Suriyeliler gerçeğinin büyük bölümünü kamp dışında yaşayan ve 1milyon 700 bin civarındaki olduğu tahmin edilen mülteciler grubu oluşturmaktadır. Kamp dışında yaşayan Suriyelilerin yaklaşık yarısının kampların bulunduğu sınır illerinde yaşamlarını sürdürdükleri ve geri kalanının ise başta İstanbul, Ankara, Mersin, Konya, Eskişehir ve İzmir olmak üzere Türkiye geneline yayıldıkları tahmin edilmektedir. Bununla birlikte, ORSAM'ın yapmış olduğu araştırmaya göre, kamp dışındakilerin kampları tercih etmemesinin beş nedeni vardır (ORSAM, 2014: 15): a) Ülkeye kaçak giriş yapan ve herhangi biryere kaydolmayan veya olmak istemeyenlerin varlığı, b) kamp yaşamına uyum sağlayamayan ve ayrılanlar, c) maddi durumu iyi olan yada özel nedenlerle kamp dışı yaşamı tercih edenler, d) kampların kapasitesinin dolması, e) akrabalık ilişkileri nedeniyle kamplar yerine akrabalarının yakınında yaşamayı tercih edenler.

GÖÇDER (Göç Edenler Sosyal Yardımlaşma ve Kültür Derneği) ve ESHİD (Eşit Haklar İçin İzleme Derneği)'in ortak araştırmasında ise kampları tercih etmeyen sığınmacılar aşağıdaki kaygı ve düşüncelerini ifade etmişlerdir (GÖÇDER ve ESHİD, 2013: 9): a) *Fiziki koşullar ve güvenlik:* Kamplar kapasite olarak gelen talebi karşılayamamakta ve fiziki koşullar kamptan kampa değişiklik göstermektedir. Bazı kamplarda maddi olanakların yetersizliği nedeniyle aynı çadır veya konteynırda birden fazla aile barınmak zorunda kalmaktadır. b) *İzolasyon ve hareket özgürlüğünün engellenmesi:* Kamplardaki giriş çıkışların, dışarıyla ilişkinin kontrol altında tutulması merkezlerin en büyük dezavantajını oluşturmaktadır. c) *Etnik ve dini kökene dayalı ayrımcılık riski:* Farklı etnik kökene veya dini inanca sahip Suriyeli sığınmacılar ayrımcılığa uğrama riski nedeniyle kamplarda kalmamaktadır. Örneğin Hristiyanlar, Kürtler, Romanlar ve Çerkezler bu gruplar arasındadır. d) *Cinsiyete yönelik ayrımcılık ve şiddet riski:* Kamp ortamının kadın ve kız çocukları bakımından cinsel istismar, taciz, tecavüz ve şiddete uğrama risklerine açık olması, özellikle yalnız kadınlar ve çocuklarıyla olan sığınmacıları kamplara gitme fikrinden uzaklaştırmaktadır.

Eğitim Sorunu

Türkiye'deki Suriyeli sığınmacıların % 50'den fazlasını eğitim çağındaki 0-18 yaş grubu oluşturmaktadır (AFAD, 2013). Bu da bir milyona yakın Suriyeli öğrencinin eğitimine bir şekilde devam etmesi gerçeğini ortaya çıkarmaktadır. Bu rakama 18 yaş üstü üniversite eğitimi yarıda kalanlar ile üniversite çağına gelenleri de eklediğimizde sorunun ciddiyeti daha açık görülmektedir. Türkiye'de Eğitim Bakanlığı ve YÖK genelgelerle Suriyeli öğrencilerin ilkokul, orta okul, lise ve üniversitelere intibakının sağlanması yönünde çalışmalarını sürdürmektedir. Bu alanda öncelikli sorun ciddi bir öğrenci sayısının varlığı, anadilde eğitim ve dil sorunudur. Büyük bir çoğunluk Türkçe bilmemektedir. Ayrıca Türkiye'deki eğitim kurumlarının bu yükü ne ölçüde kaldırabileceği hususu da ayrı bir tartışma konusudur. Bazı araştırmacılara göre (Yonca, 2014:31), halihazırda kamplarda yaşayan çocukların % 80'i, kamp dışında yaşayan çocukların ise ancak %14'ü eğitim görebilmektedir.

AFAD'ın (AFAD, 2013: 26) Suriye raporuna göre, kamplarda yaşayan Suriyeli sığınmacıların yüzde 12'si okuma-yazma bilmezken, kamp dışında bu oran yüzde 19 seviyesindedir. Okuma-yazma bildiğini ifade edenler kamplarda % 5.5, kamp dışında % 9, ilkokul mezunu olanlar ise sırasıyla % 37 ve % 33, orta öğretim mezunları ise % 25 ve % 19'dur. Dolayısıyla, Türkiye'deki Suriyeli sığınmacıların yarıdan fazlası ya okur-yazar değil, ya da ilkokul mezunudur. Mevcut veriler çerçevesinde Suriyeli göçmenlerin ciddi bir eğitim sorununun olduğu açıktır. Bu çerçevede Suriyeli çocukların eğitim sorunlarının aşılabilmesi için mümkün olduğu kadar ülkedeki eğitim kurumlarına yerleştirilmeleri ve uyum çalışmalarının tamamlanması önem arzetmektedir. Aynı zamanda uluslararası işbirliği içinde her düzeyde yeni eğitim kurumlarının açılması ve bu kurumlarda hem sığınmacıların kendi dilerinde eğitim verecek eğitimcilerin istihdam edilmesi, hem de Türkçe dil probleminin çözülmesi yönünde atılacak adımlar eğitim alanındaki öncelikli hususlar olarak karşımıza çıkmaktadır.

İstihdam Sorunu

Türkiye'de Suriyeli göçmenlerin yaklaşık yarısını çalışma çağındaki nüfus oluşturmaktadır. Bu bağlamda, Suriyeli göçmenlerin Türkiye'de kalış süresi uzadıkça özellikle kamp dışında yaşayanların büyük ekseriyeti açısından yaşamlarını sürdürebilmeleri için istihdam konusu giderek zorunlu bir hal almaktadır. Ancak iş bulma ve çalışma konusunda mevzuat, statü, dil ve eğitim düzeyi sorunu yanında Türkiye'nin kendi vatandaşları için de genel olarak işsizlik sorununun var oluşu ve bu çerçevede iş bulmanın zorluğu gibi güçlükler söz konusudur. Bu güçlükler yanında yukarıda da ifade edildiği gibi, Suriyeli göçmenlerin büyük bir yüzdesi ya okur-yazar değil ya da sadece ilkokul eğimi almış durumda ve bu da niteliksiz bir işgücü demek. Oysa, niteliksiz işgücü olgusu zaten Türkiye'nin temel sorunlarından bir tanesi. Dolayısıyla, iş bulan ve çalışan geçici sığınmacıların büyük çoğunluğu düşük ücretle niteliksiz işlerde illegal-kaçak çalışmakta ve sosyal güvenlikten de yararlanamamaktadırlar. Özetle, Türkiye'de

Suriyeli göçmenlerin geçici sığınmacı statüleriyle yasal olarak çalışma hakları bulunmamaktadır. Ancak Ekim 2014 tarihli Geçici Koruma Yönetmeliği'nin 29. Maddesi, Göç İdaresi Genel Müdürlüğü'ne yeni kayıt olan ve bu kurumun verdiği kimlik kartlarına sahip olan Suriyeli sığınmacılara önceden ikamet izni almış olma şartı aranmaksızın Bakanlar Kurulu tarafından belirlenecek sektör ve yerlerde çalışma izni alabilmelerinin yolunu açmış bulunmaktadır (Geçici Koruma Yönetmeliği, 2014).

Sağlık Sorunu

Türkiye'de Sağlık Bakanlığı Suriyeli mültecilerin sağlık hizmetlerini Başbakanlık Afet ve Acil Durum Yönetimi Başkanlığı tarafından 2013 yılında yayımlanan 2013/8 sayılı genelge doğrultusunda yerine getirmektedir. Bu çerçevede Türkiye Cumhuriyeti Devleti, Suriyeli mültecilere tüm kamu hastanelerine ulaşabilme ve hizmet alabilme imkanı vererek bunun için de bir fon ayırmıştır. Türk Tabipler Birliğinin 2014 yılında yapmış olduğu araştırmaya göre, sadece kamplarda bugüne kadar 6.051 doğum gerçekleşmiştir. Sunulan toplam poliklinik hizmeti sayısı ise 1.5 milyonu aşmaktadır. Bununla birlikte, Türkiyede'ki Suriyeli mültecilerin sağlık hizmetleri ve sağlık durumları, ülkemiz için de önemli bir halk sağlığı sorunu potansiyeli taşımaktadır. Özellikle Doğu ve Güneydoğu Anadolu Bölgelerinde kızamık da dahil olmak üzere, anne ve bebek ölüm hızı gibi konularda sorunlar yaşandığı bilinmektedir. Bölgede kişi başına düşen hekim ve hemşire sayıları da Türkiye ortalamasının çok altındadır. Dünya Sağlık Örgütü'nün Suriyeli çocuklar arasında çocuk felci vakalarına rastlandığına dair açıklamasından bu yana Türkiye kamplarda ve sınır bölgelerinde aşılama kampanyası yürütmektedir (Kirişçi, 2014: 37).

Sonuç: Sığınmacıların Türkiye'ye Etkileri ve Potansiyel Sorun Alanları

Türkiye'de bugün iki milyon civarındaki Suriyeli sığınmacının yaklaşık bir milyonu sınır bölgesi illerinde yaşamını sürdürürken bir milyonu da ülke geneline yayılmış durumdadır. Sığınmacıların büyük çoğunluğu kamp dışında yaşamaktadır. Göç İdaresi'nin kayıt altına alma işlemleri ise devam etmektedir. Sonuçlar kamuoyu ile paylaşıldığında ülke genelindeki dağılımı daha net görmek mümkün olacaktır. Öte yandan, Suriyeli sığınmacılar nedeniyle kısa sürede ülke nüfusunun 2 milyona yaklaşan bir oranda artması temel kamusal hizmetlerin sunumunu nicelik ve nitelik yönüyle olumsuz etkilemektedir. Bu çerçevede Güneydeki bir milyon sığınmacının bölgede provakasyon, terör ve güvenlik endişesi yanında temel kamu hizmetleri bakımından büyük bir baskı oluşturduğunun altı çizilmelidir. Ülke geneline yayılan sığınmacılar konusu da sosyal, ekonomik, kültürel, güvenlik ve entegrasyon boyutlarıyla önemli potansiyel riskler taşımaktadır.

Suriyeli sığınmacıların Türkiye'de bölgesel ve ulusal çapta göreceli olarak neden oldukları temel sorunlar güvenlik riski, işsizlik, konut kira artışı, kaçak işçilik, eğitim ve sağlık hizmetlerinde kalite kaybı ve işçi ücretlerindeki düşüşler bağlamında analiz edilebilir. Suriyeli mültecilerle bağlantılı Türkiye'de oluşması muhtemel en ciddi sorunların başında güvenlik riski ve prokovasyon ihtimali gelmektedir. Bu bağlamda, geçmişte Hatay'da yaşanan olaylar ve gerilimler yanında 2014 yılında Kahramanmaraş ve Gaziantep'te bir çok kişinin yaralanması örneğinde olduğu gibi mültecilerle yerel halk arasında zaman zaman ortaya çıkan gerginliklerin kitlesel bir hal alması riski tehlike arz etmektedir. Yine, en büyük risklerden birisi bölgenin terör saldırılarına açık olmasıdır. Öte yandan özellikle kamp dışında yaşayan sığınmacı çocukların eğitime ve öğretime yeteri kadar yönlendirilememesi bir diğer önemli sorun alanı ve kayıp nesil riski olarak karşımıza çıkmaktadır. Eğitime yönlendirilemeyen çocukların orta vadede illegal kişi ve gruplarında etkisi ile suça itilmesi ve suç işleme eğiliminin artması olasılığı üzerinde düşünülmesi gereken ciddi bir sorun alanıdır.

Ayrıca, mültecilere verilen eğitimin kendi yerel dillerinde olması ve uzun süre Türkiye'de kalmaları durumunda Türkiye'ye uyum sorununu ortaya çıkabilecektir. Yine bir diğer sorunu emek piyasasında ücret dengesinin bozulması hususu oluşturmaktadır. Örneğin, Suriyeli mültecilerin yoğun olarak yaşadığı Kahramanmaraş, Gaziantep, Şanlıurfa gibi şehirlerde işçi ücretlerindeki gerileme yerel işçileri ciddi anlamda rahatsız etmekte ve endişelendirmektedir. Sınır bölgesi illerinde konut fiyatlarının ve kiraların normal değerlerinin üstünde seyretmesi ve bu durumun süreklilik arz ederek bir kira enflasyonu oluşturma ihtimali de bir diğer sorun alanı olarak belirmektedir. Ayrıca mevcut imkanlar çerçevesinde hastane, doktor ve hemşire yetersizliğinden dolayı sağlık hizmetlerinin arzu edilen standartlarda verilememesi ve bunun sonucunda özellikle sınır bölgelerinde bulaşıcı hastalık riskinin ortaya çıkması da ciddi bir sorundur. Aynı zamanda, Suriyeli mülteci kadın ve çocuklara yönelik cinsel istismar riski ve mülteci kadınlarla özellikle Güney ve Güneydoğu'da ikinci ve üçüncü evlilik vakıaları aile boyutu ile üzerinde durulması gereken bir diğer konudur.

Özetle; Suriye'deki iç savaş ve çatışma ortamı dört yılını geride bıraktı ve sığınmacılar için henüz geri dönüş ümidi söz konusu değil. Dört yıllık süreçte özellikle oluşturulan kamplar bağlamında Türkiye'nin diğer ülkelere göre daha iyi bir sınav verdiği açık. Ancak bundan sonrası için atılacak adımlar ve sorunun yönetimi büyük bir önem taşımaktadır. Çünkü süre uzadıkça barınma sorunundan eğitim, sağlık ve istihdama kadar sığınmacıların önemli bir kısmının içinde bulunduğu durum daha katlanılmaz bir hale gelecektir. Bu da entegrasyon konusunu ve daha kalıcı çözümlere duyulan ihtiyacı arttıracaktır. Burada özellikle BM ve AB'nin daha ciddi katkısı gereklidir. Çünkü bu sorun sadece Türkiye'nin çözmesi gereken bir sorun değildir. Türkiye dışına AB ülkelerine de yansımaları olacaktır.

Kaynaklar

AFAD (2013). Türkiye'deki Suriyeli Sığınmacılar: 2013 Saha Araştırması Sonuçları, https://www.afad.gov.tr/Dokuman/TR/60-2013123015491-syrian-refugees-in-turkey-2013_baski_30.12.2013_tr.pdf, Erişim: 10.02.2015.

AFAD (2015). 29 Haziran 2015 İtibariyle Barınma Merkezlerinde Son Durum, https://www.afad.gov.tr/tr/IcerikDetay1.aspx?IcerikID=848&ID=16, Erişim, 30.06.2015.

Geçici Koruma Yönetmeliği (2014). http://www.resmigazete.gov.tr/eskiler/2014/10/20141022-15-1.pdf).

GÖÇDER ve ESHİD (2013). Göz Ardı Edilenler İstanbul'da Yaşayan Suriyeli Sığınmacılar, İstanbul, 13 Mart 2013.

Kirişçi K. (2014). Misafirliğin Ötesine Geçerken Türkiye'nin "Suriyeli Mülteciler" Sınavı Raporu, Uluslararası Stratejik Araştırmalar Kurumu & Brookings Enstitüsü, Haziran 2014.

Medda-Windischer, R., Danson, M., Morén-Alegret, R., & Gaye, M. (2012). Social Mobility and Migration, *Migration Letters*, 9(3), 193-199.

ORSAM (2014), Suriye'ye Komşu Ülkelerde Suriyeli Mültecilerin Durumu: Bulgular, Sonuçlar ve Öneriler, Rapor No:189, s:11.

Resmi Gazete (2013). Suriyeli Misafirlerin Sağlık ve Diğer Hizmetleri Hakkında Genelge, 2013/8,09/09/2013, https://www.afad.gov.tr/UserFiles/File/Mevzuat/Genelgeler/saglik_genelgesi.tif

Sirkeci, İ. (2012), Transnasyonal Mobilite ve Çatışma, *Migration Letters*, 9 (4), 353-363.

Sirkeci, İ., Erdoğan, M. (2012). Göç ve Türkiye, *Migration Letters*, 9 (4), 297-302.

Türk Tabipleri Birliği (2014). Suriyeli Sığınmacılar ve Sağlık Hizmetleri Raporu, Birinci Baskı, Ankara Türk Tabipleri Birliği Yayınları, Ocak 2014, s. 16-18.

UNHCR (2014), Asylum Trends 2014 Levels and Trends in İndustrialized Countries, http://www.unhcr.org/551128679.html. Erişim: 10.06.2015.

Vergil, H., Yıldırım, H., Sezer, Ö., vd, (2014). Zonguldak İlindeki Göçün Sosyo-Ekonomik Nedenleri ve Alınabilecek Tedbirler, Bülent Ecevit Üniversitesi Yayınları No :1, Zonguldak.

Yonca. A.V. (2014). Suriyeli Göçmenlerin Sorunları Çalıştayı Sonuç Raporu, Mersin Üniversitesi Bölgesel İzleme Uygulama Araştırma Merkezi, 27 Ekim, s.31

Türkiye'deki İllerin Gelişmişlik Göstergelerinin Göç Üzerine Etkisinin İncelenmesi

Sibel Selim[310] Rıdvan Keskin[311] Sibel Aybarç Bursalıoğlu [312] Hasan Selim[313]

Giriş

Göç; bir toplumun ya da bireylerin belli bir zaman diliminde ortaya çıkan doğal, sosyal, ekonomik, politik ve kültürel faktörlerdeki değişmeler sonucunda ülke içinde veya ülkeler arasında, isteğe bağlı veya zorunlu olarak yer değiştirme hareketliliği olarak tanımlanabilir. Bu hareketlilik sonucunda, göç eden bireyler ya da toplum etkilendiği gibi göç edilen bölgedeki bireyler de etkilenmektedir. Bu nedenle göç, neden-sonuç ilişkisi bakımından pozitif ve negatif etkilerinin incelenmesi gereken oldukça önemli bir konudur.

İtme-çekme teorisi (Lee, 1966)'ne göre göçün başlangıç ve varış noktaları arasında anlamlı bir ilişki bulunmaktadır. Göçler daha çok büyük şehirlere doğru olurken, bazen yaşanılan kırsal alanların bağlı olduğu il ve ilçe merkezlerine, bazen de farklı kırsal alanlara doğru olabilmektedir. Göç hareketliliğinde, kentlerin çekme güçleri, kırsal bölgelerin ise itme güçleri olduğu görülmektedir. Nüfusu kente iten etkenlerden bazıları, köyden kente artan nüfus baskısı, adil olmayan toprak dağılımı, düşük verimlilik, doğal afetler, kan davaları, toprağın mirasla parçalanması, tarımda makineleşme sonucu işsizliğin artması ve güvenliktir. Nüfusu kente çeken önemli bazı etkenler ise köy-kent gelir farklılıkları, daha iyi eğitim olanakları, iş bulma ümidi, daha yüksek yaşam standardı, ulaşım olanakları, kentlerdeki sosyal ve kültürel olanaklardan faydalanma isteğidir.

Sosyo-ekonomik gelişmişlik göstergelerinin göç üzerinde etkisi olduğu açıktır. Bu nedenle, ülke genelinde bölgelerin, illerin ve ilçelerin sosyo-ekonomik gelişmişlik seviyelerinin belirlenmesi oldukça önemlidir. Böylece, yörelere ilişkin sosyo-ekonomik yelpaze ortaya çıkmakta ve bu yapı dikkate alınarak nüfus hareketliliği incelenebilmektedir.

Bu çalışmanın amacı, Türkiye'deki illere ilişkin gelişmişlik göstergelerinin bu illerin aldığı göç üzerindeki etkisinin incelenmesidir. Bu amaca yönelik analizlerde 2008-2013 dönemi ele alınmış ve Negatif Binom Regresyon Modeli (NBRM) kullanılmıştır. İlgili literatürde, NBRM'nin kullanıldığı sınırlı sayıda çalışma olup, Türkiye'deki göç konusunu bu model ile analiz eden herhangi bir çalışma bulunmamaktadır.

[310] Celal Bayar Üniversitesi, İktisadi ve İdari Bilimler Fakültesi, Ekonometri Bölümü, sibel.selim@cbu.edu.tr
[311] Celal Bayar Üniversitesi, İktisadi ve İdari Bilimler Fakültesi, Ekonometri Bölümü, ridvan.keskin@cbu.edu.tr
[312]Celal Bayar Üniversitesi, Ahmetli Meslek Yüksek Okulu, Muhasebe ve Vergi Uygulamaları Bölümü, sibel.aybarc.bursalioglu@gmail.com
[313] Dokuz Eylül Üniversitesi, Mühendislik Fakültesi, Endüstri Mühendisliği Bölümü, hasan.selim@deu.edu.tr

İlgili literatür

Bu çalışmada, illerin gelişmişlik düzeyinin illerin aldığı göç üzerine etkisi sayma veri modellerinden NBRM ile incelenmiştir. Bu bölümde, konuyla ilgili sınırlı sayıdaki çalışma özetle sunulmaktadır. Devillanova ve Garcia-Fontes (2004), 1978-1992 döneminde İspanya'daki iç göçün işgücü piyasası üzerine etkisini incelemiştir. Çalışmada, genişletilmiş çekim modeli çerçevesinde, iller arasındaki toplam göç akımına ilişkin genelleştirilmiş NBRM tahmin edilmiştir. Yerel işgücü piyasası dengesizliğinin işçi hareketliliği üzerindeki etkisini tespit etmeyi amaçlayan çalışma, İspanya'daki iç göçün dengeleyici rolünü de tartışmaktadır. Analiz bulgularına göre, 1984 sonrası göçmenlerin ekonomik koşullara karşı daha duyarlı hale geldiği ve istihdam olanaklarının ilgili dönemde arttığı ortaya çıkmıştır. Çalışmanın diğer önemli bulgularından biri, İspanyol işgücü piyasasına yönelik önceki çalışmalara paralel olacak şekilde, kalifiye personelin daha büyük iç göç hareketliliğine sahip olduğudur. Stillwell (2005), genel olarak uygulanabilecek bir göç modeli oluşturmak amacıyla açıklayıcı ve planlayıcı modeller arasındaki faklılıkları esas alan bir çalışma yapmıştır. Çalışma, mikro yaklaşımlar ile makro yaklaşımlar, matematiksel ve istatistiki modeller arasındaki ayrımı vurgulamaktadır. Çalışma, İngiltere'de politik bağlamda kullanım için geliştirilen yeni iki aşamalı Poisson regresyon modele dikkat çekerken, bu model ile Avrupa Birliği'nde göç projeksiyonu için kullanılan ve çok aşamalı demografi bağlamında geliştirilen modelleri karşılaştırmaktadır. Bülbül ve Köse (2010), 2008 yılında Türkiye'de 12 bölgenin demografik özellikleri, sosyo-ekonomik göstergeleri ve göç verileri bakımından birbirlerine göre konumlarını incelemek ve aralarındaki benzerlikler ve farklılıkları tespit etmek amacıyla çok boyutlu ölçekleme analizi uygulamıştır. Elde edilen bulgulara göre, İstanbul ve Kuzeydoğu Anadolu Bölgeleri diğer bölgelere nazaran anlamlı olarak farklı konumdadır. Birbirine en yakın bölgeler ise Batı Marmara, Doğu Marmara ve Batı Anadolu Bölgeleridir. Yakar (2010), Afyonkarahisar iline ilişkin olarak iller arası net göç dağılımını tespit etmek amacıyla illere göre net göç değerlerinin bağımlı değişken ve göçlere etkisi olduğu öngörülen gelişmişlik endekslerinin bağımsız değişken olarak belirlendiği çeşitli istatistiksel analizler yapmıştır. Elde edilen bulgular, iller arasındaki net göç üzerinde en çok sosyo-ekonomik gelişmişlik endeksinin etkili olduğunu ve Afyonkarahisar'ın net göç aldığı illerin daha düşük seviyede, net göç verdiği illerin ise daha yüksek seviyede gelişmişlik endeks değerine sahip olduğunu ortaya koymuştur. Amirault, Munnik ve Miller (2012), Kanada'da 1991-2006 dönemine ilişkin ekonomik bölge düzeyindeki nüfus sayımı verilerini kullanarak göçü etkileyen faktörleri incelemiştir. Poisson modelini ve NBRM'ni içeren analizlerden elde edilen sonuçlara göre ilin büyüklüğü göçü istatistiki açıdan anlamlı olarak etkilemekte, ancak bu etkinin önemi model özelliklerinde farklılaşmaktadır. Regresyon sonuçları, istihdam oranlarındaki farklılıkların, hanehalkı gelirlerinin ve dilin Kanada'nın ekonomik bölgeleri arasındaki göç hareketlerinin açıklanmasındaki önemini de ortaya koymaktadır. Çalışmada ayrıca, iller arasındaki uzaklığın göç üzerindeki negatif etkisinin zamanla azalacağı tespit edilmiştir. Yakar (2013), 2007-2012 dönemine ilişkin olarak Türkiye'deki illerin gelişmişlik farklılığının iller arası göçleri nerelerde ve ne düzeyde etkilediğini tespit etmek amacıyla Adrese Dayalı Nüfus Kayıt Sistemi (ADNKS)'den elde edilen göç verileri ve Sosyo-Ekonomik Gelişmişlik Sıralaması (SEGE) değerlerini kullanarak Coğrafi Ağırlıklı Regresyon analizi yapmıştır. Çalışmada elde edilen bulgulara göre, iller arasındaki net göç ile illerin sosyo-ekonomik gelişmişlik düzeyi arasında pozitif ve güçlü bir korelasyon bulunmaktadır ve net göçlerin %64'ünü illerin sosyo-ekonomik gelişmişlik düzeyi belirlemektedir. Çalışmada, illerin sosyo-ekonomik gelişmişlik seviyesinin iller arasındaki net göçü en iyi Marmara Bölgesi ve çevresi için açıkladığı, Doğu ve Güneydoğu Anadolu Bölgelerinde ise bu ilişkinin zayıfladığı tespiti de yapılmıştır. Üzümcü ve Özyakışır (2013), 1996-2012 dönemine ilişkin SEGE değerlerinden yararlanarak Ağrı, Ardahan, Kars ve Iğdır illerini kapsayan TRA2 bölgesinden gerçekleşen göç hareketlerini incelemiştir. Elde edilen bulgulara göre, bölge illerine ait SEGE değerleri ile bölgeden gerçekleşen göç hareketleri arasında yakın bir ilişki bulunmaktadır. Cheng, Young ve Zhang (2014), Avrupa Birliği ve Çin'deki iç göçü karşılaştıran ilk kapsamlı analizi gerçekleştirmişlerdir. Çalışmada göç hareketliliği modeli, eşitsizlik, dağılım ve etkinliği kapsayan seçilmiş göstergeler ile ölçülmektedir. Ardından mekansal yakınlık, uzaklık, ekonomik beklentiler, işgücü piyasası, göçmen ağı ve göç politikası gibi çeşitli faktörler arasından iç göç elastikiyetine karşılık gelecek şekilde "göç süreci" ölçülmüştür. İlk karşılaştırmalı sonuçlar için sabit etkiler NBRM ve çeşitli veri kaynakları kullanılarak toplam göç akımı modelleri oluşturulmuştur.

Metodoloji

Sayma (count) değişken, negatif olmayan tam sayı değerleri alan ve tekrar sayısını içeren bir değişkendir. Bir günde içilen sigara sayısı, bir firmanın bir yıl boyunca yaptığı patent başvurusu sayısı ve acil servislerde bir hafta içinde müdahale edilen hasta sayısı (bkz. Silva ve Windmeijer, 2001; Winkelmann, 2001; Deb ve Trivedi, 2002) sayma değişkene verilebilecek örneklerden bazılarıdır. Sayma değişkenler sık sık sürekli değişken olarak ele alınır ve bu değişkenlerin çıktıları için doğrusal regresyon modeli kullanılır. Ancak, doğrusal regresyon modelinin kullanımı etkin olmayan, tutarsız ve sapmalı tahminlerle sonuçlanabilir. Bu durumu dikkate alarak, sayma değişkenlerin çıktılarının özelliklerini açık bir şekilde ele alan farklı modeller oluşturulmuştur (Long, 1997:217). Sayma veri regresyon modelleme teknikleri oldukça yeni olmasına rağmen sayma verilerin istatistiksel analizleri oldukça uzun ve zengin bir tarihe sahiptir. Sayma veri modelleri içerisinde Poisson Regresyon Modeli (PRM) en temel modeldir. PRM'de olay sayısı (y), aşağıda verilen koşullu ortalamaya sahip Poisson dağılımı gösterir.

$$\lambda_i = E(y_i / x_i) = \exp(x_i \beta). \tag{1}$$

λ arttığı zaman, y'nin koşullu varyansının arttığı, tahminlenen sıfırların oranının azaldığı ve dağılımın normale yaklaştığı görülür. Bu model, çıktının koşullu ortalamasının koşullu varyansına eşit olduğu tanımlayıcı karakteristiklere sahiptir. Uygulamada, koşullu varyans sık sık koşullu ortalamayı aşar. Bu problem, varyansın ortalamayı aşmasına izin verildiği bir NBRM'nin kullanılmasına neden olur. NBRM, aşırı yayılım durumunda PRM'ne bir alternatiftir (Wang ve Famoye, 1997, 274; Rock, Sedo ve Willenborg, 2001, 357). Bu model, PRM'nin "ortalama" parametresini modelleyerek heterojenliği hesaba katmaktadır (Carrivick, Lee ve Yau, 2003:55). Chesher (1984) ve Bauer, Million ve Rotte (1999) ihmal edilen heterojenliğin tutarsız veya etkin olmayan parametre tahmincilerine yol açtığını ileri sürmüşlerdir. Gözlenemeyen heterojenlik durumunda olaylar arasındaki pozitif korelasyon aşırı yayılıma yol açmaktadır (Bauer, Million ve Rotte, 1999:11; Greene, 1997:4-7). Gözlenemeyen heterojenlik aşağıdaki regresyonda bir random etki yoluyla ifade edilmektedir.

$$\widetilde{\lambda} = \exp(x_i \beta + \varepsilon_i)$$ (2)

Bu modelde random etki olmasına rağmen y sayma değişkeni hala λ parametreli Poisson dağılımına sahip olmaktadır. Random etkinin varlığı, y'nin koşullu beklenen değerini değiştirmez. Yani, E[y/x, ε] ve E[y/x] eşit olmaktadır. Bu nedenle, ε'nun dağılımı bilinmese bile β değerleri genelleştirilmiş momentler metodu ile tutarlı bir şekilde tahmin edilmektedir (Silva, 1997:219).

Sayma veri modelleri doğrusal olmadığından katsayılar doğrudan yorumlanamaz. Ancak, marjinal etkiler yoluyla katsayıları yorumlamak mümkündür. Marjinal etkiler aşağıdaki gibi hesaplanabilir.

$$\frac{\partial E(y \mid x)}{\partial x_k} = \frac{\partial \exp(x\beta)}{\partial x\beta} \frac{\partial x\beta}{\partial x_k} = \exp(x\beta)\beta_k = E(y \mid x)\beta_k.$$ (3)

Bu model doğrusal olmadığından, marjinal etkinin değeri hem x_k' nın katsayısı hem de belli bir x için y'nin beklenen değerine dayanmaktadır. E(y|x)'in değeri ne kadar büyük olursa, E(y|x)'deki değişim oranı o kadar büyük olmaktadır.

Ekonometrik analiz

Veriler ve Tanımlayıcı İstatistikler

Bu çalışmada, ekonomik, sosyal ve fiziksel altyapı göstergeleri kullanılarak, 2008-2013 döneminde Türkiye'deki 81 ilin gelişmişlik göstergelerinin illerin aldığı göç üzerindeki etkisi NBRM ile analiz edilmiştir. Modelde kullanılan veriler 2008-2013 dönemine ilişkin ortalama değerler olup bu veriler Teşvik Uygulama ve Yabancı Sermaye Genel Müdürlüğü, Bankalar Birliği, Türkiye İstatistik Kurumu ve Maliye Bakanlığı'ndan temin edilmiştir. Modelde yer alan bağımlı değişken "illerin almış olduğu göç" olup, bağımsız değişkenler ise illere yapılmış olan teşviklerle elde edilen istihdam, merkezi yönetim bütçe harcamaları, köy yolu uzunluğu, değişim katsayısına göre işsizlik oranı, kütüphane sayısı, kişi başına sanayi elektrik kullanımı, ilköğretim okulu sayısı, şehirleşme oranı, lisans ve ön lisans mezun sayısı, kişi başına tarımsal üretim değeri, tarımda kullanılan makine sayısı ve toplam banka kredileridir. Bu çalışmada hastane yatak sayıları, hekim sayısı ve hastane sayısı gibi sağlık göstergeleri iktisadi açıdan anlamsız bulunduğundan modelde yer almamıştır. Türkiye'de 2008-2013 döneminde en çok göç alan on il Şekil 1'de gösterilmiştir.

Şekil 1. Türkiye'de 2008-2013 döneminde en çok göç alan on il

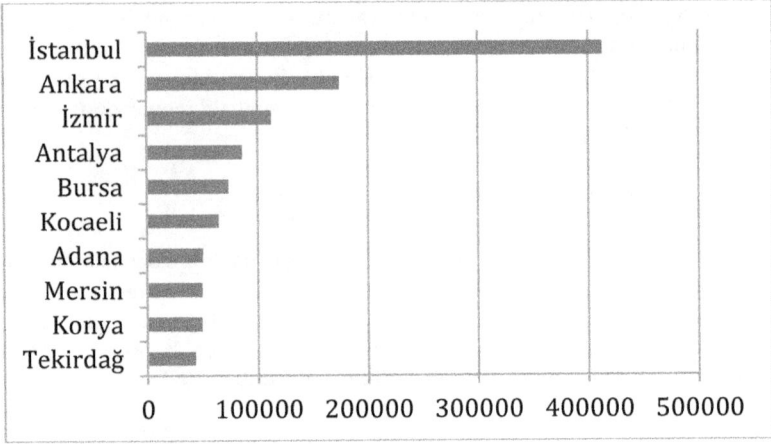

Tablo 1, modelde kullanılan değişkenlere ilişkin tanımlayıcı istatistikleri içermektedir. 2008-2013 döneminde 81 ilin aldığı ortalama göç 29,100.47'dir. İllere yapılmış olan teşviklerle elde edilen istihdam 1262.187 kişidir. Değişim katsayısına göre işsizlik oranı %9.96 olup şehirleşme oranı %65.745'dir. Ortalama kütüphane sayısı yaklaşık 14'tür. İllerin merkezi yönetim bütçe harcamaları ortalama 1,570,209,000 TL'dir. Tarımda kullanılan makine sayısı 153,550.8 olup, kişi başına tarımsal üretim değeri 195,671.2'dir. Toplam banka kredileri ise 981,223,000 TL'dir.

Tablo 1. Tanımlayıcı istatistikler

Değişkenler	Ortalama	Standart sapma
İlerin aldığı göç	29,100.470	49848.480
Teşvikli istihdam	1262.187	1893.691
Merkezi yönetim bütçe harcamaları	1,570,209,000	2925627.000
Köy yolu uzunluğu	3,780.778	2269.385
Değişim katsayısına göre işsizlik oranı	9.959	3.028
Kütüphane sayısı	13.969	9.018
Kişi başı sanayi elektrik kullanımı	1079.403	1053.477
İlköğretim okul sayısı	701.358	599.184
Şehirleşme oranı	65.745	13.847
Lisans ve ön lisans mezun sayısı	6368.621	18219.960
Kişi başı tarımsal üretim değeri	195,671.200	161865.800
Tarımda kullanılan makine sayısı	153,550.800	269424.700
Toplam banka kredileri	981,223,000	3813663.000

Bulgular

Yayılım parametresi olan $\sigma2$ değeri 1'den büyük olduğundan aşırı yayılım söz konusudur ve NBRM'nin kullanılması gerekmektedir. LR testinin sonucu da bu durumu doğrulamaktadır. Model katsayılarının yorumlanması için gerekli olan marjinal etkiler Tablo 2'de sunulmuştur. Elde edilen sonuçlara göre, illerin göç almasında etkisi olan en önemli değişkenler 1'den büyük marjinal etki değerine sahip olan *teşvik belgeli yatırımlarla istihdam edilen ortalama kişi sayısı, işsizlik oranı, kütüphane sayısı, kişi başına sanayi elektrik kullanımı, ilköğretim okul sayısı* ve *şehirleşme oranı*dır. İllere ilişkin teşviklerle elde edilen istihdamdaki bir birimlik artış ilin göç almasını 4.68 kat arttırmaktadır. Türkiye'deki teşvik belgeli sabit sermaye yatırımlarına bakıldığında, Marmara bölgesinin yıllık ortalama %43.4 oranı ile neredeyse diğer bölgelerin toplamına yakın bir pay aldığı görülmektedir. Marmara bölgesini Ege, Akdeniz ve İç Anadolu Bölgeleri izlemektedir (Eşiyok, 2005).

Tablo 2. Negatif Binom Regresyon Modeli

Bağımsız Değişkenler	Katsayı	z değeri	Olasılık değeri	Marjinal etkiler
Teşvikli istihdam	0.000245	5.190	0.000*	4.681979
Merkezi yönetim bütçe harcamaları	3.01E-08	2.190	0.028**	0.000575
Köy yolu uzunluğu	0.000046	3.220	0.001*	0.871726
İşsizlik oranı	-0.061528	-5.270	0.000*	-1176.04
Kütüphane sayısı	0.007651	1.730	0.083***	146.2382
Kişi başı sanayi elektrik kullanımı	0.000067	2.480	0.013**	1.275141
İlköğretim okul sayısı	0.000417	3.490	0.000*	7.969847
Şehirleşme oranı	0.004526	1.700	0.089***	86.50259
Lisans ve ön lisans mezun sayısı	2.38E-06	1.620	0.106***	0.045397
Kişi başı tarımsal üretim değeri	4.14E-07	1.670	0.095***	0.007907
Tarımda kullanılan makine sayısı	-1.19E-06	-2.730	0.006*	-0.02275
Toplam banka kredileri	-1.83E-09	-0.270	0.784	-3.5E-05
Sabit	9.26168	36.210	0.000*	
$\hat{\sigma}^2$	1143.400			
Pearson $\chi 2$ istatistiği	80037.92			
Prob > $\chi 2$ (70)	0.000			
Likelihood-ratio test				
$\chi^2(01)$	7.8e+04		0.000	

*,**, *** sırasıyla %1, %5 ve %10 önem seviyesinde istatistiksel olarak anlamlılığı ifade etmektedir.

Ekonomik gelişmişlik düzeylerinin karşılaştırılmasında kullanılan en önemli mali göstergeler arasında merkezi yönetim bütçe harcamaları yer almaktadır. Özellikle altyapıya yönelik yatırımları kapsayan kamu yatırım harcamaları sosyoekonomik gelişmeyi hızlandıran unsurlar arasındadır. Merkezi yönetim bütçe harcamaları arttıkça illerin aldığı göç miktarı artmaktadır. Ayrıca, toplam banka kredileri de illerin mali gelişmişlik göstergeleri arasındadır. Kullanılan model sonucuna göre banka kredilerinin illerin aldığı göç üzerindeki etkisi anlamsızdır. Sosyoekonomik kalkınmanın temel girdilerinden biri de enerjidir. Çünkü, gelişme ile enerji tüketimi arasında yakın bir ilişki vardır (Albayrak, 2003). Yaşam standardının yükselmesi ve gelişen teknolojinin insanlara sunduğu konfor her geçen gün daha fazla enerjiye ihtiyaç duyulmasına sebep olmaktadır. Elektrik enerjisi sanayinin temel girdisi olması nedeniyle ülkelerin gelişmişlik göstergelerinden biri olarak önemini korumaktadır. Bu çalışmada elde edilen sonuçlara göre, kişi başı sanayi elektrik kullanımı arttıkça ilin almış olduğu göç miktarı da artış göstermektedir.

Az gelişmiş bölgeler çoğunlukla ülke düzeyinde gerçekleşen istihdamdaki büyümeden pay alamayan yörelerdir ve bu da dikkatleri bölgesel işsizlik düzeylerine çekmektedir. Gelişmiş bölgelerin aksine geri kalmış bölgeler, endüstriyel yeşermenin olmadığı ve işsizlik oranının çok yüksek olduğu bölgelerdir. İşgücünün eksik istihdamı ve açık ve gizli işsizliğin büyük oranlarda olması bu bölgelerden gelişmiş bölgelere göçü teşvik eden bir unsurdur (Bozdoğan, 2008:15). Bu durumda, gelişmiş bölgelere işgücü gönderen bölgelerde nitelikli insan kaynağı noksanlığının baş göstermesi bölgesel kalkınmayı engellemektedir (Kulaksız, 2008). Bu çalışma elde edilen sonuçlara göre, işsizlik oranının artması ile illerin aldığı göç azalmaktadır. Sosyoekonomik aktiviteler açısından çeşitlilik gösteren gelişmiş iller, yüksek öğrenim görmüş nitelikli işgücü için çekim merkezi olmaktadır. Dolayısıyla, sosyoekonomik gelişmişlik düzeyinin artmasına paralel olarak yüksek öğrenim görmüş nüfus oranı da artmaktadır (Albayrak, 2003:15). Bu çalışmada elde edilen sonuçlarda görüldüğü gibi, lisans ve ön lisans mezunlarındaki bir artış söz konusu ilin daha fazla göç almasını sağlamaktadır. Diğer yandan, *kişi başına tarımsal üretim değeri* değişkeni tarım sektöründe çalışan kesimin gelir düzeyini ve verimliliğini yansıtmaktadır. Tarımda makineleşme ise tarımsal verimliliği belirleyen önemli bir faktördür. Tablo 2'de sunulan model sonuçlarına göre, kişi başına tarımsal üretim değeri illerin aldığı göçü arttırırken tarımda makineleşme illerin aldığı göçü azaltmaktadır. Ayrıca, köy yolu uzunluğu, ilköğretim okulu sayısı ve kütüphane sayısının illerin aldığı göç üzerindeki etkisinin anlamlı ve pozitif olduğu görülmektedir.

Sonuç

Bu çalışmada amaç, illerin sosyal, ekonomik ve fiziksel altyapı göstergeleri kullanılarak, Türkiye'deki 81 ilin gelişmişlik göstergelerinin illerin aldığı göç üzerindeki etkisinin analiz edilmesidir. Bu amaca yönelik analizlerde 2008-2013 dönemi ele alınmış ve Negatif Binom Regresyon Modeli (NBRM) kullanılmıştır. Elde edilen sonuçlara göre, illerin almış olduğu göç üzerinde en önemli etkiye sahip göstergelerin, *teşvik belgeli yatırımlarla istihdam edilen ortalama kişi sayısı, işsizlik oranı, kütüphane sayısı, kişi başı sanayi elektrik kullanımı, ilköğretim okul sayısı* ve *şehirleşme oranı* olduğu görülmektedir. Bu göstergeler içerisinde de en önemli olanı *işsizlik oranı*dır. İşsizlik oranındaki artış illerin göç almasını çok büyük miktarda azaltmaktadır. Bu göstergeyi sırasıyla *kütüphane sayısı* ve *şehirleşme oranı* izlemektedir. Gelişmekte olan bir ülke olarak Türkiye, hem ekonomik hem de sosyal sorunları olan ve bu sorunları sahip olduğu sınırlı kaynakları en uygun biçimde kullanarak çözmeye çalışan bir ülkedir. Bölgeler arası dengeli kalkınmanın sağlanamaması sonucu ortaya çıkan gelişmişlik farklılıkları gelişmiş ve gelişmekte olan birçok ülkede olduğu gibi ülkemizde de görülmektedir. Üretim kaynaklarının yetersizliği ve dağılımındaki dengesizliklerin yanında diğer bazı ekonomik olanaksızlıklar Türkiye'de bölgeler hatta iller arası dengesiz gelişmeye yol açmaktadır (Albayrak, 2003). Bu dengesizlikler ise illerin aldığı ve verdiği göçü etkilemektedir. Göreceli olarak gelişmiş ve gelişmekte olan iller, sağladıkları olanak ve kolaylıklar bakımından göç çekim merkezi olma özelliği taşımaktadır.

Kaynakça

Albayrak, A. S. (2003). Türkiye'de İllerin Sosyoekonomik Gelişmişlik Düzeylerinin Çok Değişkenli İstatistik Yöntemlerle İncelenmesi. İstanbul Üniversitesi Sosyal Bilimler Enstitüsü İşletme Anabilim Dalı Doktora Tezi.

Amirault, D., Munnik, D., & Miller, S. (2012). What Drags and Drives Mobility: Explaining Canada's Aggregate Migration Patterns. Bank of Canada Working Paper, No: 2012-28, Erişim: 14.02.2015.

Bauer, T., Million, A., Rotte, R., & Zimmermann, K. F. (1999). Immigrant Labor and Workplace Safety. IZA, Discussion Paper No: 16.

Bozdoğan, M. N.(2008). Bölgesel Kalkınmanın Sağlanmasına Yönelik Vergi Özendirme Önlemlerinin Türkiye Açısından İncelenmesi ve Etkinliğinin Analizi, TOBB, Ankara.

Bülbül, S., & Köse, A. (2010). Türkiye'de Bölgelerarası İç Göç Hareketlerinin Çok Boyutlu Ölçekleme Yöntemi İle İncelenmesi. İstanbul Üniversitesi İşletme Fakültesi Dergisi, C. 39, S. 1, 75-94.

Carrivick, P. J. W., Lee, A. H., & Yau, K. K. W. (2003). Zero- Inflated Poisson Modelling to Evaluate Occupational Safety Intervention. Safety Science, 41:53-63.

Cheng, J., Young, C., Zhang, X., & Owusu, K. (2014). Comparing inter-migration within the European Union and China: An initial exploration. Migration Studies, Vol. 2, I. 3, 340-368.

Chesher, A. (1984). Testing for Neglected Heterogeneity. Econometrica, 52(4).

Deb, P., & Trivedi, P. K. (2002). The Structure of Demand for Health Care: Latent Class Versus Two-Part Models. Journal of Health Economics, 21:601-625.

Devillanova, C., & Garcia-Fontes, W. (2004). Migration Across Spanish Provinces: Evidence From The Social Security Records (1978-1992). Investigaciones Económicas, Vol. XXVIII (3), 461-487.

Eşiyok, A.(2005). AB Sürecinde Türkiye'de Bölgesel Kalkınma Farklılıkları, Büyüme Kutupları, Sanayinin Mekansal Dağılımı ve Bölgesel Gelir, Türkiye Kalkınma Bankası, Ankara.

Greene, W. H. (1997). FIML Estimation of Sample Selection Models for Count Data. Steern School of Business, New York University, Manuscript.

Kulaksız, Y. (2008). Türkiye'de Bölgesel Gelişmişlik Farkları, İstihdam ve Kurum Hizmetlerinin Çeşitlendirilmesi. Çalışma ve Sosyal Güvenlik Bakanlığı Türkiye İş Kurumu Genel Müdürlüğü, Uzmanlık Tezi.

Lee, E. S.(1966). A Theory of Migration. Demography, 3(1): 47-57.

Long, J. S., (1997). Regression Models for Categorical and Limited Dependent Variables, Thousand Oaks, CA: Sage Publication .

Rock, S., Sedo, S., & Willenborg, M. (2001). Analyst Following and Count Data Econometrics. Journal of Accounting and Economics, 30:351-373.

Silva, J. M. C. S. (1997). Unobservables in Count data Models for on-site Samples. Economics Letters, 54:217-220.

Silva J. M. C. S., & Windmeijer, F. (2001). Two-part Multiple Spell Models for Health Care Demand. Journal of Econometrics, 104: 67-89.

Stillwell, J. (2005). Inter-regional Migration Modelling: A Review and Assessment. 45th Congress of the European Regional Science Association, Vrije Universiteit Amsterdam, The Netherlands, 23-27 August 2005, Erişim: 14.02.2015 <www.ekf.vsb.cz/export/sites/ekf/projekty/cs/weby/esf-0116/databaze-prispevku/clanky_ERSA__2005/770.pdf>.

Üzümcü, A., & Özyakışır, D. (2013). TRA2 Bölgesinde Sosyo-Ekonomik Gelişmişlik Düzeyi ve Göç İlişkisi (1996-2012). 2. Uluslararası Bölgesel Kalkınma Konferansı, 16-17 Mayıs 2013-Elazığ, 1-21.

Wang, W., & Famoye, F. (1997). Modelling Houshold Fertility Decisions with Generalized Poisson Regression. Journal of Population Economics, 10:273-283.

Winkelmann, R. (2001). Healthcare Reform and the Number of Doctor Visits-An Econometric Analysis. Discussion Paper, No:317, Erişim: 05.06.2003 ftp://repec.iza.org/RePEc/Discussion paper/dp317.pdf.

Yakar, M., Saraçlı, S., & Yazıcı, H. (2010). Afyonkarahisar İlinde İller Arası Göçlerin Gelişmişlik Endeksleriyle Analizi. Doğu Coğrafya Dergisi, S. 24, 255 - 272.

Yakar, M. (2013). Türkiye'de İller Arası Net Göçlerle Sosyo-Ekonomik Gelişmişlik Arasındaki İlişkinin Coğrafi Ağırlıklı Regresyon İle Analizi. Ege Coğrafya Dergisi, C. 22, S. 1, 27-43.

Göç yollarında ulaşım araçları (1968 öncesinde)

Yılmaz Büktel

Giriş

1968 yılı, bu bildiri için iki farklı önemli noktaya işaret eder. İlki Mercedes – Benz lisansıyla Türkiye'de ilk defa fabrikasyon olarak şehirlerarası ve şehiriçi otobüs imalatının başladığını gösteren bir kuruluşun faaliyete geçmesidir. İkincisi ise Yaşar Kemal'in eserinden uyarlanan 1968 yılı yapımı Urfa – İstanbul filmidir.[314] Bu filmde günün şartlarında ve günün ulaşım araçlarıyla yaşanan bir kaçma-kovalama öyküsü perdeye aktarılmıştır. Konumuz itibarı ile bizi filmde kullanılan ulaşım araçları ilgilendirir.

Bildiri genelinde ise amaçlanan, 1950 yılında tek parti iktidarının değişimiyle başta "Taşı Toprağı Altın Şehir" İstanbul olmak üzere Anadolu'nun büyük illerine doğru yoğunlaşmaya başlayan göç yolları ve göç araçları üzerinde durarak 50'li ve 60'lı yıllarda Türkiye'nin ulaşım koşullarını (hava - deniz ve kara yolları) irdelemektir.

Türkiye'de 1968 öncesinde yabancı motor ve şasilerle olsa da fabrikasyon otobüs imalatı girişimleri olmuştur. Ancak kalıcı olan ve bugün dahi üretimini sürdüren kuruluş 1968 de faaliyete geçtiği için bu tarihin Türkiye'nin karayolu taşımacılığı için bir milat olduğu düşüncesindeyiz. Bu konuda günümüze baktığımızda daha çok imalatçı ve daha çok marka model ile Şehirlerarası ve şehiriçi ulaşımında çok yol katedildiğini görmek mümkün olabilir. Ancak bizim amacımız bu gelişmeyi anlatmak değil, 1968 tarihi öncesindeki yaklaşık 20 yıl bir süreçte ülkemizin kara-demir-hava ve deniz yollarının durumunu irdelemektir. Göç konusuyla bu durumun ilgisi işe 50li yılların başında, çok partili dönemin başlangıcıyla, iş ve aş bulmak için başlayan ve esasen halen de süregelen yurtiçi hareketliliğinin güçlüklerini göz önüne koyan bir çalışma yapmaktı.

Bu durumun olgularına tamamen değil ama uzantılarına, yaş itibari ile o dönemin araçlarını kullanarak, kısmen yaşamış biri olarak vakıftım. Ancak 1968 yılı yapımı **Urfa–İstanbul** ve devamı niteliğindeki aynı yıl yapımı **Beşikteki Miras**[315] filmleri, aslında bir anlamda macera - takip filmi olmasına karşın aynı zamanda bir yol filmi niteliği de taşıyor ve söz konusu 20 yıllık sürecin sıkıntılarını görselleriyle izleten bir özellik taşıyordu. Türk sineması, yaygın adıyla Yeşilçam'ın listesinde göçü konu eden pek çok filmde[316], esas konu, sıladan gurbete olan yolu değil, gurbette göçün ya da diğer bir anlatımla büyük şehirde varolma - yokoluş öykülerinin sergilendiği çalışmalar olarak görülür. Söz konusu ettiğimiz iki film ise asıl konusu Göç olmamakla beraber bir yol filmi niteliği taşıdıkları için bize, 1968 yılında kara ve demiryolu araçlarının durumunu gösterir.

Bu iki film bize, başka görsel kaynakları kullanarak, eksikleri tamamlayarak hava ve deniz yolu araçlarının da durumuna değinen, 20 yıllık sürecin, özellikler ve

---

[314] Urfa – İstanbul, 1968, Yön.O.Nuri Ergün
[315] Beşikteki Miras, 1968, O.Nuri Ergün
[316] Bu konuda örnek film sayılamayacak kadar çoktur. Sadece tanınmış birkaç örnekten söz edersek: Gurbet Kuşları, 1964, Halit Refiğ; Düğün,1973, Ömer L.Akad; Gelin, 1973, Ömer L.Akad; Diyet 1974, Ömer L.Akad.

anılarla desteklenen, görsellerle zenginleştirilmiş panoramasını oluşturma amaçlı bir çalışma yapma düşüncesini verdi. Dolayısıyla söz konusu olan fabrikanın kuruluşu ve iki film, bildirinin amacını değil, 1968'den geriye doğru uzanan görsel bir yolculuğun başlangıcını oluşturmaktalar.

50li yıllardan 60lı yılların sonuna kadar olan süreçte ulaşım kanalları açısından Türkiye'ye baktığımızda manzara genel itibarı ile şudur:

Kıyı kentleri batının büyük illerine deniz yolu ile bağlanmaktadır. Doğu, Güney doğu bölgeleri ise Ankara üzerinden demiryolu hatlarıyla Batı illerine ulaşmaktadır. Ücret analizleri yapma olanağı bulamadım ancak 60lı yılları kısmen yaşadığım için bu ücretler makul olsa da halkın alım gücüyle kıyaslandığında o kadar da ucuz görünmüyordu. Yani insanlar genellikle doğdukları yerlerde yaşamak zorundaydı. Kalabalık bir ailenin İstanbul ve İzmir'i bırakın Ankara'ya hatta Adana'ya bile gelebilmesi önemli bir bütçeyi gerektiriyordu.

Deniz yolu ve Demir yolu bu durumdayken halkın uçak kullanmasını beklemek zaten abesle iştigal olurdu. İşte Kara yolu bu koşullarda ucuz bir alternatif olarak ortaya çıktı. Aslında zaten vardı ama Deniz ve Demir yollarına alternatif olmasıyla gerçek anlamda doğmuş oldu. Bu bildirinin bir amacı da anılan tarihlerde gerçekleşen göç hareketlerinin, şehirlerarası karayolu taşımacılığının bir sektöre dönüşmesine neden olduğunu göstermektir.

Deniz Yolları

1930 yılından başlayarak Deniz Yollarında çalışan gemilerin çoğu ülkemiz adına yurtdışı tersanelerinde inşa ettirilen gemilerdi. Bu gemiler tek tek değil ikili üçlü gruplar halinde imal edilen kardeş gemilerdi. Bunların yanı sıra hibe olarak ya da 1930 öncesinde satın alınarak gelen ikinci el gemiler de filomuzda yer alıyordu.

İlk akla gelen deniz yolu hatlarımız 6-7 günlük periyotları olan İstanbul kalkışlı Karadeniz ve Akdeniz postaları idi. Bunun yanında Marmara'da Bandırma ve adalara ulaşmayı amaçlayan nispeten kısa erimli hatlar da vardı.

Bu dönemde kullanılan gemilerin hepsi yük ve yolcu taşımak için dizayn edilmiş gemilerdi. Gemiler yoğun zamanlarda yükünü ve kamara yolcusunu aldıktan sonra limitler dahilinde açık güverte yolcusu da alırdı.[317]

TARI, AKSU ve GÜNEYSU: Tarı, 1908'de İngiltere, Hartlepool'de, Furness, Withy & Co. Ltd. tezgahlarında inşa edilmişti. Önce Tadla, sonra Frankenvald adıyla çalıştı. 4.026 gros tonluktu. Uzunluğu: 121 metre, genişliği 14 metre, su kesimi: 74 metre idi. 2.500 beygir gücündeki makinesiyle 14 mil hız yapabiliyordu. 1967 yılının 1 Şubat günü satıldı. Güneysu, 1908'de Avusturya-Macaristan İmparatorluğu'nun Trieste'deki Austriaco tezgahlarında inşa edilmişti. Önceleri Graz ve sonra da Bulgaria adı altında çalıştı. 3.845 gros tonluktu. Uzunluğu: 121 metre, genişligi: 14,5 metre, su kesimi: 6,6 metre idi. Makinesi 3.500 beygir gücündeydi. 29 kasım 1961 günü, 123.494 dolara hurdaya gitti. (Aksu ile Güneysu birbirinin eşi gemilerdi)

Tarı, Aksu ve Güneysu ile birlikte 1930 yıllarına kadar Vapurculuk Şirketi adına çalıştı. Sonra Millileştirildi. Millileştirme zamanın başbakanı İsmet

---

[317] Deniz yollarında çalışan gemilerin fotoğrafları kişisel arşivimden ve aşağıda linkini verdiğim forum başlığındaki resimlerden seçilerek temin edilmiştir. Vapurlarla ilgili olarak verilen bilgi dipnotları çoğunlukla Wowturkey sitesindeki ilgili yazarlara yönlendirecektir. http://wowturkey.com/forum/viewtopic.php?t=15063

İnönü'nün bir politikası idi o gemiler o zaman milleştirilmeyip o şirketler ki sayıları beşten fazla bu güne kadar gelseydi acaba Türkiye yolcu gemisi bakımından bu gün nerelerde olabilirdi acaba iyi araştırma yapmak lazım gelir bu konuyu.(Ali Bozoğlu)[318]

TIRHAN, ETRÜSK, ve KADEŞ: Üçü de Denizyolları'nın, filosunu gençleştirmek amacıyla Almanya'da inşaa ettirdiği birbirinin eşi yolcu ve yük gemileriydiler. içlerinden Etrüsk'ün tonajı, her nedense öteki iki kardeşinden biraz daha azdı. Üçüne birden 136.296 İngiliz Sterlini ödenmişti.

1938 yılının güzel bir bahar günü İstanbul sularına geldiler. Üçü de modern teknolojiyle inşaa edildikleri için, rahat, kullanışlı ayrıca da estetiği olan bembeyaz gemilerdi. 3.088 gros tonluktular. Boyları 107 m, genişlikleri de 14,5 m idi. Çift uskurlu idiler. Saatte 12 mil hız yapacağının ileri sürülmesine karşılık, hiç bir zaman 10 milin üstüne çıkamadılar.

Gelir gelmez üçü de hizmete kondu. Ne var ki, çok geçmeden İkinci Dünya Savaşı'nın amansız rüzgarları Avrupa'yı kasıp kavurmaya başlayınca, Türkiye'de olanakları el verdiğince bir takım önlemler alma gereği gördü. Bu üç gemiden Etrüsk ile Kadeş hastane gemisi olarak kullanılmak üzere Donanmanın emrine verildi. Üçüncü kardeş Tırhan'ı ise iç hatlarda çalıştırmaya devam ettiler. 40 ve 41 yılları arasında Donanma'nın hizmetinde kalan iki gemi, daha sonradan tekrar Denizyolları'na teslim edildi.

Bir süre sonra siyaha boyanan bu üç gemi yıllarca Karadeniz postası, Bandırma postası gibi iç hatlarda çalıştırıldılar. Geceleyin 21:00 da Tophane Rıhtımından hareket ediyor, neredeyse yarım yolla seyrederek sabahleyin gün ışırken Bandırma'ya yanaşıyordu. Yolcularının büyük bir bölümü hep trenle İzmir'e gidecek kimselerdi. Yıllarca yolcu ve yük taşıdılar. 29 yıllık yorgun bir gemi oluncaya kadar yaz demeden, kış demeden her türlü havada Marmara ve Ege kasabalarının İstanbul'a bağlantısını sağladılar.

Bunlardan Tırhan 1967'ye gelindiğinde seferden alınıp Haliç'te Camialtı Tersanesi'ne bağlandı. Sekiz yıla yakın bir süre Haliç'in boz bulanık sularında yattı. 1975'te sökülmek üzere 5.750.000 liraya hurda olarak Kalkavanlara satıldı. Bu üç gemiden de günümüze, ne yazık ki soluk birkaç fotoğraftan başka bir şey kalmadı. (Eser Tütel)[319]

Bunlar aslında 3 degil 4 gemi olarak siparis edilmislerdi,ve 4.süne Salon adi verilmisti. Ancak bu 4.gemi II.Dunya savasinin baslamasi nedeni ile Turkiye'ye teslim edilememis ve II.Dunya savasi sirasinda Alman donanmasinda hizmet vermis, savastan sonra ise Sovyetler Birligine verilmistir, Bu gemi 60 li yillarin sonuna kadar Sovyet ticaret filosunda hizmet gormustur.[320]

MARAKAZ, SUS ve TRAK: Marakaz, Sus ve Trak, 1938'de Almanya, Kiel'de Frd. Krupp Germ. A. G tezgahlarında yapılan yük ve yolcu gemileriydi. Bu 3 gemi de, Kadeş, Tırhan ve Etrüsk gibi kardeş gemilerdiler Daha küçük boyutlu oldukları için Marmara içinde çalıştılar. Trak 1944 yılında Bandırma açıklarında kayalara çarparak battı. Bu altı geminin en büyük özelliklerinden birisi isimlerin, Mustafa Kemal ATATÜRK tarafından verilmiş olmasıdır. Ayrıca bu gemiler o zamana kadar Denizyolları İşletmesi tarafından sipariş verilerek yaptırılan ilk

[318] http://wowturkey.com/forum/viewtopic.php?p=428670#428670
[319] Tütel Eser. İstanbul'un Unutulmayan gemileri, İstanbul 2006, ISBN975640390X
[320] http://wowturkey.com/forum/viewtopic.php?p=376354#376354

gemilerdir. O zamana kadar Denizyolları İşletmesi gemilerini hep ikinci el olarak temin etmiştir.[321]

TRABZON, ORDU ve GİRESUN: Trabzon,Ordu ve Giresun kardeş gemiler olup 1938 Danimarka yapimidir. II. Dunya Savasindan sonra filoya katilmislardir. (yanilmiyorsam 1949 da)[322]

Trabzon gemisi 1938'de, Danimarka, Nakskov'da Nakskov Skibs AlS tezgahlarında motorlu yolcu gemisi olarak inşa edilmişti. 6.790 gros, 4.803 net tonluktu. Uzunluğu: 134,2 metre, genişligi: 17,7 metre, su kesimi: 10,3 metre idi. İtalya, Torino,Fiat Grandi Motori yapımı, 6.000 beygir gücünde dizel motoru vardı. Tek uskurluydu. 14 mil hız yapıyor, 528 yolcu alabiliyordu. Önce Elazığ adı verildiyse de sonra Trabzon olarak değiştirildi. 1970'te Deniz Kuvvetleri Komutanlığı tarafın dan satın alınınca Erkin II adını aldı. 1983'te Aliağa'da söküldü.[323]

Ordu Gemisi, M/S CAPOAPO adı ile 2 Ekim 1937 Danimarka yapısı, Naskov Skibs AlS Tersanesinden kızaktan indi.10449 groston, 6302 net ton ve azami yük kapasitesi 6200 ton. Boy: 134..20 m., en 17:60.m., derinlik 7.1 m. Yolcu kapasitesi 1155. Ana taban (iskelet) yapıldı. Bu bölüm yakıt ve su balastı taşımak için 6 tanka bölündü. 5 kargo bölümünün 1,2,4 ve 5 numaraları genel kargo, 3 numarası tamamen soğutuculuydu ve 1 ve 2 numaralı güverte arasında soğuk taşınacak yükler için bulunacaktı. Soğutucu makineleri Danimarka'daki Thomas Ths. Sabroe & Co. Aarbus firmasından temin edildi.(Ali Bozoğlu)

Bu üç gemi, genellikle Karadeniz ve İzmir hatlarında dönüşümlü olarak çalışmaya başladılar Bunlardan Karadeniz Sürat Postası her hafta salı günü saat 10,00'te İstanbul'dan kalkar Zonguldak, Samsun, Ordu, Giresun, Trabzon ve Hopa'ya uğrar, yükünü, yolcusunu çıkarır, Hopa' dan dönüşe geç ve aynı limanlardan yük yolcu alıp aynı haftanın pazar günü İstanbul'a dönerdi. Bir diğeri ise İstanbul, Akçakoca, Ereğli, Zonguldak, Amasra, Kurucaşile, Cide, İnebolu, İlişi, Abana, Çatalzeytin, Türkeli, Ayancık, Sinop, Samsun, Ordu, Ünye, Fatsa; Görele, Tirebolu, Rize, Hopa'ya uğrayan Karadeniz Aralık Postası yapardı. Bu Posta 14 gün sürerdi. Bir diğeri ise İstanbul-İzmir Seferi yapardı. [324]

İSKENDERUN ve SAMSUN: İskenderun gemisi, 1950'de, İtalya, Cenova;da S.A. Ansaldo tezgahlarında buharlı yolcu gemisi olarak inşa edildi. 6.570 gros, 3.624 net tonluktu. Uzunluğu: 132metre, genişliği: 17,5 metre, su kesimi: 10,2 metre idi. S.A. Ansaldo yapımı, her biri 4.400 beygir gücünde 2 adet buhar türbini vardı. Çift uskurluydu. 19 mil hız yapabiliyordu. Yeni olarak alındı. Güzel ve hızlı bir gemiydi. Yüzme havuzu vardı. 1964'te, kazanları ve yardımcı makineleri Hollanda'da yenilendi. 1982 Ekim'inde satıldı.

Samsun gemisi 1951'de, İtalya, Cenova'da S.A. Ansaldo tezgahlarında buharlı yolcu gemisi olarak inşa edildi. 6.543 gros, 3.558 net tonluktu. Uzunlugu: 132 metre,genişliği: 17,3 metre, su kesimi: 10,3 metre idi. S.A. Ansaldo yapımı, her biri 4.400 beygir gücünde iki buhar türbini vardı. Çift uskurluydu. 19 mil hız yapabiliyordu. Yeni olarak alındı. Biçimli ve yollu bir gemiydi. Yüzme havuzu

[321] http://wowturkey.com/forum/viewtopic.php?p=428689#428689
[322] http://wowturkey.com/forum/viewtopic.php?p=132767#132767
[323] http://wowturkey.com/forum/viewtopic.php?p=428696#428696
[324] http://www.denizhaber.com/index.php?sayfa=yazar&id=28&yazi_id=100313

vardı. 1964'te, kazanları ve yardımcı makineleri Hollanda'da yenilendi. 1982 Ekim'inde satıldı

İskenderun ve Samsun gemileri ile ilgili olarak sevgili büyüğümüz Eser Tutel'in 07 Aralık 2006 tarihinde Dünya Gazetesi ekinde verilen Denizcilik ekinde çıkan yazısı (Bu Ek her perşembe günü verilmektedir.)[325]

ANKARA: Ankara, II. Dünya savaşı sonrasında Amerika tarafından ülkemize hibe edilen, oldukça ilginç hikayesi olan bir gemidir: "Newport News Ship building& Dry .Dock.Co tersanesinde 1927 yılında bir Kızılderili kabilesinin adı olan " IROQUOIS " adı ile inşa edildi. Boyu 124,76 Metre 19.08 Metre derinliği 6.25 metre İlk sahipleri New York and Miami Steamship Corp. Daha sonra 1933'de Clyde Mallory Steamship Line. New York'ta firmasınca satın alınıyor ve Bu arada İkinci Dünya Savaşı başlıyor ve gemi Teselli anlamına gelen "SOLACE AH 5" ismi ile Amerikan Deniz Kuvvetleri'nde hastane gemisi oluyor. Yıl1946.

İki yanına kocaman birer kırmızı haç işareti boyanmıştı. Artık Pasifik sularındaydı. Pearl Harbour baskınında, bu kırmızı haçlar sayesinde Japon uçaklarının müthiş saldırısından kurtulmayı başarmıştı. Adalarda sürüp giden kanlı savaşlarda yaralananları San Francisco'ya taşıyordu.

Modern bir ameliyathanesi vardı. Sağladığı imkân ve verdiği hizmetlerle 25.000 Amerikan askerinin kurtarılmasını sağlamıştı. Bu güzel ve biçimli gemi, 1948 yılı Ekim'inde Devlet Denizyolları ve Limanları Umum Müdürlüğü tarafından satın alındıktan sonra yapılan tadilatla 25 adet lüks mevki, 89 adet birinci mevki, 40 adet ikinci mevki, 5 adet de turistik kamaralı bir yolcu gemisi haline getirildi.

Bu güzel gemiye idarece ne isim verilmesi hususunda görüşmeler yapılırken bu güzel gemiye " ANKARA " ismi verilmesi gündeme geliyor fakat bir sorun vardır filoda ANKARA isimli bir gemi vardır eski S/S ANKARA gemisinin ismi S/S ÇORUM olarak değiştirildi ve yeni gemiye S/S ANKARA ismi verildi.

Bulunduğu tersanede tepeden tırnağa bakım ve onarım gördükten sonra İşletmenin tecrübeli Kaptanlarından 551 sicil sayılı Kaptan Seyfi GEZER tarafından İstanbul'a getirildi. Önceleri siyah renkli idi sonra Beyaz'a boyandı. . Geminin yolcuları için ayrılan kısmı, tüm hacminin %80'ine yaklaşıyordu. Geniş bir sigara salonu, büyük bir barı, rahat yemek salonları ile S/S ANKARA ferah bir gemiydi. Ayrıca garajı da olduğundan yolcuların arabaları yan taraftaki kapaklardan içeriye alınabiliyordu." (Ali Bozoğlu) [326]

Deniz yollarının gemileri 50 li 60 lı yıllarda ve öncesinde de Halkın yaşamında hep varolmuş, halkın söylencelerinde yer almıştır. Bu türden çok öykü bulunabilir ama buraya bir kaçını almakla yetiniyoruz:

"Görenler esmerliğimden yanlış tahminlerde bulunur hep, ama aslen Trabzonluyum. Yavaş yürüdüğümde, uyuşuk ya da uykusuz olduğum zaman babannem " hayde hayde yürü! eylenma(oyalanmak) Tarı vaporu gibi!" der. Başkalarından da duymuştum bunu. Ben eskiden Tarı'nın geminin türü , taşıdığı malzeme (Darı kelimesiyle ses benzerliğini düşünüp bu kanıya varmıştım. insan karadenizli olmaya görsün) Daha sonra bir gün sorduğumda "Uşaam evelden bi Tarı vaporu vardi, eyleni durudu. Her limana girerdi , altı güne anca varırdi" dedi.

[325] http://wowturkey.com/forum/viewtopic.php?p=388388#388388
[326] http://freeshipplans.com/scale-model-articles/ss-ankara-ah-5-solace-ss-iroquois/

Bir geminin bir halkın kültürüyle nasıl kaynaştığına güzel bir örnek bence. Keşke eskisi kadar sahiplenilse herşey, anında tüketilmeye maruz kalmasa... Bu arada gemi aslında o kadar da yavaş değilmiş, sanırım limanlarda yük ve yolcu nakli uzun sürdüğünden sefer bu kadar uzuyormuş. Zira çoğu yerde rıhtım değil mavnalar varmış... Olsun, hala yaşıyor Tarı gemisi; bana da paylaşmak düşer...

Bir de allah uzun ömür versin, 100 yaşın üstünde bir nenemiz var. Babamın amcasının karısı, namı değer "Tonya Kızı". Dinlemeyi çok severim onu, yarım diş kalmış ağzından saatlerce hikayeler dökülür. Güncel olanlar dışında anlattığı her hikayenin başı aynıdır: "Eeeeeey gidi uşaam evelden yol yoğudi, iz yoğudi. Trabzon'dan vaborlan geliduk Zonguldak'a ordan buriya heeeğp yörüme. Haburalar hep gafulluğudi..." Anlattığına göre ineklerini bile getirmiş Trabzon'dan gemiyle."(Emrak)[327]

Anlatılanlar hem keyif verici, hem de günün ulaşım gerçeklerini sergiler bir nitelik taşımıyor mu?

Demir yolları

Ülkemizde demiryolu ulaşımı başladığından bu yana trenlere hareket veren güç, halkın "kara tren" diye tanımladığı buharlı lokomotifler olmuştur.

Başlangıçta İzmir-Aydın güzergahı ile ilk atılımı yapan idare, 50li 60lı yıllarda çok daha fazla büyük bir demiryoluna ağına sahip olmuşsa da bu gelişme güç veren araçlara yani lokomotiflere yansımamıştır. Görebildiğimiz kadarı ile anılan tarihlerde değineceğimiz modellerle yeni araçlar alımı başlamış ama bu kez de ulaşım ağının gelişimi durdurulmuş gibidir. Ancak son yıllarda olumlu bir gelişme olarak her iki alanda da(Hat bakımı ve araçlar) çalışmalar yapıldığını görüyoruz.

Buharlı lokomotifler ve 50li 60lı yıllarda ülkemizde görülen diğer trenler hakkındaki fotoğraf ve bilgiler için yine kaynağımız aynı.[328]

Buharlı lokomotiflerini uzun uzun anlatmaya gerek yok ancak genellikle batı bölgelerinde çalışan dizel motorlu trenlerin ya da kısaca motorlu trenlerin model ve markalarına kısaca değinmek gerekiyor.

Man motorlu trenler: Ülkemizde farklı motor çeşitlemeleriyle çalışan Man motorlu trenlerin iki farklı modelini görüyoruz. Bunlardan ilki , orta kısmındaki restoran bölümü ile daha lüks olan 3 vagonlu olanı (MT5200 ve MT5300) ve diğeri daha sade iki vagonlu (MT5400 ve MAN 21 25) araçlardır. Bu ikincinin halk arasındaki adı motorlu tren değil de oturay veya otoraydır. Oturaylar ülkemize daha sonradan gelecek olan raybüslerin öncüsü gibi ince yapılı ve pratik araçlardır.

Üçüncü tip diyebileceğimiz Motorlu trenler Fiat motorludur (MT5500) ve yapı ve hacım olarak üç vagonlu Man motorlu trenlere benzerler.

Hava Yolları

Bugünkü Türk Hava Yollarının kuruluşu öncesinde, Ulusal Hava yolu ağımızda önce THP ve sonrasında DHY uçaklarının uçtuğunu biliyoruz.

---

[327]
http://wowturkey.com/forum/viewtopic.php?p=992592&sid=9c6b7e58f7d8a0da7e791b53d94e309b#992592
[328] http://wowturkey.com/forum/viewtopic.php?t=22187

"20 Mayıs 1933 tarihinde 2186 sayılı kanunla, "Hava Yolları Devlet İşletme İdaresi" adı altında Milli Savunma Bakanlığı'na bağlı olarak 180,859 TL sermayeyle ve 24 personelle kurulan DHY, 3 Haziran 1938 tarihinde, 3424 sayılı kanunla "Devlet Hava Yolları Umum Müdürlüğü" haline getirilerek, 27 Mayıs 1939 tarihinde 3613 sayılı kanunla Ulaştırma Bakanlığı'na bağlanmıştır. DHY'nin hızla gelişmeye çalıştığı dönemde patlak veren İkinci Dünya Savaşı, bütün planları alt üst etmiş, ülkemizdeki birçok bölgeye stratejik amaçlı havaalanlarının inşa edilmesini zorunlu hale getirmiştir. Bu durum savaşa rağmen, DHY için avantaj olmuş ve bu sayede çok sayıda şehre uçulabilir hale gelinmiştir. İkinci Dünya Savaşı'nın en zor günlerinde DHY aralıksız seferlerine devam etmiş, ordu birliklerine paraşütçülüğü tanıtmak ve öğretmek amacıyla da, tayyarelerini THK ile müştereken kullanmıştır. 1941 ve 1942 yıllarında Samsun, Elazığ ve Van gibi yeni uçuş hatları açılmıştır. ...

... Demokrat Parti Hükümeti döneminde alınan karar gereği, 21 Mayıs 1955 tarihli ve 6623 no'lu meclis kararıyla, TÜRK HAVA YOLLARI ANONİM ORTAKLIĞI KANUNU adı altında hazırlanan kanun hükmündeki kararname uyarınca, THY A.O'nun ilk temeli atılır. THY A.O'nın ana sözleşmesinin, 20 Şubat 1956 tarihinde Bakanlar Kurulu tarafından onaylanması sonrasında, TÜRK HAVA YOLLARI ANONİM ORTAKLIĞI, 1 Mart 1956 tarihinden itibaren Resmi olarak faaliyete geçer."(Firuz Altıngöz) [329]

50li 60 lı yıllar hem DHY hem de THY dönemine denk gelir. Biz bu süreçte kullanılan 3 uçak modeline bakacağız.

DC-3 uçakları: Filoya 1945 yılında giren bu uçakların toplam rakamı 30 adet idi. "DC-3 ve C-47 DAKOTA'lar, 2 Ağustos 1932'de Donald W.Douglas'ın kurmuş olduğu Douglas Aircraft Company tarafından atası, DC-1 ve DC-2 tayyarelerinin gelişmiş modeli olarak üretilmiş ve ilk uçuşunu, 17 Aralık 1935 tarihinde gerçekleştirmiştir. DC-3'lerin Dünya Havacılık tarihindeki popülaritesi, askeri versiyonu olan C-47'lerin İkinci Dünya Savaşı sırasında malzeme, personel taşıma ve de yaralı naklinde ambulans uçak olarak ifa ettiği görevlerindeki başarısından kaynaklanmaktadır. DC-3 ve C-47'ler, halen dünyada en fazla üretilme unvanına sahip olan tayyarelerdir. Askeri ve sivil versiyonları dahil olmak üzere değişik tip ve modelde toplam 10.819 adet üretilmiştir"(Firuz Altıngöz) [330]

Vickers Viscount: İmalatı ilk kez İngiltere'de 1948 yılında başlayan bu uçakların, DHY için sipariş edilen ve 794D olarak tescil edilen 5 uçağın ilki 1958 yılında ülkemize ülkemize gelmiştir.(Zafer Orbay) [331]

F(okker) – 27: Filoya 1960 yılında 5 ve 1961 yılında 2 olmak üzere toplamda 7 adet F-27 uçağı alınmıştır. "Bir 50li yıllar dizayni olan F-27 ler C-130 lar ile birlikte dunyanin en basarili turboprop ucaklari sayilirlar.Gerek orijinal F-27 ler gerekse de onların modernize edilmis yeni modelleri bugunde dunyanin zor sartlar hukum suren bircok bolgesinde gerek yolcu ucagi, gerekse askeri nakliye ucagi veya yardim kuruluslarina malzerme tasiyan ucaklar olarak basari ile

---

[329] Konu ile ilgili daha geniş bilgi için: http://wowturkey.com/forum/viewtopic.php?p=352669#352669
[330] http://wowturkey.com/forum/viewtopic.php?p=352669#352669
[331] http://kokpit.aero/index.php?route=article/article&article_id=4815

calismaktadirlar. F-27 ler toprak pistlere inip kalkabilecek sekilde dizayn edilmislerdir ,saglam ve bakimi kolay tayyareler olarak bilinirler. "(Ümit I)[332]

Uçakların rakamsal durumuna bakarsak burada değinmediğimiz modellerle beraber 50 civarında bir Uçak filomuz olduğunu görebiliriz. Bu uçakların kendi özelliklerinin yanısıra hepsinde kolayca görülebilen ortak özellikleri pervaneli(pervanesi dışta olan) oluşları ve 30 – 40 arası yolcu kapasitelerinin olmasıdır. THY, 1967 yılında yılında kiralayarak filosuna kattığı ilk DC-9 uçağı ile pervaneli uçak alımı dönemini kapatmış ve jet uçaklarına geçiş yapmıştır.

Kara Yolları

Karayolunu taşımacılığının başına **şehirlerarası** sıfatını özellikle ilave etmek gerekir. Çünkü 50li yılların başlarında Batıda o kadar fazla olmasa da Doğu bölgelerimizde mevcut araçlarla şehirlerarası yolculuk yapmak macera yaşamak olarak değerlendirilebilir. Bu dönemde Türkiye'de otoyolları, duble yolları bırakın köy yolu niteliği taşıyan yollar bulabilmek bile büyük bir şanstı. Mevcut araçlar olarak tanımladığım otobüsler (aslında bunlara kaptı kaçtı, otobüsçük demek daha doğru olur) kamyon şasileri üzerine yapılmış yapma kasa araçlardır ve başlangıçta bu kasalar ahşaptan yapılmıştır ve araçlar hiçte şehirlerarası yolculuklara uygun değildir. Ancak eldeki olanaklar budur ve aslında uzun yola uygun olmayan bu araçlar yukarıda değindiğim nedenlerden ötürü deniz ve demir yollarına alternatif bir yol olarak halk tarafından bir anlamda zorunlu olarak seçilmişti. Çağına göre gelişmiş araçlar olan Gemi ve Trenle yolculuk yapmak yerine daha düşük bir bütçe gerektireceği için bu uygunsuz araçlarla sıkıntılı yolculuklara katlanmak halkın tercih nedeni olmuştu.

Bu tercih kısa zamanda tüm ülke boyutunda yaygınlık kazanmış ve Karayolu taşımacılığı cazip bir sektör haline dönüşmenin ilk adımlarını atmaya başlamıştır. Ancak doğru dürüst yolları ve araçları olmayan ülkede bu adımların ilerletilmesi o kadar da kolay değildi. Ancak halkın tercihi bu adımların gerçekleştirilmesine yardımcı oldu. Yapma kasa ustaları işlerinde uzmanlaştı, ahşap kasalardan sac kasaların yapımcılığına geçtiler, Ustalık maharetiyle yapılan ahşap kasalardan, proje tasarımlarıyla yapılan kasalara geçtiler. Kasa yapımı için seçilen ekonomik ömrünü tamamlamış kamyon şasilerinden, bu iş için özel olarak ithal edilen kamyon şasilerini kullanmaya başladılar. Yine ustalık marifetiyle yapılan kasalar yerine aracın motor gücü-taşıma kapasitesine uygun kasalar planlanmaya başlandı. Ancak tüm bu gelişmeler halkın tercih ve taleplerini karşılamaya yetmiyordu.

Pasta büyüyünce bundan büyük dilimler kapmak isteyen 2-3 araçtan oluşan bireysel işletmeciler bir araya gelip firmalar kurarak güçlenmeye başladılar[333] ve palazlanan firmalar araç yetersizliğine otobüs ithali ile çare bulmaya çalıştılar. Bu çare ithal araç sahibi firmaların yolcu kapma yarışında öne geçmelerini sağladı. Ancak İthal araçların bozulan parçalarını değiştirerek yenilemek, motor arızalarını gidermek büyük harcamalar gerektiriyordu, yani ithal otobüs almak, konunun yasal

---

[332] http://wowturkey.com/forum/viewtopic.php?p=193835#193835
[333] Palazlanan firmaların bir de güç mücadelesi vardı ki bu daha çok yolcu kapma yarışı gibi gözükse de bazen silahlı çatışmalara dönüşebiliyor ve kanda dökülüyordu. Gelişimin bu kanlı yönünü de işleyen bir film olarak Halit Refiğ yapımı 1967 yılı yapımı Ayhan Işık'ın başrolde olduğu"Aslan Pençesi" filmini gösterebiliriz: Halit Refiğ; Aslan Pençesi,1967

düzenlemeleri tam olarak netleşmediğinden bazen astarı yüzünden pahalı sonuçlara yol açabiliyordu.

Yapma kasa üreticileri Türkiye'nin pek çok yanında vardı ama bu konuda Bursa ilinin tartışmasız bir öncülüğü vardı. İthal araç alımını önlemek ya da en azından sınırlayarak, pazarlarının küçülmemesini isteyen bu girişimciler birleşerek otobüs fabrikaları kurma çalışmalarına başladılar. Ancak ilk girişimler hüsranla sonuçlandı: Yeterli bilimsel alt yapısı olmayan, dışarıdan gelen motor ve şasilere bağlı bu kasa yapıcı firmalar (bunlar beni aşan ayrı bir çalışma konusudur) kötü dizaynlar, üretilen araçlarda baş gösteren arızalar ve malzeme temininde güçlüklerden ötürü zamanında yetiştirilemeyen siparişler gibi nedenlerle kepenk kapamak zorunda kalsalar da imalatta iz bırakmış bazı firmalar ortaya çıktı.

Bu süreç 1968 yılında kurulan Alman ortaklı **Otomarsan** fabrikasıyla sonunda istenilen başarıyı yakaladı ve Fabrika günümüze kadar olan süreçte kendini geliştirerek binlerce otobüs-kamyon üreterek bunların önemli bir bölümünü ihraç etme başarısını da gösterdi. Hatta ülkemizdeki ucuz işçilik nedeniyle motor ihtiyaçlarını karşılayan Mersedes ve Man firmalarının bulunduğu Almanya'ya bile **Mersedes** ve **Man** marka araçlar ihraç edildi. 50li yılların başından 60lı yılların sonuna kadar olan 20 yıllık bir süreçte Ülkemiz girişimcileri, halkın tercihini kullanarak bireysel ustaların yaptığı yapma kasalardan, ulaşım dünyasında ve halk arasında **0302 efsanesi** olarak tanınan ve Türk izlerini üzerinde barındıran bir imalatı gerçekleştirecek düzeye gelmiştir.

Bütün bu süreçte otobüs yapımı hızla gelişirken, bu hıza ayak uyduramayan olgu ise karayollarının yapımıdır. 70li yılların başında bile Türkiye yolları "köstebek yuvası" "tarla" gibi sıfatlarla tanımlanırdı

Değerlendirme

Bu satırların, Karayolu taşımacılığının başarısını dile getirmek için yazıldığını düşünmeyin. Karayolu taşımacılığı yukarıda da belirtildiği gibi 50 li yıllarda halkın umutlarına çare olmak için düşünülmüş bir ara çözümdü ve girişimciler bu çözümü fırsata dönüştürdüler.

Konuya, günümüze uzanan geniş bir perspektifle baktığımızda 50-60lar dönemi Deniz yolu araçlarının kullanımdan kalktığını, yerini nesil araçların aldığını ancak bu yeni nesil araçların seferden çekilenlerin yerine, işletmenin yeni araçlarla donatılmayıp sürekli kan kaybettiğini gördük ki bu da üç tarafı denizlerle çevrili ülkemizde deniz yollarının işlevinin bittiğine işaret etmektedir.

Demiryolu araçlarının başını çeken kara trenin buharlı lokomotifi artık müzelerde[334] ve eski istasyonlar önünde sergilenmektedir. Onların yerini alan dizel ve elektrikli lokomotiflerde miadını doldurmakta ve yerini hızlı trenler almakta gibi görünse de bu gelişmeler tamamen dışa bağımlı ve çağın teknolojisine pekte uymayan yatırımlar olarak görünür.

Hava yolları ise özellikle 90 lı yıllarda özel havayollarının pazardan pay almaya başlamasıyla ciddi bir gelişim göstermiş[335] ve Milli havayolumuz THY kadar diğer firmalarda hava yollarında söz sahibi olurken uçak filoları sürekli olarak yenilenmiş

---

[334] Çamlık, Selçuk, İzmir. Çamlık Buharlı Lokomotif Müzesi
[335] İlk özel hava yolu olarak kabul edebileceğimiz Pegasus'un kuruluş öyküsü için bkz. http://tr.wikipedia.org/wiki/Pegasus_Hava_Yolları

ve büyümüştür. Bu gelişim beraberinde ucuz bilet kampanyalarını da getirerek orta sınıf halkın da hava yollarını tercih etmesi sonucunu doğurmuştur ki bu da hava yolları pastasının büyürken Karayolu pastasının da giderek küçülmesine yol açmaktadır.

Bu gelişmeler karşısında otobüsle ulaşımın geleceği karanlık ya da kararsız görülmektedir. Halk erken uçak bileti alımlarıyla uzun mesafeli yolculuklarını otobüslerden daha ucuza ve 1-2 saat içinde yapmayı doğal olarak tercih etmektedir. Otobüs ulaşımı, uzun mesafe yolculuklarında kan kaybederken yönünü işlek kısa güzergâhlar üzerine çevirmekte, ancak ayakta kalabilmek içinde yol ücretlerinden taviz vermemektedirler. Otobüsle ulaşımın diğer bir tehlikesi, büyük firmaların, çok da legal olmayan yollarla küçük firmaları yutmasıdır ki otobüs yolcusu onları bırakma eğilimine girdiği takdirde bu büyük firmaların fırtına önündeki genç fidanlar gibi kırılması şaşırtıcı olmaz. Aklı başında ulaşım firmaları ise hava yollarındaki gelişmeleri görerek sektör değiştirmeye hevesli olmakla beraber henüz bu değişimi gerçekleştiren bir firma çıkmamıştır.

Vardığım sonuçların ve ortaya koymaya çalıştığım tüm iyi-kötü gelişmelerin nedeni, bildiriye konu olan süreçteki iç göç hareketleridir. T.C hükümetlerinin yatırımlarını ülke sathına eşit olarak yaymaması, yaşadığı yerde geçimini sağlamayan halkı, olmayan imkanları ile batıya göçe zorlamıştır, Bu iç göç olgusu insanların doğal yaşam çevrelerinden kopmasına, kültür erozyonuna ve ailelerin bölünmesine neden olmuştur. Günümüzde şehirli köylü ayrımı yoktur, bu güzel bir sonuç gibi görülebilir. Ama ayrımın olmaması burada iyi bir şey olarak sunulamaz çünkü aslında yok olan şehirlinin ve köylünün ta kendisidir. Bugün nice insanımız köylülük ve şehirliliği bedenlerinde beraberce ve iliklerine kadar hissetmektedir.

Bu çerçevede, Karayolu gelişimi evet bir gelişmedir ama ülkemizin önünü açan bir gelişme değildir ve umalım ki bu tercihler bir yarışsa halkımız için hayırlı olan kazansın.

Göç/göçer yazını incelemelerinde *Çatışma ve Göç Kültürü Modeli*

Ali Tilbe[336]

Giriş

Kökleri çok eskilere uzanan göç ya da sürgün olgusu, özellikle içinde bulunduğumuz çağın, evrensel sorunsal konularından birisi olarak değerlendirilebilir. Cumhuriyetimizin kuruluşunu izleyen yıllarda, özellikle ellili yıllardan sonra yurtiçinde Doğu'dan Batı'ya, kırsaldan kente göçlerle birlikte, ülkemizdeki kenter sayısı her geçen gün artmakta ve bu göç dalgası günümüzde de sürmektedir. Altmışlı yıllardan sonra, Almanya ve Fransa gibi Avrupa ülkeleri başta olmak üzere, Türkiye'den dünyanın birçok ülkesine göçler yaşanmış, sayısı birkaç milyonu bulan ulusötesi Türk göçer nüfusu ile Türkiye dışgöç olgusunu deneyimlemiştir. Görüldüğü üzere, göç olgusu, göçebe geleneğinden gelen Anadolu insanı için günümüzde de en temel sorunsallardan birisi olarak belirmektedir.

Türk Dil Kurumu *Büyük Türkçe Sözlük*te Göç olgusu; "ekonomik, toplumsal, siyasi sebeplerle bireylerin veya toplulukların bir ülkeden başka bir ülkeye, bir yerleşim yerinden başka bir yerleşim yerine gitme işi, taşınma, hicret, muhaceret" olarak tanımlanmaktadır. Kuşkusuz ekonomik, toplumsal, siyasal ya da ekinsel çok değişik nedenlerden dolayı insanlar, yaşamlarının geri kalan süresini ya da bir bölümünü geçirmek üzere, doğdukları ya da yaşadıkları uzamlardan, köylerden, kentlerden ya da ülkelerden bireysel ya da toplu olarak kesin bir biçimde ya da geçici bir süreyle ayrılmak durumunda kalmaktadırlar. Bu devinimle birlikte göç olgusu da başlamış olmaktadır.

Göçerleri yani göç eden insanları, yeni yerleşim uzamlarında çok çeşitli sorunlar beklemektedir. Özellikle ulusötesi göçerlerin en başat sorunu, öncelikle dil/iletişim konusudur. Bunun yanında iki dillilik (İng. bilingualism), kimlik arayışı (İng. identity), ekinsel parçalanma (İng. cultural fragmentation), toplumsal uyum (İng. social harmony), bütünleşme (İng. integration), yalnızlık, (İng. loneliness), benzeşim (assimilation) ya da yabancılaşma (İng. alienation) gibi konular öne çıkmaktadır (Tilbe ve Sirkeci, 2015, ss. 1-2). Aşmakta zorlandıkları bütün bu sorunlara bağlı olarak, ulusötesi göçerler çoğunlukla bir iyelik, yabansılık, yoksunluk ya da dışlanmışlık duygularıyla iki ekin, yeni değer yargıları ve toplumsal düzen arasında bocalar ve bir başkaldırı ve reddetme duygusuyla içe kapanarak kendi özdeğerlerini ve ekinlerini yeniden kurma ve sürdürme çabasına girerler. Bu arayış, onların yeni yerleşim uzamlarına uyum ve bütünleşme süreçlerini zora sokar. Kuşkusuz benzer sorunların, belli ölçüde yurtiçi göçerler için de geçerli olduğu söylenebilir. Ancak, sonraki kuşak göçerlerde büyük ölçüde olmasa da, bir bütünleşme, uyum ya da benzeşim durumları görülebilmektedir. Doğal olarak bu döngü karşılıklı etkileşimle sürüp gidecektir.

[336] Doç. Dr. Ali Tilbe Namık Kemal Üniversitesi, Fransız Dili ve Edebiyatı Bölümü'nde öğretim üyesidir. 2014-2015 yılları arasında bir yıl süreyle Londra Regent's Üniversitesi, Regent's Ulusötesi Araştırmalar Merkezi'nde doktora sonrası misafir araştırmacı olarak çalışmıştır. E-posta: alitilbe@hotmail.com.

Biz bu çalışmada, ilk olarak kamuoyunda çağrıştırdığı bir takım olumsuz anlamlardan dolayı göçmen sözcüğünü tartışmaya açmak ve İbrahim Sirkeci ile Jeffrey Cohen'in "Not Migrants and Immigration, but Mobility and Movement" adlı ortak makalede; 'göçmen (İng. migrants) ile göç (İng. immigration)' sözcüklerinin yerine önerdikleri, 'göçer / yer değiştiren (İng. movers) ile devinim / hareketlilik (İng. mobilitiy)' kavramlarını kullanmayı yeğlediğimizi vurgulamak istiyoruz.

Göç yazınına genel bir bakış

'Yazın, toplumun bir anlatımıdır' savsözünden devinimle, göçerlerin deneyimlediği bu duygular ile yaşanan bu ve benzeri sorunların anlatımını bulduğu önemli alanlardan birisinin, kuşkusuz yazın ya da sanat uzamı olduğunu görüyoruz. Yazar, düşünür ve sanatçılar, içinden çıktıkları toplumsal belleği ve ortak olası en üst bilinci en iyi biçimde yansıtmayı başarabilmelerinden ötürü, bu yeni yerleşim uzamlarında, kendi sanat, müzik ve yazınlarını yaratmaktan geri kalmamışlardır. Bu yeni yaratı alanı, hem ülke sınırlarında gelişen göç yazınında, hem de ulusötesi göçer yazınında karşılığını bulmuştur. Türk göçünü kapsayan bu yeni yaratı alanı, eleştirmenlerce göç, sürgün, göçmen, yerli ya da konuk işçi yazını gibi değişik adlandırmalarla anılmış ve göç ile yazın ilişkisi bu araştırmalarda ilgi odağı olmaya başlamıştır.

Türkiye'de 50'li yıllara kadar romanlarda daha çok köy ya da kırsal yaşam izlekleri öne çıkmıştır. 50 sonrası endüstri yatırımlarının Batı'ya yönelmesi sonucu olarak, kırsal alanlardan kentlere göç dalgaları başlamış, bu yeni toplumsal durum da Orhan Kemal, Fakir Baykurt gibi toplumcu gerçekçi yazarlarımızın romanlarında göç izleği olarak işlenmiştir. Belli sayıda çağdaş Türk yazarı da iç göç izlekli romanlar yazmayı sürdürmektedir.

Almanya'da yaşayan Türkiye kökenli yazarların çok kısa süre içinde bir yazın geleneği kurduklarını söyleyen, İngiltere'de Swansea Üniversitesi'nden Tom Cheesman[337], 'Novels of Türkich German Settlement': 'Türk-Alman Yerlilerin Romanları' adlı incelemesinde şöyle diyor;

> "bu yazın, 'öteki yazın'dan ayrıldığında metinleri ve yazarları yaşamöyküsel, ulusal ya da etnik köken gibi yazınsal olmayan bir öğeye indirgenir. Bir yazınsal yapıt için bu çok da ilginç değildir. İlginç olduğunda ise bu bir yapıt için en kötüsüdür! Buna karşın 'etnik azınlıktan' birçok yazar, bu topluluğun temsilcisi olma rolünü benimsiyor ya da bu rolü benimsemeye zorlanıyor. Eleştirmen, araştırmacı olarak buna dikkat etmek gerekiyor. Ben kitabımda 'Literature of settlement' kavramını kullandım. 'Settlement', 'yerli' anlamına geliyor. Bu kavramı 'Göçmen Edebiyatı'nın karşıtı olarak kullandım. Bundan başka, göçmen kökenli yeni yazarlar kuşağı göç etmemiş, tersine Almanya'da büyümüş, burada okula ve üniversiteye gitmişlerdir. Bunlar nesnel ve yasal olduğu gibi öznel ve yazınsal olarak ta buraya üyedirler. Kuşkusuz ki, göç süreci hala sürüyor, ancak ekinsel olarak çoktandır başka bir şey yaşanıyor".

Görüldüğü gibi, burada dile getirilmek istenen, izleksel odaklı yazınsal ürünler bütüncesi değil, yeni bir yazın uzamıdır göç/göçer yazını olgusu. Uzama ilişkin kavramsal ayrıklıkların önüne geçmek ve bütüncül bir yapı oluşturmak için tüm bu

---

[337] http://www.yenihayat.de/kutur/yeni-bir-edebiyat-gelenegi-yarattilar

kavramlar ile bu uzamı *göç yazını*, ulusötesinde gelişen yazını da *göçmen* yerine *göçer yazını* olarak adlandırmanın kapsayıcı olacağını düşünmekteyiz.

Günümüzde Almanya'da *göçmen yazını* olarak tanımlanan bu uzamda, 200'den fazla Türkiye kökenli yazar yazınsal ürün vermektedir. Çok değişik izleklerin ele alındığı romanlarda 'delilik, kimlik yitimi, ölüm, hapishane, sınır dışı edilme,' "özlem, vatan sevgisi, ana dili bilinci, barış, özgürlük, asimilasyon karşıtı tutumla paralel gelişme gösteren milliyet bilinci, birlikte yaşama bilinci, ötekileştirme eleştirisi" (Akgün, 2015, s. 80) gibi izlekler öne çıkmaktadır

Buna koşut olarak Almanya, Fransa ve öteki Avrupa ülkelerinde Türkçe yapıtlarıyla tanınan Nedim Gürsel, Yüksel Pazarkaya, Aras Ören, Güney Dal, Levent Aktoprak, Tamer Çağlayan, Aysel Özakın, Gültekin Emre, Yücel Feyzioğlu ile çeşitli nedenlerden dolayı Avrupa'da bulunmak durumunda kalan ve uzun süre o uzamda yazınsal etkinliklerini sürdüren, Zülfü Livaneli, Demir Özlü, Fethi Savaşçı, Fakir Baykurt, Yusuf Ziya Bahadınlı ve Dursun Akçam gibi çok sayıda Türkiye kökenli yazar ve şairimizin yarattığı bir göçer/göçmen/sürgün yazar/yazını da söz konusudur. Öte yandan Almanya'da doğup, büyümüş; Emine Sevgi Özdamar, Renan Demirkan, Saliha Schienhardt, Zafer Şenocak, Zehra Çırak, Metin Fakoğlu, Şinasi Dikmen, Feridun Zaimoğlu, Selim Özdoğan, Serdar Somuncu gibi yapıtlarını Almanca yazanlar ile Belçika'da doğup büyüyen ve yapıtlarını Fransızca yazan Kenan Görgün gibi çok sayıda ikinci kuşak yazar, hem Türk, hem de yabancı okurlar tarafından beğeniyle okunmakta ve saygın yazın ödülleri kazanmaktadırlar. Günümüzde göçer yazını üretiminin büyük bir birikime ulaştığını rahatlıkla söylenebilir.

Göç yazını: yazın toplumbilimsel bağlamda *çatışma ve göç kültürü modeli*

Yazın ve göç ilişkisini ortaya koymak için, göç izlekli yapıtları ele alırken, öncelikli devinim noktasının, yazının toplumsallığını ve bilgilendirme işlevine iye olduğunu kesinlemek gerekir. Doğal olarak bir göç yapıtını anlamak ve açıklamak için, toplumsalcı bir bakış açısıyla yaklaşmak tutarlı ve birlikçi bir çözümlemeye götürebilir yazın eleştirmenlerini. Karşı durumunda yapılacak çalışmalar, izleksel bir bütünce oluşturmaktan öteye gidemez. Marksçı yazının, "yapıt bireyin değil, toplumun bir anlatımıdır" (Tilbe-Tilbe, 2015, s. 188) savından devinimle, üretilen yapıt ile üretimin içinden çıktığı toplumsal yapı arasında var olan yadsınamaz türdeşlikleri ortaya koymak, bunu yaparken de değişik yazınsal ve toplumsal eleştiri yöntemlerinden ve uygulayımlarından yararlanmak özgün bir çözümlemeye götürebilecektir eleştirmeni. Yazın ile toplumun birbirinden bağımsız olarak anlaşılması olası değildir. Kuşkusuz yazının, bir kurmaca evrenin parçası olduğu gerçeğini unutmaksızın, birebir toplumsal gerçekliği öykülediğini ileri sürmek bizi çeşitli gerçeklik ve kurmaca arasında örüntülenen yanılgılara götürebilir. Ancak yazın kurmaca nitelikli olsa bile, inceleme nesnesi toplumsal yapı ile ilintili olmak ve ondan etkilenmek durumundadır. Bu bağlamda yazın toplumbilimi, ya da yaygın deyişle edebiyat sosyolojisi kuramı göç araştırmacıları için bir inceleme yöntemi olarak birçok olanak sunacaktır.

Bunun yanında göç yapıtlarının çözümlenmesinde genel göç kuram ve inceleme yöntemlerinin de eleştirmenlere yöntemsel ve uygulayımsal olanaklar sunacağı açıktır. Bu bağlamda genel kuramsal yaklaşımlardan devinimle yeni karma bir eleştirel yaklaşım benimsemek göç yazını incelemeleri için bir gereklilik olarak görünmektedir. Göç kavramının yalnızca toplumsal bir devinim olmadığı, bireysel devinimlerin de belirleyici olduğu düşünüldüğünde, Sirkeci ve Cohen'in, Alman toplumbilimci Ralf Dahrendorf'un (1929-2009) (*Sanayi Toplumunda Sınıf ve Sınıf Çatışması*, 1959), şiddetle eşanlamlı olmayan çatışma tanımından devinimle geliştirmiş oldukları; "hayata karşı bir itirazı, beklentisi ve mücadelesi olan insanların ortaya koyduğu göç, dikkate değer bir meydan okumadır" (Sirkeci ve Erdoğan, 2012, s. 298) varsayımına dayanan *çatışma ve göç kültürü* modelinin, bütün göç kuramları içinde; özelde ulusötesi, genelde tüm göç romanlarının çözümlenmesi bağlamında açıklayıcı olacağını düşünmekteyiz. Bu yaklaşımımızla, araştırmaların alanlar arası karşılıklı etkileşiminin altını çizmek isteriz. Kanımızca, genel göç kuramları içinde ulusötesi bireysel ve toplumsal göç devinimlerini en tutarlı biçimde açıklayabileceğini varsaydığımız eğilimdir çatışma modeli. Kuşkusuz bu model ile çözümleme yaparken, yazın toplumbilimi ile görüngübilimin eleştirel olanaklarından da yararlanarak modeli yazın incelemelerine uyarlamak gerekecektir. Sirkeci bu modelin öteki göç kuramlarına göre üstünlüğünü şöyle sıralar:

> "*a) Göçü iki yer arasındaki görece çekiciliğin sonucu olarak bir yerden bir yere hareket olarak gören 'itme-çekme' modelinin sıkıcılığından, b) ağ modellerinin kendi kendini doğrulama yanılgısından (Mertofl, 1959:423), c) uluslararası göçün bürokratik olarak 12 aydan daha fazla süreyle ikamet değişikliği olarak tanımlanmasından, d) göçmenler-göç etmeyenler gibi karşıtlıklardan, e) gönüllü-zorunlu göç, ekonomik-siyasi göç gibi kuramsal olarak göç davranışını anlamamıza katkısı olmayan yaklaşımlardan uzaklaşma olanağı ve alanı sağlar*" (Sirkeci, 2012 ss. 353-354).

Görüldüğü gibi, bu kuram; "zorunlu ve gönüllü göç ayrımını reddederek, her düzeydeki çatışmaların, gerilimlerin, zorluk ve anlaşmazlıkların insanların ve grupların yer değiştirmesine neden olduğu gerçeğinden hareketle, her göçün şu veya bu biçimde bir çatışma üzerine kurulduğunu" (Tilbe ve Sirkeci, 2015, s. 1) varsaymaktadır. Şurası bir gerçektir ki, "kökleri çok eskilere uzanan göç ve sürgün olguları, özellikle içinde bulunduğumuz çağda süregiden savaşlar ve gerilimler ile devinerek karşımıza çıkmaya devam edecek gibi" (s. 1) görünmektedir. Tarihin çeşitli dönemlerinde ulusal, dinsel, siyasal, ırksal ve benzeri çok sayıda çatışma biçimi, insanlarda bulundukları uzamlarda güvensizlik duygusu uyandırarak, bireysel ya da toplu göçleri tetiklemiş ve büyük acılara yok açmıştır. Bunun en son örneğini, günümüzde süren Irak ve Suriye iç çatışmaları sırasında, milyonlarca kişinin göç etmek zorunda kalmasında görebiliyoruz. Devingen ve karmaşık bir olgu olan göç devinimini, Türkiye içinde ve Türkiye'den Avrupa'ya yoğun olarak yaşanmış olan göçlerde görmemiz olasıdır. Çatışmanın sonucu olarak beliren göç etme olgusu üzerine kurgulanan romanlarda uygulanabilecek olan bu modelinin yazın araştırmaları için tutarlı görünmektedir.

Bu modelde öne çıkan anahtar sözcük, ulusötesilik ve güvensizlik kavramlarıdır. Sirkeci'ye göre;

> "*Ulusötesilik, "lineer göç modellerinden sınır aşan insan hareketlerinin sirküler, dalgalanan ve dinamik bağlar oluşturan bir kuramsal çerçeveye yönelmemize imkan sağlamaktadır. Bu sayede varılan yer yerine, çoklu hem burada hem orada durumları kavramsallaştırılabilmektedir. Transnasyonalizm süreç ve hareketliliğe vurgu yaparken*

ulusu ademi merkeziyetleştirerek yerellik ötesine geçen, farklı yerellikleri birleştiren aidiyet ve kimliklere referans verir. (Werbner 1999- Wimmer ve Glick-Schiller, 2003). Bunun gelecekte göçerler için temel aidiyet normu olacağı iddia edilmektedir (Castles, 2002, s. 1158)" (Sirkeci, 2012, s. 354).

Ulusötesi göçerler, ulus devletlerin ulus devletlerin yönetme gücünü zora sokmakta, "devletlerin sınırlarını, ulusal kimliklerini ve kendi vatandaşlarını kontrol etme yeteneğine meydan okumaktadırlar" (Koser, 2007: 242, aktaran, Sirkeci, 2012, s. 354). Ulusötesilik kavramı özellikle göçer yazın alanını sarıp sarmalayan bir olgudur. Modelde söz edildiği gibi, ikidillilik, ikiekinlilik ve hem orada hem burada olma durumu ile ilintili iyelik ve kimlik sorunları söz konusu olmaktadır. Bu durum, sınırlarını korumak için her çeşit önlemi almaya çalışan ulus devletleri sarsmaktadır.

İnsan güvenliği denilince hemen usa tolum ve devlet güvenliği gelmektedir. Ancak devletin güvenli olması insanın güvende olması anlamına gelmemektedir. Özellikle baskıcı dizgelerde, devlet güvendedir ancak baskıya uğrayan kişi ve toplumlar büyük güvenlik sorunu yaşamaktadırlar. İnsani güvenlik kavramının öncülerinden Amartya Sen'e göre; insan güvenliği, "hayatta kalma, günlük hayat ve onurlu bir yaşama hakkına yönelik tehditlere ve bu tehditlerle baş etme çabalarıyla" (2000:1) ilişkilidir (Aktaran, Sirkeci, 2012, s. 355).

Abraham Maslow'a göre; gereksinimler önem sırasına göre sıralanırken, temel gereksinimler olan *"hava, gıda, barınma ve seksten"* (1943) hemen sonra güvenlik ve korunma gelir (Aktaran, Sirkeci, 2012, s. 355). Toplumsal gönenç insan güvenliği için temel olgudur, yoksulluk ve derinleşen eşitsizlik ve işsizlik güvenliği tehlikeye atacak temel kaygılardır. İnsani Güvensizlik Endeksinde, "insani güvenliğini tehlikeye atanın sadece askeri tehditler değil aynı zamanda kaynak yetersizliği, hızlı nüfus artışı, insan hakları ihlalleri, salgın hastalıklar, çevre kirliliği, kirlenme ve biyolojik çeşitliliğin yok olması" (Homer-Dixon, 1994, aktaran, Sirkeci, 2012, s. 355) gibi nedenlere vurgu yapılır. Sirkeci'ye göre; "insani güvensizlik belli bir yerde, belli bir durumdaki belli bir insan topluluğu ve/veya bireyler için çatışmanın bir tür yoksunluk, yoksulluk hissi yaratması olarak görülebilir" (Sirkeci, 2012, s. 355).

Kuşkusuz güven ve güvensizlik algısı göreli ve özneldir, özdeksel ve özdeksel olmayan nedenlerden ötürü kişiden kişiye, aileden aileye, toplumdan topluma dünya görüşlerine ve toplumsal konumlarına göre değişiklik gösterir. Sivil ve toplumsal çatışmalar, savaşlar, çevresel yıkımlar, azınlık grubu üyeleri için kendini, anadilini, ekinini ve dinsel törenlerini özgürce gerçekleştirememe gibi siyasal, dinsel ve ekinsel nedenlerden dolayı baskı ve huzursuzluk duyumsama, artırımsal olanakların ve fırsatların yetersizliği, yüksek işsizlik oranları, düşük gelir, tsunami ve kuraklık gibi doğal yıkımlar, varsıllar ile yoksullar arasında beliren sınıfsal çatışmalar gibi çok sayıda etkenden söz edilebilir. Kimi zaman da bu sayılan olayların birçoğu bir arada görülebilir ve çatışma tehlikesini artırabilir.

Görüldüğü gibi, ulusötesi göçlerdeki temel etkenin insanların güvenlik arayışı olan güvensizlik ortamından güvenlik ortamına doğru nüfus akımları olması, başka bir deyişle "algılanan (insani) güvensizlikten kaçınma olarak formüle edilebilir" (Sirkeci, 2012, s. 356). Bu bağlamda, itme-çekme modeline göre de güvensizliği itme, güvenliği de çekme etkeni olarak ilişkilendirmek olasıdır.

Sirkeci'nin tanımı, en gizli ve örtülü gerilimlerden en şiddetli çatışmalara kadar toplumsal yapı içinde ereklerin uyuşmadığı tüm ilişkileri kapsar. "Bu çatışmalar da etnik ve veya dinsel, politik nedeni: olmak zorunda değil. Ona göre çatışma sadece —isyanlar, savaşlar, silahlı çatışmalar gibi- deklare edilmiş karşılaşmalarda değil aynı zamanda yarışmalarda, kapışmalarda, anlaşmazlıklarda ve gerilimlerde de vardır" (Aktaran, Sirkeci, 2012, s. 356).

Şekil 1: İnsani güvenlik ve çatışma eksenleri

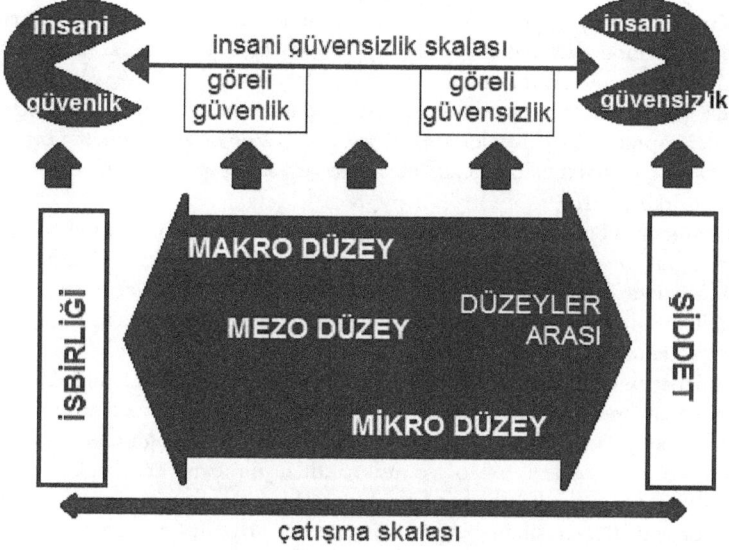

Kaynak: Sirkeci, 2012

Sirkeci, çatışmayı bir süreklilik gösterge çizelgesi üzerinde tanımlar. Bir uçta insani güvenliğin sağlandığı, anlaşma ve işbirliğine dayalı eşitlik durumu, öteki uçta ise uzlaşmanın yerini şiddete bıraktığı güvensizlik yani çatışma durumu söz konusudur. Sirkeci bu durumu aşağıdaki çizelgede görselleştirmiştir (s. 357). Uluslararası işçi değişim anlaşmaları işbirliğine, savaş ve çatışma bölgelerinde kaçan sığınmacı krizleri de şiddet ve çatışma durumuna örnek olarak verilebilir.

Bu gösterge çizelgesine göre, göç bir insani güvenlik arayışı anlamıma gelmektedir. Ulusötesi alan *"çatışma potansiyeli ile örülü bir çatışma alanıdır"* (Rummell, 1976, aktaran, Sirkeci, 2012, s. 357). Sürekli bir göç olgusuyla karşı karşıya kalan ulusötesi alan, her an çatışmaya açıktır ve sürekli çatışma ve değişime uğrayan yeni göç yolları ile dönüşmektedir.

İnsani güvensizlik ortamına uğrayan insanların önünde iki seçenek vardır: "statükoyu devam ettirmek ve b) çıkış. Statüko opsiyonunu seçenler temel olarak oldukları yerde kalırlar ve hakim olan görüş, taraf, etnisite ve/veya hükümetle uzlaşırlar ya da onu kabul ederler; çıkış seçeneği ise isyancılara katılmak ve göçü de içeren çatışma bölgesini terk etmeyi içerir" (Sirkeci, 2006) Bunların arasında birey, aile ve toplulukların başvurduğu karma yöntemler de görülebilir.

Şurası bir gerçektir ki, insani güvensizlik algısı her zaman göçle sonuçlanmayabilir. Göç insani güvensizlik ortamına (İGO) (Sirkeci, 2006, 2007,

Cohen ve Sirkeci, 2011) uğrayanlar için önemli seçeneklerden yalnızca birisidir. İGO maddi "(örn. silahlı çatışma, yoksulluk, işsizlik, kötü altyapı) ve maddi olmayan (örn. ayrımcılık, baskı, insan hakları ihlalleri, cezalandırılma korkusu, anadil sınırlamaları)" (Sirkeci, 2012, s. 358) güvensizlik öğeleri içerir (Sirkeci, 2006, 2005a) ve bunlar çoğunlukla çatışmalardan ileri gelir.

Bu modelde temel olarak 3 çatışma düzeyi tanımlanmaktadır:

Makro (örn. Gönderen, transit ve göç alan ülkelerin çatışan siyasi tercihleri), *mezo* (örn. Göç eden ve göç etmeyen haneler arası gerilimler, hanehalkı içerisinde cinsiyet rollerinden kaynaklı gerilimler), *mikro* (örn. Bireyler arası çatışmalar, göçmenler ile göçmen olmayanlar arası gerilimler) ve de *bu düzeyler arası* (örn. Sınır güvenlik görevlileri, vize görevlileri vb. ve göç eden bireyler arası gerilimler). Bu çatışmalar çapraz -yani düzeyler arası da olabilir. Örneğin devlete karşı birey veya bireye karşı hanehalkı/aile (mezo) veya bireye karşı birey (mikro) düzeylerinde olabilir" (Sirkeci, 2012, s. 359).

Bir çatışmaya bağlı olarak gelişen makro düzeyde göçleri yönetmek için, göçer akınına uğrayan ülkelerin oluşturmaya çalıştığı bir ulusötesi yönetim birimi kurulması girişimleri söz konusudur. Bu karşılıklı uzlaşma çabalarının sonucu olsa da genellikle bir makro çatışmaya her an açık alandır. Romanlarda genellikle bu düzeyde izlekler sıklıkla görülmekte, Yahudi ve Türk göçlerinde bu durumlar deneyimlenmektedir. Köken ülkelerde azınlık gruplarının kimi istekleri ile ulusal çıkarlar çatıştığında zorunlu göçler söz konusu olabilir. Ulusötesi göçlerin bir sonucu olarak geride kalan aile bireyleri arasında cinsiyete bağlı olarak aile içinde yönetim kurma istekleri mezo ve mikro düzeyde cinsiyete bağlı çatışmaları tetikleyebilir. Eşini bırakarak yurtdışına çıkan bir aile reisinin işlevini üstlenmek için geride kalanlar arasında bir çatışma çıkabilir. Bunun gibi çok sayıda örnek vermek olasıdır.

Kuşkusuz modelde belirlenen bu düzeysel ayrımlar, yazın araştırmacılarının incelemelerini konumlandırabilmeleri için çok yol gösterici işlev üstlenmektedir. Özellikle romanlarda ele alınan göç durumu ve konulara göre kolaylıkla düzeyler belirlenebilir ve anlatı yerlemleri ile olay örgüsü bu düzlemde incelenerek açıklayıcı sonuçlar elde edilebilir. Bu modelden devinimle, romanların ulamlandırılması da kolaylaşacaktır.

Bu bağlamda, göç yapıtlarının incelemesinde, Lucien Goldmann'ın (bkz, *Roman Sosyolojisi*, 2005) yazın toplumbilimsel metinleri çözümlemek için de kullanılan, görüngübilimsel *anlama* ve *açıklama* düzeylerinden oluşacak iki aşamalı bir çözümleme yöntemi öneriyoruz:

Tablo. 1

Anlama Aşaması > İçkin Çözümleme ↓	Açıklama Aşaması > Aşkın Çözümleme ↓
Anlatı Yerlemleri → Kişi, Süre, Uzam	Dönemsel Göç Devinimleri ve Toplumsal Yapı
Anlatının Yapısı → Bakış Açıları; Anlatım Uygulayımları	Öne Çıkan Temel İzlekler

Mikro, Mezo, Makro Düzeylerin Belirlenmesi→ Göçten Önceki Toplumsal Konum	Göçten Sonraki Toplumsal Konum
Göç Olgusu → Göreli Güvensizlik Uzamı; Çatışma ve Göç Devinimi	Göreli Güvenlik Uzamı → İşbirliği mi? Bütünleşme mi? Ayrışma mı?

Bu yönteme göre, birinci aşama anlama düzeyi, yapısalcı bir yaklaşımla metne içkin olarak gerçekleştirilir ve metinde yer alan anlatı yerlemleri ile anlatısal uygulayımlar incelendikten sonra, çatışma modeline göre; göçer toplumsal yapı ve ilişkilerden oluşan yapıtın özü ve iç tutarlılığı çözümlenir, metne aşkın olan açıklama aşamasında ise; metinde söz edilen göç olgusu/izleği, çatışma modeli temelinde, yapıtı aşan ve çevreleyen toplumsal, ekonomik ve siyasal dışsal bağlanımlarıyla güvensizlik ◇ güvenlik düzleminde açıklanır ve tutarlı bir eleştirel yaklaşım ortaya konulabilir. Bunun sonucunda da göç metinleri, salt izleksel çözümlemeler olmak yerine, dizgesel bir eleştirel yaklaşıma kavuşmuş olabilecektir. Bu çözümleme önerisi, Sirkeci ve Cohen'in *çatışma ve göç kültürü modeli* ile Goldmann'ın *oluşumsal yapısalcılık* adını verdiği yazın toplumbilimi inceleme yöntemine dayandırılan karma bir yaklaşımdır.

Sonuç

İnceleme nesnesinin salt bir izlek ya da ileti aracı olarak görülmemesi, onun yazınsal bir olgu olduğunu unutmadan, o nesnenin yazınsal değer ve niteliğinin yazınsal inceleme uygulayım ve yöntemleri aracılığıyla ortaya konması önemlidir. Şurası unutulmamalıdır ki, her değerli yazınsal ürünün, yazın eleştirisinin genel geçer kurallarına uygun olarak oluşturulması önceliklidir. Doğal olarak her göç izlekli yapıtı, göç yazını çerçevesi içine almak yazınsal bağlamda olanaklı olmayacaktır. Bu bağlamda bir ulamsal değerlendirme ile bu yapıtların ele alınması gerekir. Kuşkusuz bu nitelik sorunu daha çok, ulusötesi Türk göçer yazını bağlamında düşünülmelidir. Fakir Baykurt, Nedim Gürsel, Zülfü Livaneli gibi Türkiye'de yazın geleneği içinde yer alan yazarların yapıtları, genel olarak yazınsal kurgu bağlamında yüksek nitelikli olarak değerlendirilebilir. Bu sorun daha çok ulusötesi göçten sonra, karşı uzamlarda sonradan yazarlık serüvenine atılanların yapıtlarında daha belirgin olarak görülebilir. Bütün bu değerlendirmeleri, yazın toplumsal bir yaklaşımla çatışma ve göç kültürü modeli çerçevesinde kurgulayarak gerçekleştirmek, hem biçimsel, hem de biçemsel ve izleksel olarak romanların iyi anlanmasına ve açıklanmasına olanak vermesi, göç yazını araştırmalarına yeni bir açılım getirebilmesi umulmaktadır.

Kaynakça

Akgün, A. (2015). "Türk Edebiyatı Bağlamında Edebiyat-Göç İlişkisi ve Göçmen Edebiyatları Üzerine Bir Değerlendirme", *Göç Dergisi*, Cilt: 2, Sayı: 1, ss. 69 – 84.
Cheesman T. (2015). 'Novels of Türkich German Settlement'. http://www.yenihayat.de/kutur/yeni-bir-edebiyat-gelenegi-yarattilar, Erişim Tarihi: 05.04.2015.
Goldmann, L. (2005). *Roman Sosyolojisi*. (çev. Ayberk Erkay). Ankara: Birleşik Kitabevi.
Sirkeci, I. (2006). *The Environment of Insecurity in Turkey and the Emigration of Turkish Kurds to Germany*. New York, US: Edwin Mellen Press.

Sirkeci, İ. (December 2012). "Transnasyonal mobilite ve çatışma", *Migration Letters*, Volume: 9, No: 4, pp. 353 – 363.

Sirkeci, İ. ve Cohen, J.H. (July 2013) "Not Migrants and Immigration, but Mobility and Movement". Erişim Tarihi: 07.05.2015, http://citiesofmigration.ca/ezine_stories/not-migrants-and-immigration-but-mobility-and-movement/

Sirkeci, İ. ve Erdoğan, M-M. (December 2012). "Editoryal: Göç ve Türkiye", *Migration Letters*, Volume: 9, No: 4, pp. 297 – 302.

Tibe, A. ve Tilbe F. (2015). "Reşat Enis Aygen'in Afrodit Buhurdanında Bir Kadın Adlı Romanında Çalışma İlişkileri: Yazıntoplumbilimsel Oluşumsal Yapısalcı Bir İnceleme". *Humanitas - Uluslararası Sosyal Bilimler Dergisi / Humanitas - International Journal of Social Sciences*, Bahar / Spring, Sayı / Number 5, pp. 187-216 , TEKİRDAĞ.

Büyük Türkçe Sözlük, Türk Dil Kurumu. Erişim Tarihi: 07.06.2015, http://www.tdk.org.tr/index.php?option=com_bts&arama=kelime&guid=TDK.GTS.55eb2f1 1c29c80.64053286

Menekşe Toprak'ın Öykülerinde Almanya'ya Göç'ün Farklı Yüzleri

Nesime Ceyhan Akca[338]

Giriş

Göç, insanlık tarihinin hiçbir döneminde yok olmamış, çeşitli sebeplerle varlığını daima korumuş bir olgudur. Yaşamı başka yerde sürdürme kararı kolay bir karar değildir. Savaşlar, tabii afetler, can ve mala dair emniyetsizlik, geçim sıkıntıları, siyasal baskılar, daha özgür yaşama arzusu, göç için, bilhassa kitlesel göç hareketleri için temel sebeplerdir ve kişilerin çoğu kez bu hallerde fazla düşünme şansları yoktur. Sürgün de kişilerin yahut kitlelerin üzerinde fazla düşünme şansının olmadığı bir tür göçtür. Bir de başka bir mekânda hayatı devam ettirmeyi arzulayan, tamamen şahsın iç dünyasının arzusuna göre şekillenen mekân değiştirmeler vardır. Daha çok ferden (yahut eş ve çocuklarla) gerçekleşen bu yer değiştirmeler de bu gruplar içerisinde anılabilirler; çünkü neticeleri itibariyle kültürleşme, entegrasyon, kimlik sorunları vs. bu göçlerde de benzer sorunlar olarak ortaya çıkar.

Orta Asya bozkırlarından Avrupa ortalarına kadar ilerleyen Türklerin göç'le ne kadar içli dışlı oldukları ortadadır. Moğol akınları yahut coğrafi şartların elverişsizliği sebepleri dışında yeni yurtlara açılmayı İlây-ı Kelimetullah (Allah'ın adını yeryüzüne yayma, fetih) ya da Kızıl Elma'ya ulaşmak gibi ideallerle beslenen bir toplumun mekân değiştirmenin güçlüklerini psikolojik olarak kolaylaştırmış olduğunu düşünebiliriz.

Türklerin 20. Yüzyılın ikinci yarısında en büyük kitlesel göçünün Avrupa'ya, özellikle de Almanya'ya işçi göçü olarak gerçekleştiğini söylemeliyiz. İkinci Dünya Savaşı ardından yerle bir olan Avrupa ülkelerinin sanayide ve yıkımların tadilinde çalıştırmak üzere birbiri ardınca Akdeniz ülkelerine (İtalya, Yunanistan, İspanya) gönderdikleri işçi davetlerine ve devletlerarası işçi kabulü antlaşmalarına Türkiye de (1961) dâhil olur. 1950'li yıllarda elemeği ihtiyacı en üst seviyede olan Avrupa ülkeleri göçmen işçi kabulünün geçici bir müddet süreceğini öngörmüş; ancak süreç, beklenenin dışında ihtiyaç azaldığı yahut ortadan kalktığı 1970'li yıllarda ve sonrasında da engellenememiştir.

Türkler 1955 sonrası birçok Avrupa ülkesine (Hollanda, Belçika, Danimarka, Avusturya, İsveç, İsviçre, İngiltere, Fransa) işçi göndermekle birlikte göçün en fazla gerçekleştiği ülke Almanya'dır. Cemâl Yalçın'ın Göç Sosyolojisi adlı eserine göre 1960 yılında Almanya'ya giden Türk işçilerin sayısı 2 700 iken bu sayı 1963'te 10 katına çıkarak 27.500 olmuş ve 1973 yılına gelindiğinde ise yarım milyonu çoktan geçmiştir (Yalçın, 2004, s. 134). "Günümüzde Almanya'da yaşayan yaklaşık 2.700.000 Türk'ün Almanya'ya entegrasyonu, sosyolojik, siyasi ve ekonomik açıdan önemli bir konudur." (Şahin, 2010, s. 105).

---

[338] Doç.Dr., Çankırı Karatekin Üniversitesi Edebiyat Fakültesi, Türk Dili ve Edebiyatı Bölümü, 18100 Çankırı, Türkiye. E-mail: nesimeceyhan@hotmail.com

Başlangıçta, biraz kazanıp memlekete geri dönmek niyetiyle başlayan ve ailelerini geride bırakarak gerçekleşen göç, 70'li yıllarda eşlerin ve çocukların Almanya'ya getirilmesiyle yeni bir sürece evrilmiştir. Bu durum, misafirliğin uzayacağını haber verir. Ailelerin birleşmesi, gelen çocukların ve Almanya'da doğacak olan çocukların problemlerine (sağlık, eğitim, entegrasyon) başlangıç olarak görülür.

Cemal Yalçın, yabancı ülkelerde yaşayan ikinci ve sonraki kuşak Türklerin sorunlarına dair iki genel yaklaşımdan söz eder. Klasik yaklaşım olarak da anılan birinci yaklaşım, ikinci kuşağın yaşadığı kültürel farklılıkların tehlikeli bir gelişme kaydettiği yönündedir. Çok az Türk kültürü, buna karşılık yabancı kültürden fazlaca etkilenme bunun neticesi olarak karşı kültüre daha fazla yaklaşma ve benzeme olarak özetlenen ilk yaklaşım, acilen Türk toplumunun Türk kültürü eğitimi alacak imkânlara kavuşturulmasını tavsiye eder.

"İkinci yaklaşım, daha çok melez kimlikler üzerinde yoğunlaşmakta, ikinci ve sonraki kuşak yurtdışında yaşayan Türklerin hem yaşadıkları ülkenin kültüründen hem de Türk kültüründen parçalar taşıdıklarına ve dolayısıyla kendilerini tarif etmek için melez kimlikler geliştirdiklerine dikkat çekmektedir. Bu yaklaşım, durumun aslında korkulacak bir şey olmadığını iddia etmektedir." (Yalçın, 2004, s. 168).

Almanya'ya giden ilk kuşağın yaşadığı birçok talihsizlikle bu ikinci kuşak tabii olarak karşılaşmayacaktır. İlk gidenlerin nasıl olsa dönecekler düşüncesiyle toplumdan yalıtılmaları, yok sayılmaları, vasıflarının çok altında işlerde çalıştırılmaları, temel insanî ihtiyaçlarının karşılanmasında ağırdan alınması; ikinci ve sonraki neslin bilhassa dil bilmesi ve Alman kültürünü tanıması, haklarını sorgulamaya başlamaları sebebiyle oldukça azalmıştır; ancak bu durum, yeni neslin ırkçı fiili saldırılar yaşamaları sürecini de artırmıştır. İlk neslin yazdıkları edebî metinler yaşadıkları yabancı toplumunun ilgisini çekmezken, ikinci ve sonraki kuşak Türk yazarların yazdıkları ev sahibi toplumlarda ilgi çekmeye bilhassa iki kültürlü gözün penceresinden kendi toplumlarını görme ihtiyacı belirmeye başlamıştır.

"Nuran Özyer, Almanya'da yazan Türkler tarafından yaratılan edebiyatı artık; konuk işçilerden oluşan yazarların, entelektüel göçmen yazarların, entelektüel konuk işçilerin ve konuk işçilerin çocukları olan genç yazarlar kuşağının yazdığı edebiyat olmak üzere dört grup altında toplayabileceğimizi ifade etmektedir. 60'lı yıllarda yazmaya başlayan Türkleri, içinde yaşadığı toplumun dilini ana dilinden daha iyi konuşan, o toplumun okullarında eğitim görmüş ve o toplumun kültürüne daha yakın yetişmiş ikinci, üçüncü kuşak izler. İkinci kuşak yazarlar, birinci kuşağa oranla yaşadıkları ve yazdıkları toplumun içinde daha fazla ilgi çekmektedirler." (Özbakır, 2000, s. 212).

Makalemize eserleriyle esas teşkil edecek olan Menekşe Toprak, yukarıdaki sınıflamada "konuk işçilerin çocukları" grubuna dâhil edilebilir.

Menekşe Toprak'ın hikâyelerinde göç'ün farkli halleri

Menekşe Toprak, 1970 yılında Kayseri'de dünyaya gelmiştir. Anne ve babası Almanya'ya giden ilk kuşak işçilerdendir. İlk ve ortaöğrenimini Köln ve Ankara'da yapar. Başlangıçta köyde akrabaları yanında bırakılan tipik bir Almancı işçi ailesi çocuğudur. İlerleyen senelerde (9 yaşında) o da Almanya'ya alınır. Almanca bilmediği için iki yıl Türk sınıfında eğitim alır. Lise bitince Türkiye'de üniversite okumasının daha iyi olacağı düşünülerek tekrar Türkiye'ye teyzelerinin yanına gönderilir. Ankara'da Ankara Üniversitesi Siyasal Bilgiler Fakültesini bitirdikten sonra Ankara ve Berlin'de dört yıl kadar bir bankanın elemanı olarak çalışır. 2002 yılından günümüze gazetecilik ve çevirmenlik yapan yazar, Berlin ve İstanbul'da yaşamaktadır. Hikâyeleri Almanca, Fransızca, İtalyanca ve İngilizceye çevrilen genç yazar, bu ülkelerin edebiyat dergilerinde ve öykü antolojilerinde yer almıştır. Hâlihazırda iki öykü kitabı (Valizdeki Mektup, YKY 2007; Hangi Dildedir Aşk, YKY 2009) ve iki romanı (Temmuz Çocukları, YKY 2011; Ağıtın Sonu, İletişim 2014) vardır (Kahraman, 2013). Biz burada ağırlıklı olarak iki hikâye kitabına odaklanacağız.

Gürsel Aytaç, ikinci kuşak Türk genç yazarların yazdıklarında azınlık ve kimlik gibi problemlerin ön sıralarda ele alınsalar bile, salt evrensel ve insana ilişkin konuların da dile getirildiğine işaret ediyor (Aytaç, 1991, s. 155). Menekşe Toprak, bu çerçeveye rahatlıkla oturtulabilecek bir kadın yazardır. Hikâyelerinde iki kültür ve toplum arasında sürekli gidip gelse de bilhassa kadın duyarlılıklarını, kültürlerin üzerinden, salt kadın kimliği olarak yakalayabilmiş olması önemli görünüyor. Bir başka nokta ise içerisinde göçmen sıfatıyla bulunduğu Alman toplumuna yahut devletine herhangi bir suçlayıcı bakışın eserlerinde görülmemesidir. Türkler de Almanlar da eşit insanî zaaf ve eksikliklerle ele alınmışlardır.

Hikâyelerde toplumsal cinsiyet, göç ve kadın kimliği

Öncelikle söylememiz gereken Menekşe Toprak'ın kadın kimliğini merkeze alarak yazdığıdır. Hikâyelerinin birçoğunun otobiyografik özellikte olması da yazarın kendinden hareketle ve kadın duyarlılığını öne alarak yazdığını işaret ediyor. Yabancı bir toplumun içinde tüm kadınlıklarıyla var olmaya çalışan kadınların hikâyeleridir elimizdekiler. Hikâyelerdeki kadın kahramanların çoğu bekârdır, eşini yahut sevgilisini ya terk etmiş yahut terk edilmişlerdir. Bu kadınlar, bir Alman'a âşık olmaktan yahut bir Alman'la beraber olmaktan/evlenmekten/birlikte yaşamaktan çekinmezler. "Valizdeki Mektup", adlı hikâyede kahraman genç kız, Peter adlı bir Alman gence âşıktır ve onunla mektuplaşmaktadır. "Yokuştaki Kız" ve "Doğuda Bir Yerde" hikâyelerinde geçen Berlin'de doğup büyümüş Türk kızı Aylin de Sevim de, erkeklerini terk etmiştir. "Ah! Şarap İçerken Bir de Gazete Okusam" adlı hikâyenin kahramanı Maraşlı Emine, eşi Türkiye'de ve hâlâ nikâhlı kocası konumunda iken senelerce Franz'la birlikte yaşar.

Hikâyelerine odaklanılan Türk kadınların Almanlar içerisinde geleneksel Türk kadınını temsil etmedikleri açıktır; buna rağmen Almanların geleneksel Türk kadını anlayışından haberdar olarak Türk kadınlarını "namus budalaları" olarak görmeleri hikâyelere yansır. Yazar, "Eve Dönüş" adlı hikâyesinde bir Alman kadın kahramanına "Türk kadınları namus budalaları olarak bilindiklerine göre, kadının bakire olması işten bile değil." (Toprak, 2007, s. 37) dedirterek yaşı geçkin ve bekâr bir Türk kızı hakkında Alman toplumunun muhtemel düşüncelerini aktarır.

Türk kadını için Alman toplumu bekâret meselesini bu şekilde aşağılarken, Türk toplumu kadınlarına farklı sorumluluklar yüklemektedir. Bekâret, önemli bir sosyal baskı ve kontrol unsurudur. "Güzel Bir Gün" adlı hikâyede kahramanın ablası bekâretini koruyabilmek için gizli ilişkisini sürdürürken sağlığını hiçe sayan yollara başvuruyor; kahraman genç kız ise ablasının aksine ailesi hatırına sevdiği adamla el değmeden evleniyor; baba ve anne kızlarıyla gurur duyuyor. Aynı hikâyede eşinden ayrılan halanın mastürbasyonu aktarılarak ailenin kadın cephesinden bir başka trajik yanı ifade buluyor.

Genel olarak Türk aileler, çocuklarının gayrı meşru ilişkilerinden hoşnut değildirler. "Valizdeki Mektup", adlı hikâyede Meryem Teyze'nin eşi öldükten sonra yetiştirdiği çocuklarından söz edilirken, yabancı biriyle birlikte yaşayan kızı üzeri örtülerek anılır:

"Meryem Teyze 1961 yılında kocasından da önce gelenlerdendi. Çok iyi Almanca konuşuyordu. Kocası yıllar önce genç yaşta kanserden ölmüş, o da bir daha evlenmemişti. Benim Memo Abi dediğim oğlu ve biri Türkiye'de evlenip orada kalan, diğeri de –o sözünü pek etmese de herkes biliyordu- bir Alman'la yaşayan kızlarını tek başına yetiştirmişti. Hep canlı, neşeli, harika hikâyeler anlatan, ak pak, şişmanca bir kadındı." (Toprak, 2007, s. 14).

"Ah! Şarap İçerken Bir de Gazete Okusam" adlı hikâyedeki Emine, ise Alman Franz'la uzun yıllar bir Alman gibi yaşaması noktasında ailesi tarafından eleştirilmiş, daha fenası tüm aile, bir kız kardeşi hariç, Emine ile irtibatı kesmiştir: "Ailesi içinde tek görüştüğü kimse olan kız kardeşi, tam bir Alman olup çıktığını söyleyıp dururdu her fırsatta kendisine." (Toprak, 2007: 105). Görüldüğü gibi Türk kadınları için yaşadıkları toplumla aile çevresinin ve Türk toplumunun toplumsal cinsiyet noktasında yüklediği roller birbiriyle çelişmektedir. Bu durumda kadınlar, iki toplumdan birinin beklentilerini görmezden gelmeye başlarlar.

Menekşe Toprak'ın kadınları Almanya'da hayata dahil olmaya kararlı ve bunu başarabilmiş kadınlardır. "Valizdeki Mektup"un kahramanı genç kadının ilk göçmen kuşağı temsil eden annesi bunlardan biridir: *"Dilini bilmediği, öğrenmemek için büyük bir aşkla direndiği bu ülkede babam hep bir yabancı olarak kalmış; bu yabancılığıyla da içe kapanık, beceriksiz adam kimliğine bürünüvermişti. Hata yapmaktan korkmayan, gözü kara bir kadın olduğu için, annemin dil sorunu hemen hemen hiç yoktu. Her yere giren çıkan annem, çalıştığı fabrikadaki kadınlarla dedikodu yapıp bundan keyif alacak kadar öğrenmişti buranın dilini." (Toprak, 2007, s. 10).*

"Ah! Şarap İçerken Bir de Gazete Okusam" adlı hikâyenin kahramanı Maraşlı Emine ise Almanya'ya giden ilk kuşak işçiler içerisinde varoluş savaşı veren ve kendince bunu başarabilmiş farklı bir kadındır. Bu kadın, adeta kendini var etmenin şartının kendisinden ve değerlerinden kopmak olduğuna inanmıştır. 14 yaşına girmeden istemediği bir adamla evlendirilen Emine, 16 yaşında anne olmuştur. Okuma yazma dahi bilmeyen Emine'nin Almanya'ya gidişi bu kaderden kaçıştır her şeyden önce. Ona "Korkmadın mı?" diye sorulur sıklıkla:

"Onlara hep hayır korkmadım, kocamı bırakıp tek başıma Almanya'ya gelirken de, üzerimdeki çullardan örtülerden sıyrılırken de, öldükten sonra insanı bekleyen o cehennem ateşini unuturken de korkmadım, demişti." (Toprak, 2007, s. 99).

Emine, onu Maraş'a ve sevmediği eşi Hasan'a bağlayan bütün değerlerden sıyrılarak Almanya'ya yönelmiştir. Artık tek hedefi vardır; çok para biriktirip zengin olmak, Türkiye'de kendi mülkünde özgürce istediği eşle yaşamak.

'Köln'deki ilk aylarında yol bilmez, iz bilmez bir halde beş kadınla aynı odayı paylaştığı yurtta, fabrikada eline geçen 800 Mark'ın tek feniğini harcarken bile nasıl da keyfi kaçıyordu. Eli varmıyordu para harcamaya. Öyle ki bu yüzden açlık çektiği bile oluyordu. Kurulu sofraların, şifon geceliklerin, kadife perdelerin, içlerinde kristal vazoların, porselenlerin dizili camlı kocaman vitrinlerin hayaliyle dolup taşarak biriktiriyordu paralarını. Ama Köln'e

geldiğinin altıncı ayında, açlığa dayanamamış ve bandın yanına düşüp kalmıştı." (Toprak, 2007, s. 101-102).

Emine'yi Franz iyi eder. Franz'ın evine taşınır, onun hazırladığı domuz bifteklerini, köftelerini yer. Menekşe Toprak, "domuz biftekleri"ni boşuna söylememiştir. Çünkü Almanya'daki Türklerin en hassas oldukları dini/kültürel unsurlardan biri domuz etine dairdir. Domuz etinden uzak durmak, kültürel kodların muhafazasını gösterir. Franz, Emine'ye para harcatmaz; Emine ise Franz'ın bazen sınırların dışına çıkan cinsel isteklerine cevap verir.

Emine, hikâyenin sonunda iki hafta önce Almanya'dan emekli olmuş, Türkiye'de bir sahil şehrine yerleşmiş olarak karşımıza çıkar. 57 yaşında iken 41 yaşındaki yeni sevgilisiyle mektuplaşabilmek için okuma yazma öğrenmiştir ve genç aşığına para yedirdiği sözlerine aldırmadan şarabını yudumlamaktadır.

Menekşe Toprak'ın kahraman kadınlarının millî ve dini kimliklerini muhafaza etmeye yönelik bir kaygılarının olmadığını görürüz. Yukarıda da söylendiği gibi yazar, Türk ailesi içerisinde kadınların muhafazasına yönelik yapıya işaret eder; ancak bunun doğruluğu ya da yanlışlığını tartışmaz. Kahramanları ise adeta bu muhafaza duygusundan kaçarlar. Yazarı, göçmen edebiyatı içerisinde farklı bir yere koymamızda hikâyelerindeki bu duruşun etkisi vardır. Özellikle Türk edebiyatı içerisinde göçmen edebiyatı Almanya alt başlığında değerlendirildiğinde kültürel kodların muhafazasının ve kimlik muhafazasının öne çıkarıldığını, entegre oluşun, Almanlara benzemenin yadırganarak vurgulandığını görürüz. Oysa Menekşe Toprak, bireyin varoluşuna ve kendini inşasına odaklanmıştır. Bu sebeple küçük insanın hallerini açarak yargılamadan ve taraf tutmadan "kadın"ı anlatmıştır. "Park" adlı hikâyenin kahramanı genç kadının Türk olup olmadığı üzerinde durmayız bile. Köpeğiyle meşgul bu genç kadın Almanların istediği ölçüde entegre bir tiptir.

Menekşe Toprak'ın kadınları terk etme ve edilme duygularının ardından anlatılırlar hep. Neredeyse hikâyelerinin bütününe yayılan terk etme/edilme duygusu Menekşe Toprak'ın 9 yaşına kadar anne babası tarafından köylerinde bırakılması ile ilintili olabilir. Yazar, ilk çocukluk evresinde senede ancak bir kez (bir ay) görebildiği ailesinin yokluğuna dair izler metinlerine yansıyor olabilir.

Göç ve çocuk

Türkiye'den Almanya'ya gerçekleşen işçi göçünün etkilediği en önemli insan grubu çocuklardır. İşçi ailelerinin çocuklarının bilhassa ilk dönemlerde Alman bakıcılar elinde kalması; anne babaların sürekli çalışmaları ve çocukların anaokulundan itibaren vakitlerinin önemli bir kısmını Almanlarla geçirmeleri sebebiyle Almanlara daha fazla benzemeleri ve asıl kültürlerinden süratle uzaklaşmaları; aile içi problemler yaşandığında (şiddet/ geçimsizlik) Alman makamlarınca çocukların ailelerinden koparılarak çocuk yurtlarına yahut koruyucu Alman ailelere verilmesi; çocukların Almanya'da Türk, Türkiye'de Almancı aşağılamalarına muhatap olmaları, daima öteki olarak görülmeleri çocuk dünyaları için önemli güçlüklerdir. Göçün ilk güçlüklerini karşılayan bu çocuklar, 2. Kuşak Türkleri meydana getireceklerdir.

Bu çocukların birçoğu için "memleket", anne babalarının anladıkları ve algıladıkları memleket değildir:

"Babam üşengeç bir adamdı, biraz. Öyle sanıyordum, ama çok sonraları, bunun aslında bilmediği bir dilde derdini anlatamadığından kaynaklandığını memlekete (sadece tatillerde gördüğüm, bana pek bir şey ifade etmeyen, doğup büyüdükleri ülkeleri için hep böyle derlerdi) gittiğimizde fark etmiştim." (Toprak, 2007, s. 10).

Menekşe Toprak'ın hikâyelerinde rastladığımız ve "göç edebiyatı" içerisinde adeta unutulmuş olduğunu gördüğümüz bir noktaya; "geride bırakılan çocuk" olgusuna değinmeliyiz. Özellikle birinci kuşak işçi ailelerinde çocukların biri yahut bir kısmının anane, babaanne, teyze, hala gibi birinci dereceden aile yakınları yanına bırakılmaları ve senelik izinler dışında çocuklarla irtibat kurulmaması, bu sıkıntının sebebidir. Almanya'da işler yoluna girince birkaç yıl sonra çocuklar aileleri yanına alınsalar da bebeklik yahut ilk çocukluk evresinde yaşanan ayrılık, travmaya yol açabilmektedir. Bireysel ve toplumsal psikoloji bakımından etki alanı geniş sonuçlara yol açan "geride bırakılma/terk edilme" travması, çocuğun yetişkinliği sırasında da çoklukla atlatılamamaktadır. Çocuklarda ailesine ısınamama, ailesini suçlama, tercih edilip yanlarında götürülen kardeşe karşı öfke; ilerleyen yaşlarda bağlanma sorunu (sabit bir işe veya eşe), intikam alma hissi vb. sorunlar kendini hissettirmektedir.

Menekşe Toprak da "geride bırakılan çocuklar"dandır. Anne babası onu 9 yaşına kadar yakınları yanına bırakmış, 9 yaşında yanlarına almışlardır. Yazarın hikâyeleri, bu yaşanmışlığın izlerine açıktır. Menekşe Toprak'ın Temmuz Çocukları romanı da direkt bu soruna parmak basar. Romanın aile içinde sorunlu kadın kahramanı da küçük yaşlarda altı yıl anne babası tarafından Türkiye'de bırakılmıştır. Ve hayatı, esas itibariyle bu suçun diyetini ailesine ödetmekle geçer. Yazarın "temmuz çocukları" tanımlaması, yazları bir ay yıllık izne gelen Almancı ailelerin çocuklarını tanımlar.

Menekşe Toprak'ın "Yokuştaki Kız", adlı hikâyesi, bu meseleye işaret eder. Eşini neredeyse sebepsiz terk eden Sevim'i aramak ve anlamak üzere Berlin'den yola çıkan kahramanımız, bir köy fotoğrafı ve kırık dökük bilgi kırıntılarıyla Anadolu'da Alevi bir Kürt köyüne kadar gelir. Berlin'de tanıdığı, sevdiği ve evlendiği doktoralı entelektüel kadın, bu metruk köyde mi sekiz yaşına kadar yaşamıştır? Babaanne yanında bırakılan Sevim'i anlamak için çıkılan yolculukta bu köyden işe başlanması çok doğrudur. Yıllar sonra hiçbir şey ifade etmediği zannedilen bu köy, Sevim'in şahsiyetine terk edilmişliği kazımıştır.

"Okula bakan bu yokuşta niye tek başına oturduğunu soranlara, hiç, diyor sadece. Ama yıllar sonra, on dört on beş yaşlarındayken bu yokuşun ne anlama geldiğini bulup çıkarıyor küçük kız. Her yaz, şehre bağlanan bu yoldan anne babası birden çıkıverirler; annesinin kendisine bakarken, kucağına alıp koklarken sessizce yanaklarından süzülen yaşlar korkutur, boğazına düğümlenen bir ağlamaya dönüşür. Tam alışırken sıcaklığına, kokusuna; her şey yolundaymış gibi görünürken, çekip giderler yine bu yoldan. Annesinin günbegün yüzüne yerleşen hüznünden, kendilerinden özür dileyen bakışlarından anlar ne zaman gideceklerini. Onlar gittikten sonra da günlerce yolun sağına düşen bu tepelikteki taşın üzerinde oturur, tarlalar arasından kıvrıla kıvrıla giden yola kendisi de çıksa, onlara ulaşacaklarını düşler." (Toprak, 2007, s. 69-70).

Küçük kız babaannesi ile bırakılmıştır. Anne babası her ay düzenli olarak para gönderseler de kızın bakımı, umdukları şekilde değildir: *"(...) yepyeni güzelim önlüğünü yaktığını babaannesine söylemeye korkacağını da. Her ay oğlu ve gelininin çocukları için gönderdiği paraları harcayamadığı, belki de ortalıkta dolanan büyük oğlundan kalma boy boy öksüz diğer beş torununa da bakabilme derdiyle her geçen gün biraz daha cimrileşen, nice kıtlıklar yaşamış babaannesinin onu azarlayacağını, tıpkı aç yatmamak için bazen ekmek çalıp gizli gizli yediğini fark ettiğinde yaptığı gibi küplere bineceğini, kollarına sert çimdikler atacağını da düşünmüyor." (Toprak, 2007, s. 70-71).*

Yetişkin Sevim, tüm bu çocukluk hikâyelerinin toplamıdır. Kendisini seven ve aralarındaki kopuşu bir türlü anlamlandıramayan eşinin onu arayışında sebeplerle neticeyi birleştirmeye çalışırız.

Menekşe Toprak'ın çocuklara dair kısaca değindiği bir göç halini de "Hangi Dildedir Aşk" adlı hikâyede yakalıyoruz. Almanya'ya gitmiş, orada bir müddet yaşamış ve ailesiyle dönerek Türkiye'de hayatına devam eden çocuklar ve bu çocukların yetişkinliklerine sarkan Almanya özlemi...

"Çocukluğunu Hamburg yakınında, elma ağaçlarının yeşillikleri içinde bir köyde geçirmiş, on dört yaşında ailesiyle beraber İstanbul'a yerleşmiş olan Ziya'nın Almanya özlemi, çocukluğundaki o köye ulanıyordu. Nasıl da içi giderek anıyordu Ziya bu köyü. Eski okulunu, köyün girişindeki dereyi, yeşilliği... Ormanlarında akranlarıyla savaş oyunları oynadıkları o yerleri bir kez daha görmek için vize alamayışına nasıl da içerliyordu. Ziya, Almanya'yı seviyordu, ama asıl aradığı, çocukluğundaki o korunaklı köydü. Sözünü ettiği komşularının evinden yükselen çörek kokularıydı, yaşıtlarıyla silahşorluk oyunlarına daldığı kızılağaç ormanıydı." (Toprak, 2009, s. 38).

Özlenen bir Alman köyüdür; ancak Almanya'da köylerin, imarından, marketlerinden, sağlık ve eğitim imkânlarına kadar şehirler kadar mamur olduğunu biliyoruz. Bundan otuz kırk sene önce Almanya'da bir köyden, Türkiye'de büyük şehirlerimize gelen kişilerin dahi özellikle imar noktasında büyük hayal kırıklıkları yaşadıkları bir vakıadır.

Melezlik sorunu

Menekşe Toprak'ı "göç edebiyatı" içerisinde farklı hassasiyetleri yakalamış bir yazar olarak görmemizi sağlayan diğer bir dikkati ise "melezlik" meselesine değinmesidir.

"Literatürde melez kimliklerin nasıl ortaya çıktığına ilişkin verilen cevaplarda daha çok, iki farklı kültüre sahip bireylerin evliliklerinden dünyaya gelen çocuklar konu edinilmekte ve eşlerin ırksal farklılıkları sebebiyle (beyaz, zenci vb.) bu çocuklarda ortaya çıkacak melez kimliklerin problemli olacağı tartışılmaktadır. Elbette ki yurtdışında yaşayan Türklerden bazıları yabancı eşlerle evlenmiş ve çocuk sahibi olmuştur. Dolayısıyla bu çocukların melez kimlik geliştirmeleri beklenen bir sonuçtur; fakat tamamen Türk ailelerin çocuklarında da bu türden tanımlamalara rastlanması ilk bakışta şaşırtıcı görünse de normal karşılanması gereken bir gelişmedir." (Yalçın, 2004, s. 169).

Menekşe Toprak'ın hikâyelerinde "melezlik" kavramının yukarıda anılan iki boyutu da dillendirilir. Bunun aynı hikâye içinde vurgulanması tesadüfi olmamalı.

"Hangi Dildedir Aşk" adlı hikâyede vaktiyle Almanya'ya gelerek annesiyle evlenmiş ve annesinin hamile olduğunu öğrendiğinde onu terk ederek Türkiye'ye kaçmış babasının peşine düşen genç bir kadın anlatılır. Babası hakkında çok az bilgisi olan genç kızın hafızasında

geçmişte bir fotoğraftan gördüğü silik bir yüz ile babasının İstanbul'da oturduğu semte dair bazı malumat vardır.

"Çocukken o çok merak ettiği, ergenlik çağında sadece bir kinle andığı, sonradan ise hafızasından sildiği, kendisi henüz annesinin karnındayken İstanbul'a dönen ve bir daha geri gelmeyen babası Mustafa Şahin hakkında bildiği tek şey, yakışıklı olmasıydı. Tek başına görüntü aşk için yeterli olamazdı, değildi. Doğacağından haberdar olduğu halde onu bir kez dahi görme gereği duymadan hayatlarından çekip gitmişti. (…) Tanımadığı yabancı bir adama niçin özlem duyuyordu ki! (…) Bu, babasını merak eden, yaşıtlarının "bir babaya sahip olma" halini kıskanan küçük kızın hüznüydü. Ya da soluk renkli poloroid fotoğrafta gülümseyerek bakan genç, esmer, uzun boylu adamın şimdi içine girdiğini sandığı dünyasını keşfetmenin getirdiği duygu seli." (Toprak, 2009, s. 44).

Genç kız art arda çocukluğunu ve annesinin ailesinin babası hakkındaki düşüncelerini anımsar. Ananesinin öfkelendikçe babasına hakaret ettiğini, kendisi için "Türk piçi" deyişini, babasının gidişine çocuğun Türkleşmediği için memnun oluşunu hatırlar. Kendisi Türkçe ve Türk kültürüne dair hiçbir şey bilmez. Ama yaşı oturdukça ve insanları anlamaya başladıkça babasına da öfkesi azalmıştır. Babasına doğru çıktığı yolculuk onu babasına kavuşturmasa da ona insana dair başka şeyler öğretecektir.

Aynı hikâyenin diğer kahramanı Aylin ise melezliğin ikinci cephesini temsil eder. Aylin, Almanya'da yetişmiş bir genç kadındır ve Türk-Alman karışımı bir kimlik sergiler. İstanbul'un Alman ahalisi ile çok iyi anlaşır, Türkleri tanır; ama Türklerle Almanlar kadar rahat iletişim kuramaz.

"Söz konusu bu melez kimliklerde dikkat çekici en önemli nokta, iki kültürden öğeler taşıyan insanların kendi aralarındaki iletişimlerinin iki dilin karışımından oluşmasıdır. Cümlelerine Türkçe başladıklarında, yaşadıkları ülkenin diliyle bitirmeleri veya konuşmaları sırasında dilden dile spontane olarak geçiş yapmaları, sadece kendilerine özgü bir durumdur ve bu şekilde iletişimleri hem Türkiye'deki bir Türk için hem de o ülke yerlilerinden biri için anlaşmaz ya da az anlaşılır bir özellik taşımaktadır; fakat bunların hiçbiri, bu kuşaklardaki Türklük bilinçlerinin yok olacağı anlamına gelmemeli." (Yalçın, 2004, s. 170-171).

Cemâl Yalçın'ın yukarıdaki tespiti adeta Aylin'i anlatır. "Aylin'in Almanca konuştuğu anki haliyle Türkçe konuşurkenki hali arasında dağlar kadar fark vardı. Almanca konuşurken adeta rahatlıyor, gülümsemesi çok daha sahici oluyordu. Şimdi de öyleydi. (…)" (Toprak, 2009, s. 45).

"Adam çoğunlukla Türkçe konuşurken, Aylin'in dili sürekli Almancaya kayıyor, iyice gerilip sesleri yükseldiğinde ise bütünüyle Almancaya sarılıyordu." (Toprak, 2009, s. 35).

Aylin babasının izini arayan kadına "melez misin sen, ailenin bir tarafı esmer miydi, saf kan Almanlara benzemiyorsun" diye soracaktır. Diğeri soruyu geçiştirse de Menekşe Toprak, melezlik üzerine duygusunu bir vesile kahramanlarına söyletir:

"Doğulu gözler, batılı bakışlar… Niye şaşırıyorum ki, dünya melezleşmedi mi zaten? Melezlik de bir ırk değil mi?" (Toprak, 2009, s. 53).

Sonuç yerine

"Almanya'daki göçmen edebiyatı, yaşanılan sorunların ve toplumsal gerçeklerin bir yansıması olarak ortaya çıkmıştır. Göç sürecinde yaşanan ötekileştirme, kültür ve kimlik çatışması, yalnızlık, dışlanma, uyum, iki kültürlülük, kuşaklar arası farklılaşma, getto hayatı, Türkiye ile ilişkili durumlar vb. birçok sorun aslında bu edebiyatın zeminini hazırlamıştır. Birlikte yaşama sürecinde orijin kökenli kültürel kodlar ile göç edilen ülkenin kültürel kodlarının uyuşmaması neticesinde yaşanan iki taraflı aksiyoner ve reaksiyoner tavırlar ile birlikte kültürel ve kimliksel çatışma alanları ve iki dilli, iki kültürlü melez kimlikler oluşmakta ve bu durum oluşan edebiyata yansımaktadır." (Güllü, 2015, s. 141).

Menekşe Toprak'ın otobiyografik diyebileceğimiz hikâyelerinde Almanya göçünün edebiyatımız yansıyan genel meselelerinden farklı olarak yabancı bir toplumda kendini gerçekleştirmeye çalışan kadın, önemli bir yer tutar. Klasik bakışla kültürü ve inançları arasında bunalan ve doğruyu arayan, vicdan azapları çeken kadınlar değillerdir bunlar. Ayrıca kültürün ve inançların taşıyıcıları olarak da görünmezler. Düşünce dünyalarında var olma ve tutunma esastır. İkinci orijinal yaklaşım Türkiye'de bırakılan çocuklarla ilgilidir ki netice itibariyle tutunamayan tutunmaya çalışan kadının kökeni de bu travmaya bağlanır. Ve bir tutunma arzusu da Türk erkeklerin Alman eşlerden doğan çocukları ile ilgilidir. Babası tarafından kabul görmeyen yarı Türk yarı Alman bir nesil vardır ve bu nesil, göç mağduru bir başka grubu temsil eder.

Tüm bu dikkatleri ile Menekşe Toprak, insan'dan doğan yanlışların acılarını işler. Almanlara karşı bir duruşu olmadığı gibi Türkleri de suçlamaz. Hikâyelerinde insan'ın evrensel yanlışları ve bunların neticeleri vardır. Edebiyat ise iç dünyamızın ve dış dünyamızın en masum şahididir.

Kaynakça

Aytaç, G. (1991). Edebiyat yazıları II, Gündoğan Yayınları, Ankara.

Güllü, İ. (2015). Göçmen edebiyatında din ve kimlik yansımaları: Fakir Baykurt'un Yarım Ekmek romanında din ve gelenek, Göç Dergisi, 2(1), 117-145.

Kahraman, B. (2013). (Menekşe Toprak'la röportaj)"Yazmak cesaret gerektirir", Aydınlık KİTAP, 2 Ağustos.

Özbakır, İ. (2000). Almanya "Konuk işçi edebiyatı"nın bir Türk temsilcisi Renan Demirkan'ın "Üç şekerli demli çay"ında kimlik problemi", Türklük Bilimi Araştırmaları –IX-/2000.

Şahin, B. (2010). Almanya'daki Türk göçmenlerin sosyal entegrasyonunun kuşaklar arası karşılaştırması: Kültürleşme", Bilig, 55, 103-134.

Toprak, M. (2007). Valizdeki mektup, YKY, İstanbul.

Toprak, M. (2009). Hangi dildedir aşk, YKY, İstanbul.

Toprak, M. (2011). Temmuz çocukları, YKY, İstanbul.

Yalçın, C. (2004). Göç sosyolojisi, Anı Yayınları, Ankara.

Cumhuriyet Dönemi Romanlarında Ekonomik Nedenlere Bağlı İç Göçe Dair Bir Tahlil Denemesi

Polat Sel[339]

Ekonomik Nedenler

İç göç hareketi, bireylerin herhangi bir yerleşim biriminden (köy, kasaba, şehir) bir diğer yerleşim birimine geçici veya kalıcı bir süre için gelmeleridir. İç göçün yönü bakımından dört alt kategori içinde yer aldığı bilinmektedir: Kırdan-kente, kentten-kente, kentten-kıra, kırdan-kıra (Akkayan,1979, s. 23-25).

Türkiye'de bu dört tip göç yönünden en fazla görüleni kırdan-kente doğru olan göç olmakla birlikte son zamanlarda kentten-kıra doğru da bir geri dönüşümün yaşanmaya başlandığı hissedilmektedir. Orhan Türkdoğan sahada yapmış olduğu araştırmalar neticesinde vardığı çıkarsamalarda iç göç hareketinin gerekleşmesinde yeterli toprağa sahip olamama, geçim sıkıntısı, nüfus artışı, yine araştırma yapılan bölgenin karakteristik yapısına bağlı olarak ortaya çıkan kan davası, ağa zulmü gibi faktörlerin önemli ölçüde rol oynadığı sonucuna varmıştır. Bunun yanı sıra mevcut itici faktörlerin yanında sanayileşme ve kentleşmenin de kırsal alandan çıkmak isteyen bireyler için çekici bir faktör haline geldiğini de belirtmiştir (Türkdoğan, 1977, s. 322). Kemal H. Karpat da Türkdoğan'ın görüşüne katılarak kırdan kente olan göçte itici unsur olarak yoksulluğu, gelir düşüklüğünü gösterir. Ayrıca eğitim ve sağlık olanaklarının şehirde bulunmasının da yine göç hareketine olumlu yönde katkıda bulunduğunu ifade eder. Karpat, bireylerin kırdan kente gelmesinde etkili unsur olarak da iş ve istihdam olanaklarıyla, eğitim ve sağlık alanında sunulan olanakların büyük bir etki yarattığı kanısındadır (Karpat, 2003, s. 45). Söz konusu sebeplerin sadece ülkemiz için değil dünyanın birçok yerinde göç etmiş genel insan profili için de geçerli olduğunu belirtir. Onların da göç etmelerinde toprak yokluğu, toprak verimsizliği, fazla nüfustan kaynaklanan yoksulluk gibi benzer ekonomik nedenlerin ön planda olduğunu açıklar (Karpat, 2003, s. 56-57).

Ruşen Keleş'e göre de kırdan kente bireylerin göç etmesinde tarımda verimin yeterli olmayışı, tarım topraklarının artan nüfusla birlikte giderek küçülmesi gibi sebeplerin yanında tarımda makineleşme, iklim koşulları ve erozyon da etkilidir (Keleş, 1972, s. 37). Cavit Orhan Tütengil'e göre de köyden kente göçte makineleşmenin, topraksız ya da yeterli düzeyde toprağı olmayan köylünün sayısının artmasının etkisi vardır. Ayrıca Tütengil 1950'li yıllardan sonra ekilebilir toprakların sınırlarına erişilmesiyle, kara ulaşım ağındaki gelişmelerin de kırdan kente doğru olan ivmeyi artırdığı görüşündedir (Tütengil, 1979, s. 165). Bu doğrultuda yazarların çoğu birbirine yakın görüşler ileri sürmüşler ve ağırlıklı olarak ekonomik etmenlerin iç göçte yaratmış olduğu yansımaya dikkat çekmişlerdir.

Bu çalışmada incelenecek olan eserlerde iç göçün belirleyici unsurları arasında yer alan ekonomik etmenlerin kurgusal bir düzlem olan roman sahasındaki

---

[339] Arş. Gör. Polat SEL, Trakya Üniversitesi, Balkan Yerleşkesi, Edebiyat Fakültesi, B Blok, Merkez-Edirne. E-mail: polatsel@trakya.edu.tr

yansımalarının nasıl olduğu hususunda karşılaştırma ve metin çözümleme yöntemlerine başvurarak bir sonuca varılacaktır. Bu bağlamda seçilmiş olan romanlarda yapılan araştırmalar neticesinde iç göçün gerçekleşmesinde itici etmen olarak rol oynayan birçok ekonomik nedenin roman düzleminde ele alındığı ortaya çıkmıştır.

Nüfus artışı sonucu toprakların küçülmesi

Türkiye'de özellikle Türk çiftçisinin sahip olduğu toprak miktarına bakıldığında diğer Batı ülkeleri ve Amerika'daki çiftçilerle karşılaştırıldığı zaman onlarla aynı ölçüde teknolojik imkânlara ve girdilere sahip olsalar bile çiftçi başına düşen toprağın az olması sebebiyle ekonomik anlamda sıkıntı içinde oldukları görülür. Bunun yanı sıra aynı ölçüde tarım alanına sahip olmaları durumunda dahi bu sefer de toprağın yeterli ölçüde verimli olmamasından dolayı aynı ölçüde kazanca sahip olmaları oldukça zordur.

Tarımla uğraşan çiftçi ailelerde kişi başına düşen toprak alanının az olması Türkiye'de başlı başına bir sorun teşkil etmektedir. Bu durumun doğal bir sonucu olarak mevcut tarım alanının artan nüfusla parçalanması geçim sıkıntısını da beraberinde getirir. Bu da aile üyelerinden birkaçının gittikçe parçalanan ve küçülen toprak alanı sebebiyle daha iyi bir kazanca sahip olmak arzusuyla kente göç etmelerine neden olur (Çakman, 1996, s. 30-33).

Alper Aksoy *Ümraniye İçinde Vurdular Bizi* adlı romanında Giresun'un Göbele ilçesinden İstanbul'a gelmek zorunda kalan beş arkadaştan bahsederken temel göç nedeni olarak ekonomik sebepleri gerekçe gösterir. Durmaksızın artan nüfus artışı neticesinde aynı boyutta kalan toprakların, gittikçe küçük paylara ayrılması sonucunda, ailelerin temel geçim standartlarını karşılamaktan yoksun hale gelmesiyle beraber göç kaçınılmaz bir hale gelir.

Atalarını varlık içinde yaşatan toprağın artan nüfusla beraber gittikçe daha küçük parçalara ayrılması sonucunda ailelerde geçim sıkıntısı ortaya çıkar. Yazar yaşanılan bu trajik durumu henüz romanın başında "Ver Elini Gurbet" adlı bölümde şu şekilde anlatmıştır:

"Dedeleri bu cömert topraklarda yoksulluk nedir bilmeden ömür sürdüler. Babalarının gençliği de bu cömertliğin nimetleri arasında geçti. Fakat her aileyi geçindiren topraklar, şimdi, dörde, beşe, altıya bölünmek durumundaydı. Hatta yediye, sekize, dokuza... Ocaklar çoğalmış... Ama toprak aynı toprak. Ve bölündü topraklar. Şimdi her ailenin geçim umudu bir arsa kadar küçülmüştür. Bu arsayı dişle, tırnakla kazmak, yoğurmak, geçimlerini -yoksulluk içinde de olsa- sürdürmelerini sağlayabilirdi. Ama sırada başka altılar, yediler, sekizler var. Ya onlar, ya onların rızkı?... Bu avuç içi kadar yerden mi sağlanacak? Bunu düşündüklerinde keskin bir acı oynar yüreklerinde..." (Aksoy, 1983, s. 5-6)

Artan nüfus, gençlik zamanları geçip gittikten sonra yaşanacak geçim sıkıntısı karşısında tek çıkış noktası vardır: Gurbete göç etmek. Nitekim Göreleli beş arkadaş da gelecekte içinde bulunabilecekleri bu karamsar tablo karşısında çok geçmeden göç etme kararı alırlar. Yazar onların göç kararını alırken içine düştükleri çıkmazı romanda şöyle yansıtır:

"Altıların, yedilerin, sekizlerin ilk ucu göründü. Kimi ocaklar üçü aşmış, dördüncüyü gözlemekte. Şimdi kuvvet var kollarında, gençlik var bedenlerinde. Ya bir de yitip gidince bunlar? İşte o zaman "Ah"lar çare olmaz dertlerine. 'Senin gibi atanın,

ta yedi ceddine, yedi ceddiyin yedi göbek ötesine…'diye başlanır söze. N'etmeli, neylemeli? Tutulacak yol tektir; bu yol başkalarınca da tutulmuştur: 'Ver elini gurbet!" (Aksoy, 1983, s. 5)

Toprak reformu

Cumhuriyet dönemi Türk romanlarına genel olarak bakıldığında ekonomik nedenler arasında yer alan bir diğer önemli husus da toprak reformudur. Toprak reformu neticesinde birçok ağa bulunduğu yerlerden topraklarının kamulaştırılması sebebiyle başka yerlere gitmek zorunda kalmışlardır.

Alev Alatlı'nın *İşkenceci* adlı romanında Abdurrahman Ağa'nın başlangıçta 55'lilerden olduğu gerekçesiyle tutuklandığını, sonradan onlardan olmadığı anlaşılınca serbest bırakıldığını ancak onların 18 Ekim 1960[340] tarihli yasayla tehcir edilmelerine bağlı olarak kendisinin de izleyen 4753 sayılı kanun uyarınca topraklarının kamulaştırıldığını anlatır. Böylece Abdurrahman Ağa'nın uzun zamandır kan davalısı olduğu Sarılar, kamulaştırılan toprakların da sahibi olur. Bu içine düşülen çıkmaz karşısında Abdurrahman Ağa'nın yaşadığı hayal kırıklığı romanda şöyle anlatılır:

"Yeni koşullar kurşun oldu, üstüne üstüne yağdı Abdurrahman Ağa'nın. Körebe oldu, koordinatlarını yitirdi. Ne siper alabildi ne de öldürücü kurşunla kucaklaştı… Başına gelenleri doğal afetler sınıfına soktu. Seçimler, tarih, devrim, düzen, yasalar, anayasalar, haklar, haksızlıklar, mahkemeler, tapular, sistem dışı, başlarına buyruk değişkenler oldular. Ölüm kaderse, düşmek de kaderdi… Vazgeçemeyeceklerini toparladı, meçhule göçtü. Meçhule, yani İstanbul'a." (Alatlı, 1995, s. 34)

Toprağın verimsizliği

İsmail Cem, *Türkiye'nin Geri Kalmışlığının Tarihi* adlı eserinde toprağın verimsizliğine ve şişkinliğine de değinir. Ülkemizdeki topraklardan istenen verimin elde edilememesini toprakların gereğinden fazla parçalanmış oluşuna bağlar. Ayrıca topraktan istenilen düzeyde ürünün ve yüksek düzeyde faydanın sağlanması için en az 75 hektar toprağın olması gerektiğini belirtir. Devamında ülkemizle diğer ülkelerdeki toprağın verimlilik düzeyi karşılaştırıldığında hektar başına alınan ürün açısından diğer ülkelerin bize oranla aynı birimden 3 kat fazla ürün aldığı tespitinde bulunur (Cem, 1982, s. 435-437).

Türkiye'deki toprağın verimsizliği bu genel durumu roman düzleminde ortaya koyan yazarların da gözünden kaçmamıştır. Kemal Ateş *Toprak Kovgunları* adlı romanında Kırşehir'in Kaman kırsalından Ankara'nın Elmadağ semti civarlarına göç eden ailelerin burada verdikleri yaşam mücadelesini anlatır. Buradaki gecekondu yaşamına ağırlık verilir. Yazar, eserinde şahısların köyden şehre göç etmelerinde etki eden temel sebepleri belirtirken metinde farklı gerekçelerin de yer aldığı görülmekle beraber, ilk sırada yine ekonomik sebepler kendisini gösterir. Romanın önemli şahıslarından birisi olan Emin'in göç kararının en temel sebebi toprağın verimsizleşmesi sonucu artık eskisi kadar ürün vermemesidir.

---

[340] 18 Ekim 1960 tarihinde, "mülk ve nüfuzunu kullanarak zararlı faaliyetleri tespit edilen kişilerin Bakanlar Kurulu kararıyla bulundukları illerden başka illere nakledilip, topraklarının kamulaştırılması" kararlaştırıldı. Akdağ, Y., Toprak ve Tarım Politikası ve Toprak Talebi, http://www.ozgurlukdunyasi.org/arsiv/132-sayi-207/409-toprak-ve-tarim-politikasi-ve-toprak-talebi sitesinden alınmıştır. Erişim tarihi: (3.06.2014).

Nitekim topraktan gelen ürünün azalması kazancı da etkilemiş, aileler ihtiyaçlarını karşılayamaz duruma gelmiştir. Emin ve ailesi için de göç etmek keyfi bir seçenek değil, biraz da zorunlulukların doğurduğu bir sonuçtur. Yazar romanda Emin'in ağzından içinde bulundukları ekonomik çıkmazı şu şekilde yansıtır:

"Geçinemeyip terk ettikleri köylerini düşünüyordu Emin. O yıllar birçok insan baba evinden ayrılmış, kendi başına bir iş tutmaya başlamıştı. Kimi yumurtacılık yapıyor, kimi tavukçuluk, kimi kap kacak alıp satıyor. Herkes çerçi oldu, herkes bişey alıp satıyor. Toprak doyurmuyordu insanları. Yıllardır atalarını doyuran toprak, 'Artık sizi doyuramam, bırakın yakamı' diyordu. Çaresiz, onlar da bıraktılar toprağı. Başka ne yapabilirlerdi ki? Zorla güzellik olmaz. Vermiyor işte toprak! Harman sonu elleri boş dönüyorlar, ektikleri tohumu bile alamıyorlardı. Bir yıl çalış, didin, ek, biç, sonunda da boş çuvallarla dön evine. Köylülerin yüzünden düşen bin parça oluyordu. Her hasat sonu toprak, bu acı gerçeği yüzlerine haykırıyordu: 'Sizi doyuramayacağım, bırakın benim yakamı! Bırakıyordu köylüler. Başka ne yapabilirlerdi ki?" (Ateş, 1999, s. 295)

Muttalip Canbazoğlu'nun *Gurbetlerin Çocuğu* adlı romanının başkahramanı olan Talip'in yaşadığı köyden Ankara'ya gitme düşüncesinin belirmesinde özellikle başta abisi Hayri ve yengesi olmak üzere aile fertlerinin önemli ölçüde rol oynamasının yanında, toprağın verimsizliği ve aile fertlerinin geçimlerini topraktan çıkarmak için verdikleri amansız mücadeleye şahit olması da etkili olur. Abisi Hayri yapmış oldukları mücadeleye karşın sevdikleri insanları yitirmeleri ve topraktan da umulan verimi alamamaları üzerine zaman zaman mevcut duruma isyan ederek kardeşine büyük şehre gitmesi tavsiyesinde bulunur:

"... Aldığımız ne sonra bu verimsiz kıraç topraklardan? Hiç... Hiç. Kendimi bildim bileli toprağın esiriyim. Evet, tam kendisi, benim, bizim yaşamımız esaretten farklı değildir. Biz bütün Anadolu toprağın, yokluğun esirleriyiz. Bebemiz yiter, karımız yiter, anamız, bacımız yiter... Ne yaparsın bütün Anadolu'nun, köylülerin alın yazısı bu. Verimsiz toprakla, sıcakla savaşacaksın. Canın damla damla toprağa akacak sonra karşılığında kışı zor yetirecek buğday, arpa alacaksın. Vallahi yaşamak değil bu. Billâhi yaşamak değil bu." (Canbazoğlu, 1966, s. 90-100)

Talip gerek abisi Hilmi'nin, gerek yengesinin, gerekse annesi ve diğer kardeşlerinin içinde bulundukları durumu yakından görmekle kalmaz; yaşı büyüyüp de o da toprakla uğraşmaya başlayınca içine girdiği işin zorluğunu kavrar. Ürünü elde etmek için verilen emeğin ve hasat zamanına kadar çekilen çilenin her aşamasını yaşayarak durumun zorluğunu anlar. Ölen babasını düşünür:

"Arpalar yolunurken canımızdan birazını daha verdik toprağa. Bizim taşlı tarlalar insanı eritiyor, çürütüyor, yakıyor. Orakla biçemezsin ki... Taş her taraf taş... Bu taşların içinden çıkanla çocukların doyacak! Ocağın tütecek... Babamın genç yaşında göçüşündeki sebebi şimdi daha çok anlıyorum. Bu verimsiz topraklar, bu taşlı tarlalar göçürtmüş onu." (Canbazoğlu, 1966, s. 107)

Tarımda makineleşme

1950 yılında Demokrat Parti'nin iktidara gelmesiyle birlikte hükümetin temel hedefi oyların büyük bir kısmını aldığı köye ve köylüye olan minnet borcunu ödemek amacıyla tarım sektöründe yatırım yapmak ve yenilikler getirmektir. Bu politika sadece Türk hükümetinin politikası olmayıp Amerika tarafından da desteklenmekte ve Marshall Planı kapsamında Türkiye'nin sanayileşmesinden çok bir tarım üreticisi olarak kalması düşünülmektedir. Hükümet Amerika'dan da aldığı destekle hem tarım alanlarını genişletme yolunu açar hem de ilkel denilebilecek eski tarım araçlarını tedavülden kaldırmak suretiyle tarım sektöründe makineleşmeye gider. Böylece mevcut hükümetin ve Amerikan sermayesinin de desteğiyle ülkeye traktör ve pulluk sevkiyatı başlar. 1946 ile 1954 yılları arasında traktör sayısında büyük bir artış yaşanır. Bu da toprakların genişlemesiyle birlikte traktörü olmayan ve ortakçılıkla geçimini sağlayan ailelerin, bulunduğu yeri geçici ya da kalıcı olarak terk etmesine sebep olur (Oktar ve Varlı, s.9-15).

Tarımda makineleşme ve ortakçılığın bitmesi, Behzat Ay'ın *Dor Ali* adlı romanında ele alınır. Yazar, en başta bu gibi nedenlerden dolayı bulunduğu yer olan Düzlek köyünden Samsun'a göç ederek, şehirde var olma mücadelesi veren bir köylü ailesinin hayat hikâyesini gözler önüne serer.

Dor Ali, köyün öğretmeniyle yapmış olduğu görüşmede göç etmesine sebep olan faktörler arasında tarımda makineleşme ve beraberinde getirdiği geçim sıkıntısını gösterir ve başta kendisi olmak üzere köylüler üzerindeki olumsuz etkisini şu şekilde anlatır:

"Bizimki ayrı... Biz karnımızı doyuramıyoruz. Doyursak bile köylerde yaşamak geçti bizlerden... Her gün biraz daha yoksullaşıyoruz. Sıkıntılarımız gün geçtikçe çoğalıyor... Önceleri yarıcılık yapıyorduk, günlükçülük yapıyorduk... Şimdi bu işler galmadı. Gözünü açanlar, topraklarını genişletti öğretmenim... Genişleyen topraklarını sürmeye traktör aldılar: biçmeye, biçerdöğer aldılar. Makineleşti eloğlu. Bizim gücümüze gufatımıza hacet galmadı. Böylece günlükçülük yapamaz olduk..." (Ay, 1966, s. 32)

Yazar, başlangıçtan beri var olan ve tarımda etkili olmaya başlayan ekonomik etkenlerin birleşmesi neticesinde Dor Ali'nin göç etmekten başka bir çaresinin kalmadığını onun ağzından okuyucuya şöyle aktarır:

"Şu zamanda üç dönümlük toprakla köyde geçim olmaz. Önceleri anlattığım durumlar yoktu da oluyordu. Traktör yoktu, biçerdöver yoktu, sulama makinesi yoktu; biz vardık! Şimdi onlar olunca biz açıkta kaldık. Bakakaldık. Bütün gün kahvedeyiz. Kağıt oynuyoruz, dedikodu yapıyoruz, kötü kötü düşünüyoruz... Hasta goyunlar gibi olduk..." (Ay, 1966, s. 33)

Dor Ali'nin samimi arkadaşlarından Yusuf ve Mustafa da onun içinde bulunduğu sıkıntıyı ve tepkisini aynen paylaşırlar. Onlara göre Dor Ali haklıdır. Devir artık eski devir değildir. Tarımda makineleşmeyle beraber, sadece Dor Ali değil; onun gibi çalışan birçok köylü işsiz kalma tehlikesiyle karşı karşıyadır. Artık iki üç dönüm tarlayla aile geçindirmek mümkün değildir. Bu yenilikler sadece geniş toprak sahiplerine yaramış, onları biraz daha varlıklı hale getirmiştir:

"Doğru Ali'nin söyledikleri. Bizlerin köyde kalması geçti artık. Dünya değişti, çiftçilik de değişti. İki dönüm tarlayla Düzlek düzleğinde çiftçilik yapılmaz. Düzlek, ikişer, üçer bin dönüm toprağı olup, bu toprağı makine sesleriyle şenlendirenlerin olsun! Onların traktörleri bizi Düzlekten kovuyor. Onların makinaları bizi bu topraklardan atarken, sahıplarının göbeğini şişiriyor... Sahıplarının cüzdanlarını dolduruyor..." (Ay, 1966, s. 34)

Geçim sıkıntısı ve işsizlik

Cumhuriyet dönemi Türk romanlarının geneline bakıldığında işsizlik, ekonomik olarak göç sebepleri arasında yer alan temel sorunlardan birisidir. Ailelerin, bireylerin bulundukları yeri terk etmelerinin bir diğer sebebi de düzenli bir iş sahibi olmamaları ve çalıştıkları işlerden yeterli gelir sağlayamamalarıdır.

Talip Apaydın'ın *Kente İndi İdris* adlı romanı incelendiğinde, köyden şehre göç sebebi olarak en başta geçim sıkıntısının geldiği anlaşılır. Eserde içinde bulunduğu durumdan hoşnut olmayan İdris'in, şehirden köye gelen Kara Ömer'in kılık kıyafetinden, şehirdeki rahat yaşamından bahsetmesi üzerine daha iyi bir yaşantıya kavuşmak için ailesini de ikna ederek şehre göç etmesi ve sonrasında şehirde iş buluncaya kadar çektiği sıkıntıları anlatılır. Fabrikada iş bulmasından sonra burada yer alan sendikalar arasındaki çekişme ve işçilerin tuttukları sendikalara göre kendi aralarında gruplaşmaları, işçi-patron çatışması eserde işlenen diğer konulardır.

Yazar henüz romanın daha giriş bölümünde romanın başkarakteri İdris'in içinde bulunduğu kötü durumu şu şekilde yansıtır:

"Üstü başı dökülüyor İdris'in. Ayağında kara lastikler delik, başında kasket yamalı. Omzunda bel kürek, işten geliyor. Bir yılgın, bir bıkkın. Yüzünde kara düşünceler. Dünya yıkılmış, biz altında kalmışız. Çalış çalış sonu yok. Eşeğin kuyruğu gibi ne uzarsın, ne kısalırsın. Köylülük değişmez bir yaşam. Ek, biç, kaldır. Karnın yarı doyar yarı doymaz. Bugün yediğini yarın da yersin, bu yıl giydiğini gelecek yıl da giyersin. Yıllar geçer, hiç değişiklik yok, Aynı evler, aynı sokaklar, aynı insanların yüzleri, Konuştuğun şeyler bile aynı. Uyuşuyor insan, usanıyor, uykusu geliyor." (Apaydın, 1991, s. 3)

Köye gelen arkadaşı Kara Ömer'in şehirde rahatının yerinde olması, kılık-kıyafet olarak değişmesi, gecekondusunu yaptırıp çocuklarını da okula verdiğini söylemesi geçim sıkıntısı çeken İdris'in radikal bir karar alarak köyü terk etmesinde etkili olur:

"Köy yerinde çalış çalış sonu yok. Hep gidenler Kara Ömer gibi adam oluyor. Arada bir geliyorlar, yüzleri güleç. Şehir şehir diye ağızlarından sular akıyor. İşim iyi, halimden memnunum. Gecekondumu da yaptım. Keyfime diyecek yok. Ulen İdris, herkesin kötüsü sen misin? Herkes becerir de sen niye beceremeyeceksin? Köyde çalış çalış... ne geçti eline?..." (Apaydın, 1991, s. 5)

Ali Bilhan'ın *Alicik* adlı romanında ise romanın kahramanlarından Ali'nin bir dağ köyü olan Yukarı Alan'dan Hatay'ın Amik ovasına göç etmek istemesinin altında yatan nedenler yine ekonomik temellere dayanır. İçinde bulunduğu köyde geçim sıkıntısının olması, köyden şehre gidenlerin orada bir düzen tutturup, daha iyi bir yaşam sürmeleri, kendisini köyden ayrılmak konusunda teşvik eden faktörler arasında yer alır. Nitekim Alicik'in içinde bulunduğu sıkıntılı durumda kafasından geçenleri yazar, okuyucuya şu şekilde aktarır:

"Babası, amcası, dayısı kısaca bugüne dek yaşayıp gelen tüm geçmişi ortadaydı. İki baş keçiylen birkaç kök bağın derdine ömür bitirmişler. Kim var şimdi ortada? Kime ne kaldı? Yukarı Alanlılar'a ne kaldı? Sürüp giden aynı tasa aynı görenek. Obur Osman şehre gitti, bir bekçilik buldu. Hem de ev-bark sahibi oldu, avrat sahibi oldu. Cemil'in oğlu berber çıraklığına girdi. Yarın ustası gibi olacak, temiz temiz beğleri tıraş edecek... Yukarı Alan'ın yaşatma verimi kalmadı. İki kök bağla beş-on keçinin götünü beklemek yetmiyor gayri..." (Bilhan, 1987, s. 3-4)

Böylece Alicik, romanın ilerleyen sayfalarında Zortuk Ağa'nın çiftliğine giderek ona Veli emmisinin selamını iletir. Kendisine bir iş vermesini rica eder. Zortuk Ağa kendisinden iş istenmesine başta kızsa da sonradan kâhyaya emir vererek Alicik'i yanına azap olarak alır.

Buraya kadar seçmiş olduğumuz örnek romanlar üzerinde yaptığımız incelemelerden de açıkca görülmektedir ki; roman sahasında kalem oynatan yazarlar da içinde yaşadıkları toplumun bir parçası olarak bireyleri etkileyen ve onların göç etmelerinde önemli bir rol oynayan ekonomik etmenlere karşı duyarsız kalmamış, kurgusal bir dünya olan roman içerisinde yaratmış oldukları karakterler vasıtasıyla ekonomik nedenlerin bireyin göç kararı almasında ne kadar etkili bir itici faktör olduğunu başarıyla yansıtmışlardır.

Kaynakça

Akdağ, Y. Toprak ve Tarım Politikası ve Toprak Talebi.
  http://www.ozgurlukdunyasi.org/arsiv/132-sayi-207/409-toprak-ve-tarim-politikasi-ve-toprak talebi sitesinden alınmıştır. Erişim tarihi: (3.06.2014).
Akkayan, T. (1979). Göç ve Değişme. Edebiyat Fakültesi Basımevi. İstanbul.
Aksoy, A. (1983). Ümraniye İçinde Vurdular Bizi. Ocak Yayınları. Ankara.
Alatlı, A. (1995). İşkenceci. Boyut Yayınevi. İstanbul.
Ateş, K. (1999). Toprak Kovgunları. Doğan Kitapçılık. İstanbul.
Apaydın, T. (1991). Kente İndi İdris, Başak Basın Yayım. Ankara.
Ay, B. (1966). Dor Ali. Remzi Kitapevi. İstanbul.
Bilhan, A. (1987). Alicik. Sanat-Koop Yayınları. İzmir.
Canbazoğlu, M. (1966). Gurbetlerin Çocuğu. Gündüz Yayınları. Ankara.
Cem, İ. (1982). Türkiye'nin Geri Kalmışlığının Tarihi. Cem Yayınları. İstanbul.
Çakman, M. K. (1996). Toprak, Tarım ve Nüfus. Ekonomik Yaklaşım, Cilt: 7, Sayı: 22.
Karpat, K. (2003). Türkiye'de Toplumsal Dönüşüm. İmge Kitapevi. Ankara.
Keleş, R. (1972). Türkiye'de Şehirleşme, Konut ve Gecekondu. Gerçek Yayınevi. İstanbul.
Oktar, S., & Varlı, A. (2010). Türkiye'de 1950-1954 döneminde Demokrat Parti'nin Tarım Politikası.
  M.Ü. İktisadi ve İdari Bilimler Fakültesi, Cilt: XXVIII, Sayı I, s. 1-22.
Türkdoğan, O. (1977). Köy Sosyolojisinin Temel Sorunları. Dede Korkut Yayınları. İstanbul.
Tütengil, C. O. (1979). Kırsal Türkiye'nin Yapısı ve Sorunları. Gerçek Yayınevi. İstanbul.

Türkistan'dan Balkanlara son Türk göçünü gerçekleştiren Peçenek, Uz ve Kumanların göç yolları ve kültürel etkileri

Fatma Rodoplu[341]

Giriş

Türkistan'dan batı istikametine Türkler tarafından gerçekleştirilen büyük göçlerin son halkasını Peçenek, Uz ve Kumanlar oluşturur. IX-XII yüzyıllar arasında gerçekleşen göçlerin özelliği aynı yolu takip ederek birbirlerinin ardılları olmaları ve birbirlerini etkilemiş olmalarıdır. En doğuda bulunan Kumanlar önlerindeki Uzları tazyik etmişler, Uzlar da Peçenekleri baskı altına alarak göç hareketinin yönünü sahasını genişletmiştir.

Peçenek, Uz ve Kumanların Ortaya Çıktığı Coğrafyalar ve Başlıca Göç İstikametleri

Göktürk Hakanlığı'na bağlı boylardan olan Peçenekler VIII. yy. ortalarında Issık Göl ve Balkaş Gölü yakınlarında yaşadıkları düşünülmektedir. Batı Göktürk Devleti'nin zayıflaması ve dağılmasıyla Peçenekler bulundukları yerlerden batı istikametine doğru yönelmişler Talas boyundan Sır Derya'nın aşağı tarafına geçmişlerdir. Ayrıca Oğuz boylarının birçoğunun Sır Derya yönünde ilerlemeleri Peçeneklerin yeniden yer değiştirmesine ve Hazar Hakanlığı'na yaklaşmalarına sebep olmuştur. (*Yücel, 2007, s. 36*) 860-880 yılları arasında (İdil) Volga nehrinin batı tarafına gitmişlerdir. Peçenekler Volga'nın kuzeyine geçtiklerinde Karadeniz'in kuzeyindeki bozkırlar oldukça tenhaydı. Peçeneklerin Volga bölgesine geldikleri esnada bölgede bulunan ve Hazarlara tabi olan Macarların büyük bölümü Donets nehri sahasında bulunmaktaydı. (*Yücel, 2007, s. 34*) Peçenekler Macarları Dinyeper ve Don arasındaki Rus bozkırlarının batı yakasında bulunan Atelkuzu'dan çıkararak batı istikametine doğru göç ettiler. (*Grousst, 2010, s. 211*)

Peçeneklerin Don ve Kuban boyları, Orta ve Aşağı Dinyeper, Kırım ve Tuna'ya kadar 2000 kilometreden daha geniş bir alana yayılmışlardır. Peçeneklerin Rus bozkırlarına ilk geliş tarihi 915 yılıdır. Peçeneklerin bulunduğu saha Kiev Rusya'sının güneyidir. (*Yücel, 2007, s. 35*)

Peçenekler Karadeniz'in kuzeyindeki bozkırlarda yüzyıldan fazla bir süre rahat bir hayat yaşamışlardır. Bu sırada doğuda bulunan Peçenekler ise kendilerini Volga ötesinden çıkaran ve batıya doğru ilerlemelerine sebep olan Uzların baskılarına maruz kalmaktaydılar. XI. yüzyılın başlarında, Uzların esas kitlesi doğudan gelen Kumanların baskısı ile Volga'nın batı tarafına geçmiş ve Don boylarını işgale başlamışlardır. Bu sırada Peçenekler de Dinyeper'e doğru kaymaya başlamışlardır. X. yüzyılın ortalarında Peçenekler kalabalık zümreler halinde Macaristan topraklarına yerleşmişlerdir. Ancak esas kütle Dinyeper'in sağ tarafındaki Dinyester boyuna, günümüz Basarabya'sına gitmiştir. 1036 yılında Kiev

---

[341] Arş. Gör. Fatma Rodoplu, Trakya Üniversitesi, Balkan Araştırma Enstitüsü, Balkan Tarihi Anabilim Dalı, Edirne. İletişim E-mail: fatmarodoplu@trakya.edu.tr

Rusya'sından ağır bir yenilgi alan Peçeneklerin esas kitlesi Aşağı Turla ve Tuna boyuna gitmiştir.

Peçeneklerin göç sahalarının sınırları tam olarak tespit edilememiştir. (İdil) Volga'yı geçip batıya giden sekiz Peçenek uruğu Dinyeper nehrinin sağ ve sol tarafına olmak üzere iki sahaya bölünmüştür. Doğu tarafında bulunanlar Hazar sınırı, Kuban boyu ve Kırım'da meskûn iken, Dinyeper'in batısında ise Bulgaristan (Aşağı Tuna boyu), Macaristan (Karpatların eteklerinde) ve Kiev Rusya'sı yakınında görülmüşlerdir. 1016'dan itibaren Peçeneklerin esas kitlesi Aşağı Tuna boyuna geçmiştir. Aral Gölü'nün kuzeyinde yaşayan Oğuzların bir kolu olan Uz baskısının artması üzerine Peçeneklerin Balkanlara geçmesi adeta bir zorunluluk haline gelmiştir. (*Grousst, 2010, s.211*)

1048'de Uzların Don boyundan Dinyeper Nehri'ne doğru Kiev Rusya'sının güneyine kadar yayıldıkları görülmektedir. Kuman baskısına maruz kalan Uzların bir süre sonra Orta Dinyeper boyunda kalabalık bir zümreyi teşkil ettiği görülmektedir. Peçeneklerin ardı sıra Bizans ve Bulgar mukavemetini kırarak 1065'de Tuna'yı geçmişler, Trakya ve Makedonya, Selanik ve Mora'ya kadar gelmişlerdir. (Yücel, 2007, s. 47)

V. Minorsky Kıpçakları, sınırlarını doğuda Kırgızlar, güneyde Artuş ve Atil nehirleriyle çizdiği Kimeklerin bir kolu olarak tanımlar. *(Minorsky, 2008, s.54-58)* Kimek ikili federasyonu içerisinde bulunan Kıpçak kolu güneyden gelen Kun (Kuman) göçleri ile daha da güçlenerek, birlikte Volga üzerinden batıya yönelmiştir. Önlerindeki Uz kütleleri Balkanlara çekilince Güney Rusya sahaları onların yerleşmesine müsait bir hale gelmiştir. Kumanlar XI. yüzyılın sonlarından itibaren Don-Dinyester ağırlık merkezi olmak üzere, Balkaş Gölü-Talas havalisinden Tuna ağzına kadar yayılmışlardır. Kafkaslarda Kuban bölgesini de içine alan bu arazi, kuzeyde Oka-Sura nehirleri boyunca yani Bulgarları sınırlarına kadar uzanıyordu. Kumanlar 1091'de Macaristan, 1092'de Lehistan yönünde ilerleyerek nihayetinde Bizans topraklarında görünmüşlerdir. Don-Kuban Kumanlarının bir kısmı Gürcistan'a geçerek Çoruh ve Kür dolaylarına yerleşmiştir.

2. Peçenek, Uz ve Kumanların Bıraktığı Bazı Kültürel İzler

Görüldüğü gibi oldukça geniş bir coğrafyada uzun yıllar etkili olan Türk kavimlerinin geçtikleri yollar üzerinde, yaşadıkları coğrafyalarda kendilerinden izler bırakmamış olmaları olası değildir. Bunların başında edebiyata olan etkisi gelir. Özgün Rus edebiyatının ilk örneklerinde konular arasında sürekli mücadele halinde oldukları Türkler ön sıralardadır. Bu dönemde yazılmaya başlanan vakayiname türünün ilk örneği olan "Geçmiş yılların öyküsü" adlı eserde Peçeneklerle olan mücadelelerine geniş yer verilmektedir. 997 yılında: *Vladimir Novgorod'a gitti. Knezin olmadığını öğrenen Peçenekler Belgorod şehrine geldi ve burada kaldı. Şehirden kimsenin çıkmasına izin vermediler ve şehirde büyük bir kıtlık ve açlık yaşandı. Vladimir kendinden oldukça fazla miktarda savaşçısı olan Peçenekler karşısında şehre yardım edemedi. Uzun kuşatma büyük bir açlığa sebep oldu. Toplanan halk "Yakında nasıl olsa açlıktan öleceğiz, hala knezden bir yardım yok. Bizim için hangi ölüm daha iyi? Peçeneklere teslim olup bazılarımızın ölüp bazılarımızın hayatta kalması mı yoksa açlıktan ölmek mi? Hepsi aynı bizim için" dedi (http://www.narodrusi.ru/publ/10-1-0-12)*

Rus halk edebiyatının önde gelen eseri "İgor seferi destanı" Novgorod-Seversk Knezi İgor'un Kumanlar üzerine çıktığı seferi konu almaktadır. Rus birliklerinin Kumanlarla girdiği acınası mücadeleyi şu dizelerle dile getirir yazar:

Бился день,
Бился другой,
На третий день к полудню пали стяги Игоревы.
Тут два брата разлучились на берегу быстрой Каялы;
Тут кровавого вина не достало;
Тут пир закончили храбрые русичи:
Сватов напоили, а сами полегли за землю Русскую.
Никнет трава от жалости,
А дерево с горем к земле приклонилось

Gün boyu savaşıldı,
Ertesi gün yine savaşıldı,
Üçüncü gün öğlen saatinde İgor düştü.
İki kardeş Kayala kıyısında hemen ayrıldı;
Buradaki kan şarabı bitti;
İşte cesur Rusların bayramı bitti:
Kendilerini Rus toprağı için helak ettiler,
Otlar kederden boynunu büktü,
Ağaçlar üzüntüyle yere eğildi.

İgor Seferi destanının 1800 yılında ilk basımından sonra Rus ve Avrupalı dilci, edebiyatçı, folklorist ve tarihçiler bu halk destanındaki Türk (Kuman) kökenli kelimelerin varlığı üzerine çeşitli münakaşalara girmişlerdir. Platon Mihayloviç Melioranski "boyarin, kogan, saltan, haralug, şereşir" gibi kelimelerin Türk kökenli olduğunu iddia eder. (Stoyanov, 2009, s.164-166)

Kıpçaklardan kalan bir diğer yazılı eser de Avrupalılara Kıpçak dilini öğretme amacıyla yazılan Codex Cumanicus adlı sözlüktür. Latince-Farsça-Kumanca sözlük Kırım, Kerç, Taman çevresindeki Kıpçak dili hakkında fikir vermektedir. (Yücel, 2007, s. 65) Codex Cumanicus'un Kıpçak Türkçesine ait kelime hazinesi ile Kıpçak grubuna giren çağdaş Türk lehçelerinden Kazan Tatarcası ve Karaimce arasındaki benzerlik ve paralellikler konusunda çeşitli araştırmalar yapılmıştır. Kafkasya'da konuşulan Kıpçak lehçelerinden Karaçay-Malkar Türkçesi de aynı mirası paylaşan bir Türk lehçesi olması sebebiyle Codex Cumanicus ile büyük benzerlik ve paralellikler taşımaktadır. (Tavkul, 2003, s. 45-81)

İrtiş boyundan başlayarak Tuna nehrine kadar uzanan geniş bir coğrafyada yaşayan Kumanların kullandığı Kuman-Kıpçak Türkçesi Batı Türkçesi veya Orta Türkçe adıyla anılmıştır. Dilin özelliklerini ve kurallarını en iyi Divan-ı Lugat-it Türk ile Kaşgarlı Mahmud yansıtmıştır.

Peçenek, Uz ve Kumanlar özellikle Balkanlarda yer adlarıyla yaşamaya devam etmektedir. Romanya ve Bulgaristan'da ağırlıklı olmak üzere çeşitli Balkan ülkelerinde ortaçağ Türklerine ait toponimler mevcuttur. Özellikle Sofya ve kuzey Bulgaristan ile Dobruca bölgesinde Kuman kalıntıları daha fazladır. M. Türker Acaroğlu'nun verdiği Türk menşeli olan bazı yer adları ve bulundukları yerler şu şekildedir:

Al-Timir: Sofya'ya bağlı eski bir Türk köyü olan Al-Timir Bulgar-Türk hanı Terter'in kardeşinin adından gelmektedir.

Asen (Hısen): Lofça ilinin Tetevan ilçesine bağlı köydür. İkinci Bulgar Devleti'nin kurucusu olan Kuman kökenli Asen hanedanının adını taşımaktadır.

Aşağı Turgan: Sofya ilinin Radomir ilçesine bağlı eski bir Türk köyü. Turgan, Peçenek-Kuman dilinde durgun su anlamına gelir.

Basarabya: Ülkenin kurucusu olan Basaraba'nın Kuman kökenli bir Türk olduğu bilinmektedir. "Basar" Türkçe "yenmek, galip gelmek" anlamına gelen "bas" kökünden gelmektedir.

Batak: Tırnova ilinin Ziştovi ilçesinde köy adı. Adının Peçenek, Kuman ya da Uz Türklerinden kaldığı kesindir. Köy bataklık bir alanda kurulduğu için bu adı almıştır.

Batişniçe: Ruçuk'a bağlı olan köy adının sonuna –itsa eki getirilerek Slavcalaştırılmıştır.

Bejanova: Lofça Lukovit'te bir Türk köyüdür. Bejan Peçenek adının Macarca biçimidir. Peçenek Türk kökenli olduğu anlaşılmaktadır.

Berende: Safya'ya bağlı Türk köyüdür. Bu yer adı Peçenek soyundan Berende boyunu anımsattığı ileri sürülmektedir.

Borilofça: Vidin'e bağlı eski bir Türk köyü. Kuman-Peçenek kökenli Boril kişi adının sonuna ek getirilmek suretiyle Slavcalaştırılmıştır. Kaloyanın ölümünden sonra tahta üç kardeşin ablasının oğlu Boril çıktı. (Vasary, 2008, s. 69.)

Çekan: Sofya'ya bağlı Türk köyü. Kumanca çekan, çakan: ağaç-kakan anlamına gelir. Eski Yugoslavya'da da Dimitrovgrad ilçesine bağlı da bir Çekan köyü vardır.

Korman: Lofça ilinin Selvi ilçesine bağlı eski bir Türk köyüdür. Kuman kökenli olduğu düşünülmektedir. Günümüzde de Korman şahıs ismi olarak kullanılmaya devam etmektedir.

Şoplar: Lofça'da bulunan bir Türk köyüdür. Peçenek-Kuman kökenlidir.

Terter: Hezargrad'a bağlı bir Türk köyü olan Terter'in adı İkinci Bulgar devleti hanedanlarından gelmektedir.

Uzlar: Hacıoğlu Pazarcık ilinin Balçık ilçesine bağlı Türk köyü. Adından da anlaşılacağı üzere Uz Türklerinin adını taşır.

Kaloyan: Hacı Dima ve Dospat kentleri arasında kalan arazi adı. II. Bulgar devletinin kurucusu Asen'in kardeşinin adını taşımaktadır.

Kaspi-çan: Şumnu Yenipazar'da bir kasaba adıdır. Uz Türklerinin başbuğlarından birinin adı olduğu düşünülmektedir.

Bulgaristan, Romanya, Makedonya gibi Balkan ülkelerinde bulunan yukarıda saydığımız Kuman, Kıpçak, Uz yer adlarının yanı sıra "Kuman, Kumaniçe, Kuman deresi, Kumanova, Kuman çayırı, Kuman mezarı, Kumantepe, Peçenek, Peçinska, Peçenyaga" gibi tamamen menşeini belli eden sayısız yer adı bulunmaktadır.

Sonuç

Türkler ilk ortaya çıktıkları yerlerden çok uzak topraklara kadar uzanan birçok göç hareketi gerçekleştirmişlerdir. Yeni yerleştikleri yerlere, coğrafi özelliklerine uygun olarak geldikleri yerlerin adlarını, boy ve boy beylerinin ve kahramanlarının adlarını vermişlerdir. Bugün idari olarak farklı milletlerin egemenliğinde olsa da Rus, Balkan ve Orta Avrupa topraklarında Türk kültürünün izine rastlamak oldukça olağandır. Yüzyıllarca gerek askeri, gerek idari ve gerekse de sosyal alandaki birçok uygulamada Türk etkisi izlenmektedir.

Kaynakça

Acaroğlu, M. T. (2006). Bulgaristan'da Türkçe Yer adları kılavuzu, Ankara.

Acaroğlu, M. T. (2006). Balkanlarda Türkçe Yer Adları Kılavuzu, İstanbul.

Ahincanov, S. (2014). Kıpçaklar, Türk Halklarının Katalizatör Boyu, çev. Kürşat Yıldırım, İstanbul.

Efendiyeva, Ç. (2003). Eski Rus "İgor Destanı" adlı eserdeki eski Türk kökenli kelimeler üzerine bir inceleme, Bilig, S. 24, Kış, Ankara.

Golubovski, P. (1884). Peçenegi, Torki i Polovtsi do naşestviye tatar, , Kiev.

Grousst, R. (2010). Bozkır İmparatorluğu, çev. Dr. M. Reşat Uzmen, İstanbul.

Miçev N.-Koledarov P. (1989). Reçnik na seliştata i seliştnite imena v Bılgariya, Sofya.

Minorsky V. (2008). Hududul Alem Minel-Meşrik İle'l-Magrib, çev. Abdullah Duman-Murat Ağarı, İstanbul.

Stoyanov, V. (2009). Kumanologiya I-II, Sofya.

Tavkul, U. (Bahar 2003). Codex Cumanicus ve Karaçay-Malkar Türkçesi Türk Dünyası Dil ve Edebiyat Dergisi, (15).

Vasary, İ. (2008). Kumanlar ve Tatarlar, çev. Ali Cevat Akkoyunlu, İstanbul.

Yücel, M. U. (2007). İlk Rus Yıllıklarına Göre Türkler, Ankara.

Yücel, M. U. (2006). "Kuman Kıpçakların Tarihinde İgor Destanı'nın Yeri ve Önemi", Belleten, C. LXX, S. 258, Ankara.

Rus Yıllıkları
Povesti Vremennih Let
İpatiyevskaya Letapis
Lavrentiyevskaya Letapis

Yahya Kemal'de yolculuk ve şiirin varoluş serüveni

Pınar Aka

Yahya Kemal, 1903 senesinde, o sırada padişah olan Abdülhamid'in baskıcı rejiminden kaçmak düşüncesiyle İstanbul'dan tek başına bindiği gemiyle Marsilya'ya doğru yola çıktığında henüz on sekiz yaşındadır. Şair, oradan geçtiği ve o sırada Batı medeniyetinin ve modernitenin başkenti olarak görülen Paris'te dokuz sene kalacaktır. Peki onu genç yaşta böyle bir maceraya iten ne olmuştur?

"En vahşi, en uzak olan herhangi bir toprak, yeniden bulunan bir vatan gibidir" der Lamartine (2008, s. 551). Yahya Kemal, Batı'ya ve Paris'e doğru yolculuğunun sebeplerini nasıl açıklarsa açıklasın onu, on üç yaşındayken kaybettiği annesinin ölümünü hatırlatan topraklardan uzaklaşıp denize açılmaya iten dürtüyü anlamak zor değildir.

Yahya Kemal'de 'gurbet' kavramı da ölümle yakından ilişkilidir ve tıpkı ölüm gibi şairin şiirlerinde muğlaklığın yoğunlaştığı alanlardan biri olur. "Hüzün ve Hâtıra" şiirinden alınmış olan "Gurbette duyduğum sonu gelmez hüzünleri,/ Yaprakların döküldüğü hicranlı günleri,/ Andım birer birer, acıdım kendi hâlime" (Beyatlı, 1967, s. 116) dizelerinde gurbette olmanın yarattığı derin hüzün ortaya konurken "Gurbet" şiirinde bu durumun yarattığı sıkıntı ve acılar sıralandıktan sonra 'gidilen menfâ'nın neresi olduğu konusunda bir muğlaklık oluşturulur. Bu, dünya üzerinde gerçek bir yer olabileceği gibi ölüm diyârı da olabilir.

> *Gurbet nedir bilir mi o menfâya gitmiyen?*
> *Ey gurbet, ey gurûbu ufuklarda bitmiyen*
> *Ömrün derinliğinde süren kaygı günleri!*
> *Yıllarca, fakr içinde, hayâtın hüzünleri.*
> *Bir çöl çoraklığında hayâlin susuzluğu;*
> *Hem uyku ihtiyaçları, hem uykusuzluğu.*
> *En sinsi bir ezâ gibidir geçmiyen zaman;*
> *Bin türlü başka cevri de vardır ki bî-aman;*
> *Yalnızlığın azâbı her işkenceden beter;*
> *Yalnız bu kahrı insanı tahrîb için yeter. (Beyatlı, 1967, s. 115)*

Yahya Kemal'in "Açık Deniz" şiirinden alınmış olan "Çıktım sürekli gurbete, gezdim diyar diyar;/ Gittim o son diyâra ki serhaddidir yerin," (Beyatlı, 1967, s. 15) dizelerinde gurbetin bu kez daha somut bir anlamı olduğu anlaşılmakta, bu dizeler, şairin Doğu'dan Batı'ya doğru yaptığı gemi yolculuğunu çağrıştırmaktadır. Şair, annesinin öldüğü toprakları terk edip denize açılmış, bu yolculuk sonucunda dokuz sene boyunca vatanından uzakta, "gurbette" kalmıştır. Ancak yolculuğunun sonunda vardığı Avrupa toprakları simgesel olarak bir sınır noktasıdır. Zira bu nokta, belki de yalnızca Doğu'yla Batı değil, bu dünyayla öte-dünya arasındaki sınır noktasıdır.

Yahya Kemal'de 'deniz', 'su' ve 'yolculuk' imgelerinin öne çıkması bu açıdan bakıldığında şaşırtıcı değil. Yolculuk, şiirin varoluş serüvenini ortaya koymak için uygun bir metafordur. Deniz-ses ilişkisini gözler önüne seren dizeler ve şiirlerse, söz konusu serüvenin Yahya Kemal'in şiirinin oluşumundaki temel işlevini gösterecektir. "Deniz" şiirinden alınmış olan "Sesler denizin ufkunu uçtan uca sardı," (Beyatlı, 1967, s. 133) ve "Sesler geliyor sandım ilâhî sulardan," (Beyatlı, 1967, s. 133) dizelerinde sözünü ettiğimiz ilişki açıktır. Ancak deniz-ses ilişkisi ve sesin taşıdığı anlam bağlamında bu şiirin tamamına yakından bakmak gerekmektedir. Şiirinin birinci bölümünde ortaya konan "ölümün şiiri" ve "ölülerden gelen âhenk" kavramları özellikle dikkat çekicidir.

> *Bir gün deniz ölgündü. Bir oltayla balıkta,*
> *Kuşlar gibi yalnız, yapayalnızdım açıkta.*
> *Şehrin eleminden bir uzak merhaledeydim,*
> *Fânîleri gökten ayıran perdeye değdim.*
> *Rüzgârlara benzer bir uğultuyla sulardan,*
> *Sesler geliyor sandım ilâhî sulardan,*
> *Her an daha coşkun, daha yüksek, daha gergin,*
> *Binlerce ağızdan bir ilâhî gibi engin*
> *Sesler denizin ufkunu uçtan uca sardı,*
> *Benzim, ölümün şi'ri yayıldıkça, sarardı.*
> *Kalbimse bu hengâmede kuşlar gibi ürkek,*
> *Kalbim heyecandan dedi : "Artık dönelim, çek!*
> *Kâfî!.. Ölülerden gelen âhenge kapılma!" (Beyatlı, 1967, s. 133-134)*

"Sessiz Gemi" şiirini anımsatan ve bir kez daha yolculuk metaforu etrafında inşa edilen "Gece" şiirinde "Gittik... Bahs açmadık dönüşten" dizesinin varlığı, bunun bir ölüm yolculuğu olduğu konusunda kuşkuya yer bırakmaz. Sözü edilen yolcuğun, "Gitmiş kaybolmuşuz uzakta,/ Rü'yâ sona ermeden şafakta..." (Beyatlı, 1967, s. 54) dizelerinin de ortaya koyduğu gibi bir rüya boyunca gerçekleşmesiyse, rüya–ölüm ilişkilendirmesine olanak sağlayacaktır.

"Akşam Mûsıkîsi" şiirinde yer alan "Artık ne gelen, ne beklenen var" (Beyatlı, 1967, s. 55) dizesi, ölüm diyârına uğurlanmış bir ölüden söz edildiğini imâ etmektedir. Aynı şiirden alınmış "Gözlerden uzaklaşınca dünyâ/ Bin bir geceden birinde gûyâ/ Başlar rü'yâ içinde rü'yâ" (Beyatlı, 1967, s. 56) dizeleriyse dünyayla rüya arasında kalmışlık durumunu çağrıştırırken, Yahya Kemal'in şiirlerinde rüya ile ölüm âlemi arasında kurulan yakınlığı belirginleştirir.

"O Taraf" şiirinde, rüyayla ölüm âlemi arasında kurulan bir yakınlığın ötesinde, bir örtüşmeden söz etmek mümkündür. Bu şiirin öznesi, sözü edilen rüya yolculuğunu öte-dünyayı keşfedecek kadar ileri bir noktaya götürür: "Gördüm ölüm diyârını rü'yâda bir gece" (Beyatlı, 1967, s. 110).

Yahya Kemal'in şiirlerinde ses bağlamında bir muğlaklık söz konusudur. Ses, hem yaşamla, hem de ölümle ilişkilendirilebilir. Sessizlikte böyle bir muğlaklık yoktur. "Nazar" şiirinde Leylâ ölürken sessizce solar: "Soldu, günden güne sessiz, soldu!/ Dediler hep: "Kıza bir hâl oldu!" (Beyatlı, 1967, s. 150). "O Taraf" şiirinde rüyada ölüm diyârını gören özne, "[s]essizlik ortasında gezindim" (Beyatlı, 1967, s. 110) diyecektir. Şiirin devamında ölüler, sessizlikleriyle tanımlanır: "Allâha şükredip duruyorlar ve kol kola,/ Sessiz, yavaş yavaş dalıyorlardı bir yola" (Beyatlı, 1967, s. 111). "Sessiz Gemi" ise sessizlikle ölüm arasında kurulan ilişkiyi belirginleştirir.

"Koca Mustâpaşa"da "Gitme! Kal! Sen bu taraf halkına dost insansın;/ Onların meşrebi, iklîmi ve ırkındansın" (Beyatlı, 1967, s. 51) diyen ses, 'yaşam dürtüsü'nün aracı gibi görünmektedir. Oysa "Deniz"de, gerçek dünyaya ait olmayan ve başka bir dünyadan geldiği izlenimini veren bazı sesler vardır: " Sesler geliyor sandım ilâhî kuğulardan " (Beyatlı, 1967, s. 133). Bu sesleri, şiirin öznesinin, "Fânîleri gökten ayıran perdeye değdim" (Beyatlı, 1967, s. 133) dediği noktada işitmesi anlamlıdır. Nitekim "Süleymaniye'de Bayram Sabahı" şiirinde de ses, bu dünyaya ait olanla öte-dünyaya ait olan unsurları bir araya getirir: "Duyulan gökte kanad, yerde ayak sesleridir" (Beyatlı, 1967, s. 9).

Diğer taraftan, "Deniz" şiirinde özneye maddi dünyadan kurtulup özgür bir ruh olmasını tavsiye eden 'öteki ses', özneyi rüyaya doğru çağıran bir sesi akla getirmektedir. Bu ses, ölüme çağırıyor olabileceği gibi şiire çağırıyor da olabilir.

"Ses" şiirinde bu bağlamda muğlaklığın ortadan kalktığı söylenebilir. Zira burada ses, yaşamı imleyen 'yaz' metaforuyla ilişkilendirilir. Bu noktada Yahya kemal'in şiirlerinde sıkça karşımıza çıkan bu metafora daha yakından bakmakta yarar var. Bu metaforun sadece "Geçmiş Yaz" şiirinde değil, diğer şiirlerde de neredeyse hep geçmişle ilişkilendirildiği görülecektir. Örneğin "Özleyen" şiirinden alınmış "Sen nerdesin, ey sevgili, yaz günleri nerde!" (Beyatlı, 1967, s. 151) dizesinde 'yaz', başta anne olmak üzere sevilen ve özlenenleri akla getirir. "Açık Deniz" şiirinde geçen "Her yaz şimâle doğru asırlarca bir koşu/ Bağrımda bir akis gibi kalmış uğultulu" (Beyatlı, 1967, s. 14) ve "Akıncı" şiirinde geçen "Bir yaz günü geçtik Tuna'dan kaafilelerle" (Beyatlı, 1967, s. 22) dizelerinde Osmanlı'nın fetihlerinde muzaffer olduğu bir zamana göndermede bulunulur. "Yol Düşüncesi" şiirinin son dizeleri ise vatanın bütünlüklü haline duyulan özlemi "bitmeyen bir yaz" metaforuyla somutlar:

Vatan şehirleri karşımda, her saat, bir bir,
Fetihler ufku Tekirdağ ve sevdiğim İzmir,
Şerefli kubbeler iklîmi, Marmara'yla Boğaz,
Üzerlerinde bulutsuz ve bitmiyen bir yaz,
Bütün eserlerimiz, halkımız ve askerimiz,
Birer birer görünen anlı şanlı cedlerimiz,
İçimde dalgalı Tekbîr'i en güzel dînin,
Zaman zaman da Nevâ-Kâr'ı, doğsun, Itrî'nin.
Ölüm yabancı bir âlemde bir geceyse bile,
Tahayyülümde vatan kalsın eski hâliyle. (Beyatlı1967, s. 84)

Yahya Kemal'de 'yaz'ın her zaman yaşamı imlediği anlaşılmaktadır. Bu bağlamda 'yaz'ın 'sonbahar'la oluşturduğu karşıtlık, "Sonbahar" şiirinden alınmış olan "Fânî ömür biter, bir uzun sonbahar olur" (Beyatlı, 1967, s. 85) ve "Düşünce" şiirinden alınmış "Bitsin, hayırlısıyle, bu beyhûde sonbahar!" (Beyatlı, 1967, s. 88) dizelerinin de ortaya koyduğu gibi bu görüşümüzü destekler niteliktedir. "Kaybolan Şehir" şiirinde geçen "Bir sonbaharda annemi gömdük o toprağa" (Beyatlı, 1967, s. 77) dizesindeyse, şairin muhayyilesinde annenin ölümüyle sonbahar arasında kurulan ilişki açıkça ortaya konur.

Diğer taraftan, "Geçmiş Yaz" şiirinde gördüğümüz gibi 'yaz' geçmişi muhafaza etmekle kalmaz, aynı zamanda estetize de eder. "Mevsimler" şiirinden alınmış "Biten yazla başlar keder mûsıkîsi" (Beyatlı, 1967, s. 44) dizesi ve "Ses" şiirinden alınmış "Bir lâhzada bir pancur açılmış gibi yazdan/ Bir bestenin engin sesi yükseldi Boğaz'dan" (Beyatlı, 1967, s. 132) dizelerinde görüldüğü gibi bu estetizasyonun aracı, "Geçmiş Yaz" şiirinde olduğu gibi rüya ve şiir değil, bu kez müziktir.

Bu noktada 'yaz' sözcüğünün hem mevsimi hem de 'yazmak' fiilinin emir kipini imlediğini belirtmekte yarar var. Yahya Kemal'in şiirlerinde de dille ve şiirle olan bağı açıkça ortaya konan 'yaz' imgesi, kaybedilmiş ve ölüme uğurlanmış olanları şiir yoluyla canlandırmanın bir aracına dönüşür.

Böylece, geçmişle gelecek arasında kalmışlık durumu, geçmişe ve hatırlananlara gönderme yapan 'yaz' imgesiyle geleceğe ve ölüme gönderme yapan 'rüya' imgesinde bulur şiirsel karşılığını. İlginç bir şekilde, gerek 'yaz' imgesi etrafında örülen geçmişi bellekte canlandıran, gerekse ölüm diyarını hayâl eden şiirlerde donmuş bir zaman tasavvuruna varılır. Oysa Yahya Kemal'in gerek kültürel konularda gerekse şiir bağlamında çok önemsediği 'imtidâd' kavramı sürekli bir değişimi, dönüşümü ve yinelenmeyi, dolayısıyla da geçmişten kopmadan da olsa akıp giden bir zaman tasavvurunu kaçınılmaz kılmaktadır. Geçmişle gelecek arasında bulunan ve Henri Bergson'un 'durée' kavramıyla örtüşen, böyle bir zamandır ve şiirsel karşılığını 'akşam' imgesinde bulur. Bergson'a göre, "bir algı ne kadar kısa olursa olsun, gerçekte her zaman belli bir süreyi işgal eder ve dolayısıyla da, birçok anı birinden diğerine uzatan hafızanın bir çabasını zorunlu kılar" (1999, s.30-31). İşte hafızanın geçmişini, algının eyleme dönük geleceğine doğru uzatan da bu süre, 'durée'dir.

Yahya Kemal'de gündüzle gece arasında bir ara zamanı imleyen 'akşam', ölüm-öncesi bir zamanı imlemekle birlikte, hep ölümü ima eder şekilde kullanılır. "Mehlika Sultan" şiirinden alınmış "Dediler: 'Belki son akşamdır bu" (Beyatlı, 1967, s. 122) dizesi ve "Deniz Türküsü" şiirinden alınmış "Gidişin seçtiğin akşam saatinden belli./ Ömrünün geçtiği sâhilden uzaklaştıkça/ Ve hayâlinde doğan âleme yaklaştıkça," (Beyatlı, 1967, s. 96) dizeleri bunu açıkça ortaya koyar. 'Akşam', "Rindlerin Akşamı" şiirinde, bu kez sınırda olma durumunun en belirgin imgelerinden 'ufuk'la birlikte anılır ve tıpkı bu imge gibi, yaşamla ölüm arasında olmanın ötesinde, ölüme doğru bir eğilimi, hatta gidişi imler:

Dönülmez akşamın ufkundayız. Vakit çok geç;
Bu son fasıldır ey ömrüm, nasıl geçersen geç!
Cihâna bir daha gelmek hayâl edilse bile,
Avunmak istemeyiz öyle bir teselliyle.
Geniş kanatları boşlukta simsiyâh açılan
Ve arkasında güneş doğmıyan büyük kapıdan
Geçince başlıyacak bitmeyen sükûnlu gece.
Gurûba karşı bu son bahçelerde, keyfince,
Ya şevk içinde harâb ol, ya aşk içinde gönül!
Ya lâle açmalıdır göğsümüzde yâhud gül. (Beyatlı, 1967, s. 92)

Dikkat edilirse, şiirin son bölümünde ölüme geçişin tamamlanmasından sonra bile "O Taraf" şiirindeki gibi donmuş bir zaman tasavvuruna varılmaz. Divan edebiyatının şiiri imleyen mazmunu 'gül'ün açması, zaman bağlamında devamın ve 'imtidâd'ın şiirle gerçekleştiğinin göstergesidir. Böylece 'akşam' imgesi, ölümün gerçekliğinden ölümün şiirine geçmeyi sağlayan bir köprü işlevi görür.

Bu noktada yukarda sözünü ettiğimiz "Akşam Mûsıkîsi" şiirine daha yakından bakmakta yarar var. Bu şiirde, 'akşam' imgesi, yaşamla ölüm ve geçmişle gelecek arasında olma durumunu imlemekle kalmaz, bu uçları bir araya getirerek şiirsel 'imtidâd'a da olanak sağlar. Gerçekten de bir hatırlama eylemiyle başlayan şiir, dünyanın gözden kaybolmasıyla birlikte, ölümü imleyen rüyanın başlamasıyla sona erer. Bu şiirde, benzer bir durumun görüldüğü "Bir Dosta Mısralar" şiirinden farklı olarak, geçmişle gelecek arasındaki ara zaman yok sayılmaz. Ancak bu ara bölgede, şiirin sonunda sözü edilen "rüya içinde rüya" ile uyumlu bir şekilde 'zaman içinde zaman' diye adlandırabileceğimiz bir kavramdan söz etmek mümkündür.

Kandilli'de, eski bahçelerde,
Akşam kapanınca perde perde,
Bir hâtıra zevki var kederde.

Artık ne gelen, ne beklenen var;
Tenhâ yolun ortasında rüzgâr
Teşrin yapraklarıyle oynar.

Gittikçe derinleşir saatler,
Rikkatle, yavaş yavaş ve yer yer
Sessizlik dâimâ ilerler.

Ürperme verir hayâle sık sık,
Her bir kapıdan giren karanlık,
Çok belli ayak sesinden artık.

Gözlerden uzaklaşınca dünyâ
Bin bir geceden birinde gûyâ
Başlar rü'yâ içinde rü'yâ. (Beyatlı, 1967, s. 55-56)

"Musikî daima oluş hâlindedir. Zaman gibi ve onun nizamıyle kendi kendisini yiyerek büyür, kendinde doğar ve kendinde kaybolur" (1998, s. 36) diyen Ahmet Hamdi Tanpınar, Yahya Kemal'in şiirinde ortaya çıkan, 'şiirsel zaman' olarak tanımlayabileceğimiz ve gerçek zamandan farklı olan bu zaman tasavvurunun müzikle olan ilişkisini ortaya koyar. "Musikî giydirilmiş zamandır" (Tanpınar, 1998, s. 37) sözüyle ise Tanpınar müzikle bu zamanı örtüştürür.

Diğer sanatların hemen hepsinde tabiattan bir şey var. Musikî sadece alır; zaman gibi onu da her şeyle durdurabilirsiniz. Maddesizdir, sesten yani heyecanların en iptidaî işaretinden yapılmıştır. Onun için daima iptidaîdir. Düşünceyi değil, nabzı idare eder. (Tanpınar, 1998, s. 37)

Zaman meselesinin müzikle olan bu iç içeliği, Yahya Kemal'in şiirinin lirizminin sessel boyutunun "imtidâd" bakımından taşıdığı önemi gözler önüne seriyor. "Ses" adlı rubâîsinde "Yâ Rab bana bir ses yaratan kudreti ver" (Beyatlı, 2004, s. 36) diyen şairin, şiirin bu ses boyutunu her şeyden fazla önemsediği anlaşılmakta. Nitekim bir başka rubâîsinde "Bir bitmiyecek şevk verirken beste/ Bir tel kopar âhenk ebediyyen kesilir" (Beyatlı, 2004, s. 39) dizelerinde sesin ve müziğin yokluğunu ölümle ilişkilendirir.

Bu noktada şunu vurgulamak gerekiyor: Şiirin ve lirizmin sessel boyutunun yanında görsel bir boyutu da vardır. "Akşam Mûsıkîsi" şiirinde geçen "rüya içinde rüya" kavramı bu boyutu gözler önüne serer. Ancak Yahya Kemal'in şiirinin görsel boyutunu sessel boyutundan bağımsız olarak ele almak pek mümkün değil. Nitekim Tanpınar'ın şu sözleri de rüyanın görsel imgelerinden ziyade 'atmosfer'ini öne çıkararak onu, anlamını yarattığı atmosferde bulan müzikle ilişkilendirmemize olanak sağlar:

> Rüyaların tesiri üzerinde az çok duranlar onlarda bu tesiri yapan şeyin birbirini takip eden hayallerden ziyade beraberinde yürüyen hava olduğunu kabul ederler. Her rüya kendi hususî atmosferi içindedir; onu sırasına göre eğlenceli, zâlim, mesut, bedbaht, mukaddes veya günahkâr yapar. Bu, rüyanın ruh hâleti, duygusudur. (Tanpınar, 1998, s. 32)

Peki Yahya Kemal'in "rüya içinde rüya" metaforuyla tanımlamaya çalıştığı şey nedir? "O Taraf" şiirinde rüyanın öte-dünyaya gitmenin ve bu âlemi seyretmenin bir aracı olduğu hatırlandığında, "rüya içinde rüya" metaforu bir kez daha "Deniz" şiirinde geçen "ölümün şiiri" kavramını çağrıştırır. Ancak bu kavram nasıl temellendirilebilir?

Bu noktada Tanpınar'ın, Gaston Bachelard'ın bahsettiğini söylediği "ölümün sentaksına" değinmek anlamlı olabilir. Gerçekten de Bachelard *L'Eau et les rêves* (Su ve rüyalar) adlı kitabında, Mme Bonaparte'ın "Edgar Poe'nun poetikasında egemen olan imgenin, ölen bir anne imgesi" olduğunu gösterdiğini belirtir (1942, s. 58). Ona göre, "Poe'yu okurken, ölü suların garip hayatını daha yakından anlarız ve dil, en korkunç sentaksı, ölen şeylerin sentaksını öğrenir" (Bachelard, 1942, s. 20).

Tanpınar, suyun "'ölümün sentaksı ile konuşması' hususiyeti"ne (1995, s. 197) Yahya Kemal'in eserinde sık sık rastlandığını belirttikten sonra, şairin "[i]lk şiirlerinden biri olan 'Mehlika Sultan'dan itibaren biz bu konuşmaya, bazan suyun daveti, bazan sadece telkini olarak [....] ve bazan da 'Deniz' manzumesinde görüldüğü üzere, açıkça kendi sesiyle konuşması şeklinde rastlarız" (1995, s. 197-198) der.

Gerek Bachelard'ın, gerekse Tanpınar'ın sözlerine dayanarak Yahya Kemal'in şiirlerinde "ölümün sentaksı"nı temellendirmek için öncelikle ölüm teması etrafında örülmüş şiirlere ve 'su' imgesine odaklanmak gerekmektedir. Bu noktada, "Deniz" şiirinde geçen 'deniz insanı'nın sözleri bize önemli ipuçları sunabilir. Özneyi ölüme çağıran bu insanın emir kipiyle konuşması özellikle dikkat çekici.

> *Mâdem ki deniz rûhuna sır verdi sesinden,*
> *Gel kurtul o dar varlığının hendesesinden!*

Son zevkin eğer aşk ise ummâna karış, tat!
Boynundan o cânan dediğin lâşeyi silk, at!
[....]
Aldanma ki sen bir susamış rûh, o bir aç;
Sen bir susamış rûh, o bütün ten ve biraz saç.
Ummâna çıkar burda bugün beklediğin yol,
At kalbini girdâba, açıl engine, rûh ol!" (Beyatlı, 1967, s. 134)

Konuşanın bir 'deniz insanı' olması ve onun 'susamış ruh' olarak tanımladığı birine hitap etmesiyse 'ölümün sentaksı'nı suyla ilişkilendirmekte Tanpınar'ın haklı olduğunu ortaya koymaktadır. Emir kipinin 'su' imgesiyle olan yan yanalığı, Yahya Kemal'in başka şiirlerinde de karşımıza çıkar. Örneğin "Geçmiş Yaz" şiirinin öznesi şöyle bir telkinde bulunur: "Körfezdeki dalgın suya bir bak, göreceksin:/ Geçmiş gecelerden biri durmakta derinde" (Beyatlı, 1967, s. 138). "Vuslat" şiirinin âşıklarıysa "Dünyâyı unutmuş bulunurken o sularda" (Beyatlı, 1967, s. 129), şiirin öznesi, ölümü çağrıştıran vuslata ve geceye seslenir: "Ey vuslat! O âşıkları etsununa râm et!/ Ey tatlı ve ulvî gece! Yıllarca devâm et!" (Beyatlı, 1967, s. 129).

"Geçiş" şiirinde 'su' sözcüğü geçmez ancak ölümün daveti bir kez daha emir kipinin kullanıldığı bir dizede bulur ifadesini: "Râhatça dal, ölüm sonu gelmez bir uykudur" (Beyatlı, 1967, s. 105). Bu dizenin öznesinin kimliği belirsizdir ancak bu, pekâlâ ölümün kendisi de olabilir.

Bu örneklerin ışığında, Yahya Kemal'de 'ölümün sentaksı'nın, ölüm temasını ele alan şiirlerde emir kipinin kullanımında somutlandığını ifade etmek mümkün görünüyor. Böylece ölümün 'zorbalığı' bu sentaksta buluyor karşılığını.

Öte yandan, Yahya Kemal'in "Deniz" şiirinde geçen "ölümün şiiri"ni sözünü ettiğimiz 'ölümün sentaksı'yla sınırlandırmak mümkün değil. Zira bu şiiri, onun sözdağarına ve imge dünyasına dayanarak temellendirmek daha anlamlı olabilir. Tıpkı şiir dilinin, günlük konuşma dilinden farklı olduğu gibi, "ölümün şiiri" de konuşma dilininkinden farklı bir sözdağarına ve imge dünyasına sahip olmak durumunda. Bu imge dünyasındaysa 'su'yun merkezi bir konumda olduğunu söylemek mümkün. Gerek Bachelard'ın Poe için yazdıklarında, gerekse Tanpınar'ın Yahya Kemal'in şiiriyle bu bağlamda kurduğu paralelliklerde "ölümün sentaksı"nın da 'su'yla ilişkilendirilmesi bu bağlamda bir örtüşmenin olduğunu gösteriyor.

Yukarda Yahya Kemal'in şiirlerinde 'akşam' imgesinin ölümün gerçekliğinden ölümün şiirine geçişi sağlayan bir köprü işlevi gördüğünü söylemiştik. "Sonbahar" şiirinin son dörtlüğündeyse bu işlevi 'su'yun yerine getirdiğini görüyoruz. Bu şiirde su vasıtasıyla gerçekleşen ve 'anne toprak'ta somutlanan ölü annenin farketmediği "ölüm mâcerâsı" gerçek olmaktan ziyade, şiirsel bir deneyim olarak yorumlanmalıdır.

Yaprak nasıl düşerse akıp kaybolan suya,
Rûh öyle yollanır uyanılmaz bir uykuya,
Duymaz bu anda taş gibi kalbinde bir sızı;
Farketmez anne toprak ölüm mâcerâmızı. (Beyatlı, 1967, s. 86)

Suyun, sözünü ettiğimiz geçiş için 'akşam' imgesine oranla daha zengin olanaklara sahip olduğunu söylemek mümkün. Gerçekten de Bachelard, "akışkanlığın, bize göre, dil arzusunun kendisi " olduğunu söyler (1942, s. 210). "Saf hayalgücü ve şiirsel tahayyül tarafından suya hemen her zaman dişil bir özellik atfedilmesi "yle (Bachelard, 1942, s. 22) uyumlu bir şekilde Luce Irigaray, dişil dili tanımlarken 'akışkanlık' kavramından yararlanır:

> *Oysa kadın konuşuyor. Ama "aynı" değil, "tıpkı" değil , "kendiyle ya da herhangi bir x ile özdeş" değil. "Özne" değil, tabii eğer falokratizm tarafından dönüştürülmüş değilse. "Akışkan" konuşuyor, bu düzenin felç olmuş arka yüzlerinde bile ki bunlar artık akamama ya da kendine dokunamama halinin belirtileridir... (1977, s. 109)*

Bachelard da "suyun sözü" (1942, s. 209) kavramını ortaya atarak suyun dille olan ilişkisini vurguladıktan sonra şunu belirtir: "Sonuç olarak suyun sözüyle insan sözü arasında devamlılık vardır" (Bachelard, 1942, s. 24). Ona göre, "suyun sesleri neredeyse metaforik bile değildir" (Bachelard, 1942, s. 24) ve "[o]rganik olarak insan dilinin, özel bir psişik heyecan veren ve suyun imgelerini çağıran bir akışkanlığı vardır" (Bachelard, 1942, s. 24). Bütün bunlar, Bachelard'ın "suyun şiiri" (1942, s. 209) kavramını ortaya atmasına olanak sağlar.

Su, akışkan, çarpmasız, devamlı ve devam eden, ritmi gevşeten, farklı ritimleri tek biçimli bir maddeye dönüştüren dilin efendisidir. Böylece rahatlıkla, akışkan ve canlı, kaynağından akan bir şiirin değerini dile getiren ifadeye tam anlamını verebiliriz. (Bachelard, 1942, s. 209)

Suyun hem doğumu ve anneyi çağrıştıran ve hep 'dişil' olanla ilişkilendirilen, hem de dile ve şiire açılan sembolizmi, ölü anneyi şiire dönüştürme ve 'ölümün şiirini' yazma konusunda Yahya Kemal'e zengin olanaklar sunar. Diğer taraftan su, "yaşamla ölüm arasında bir tür plastik aracıdır" (Bachelard, 1942, s. 20). Suyun yaşamla ölüm arasında bir aracı görevi görmesi, onun gerek "L'Eau et les rêves" (Su ve Rüyalar) adlı kitabının başlığının da ortaya koyduğu gibi Bachelard'da, gerekse Yahya Kemal'in şiirlerinde rüyayla ilişkilendirilmesinin arkasında yatan nedenlerden biri olmalıdır. Zira Freud'un söylediğine göre, rüyanın da bir arada kalmışlık durumunu imlediğini hatırlatalım: "Rüya uykuyla uyanıklık arasında bir ara konum olarak görünmektedir" (s. 74). Diğer taraftan, "uyku, ölümün ilk ampirik görünümüdür. Uyku ve ölüm kardeştir der Homeros" (Morin, 1970, s.139).

Bu noktada "Mehlika Sultan" şiirinde ortaya konan, sudan rüyaya doğru gerçekleşen açılımı ele almakta yarar var. Suyun "akışkanlık" kavramı bağlamında dille olan ilişkisi göz önüne alındığında, onu aynı zamanda lirizmle ilişkilendirmek de mümkün görünmekte. Ancak suyun lirizminin daha ziyade ses-merkezli ve müzikle ilişkili bir lirizme yakın göründüğü söylenebilir. Yahya Kemal'in şiirinde suyun rüyayla yan yanalığı ve iki sözcük-imge arasında ortaya konan etkileşim, rüyanın da daha ziyade görsel imge-merkezli bir lirizmi temsil ettiğini düşündürür.

Gerçekten de Yahya Kemal'in pek çok dizesinde rüyanın görme algısıyla ilişkilendirildiğini gözlemlemek mümkün: "Senelerden beri rü'yâda görüp özlediğim/ Cedlerin mağfiret iklimine girmiş gibiyim" (Beyatlı, 1967, s. 11); "Üsküdar, bir ulu rü'yâyı görenler şehri!" (Beyatlı, 1967, s. 28); "Sanki halkın uyanık gördüğü rü'yâ idi o!" (Beyatlı, 1967, s. 28); "Dünya güzel göründü resimleşmiş uykuda" (Beyatlı, 1967, s. 58); "Hilkatın gördüğü rüya biter, etraf ağarır" (Beyatlı, 1967, s. 97); "Gördüm ölüm diyârını rü'yâda bir gece" (Beyatlı,

1967, s. 111); "Naklettiğim gibiydi rü'yâda gördüğüm" (Beyatlı, 1967, s. 111); "Gördükleri rü'yâ ezeli bahçedir aşka" (Beyatlı, 1967, s. 127).

Burada Bachelard'ın sözlerini hatırlayalım: "Rüya gören göz, görmez, ya da en azından farklı bir şekilde görür" (1999, s. 149). Ancak Yahya Kemal'in şiirlerindeki özne, ortaya konan rüya atmosferinde farklı bir şekilde görmekle kalmaz, "Gördüm ölüm diyârını rü'yâda bir gece" (Beyatlı, 1967, s. 111) dizesinin ortaya koyduğu gibi farklı bir dünyayı görür. Bu durum, Yahya Kemal'de rüyanın daha ziyade ölüme yakın olduğunu belirtmemize olanak sağlar. Ancak bu konuda bir muğlaklıktan söz etmek de mümkündür. Zira arada kalmışlığı imlemesiyle uyumlu bir şekilde, rüyanın yaşamı ve ölümü imleyen imgelerin yanı başında yer alarak bunlara eşit mesafede durduğu durumlar da yok değildir. Örneğin "Bir Tepeden" şiirinden alınmış olan "Rüya gibi bir akşamı seyretmeğe geldin" (Beyatlı, 1967, s. 20) dizesi, "Rü'ya gibi bir yazdı. Yarattın hevesinle" (Beyatlı, 1967, s. 138) dizesinin yankısı gibidir. Önceden belirttiğimiz gibi, Yahya Kemal'de 'yaz' daha ziyade yaşama, 'akşam'sa daha ziyade ölüme yakın görünen imgelerdir.

Ancak gerek 'su' imgesinin, gerekse Yahya Kemal'in lirizm anlayışının, hem sessel hem de imgesel olanı kapsadığını gözardı etmemek gerekiyor. Nitekim şairin şiirlerinde su, şiire ait olan her şeyi kendinde toplayan bir unsur olmakta. "O açılır, alır, muhafaza eder, sonra kendi üstünde dönerek geriye verir. Bu, akan su ile denizin arasındaki farktır" der Tanpınar (1995, s. 178). Nitekim "Geçmiş Yaz" şiirinde su, geçmişi bir şiir olarak estetize ettikten sonra bir rüya biçiminde muhafaza eder.

Suyun estetize edici gücü, Yahya Kemal'in başka şiirlerinde de karşımıza çıkar. "İstinye" şiirinde yer alan "Durgunlaşıp bir ayna kadar parlıyan suda,/ Dünyâ güzel göründü resimleşmiş uykuda" (Beyatlı, 1967, s. 57) dizeleri bu konuda bir örnek oluşturur. Suyun estetize etme özelliği, 'ayna' imgesiyle arasındaki yakınlıkta da somutlanmaktadır. "Hayâl Şehir" şiirinden alınmış olan "Gece, birçok fıkarâ evlerinin lâmbaları/ En sahîh aynadan aksettiriyor Üsküdar'ı" (Beyatlı, 1967, s. 31) dizeleri, 'ayna' imgesinin bu dönüştürücü gücünü bir kez daha ortaya koyarken, bu bağlamda Yahya Kemal'le Baudelaire'le arasında kurulan bir ilişkiden söz etmemize de olanak sağlar. Zira "La Beauté" (Güzellik) şiirinden alınmış olan " O uysal âşıkları kendime çekecek/ Saf aynalarım var, her şeyi en güzel kılan" (Baudelaire, 1996, s. 49) dizelerinde 'ayna'nın, tıpkı Yahya Kemal'de olduğu gibi, estetize etme işlevi olduğu görülmektedir.

"Madrid'de Kahvehâne" şiirinden alınmış olan "Bâzan gönül dalar suların mûsikîsine" (Beyatlı, 1967, s. 172) dizesiyse, suyun estetize etme gücünün sessel yönünü ortaya koyar. Zira "resimleşmiş uyku" ifadesinde bu gücün daha ziyade görsel yönü vurgulanırken, bu şiirde bir dönüştürüme uğratılarak müziğe çevrilen, sestir. Böylece su, bir kez daha görsel olanla sessel olanı bir araya getiren bir unsur olur.

Böylece, geçmişle gelecek, yaşamla ölüm ve imge-merkezli ve ses-merkezli lirizm arasındaki geçişlere olanak sağlayan suyun sembolizmi, Yahya Kemal'in şiirindeki dinamizmin başlıca kaynağıdır. Zamanın donmuşluktan kurtulup geleceğe doğru uzanmasını sağlayan ve şiirsel 'imtidâd'ı olanaklı kılan da yine su olur. Ancak Yahya Kemal'de gelecek, ölüm-sonrasını da kapsamaktadır. Su imgesi etrafında inşa edilen "suyun şiiri" ise şairin "ölümün şiiri" olarak tanımladığı şiirle örtüşür.

Kaynakça

Bachelard, G. (1942). *L'eau et les rêves.* Paris: José Corti.

___. (1999). *La poétique de la rêverie.* Paris: Quadrige, 1999.

Baudelaire, C. (1996). *Kötülük Çiçekleri* (S. Maden, Çev.). İstanbul: Çekirdek Yayınları.

Bergson, H. (1999). *Matière et mémoire.* Paris: Quadrige.

Beyatlı, Y. K. (1967). *Kendi Gökkubbemiz.* İstanbul: İstanbul Fetih Cemiyeti.

___. (2004). Rubâîler ve Hayyam Rubâîlerini Türkçe Söyleyiş. İstanbul: Yapı Kredi.

Freud, S. (t. y.) *Introduction à la Psychanalyse.* Paris: Petite Bibliothèque Payot.

Irigaray, L. (1977). *Ce sexe qui n'en est pas un.* Paris: Editions de Minuit.

Lamartine, A. de. (2008). *Voyage en Orient.* Paris: Arlea.

Morin, E. (1970). *L'homme et la mort.* Paris: Editions du Seuil.

Tanpınar, A. H. (1995). *Yahya Kemal.* İstanbul: Dergâh Yayınları.

___. (1998). *Edebiyat Üzerine Makaleler* (Z. Kerman, Haz.). İstanbul: Dergâh Yayınları.

Göçmen Bir Yazar Olan Murat Tuncel'in Kaleminden
Maviydi Adalet Sarayı ve *Gölge Kız*

Ayla Kaşoğlu[342]

Giriş

Göçmen Edebiyatı söz konusu olduğunda, Almanya'ya kıyasla Hollanda'daki Türk yazarların çalışmalarına daha az ilgi gösterilmiştir. Bu yazarlardan biri de Murat Tuncel'dir. 1952 doğumlu Tuncel, İstanbul Atatürk Eğitim Enstitüsü Türkçe Bölümü'nü bitirdikten sonra Anadolu'nun çeşitli yerlerinde öğretmenlik yapmış ve 1989 yılında Türkçe dersleri vermek üzere Hollanda'ya gitmiştir; halen yaşamını orada sürdürmektedir. Ülkemizde pek tanınmayan ve yapıtları üzerine akademik bağlamda bir çalışmaya rastlamadığımız Tuncel'in 1994 yılında Şükrü Gümüş Roman ödülünü alan *Maviydi Adalet Sarayı* ve 2000 yılında Orhan Kemal Öykü Ödülünü alan *Gölge Kız* adlı yapıtlarında dış göç olgusu ele alınır.

Murat Tuncel'e göre göç olgusu bir arayış eylemidir ve iki şekilde gerçekleşir. Birincisi gidiş dönüşlerle, ikincisi ise dönüşü olmayan bir gidiştir. Yaşanılan değişimler bireyi isteğe bağlı ve zorunlu göç olmak üzere iki türlü göçe zorlar. İsteğe bağlı göç, daha iyi yaşam umuduyla çıkılan bir arayıştır. Umut edilen yaşamın bulunup bulunmayacağı bilinmez, ama bir umut büyütüldüğü/beslendiği için bu tür göç eden kişi sonucu ne olursa olsun, bu eylemden karlı çıkar, ya da kendini zenginleştirdiğini düşünerek mutluluğunu çoğaltabilir. Zorunlu göç ise adı üstünde bir zorunluluktan kaynaklanır. Ancak sebebi ne olursa olsun bu göçün sonucu kişide büyük yıkım ve değişimlere neden olabilir. Çünkü göç eden insanın yaşamı kökten bir değişime uğrayabilir; zorunlu göç bireyi yaşama yeniden ve sıfır noktasından başlatır adeta. Dolayısıyla bu zorunlu göç herkesin başlayabileceği ve başarabileceği bir şey değildir ve bedeli de ağır olabilmektedir.

Göç konusunda genelde Avrupa'ya özelde Hollanda'ya baktığımızda ise Hollanda Merkez İstatistik Bürosu (CBS) raporlarına göre, Hollanda'ya göç resmi olarak altmışlı yılların sonu ve yetmişli yılların başında başlamıştır. Diğer Avrupa ülkelerine göçten ayrı bir karakter taşımasına ve ayrı yöntemlerle yapıldığı için kendine özgü olmasına rağmen bu göç, Almanya göçüyle iç içe anılmakta ve genellikle Hollanda'dan gelenlere de Türkiye'de

"Almancı/Alamancı" yakıştırması yapılmaktadır (Tuncel, 2012, s.184). Her yurt dışına gidip gelen işçinin -ister Hollanda, ister Belçika ya da Danimarka'ya olsun- "Almancı/Alamancı" olarak nitelendirilmesinin kaynağında ilk işçi göçünün Almanya'ya yapılması ve nicelik olarak da yoğunluğun bu coğrafyada olması yatmaktadır (Turan, 2012, s.10). Murat Tuncel, bu şekilde adlandırılmasının nedenlerini şöyle sıralar:

- Hollanda'ya ilk göç edenlerin tamamı işçi olarak ilkin Almanya'ya gider, oradaki işyerlerinde çalışma olanağı bulamayınca Hollanda'ya geçer ve orada iş bulup kalırlar.

---
[342] Prof. Dr., Gazi Üniversitesi Edebiyat Fakültesi Rus Dili ve Edebiyatı Bölümü, akasoglu@gazi.edu.tr.

- Hollanda'ya giden ikinci dalga işçi akımı da iş bulma amacıyla Almanya'ya gelen turist işçilerdir. Onlar, Almanya'nın göçmen işçi yasalarındaki standartlara uymadıkları için Almanya'da iş bulamazlar, tanıdıklarının tavsiyeleri ya da aracılığıyla Hollanda'ya giderler. Hollanda hükümetinin tanıdığı olanaklarla iş bulunca turist kimliklerini yok edip Hollanda'da kalırlar.

- Almancı/Alamancı olarak adlandırılmalarının bir başka nedeni ise Türkiye'deki insanın kolaycı bir anlayışla Avrupa'ya giden herkesi fark gözetmeksizin aynı potada eritmesidir (Tuncel, 2012, s.184).

Yine Tuncel'e göre Hollanda'nın "gast arbeiders" konuk işçi alımına karar vermesinden sonra durum biraz değişir. Almanya'ya olan işçi göçünden farklı bir boyutta gelişim gösterir:

- O yıllarda Almanya'ya göç edenlerin çoğunluğunu kent kökenli ya da kentlerde işçi olarak çalışan insanlar oluşturur. Ama Hollanda'ya göç edenlerin neredeyse tamamı köy kökenli ve hiç işçilik deneyimi olmayan insanlardı. Bunun nedeni ise Hollanda hükümetinin bilinçli ve baştan pazarlıklı göç politikasından kaynaklanır, yani Hollanda hükümeti ülkeye gelecek "gast arbeiders"ların uzun dönemde ülkede kalıcı olmasını istemediğinden alınan işçilerin özellikle köy kökenli, vasıfsız ve okur yazar olmayanlar arasından seçilmesini ister. İş bulma kurumlarındaki alım komisyonlarında da bu duruma özellikle özen gösterilir. Çünkü bu niteliklere sahip işçiler kolay uyum sağlayamayacak, biraz para kazanınca ülkelerine geri dönecekler ve böylece ileride Hollanda için de sorun yaratmayacaklardır.

- Almanya'ya göç sistemli ve belirli periyotlarla sürerken, Hollanda'ya göçün düzeni de zamanı da pek belli değildir, çünkü oraya çoğunlukla mevsimlik işçiler gereklidir. Böyle olunca da perakende ve düzensiz işçi alımı en geçerli yoldur. Bu şekildeki işçiler işverenlere de, hükümete de ekonomik açıdan fazla yük getirmeyecektir. (Tuncel, 2012, s.184-185).

Hollanda'ya göç, 1970'li yılların sonuna doğru farklı bir gelişim gösterir. Bunun nedeni de insanların doymaya geldikleri bu ülkenin artık doğdukları ülkeden daha çok yaşamlarına girdiğinin farkına varmalarıdır. Söz konusu duruma her iki taraf da hazırlıksız yakalanır. Hollandalı yetkililer "bize sorun yaratmasınlar, problemlerini kendi aralarında çözsünler", göçmenler ise "yakın olalım birbirimizin yanında olalım, kendi problemlerimizi kendimiz çözelim" diyerek aynı mahallelerde kendilerine verilen evlere yerleşince gettoların temeli atılmış olur. Zamanla göçmenler bu mahallelerde çoğalınca mahallenin eski sahipleri kültürlerini tanımadıkları bu insanlarla yaşamak istemeyip mahallelerini terkedince Batı Avrupa'da olduğu gibi Hollanda'da da neredeyse kentin yarısını kaplayan gettolar oluşur. Tuncel, bu noktada gettoların oluşumuna adeta çanak tutan politikacıları ve onların "uyum sorunumuz var" söylemlerini eleştirir. Çünkü ona göre göçmenleri yalnızca konuk olarak görüp, onları kültürleriyle kabullenilmeyip tek taraflı bir uyumda ısrar edildiği sürece problemler de bitmeyecektir.

70'li yılların sonu 80'li yılların başında yeni bir genç kuşağın göçü başlar Hollanda'ya. Bu son gelenlerin çoğunluğu ilk kuşağın orta seviyede eğitimli çocuklarından oluşur. Hatta bir kısmı üniversite eğitimlerini yarıda bırakarak göç ederler. Bunlara 12 Eylül darbesiyle zorunlu göç eden eğitimli göçmenler de katılınca durum her iki taraf için de olumlu yönde değişiklik gösterir. Bir yandan yerlilerle göçmenler arasında bağlantıyı sağlayan bu grup diğer bir yandan ise kendi kültürünü göç ettiği topluma anlatacak kadar iyi tanıyamadığı ve anlatım metodunu bilmediği için aradaki sanatsal bağlantıyı kuramaz, bilgisiz ve deneyimsizlikle birlikte aldığı kararlarda genellikle taraflı davranır. Böylece tercih ettiği tarafın sanatsal yaşamıyla bağlarını güçlendirirken, diğer tarafla zayıflatır (Tuncel, 2012, s.186). Burada Berry'nin *bütünleşme, ayrışma, asimilasyon* ve *marjinalleşme* olmak üzere dört farklı kültürlenme stratejisinden *asimilasyon* akla gelir. Birey, yerleştiği yeni uzamın kültürünü benimseyip kendi kültürünü ikinci plana iterse bir asimilasyona maruz kalır (Er, 2015, s.46).

Tuncel'in *Gölge Kız* (2003) adlı öykü kitabında Anadolu'dan Hollanda'ya uzanan yolculukta göç ve göçmenliğin izi sürülür. *Bahar Kuşu, Gölge Kız, Sığırcığın Ölümü, Cennet de Bitti, Çilli Tinike ile Çakır İsmail, Şükriye Kireç, Önemli Mektup, Suskun Korkular, Gözbebeğim* ve *Son Öykü* başlıklı toplam on öyküden oluşan kitapta Hollanda'ya gidiş hikayeleri, fotoğrafları değiştirilerek hazırlanan kimlikler, büyük bir umutla davet edilen yakınlar ve sonrasında yüzüstü bırakmalar. Bunlar gurbetin gerçekleridir. Gidilmiştir bir kere, dönüşü yoktur. Tuncel'in "kebap kokusuna gittim, baktım eşek dağlıyorlar" deyimini kitabının girişine koymuş olması tüm kitabı özetler niteliktedir (Turan, 2012, s.13-14). Yine kitabın epigrafında Tuncel'in "bu öyküleri Anadolu'dan çok uzaktaki bir başka Anadolu'da yazdım" sözleriyle alışılagelen göçmen öyküleri yerine yurtdışındaki Anadolu'nun betimlendiğine dair ipuçları verilir. Yurt dışı göçün nedenleri, göç biçimleri ve göç sonrası yaşananlar dillendirilir öykülerde. Bu öykülerde göçe dair başlıca hususlar şöyle sıralanabilir:

-Yurtdışındaki yakınlara, akraba ve arkadaşlara imrenilir; kırsalın itici gurbetin çekici faktörü; eşle bile vedalaşmadan annenin karşı çıkışına rağmen köyden bir an önce çıkıp Hollanda'ya akrabanın/tanıdığın yanına gitmeye uğraşılır.

-Yurt dışına gitmek için aracı bulunur. Kaçak yollarla gitmeye çalışılır. Bir bölümü saclarla ayrılıp silindir şeklinde küçücük bir odaya dönüştürülen koca bir tanker iletici faktör işlevi görür (*Gölge Kız*, s. 29).

Hollanda'ya gidince yaşananlar:

-Anadolu insanının saflığının yanısıra kurnazlığı; 1997 yılında Hollanda NPS Radyo 5 Türkse Redaksi Öykü Ödülü alan *Cennette Bitti* adlı öyküde Türkiye'den Hollanda'ya çocukluk arkadaşının yanına gelen Veli'nin cebindeki paralar suyunu çekince Veli, bir fırında çalışmaya başlar, kalacak yeri olmadığı için işyerinde yatıp kalkar, çocukluk arkadaşı Celil ise her hafta sonu gelip Veli'nin haftalığının yarısını alır, vermediği bir seferde onu polise ihbar eder. Neticede iyi niyet suistimal edilip kötüye kullanılır, güven sarsılır ve umutlar boşa çıkar (*Gölge Kız*, s.39).

- Anadolu insanının çaresizliği; Çakır İsmail'in "sanki yapacağım başka bir iş var. Diploma yok, bir şey yok" (*Gölge Kız*, s.40) sözleri bu çaresizliği, yeni uzamdaki şartlara, düzene katlanmaktan, adeta boyun eğmekten başka seçeneğin olmadığını gözler önüne serer.

-Hollanda'da memlekette beğenilmeyen hatta tenezzül edilmeyen bağda, bahçede, tarlada çalışmak zorunda kalınır, ancak memlekete gidilince gururdan dolayı yapılan iş gizlenir ve fabrikada çalışıldığı söylenir.

-Çalışma şartları düşünüldüğü gibi rahat değildir, çiçek toplarken bir tanesinin başına bir şey gelse bahçeciden hesap sorulur, kim zarar vermiş ise-yirmi beş sent bile olsa- ilk haftalığından verdiği zararın karşılığı kesilir. Hatta bununla da yetinmeyip kendine başka bir iş araması bile söylenebilir. İşsiz kalma korkusu gurbetçinin- özellikle çoluk çocuğunu getirenler için- en büyük kabusudur.

-Çocuklarını küçük yaşta getirenler bir nebze daha umutludur, çünkü onların dil öğrenmeleri ve okumaları mümkündür; hiçbiri çocuklarının kaderinin kendilerine benzemesini istemez. (*Gölge Kız*, s.41).

- Zaman zaman pişmanlık duyguları yaşanır. Çakır İsmail'in: "keşke babamızdan gördüğümüzü yapsaydık da buralara gelmeseydik. Kendi tarlalarımızda burada çalıştığımızın yarısını çalışsaydım ezilip büzülmeden yaşardım. Bunların hepsi bir heves ama ağırlığı taşınamayacak kadar ağır. Çocuklarımızı şehirde okutalım diye, çekip buralara geldik. Ama bunca yıldır ne şehir bize, ne de biz şehre alışabildik" (*Gölge Kız*, s.44) sözleri gurbette uyum sağlayamamanın, bir yere ait olamamanın acı gerçeğini ortaya koyar.

-Hep yalnızlık çekilir gurbette; kendine bile saklanılan sırlar kimseyle kolay kolay paylaşılmaz. Gurbet ve memleket arasında gidip gelmelerde hiç bir yere uyum sağlayamamanın acısı, en yakın tanıdıkların bile zamanla uzaklaştığı, o sıcacık sevgilerin giderek soğuduğu iliklere kadar hissedilir.

-Dil bilinmediği için resmi bir kurumdan gelen mektubu okuyacak uygun biri bulunamaz ve bunun güçlüğü *Önemli Mektup* öyküsünde vurgulanır.

- Türklerin gurbette ilk karşılanışları övgüyle, gururla anlatılagelmiştir yıllarca. İşte *Son Öykü*'deki Göcük İsmail'in karısı da "sizi bandoyla karşılamışlar, şimdikileri de şu adam nereden geldi dercesine karşılıyorlar" sözü üzerine Göcük İsmail kızar ve şöyle der: "Bizi kimse bandoyla mandoyla karşılamadı. Delinin biri uydurdu bunu, siz de inandınız. Hepsi yalan, hepsi bir şapşalın uydurması. Kim, ekmeğini bölecek insanları bandoyla karşılar? Bugün nasıl karşılanıyorsak, otuz yıl önce de öyleydi" (*Gölge Kız*, s.95).

- Tüm ayrılıklar aslında eşin, çocukların daha rahat yaşamaları içindir ve çocukların kendileri gibi işçi olmaması düşüncesiyle gurbete götürülmezler; orada doğup büyüyenler bile okullarını bitiremez iken gurbette okumak, okuyabilmek çok zordur. Ailesini yanına aldırmadığı için tepki çeken baba Göcük İsmail'in "ben de sizlerle birlik olmak, uyandığım zaman çevremde sizleri görmek, hasta olduğum zaman bir bardak su verecek, üzerim açıldığında yorganımı örtecek ya da bomboş evde yanımda nefesini duyacağım birisinin bulunmasını istiyorum, ama durum ne sizin bildiğiniz, ne de düşündüğünüz gibi. Siz orada olursanız kazancım yetmez. Orada kazanıp buraya gönderince ancak yetirebiliyorum" der. Ancak ısrarlar neticesinde ailesini yanına aldırınca "Bir yanım konuk işçi, bir yanım gurbetçi işçi. İşçinin konuğu mu olurmuş bilmiyorum ama bize öyle diyorlar(...) daha çocukluktan yeni kurtulmuştum ki evlendim. Evliliğimden mutsuz değilim, ama benden aldığı gençliğimi bana borçlu olduğunu düşünüyorum. Köyde yaşasaydım bunları düşünmezdim, ama artık burada yaşıyorum, yeni öğrendiklerim daha çok düşünmemi sağlıyor (...) orada düşündüğünüz Hollanda'yı belki hiç bir zaman bulamayacaksınız. Çünkü oradan bakınca burasının gri bulutları görünmüyor. Aydan aya alacağım üç-beş kuruşla sefil olmayız, ancak her istediğimizi de alamayız. (...). Madem burada yaşamayı seçtiniz, buradaki zorluklara da katlanacaksınız. Bir de bir-iki yıl izne gitmeyi unutup buralı olmaya çalışın" (*Gölge Kız*, s.92) sözleri gurbette çalışmanın zorluğuna ve

Hollanda'da yaşayabilmek için uyum sağlamanın gerekliliğine dikkat çekmektedir.

Murat Tuncel'in çeşitli dillere kazandırılan yapıtları arasında *Maviydi Adalet Sarayı*, 2003-2004 yıllarında *Sahte Umut* adıyla Hollandaca'ya (*Valse Hoop)* çevrilir (İpek, 2008). Yapıtta göçe dair dikkat çeken başlıca hususlar şöyle sıralanabilir:

-Hollanda'da ev, oda bulmak hiç de kolay değildir. Ellerindekini pansiyon olarak kiraya veren ve bu işi meslek haline getiren Türkler bulunmaktadır, bunlardan biri de Hacı Bülbül'dür. Doktora yalan söyleyerek emekli olan Hacı Bülbül, altmış yaşında sosyal ödenek almak için karısından ayrılır; belediyeyi kandırıp ikinci bir ev alır ve o evi pansiyon olarak işletir, pansiyondaki kişilerin parasının üstüne yatar, ya da türlü bahanelerle onları gece yarısı sokağa atar, dini para hırsıyla dolu nefsine alet eden Hacı Bülbül'e bu da yetmez, cami derneğinde biriktirdiği bağış paralarıyla Arnavutköy'de sekiz katlı bir apartman yaptırır. Kısa yoldan para kazanma eğiliminde olan Hacı Bülbül gibi dolandırıcılar yüzünden namuslu vatandaşlar yasal haklarını alamazlar, üç dört Türk ve Hollandalı bir olup turistlere oturumları varmış gibi sahte evrak düzenler ve turistlerin çocuk paralarını alıp aralarında paylaşırlar, neticede çocuk yardımı veren kurumu iki milyon zarara uğrar, bir yahut birkaç kişiden yola çıkarak kolayca tüm Türkler suçlanabilmektedir (*Maviydi Adalet Sarayı* , s. 32-33).

-Gurbettekilerin çoğu parasızlıktan şikayet eder, ama birçoğunun memlekette birkaç katlı evi vardır, çoluğunun çocuğunun rızkını kesip memlekette yatırım yaparlar, oysa ki Hollanda'da devlet çocuklarına iyi baksın diye çocuk parası vermektedir. Hiçbiri çocuğuna doğru düzgün bir şey almaz. İşleri güçleri memlekete gidip hava atmak ve ev almaktır. Memlekette ise evlerini kiraya verirler, ama kira alamazlar, ortak iş yaparlar, paralarını alamazlar. Konu, komşu, akraba, dost izne gelenlerin ne yaptığını gözlemler. Bir eksikleri olduğunda dilden dile dolaşır. Oysa memleketekilerin çoğu kasabadan öteye geçememiştir, ancak gurbetçilerden daha iyi bilirler dünya halini. Hatta onların kazançları, harcamaları, birikimleri bile konu edinilir.

-Gurbete alışmadan önce "ertesi yıl döneceğim" denilir durur, ancak o ertesi yıl bir türlü gelmez, bir iki izinden sonra ise "dönme" sözcüğü bir daha ağza alınmaz olur. Aslında gurbette zaman durdurulmuş gibidir, gidilen yıllarda yaşanılır hep.

-Oturum izni alıncaya kadar sahte kimlikle dolaşılır. Yapıttaki siyasi suçlu-memlekette Stalin yanlısı kitaplar okuduğu gerekçesiyle altı yıl hapiste yatmıştır-Arsen'in de henüz oturum izni yoktur.

-Mercedes ve BMW kullanıcıları "memleketinde Mercedes'e mi biniyordun?" düşüncesinden hareketle Hollanda polisi tarafından kaçakçılıkla itham edilir.

- Kaçaklar için polis Hollanda ile eşanlamlıdır.

- Kaçak gelenler, kendi başlarına hiçbir şey yapamazlar, sabah iş, akşam pansiyon arasında mekik dokurlar. Yakalanma korkusuyla belli bir saatten sonra dışarı çıkamazlar. İş koşulları da berbattır, sekiz saat içerisinde on altı saatlik bir güç sarf etmek zorundadırlar. Genelde kimsenin çalışmak istemeyeceği işlerde, zor şartlar altında ve yoğun olarak çalışırlar. Dil bilen gurbetçiler için hayat daha kolay iken, bilmeyenler için ise çark ev-pansiyon, iş arasında döner durur. (*Maviydi Adalet Sarayı*, s. 27).

- Hollanda'daki haklarını kaybetmek istemeyen, henüz askerliğini yapmamış ve askerliğin kısalmasını bekleyen gençler Satılmış karakteri üzerinden aktarılır. (*Maviydi Adalet Sarayı*, s.10). Satılmış, asker kaçağı olduğu için yakalanma korkusuyla babasının cenazesine bile gidememiştir. Ailesini yanına aldırmayan Satılmış, onlara hasret, özlem duyar ve günün birinde şirket kurup zengin olma hayaliyle yaşar.

- Oturma izninin ardından güzel bir gelecek kurma düşüncesiyle ailesini yanına aldıran Ömer'in bir süre sonra karısının ve oğlunun cinsel tercihlerindeki değişiklikten dolayı yuvası dağılır.

-Hollanda polisi, Türk erkeklerinin karılarını, çocuklarını dövdükleri, ve Türk ailelerin komşularıyla geçinemedikleri, gürültü yaptıkları ön yargısı içindedir ve bu sebeple tüm Türkleri aynı kefeye koyar. Aslında bir anlamda Hollanda polisinin bu düşünceyi edinmelerine gurbetçiler kendileri sebebiyet vermişlerdir. Ve Hollanda polisine göre tüm mülteciler yalancıdır. Siyasi suçlu Arsen'e de bu gözle bakılır. Verdiği belgeler ve ifadesi mülteci olmaya yeterli kanıt taşımadığı gerekçesiyle Hollanda'da yaşama isteği reddedilir. Bunun üzerine Arsen, kendisini göçmen olarak kabul etmiş olan ve orada kendini yalancı hissetmeyeceği İsveç'e gider. Bu noktada Hollandalı Bayan Carolien aracılığıyla Hollanda'nın göçmen politikası eleştirilir: (...) başka ülkeler için demokrasi isteyeceksin, işkenceleri durdurun diye bağıracaksın, kendi ülkene geleni de geri göndermeye çalışacaksın. Kim inanır senin yaptıklarına" (*Maviydi Adalet Sarayı*, s. 110).

-Gurbette yalnızca Türklerin hayatı zor değildir, Macaristan gelen Saskia'nın da hayatı ilk geldiğinde hiç de kolay olmamıştır. Elindeki avucundakini kendisini Almanya sınırını geçirenlere verince Hollanda'ya geldiği ilk zamanlar parasız kalır ve kalacak bir yeri olmadığı için parkta yatar, parkın içindeki küçük çiftliğe gelen ziyaretçilerin hayvanlara attıkları yiyecekleri toplayarak hayatta kalma mücadelesi verir.

Sonuç itibarıyla *Maviydi Adalet Sarayı* ve *Gölge Kız*'da, gurbetçileri/mültecileri sınır ötesine zorlayan nedenler ve gittikleri yerde var olma, tutunabilme mücadeleleri çarpıcı ve gerçekçi bir dille anlatılır. Yabancı olmanın zorluğu, dil bilmeme, hiçbir yere ait olamama, uyum sağlayamama, oturma izni alamama korkusunun yanı sıra memleket hasreti, aile özlemi ve aile parçalanması yaşanılan yerde göçmene olan bakış açıları ekseninde ortaya konulur. Her iki yapıtta da Anadolu'dan Hollanda'ya giden insanların Anadolu ile aralarındaki kopmaz bağları, küçük dünyaları ve bu küçük dünyaların zamanla nasıl sömürüldüğü düş, çağrışım ve geriye dönüşlerle aktarılır. Farklı öykülerden oluşan *Gölge Kız* yapıtında göçün ardından yaşanılan korkular, sıkıntılar, endişe ve kabuslar dile getirilir. Benzer duyguların, sıkıntıların yaşanmasının yanı sıra *Maviydi Adalet Sarayı*'nda dünyaya adalet dağıtan Den Haag (Lahey) kenti adaletinin bu göçmenlere ulaşmadığı ve hiçbir vakit de ulaşmayacağı korkusu eklenir. Her iki yapıtta da vurgulandığı gibi yabancı bir ülkeye gelip başka insanların vatan edindikleri topraklarda kalabilme, yaşayabilme hiç kolay değildir. Niyet, ne kimsenin yurdunu ne de başkasının ekmeğini elinden almaktır; tüm gaye emeğinin karşılığını alabilme ve insanca yaşayabilme isteğidir yalnızca.

Kaynakça

Turan, M. (2012). Almanya'ya Göçün 50. Yılında Göç, Kimlik ve Edebiyat. *Ankara: KIBATEK* .s.7-15.

Tuncel, M. (2002). *Gölge Kız*. Varlık Yayınları, İstanbul: Varlık Yayınları.

Tuncel, M. (1994). *Maviydi Adalet Sarayı*. İstanbul: Pencere Yayınları.

Tuncel, M. (2012). Hollanda'ya Göç, Gettolar ve Göçmenlerin Sanatla İlişkileri. *Ankara: KIBATEK*. s.183-188.

Er, A. (2015). "İtici" ve "Çekici" Faktörler Bağlamında İç Göç:Gaye Hiçyılmaz'dan Fırtınaya Karşı.
Göç Dergisi, 2(1), 43-58.

İpek, A. (2008). Yediden Yetmişe Herkesin Okuduğu Yazar: Murat Tuncel.
http://www.odasanat.org/index.php/2008/10/yediden-yetmise-herkesin-okudugu-yazar-murat-tuncel. Erişim tarihi: 15.05.2015.

Arafta Üretilen Yazınsal Metinler

Füsun Ataseven[343]

Giriş

Göçler, insanlık tarihinin bütün dönemleri boyunca var olmuş; kişilerin yaşamak, yerleşmek amacıyla bir yerden başka bir yere gitmeleri hareketine verilen genel addır. Bu hareket ülke içinde olursa iç göç, ülkeler arasında olursa dış göç veya uluslararası göç olarak adlandırılır.

Göç edenler amaçlarına göre çeşitlilik gösterirler: Yüksek vasıflı göçmenler, eski deyimle beyin göçü yapanlar, bugün küreselleşen ekonomiyle beraber çokuluslu şirketlerin yönetim kademelerinde çalışan ve bu görevleri kapsamında başka bir ülkeye göç eden yüksek eğitimli, yüksek ücretli işlerde çalışan kişilerdir. Bu grupta üst düzey yöneticiler, yabancı öğretmenler, sanatçılar gibi kesimler bulunmaktadır. Mülteciler: Ülkelerindeki savaş ve çatışma ortamından kaçıp başka bir devlete sığınan ve uluslararası anlaşmalarla korunan kişilerdir. Kayıtsız göçmenler: Pasaport veya vizeleri olmadan giriş yapan veya gerekli ikamet ve çalışma iznine sahip olmadan başka bir ülkede bulunan yabancılar, medyadaki yaygın ifadeyle kaçak göçmenlerdir. Transit göçmenler: Ülkelerinden ayrılmış ama son hedeflerine varmadan önce belirsiz ve çoğu zaman oldukça uzun bir süre ara duraklarda bekleyen, çoğu zaman kayıtsız olan göçmenlerdir. Kadın göçmenler: Bir emek göçü hareketi olarak, özellikle bakım sektöründe çalışmak amacıyla başka bir ülkeye göç eden kadınlardır. Örn. Türkiye'nin büyük kentlerinde eski Sovyet ülkelerinden gelen çocuk, yaşlı ve hasta bakıcılara verilen addır. Öğrenciler: Erasmus gibi değişim programları veya ülkeler arası anlaşmalarla geçici süreliğine başka ülkelerde okuyan gençlerdir. Emekliler: Güneş göçü de denilen Avrupa'nın güneyindeki iklim ve yaşam koşulları daha uygun olan yerlere giden Kuzey Avrupalı emekliler; örn. Ege ve Akdeniz kıyılarındaki İngiliz, Alman emekliler.

II. Dünya Savaşı'nın yarattığı ekonomik bunalımdan sonra 1950'li yıllarda Alman ekonomisi kalkınmaya başladığında yeni bir iş gücüne ihtiyaç doğdu ve Almanya bu iş gücünü başta Portekiz, İtalya, Yunanistan ve Türkiye'den karşıladı. Bundan dolayı büyük oranda kol emeğine ifa eden göçmen işçiler kitleler halinde Almanya'ya gittiler. Bu göç, dalgası özellikle 1960'lı yılların başında yoğun olarak görülmüştür. Yığınlar halinde Almanya'ya göç eden işçiler öncelikli olarak sadece geçici bir süre için gittiklerini düşündüler. (Zengin, 2010, s:329-349)

Göç ve göçmenlik, yazın dünyasında, 1990 yıllarına değin Almanya üzerine odaklaşır. Çünkü, ilk işçi göçünün Almanya'ya olmasının yanı sıra, nicelik olarak da yoğunluk Almanya'ya doğrudur. İster Hollanda, ister Belçika, isterse Danimarka olsun her yurtdışına gidip gelen işçiye Alamancı denilmektedir. Türklerin Almanya'da karşılaştıkları güçlükleri, ağır çalışma koşullarının yanı sıra yalnızlık, itilmişlik, kültürel çatışma en uç noktalarda yaşanır.(Bekir Yıldız, 1975)

Yüksel Pazarkaya o dönemin yazarlarını ve eserlerini işledikleri konu ve biçem bakımından şu şekilde betimlemektedir :"*Almanya'daki Türk edebiyatının ilk*

---

[343] Prof. Dr. Füsun Bilir Ataseven, Yıldız Teknik Üniversitesi, Batı Dilleri ve Edebiyatları fusunataseven@gmail.com

temsilcileri, geldikleri ülkeye hep yabancı kalmışlar, yabancı gözüyle bakmışlardır. Onlar için, göç kavramından çok gurbet kavramı geçerli olmuştur". (Pazarkaya, 2010)

Almanya'yı üç beş kuruş para kazanılacak geçici bir yer olarak gören, mutlaka geri dönmeyi düşünen insanların belki de en acılı yılları bu dönemde geçmiştir. Eşler, çocuklar Almanya'ya getirilmemiş,birçok aile parçalanmıştır. Gurbetçiliğin bin bir türlü zorluğu, topluma uyamamanın derin acıları yaşanmıştır. Almanya acı vatan döneminin edebiyatı hep gurbet, hasret, acıma, acındırma, uyumsuzluk, sabır, geri dönüş gibi konularını işlemiştir. Bu dönemin edebiyatına acı vatan edebiyatı denilebilir.

Metod

Bu araştırmada söz konusu edilen konu, ilk kuşak göçmenlerin kendi durumlarını, acı vatanda yaşadıklarını dile getirmek amacıyla yazdıkları metinlerle tanışmaktır. Sözlü bir kültürden çıkan göçmenlerin sıkıntılarını paylaşmak ve seslerini duyurabilmek için ne denli renkli metinler ürettiklerine tanıklık etmektir. Yerini yurdunu bırakıp gönüllü bir sürgünlük ya da gönüllü bir göç yoluna gitme durumunun yanında bir de arkada bırakılanların yazıya sığınmaları ister istemez sıklıkla karşımıza çıkar. Bu araştırmada elde edilen veriler çok çeşitli taramalar sonunda elde edilen yazılı metinlerden elde edilmiştir. Betimleyici ve niteliksel yöntemler kullanılmış ve tematik kategoriler yoluyla sizlerin tanıklığınıza sunulmuştur.

"Acı vatan", "arafta yaşamak", "asimilasyon", "entegrasyon" politikaları gibi kavramları; "göçmenlerin hissettikleri ve yansıttıkları" yollar ve kullandıkları diller maniler, şiirler ve düz yazı örnekleriyle tartışmaya açılmıştır.

1980'li yıllarda biyografik, etnografik teknikler eklektik bir biçimde birlikte kullanılmaktadırlar. Göçmenlerin kendi göç öykülerini yarattıkları manilerde, türkülerde, şarkı sözlerinde ifade ettikleri görülmektedir. Göç araştırmalarında kullanılan niteliksel yöntemlerle göç deneyimini yaşayanların kendi ifadelerinde değerlendirmek ve etnografik yöntemi sözlü ifadeler sonucunda elde edilen verilerde araştırmak gerçekçi olmaktadır. Her göç deneyimi biriciktir ve o anı, o yaşananları anlatmaktadır, araştırmacı sadece tanıklık edendir. Gerçek insanlar, gerçek durumlar ve gerçek duygular hakkında düşünceleri, görüşleri ve bilgileri toplamaktır esas olan. Böylesi çalışmalarda göç eden kişinin sesinin duyurulması da mümkün olabilmektedir.

Acı Vatan

1950'li yılların ikinci yarısından itibaren bireysel girişimler ve özel aracılar yoluyla Avrupa'ya yönelen Türk dış göç hareketi, 1960'lı yıllarda Almanya ile yapılan anlaşmalara dayanılarak devlet eliyle düzenlenen işgücü ihracı biçimini alır. Türkiye kökenli göçmenlerin acı vatanla tanışması, Türk dış göçünün önemli bir aşamasını oluşturur. 1965'te Fransa ile imzalanan işgücü anlaşması, göçmenlerin özellikle inşaat ve otomotiv sektörü için Fransa'ya misafir işçi sıfatıyla girmesiyle sonuçlanır. Başta geçici olarak gördükleri bu misafir işçilik deneyimi edebiyattan müziğe pek çok alana yansımıştır. İlk kuşak göçmenlerin kendilerini yazılı veya sözlü ifade ettikleri dil göç ettikleri ülkenin dili değildir.

Zamanla bulundukları ortama uyum sağlamaya çabalarken, getirdikleri kültüre ve hemşerilerine yabancılaşma olgusu gündeme gelir. Ne Almanlara ne de Türklere yaranamama, kimseyi memnun edememe engeliyle karşı karşıya kalırlar.

Yurdumuzda Alamanyalı
Almanya'da yabancıyız
Bir garib vatandaşız
Ne kardeşiz ne bacı   (A. Mahir Ofcan, in. Öztürk, 2015)

Trenin yolları demir değil mi?
İşçiye verilen emir değil mi?
Sılaya kavuşmak nasip değil mi?
Mezarım yad elde kaldı neyleyim?

İçmeden olmuşum içimde sarhoş
Rüya mısın serap mısın söyle Almanya
İnsanlıktan yana içerin bomboş
Senin merhametin yok mu Almanya (Yüksel Özkasap, in. Öztürk, 2015)

Acı Vatana Kırgınlık

Almanya'da yabancılara uygulanan özel kanunlar, aynı zamanda Alman toplumunda görülen değişmelerin göstergesi olarak gösterilir.

Yüzümüze güldü durdu
Bizi canevimizden vurdu
Son zamanlarda kudurdu
Yuh olsun şu Almanlara   (Adnan Varveren, in. Öztürk, 2015)

Fırınlar yaktığın çağa doğru mu?
Yolculuk nereye Alman efendi?
Kasaplık yaptığın çağa doğru mu?
Yolculuk nereye Alman efendi?
Hitler de küçüktü sonra büyüdü,
Kurdu orduları aldı yürüdü.
İnsanlık üstünde kurşun eridi
Yolculuk nereye Alman efendi?   (Derdiyoklar, in. Öztürk, 2015)

Arafta Yaşamak

Yabancılara özel kanun çıkarılarak, Türklerin Almanya'ya gelmeleri önlenmeye çalışılınca, gurbet kahrı çeken göçmenlerin derdi gittikçe ağırlaşır. Kalkınmasına onca katkıda bulundukları Almanya'yı nankör sayarlar ve ne denli güvenilmez olduğunun altını çizerler :

Uzun yıllar oynadılar oyunu
Bize çıktı yabancılar kanunu
Alın terimizin mükafatı bu
Yurda dön hemşerimin yurda dön yurda
Kemteri halktandır halkın ozanı

Geç anladık bize kuyu kazanı
İşte budur Almanya'nın düzeni
Yurda dön gardaşım yurda dön yurda   (Aşık Kemteri, in. Öztürk, 2015)

Zamanla bulundukları ortama uyum sağlamaya çabalarken, getirdikleri kültüre ve hemşerilerine yabancılaşma olgusu gündeme gelir. Ne Almanlara ne de Türklere yaranamama, kimseyi memnun edememe handikapıyla karşı karşıya kalır, kendilerini cinsiyeti olayan bir insan gibi görmeye başlarlar.

Yurdumuzda Almanyalı
Almanya'da yabancıyız
Bir garib vatandaşız
Ne kardeşiz ne bacı   (A. Mahir Ofcan, in. Öztürk, 2015)

Almanları, köle tüccarı olarak nitelemeye başlarlar. Alman tarihine gönderme yapmaktan çekinmez, üslupta pervasızlaşırlar :

İçmeden olmuşum içimde sarhoş
Rüya mısın serap mısın söyle Almanya
İnsanlıktan yana içerim bomboş
Senin merhametin yok mu Almanya (Yüksel Özkasap, in. Öztürk, 2015)
Fikrin karıştırmaksa dünyayı
Hayvanat cinsinden suyun var senin
(...)
Biz insanız bize yular takarsın
Gördüm pek acaip huyun var senin   (Aşık Metin Türköz, in. Öztürk, 2015)

Yabancılar kanunu Almanya'nın nankörlüğünün değil, aynı zamanda güvenilmezliğinin bir belgesi olarak görülür. Türkü ve maniler işçilerin sorunlarına uyan bir tema seçerler ve ezgilerinde çoğunlukla hareketli ama hiciv ve ironi üslubunu benimserler.

Şimdi bir de vize çıktı
Nice gönülleri yıktı
Gurbetçiler dertten bıktı
Gülerek yaşamak varken   (Derdiyoklar, in. Öztürk, 2015)

Uzun yıllar oynadılar oyunu
Bize çıktı yabancılar kanunu
Alın terimizin mükafatı bu
Yurda dön hemşerimin yurda dön yurda
Kemteri halktandır halkın ozanı
Geç anladık bize kuyu kazanı
İşte budur Almanya'nın düzeni
Yurda dön gardaşım yurda dön yurda   (Aşık Kemteri, in. Öztürk, 2015)

Asimilasyon

Asimilasyon Axel Honneth geriye dönüp Hegel'in tanınma adına savaşmak fikrini kullanarak, normatif bir değeri olan tanınma kuramını toplumsal bir kuram haline getirmeyi hedeflemiş ve şu kanıya varmıştır.

Toplumların her türlü sosyal entegrasyonu, birbirlerini belli bir düzen içinde karşılıklı tanımaları (kabullenmeleri) gereğine dayalıdır. Eğer bunun gerçekleşmesine ilişkin bir yetersizlik veya eksiklik varsa, aşağı görme duyguları kök salar". (Savaşçın, 2006)

O halde bireylerin adaletsizliğin bu türlüsüne kah yüksek sesle kah alçak sesle karşı çıkmasının nedeni, kabule/tanınmaya layık görülmemiş olmaktan dolayı duyulan öfkedir.

Göç ettikleri yörenin dilini kullanırlar. Eşler kendi aralarında ve çocuklarıyla anadillerini kullanırlar. Dil kullanmayı içlerini dökmek için bir araç olarak kullanmaya kalkışanlar da anılar, şarkılar, maniler, şiirler öyküler vs. yazmaya ve yayınlamaya başlamışlardır.

Bundan sonrası ev sahibi ülkenin tutumuna kalmıştır, bazıları destekleyici, özendirici olup, oralarda göçmenlerin seslerini duyurmalarını sağlamıştır. *Göç Şarkıları* adlı kitabının önsözünde Tülin Erbaş şöyle yazmaktadır:

Tren Avrupa yönüne Göç yıllarında Yaşam Borcu için uzanıyor.
Hasret-gurbet-sıla-özlem ezgileriyle. Gelecek kimbilir neler alıp götürecek, neler getirecek?
İlk yıllarda Türkçe'yi unutuyoruz korkularıyla basını, kasetleri evlere taşıyorduk. Derken teknolojinin nimetleri: Uydularla Türk Kanalları, İnternet kolaylıkları...
Ve şimdi de Dünya Küçüldü avuntularıyla hemen her yıl bir koşu; Vatan Özlemi. (...)
(Erbaş, 2004, s.1)

Entegrasyon

1970'lerden 1990'ların sonuna dek göç ve beraberinde getirdiği çeşitlilik gitgide artarak devam etmiştir. Entegrasyon kavramı bu çeşitlilik sonrası ortaya çıkan kimlik kaygılarından doğmuştur. Çeşitliliğe karşı bir tepki olarak gelişir ve kendisini bir tehdit altında hisseden göç ülke tarafından alınan tedbirleri içinde barındırır.

Göçmenlerin içinde yaşadıkları topluma entegre olmaları olumlu bir söylem olarak kabul görür.

Ülkenin dilini bilmek, entegrasyonun ilk anahtarıdır. Dili konuşabilmek ile topluma katılmak arasında sıkı bir bağlantı bulunmaktadır. Bourdieu'ye göre, iletişim ilişkileri aynı zamanda sembolik olarak konuşan kişiler ile temsil ettikleri gruplar arasındaki güç ilişkilerini de güncellemektedir. Bu demektedir ki, her konuşma eylemi konuşanlar arasında bir ilişki kurar ve bunu günceller. Konuşan kişinin dile teknik anlamdaki hakimiyeti, yani dinlenebilir cümleler kurma yetisi çok önemlidir. Bedenselleşmiş kültürel sermayenin en önemli unsuru dildir. Bu yüzden göç edilen ülke göçmenlere zorunlu dil kursları sunar. Bu tip kursların adı entegrasyon kurslarıdır. Göçmenin sahip olduğu kültürel sermaye içinde bulunduğu topluluğa uygun günlük yaşamını sürdürebilmesi için gereken tüm özellikleri kapsar. (Bourdieu, 1979).

Geniş olur Almanya'nın yolları
Nasıl iştir anlaşılmaz dilleri (Aşık Hasan Yılmaz, in. Öztürk, 2015)

gibi yakınmalardan sonra zaman içinde Almanca öğrenip anadilini unutanların yakınması da son dönem türkülerde, geri dön çağrılarına bir gerekçe oluşturur.

Unutturdular sana ana dilini
Makinaya nikahladık gelini
Çöktük aha bükecekler belini,

Yurda dön hey bacım yurda dön yurda! (Aşık Kemteri, in. Öztürk, 2015)

Dil sorununu, Türk işçisi kişiselleştirir ve onu bir düşman gibi görür:
Ulan Almanca germanca
Konuşup anlayamadım seni
Boğazımda laflar tıkanır kalır
Meister başlar dır dır dır.   (Rıza Taner, in. Öztürk, 2015)

İşyerinde doğrudan muhatap olunan Meister (ustabaşı), işçinin en çok yakındığı kişilerdendir.
Meister'in yüzü gülmez
İşçinin derdini bilmez
Yabancıyı Alman sevmez
Karakter sıfıra inmiş
İnsanlıktan geri kalmış
Hiç utanmaz meisterler *(Mustafa Çiftçi, in. Öztürk, 2015)*

Sonuç ve tartışma

Göçmek ne denli zorsa, geri dönüş projesi de o kadar zor ve karmaşıktır. Sosyal, ekonomik, kültürel ve psikolojik bir çok yönden başarılı sonlandırılması gereken zor bir süreçtir. Göç uyum süreci kadar hatta bir misli daha önemli olmaktadır geri dönüşün başarılı olması. Geriye dönüş kararını etkileyen nedenler, geri dönüşte elde edinilen destek ve teşvikin göçmen için ifade ettiği anlam çok önemli olmaktadır. Geri dönüş gönülle de olsa döndüğünde aradığı bulabilme, yeniden bir uyum süreci geçirmek kaçınılmazdır.

Göçmenler, göç edenler, uyum sağlayanlar, uyum sağlayamayıp mutsuz olanlar vs. hepsinin hakkında çok değişik dokümanların incelemelerinden oluşan bu nitel araştırmayı sonlandırmak için galiba en doğrusu göçmenlerin kültürel sermayelerinin iş gücü piyasasına geçişlerini sağlamakla yükümlü olan sorumlulara seslenmek olacaktır.

Göçmenleri davet ettikten sonra onları unutmak yerine entegrasyonlarına ciddi olarak olanak sağlamak göç alan ülkelerin geleceği için de sağlıklı olacaktır.

Entegrasyon sadece dil kursları düzenlemekle çözümlenecek bir sorun değildir.

Anlamlı bir entegrasyon çalışmasında, söz konusu olan her göçmenin kim olduğu, neler yapabildiği, beraberinde neler getirdiği ve hangi yöne doğru ilerlemesi gerektiğini saptamak gerekir.

Kaldı ki entegrasyon söylem ve politikaları her ülkede farklı şekillerde ortaya atılır. Ayrıca entegrasyon durağan bir kavram olarak ele alınmamalıdır. Devinim içinde, içinde bulunduğu tarihsel, siyasi, sosyal ve hukuksal bağlam ve şartlara sıkı sıkıya bağlı siyasi bir proje olarak ele alınmalıdır.

Sözü edilen önerilerin tümü acı vatanı olduğu kadar ana vatanı da ilgilenmektedir.

Son söz olarak da unutulmaması gereken bir diğer önemli kavram ulus-ötesi kimliklerin varlıklarıdır. Artık göçmenler çoklu sosyal, siyasal, ekonomik ve kültürel ilişkiler geliştirmişlerdir. Buna göre acı vatan da, anavatan da göçmenleri edilgen değil göç sürecinin karar alıcı, etken, sosyal bireyler olarak değerlendirmelidirler.

Ulus ötesi göçmenler, en az iki toplumun bir parçasıdırlar. Tek bir ülkede değil, geri dönüşte yapsalar iki ülkede birden yaşamaktadırlar. Acı vatanla, anavatan arasında bir köprü oluşturmaktadırlar.

Gelecek artık uluslar ötesi, sınırların saydamlaştığı ve uyum süreçlerinin kısaldığı projelerde gizli olanlıdır ve araştırmalar da bu yönde geliştirilmelidir.

Kaynakça

Arnd-Michael Nohl, Karin Schittenhelm, Oliver Schmidtke, Anja Weiß, Çevirisi Türkis Noyan, (ed.). (2010). *Göç Ve Sermaye*. Türkiye, Almanya, Kanada ve Büyük Britanya'da Yüksek Vasıflı Göçmenler, İstanbul: Kitap Yayınevi

Aytaç, G. (1991). *Edebiyat Yazıları*. Ankara: Gündoğan Yayınları

Baypınar, Y. (....). *İstanbul Üniversitesi Mukayeseli Hukuk dergisi*. Received from www.journals.istanbul.edu.tr/iuaded/article/download/

Bourdieu, P. (1979). *La Diztinction: critique sociale du jugement*, Paris:Editrion de Minuit

Danış, D., İrtiş, V. (der.) (2008). *Entegrasyonun Ötesinde Türkiye'den Fransa'ya Göç ve Göçmenlik Halleri*. İstanbul: Bilgi Üniversitesi Yayınları

Erbaş, T. (2004). *Göç Şarkıları*. İstanbul: Babıali Yayıncılık

Ihlamur-Öner. S,G.;Şirin-Öner. N,A. (der.) (2012). *Küreselleşme Çağında Göç, Kavramlar Tartışmalar*. İstanbul: İletişim Yayınlar

Nasrattınoğlu, İ, Ü. (1997). *Batı Avrupadaki yaşayan Türk Aşıklık Geleneği V*. Milletlerarası Türk Halk Kültürü Kongresi. Halk Edebiyatı Seksiyon Bildirileri. cilt 11. Ankara: Kültür Yayınları

Öztürk, A.,O. (2015). *Göçmen Edebiyatı Olarak Almanya Türküleri Üzerine*. Received from http://www.turkuler.com/yazi/gocmenedebiyati.asp. Almanya

Öztürk, A, O. (2007). *Alamanya Türküleri*. Ankara:Türk Göçmen Edebiyatının Sözlü/Öncü Kolu, Kültür Bakanlığı Yayınları. Kültür Eserleri : 322

Özyer. (1994). *Edebiyat Üzerine*. Ankara: Gündoğan Yayınları

Pazarkaya, Y. (1995). *Ben Aranyor*. Cem Yayınevi. İstanbul: Açı Yayıncılık

Pazarkaya, Y. (2007). Konuk işçiden kült yazarlara: Almanyalı Türklerin edebiyatı. Received from http://tr.qantara.de/webcom/show_article.php/_c-671/_nr-7/_p-1/i.html

Savaşçın, Z. (2006). *Lapsus Dergisi*. Galatasaray Üniversitesi, İstanbul

Yıldız, B. (2010). in Y. Pazarkaya, Turkish Studies International Periodical For The Languages, Literature and History of Turkish or Turkic Volume 5/2 Spring

Yıldız, B. (1975). *Alman Ekmeği*. İstanbul: İshak Matbaası.

Zengin, E. (2010). Türk-Alman Edebiyatına tarihsel Bir Bakış ve Bu Edebiyata İlişkin Kavramlar, Hacettepe Üniversitesi Türkiyat araştırmaları Dergisi. Bahar.2. Ankara

Günümüzün göç edebiyatı nedir?[*]

S. Seza Yılancıoğlu[344]

Giriş

Göç, basit anlamda fiziksel yer değiştirme değil, insanın içinde "doğduğu sosyalleştiği/sosyalleşeceği," (Akıncı:2014, 30) ortamı terk ederek yeni bir çevreye yeni bir dünyaya gitmesidir. Göç edenlerin, göç nedenleri ne olursa olsun, gittikleri ülkelerde ne şekilde karşılanırlarsa karşılansınlar, kabul edildikleri ülkelerde farklı derecelerde uyum güçlükleri yaşarlar. Göç edenler yalnızca yeni bir dil öğrenmek değil aynı zamanda yeni bir kültüre, düzene, ortama, davranış biçimlerine uyum sağlamak zorundadırlar. Bu nedenle, bireyler başka bir kültürle tanıştıklarında ister istemez kültürel bir değişime uğrarlar.

Göç, XX. yüzyılın ikinci yarısına, damgasını vuran en önemli ekonomik ve sosyo-kültürel olaydır. Yaşam koşullarını iyileştirmek amacıyla girişilen göç olayının temeli genellikle tüm toplumlarda ekonomiktir.

1960'lı yıllardan itibaren, bağımsızlıklarını kazanan eski sömürge devletlerin halkları, Avrupa'da özelikle, Fransa, İngiltere ve Belçika'ya göç ederler. Bunların yanında, 1960 ve 1970'li yıllarda, Türkiye'den de Batı Avrupa ülkelerine bir göç hareketi başlar. Bu ülkelerde, XXI. yüzyılın başında bu göçün özellikle kimlik bağlamında sosyo-kültürel boyutu öne çıkar. Öte yandan yine 1970'li ve 1980'li yıllardan itibaren Akdeniz havzası ülkelerinden Kanada'ya olan göçün boyutu yukarıda söz ettiğimiz ülkelere yapılan göçten daha farklıdır; bu coğrafyaya olan göç isteği ise eğitimli kitlelerden gelir. Bu grup içinde yer alan bireylerin amacı, refah düzeyi yüksek, din, dil, ırk ayrımı olmadan eşitlik ilkeleriyle yapılanmış bir ülkede yaşamaktır.

Ülkeler ve kıtalar arası göçler, XXI. yüzyılın başından itibaren yukarıda söz ettiğimiz ülkeler başta olmak üzere çokkültürlü ve çokkimlikli bireylerden oluşan yeni toplum modelleri oluşturur. Toplumlardaki bu değişimler yazınsal alanda "göç edebiyatı" (écritue migrante)'nı yaratır ve bu yazınsal hareket ilk defa, yüzyılın başında "Kanada" edebiyatı"nda kendini gösterir. Söz konusu edebiyatın çekirdeğini oluşturan en önemli sosyal unsur göç hareketleridir. Bu hareketlerle eş zamanlı olarak göçmen kültürleri ve diasporaları doğar, küresel etkileşim ve birbirleriyle ilişkilerinden doğan "kimlikler üstü" oluşur.

Türk Edebiyatında "Göç"

Türk Edebiyatında bu yazın türünü açıklamak için ülkenin 1960 sonrasındaki siyasal ve sosyo-ekonomik yapılarını kısaca anımsamak gerekir; 1964 yılında Türkiye'nin özellikle Almanya, Hollanda, Belçika ve Fransa gibi çeşitli Avrupa ülkeleriyle yaptığı antlaşmalar sonucu, bu ülkeler, II. Dünya Savaşı sonrasında ekonomik dinamiklerini güçlendirmek, Eski Avrupa'ya yeni ivme kazandırmak ve iş gücü açıklarını kapatmak amacıyla Anadolu köylülerine kapılarını aralarlar. Böylece Türkiye'den önce Almanya'ya daha sonra yukarıda belirttiğimiz ülkelere,

---

[*] Bu çalışma Galatasaray Üniversitesi Bilimsel Araştırma Projeleri tarafından desteklenmiştir.
[344] Galatasaray Üniversitesi, E-posa: seza.yilancioglu@gmail.com

"ekonomik nedenli göç başlar. Gittikleri ülkelerde, tek amaçları para biriktirmek, belli bir süre sonra köylerine, kasabalarına, daha iyi "ekonomik" koşullarla geri dönmektir.

Ne var ki, erkek göçmenler, bir süre sonra geride kalan eşleri ve çocukları yetiştirmede bazı sorunlarla karşılaşınca, ailelerini yanlarına almaya başlarlar; böylece aile birleşimiyle konuk eden ülkelere 1970'li yıllarda ll. Kuşak göç (Canatan: 1990, 27) başlar. Birçokları yaşamlarını konuk eden ülkelerde devam ederken, bazıları 1990'lı yıllardan itibaren, emeklilik haklarını kazanır kazanmaz, çocuklarını, torunlarını oralarda bırakarak anayurtlarına geri dönerler.

Unutulmaz anılarla dolu yirmi-otuz yıllık bu dönemin serüvenleri 1975'li yıllardan itibaren Türk Edebiyatında da yerini alır.

Bu sosyo-ekonomik yapının hazırladığı zorunlu göçün yanında, Türkiye'nin siyasal tarihinde 1971 Askeri Muhtırası ve 1980 Askeri Darbesinin ardından, siyasal düşüncelerinden dolayı, sol kökenli pek çok yazar, düşünür ve sanatçı ülkelerini terk ederek çeşitli Avrupa kentlerine kaçmak ve yerleşmek zorunda kalır.

Bu defa, bu göç, siyasal nitelikli olduğundan sürgüne dönüşür. Böylelikle 1990'lı yıllarda Türk edebiyatında "göç" ve "sürgün" izlekleri iç içe girer.

Bu bağlamda, Türk Edebiyatı'nın dünya edebiyatındaki yeri nedir sorusunu düşünmemiz olağandır.

Yazında Göç

Türk edebiyatında "göç" ve "sürgün" izleklerini daha iyi anlayabilmek adına, incelememi kuşaklar arasındaki farklılığı ve buna bağlı olarak yazınsal kuramlardaki değişimi irdelemek amacıyla iki Türk kökenli frankofon yazar; Nedim Gürsel ve Kenan Görgün'ün yapıtlarından yola çıkarak açıklamak istiyorum. *Kültürel ve dilsel değişiklikler*, Avrupa ülkelerindeki göçmenlerin psikolojik, sosyokültürel ve dilsel uyumları üzerine yapılan araştırma sonuçlarında öne çıkan en önemli unsurlardır ve *kültürel uyum (acculturation), kültürel erime (assimilation)* ve *uyum (integration)* süreçlerinden oluşur. Mehmet Ali Akıncı'nın "Fransa'daki Türk Göçmenlerinin Etnik ve Dini Kimlik Algıları" başlıklı makalesinde, kültürel ve dilsel değişim uyum sürecini ikiye ayırır: "a) *kabul*, kişinin eski kültürden gelen mirasının büyük kısmının kaybı ve yaşadığı yeni ülkenin değer yargıları ve kültürel davranışlarını kabul etmesi, yeni kültürün büyük bir ölçüde benimsenmesi, b) *tepki*, köken ülkenin kültürel değer yargıları ve inançlarının korunması, kültürel uyuma direnme hareketidir." (Phinney: 2001 in Akıncı: 2014, 31). Her iki yazarın yapıtlarının incelenmesinde bu şematik sınıflandırma esas alınacaktır.

Nedim Gürsel: göç ve sürgün

Nedim Gürsel, 1980 askeri darbesinden sonra pek çok sol eğilimli düşünür gibi Marx ve Gorki üzerine yazdığı bir makale nedeniyle hakkında soruşturma açılır, soruşturmadan kaçmak ve Fransız hükümetinden aldığı bursu kullanarak üniversite öğrenimine Fransa'da devam eder. Hakkında açılan davadan dolayı iki yıl kadar ülkesine dönemez. Anayurdundan, yakınlarından, anadilinden, ülkesinden uzakta pek çok göçmen gibi bir sürgün yaşamı sürer. Konuk eden ülkenin diline çok iyi bilmesine rağmen yaşadığı kültürel değişim o döneme ait yazınsal ürünlerine yansır. Yazarın Paris'teki yaşamı genellikle kentin sol tarafı olan "Rive Gauche"'da geçer. Burada onun en çok uğrak yerleri üniversite ya da belediye kütüphaneleridir. Yaşantısı Paris'in belli semtlerinde, kendisiyle aynı yıllarda bu ülkeye göç eden Türkler ve diğer ülke vatandaşlarıyla sınırlıdır. Yazar bu dönemde, önceki yıllarda Paris'de yaşayan anne ve babasının izini de sürer "Seine" nehrinin sol tarafında bulunana mahalle ve sokaklarda.

Yazar Nedim Gürsel, konuk eden ülkedeki *kültürel uyum (acculturation)* sürecini 1980'li, *uyum (intégration)* sürecini ise 1990'lı yıllarda tamamlar. Bu bağlamda, Gürsel'in hem kendi kültüründe hem de Fransız kültüründe etkili işlevsellik sergileyen birey olarak *iki kültürlü kimliği* benimseyen bir kimlik geliştirdiği söylenebilir.

Nedim Gürsel, Fransa'ya gelen göçmenlerin yaşam kesitlerinden esinlenerek 1990'lı yıllarda yazdığı öyküleri "sürgün" ve "aşk" izlekleri adı altında 1991'de yayımlanan *Son Tramvay* adlı öykü kitabında daha sonra da 2002 yılında yayımlanan *Cicipapa* - (Toplu öyküler 1967-1990) adlı kitapta bir araya getirir. Bu öykülerin ana izleği, Fransa'ya 1970-1980'li yıllarda "para kazanmak" amacıyla Anadolu'dan gelen Türk işçilerinin hüzünlü yaşamlarıdır. Bu öyküler, aynı zamanda "kimlik gelişimi ve etnik kimlik algısını" incelemek açısından önemli yazınsal belgelerdir. Konuyu irdelemek için iki öykü seçilmiştir:

"Pınar"

Pınar adlı öyküde, anlatıcı-kahraman, Fransa'ya, beş yaşında gelen, bir işçi ailesinin genç kızıyla, Paris'te bir Türk lokantasında tanışmasını ve daha sonra otel odasındaki gizli buluşmalarını anlatır. Pınar'ın babası duvar işçisi, annesi, bir hazır giyim atölyesinde terzidir. Anne, çok kısa bir süre sonra yaşamını bu gurbet ellerde yitirir, Pınar annesiz kalır, babası bir Fransız ile evlenince evdeki erkek kardeşine bakmak için okulu terk eder.

Yazarın, bu öyküde ele aldığı en önemli öğe, Pınar'ın yaşadığı kültürel değişimin, anadil bağlamında yansıtılmasıdır. Pınar, Fransızcayı çok iyi konuşur ve bir hazır giyim atölyesinde ütücüdür. Fransızca'sı mükemmeldi. Pasajdaki atölyelerden birinde "ütü geçiyordu".

Evet ütü yapmıyor, geçiyordu. Yanlışını düzeltmek için onu benimle Türkçe konuşmaya zorladım. Önce direndi, sonra razı oldu. "Geçmeyip", "bastığını" söyledi. Gülmeye başladım. Kızdı. Bir daha Türkçe konuşmadı benimle." (Gürsel, 2002, s. 326).

Bu öyküde Pınar'ın anadil sorununu, bir yandan, Derrida'nın ortaya koyduğu; kişinin ne tek dilli, ne çift dilli ne de çok dilli olmasıyla değil, bir kültürde kökleşmemiş "dile sahip olması" ilkesiyle açıklanabilir (Derrida, 1996, 55). Öte yandan ise, göçmen Pınar'ın kültürel ve dilsel bağlamdaki kültürel uyumu "kabul" boyutludur: Pınar, eski kültüründen gelen mirasının büyük bir kısmının kaybederek, yaşadığı yeni ülkenin değer yargılarını ve kültürel davranışlarını kabul ederek, yeni kültürü büyük ölçüde benimser. Aynı tepkiyi Pınar'ın babası da verir, annesinin ölümünden sonra baba bir Fransız ile evlenir ve olabildiğince konuk eden ülkenin kültürünü benimseyerek yaşamına devam eder.

Oysa, Pınar'ın annesi, ekonomik nedenli göç serüveninin faturasını ağır bir şekilde yaşamıyla öder. Annenin kültürel uyumu "tepki" boyutludur. Köken ülkenin kültürel değer yargıları ve inançlarından kopamadığı için kültürleşmeye tepki verir ve bu tepki de ölümdür.

Pınar ve babası, köklerinden hemen kopmayı başarır; ölen eşinin ardından bir Fransız ile evlenir ve evliliği uğruna küçük oğluna bakması için kızını okuldan alır. Babasında olduğu gibi Pınar'da da köklerinden uzaklaşma ve ana kültürüne karşı bir yabancılaşma sezilir. Her ikisi de Fransız vatandaşıdır ama Fransız olabilmişler midir?

Bu değişim, Jacques Derida'nın *Monolinguisme de l'autre* adlı yapıtında söz ettiği gibi "Kendini yeniden yapılandırma" ile kimliksel ve kültürel performativenin ortaya koyduğu tüm kimlik sorunlarına karşıtlık oluşturur (Cohen, Calle-Gruber et Vignon, 2014,160). Derrida, bir bireyin kimliğinin tanımlanmasında, yurttaşlık, bulunduğu yerin kan ölçütleri ve "konukseverlik" ilişkilerinin yeterliliği, olgusunu sorgular. (Derrida, 1996, 30). Derrida, dil, yurttaşlık, ait olduğu kültür arasında tüzüksel ve keyfiyet ilişkilerinden dolayı ayrıcalıklı bir ilişkiyi yadsır ve yurttaşlık olgusunun, bir göçmeni "konuk eden ülke" ile aynileştirmesi için yeterli olmadığını ileri sürer.

Bu son derece kırılgan yapı, aidiyet duygularının kaynağı olamaz, Pınar'ın dil sorunu, Derrida'nın yukarıda söz ettiğimiz savı gibi, anadilinin kök salmadığı bir yerde yaşamasından, kaynaklanır. Okuldan alınan Pınar, hem erkek kardeşine bakmakla hem de çalışıp para kazanarak babasına ekonomik katkı sağlamakla yükümlüdür. Pınar, kendisine çizilen bu yolda yürürken, anadilinden uzaklaştığı gibi Türkiye'li Türklerden de uzak olmayı yeğler ve Paris'te yaşayan onunla az çok aynı yazgıyı paylaşan Türklerle sıla hasretini giderir. Pınar'ın anadiliyle zayıf, kırılgan ilişkisi, "konuk eden ülke" deki yurttaşlık olgusunun da ne kadar kırılgan olduğunu gösterir. Böylece Pınar, kültürel değişim sürecini kültürel korumacılıktan adaptasyon yönünde tek boyutlu bir süreçle yaşar. Yeni kültürü elde ettikçe zamanla köken kültürünü kaybeder.

Bu öykü, "kültürleşmenin iki temel ve zıt yönlü olan kültürel korumacılık ve kültürel adaptasyon" (Akıncı.2014-31) süreçlerinin ikincisi olan "kültürel adaptasyona" iyi bir örnektir.

"Tünel"

Nedim Gürsel, *Tünel* adlı başka bir öyküsünde, kaçak yollardan Fransa'ya girmeye çalışan bir ailenin dramını vurgular. Bu öyküde de konuklayan ülkede farklı bir kimlik gelişimi karşımıza çıkar.

Seni düşünüyorum Osman! On yıl boyunca bir duvar ustası olarak yaptığın konutları, içinde oturamadığın geniş, ferah evleri düşünüyorum. (…) Bir ırmak akıp gidiyor, yıllar, ayrılıklar boyunca. Strsbourg'da, soğuk bir çatı odasındaki yalnızlığını düşünüyorum. (…) Seni köyünden, toprağından koparıp Strasbourg'da bir çatı odasının yalnızlığına, pazar günlerinin güneşli parklarına çocuksuz atlıkarıncaların mavi, kırmızı, yeşil boyalı yabancılığına savuran bir ırmak; karını, çocuklarını bozkırdan sökerek İstanbul'da bir gecekondunun sıvası dökülmüş, kırık pencereli odalarına götürüp bir tortu gibi bırakan, bıraktıktan bu yana da hiç arayıp sormayan deli ırmak işte!" (Gürsel, 2002, 240-241).

Alıntıda gördüğümüz gibi Osman, yaşam şartlarını iyileştirmeyi düşünerek önce eşi ve çocuklarıyla İstanbul'da bir gecekondu mahallesine yerleşir, daha sonra herşeyini bırakarak Fransa'ya gider. Yazarın betimlemesine göre, Osman için yaşam, sessiz akan bir ırmak değil, "bozbulanık", "delice" akan bir ırmaktır. Tam eşine ve çocuklarına kavuşmayı düşlediği sırada işini kaybeder, ailesini Fransa'ya getirtmek için vize alamaz. Osman, on yılını geçirmesine rağmen, konuk eden ülkeye tam entegre olamamasının temelinde sosyal, ekonomik, psikolojik ve siyasal değişkenler bulunur : en belirgin örneği, işini kaybettiğinden dolayı, eşi ve çocukları için vize alamamasıdır: bu da, kendisinin, konuk eden ülkede, sosyal kimliğinin ve güvencesinin olmadığını gösterir.

Bu ayrılığa son vermek için Osman karısı ve çocuklarıyla Fransa'ya kaçak yollardan İtalya üzerinden girmeye karar verir. İtalya'yı Fransa'ya bağlayan uzun Modane-Frejus tüneline girerler. Fransa'da tünelin bitiminde arkadaşı, Osman'ın iki çocuğuyla onları beklemektedir, hazin yazgıyı bilmeksizin...

Tünel çıkışında bekleyen Osman'ın iki çocuğu, tam kardeşleri, anne ve babasına kavuşacağı sırada onları taşıyan araba karşı yönden gelen trenin altında kalarak paramparça olur. Osman'ın "bozbulanık" akan yaşamı, eşi ve çocuğuyla böylece son bulur. Osman, konuk eden ülkede, sosyal güvencesi olmadan para kazanır, köken ülke ile konuk eden ülke arasındaki siyasi uygulamalar vizeyi zorunlu kılar. Vize alamayan Osman, psikolojik bunalıma girerek eşini ve çocuklarını Fransa'ya getirmek için yasadışı bir yol seçer. Kahramanın bu davranışı, kültürleşme sürecindeki *tepki* boyutuna örnektir. Köken ülkesinde yaşadığı yerel kültür dinamiklerinden esinlenerek, ailesinin Fransa'ya girebilmesi için bir çözüm üretir. Ne yazık ki bu çözüm onları ölüme götürür. Konuklayan ülkenin sosyo-kültürel dinamiklerini benimsemeyi reddeder.

Burada izlediğimiz iki öykü, bir yere aidiyet duygusunun Derrida'ya göre "takma kökenle" (prothèse d'origine), oluşan yurttaşlıkla değil, insanın içinden gelen istek ile konukseverlik bağlamında oluşan yurttaşlık ile yaşanılan yere aidiyetin oluştuğunu, gösterir. Bu öykünün kahramanları, toplumun kenarında kalan yurttaşlardır.

Pınar adlı ilk öyküde ise, babanın, yaptığı evlilikle "takma kökenin" şartlarına hemen uyum sağladığı, Pınar ise, kendini yeniden yapılandırdığı, seçtiği arkadaş çevresiyle, anlaşılır. Baba, eşinin acısını hemen unutur ve bir Fransız ile evlenerek konuk eden ülkedeki uyum sürecini hızlandırır.

Nedim Gürsel, yukarıda söz ettiğimiz öyküleri dahil tüm kurgusal anlatılarını 40 yılı aşkın süredir Fransa'da yaşamasına rağmen anadili Türkçe yazar.

Bu incelemenin ikinci yapıtı, Belçika doğumlu, frankofon yazar Kenan Görgün'ün *Anatolia Rhapsody* adlı yapıtıdır.

Kenan Görgün ve Anatolia Rhapsody

Kenan Görgün'ün babası 1967 yılında bilinen ekonomik nedenlerle eşini ve çocuklarını Türkiye'de bırakarak önce Hollanda'ya sonra da Belçika'nın Gand kentine gelir ve yerleşir, burada bir kibrit fabrikasında çalışır. 1970 yıllarda, ikinci kuşak göç akımıyla eşi ve çocuklarını yanına alarak aile bütünleşmesini sağlar ve 1977 yılında Kenan Görgün bu kentte doğar, çocukluğunu burada geçirir. Daha sonra aile Brüksel'e taşınır, babası aynı şirketin bir inşaat firmasında çalışır, otuz yıldır aynı firmada kalması, Belçika-Türkleri'nin Belçika'da aileleriyle birlikte yaşamlarını sürdürmelerinin olağan bir olguya dönüştüğünü; göçmenler ile Belçika devleti ve kurumları arasında oluşan "güvenin" göstergesidir. Baba, işi ve ailesiyle birlikte Belçika'da "kültürel uyum" ve "entegrasyon" süreçlerini *kabul* boyutunda yaşar. Zamanla köken kültürdeki değişimleri bilmeden ve bu kültürdeki bazı değerleri unutarak, konuk eden ülkenin değer yargıları ve davranış biçimlerini benimser.

Kenan Görgün, 1977'de Gand'da doğumuyla başlayan ve 2013'de İstanbul'a yerleşmesi arasındaki zaman diliminde yaşadıklarını, ailesi dahil olmak üzere diğer Türk göçmenlerin belleklerindeki olayları, tanıklıkları ve yaşanan kimliksel sorunsallarını dile getirir özyaşamöyküsel *Anatolia Rhapsody*'de. "Sürgün, ilk yer" başlıklı ilk bölümde, doğar doğmaz yaşadığı sosyal ve bireysel kimliğini şöyle dile getirir:

Dünyaya geldiğimden beri çiftim
Çift ve bölünmüş, iki tanrısal çekişme totemi.
Gereğinden fazla kimlikle yüklüyüm.
Varlığımı ağırlaştıran pek çok kabuk (Görgün, 2014, 11)345.

1990'lı yılların öykülerine, konu olan Türk göçmen işçilerinin, toplumun kenarında kalan kimlik olgusu burada çokkültürlü bir kimliğe dönüşür. O dönemin gurbetçileri yalnızca iş güçleri/el emekleriyle varlıklarını sürdürürler ve toplumdaki kimlikleri yalnızca "göçmen işçi"dir.

Oysa Kenan Görgün'ün ilk vurgusu, doğduğu, çocukluğunu ve gençliğini geçirdiği ülkede yaşadığı çokkültürlü kimliktir. Öyle ki yazar doğduğu ülkenin dilini kullanır ve anadili Türkçe'ye çok vakıf değildir. Yazar, kimliğin en önemli kültürel kodu dil olgusuyla başlar yazın hayatına; kullandığı dil ise konuk eden ülkenin dili Fransızca'dır.

Kenan Görgün, yapıtında iki kuşak (kendi ve ebeveynler) arasındaki öncelikleri ve kimliksel yapılarını dile getirir. Baba kuşağının (ailenin diğer üyeleriyle canlandırır) en büyük amacı ve ideali, yirmi-otuz yıl gurbette çalıştıktan sonra iyi paralar kazanmak, lüks araba, Türkiye ve Belçika'da, rahatlıkla oturabileceği ferah güzel evler satın almaktır. Yapılan sosyolojik bir araştırma babanın bu tavrını doğrular ve araştırmaya göre; "Belçika'da yaşamak Belçika-Türkleri'nin çoğu için normal bir olgu haline gelmiştir. Belçika ile bağları geçmişte Belçika devletinin göçü düzenleme biçiminden de kaynaklanmaktadır. Belçika göçmenlerin aileleri ile birlikte göç etmesini özendirmiştir." (Kaya-Kentel: 2008, 95)

Oysa Kenan Görgün ve kuşağına gelince durum çok farklıdır; iki kültür, iki dil, iki farklı dini görüş içinde yaşamaktadırlar. Kültürel ve sosyal bir belirsizlik içindedirler, iki dünya eşiğindedirler, biri ve öteki bir araya gelerek birbirlerini tamamlar.

Bir zenginlik edinebiliriz, ama en büyük tehlike, hiçbirine ait olmadan iki kültür arasında kaybolmaktır (Görgün, 2014, 43-44).

Kenan Görgün gibi ikinci göçmen kuşağının en önemli sorunsalı, Belçika toplumuna ya da diğer toplumlarda uyum sağlanabiliyor mu yoksa toplumdışı "gettolaşarak" mı yaşanıyor. Bu örnek ve bağlamda, Derrida'nın ortaya koyduğu "takma köken" (prothèse d'origine) kavramının, ikinci göçmen kuşağında daha farklı boyutu görürülür. Yazar, kitabında şöyle bir anısından söz eder: "ilk romanı çıktığı zaman, Belçikalı gazeteci, Kenan Görgün ile bir röportaj yapmak ister, yazar romanına duyulan ilgiden çok memnundur. Ancak gazetecinin amacı ilk Türk kökenli Frankofon yazar olması nedeniyle, yazarın Belçika toplumu hakkında

---

345 *Anatolia* Rhapsody'den alınan alıntılar S. Seza Yılancıoğlu tarafından Türkçe'ye çevrilmiştir.

düşünceleri ve topluma olan uyumunu, öğrenmektir (*Le Ligueur*: 14.01.2015). Gazetecinin yazara yaklaşımı, yaşanan ülkedeki yurttaşlık aidiyetinin, dili benimseme ve insanın içinden, bedenden gelen sevgi ve arzuyla oluştuğunu gösterir. İkinci kuşak yazar açısından baktığımız zaman, yazar, "kimliklerüstü" ve "kültürlerüstü" özellikleriyle hem Belçika toplumuna hem de Türkiye toplumuna aidiyeti "takma köken"lidir. Kenan Görgün, kendisini ve tüm göçmenleri konuk eden ülkeler için şu yorumu yapar:

> *Konuklayan ülke (tüm konuklayan ülkeler) ne benim ebeveynlerimi ne de binlerce göçmeni istemedi. Yalnızca onların iş güçlerini, daha iyi bir yaşam umutlarını istediler, yarının bugünden doğduğunu unutarak. Bizleri de ikinci, üçüncü kuşağı istediklerine de inanmıyorum. (…) Biz, göçmen çocukları, kendimiz "bölünmüş", "eksik" hissediyoruz (Görgün, 2014, 97-98).*

Yazar, göçmenlerin ikinci ya da üçüncü kuşakların kabul edildikleri ülkelerde, kendilerini bölünmüş ve eksik hissetmelerine karşın bu kuşaklar Türkiye - Türkleriyle de pek fazla uyum içinde yaşayamazlar. Onlarla birlikte oldukları zaman da farklı bir "ötekilik" yaşarlar. Kenan Görgün 2013 yılında Türkiye'ye yerleşmek üzere geldiğinde, Türk toplumu hakkındaki düşüncelerini şöyle dile getirir:

> *Lezbiyen çift el ele yürüyor. Türk mü? Ağaç altında bir bankta mısır yiyen başı örtülü kadınlar, Türk mü? Basenlerini saran dar eteğiyle, yüksek topuklu ayakkabıları üzerinde yükselen, beline kadar uzanan mısır püskülü sarı saçlı, bir elinde i-phonu diğer elinde dosya çantalı genç kadın, bir İsveç'liden daha sarı, Türk mü? Ezan okunur okunmaz camiye güruh halinde beşer onar giden, cami dolunca kaldırımda namaz kılan bu adamlar, Türk mü? (…) Buradaki Türklerin bizimle hiç alakası yok. Buranın gençleri son derece özgür ve modern! (Görgün, 2014, 111-112).*

Bu alıntıda gördüğümüz gibi Belçika'da yaşadığı iki kimlikten, iki kültürlülükten hatta iki farklı din algısından kaynaklanan kültürel ve sosyal kimlik parçalanmasını, anavatan saydığı Türkiye'ye gelince de bu parçalanmayı ya da bölünmüşlüğü gideremez. Kendini farklı bir şekilde yine "öteki" olarak görür. Bu "ötekilik" ise, onu "takma köken"li yapar.

> *İstanbul görkemli bir gözlem alanı. Sermaye, iş-kültür kavşağı, siyasal destekli güçlü sponsorların (sponsor olan siyasetçiler) hakim olduğu gayrimenkul spekülasyonun tekeli, İstanbul, on beş yıl öncesinin kenti değil artık. O dönemde, böylesine yanlış ve akıl almaz sapmaların çok uzağındaydı. Hiçbir metropol böyle olamaz. İstanbul, on beş sene içinde, Türk nüfusunun dörtte biri ve Belçika nüfusunun iki katı, kentte oturanların düşüncesi: yeni düzenlemeler çok fazla sorunlar yarattı. (….) Kent, suni modernleşmeyle Singapur ve Dubai ile yarışıyor, yöneticiler, birçok medeniyetlerin beşiği, eski Bizans başkentini, güvenliksiz, kuralsız, düzensiz pek çok cerrahi müdahalelerle, babylone-bimbo olarak görüyorlar. Görkemli, lüks, ayna camlı dış görünüşleriyle modern siteler, eski geleneksel mahalleleri yok ederek yayılıyor. (…) Bu beton bloklar arasında yeşil alanlar aramak boşuna; kilometrelerce uzanan bu bloklar arasında ne bir bahçe, ne de bir park var, ama çalışan, oradan oraya giden yirmi milyon insan, gece-gündüz, atık ve kirli havanın oluşturduğu kalın enerji bulutunu teneffüs ediyor (Görgün, 2014, 137-138).*

Her iki ülkede yaşadığı kültürel, sosyal ve kimliksel melezlikten doğan yabancılaşmayı kendi içinde yarattığı bir "kimliklerüstüyle" aşar Kenan Görgün. Bu süreçte yazar için en iyi yöntem "yazmaktır" ve yaşamını değiştiren şey; kendisi ve Fransız dili arasında kurduğu güçlü ilişkidir. Yazma edimine genç yaşta başlayan yazar, "sürgün" olarak nitelendirdiği doğduğu ülkenin kültürel hayatında yazar kimliğiyle yerini alır.

Sonuç

Anatolia Rhapsody, Kenan Görgün'ün hem özyaşmöyküsü, hem de tanıklık yazını özelliklerini taşıyan bir romandır. Yazar, iki kültürlülük, iki dillilik arasında yaşadığı bocalamayı yenebilmek için kendini yazıya verir. Tanıklık ettiği ve onu rahatsız eden her şeyi acil olarak yazıya dökerek içinde bulunduğu psikolojik kaosu aşar. Yazar, böylece, "göç ve sürgün" izleklerinden yola çıkarak, romanında, yaşadığı sosyo-kültürel ve psikolojik bağlamda kendisini etkileyen olaylardan esinlenerek yarattığı özyaşamöyküsüyle "tanıklık yazınını" harmanlar. Bu bağlamda XXI inci yüzyıl yazının en önemli izleklerinden "kimlik" sorunu, "kültürlerüstü" ve "kimliklerüstü" olgularıyla öne çıkar.

Nedim Gürsel'in öykü karakterleri, bulundukları yere olan yabancılıklarıyla dikkat çeker, yani yaşadıkları yerin yurttaşı olsalar bile, bu onlara gerçek anlamda bir aidiyet duygusu vermez., Nedim Gürsel'in Pınar, Osman, adlı kahramanları, Derrida'nın adlandırdığı "takma kökenli"dir. Kenan Görgün'e gelince, ebeveynlerini "konuk eden ülke" de doğup büyümesine rağmen yine bir kimlik, ötekilik sorunu yaşar. Bu ise XXI inci yüzyıla adını veren küreselleşmenin yarattığı kimliksel ve kültürel melezlikten kaynaklanan, çokkültürlülüğün, tekkültürlülüğe ya da yerel kültürlülüğe karşı yarattığı kültürel zenginlikten doğan bir "ötekilik"tir.

Bu çalışmada, Nedim Gürsel'in 1990'da yayımladığı sürgün izlekli iki farklı öyküsüyle, Belçika doğumlu, ikinci kuşak (göçmen) yazar, Kenan Görgün'ün 2014'de yayımlanan *Anatolia Rhapsody* arasında yapılan incelemede; XXI inci yüzyıl yazınında "sürgün ve göç edebiyatı" tanımlarının, çok dillilik, çokkültürlülük, çokkimlikle yaratılan kimliklerüstü ve kültürlerüstü olgularıyla zenginleştiği saptanır.

Kaynakça

Akıncı Mehmet Ali, "Fransa'daki Türk Göçmenlerinin Etnik ve Dini Kimlik Algıları" in *bilig*, Yaz 2014/sayı 70, 29-58.
Cohen Y.; Calle-Gruber M.; Vignon E. (2014). *Migrations maghrébines comparées : genre, ethnicité, religions*, Paris: Riveneuve Collection.
Canatan, K. (1990). *Göçmenlerin Kimlik Anlayışı*, İstanbul : Endülüs Yayınları.
Görgün, K. (2014). Kenan, *Anatolia Rhapsody*, Jutta Hepke: Vent d'ailleurs/Ici&ailleurs.
Gürsel, N. (2002). *Cicipapa*, (Toplu öyküler 1967-1990) İstanbul: Doğan Kitap.
Kaya A. ve Kentel F. (2008). *Belçika Türkleri Türkiye ile Avrupa Birliği Arasında Köprü mü?, Engel mi?* (Çev: Suna Gökçe), İstanbul: İstanbul Bilgi Üniversitesi Yayınları.
Toro de A., Zekri K., Bensmaia et Gafaiti H. (2010). *Repenser le Maghreb et l'Europe,-Hybridation-Métissage-Diasporisation*. Paris : l'Harmattan.
Torrekens. M. "Kenan Görgün en double exil" in
http://www.laligue.be/leligueur/articles/kenan-gorgun-en-son-double-exil

Edebiyatta Göçmen Kimliğine Sıradışı Bir Bakış: Kati Hirşel

Pınar Güzelyürek Çelik[346] ve Lale Arslan Özcan[347]

Giriş

Bu çalışmada Esmahan Aykol'un yurtdışında pekçok ödüle layık görülen ve çok satanlar listesinde yer alan polisiye romanlarını inceleyeceğiz: *Kitapçı Dükkanı* (2001), *Kelepir Ev* (2003), *Şüpheli bir Ölüm* (2007), *Tango İstanbul* (2012). Yazarın Almanya'da maruz kaldığı ayrımcılık ve dışlanma deneyimlerini edebiyata yöneltmesini, Sigmund Freud psikanalitiğinde açıklandığı şekliyle yüceltme mekanizması kapsamında incelerken, yazarın, roman kahramanını kendisinin "eş insanı" olarak kurgulamasını bu çerçeve içinde örnekleriyle göstermeye çalışacağız. Aynı kapsamda yazarın, göçmen kimliğini ele alış biçimiyle edebiyata getirmiş olduğu yeni soluğu ortaya koymaya gayret edeceğiz. Ardından Esmahan Aykol'un göç temasını anlatmak için polisiye roman kurgusunu seçmiş olmasıyla romanlarında eklektik bir yazın türünün örneğini oluşturduğunu tanıtlamaya çalışacağız.

Biyobibliyografya

Esmahan Aykol hukuk eğitimi gördüğü sırada *Sokak Dergisi'*nde adım atmış olduğu gazetecilik mesleğini *Güneş, Nokta* ve *Radikal İki'*de sürdürmüştür. Ardından kısa bir süre avukatlık mesleğini yapmış ancak akademik kariyerin kendisine daha uygun olduğunu düşünerek lisansüstü eğitim almak üzere 1998 yılında Berlin'e gitmiştir. "Alman ve Türk Aile Hukukunda Cinsiyet Ayrımcılığı" başlıklı teziyle Master derecesini almıştır. Doktora eğitimi sırasında yazmaya başlamış ve Kati Hirşel'in okurla buluştuğu ilk romanı *Kitapçı Dükkânı'*nın 2001'de basılmasıyla yazarlık kariyerine başlayıp hukuk kariyerine son noktayı koymuştur.

Aykol, Almanya'da doktora sırasında maruz kaldığı "ayrımcı muamelenin" kendisinde uyandırdığı incinmişlik, öfke, kızgınlık ve bu durumu net bir şekilde ispatlayamayacağını bilmesinin doğurduğu iç sıkıntısı ve bunalımı bir biçimde dışa vurma ihtiyacı olarak Kati Hirşel'i yaratmıştır. Bu nedenle romanlarındaki karakterlerde kendi yaşanmışlıklarının deneyimlenmesi için "rolleri değiştirerek" bir Almanın da aynı duyguları kurgusal bir biçimde de olsa yaşamasını sağlamak istemiştir. (Maro, 2012)

Kati Hirşel, okurun karşısına ilk kez, İstanbul'a film çekimi için gelen bir Alman yönetmenin cinayete kurban gitmesini konu eden *Kitapçı Dükkânı'*nda çıkmıştır. Her yönüyle bir azınlık karakteri olarak kurgulanan Hirşel, İstanbul'un Beyoğlu semtinde Tünel'de polisiye eserler satan bir kitapçı dükkânı işleten Yahudi asıllı bir Almandır. Kati'nin babası 2. Dünya Savaşında Alman faşizminden

---

[346] Dr., Yıldız Teknik Üniversitesi, Fen-Edebiyat Fakültesi, Fransızca Mütercim Tercümanlık Anabilim Dalı. Yıldız Teknik Üniversitesi, Fen-Edebiyat Fakültesi, Fransızca Mütercim Tercümanlık Anabilim Dalı, Davutpaşa Kampüsü, Esenler, İstanbul, Türkiye. Email: pguzelyurek@yahoo.fr
[347] Yrd. Doç. Dr., Yıldız Teknik Üniversitesi, Fen-Edebiyat Fakültesi, Fransızca Mütercim Tercümanlık Anabilim Dalı. . Yıldız Teknik Üniversitesi, Fen-Edebiyat Fakültesi, Fransızca Mütercim Tercümanlık Anabilim Dalı, Davutpaşa Kampüsü, Esenler, İstanbul, Türkiye. Email: ozcanlale@hotmail.com

kaçarak karısıyla birlikte İstanbul'a gelmiş ve burada Ceza Hukuku profesörü olarak 1965 yılına kadar yaşamıştır. Ailesinin Türkiye'de kaldığı dönemde Kati dünyaya gelmiştir. Almanya'ya geri döndükten sonra Kati, 1988 yılında bir arkadaşını ziyaret etmek üzere İstanbul'a gelmiş ve bir daha da geri dönmemiştir. (Aykol, 2001, s. 196). Bu bağlamda yazar Kati'yle ilgili olarak şöyle demektedir: *"Bana sorarsanız Kati, ne Türk ne Alman, nevi şahsına münhasır bir tip. Kendisi, 'Ne Türk ne Almanım, ben İstanbulluyum," diyordu ilk üç romanda."* (Tunaboylu, 2012)

Kati Hirşel alışılagelmiş detektiflerden farklı bir kişiliğe sahiptir. Öncelikle birincil mesleği bu değildir. Her seferinde kendini tesadüfler silsilesiyle bir cinayetin ortasında bulmakta ve merakına yenik düşerek olayların peşini bir türlü bırakamayıp, çocukluğundan beri tutkunu olduğu polisiye romanlardan esinlenerek olayı çözmeye koyulmaktadır.

2003'te yayınlanan ikinci roman *Kelepir Ev*'de Kati mafya ve rüşvetçilikle karşı karşıya kalmaktadır. Nitekim Amerika'da ödül kazanan bu kitap İngilizce'ye *Baksheesh* olarak çevrilmiştir. Romanda, herşey Kati'nin İstanbul'da Kuledibi'nde bir ev almak istemesiyle başlamakta ve İstanbul'a göç etmiş Kürt bir aile reisinin cinayete kurban gitmesiyle olaylar birbirini takip etmektedir.

Yazarın, Kati Hirşel polisiye serisinden olmayan 2006 tarihli üçüncü romanı *Savrulanlar* tam tabiriyle bir göç romanıdır. İstanbul'da başlayıp Londra'da biten bu romanda Esmahan Aykol bu kez Londra'daki göçmenlerin durumunu ele almıştır.

2007 yılında yayınlanan Kati Hirşel Polisiyesi *Şüpheli Bir Ölüm*'de yazarın deyimiyle "çevre siyaseti" ön plana çıkmaktadır. Olaylar zengin bir ailenin, çevreci bir derneğin kurucusu olan gelininin öldürülmesiyle başlamaktadır.

Son Kati Hirşel romanıysa 2012 yılında basılan *Tango İstanbul*'dur. Bu kez Kati medya camiasının kirli yüzünü keşfetmekte ve her zaman olduğunun aksine Galata çevresinden çıkıp Nişantaşı sokaklarına dalmaktadır.

Kati Hirşel romanlarının anlatı yapısı

Esmahan Aykol gerçekçi bir yazar olarak romanlarını kaleme almaktadır. Bu özelliğinin gazetecilik yıllarına dayandığını belirten yazarın romanları bize, gerek kahramanları açısından gerekse zaman, mekân ve uzam örgüsü açısından tam anlamıyla gerçek dünyadan bir kesit sunmaktadırlar. *Tango İstanbul* romanını kaleme alırken yazar Nişantaşı sokaklarını arşınladığını, restoranlarına girip çıktığını ve hatta romandaki menüleri gerçek menülerden aldığını ifade etmiştir. Keza *Savrulanlar* romanında kahramanın neler hissettiğini anlayabilmek için bizzat Londra'da iki ay garsonluk yaptığı da bilinmektedir. (Çınar, 2015)

Yazarın yapıtları aynı zamanda siyasi bir kimlik taşımakla öne çıkmaktadır. Başkahraman *Kelepir Ev*'de Türkiye'nin güncel siyasal olaylarına dair yargılarını doğrudan dile getirmektedir. Bu tavrını yalnızca Türkler söz konusu olduğunda değil aynı zamanda Alman ve İngilizler için de sürdürmektedir. Hatta kimi zaman Almanlara karşı çok sert bir tutum takınmaktadır. Ancak yazar bu yargıları, Kati'nin mizacına öylesine ustalıkla harmanlamıştır ki hiçbir şekilde göze batmayan, esprili, nutuk çeker havasına girmeyen, samimi bir toplum yergisi ortaya koymuştur.

Aykol romanlarında, olay örgüleri içinde, okura siyasal ve toplumsal bir panorama sunulur. Bu çerçevede yazar, klasik polisiye öykülerinden farklı olarak suçun toplumsal ve siyasal nedenine dair saptamalarını okuruyla buluşturur.

Kati Hirşel Romanlarında Göç Teması

"Ana temam, zaten, polisiye, aşk romanı ne olursa olsun benim kitaplarımdaki hep ana tema yabancı olmak. Bir topluma dışarıdan gelen, göç eden insan olmak ve o toplumu dışarıdan bir gözle değerlendirmek" (Çınar, 2015) sözleriyle biçemini ifade eden Aykol'un romanlarını bir göç romanı olarak nitelendirmenin yanlış olmayacağı kanısındayız. Yazar gerek göçmenliğe bakış açısı, gerek seçmiş olduğu türün özellikleriyle farklı bir sentez ortaya koymaktadır. Aykol göçmen kimliğinin sorunlarını ve dışlanmışlığı her fırsatta kaleme almaktadır: *Tango İstanbul*'da Nijeryalı temizlikçiler, Ermeni ve Rum diasporası ve Arjantin'e göç, *Kitapçı Dükkanı*'nda Türkiye'de yaşayan bir Alman göçmeni, *Kelepir Ev*'de İstanbul'a doğudan göç eden Kürtler, serinin hemen her romanında karşımıza çıkan kahramanın en yakın arkadaşı ve çalışanı, İspanyol asıllı eşcinsel Fofo. Bu bağlamda, yazarın, göçmenlik kavramını milletlerlerüstü bir düzlemde işlediği ve bu kimliği alışılagelmiş kalıplarından farklı bir duygudaşlıkla ele aldığı gözlemlenebilir.

Bu çerçeveden bakıldığında Kati Hirşel romanlarındaki göçmen vurgusunun yazarın kendisinin de deneyimlediği üzere, ötekileştirme, yabancılaştırma ve bir türlü kırılamayan önyargılar üzerinden yapıldığı açıktır:

"(...) Fakat Türklerde şair geni olduğu kesin. Allahım bu topraklar nasıl da şair kaynıyor! Fokur fokur. En normal sanılan tanıdıklar bile nasıl da gizli, keşfedilmemiş, anlaşılmamış bir şair çıkıveriyor, nasıl da insanın burnuna deri kaplı şiir defterleri dayayıveriyorlar. O utanç verici küçük pislikleri bir de gururla sunuyorlar. (...) Doğruları duymak Türkler'in kalbini kırar, ben de diyorum ya Almanlar kadar kaba değilim bir süredir. En azından Berlin'li Almanlar kadar." (Aykol, 2003, s.169)

Bütün bunlar düşünüldüğünde Esmahan Aykol'un göçmenliği anlatmak için neden polisiye roman türünü seçtiği sorusu akla gelebilir. Yazar tutkun bir polisiye roman okuru olmasının yanı sıra bu türün insan doğasını en iyi anlatma özelliği taşıdığına yürekten inanmaktadır:

"Kati Hirşel karakteri gözümün önünde belirdiğinde de onun bir polisiye kahramanı olması dışında seçenek yokmuş gibi geldi bana. Polisiye kurguyla her şey anlatılabilir, dolayısıyla çok imkânlı. Beni en çok cezbeden bu imkânlılık hali sanırım. Büyük bir aşkı da nefreti de baba katlini de polisiye kurguyla anlatmak mümkün." (Tunaboylu, 2012)

Aykol, Kati Hirşel romanlarındaki polisiye tarzını, kendi ifadeleriyle şu şekilde dile getirmektedir: *"Katilerin tarzı ne çok siyasi ne çok kan revan. Fazla dramatik şeyler olmuyor Katilerde. Kan revan benim tarzım değil. Okumam da öyle şeyler."* (Okyay, 2012)

Eş İnsan Kati Hirşel

"(...) kendilerine en geniş ve en istekli bir okuyucu kitlesi bulan romancılar, uzun ve kısa öykü yazarları üzerinde duracağız. Bu sanatçıların yaratılarında bir özellik var ki, hepsinden çok dikkatimizi çeker. Yapıtların tümünde görülen bir kahraman, okuyucuların ilgisinin odak noktasını oluşturur, sanatçı her türlü önleme başvurarak

okuyucuların bu kahramana sempati duymasını sağlamaya çalışır." (Freud, 2014, s. 110)

Eş insan karakteri edebiyatın vazgeçilmez unsurlarından biri olmuştur. Otto Rank'ın *Don Juan et le Double* adlı yapıtında belirttiği gibi genel olarak Batı edebiyatında eş insan, Dostosyevski ya da Edgar Allen Poe gibi alışılagelmişin dışında bir yaşamı olan hatta derin ruhsal sorunları olan yazarların kurgusudur (Rank, 2001, s.51). Eş insan kurgusu, en klasik haliyle Dr. Jekyll ve eş insanı Mr. Hyde örneğinde olduğu gibi birbirini tamamlayan kişilik özelliklerini ortaya koymaktadır: Eş insan, kahramanın gerçekleştiremediği tüm arzularını aktardığı, kötücül ve sonunda gerçek kahramanın yok olmasına neden olarak onun yerini alan bir karakterdir.

Ancak Kati örneğindeki eş insan daha çok yazarın olmak istediği kişiyi yansıtır niteliktedir. Aykol'daki eş insan tehdit edici olmaktan çok teskin edici hatta rehabilite edici bir rol üstlenmiştir. Aykol'un *"Berlin'de sırf Türk olmaktan ötürü uğradığı ayrımcılığa tepki olarak yarattığı bir kahraman"* (Maro, 2012) olarak tanımladığı Kati Hirşel, yazarın sıkıntılarını, Türk toplumunda aynı türden sıkıntıları çeken bir Almana yansıtması amacıyla yaratılmıştır. Örneğin Kati Hirşel özellikle *Kitapçı Dükkanı'*nda, bir Alman olarak Türkiye'de yaşadığı sıkıntılardan daha çok, roman boyunca iki toplumu karşılaştırmakta ve kendi ülkesinin insanlarına karşı acımasız eleştiriler getirmektedir:

"İstanbul'un en sevdiğim yanlarından biri de bu bakımlı olma hikayesi: Burada gündelik hayatın bir parçası hatta düpedüz bir alışkanlık olarak berbere, güzellik enstitülerine gidiliyor. Almanya'da ise (...) sokaklar zorunlu kalmadıkça yüzüne bakmayı istemeyeceğiniz insanlarla doludur. Münih farklıdır, orada göz estetiğini okşayacak birilerine rastlanır ama hele de Berlin'de bu paçozlar ordusu yüzünden insanın canı sokağa çıkmak istemez." (Aykol, 2001, s. 22).

Ancak rehabilitasyonun etkisiyle Hirşel'in *Tango İstanbul'*da bu eleştirileri yön değiştirir, bir başka deyişle Alman toplumu yergisinden uzaklaşarak dünya meselelerine eğilir ve eleştiri okları daha çok içinde bulunduğu Türk toplumuna yönelir:

"Katiller arkalarında Türk bayrağı, yanlarında polislerle objektiflere sırıtmıştı. Genç kızlar, genç erkekler, ellerinde Türk bayraklarıyla şakımıştı: 'Burası Türklerin Türkiye'si! Beğenmeyen çeksin gitsin!' İçim dondu. İstanbul artık benim şehrim değil miydi?" (Aykol, 2012, s. 249)

Sürekli birinci tekil şahısta kaleme alınan Kati karakteri tıpkı yazar gibi İstanbul'a tutkundur ve kendi ayakları üzerinde durmaktadır. Yazarla aynı sosyal statüdedir ve polisiye okumaya çocukluk yaşlarından beri tutkuyla bağlanmıştır. Hukuk her ikisinin de yaşamlarında dönüm noktası olmuş ve yazarın gazetecilik yetileri Kati'ye amatör detektiflik yetileri olarak yansımıştır. Her ikisi de toplumsal ve politik olaylara çok duyarlıdır.

Kati Hirşel karakterinin en ilgi çekici yönlerinden biri de yaşayan bir karakter olmasıdır. 1958 doğumludur ancak bakımlı olduğu için en az 10 yaş genç gösteren ufak tefek, çekici bir kadındır. Yazarın özellikle kendinden yaşça büyük bir karakter yaratmak istemesinin nedeni olgun kadınların da çekici olduklarını göstermek istemesidir (Maro, 2012). Aykol kimi röportajlarında Kati'yi arzularını, isteklerini yansıttığı eş insanı olarak yarattığını dile getirmektedir:

"*Kati Hirşel kadar girişken, rahat, hazırcevap, komik ve pervasız olmayı canı gönülden dilediğim zamanlar oluyor. Belki eskiden, roman yazmaya ilk başladığımda öyleydim de. Ama dört duvar arasına kapanıp saatler, haftalar, aylar ve yıllarca roman yazmak, insanın sosyal reflekslerini zayıflatıyor. Roman gerçekliğinde, Kati gibi bir kadının benliğinde gezinip ona komik komik, parlak laflar söyletebiliyorum da gerçek hayatta öyle biri değilim. Yaşça da benden büyük Kati Hirşel. Onu Monica Bellucci'ye benzetiyorum ya da benim çok sevdiğim Alman oyuncu İris Berben'e. Zamansız güzel, aurası olan bir kadın.*" (Çınar, 2009)

Son olarak, yazarın yapıtlarını kronolojik olarak ele aldığımızda *Kitapçı Dükkanı ve Kelepir Ev'de* kurgunun daha çok Kati'nin her iki toplumu sürekli birbiriyle karşılaştırarak hicvetmesi etrafında şekillendiğini, ancak son iki romanı *Şüpheli bir Ölüm* ve *Tango İstanbul'*da daha çok polisiye kurgunun öne çıktığını söyleyebiliriz.

Yüceltme mekanizması

Bilindiği gibi, Sigmund Freud ilgisini yaratı ve yaratının oluşum sürecine yöneltmiş ve bu anlamda Leonardo da Vinci, Michelangelo, Dostoyevski gibi sanatçıların yaratılarının kökenlerine inerek bu konuyla ilgili konferanslar vermiştir. Bu kapsamda, içgüdünün amacının toplum tarafından değerli görülen bir amaca kaydırılması ve bu uğurda gösterilen çabadan haz alınması olarak tanımlayabileceğimiz yüceltme mekanizması, Sigmund Freud psikanalitiğinde bir savunma mekanizması olarak incelenmiştir. Bununla birlikte klinik açıdan ele alındığında bastırma, gerileme, tepki oluşturma, yapıp bozma, yansıtma, içe yansıtma, yalıtma, kendine yöneltme, karşıtına çevirme şeklindeki dokuz savunma mekanizmasına ek olarak yüceltme mekanizması belirlenir ki bu da yüceltme mekanizmasının, Anna Freud'un tabiriyle "*nevrozdan çok normalliğin incelenmesine dâhil edilebilecek*" bir mekanizma olduğunu bize göstermektedir. (Freud, A. 2015, s.37)

Bu nedenle yüceltme kavramı, Sigmund Freud tarafından metapsikolojik açıdan hiçbir zaman tam olarak tanımlanmamıştır, ancak o kadar önemli bir yere sahiptir ki, yine Freud'un bakış açısıyla, nasıl baskılama çocukta yaratıcı bir alternatif oluşturuyorsa nevrozlu yetişkinde yüceltme pozitif bir çıkış yolu olabilmektedir.

Yüceltmeyle birlikte yalnızca itkinin amacı değişmemektedir aynı zamanda nesnesi de değişerek sosyal, pozitif ve değerli bir boyut kazanmaktadır: " *Bir tür amaç dönüşümü ve nesne değişimidir ve bu eylemlerde yüceltme dediğimiz sosyal değerler ölçekleri önem kazanmaktadır (Nouvelles conférences de Psychanalyse, 1932).*" (Salas, 2013) Bu çerçevede, Freud, psikolojik romanlardaki kahramana dikkat kesilerek, sanatçının yaratmış olduğu kahramanın ruhuna oturduğunu ve diğer tüm roman kişilerini de bu gözle incelediğini belirtir. Bu açıdan şu çıkarsama yapılabilir: "*Sanatçı ben'i gözlemleyerek yaratısına kendi ben'inden parçalar koyar ve böylelikle kendi ruh çatışmalarını birden çok kahramanda kişileştirerek ortaya koyar*". (Freud, 2014, s. 111)

Tüm bunlara paralel olarak, Divansız psikanalist olan yazar, Freud'a göre sezgisel bir şekilde oto-analizini yapar: "*Roman yazarı kendi ruhunun bilinçdışına dikkat kesilerek yoğunlaşır, tüm olasılıklara kulak verir ve bilincin eleştirel bakışıyla baskılamak yerine sanatsal bir ifadeye dönüştürür. Kendi iç dünyasından bizim başkalarından öğrendiğimizi öğrenir (1907) (Nouvelles conférences de Psychanalyse, 1932).*" (Salas, 2013)

Tüm bu verilerin ışığında, kanımızca, yükseköğrenim yapmak amacıyla gitmiş olduğu Almanya'da uzun yıllar kalan Esmahan Aykol, yaşadığı travmatik deneyimlerin sonucunda, maruz kaldığı ayrımcılığın yaratmış olduğu "intikam ve öfke" duygularını sosyal düzlemde kabul gören yaratıcılık alanına yönelterek yüceltmiştir: *"Kati Hirşel sayesinde bir Alman da Türkiye'de ayrımcılığa uğruyor diye düşünmeye başladım ve delirmekten kurtuldum"* (Yılmaz, 2012). Keza kendisiyle yapılan röportajlarda tam da yüceltme mekanizmasının özüne dönük olan bu boşaltımı pekçok kez ifade etmiştir: Kendisine sorulan "Polisiye romanlar yazarak içindeki zehri mi akıtıyorsun? sorusuna *" Zehir, denebilir mi bilmiyorum çünkü baş etmeyi becerebildiğime göre o kadar şiddetli bir duygu olamaz diye düşünüyorum. Ama Kati romanlarının beni daha mutlu, daha olumlu bir insan yaptığı açık."* (Çınar, 2012) şeklinde cevap vermiştir.

Esmahan Aykol'un romanlarına bu objektiften bakıldığında eleştirilerinin ilk romanlarda daha yoğunken son romanlarına gelindiğinde giderek azalmış olduğunu söyleyebiliriz. Bu da aslında yüceltme mekanizmasının bir anlamda görevini yerine getirmiş olduğunu bizlere göstermektedir. İkinci kitabı *Kelepir Ev*'de Almanların ayrımcı davranışlarına getirdiği eleştiri Kati'nin ağzından şu şekilde dökülmektedir:

"Siyasetten kaçmaya çalışsanız da yolu yok. Herkesin fışkırtmaya hazır beklettiği en az otuz tane değerli fikri var. Konuşan Türkiye. Almanlar böyle değildir. Hakkında canla başla fikir beyan ettikleri bir tek konu vardır: Ülkedeki yabancılardan nasıl kurtulunacağı." (Aykol, 2003, s.129)

Türk toplumuna yönelik eleştirilerini de son romanı *Tango İstanbul*'da parçalamış olduğu *ben*'lerinden biri olan Lale'nin ağzından şu biçimde dile getirmektedir:

"Ermeni diye Hrant Dink'i gündüz vakti sokağın ortasında vurdular. Ne oldu? Hiç! Memlekette tosuncuk kıtlığına kıran girmedi ya... iki tosuncuk da senin damarlarında dolaşan Yahudi kanını kışkırtıcı bulursa ne olacak? – Beni korkutmaya mı çalışıyorsun? diye diklendim. Diklendim ama yavaş yavaş korkmaya başlıyordum. – Hayır. Gerçekleri görmeni sağlamaya çalıyorum. Onların gözünde sen nesin biliyor musun? Mossad ajanı mı, Bundesnachrichtendienst'ten mi olduğu belli olmayan Türkiye'yi karıştırmaya gelmiş bir kaltaksın." (Aykol, 2012, s. 248)

Sonuç

Esmehan Aykol'un romanlarında karakterleri, ayrımcılığa uğramakta, hor görülmekte, sürülmekte, dışlanmakta, önyargılarla bir kalıba oturtulmakta ve hiçbir şekilde bu kalıptan çıkarılmasına izin verilmemekte hatta *"insanlığın iliklerine işleyen bir ötekileştirme"*yle (Saka, 2012) karşı karşıya kalmakta, kısacası göç olgusunun geniş bir panoramasını çizmektedirler. Yazar, romanlarında, yüceltme mekanizmasını kullanarak, ayna tekniği ve eş insan kahraman kurgusunu uygulamış ve göç ve göçmen olgusuna her iki taraftan da bakmıştır. Ayrıca, göç edebiyatı temalarını polisiye roman kurgusu içinde işleyerek eklektik bir yazın türü oluşturmuştur.

Tüm bu verilerin ışığında Esmahan Aykol'un iyiden kötüye giden ilk göç olarak tanımladığı Adem'in cennetten sürülüşüne kadar dayandırdığı göç olgusunu, millet, din ve mezhep kalıplarından çıkarıp çok daha evrensel bir insanlık durumu olarak ele aldığını saptamış bulunuyoruz. Yazara göre, ceza olarak gelen ilk zorunlu göçün ardından, insanlığın ilk zamanlarında hep iyiyi bulmaya doğru güdülenen göç yerleşik düzene geçilmesiyle birlikte sonu belirsiz bir macera olmuştur: *"Yerleşikler onları taktir etti ama hiçkimse kendisi göç eden olmak istemedi, göç hüzünle özdeş oldu. Göçün görkemli dönemi kapandı. Gidenler ağladı, kalanlar ağladı."* (Aykol, 2006, s. 250)

Kaynakça

Aykol, E. (2001). Kitapçı Dükkânı. İstanbul: Everest Yayınları.

Aykol, E. (2003). Kelepir Ev. İstanbul: Everest Yayınları.

Aykol, E. (2007). Şüpheli Bir Ölüm. İstanbul: Merkez Kitaplar.

Aykol, E. (2012). Tango İstanbul. İstanbul: Mephisto Kitaplığı.

Aykol, E. (2006). Savrulanlar. İstanbul: Merkez Kitaplar.

Çınar, S. (2015). 6 News kanalında yayınlanan, Sayım Çınar'ın yapmış olduğu Sayım'ın Bavulu: Konuk Esmahan Aykol adlı röportaj. Kaynak: https://www.youtube.com/watch?v=cXiLlXqzUpg Erişim Tarihi 05.04.2015.

Çınar, S. (21.07.2009). Esmahan Aykol ile röportaj. Kaynak: http://www.lambdaistanbul.org/s/medya/yazar-esmahan-aykol-gazetecilige-lanet-ettigim-bir-donem-oldu-bilegime-bagli-bir-tas-gibi-geldi-ga/ Erişim Tarihi: 20.04.2015.

Çınar, S. (30.10.2012). Esmahan Aykol ile röportaj. Kaynak: http://www.medyatava.com/haber/esmahan-aykol-yeni-kitabi-tango-istanbulu-anlatti-kahramanlarimin-gercek-hayatta-bir-karsiligi-var_80328 Erişim Tarihi: 15.04.2015.

Freud, A. (2015). Ben ve Savunma Mekanizmaları. (Çev. Yeşim Erim). İstanbul: Metis, 4. Basım [2002 1.basım]

Freud, S. (2014). Sanat ve Sanatçılar Üzerine, (Çev. Kâmuran Şipal). İstanbul:Yapı Kredi Yayınları

Maro, A. (28.10.2012). İstanbul Rehberi Gibi Bir Polisiye.... Milliyet. Kaynak: http://www.milliyet.com.tr/istanbul-rehberi-gibi-bir-polisiye-/pazar/haberdetay/28.10.2012/1618112/default.htm Erişim tarihi: 02.03.2015.

Okyay, S. (04.11.2012). NTV Radyo'da yayınlanan Sevin Okyay'ın hazırladığı Cinayet Masası adlı program. Kaynak: http://www.ntvradyo.com.tr/PodcastDetay/2021/22to8gle/cinayet-masasi. Erişim Tarihi: 15.04.2015.

Rank, O. (2001). Don Juan et Le Double. Paris: Editions Payot et Rivages.

Saka, F. (12.11.2012). Esmehan Aykol'l röportaj metni: "Ötekileştirme iliklerimize kadar işlemiş". Kaynak: http://vatankitap.gazetevatan.com/haber/otekilestirme_iliklerimize_kadar_islemis_/1/19346 Erişim Tarihi: 17.04.2015

Salas, C. (9.12.2013). "Approches psychanalytiques : Transmission, passe et impasse ". 9 Aralık 2013 tarihinde Troyes'de Institut Universitaire Européen Rachi gerçekleştirilen konferans metni. Kaynak: http://psy-troyes.com/2014/01/16/la-creation-litteraire/ Erişim Tarihi: 27.02.2015.

Tunaboylu, A. (18.10.2012). Kati Hirşel Polisiyeleri İstanbul Sokaklarının Fotoğrafıdır. Kaynak:http://www.bugunbugece.com/oku-bak/yazi/esmahan-aykol-kati-hirsel-polisiyeleri-istanbul-sokaklarinin-fotografidir Erişim Tarihi: 15.04.2015.

Yılmaz, İ. (24.11.2012). Kanlı Ayak İzlerinin Değil Polisiye Romanların Peşinde. Hürriyet Keyif. Kaynak: http://www.hurriyet.com.tr/keyif/22000141.asp Erişim Tarihi: 05.04.2015.

Tuna dergisi ve göç edebiyatına bir bakış - yazar ve şair Zahit Güney'in göç ile ilgili yazıları üzerine

Cahit Kahraman ve İlhan Güneş

Giriş

Bulgaristan Türkleri ve göç hep iç içe olmuş bir olgudur. Osmanlı-Rus savaşı sonrası yoğun göç dalgaları başlamış, en son 1989 göçüne kadar sürmüştür. Türkiye ve Bulgaristan arasında imzalanan ikili antlaşmalarla 1950-51 yıllarında göç devam etmiş ve bu göç sırasında parçalanan aileleri birleştirmek amacıyla 1969-1978 yılları arasında yoğun olarak sürmüştür (Akgün, 2011, s.76). Son Göç veya Büyük Göç olarak da bilinen 1989 Bulgaristan Türklerinin göçü, bu göçün canlı tanıkları yüz binlerce göçmenin hafızasında yaşamakta olduğu gibi, yüzlerce yazar ve şairin kaleminde halen canlanmaktadır. Hayriye S. Yenisoy, "1989 Bulgaristan'ın gerçekleştirdiği geniş kapsamlı zorunlu göçün sebeplerini 1984/85 olaylarında aramamız gerektiğini" belirtir (Kırcaali Haber, 16 Haziran 2010, s.3). 1989 Bulgaristan Türklerinin göçü zorunlu göç kapsamındadır ve iki ülke arasında bir antlaşma olmaması bu göçü özel ve farklı kılmaktadır.

Bulgaristan'dan gelen yazarlar Türkiye'de çeşitli yayın organları, gazete ve dergilerde eserlerini yayınlama fırsatı bulmuş, anılarını, duygularını, düşüncelerini ölümsüzleştirmişlerdir. Birçok yazar kendi şiir güldestelerini de Türkiye'de gün ışığına çıkarmış, yüz binlerce göçmenin duygu ve düşüncelerine ışık tutmuştur. Bu şiirler göçmenlerin gücüne güç katmış, onlara sabır, direnme ve umut kaynağı olmuştur. Böylece, göç ve göçmenleri konu eden zengin bir yazın edebiyatı da oluşmuştur. "Göç Edebiyatı" olarak adlandırılan bu edebiyat, "yazarlıklarını (genelde) 1989'a kadar Bulgaristan'da, bundan sonra da Türkiye'ye sığınmak zorunda kalmış olan ve bu yazın geleneğini Türkiye'de sürdüren yeteneklerin yaratmakta olduğu edebiyattır" (Çavuş, 2005, s.105). Balkan Türk Edebiyatı ve Bulgaristan Türk Edebiyatının, Türklerin Balkanlara ayak basmalarıyla oluşan Rumeli Türk Edebiyatının sözlü edebiyat geleneğinin devamı niteliğinde, zor koşullara rağmen günümüze kadar yaşatılmıştır (Canım, 2001&Buttanrı, 2005). Göç Edebiyatını ele aldığımızda, 1989 göçünü, üç döneme ayırmak mümkündür. Birinci dönem "Göç Öncesi" dönemi, ikinci dönem "Göç Süreci" dönemi ve son olarak üçüncü dönemi "Göç Sonrası" olarak adlandırmak mümkündür. Birinci dönem, Türklerin isim değişikliğinden göç sürecine kadar ki zaman dilimini kapsamaktadır. Bu dönem, Bulgaristan Türklerinin adalet arayışı ve mücadele yıllarıdır. İkinci dönem, göç sürecini ve o süreçte yaşanan olayları ele alır. Üçüncü dönem ise göç sonrası yaşananlar, özlem ve ayrılık duyguları ile geçen süreci gösterir.

Amaç

Tuna dergisi 1996 yılında Mehmet Çavuş tarafından kurulmuş, 2009 yılına kadar yayın hayatını sürdürmüştür. Dergide neşredilen konular çok geniş yelpazeli olsa da, yazarların hayatında "göç", bir dönüm noktası olduğundan, bu konu üzerine birçok eser vermişlerdir. Göç ile ilgili yazılarda, göç öncesi anılar, kısa öyküler, tarihi olaylar üzerine yazılar da olmakla beraber, göçün gerçekleşme an'ı, göç sonrası yaşananlar, duygu ve düşüncelerden meydana gelen eserler de mevcuttur. Tuna dergisi bünyesinde toplanan yazarların büyük çoğunluğu Sofya Üniversitesi Türkoloji bölümünü bitirmiş, uzun yıllar Bulgaristan'da Türkçe ve Türk edebiyatı üzerine öğretmenlik yapmış aydın kişilerden oluşurken, aynı zamanda göç olayının da bizzat canlı tanıklarıdır. Derginin kurucusu Mehmet Çavuş başta olmak üzere, Ahmet Emin Atasoy, İsa Cebeci, Zahit Güney, Ömer Osman Erendoruk, Sabri Tata ve burada ismini sayamadığımız daha birçoğu yukarıda bahsi geçen vasıflara sahiptir.

Bu çalışmamızın amacı Tuna dergisinde "89 Göçü" olarak bilinen Bulgaristan Türklerinin son göçü ile ilgili yer alan göç temalı şiirler ve şair Zahit Güney'in yazılarında göç olgusunu incelemek ve göçün çağrıştırdığı duygu ve düşünceleri göç şiirleri aracılığı ile ortaya koymak olacaktır.

Yöntem

Araştırmamızın kaynağını oluşturan Tuna dergisi 1996 yılından 2009 yılına kadar 13 yıldan fazla yayın hayatında kalmayı başarmıştır. Tekirdağ bölgesinde temsilcilikleri bulunan derginin sorumlu yazarları ile irtibata geçerek, dergi hakkında bilgi alınmıştır. Bu yazarlardan biri Çorlu temsilcisi İsa Cebeci ve diğeri de Tekirdağ temsilcisi Zahit Güney'dir.

Bu çalışmada sadece göç temalı şiirler değerlendirilmiştir. Bu şiirleri, vermek istenilen mesaj, içeriğine göre çağrıştırdıkları duygular özenle gruplandırılmıştır. Buna göre toplam 10 kategori oluşturulmuştur. Bu kategoriler sırasıyla şunlardır:

Tarihi bir olgu olarak göç

Göç şiirlerinde sıklıkla tarihi olaylar tasvir edilmiştir. Şairler, yüzyıllar öncesi başlayan şanlı ve ihtişamlı yürüyüş, şimdilerde göç ile geri dönüşün hüzünlü bir tablosunu ortaya koymaktadır. Ata yurdunu terk etmenin verdiği burukluk, acı, keder hislerini verir. Mehmet Ş. Çavuşoğlu "Tarih" şiirinde bu duyguları yansıtır.

Burada verilen şiirler dışında, Ahmet Cebeci'nin "Tuna Destanı", Nazif Öztürk'ün "Tuna da At Suladık", Galip Sertel'in "Bir Osmanlı Sedasıdır Rivayetlerde" gibi daha birçok örnekler sıralanabilir.

Göç öncesi adalet arayışı ve mücadele olgusu

Bu grupta ele alınan şiirler, göç öncesi yapılan haksızlıklar, baskılar ve bunlara karşı bir serzenişin oluştuğunu göstermektedir. Ad değişimi ile başlayan bu zorlu sürecin, Bulgaristan Türklerinin adalet arayışı ve mücadelenin başlamasına neden olmuştur. Bu dönem göç edebiyatının ilk evresi sayılır. Bu duygular Latif Karagöz'ün "Çınar ağacının Öyküsü" açıklıkla işlenmiştir. Eşref Rodoplu'nun "Kader" ve Galip Sertel'in "Ev" şiirlerinde de göç öncesi adalet arayışı ve mücadele unsurları ustalıkla işlenmiştir.

Göç etme nedeni olarak Türklük, Türkçe ve "Kimliğe" kavuşma olgusu

1989 göçünü, diğer göçlerden ayıran en önemli özelliği, "Türklük", "Türkçe" ve "kimliğe kavuşma" olgusudur. Göç, Türk kimliğine kavuşmak, Türklüğünü kanıtlamak için yapılmıştır. Son göçün ana temasını oluşturan bu düşünce olmuştur. İsim değişimi ile Türk kimliklerini kaybedenler, Türkçe konuşmaları yasaklananlar, bu göç sayesinde bunlara yeniden kavuşmanın mutluluğu ve sevinci şiirlere yansımıştır. Ahmet Emin Atasoy'un "Yanıt" şiirinde Bulgaristan Türklerinin anadili Türkçe olduğunu vurgular.

"Göç" şiirinde Haşim Akif, göçün, cebinde yepyeni kırmızı bir pasaport ve elinde bir bavul, "Türklük" uğruna yapıldığını dile getirmektedir (Akif, 1997, s. 41). İbrahim Kanberoğlu'nun "Dinmeyen Sancı" şiirinde "Türklüğü", vatanı olarak bildiği ve unutamadığı eski yuvasında cesurca dile getirdiğini anlatır (Kamberoğlu, 1999, s. 52).

Göç şiirlerinde vatan sevgisi olgusu

89 göçü şiirlerinde işlenen vatan sevgisi olgusu, göçmenlerin daha önce hiç görmedikleri, gelmedikleri, bilmedikleri, özlemini duydukları Türkiye'yi vatan olarak benimsemeleri, kabul etmeleri ve sevmeleri açıkça görülür. Bu vatan sevgisi, Bulgaristan Türklerinin hayallerinde canlandırdıkları yerin aşkı, aşkların en büyüğü olarak gösterilmiştir. Tuna dergisinde yazan aydınların sınır dışı edilerek verilmek istenen ceza, onlar için bir ödüle dönüşmüş veya öyle algılanmıştır. Göç bir ceza olarak verilmek istense de, göç edenler bunu bir ödül gibi görmüştür. Nazif Öztürk'ün "Hakkımı Yediler" şiirinde Bulgaristan'dan göç ederek anavatana kavuşmanın sevinci açıkça yansıtmıştır.

Özgürlük olgusu olarak göç

Özgürlük teması, 89 göçmenleri arasında, yeniden doğuş, kurtuluş, aynı zamanda yeni bir başlangıçtır. Göç ile özgürlüklerine kavuşan göçmenler, yeni umutlarla yeni hayatlarına başlamanın sevinci içindeler. Ahmet Emin Atasoy, "Soydaşlarımız" şiirinde göçü yeniden doğuş olarak tasvir etmektedir. Göç ile özgürlüklerine kavuşan göçmenler için, yeni bir başlangıç yaparak yeniden doğmuş gibi hissetmişlerdir.

İsa Cebeci'nin "Göçmen" şiiri, göç ve özgürlüğü ustaca anlatmıştır. Göç ve özgürlük yeniliğin simgesidir. Hayatlarında artık her şey yenilenmiştir. Özgürlük, yepyeni bir pasaportla yeniliklere açılan bir dünyadır.

Göç sonrası özlem olgusu

Göç edebiyatında özlem teması belki de en çok kaleme alınan temadır. Tuna dergisinde sayısız şiir özlem duygularını vurgular. Şiirler, doğup büyüdükleri toprakları, çocukluklarının geçtiği anıları, mutlu ve acı günleri anımsatır. Özlem, Bulgaristan'dan bir daha dönmemek üzere göç etmiş insanların duygusudur. Ömer Osman Erendoruk "Deli Özlem" şiirinde özlem duygularını yüksek sesle haykırır.

İsa Cebeci "Unutamıyorum" şiirinde, gönül sesine kulak verirken özlemle eski toprakları anar. Sadece kendi sesi değil, anne-baba mezarından gelen seslere de kulak verir. Ömer Osman Erendoruk "İlk Bahar Özlemi" şiirinde, özlem dolu yerlere hayali gezintiler yaptığını, gönüllere hudutlar olamayacağı mesajını verir.

Göç'ün getirdiği acılar, sıkıntılar ve zorluklar

Göçün getirdiği acılar, sıkıntılar ve zorluklar göç esnasında, yolculukta çekilen duyguları yansıtmaktadır. Göç şiirlerinde, göç sonrası acılardan veya zorluklardan bahsedilmemiştir. Göç sonrası adaptasyon sorunu da şiirlerde konu edilmemiştir. Daha önce de belirtildiği gibi, bu göç bir "bayram" ya da bir "ödül" olarak algılanmış, çekilen sıkıntılar unutulmuştur. Ali Bayram, "Benim Halkım" şiirinde göçmenlerin keder dolu kaderlerine göç ile çare bulduklarını belirtir.

Göç sonrası ayrılık ve yalnızlık olgusu

Göç ile gelen ayrılıklar, göç sonrası yalnızlık duyguları şiirlere konu olmuştur. Bu, insanların birbiriyle ayrılması kadar, yaşadıkları yerlerden, yuvalarından zorla koparılmaları anlatılmıştır. Arada kalan sınır, insanları ayırmıştır ancak, şairler, göçmenler, hayallerinde "O" yerlere gönüllerince seyahat ettiklerini, zamanı da aşarak gençliklerine geri dönebildiklerinden bahseder. Emine Öztürk, "Ayrılık" şiirinde göç ile gelen ayrılık sonrası yalnızlığın bir gönül sızısına dönüştüğünü ve iki ülkeyi (göç ettiği ve göçle geldiği ülkeyi) ayıran sınırın varlığından şikâyet etmektedir.

İbrahim Kamberoğlu, "Çocuklarla Hasbihal" şiirinde göç sonrası yaşanan yalnızlığı kast ederek ayrılık acısını gelecek kuşaklara tarih dersi verir. Ali Bayram, "Dostsuz Yaşam" şiirinde, göç sonrası dosta hasret yaşamın getirdiği üzüntüyü ustalıkla ifade etmektedir. Göç ile oluşan sınırlar insanların bir araya gelmesini engellemektedir. Süleyman Özgür'ün "Benim heyecanımdır yıldızların titreyişi" (Tuna 73-74, 2003, s.60) ve Nazif Öztürk'ün "Parçalanmış Ailelerin Perişanlığı" (Tuna, 39, 2000, s.29) şiirleri de bu duyguları yansıtmaktadır.

Göç ve iki vatan arasında kalma olgusu

Göç, geri dönüşü olmayan, ebedi bir ayrılıktır. Doğup büyüdüğün ve yaşadığın yerlerden sonsuza dek kopma düşüncesi, göçmenler arasında üzüntü veren duygulara neden olmuştur. İki vatan arasında kalma temalı şiirler bu dönemi yansıtır. Aidiyet hissi göç şiirlerinde sıkça işlenmiştir. Sabri İbrahim Alagöz, "İki Mezar Arasında" şiirinde, iki ayrı ülkede kalan anne ve babasının mezarları arasında olmanın kendisine bir türlü huzur vermediğini ve şair bu acıyı cehennem kuyusuna benzetir. Ahmet Emin Atasoy'un "O Yer" şiirinde şair son arzusunu aktarır. Bu çocuklarına bıraktığı son vasiyeti sayılabilir. Doğduğu topraklara gömülmek, aidiyet hissini açıkça belirtir.

Göç sonrası boş ve sahipsiz kalan yerlere ağıt

Göç sonrası terk edilen yerler, sahipsiz kalan evler, yalnızlık ve hüzün, göç şiirlerde ağıt olarak dile getirilmiştir. Asırlar boyu tarihle dolu, nesiller boyu anılarla dolu bu yöreler, şimdi kimsesiz, bir duaya bile hasret kalmıştır. Ahmet Emin Atasoy, Ömer Osman Erendoruk, Durhan Hasan Hatipoğlu ve Sabri İbrahim Alagöz'ün şiirleri bu duyguları aktarmaktadır. Ömer Osman Erendoruk, "Boş" şiirinde, göç sonrası her yerde bir yalnızlığın hakim olduğunu, kimsesiz kalmış yerlerde olmanın da artık anlamsız olduğunu vurgular.

Tuna Dergisi ve Zahit Güney

Zahit Güney, 3 Şubat 1946 yılında Dobruca'nın Kilikadı köyünde doğmuş, ortaöğretimini köyde tamamladıktan sonra liseyi Kurtpınar (Tervel) şehrinde bitirmiştir. 1970 yılında Sofya Üniversitesi Türk Filoloji bölümünden mezun olduktan sonra doğup büyüdüğü topraklara geri dönmüş ve 1989 yılına kadar öğretmenlik yapmıştır. Truden Rayon (Çalışma Bölgesi) olarak adlandırılan bir sistem sayesinde, üniversiteden mezun olanların kendi memleketlerinde öğretmenlik hakkı veren bu sistem sayesinde Zahit Güney Türk köyü olan Kilikadı köyünde Türkçe öğretmeni olarak atanmıştır. Ne yazık ki, 1974 yılında Türkçe dersleri kaldırılmış ve bu yıldan sonra Bulgarca öğretmeni olarak 1989 göçüne dek çalışmıştır. 1980-82 yılları arasında lise öğrenimi gördüğü Kurtpınar şehrinde çalışsa da 1982-89 yılları arasında tekrar kendi köyüne dönmüş ve Bulgaristan'daki iş hayatını orada tamamlamıştır. İlk yazısı, "Halk Gençliği" gazetesinde Harman diye bir makalesi yayınlanmıştır. 1964 yılında Sofya'da çıkarılan Yeni Işık gazetesinde ilk şiiri çıkar. Güvercin takma adıyla "Bayram Arifesinde" adlı bu şiir hakkında gazete, "gelecekteki parlak şairi müjdelemektedir" diye övgüyle bahsetmiştir. Bulgaristan'da 25 yıl şiir ve çeşitli yazılar yazmaya devam eden şair, 2 Haziran 1989 yılında Türkiye'ye göç ettikten sonra Tekirdağ'a yerleşmiş ve 1990 yılında Tekirdağ 50. Yıl İlköğretim Okulunda Türkçe Öğretmeni olmuş, 2007 yılında emekli olana kadar Türkçe öğretmenliği yapmıştır. Bulgaristan'dan göç ettikten sonra, hayat mücadelesine giren şair, yazılarından uzak kalmıştır. Ailenin geçim derdi, barınma derdi, tüm sorumluluk onun omuzlarındadır ve istemeden de olsa, şiirden uzak kalmıştır. *Kapıkule unutulmaz* adlı şiirde, şair olmanın zorluklarını anlatmak istemiştir.

İşçi
pazarında
Her sabah
Aynı hava,
aynı gazel:
-Aşçı varsa
gelsin;
-Şoför varsa
gelsin;
-Tornacı
varsa
gelsin...
Acı, ama
gerçek;
-Sen dur!
-Şair misin,
nesin?

Tuna dergisinin 1996 yılı kuruluşundan itibaren Tekirdağ temsilciliğini yapan Zahit Güney, dergi yazılarında da aktif rol üstlenmiştir. 1997 yılında ilk şiir kitabı "İnsan Olmak" kitabında çıkan şiirlerden dergide de zaman zaman şiirleri yayınlanmış, daha geniş kitlelere ulaşmayı başarmıştır. Daha sonra "Bölüşmek" (2002), "İnsan Yanım" (2006), ve "Yaşım Hep On Bir" (2011) olmak üzere, her beş yılda bir şiir kitabı çıkarmaya devam etmiştir. Zahit Güney, göçü tarif ederken, "dünyanın en zor yolculuğu", "Bulgaristan Türkleri göçe hep hazır durumda oldular, her an göç edecekmiş gibi mutfak dolaplarımız bile yokmuş", ve "göç, belki de biz Türkleri hayatta tutan bir şey, dinamik, değişim olmuştur" diye açıklamıştır (Zahit Güney, kişisel görüşme, 30.01.2015). Zahit Güney, "Öç" şiirinde göçü, insanlardan öç alırcasına uzun bir süreç ve durmadan devam eden bir olay olarak verir. Ecdadımız Orta Asya'dan bu yana göç ederek bu topraklara geldiği, kısa, fakat anlamlı bir göç şiiridir.

Tarihin bizden aldığı
En büyük öç
Ortaasya'dan bu yana
Hep göç
Hep göç...

(Tuna, 81-82, 2003, s.59)

Zahit Güney, "Yasaklı Şiir" şiirinde göç yolculuğunu ve o duyguları anlatır.

Zahit Güney, "Özlem-2" şiirinde, yaşadığı yerin adeta burnunda tüttüğü, göç ettiği yeri benimseyişi ve her iki yerle de özdeşleştiğini gösterir. Bu şiirler dışında, *Yer düğüme, gök ilik, Nalbantın Ağıtı, İçimdeki Tuna, Türkiyem, Bölüşmek, Göçmen kızları, Özlem-1, Yanlış Adres*, gibi şiirler de göç konusunu ele almıştır.

Sonuç

Göç konusu Bulgaristan Türk Edebiyatında sarsılmaz bir yer

Korku dolu bir yolculuktu o
Araba dolusu otobüs dolusu tren dolusu
Durmak yasak;

Kara kollarla çullanınca üstümüze gece
Hiç vakitsiz bir yaşa daha girdik
Sormak yasak;
...
Çift yürekle doğanların kartalların kanatlarında
Bayraklaştırarak onurumuzu
Bulut bulut aktık kuzeyden
Güneye;
Ağlamak yasak...
(Güney, 2004, s.28)

edinmiştir. Bulgaristan Türkleri için göç, sürekli kanayan bir yara olmuş ve olmaya devam edecektir. Ahmet Ş. Şerefli, "89 göçü ile Türkiye'ye 70 günde 345 bin insan, bavullarla geziye gidermiş gibi Anavatana geldiler" derken, yaşanan trajediyi gözler önüne sermektedir (Ahmet Şerif Şerefli, 2002, s.28.). Yaşadığı yerleri, malını, mülkünü, akrabasını, dostunu, sevdiğini bırakıp, elinde hiçbir şey olmadan yapılmış bir göçtür. İşte bu durum farkını göstermek uğuruna yazılmış bu eserler, "1989 Göçü" neden benzersiz olduğunu sergilemektedir. Bu araştırmada göç konulu şiirlerin verdiği mesajlara bakıldığında, 1989 göçünün 10 farklı olguyu çağrıştırdığı saptanmıştır. Bunları üç döneme ayırmak mümkündür. Birinci dönem: "Göç Öncesi"; İkinci dönem: "Göç Süreci"; Üçüncü dönem: "Göç Sonrası" olarak bölünebilir. Birinci dönem, isim değişikliği sonrası adalet arayışı ve mücadele yıllarını ele alan dönemdir. İkinci dönem, kazanılan göç ve göç sürecini kapsar. Üçüncü dönem ise, vatana-kimliğe kavuşma ve sonrasını işaret eder. "Tarihi bir olgu olarak göç" ve "Göç öncesi adalet ve mücadele olgusu" temaları ilk dönemi anlatmaktadır. "Göç etme nedeni olarak Türklük, Türkçe ve kimliğe kavuşma" ile "Vatan sevgisi olgusu" ve "Özgürlük olgusu" temaları ikinci dönemi, göç sürecini göstermektedir. Diğer temalar göç sonrası duygu ve düşünceleri konu etmiştir. Bunların arasında "Özlem" olgusunu içeren şiirler çoğunluktadır. Sıla özlemi, doğup büyüdükleri yerlere duyulan hasret şiir dizelerinde yaşatılmıştır. Vatan sevgisi, özgürlük, Türkçe ve Türklük, kimliğe kavuşma temaları şiirlerden hiç eksik olmamış, göçün özünü özetler. Tuna dergisinde incelenen şiirlerde de Türklük ve Türk kimliğine kavuşma konusu öne çıkmaktadır. Bütün bunlar Türk kimliğine kavuşmak, Türkçe dilini kurtarmak, özgürce dinini ifa etmek uğuruna yapılmıştır. Verilen mücadele ve adalet arayışı sonucunda kazanılan göç, kimliğe kavuşma ile taçlandırılmıştır. Bulgaristan'dan göç ederken, göçmenler, isimlerini geri almak, kimliğine ve özgürce konuşabilecekleri Türkçelerine kavuşmayı düşünmüşlerdir. Bu nedenle, Türkiye'ye vatan toprağını öperek ayak basmış, dualarla kurtulduklarına şükretmişlerdir.

Şiirlerde göçten sonraki sıkıntılardan, adaptasyon sorunlarından, vatana kavuşma sevincinden dolayı, bahsedilmemiştir. Daha çok göç öncesi ve göç esnasında karşılaşılan sıkıntılardan söz edilmektedir. İsa Cebeci'nin de dediği gibi, bu göç "bayram" olmuştur (İsa Cebeci, kişisel görüşme, 13 Şubat, 2015). Nebiye

İbrahim Akbıyık'a şiirlerinden dolayı verilen "Türkiye'ye gönderilme cezası", hem onun hem de tüm göçmenler için ödül olmuştur.

Ahmet Emin Atasoy, Zahit Güney hakkında ki bir yazısında "O umudun ve iyimserliğin şiirini yazdı, güzelliklere yöneldi, iyi ve doğruyu savundu, hoşgörü örneği sergiledi" diye bahseder (Atasoy, 2004). Güney, "yaşamının büyük bölümünü Bulgaristan'da geçirmiş, baskı ve entrikalara göğüs gererek öz benliğini, ulusal varlığını kanıtlamak ve yaşatmak davasında kişisel yaşantısının ötesinde emeği sömürülmüş, hakları gasp edilmiş, onuru incitilmiş bir topluluğun acılarını, isyanlarını, özlem ve umutlarını dile getirmenin bilincini ve sorumluluk yükünü taşıyanlardandır" diye söz etmektedir (Atasoy, 2004). İbrahim Tatarlı, Zahit Güney için, "çağdaş şiirin gözde yeteneklerinden biri olmuştur" der (Tatarlı, 2007).

Zahit Güney, göç temalı şiirlerinde özgürlük, özlem, Türkçe ve Türklük, göç esnasında karşılaşılan zorlukları tema olarak işlemiştir. Şiirlerinde yalın ve sade bir dil kullanımının yanı sıra, metaforik öğelerin kullanımı da gözlemlenmiştir. Bizzat göçün şahidi olan şair, göç öncesi ve göç sonrası yaşanan olayları ustalıkla tasvir etmiştir.

Kaynakça

Akgün, A. (2011). *Bulgaristan'dan Anadolu'ya Göçen Türkçe ve Türk Edebiyatı.* İzmir: Uluslararası Sosyal ve Ekonomik Bilimler Dergisi. 1 (75-79)
Akkayan, T. (1979). *Göç ve Değişme.* İstanbul. İstanbul Üniversitesi Basımevi.
Atasoy, A. E. (2004).*Birikmiş Yansımalar Vitrini,* İstanbul: Tuna Yayınları.
Buttanrı, M. (2005). Bulgaristan Türk Edebiyatı. *Eskişehir Osmangazi Üniversitesi Sosyal Bilimler Dergisi.* 6(2).
Canım, R. (2001). *Yirminci Asrın Başında Balkanlarda Yaşayan ve Türkçe Yazan Şairler,* Erzurum: A.Ü. Türkiyat Araştırmaları Enstitüsü Dergisi. 16. s.82.
Hacısalihoğlu, M. (2012). "89 Göçü" İle İlgili Tarih Yazımı Ve Kamuoyu Algıları, Hacısalihoğlu, Neriman E., Hacısalihoğlu, Mehmet (Ed.). 89 Göçü: Bulgaristan'da 1984-1989 Azınlık Politikaları ve Türkiye'ye Zorunlu Göç. İstanbul. Yıldız Teknik Üniversitesi BALKAR&BALMED
Haliloğlu, A. (1997). "Göç".*Balkanlarda Türk Kültürü,* 25. s.34.
Şen, H. (2009). "1989 Bulgaristan Göçmenleri ve Sorunları", [Elektronik Versiyon]. *Bulgaristan Türklerinin Sesi.* (18 Ocak 2009).
Salim, R. (2001). *Balkanların Sesi.* 12. s.20.
Şerefli, Ş. A. (2002). *Bulgaristan'daki Türkler (1879-1989),* Ankara: T.C. Kültür Bakanlığı
Tatarlı, İ. (2007) *Zahit Güney'in Şiiri.* "Hoşgörü", Razgrad.
Yenisoy, S. H. (16 Haziran 2010). Zorunlu Göçün 21. Yılı. Bulgaristan Türklerinin Sesi Kırcaali Haber.

Author Index

www.ingramcontent.com/pod-product-compliance
Lightning Source LLC
Chambersburg PA
CBHW021841020426
42334CB00013B/144